The Essays
Virginia Woolf
VOLUME IV

THE ESSAYS OF VIRGINIA WOOLF

Volume I: 1904–1912
Volume II: 1912–1918
Volume III: 1918–1924

The Essays of Virginia Woolf

VOLUME IV

1925–1928

EDITED BY

ANDREW M^CNEILLIE

A HARVEST ORIGINAL

HARCOURT, INC.

Orlando   Austin   New York   San Diego   London

Requests for permission to make copies of any part of the work
should be submitted online at www.harcourt.com/contact
or mailed to the following address: Permissions Department,
Houghton Mifflin Harcourt Publishing Company,
6277 Sea Harbor Drive, Orlando, Florida 32887-6777.

www.HarcourtBooks.com

First published in Great Britain by The Hogarth Press, 1994

Library of Congress Cataloging-in-Publication Data
available upon request
978-0-15-603522-4

Printed in the United States of America

A C E G I J H F D B

Contents

Introduction

Virginia Woolf's output on all fronts, in print and in private, during the relatively short span of 1925 to 1928 covered by the present volume was as prodigious as ever. But it was not quite as vast as this book's proportions might suggest. And this is because Volume IV includes not only her journalism for the four years concerned but also *The Common Reader* published by the Hogarth Press on 23 April 1925. (Her novel *Mrs Dalloway* appeared some three weeks later, and on that day, 14 May, she began in some detail to conceive *To the Lighthouse*.)

Reaching the milestone of her first essay collection provides a timely and valuable opportunity for retrospection.

In fact, work on *The Common Reader* belongs immediately to the period covered by the preceding volume, 1919–24. That volume collects, among much else, original versions of several articles subsequently refurbished, as Woolf liked to term it, for inclusion in *The Common Reader*. (It also includes the important experimental drafts 'Reading', written in 1919, and 'Byron & Mr Briggs'.) Volume III thus serves as a detailed introduction to *The Common Reader*. So too, at a further remove, do Volumes I and II. For *The Common Reader* is, in spirit if not in the letter, a distillation of almost a quarter of a century of eclectic publication and voracious reading. Beyond that we must also acknowledge yet more, foundational reading (historical, biographical, critical, fictional: canonical and obscure) that Woolf enjoyed in her father's library, and considerably at his inspiration, at 22 Hyde Park Gate. (Of this, and of her authorial apprenticeship, there is detailed record in her early journals.)[1] The paternal fraction of the patriarchal heritage was, when we come down to it, far from being in every respect anathema to Woolf. This bears stating if we are to answer as fully as possible the question, adapted from her famous essay, 'How Should One Read *The Common Reader?*'

Although, to take the best example, a world lies between Leslie Stephen's *Hours in a Library* and *The Common Reader*, historically, morally, and artistically, or, it might be said, quite literally temporally (his hours are by Woolf compacted into moments), the two works are not without literary and intellectual connection.[2] To state the obvious, both are predominantly biographical, or biographically orientated in their criticism. Both take their orientation from the idea of 'reading'. (See the opening of Stephen's essay on Sterne for his version of an empathetic approach which Woolf would make her own.)[3] Neither pays undue homage to a hierarchical tradition. That Woolf when reading for an essay or review habitually consulted her father's essays and contributions to the *Dictionary of National Biography* is borne out by her reading notes (see for example what is said below regarding 'Impassioned Prose'). We also have her own direct acknowledgement. She always found something in him 'to fill out; to correct; to stiffen [her] fluid vision'. He was not she said a writer for whom she had 'a natural taste' but nor did she feel her relationship with his work to be merely filial. She enjoyed 'a reader's affection for him; for his courage, his simplicity, for his strength and nonchalance, and neglect of appearances'.[4] Indeed, she shared with Stephen a common perspective upon literature as a commodity that is socially and historically conditioned, despite her belief in 'purity' and autonomy. It is a befitting irony that the extraordinary (and to some exasperating) jeu d'esprit *Orlando*, conceived, written and published (on 11 October 1928) in the years covered by this volume, and a close cousin to *The Common Reader*, itself expresses a view of English literature that is as *historical* and *social* as Stephen could have wished, for all the gendering of his critical values. (He was, as his daughter could not help but notice, more than inclined to associate sense with 'manliness'.)[5] She took pride too in being, as her father had been, a professional writer, a journalist caught up in the routine of reviewing.

As a consumer of biographies and memoirs and the author of numerous biographical essays, Woolf also enjoyed with Stephen a democratic faith in the value of all writing. The editor of the *DNB* shared something of his daughter's evaluation of what he also called the 'rubbish' heaps of literature. He even hazarded the idea that just as he made a will the sensible citizen, eminent or otherwise, should be by duty bound to write his autobiography.[6] Woolf, although she did not say so in as many words, would have rejoiced to concur with her father on this point. But we might expect that she would add the kind of twist we find in her essay on 'Miss Ormerod': 'Oh, graves in country churchyards – respectable burials – mature old gentlemen – D.C.L., L.L.D., F.R.S., F.S.A. – lots of letters come after your names, but lots of women are buried with you.'[7]

In *The Common Reader* Woolf sought not only to 'make some kind of whole – a portrait of a man, a sketch of an age, a theory of the art of writing',[8] but also in her oblique fashion to gesture towards the resurrection of women from a history written largely by men. By this and by her interest in family lives (see for example 'Taylors and Edgeworths') she anticipated, albeit in miniature studies, a movement among biographers still only embryonic to write group lives and to celebrate the spouses (Jane Welsh Carlyle), sisters (Dorothy Wordsworth), and lovers and mistresses (Elizabeth Hitchener, Harriette Wilson) of great male egos.[9]

To read the table of contents of *The Common Reader*, where we find obscurities (or relative obscurities) such as the Pastons, the Duchess of Newcastle, the family of Isaac Taylor and that of Richard Lovell Edgeworth, Laetitia Pilkington, Miss Ormerod, Miss Mitford, Dr Bentley, Lady Dorothy Nevill, Archbishop Thomson, rubbing shoulders with Chaucer, Montaigne, Defoe, Jane Austen, the Brontës, George Eliot, Joseph Conrad and the great Russians, is to be reminded just how much Woolf, from her story 'The Mark on the Wall', published in 1917, to *A Room of One's Own* (1929) and *Three Guineas* (1938), and indeed throughout her work, quarrelled with 'Whitaker's Table of Precedency', with the provoking and stultifying idea that 'the great thing is to know who follows whom'.[10] Indeed, in 'Phases of Fiction', the extended essay whose writing stands behind a significant part of the work in Volume IV, she refers to the 'common reader' as one who is 'suspicious of fixed labels and settled hierarchies'.[11] For Woolf too, it must be said, obscure lives had quite another interest. They appealed to her as a novelist. She found and appreciated in memoirs, letters and other accounts of the all but mute and inglorious Jane and John Miltons, how 'Certain scenes have the fascination which belongs rather to the abundance of fiction than to the sobriety of fact.'[12] (In her essay on 'Miss

Ormerod', indeed, the boundaries between fiction and fact are crossed and recrossed, with extraordinary liberty.)

'Literal truth-telling,' wrote Woolf, 'and finding fault with a culprit for his good are out of place in an essay, where everything should be for our good and rather for eternity than for the March number of the *Fortnightly Review*.' The precepts gathered in 'The Modern Essay' – 'the essay must be pure – pure like water or pure like wine' and so on – may serve to remind us of the aesthetics of Bloomsbury, quite as much as those of Walter Pater, and of the artistic principles that inform not only the individual pieces in *The Common Reader* but also the collection as a whole.[13]

As a reviewer Woolf was sharply conscious that 'collected essays are always the hardest to read, because, collected though they may be, it is often only the binding that joins them together'. Or, as she put it in *The Common Reader* itself, 'Journalism embalmed in a book is unreadable.'[14] In her case, however, as is borne out by many examples in this volume, and by the relatively minimal revision involved in translating journal articles into her book, the truth is that she had long ago achieved a style of essay-writing, especially in her 'leaders' in the *Times Literary Supplement*, but even as early as 1908 in the pages of the *Cornhill Magazine*, that was not only 'well-wrought' but which exhibited from essay to essay a distinct cohesion of preoccupation and point of view.

None the less, when embarking on her 'Reading book', she taxed herself with the problem of how to give it 'shape'.[15] As we have seen in Volume III she experimented no less ambitiously upon this project than she did with her fictions. Indeed, she sought ('Byron & Mr Briggs' is the clearest example) to provide a fictional frame for her book (as she had framed such essays as 'Character in Fiction'):

There could be an introductory chapter. A family which reads the papers. The thing to do wd. be to envelop each essay in its own atmosphere. To get them into a current of life, & so to shape the book; to get a stress upon some main line – but what the line is to be, I can only see by reading them through. (*II VW Diary*, 17 August 1923)

In the same diary entry she talks of embedding her essays in what she termed 'Otway conversation', the conversation between a fictitious, book-loving Penelope Otway and her friend. But in the end, inspired by Dr Johnson's observation in his 'Life of Gray' regarding the 'common reader', she settled upon a more conservative formula. It was to prove immensely successful, and yet too it divided her readers.

'I am in a state of complete bewilderment,' she wrote to Janet Case on 23 June 1925, 'as everyone seems to prefer either Mrs Dalloway to the C.R. or the other way about, and implore me to write *only* novels or *only* criticism, and I want to do both.' A little more than a year later she would still be haunted by Case's 'damned criticism' that *Mrs Dalloway* was 'all dressing' and 'technique' while *The Common Reader* had 'substance'.[16] (Yet 'substance' is precisely what some quite eminent critics were to protest Woolf's essays lacked.) Lytton Strachey, to whom the book is dedicated, Desmond MacCarthy, and Thomas Hardy were among those who published or otherwise conveyed their pleasure and praise.[17] But by far the most percipient review, among some extremely good reviews, was that by Hugh I'Anson Fausset in the *Manchester Guardian* of 14 May 1925:

... her ideas are seldom explicit: she is so fine an artist because her thought, concentrated and effective as it is, is not starkly separated from the fluid elements of experience, from her immediate human response to the life that literature and writings too humble to rank as literature embody. It is thus that she succeeds in combining keen analysis with a synthesising humanity and can disentangle the ideas which animated an individual or a people in the very process of picturing, with a selective fidelity to detail, the objective circumstances of their lives. And being thus both exact and imaginative, her intercourse with her subjects is really that of a contemporary, and not that kind of ironic intimacy which, however stealthily, betrays a detached egotism by its tendency to exploit.[18]

Fausset was quite possibly alluding here to his fellow biographer Lytton Strachey. He certainly captures the sense of emotional engagement with which Woolf's best essays are so vibrantly alive, and may remind us of her declaration, upon reading George Eliot for an anniversary article, how she could '. . . see already that no one else has ever known her as I know her'.[19] (To which she added that she always thought this whatever she read.) None the less, as she observed while reading *David Copperfield*, 'the right mood for reading' was rare and 'in its way as intense a delight as any; but for the most part pain'. There were moments when all the masterpieces did no more than 'strum upon broken strings'.[20] This was a syndrome, it may be supposed, Edmund Wilson experienced and expressed in his masterful account of the modernist movement *Axel's Castle* (1931) when making his only reference in that book to Virginia Woolf. 'Each of the essays of Strachey or Mrs Woolf,' Wilson begins, and contributes as he does so to a persistent strain of reductionism that has sought to lump Bloomsbury together and to talk of their prose as if it were all written by the same person, 'so compact yet so beautifully rounded out, is completely self-contained and does not lead to anything beyond itself; and finally, for all their brilliance, we begin to find them tiresome.' (John Gross, in another classic, *The Rise and Fall of the Man of Letters* (1969) makes a similar, if more discriminating, judgement.)[21] But there is the world of difference between Woolf's self-confessed obliquity – she called it her 'surface manner' and saw that it derived in part from her Victorian tea-table training – and Strachey's ironic *'Je n'impose rien; je ne propose rien: j'expose'*, just as there is the world of difference between his cabinet-making, 'his two semi colons; his method of understatement; & his extreme definiteness', to which Strachey confessed in 1919, and Woolf's more vigorous, if circumambulatory and circumambient approach.[22] (Like Henry James, she was an inveterate encoder, both as a novelist and as an essayist – the two did not always seem to her to be entirely distinguishable practices[23] – and the habit is one that carries its price.) For his part Strachey recognised a clear distinction. He may have been half-malicious and he may have been attempting, as Woolf suspected, 'to reserve the particular praise' he wished for himself, but still he paid her a compliment which rings true. She was, he said, not just 'the best reviewer alive' but also 'the inventor of a new prose style, & the creator of a new version of the sentence'.[24]

Publication of *The Common Reader* (by 27 June 1925 she was calling it 'a book too highly praised')[25] led inevitably to commissions; she found herself 'getting pushed into criticism' and thought it 'a great standby – this power to make large sums by formulating views on Stendhal & Swift';[26] and the market for her journalism expanded (see Appendix IV), notably in North America. The *Atlantic Monthly* approached her for the first time and, finally, in 1927, published her essay on 'The Novels of E. M. Forster' (for the full saga of which event see the opening annotation to the essay). She wrote on 'American Fiction' ('Women writers have to meet many of the same problems that beset Americans', p. 271) in the newly founded *Saturday Review of Literature*. A series of lengthy essays, including 'Poetry, Fiction, and the Future' (of which more below), and pieces on Katherine Mansfield, Ernest Hemingway (whom she provoked into a violent temper, p. 456), E. M. Forster, Shelley, Harold Nicolson and G. B. Stern appeared hard on each other's heels in the *New York Herald Tribune*. The *Yale Review* published

'How Should One Read a Book?' (later considerably revised for inclusion in the second *Common Reader*) and also her essay on 'Street
Haunting', which gives us, as she is so often to be found in her
diary, Woolf as *flâneuse*, breasting the tide of London's streets upon
the slender pretext of needing to purchase a pencil.[27] There were excursions into two New York journals, *Forum* and *Arts*, and the
New Republic continued to take proofs of her contributions to the
Nation & Athenaeum.

Leonard Woolf, despite at least one resignation and much fret-
ting, remained that paper's literary editor and Woolf made an extremely high level of contribution, great and small, to its pages.
Elsewhere on the home front she contributed to T. S. Eliot's *New
Criterion*, to *T. P.'s Weekly*, to Desmond MacCarthy's *Life and
Letters*, to the *Weekly Dispatch*, to *Vogue*, to *Time & Tide*, to the
Bermondsey Book, to something called *Now and Then*, to *Eve*, and
of course to the *TLS*. But that paper, towards which Woolf felt a
great allegiance, no longer occupied quite the same privileged position in her world. (There are only seven *TLS* contributions here, as
against almost seventy in Volume III.) Her diary entry of 23 July
1927, in which she makes a tally of her earnings, makes the position
clear:

> ... I have worked very methodically & done my due of articles, so that with luck, I
> shall have made £120 *over* my proper sum by September. That is I shall have made
> £320 by journalism, & I suppose at least £300 by my novel this year. I have
> thought too much, though on purpose, with my eyes open, of making money; &
> once we have each a nest egg I should like to let that sink into my sub-
> consciousness, & earn easily what we need. Bruce Richmond is coming to tea on
> Monday to discuss an article on Morgan; & I am going to convey to him the fact
> that I can't always refuse £60 in America for the Times' £10. If I could make easily
> £350 a year, I would: if I could get some settled job.

A settled job was hardly likely ever to be her lot, but not only did
she now discover more outlets for her work, she was also enabled as
a direct consequence to write a higher proportion of essays *tout
court*, as opposed to essay-reviews.

Although she had long ago achieved the freedom in her reviews to
approach her author at whichever angle she chose, regardless of the
book nominally in view (see as a representative example here,
'*David Copperfield*'), she had never before produced quite as many
essays upon themes (for example, 'On Being Ill', 'How Should One
Read a Book?'), subjects ('Pictures', 'The Cinema', 'Waxworks at
the Abbey') or occasions ('Street Haunting', 'The Sun and the Fish'

which describes an eclipse of the sun as seen from the Yorkshire moors). Her interest in obscure lives, which had prompted her on 20 July 1925 to talk of a recurrent idea 'to tell the whole history of England in one obscure life after another', was to lead her, 'advancing with lights across the waste of years to the rescue of some stranded ghost',[28] to write indeed on 'Sterne's Ghost', on 'Jones and Wilkinson', on John Mytton and on Harriette Wilson.

George Meredith's reputation may have plummeted precipitously since the turn of the century, when it was at its zenith (it is hard to believe now that he exerted a not inconsiderable influence on, for example, the young James Joyce),[29] but he had not quite become a total obscurity by 1928, the centenary of his birth. Woolf took stock of him in the *TLS* and also of Thomas Hardy, who died that year (and whose funeral the Woolfs attended), producing in both instances commemorative essays of a type she had long ago made an art of her own. (For essays in a similar, if more personal vein, see the amusing account of 'Julia Margaret Cameron', and also the obituary of Lady Strachey.)

'Hardy and Meredith between them very nearly did for V.', Leonard Woolf wrote to Vanessa Bell on 7 February 1928, reminding us not only of the immense burden of work she had on hand at any one time but also of the toll such intense activity could take upon her health.[30] (Remember that she wrote in addition to her journalism *To the Lighthouse* and *Orlando* in the three years covered by this volume, began *A Room of One's Own*, and drafted a great part of 'Phases of Fiction' whose perspectivist theories, incidentally, emerge in several of the essays here – notably 'Robinson Crusoe' – and were to an extent inspired by E. M. Forster's *Aspects of the Novel* (1927), discussed by Woolf in 'Is Fiction an Art?'). But in fact there was only one period of protracted illness and relative inactivity, August–December 1925. At least some of that time seems to have been engaged in the final throes of 'On Being Ill', and much of it, as we may suppose from that essay, in a kind of hothouse gestation of *To the Lighthouse*, upon which she recommended work in considerable earnest in January.

Three essays of this period relate with especial significance to Woolf's fiction. (Other links, for example, between *Orlando* and 'The New Biography' and 'Poetry, Fiction, and the Future', are abundantly detectable throughout the volume.) 'Poetry, Fiction, and the Future' (later reprinted by Leonard Woolf under the title

'The Narrow Bridge of Art') published in 1927 is the most direct manifesto Woolf ever produced, being effectively a programme for writing *The Waves* (1931), in which she envisaged a work 'written in prose, but in a prose which has many of the characteristics of poetry' (p. 435). This was cousin to the 'Impassioned Prose' of Thomas De Quincey about which Woolf had written earlier, at a key stage, while drafting the 'Time Passes' section, in the writing of *To the Lighthouse* (1927). It is especially interesting to find her actively reading and writing about De Quincey while simultaneously involved (dates in the holograph of the novel and diary and correspondence references coincide to confirm it)[31] in one of her most ambitious prose experiments, in which she sought to create a poetic interlude that telescoped ten years of history into a single night. For this prompts a recognition of De Quincey's very great importance to her and provides a direct link with the Romantic epiphany, called by Wordsworth 'spots of time' and by De Quincey 'involutes'.[32] (Woolf had already written about De Quincey quite tellingly in 1906 in 'The English Mail Coach', *I VW Essays*, Appendix I, as she would again in 'De Quincey's Autobiography', *V VW Essays* and *CR2*.)

De Quincey was something of a favourite with the Stephen family. Julia Stephen, according to her daughter, kept a copy of his *Confessions* at her bedside.[33] (Is it merely coincidence, one cannot help but wonder, that Mr Carmichael in *To the Lighthouse* is an opium eater?) Leslie Stephen wrote at length upon De Quincey and in the course of an attempt to account for the phenomenon of his prose makes the following effort at classification: 'In deciding whether a bat should be classed with birds or beasts, we have to determine the nature of the beast and the true theory of his wings. And De Quincey, if the comparison be not too quaint, is like the bat, an ambiguous character, rising on the wings of prose to the borders of the true poetical region.'[34] The idea of Virginia Woolf as 'Batwoman' may spring irresistibly to the postmodern mind. But it is perhaps more amusing to note that while she was engaged in writing the novel that would lay her father's ghost, Woolf made notes from *Hours in a Library*, notes that at one point surface almost but not quite directly in her essay. Stephen observes, in quasi-scientific mode: 'He belongs to a genus in which he is the only individual.'[35] Which Woolf renders: 'And one of De Quincey's claims to our gratitude, one of his main holds upon our interest, is that he was an exception and a solitary. He made a class for himself' (p. 363).

The third essay relatable directly to Woolf's fiction is the introduction she wrote, until now unreprinted, to the American Modern Library Edition of *Mrs Dalloway* (1928), which, with appropriate disavowals on the subject of authorial intention, provides valuable illumination concerning the novel's evolution.

Forensic reading, as in connection with her work upon De Quincey, undoubtedly helps us understand more thoroughly the kind of writer Woolf was. And what kind of writer was she? One that certainly resists at every turn our little formulations. We hardly need to be reminded that, unlike T. S. Eliot, whose *The Sacred Wood* (1920) was among the critical works she read while feeling her way towards a formula for *The Common Reader*, or I. A. Richards, whose *Principles of Literary Criticism* (1925) she subsequently read, Woolf most emphatically did not write for either academy or scholar.[36] Her hostility towards the idea that English literature should be taught was pronounced. (It informs her highly amusing account of Walter Raleigh in 'A Professor of Life' here.) In any comparison with the academically orientated critic, Woolf can appear determinedly, even quaintly, eclectic, and in an odd sense for all her brilliance and emotion, disengaged. It might for example be thought that placed as she was with her husband the literary editor of the *Nation & Athenaeum*, she would make first claim, given her interests, to review the latest Marcel Proust or Arnold Bennett. But when *Albertine Disparue* (1925) came out, Francis Birrell dealt with it while Woolf wrote about *Robinson Crusoe*, and when *Lord Raingo* (1926) was published it was reviewed by Leonard Woolf in an issue to which Woolf contributed an unsigned piece on Jerome K. Jerome's autobiography *My Life and Times*.[37] (No one could charge her with careerism.)

Similarly, in her essay on 'American Fiction' discussion of Sinclair Lewis's *Babbitt* (1922) makes no direct capital from references in that book to Shaw and Wells, or to Joseph Hergesheimer, several of whose novels Woolf had previously reviewed.[38] Nor, writing sympathetically in the same essay about Sherwood Anderson's *A Story Teller's Story* (1924) does she seize upon such an undeniably tempting and pertinent passage as: 'I am trying to give you the history of a moment and as a tale-teller I have come to think that the true history of life is but a history of moments. It is only at rare moments we live.'[39]

This apparent nonchalance with its palpable omissions, as the earnest reader might be forgiven for thinking them to be, can of course be accounted for in innumerable ways, not least in terms of contingency and the exigencies of reviewing.[40] Woolf herself made this clear, by implication, in the piece entitled 'Preferences', contributed to the *New York Herald Tribune* in the spring of 1928, in response to a request to 'name some books that have interested me during the past winter' (p. 542). There we find an account of what she has not had time to read (including those final volumes of Proust), as well as of books, a life of Conrad, Gertrude Bell's letters, she has read and read, it seems, not in order to review. Obscure biographies, read by 'chance and choice', figure in her list, as do the poems of Lady Winchilsea and of W. B. Yeats (whose *The Tower* is reviewed here).

In this context we glimpse Virginia Woolf, as often elsewhere, in her diary and letters, the common reader and hard-pressed reviewer, albeit one of quite prodigious energy and of the greatest gifts, whose love and belief in the sheer pleasure of reading was almost pathologically impassioned. For what else could have made her write (by courtesy it seems of Tennyson, p. 543), in concluding her 'Preferences', possibly the common reader's perfect epitaph, or elegy: 'But as I look through the crowded lists I feel with some distress how likely it is that in the press and scuffle the book I should most have enjoyed has been trampled under foot and will only be found reprinted when "I have lain for centuries dead"'?

1—Virginia Woolf, *A Passionate Apprentice. The Early Journals 1897–1909*, ed. Mitchell A. Leaska (The Hogarth Press, 1990).

2—Leslie Stephen, *Hours in a Library* (4 vols, Smith Elder, Duckworth and Co., 1874–1907).

3—*Ibid.*, vol. iv, 'Sterne', pp. 53–4: 'To read a book in the true sense – to read it, that is, not as the critic but in the spirit of enjoyment – is to lay aside for the moment one's own personality, and to become a part of the author.'

4—Virginia Woolf, *Moments of Being*, Revised and Enlarged Edition, ed. Jeanne Schulkind (The Hogarth Press, 1985), 'A Sketch of the Past', pp. 115–16.

5—*Ibid.*, p. 115. For a thorough summary of Stephen's gendering of virtue see Noël Annan, *Leslie Stephen. The Godless Victorian* (Weidenfeld and Nicolson, 1984), ch. 11, pp. 303–7.

6—See Leslie Stephen, *Studies of a Biographer* (4 vols, Duckworth and Co., 1898–1902), vol. i, 'National Biography', p. 4; and, for example, Virginia Woolf, *The Common Reader: 2nd series* (The Hogarth Press, 1932; 1986), 'How Should One Read a Book?', p. 263.

7—See below, *The Common Reader*, 'Lives of the Obscure', III 'Miss Ormerod', pp. 135–6.

8 – *Ibid.*, 'The Common Reader', p. 19.

9 – For VW on: 'Shelley and Elizabeth Hitchener' see *I VW Essays*; 'The Letters of Jane Welsh Carlyle', *I VW Essays* and 'Geraldine and Jane' *CR2* and *V VW Essays*; 'Dorothy Wordsworth', *CR2* and *V VW Essays*. For 'Harriette Wilson' see below.

10 – Virginia Woolf, *The Complete Shorter Fiction*, ed. Susan Dick (The Hogarth Press, 1985), 'The Mark on the Wall', p. 88.

11 – Virginia Woolf, *Granite & Rainbow* (The Hogarth Press, 1958), 'Phases of Fiction', p. 94.

12 – See below, *The Common Reader*, 'Lives of the Obscure', I 'Taylors and Edgeworths', p. 124.

13 – *Ibid.*, 'The Modern Essay', p. 217.

14 – *III VW Essays*, 'Patmore's Criticism', p. 308; and see below *The Common Reader*, 'The Patron and the Crocus', p. 214.

15 – *II VW Diary*, 23 May 1921. Nor should it be assumed that the refurbishments her articles underwent, though in most cases small, were of negligible significance, as may especially be seen in a comparison of 'Modern Novels' (*III VW Essays*) and its *Common Reader* version 'Modern Fiction' here.

16 – *III VW Letters*, no. 1563, to Janet Case, 23 June 1925; *III VW Diary*, 13 September 1926.

17 – Desmond MacCarthy reviewed *The Common Reader*, under his pen name 'Affable Hawk', in the *New Statesman*, 30 May 1925. For Thomas Hardy's praise see *III VW Diary*, 1 June 1925, and for Lytton Strachey's see *ibid.*, 18 June 1925.

18 – Hugh I'Anson Fausset's review is reprinted in *Virginia Woolf: The Critical Heritage*, ed. Robin Majumdar and Allen McLaurin (Routledge and Kegan Paul, 1975).

19 – *II VW Letters*, no. 1010, to Lady Robert Cecil, 26 January [?] 1919.

20 – *III VW Diary*, 16 June 1925.

21 – Edmund Wilson, *Axel's Castle* (1931; Fontana Library, 1962), ch. iv, 'T. S. Eliot', p. 104. John Gross, *The Rise and Fall of the Man of Letters* (Weidenfeld and Nicolson, 1969), ch. 9, 'Modern Times', p. 244: 'His [Desmond MacCarthy's] essays are far less highly wrought than those of Virginia Woolf or Lytton Strachey, but they do have the advantage of making one think about the books he discusses. The typical Virginia Woolf essay by contrast is a brilliant circular flight, which, as criticism, leads nowhere.'

22 – For Woolf's 'surface manner', see 'A Sketch of the Past', p. 150. Lytton Strachey, *Eminent Victorians* (1918; Penguin, 1948), Preface, p. 10: 'To quote the words of a Master – "*Je n'impose rien; je ne propose rien: j'expose.*"' The master in question was until quite recently held by scholars to be Voltaire, but, I am informed by S. P. Rosenbaum, the quotation is now generally believed to be Strachey's own invention.

23 – *II VW Diary*, 19 June 1923, writing about *Mrs Dalloway*: 'I daresay its true, however, that I haven't that "reality" gift. I insubstantise, wilfully to some extent, distrusting reality – its cheapness. But to get further. Have I the power of conveying the true reality? Or do I write essays about myself?'

24 – *I VW Diary*, 25 May 1919.

25 – *III VW Diary*, 27 June 1925.

26 – *Ibid.*

27 – For a brilliant account of Woolf's street haunting pursuits see Rachel Bowlby, *Still Crazy After All These Years: Women, Writing and Psychoanalysis* (Routledge, 1992), ch. 1, 'Walking, Women and Writing: Virginia Woolf as *flâneuse*', pp. 1–33.

28 – See below *The Common Reader*, 'Lives of the Obscure', I 'Taylors and Edgeworths', p. 119.

29 – See *The Critical Writings of James Joyce*, ed. Ellsworth Mason and Richard Ellmann (Faber and Faber, 1959), ch. 10, 'George Meredith', editors' headnote, p. 88.

30 – See *Letters of Leonard Woolf*, ed. Frederic Spotts (Weidenfeld and Nicolson, 1989), to Vanessa Bell, 7 February 1928, p. 230.

31 – See *Virginia Woolf. To the Lighthouse. The original holograph draft.* Transcribed and edited by Susan Dick (The Hogarth Press, 1983).

32 – De Quincey was almost certainly the first person, after Coleridge and outside the immediate Wordsworth *ménage*, to read *The Prelude*, and its influence upon his own autobiographical writing was immense.

33 – See 'A Sketch of the Past', p. 86.

34 – Leslie Stephen, *Hours in a Library*, vol. i, 'De Quincey', pp. 326–7.

35 – *Ibid.*, p. 326.

36 – See Brenda Silver, *Virginia Woolf's Reading Notebooks* (Princeton University Press, 1983), regarding Eliot and Richards. The notebooks reveal a quite startling quantity of reading and much that did not surface in or necessarily relate to either essays or reviews. Nor is there reason to believe that their record is exhaustive.

37 – See the introductory notes to Woolf's articles below, pp. 335n1 and 375n1.

38 – For Woolf on Hergesheimer see *II* and *III VW Essays*.

39 – Sherwood Anderson, *A Story Teller's Story* (1924; Jonathan Cape, 1925), p. 309.

40 – It should be said that there is much evidence to suggest that even when writing the briefest of notices Woolf did not stint to read her volume through.

Editorial Note

The present volume is compiled upon the principles already established for the edition. Of the 125 pieces it includes, twenty-six make up *The Common Reader*, published by the Hogarth Press on 23 April 1925, and sixty-two are reprinted for the first time. Variants are provided here from articles (signalled by headnotes in volume III) which were included in *The Common Reader* with relatively little revision. Headnotes are similarly given in this volume for (five) essays minimally revised for inclusion in *The Common Reader: 2nd series*, which will form part of volume V. It has not been possible to accommodate an account here of the variants arising in the corrected proofs recently made available at the William Allan Neilson Library, Smith College, Northampton, Massachusetts. But it is planned to give these in an appendix to volume VI, where, too, account will be made of the American edition of *The Common Reader*, published by Harcourt, Brace and Company, on 14 May 1925, and to which the proofs relate. The essay 'Miss Ormerod', first collected in the American edition, is, however, incorporated here as one of 'The Lives of the Obscure'. Variants between versions of essays in this volume and posthumously collected, revised texts, issued by Leonard Woolf, are to be addressed, as far as proves possible, in volume VI. That volume will also collect any newly discovered essays, reviews and notices, such as those gathered from the *Times Literary Supplement* by B. J. Kirkpatrick and published in *Modern Fiction Studies* (Volume 38, number 1, Spring 1992).

The question of variants also arises in the case of co-published articles. This is particularly so for those essays that found publication on both sides of the Atlantic, most notably in the pages of the

Nation & Athenaeum on the one side and the *New Republic* on the other. As Appendix VI shows, several other periodicals were involved, but in far fewer instances. Among them was the New York journal *Arts*, edited by Virgil Barker, in which the essay 'The Cinema' appeared, only to reappear a little later in a variant form under the title 'The Movies and Reality', in the *New Republic*, to the discomfort of Barker, and no less to the embarrassment of his author. But we may be grateful for the episode because it led to a letter to Barker (*VI VW Letters*, no. 1676a; see below p. 353 n1) in which Virginia Woolf explains how this came about. The circumstances were as follows. The *New Republic* version of 'The Cinema' did not derive from the *Arts* version but from one published in the *Nation & Athenaeum*, and the *New Republic* enjoyed an arrangement with that paper whereby it could take 'certain articles . . . sent to it in proof'. In this case, it was maintained, the secretary at the *Nation & Athenaeum* had not sent proofs of 'The Cinema' to the *New Republic* and the conclusion was, therefore, that the essay had been lifted in error. Until this letter came to light it seemed just possible that minor variants in *New Republic* versions might stem from copy-editorial intervention. The absence of variants in this instance helps perhaps to give authority to *New Republic* versions. None the less, in this edition copy texts are generally taken from the *Nation & Athenaeum*, especially as the link with that paper, through the offices of Leonard Woolf, was so direct. For the most part *New Republic* versions differ only in minor features of house style. But where they differ more significantly, variants or, in the case of 'The Cinema' complete variant versions, are provided. In one instance, in connection with the *TLS*, upon subjective grounds and only technically in observance of chronology, a *New Republic* essay, 'Dorothy Osborne's Letters', has been placed in the main body of the text and the home-based version reproduced as Appendix V (a further version occurs in *The Common Reader*: 2nd series – see volume V). The truncated *Forum* version of 'On Being Ill', published as 'Illness – An Unexploited Mine', is also appended here.

As in the previous volumes the contents follow the listing in the third edition of B. J. Kirkpatrick's indispensable bibliography, with the insertion of the following: 'Julia Margaret Cameron' (p. 375); 'The Governess of Downing Street' (effectively Kp C283.1, p. 426); 'An Introduction to *Mrs Dalloway*' (p. 548). The essay 'Poetry, Fiction and the Future' retains its original title as opposed to the posthumous 'The Narrow Bridge of Art'. Like its predecessors too, the volume errs on the side of duplication. Rather than attempt to account for second *Common Reader* revision with an over-elaborate apparatus in the next volume, a number of marginal candidates for such treatment are printed in full here. The essay 'The Niece of an Earl' is included here to emphasise its chronological importance in the development and disclosure of Woolf's views on class and democracy. It will be duplicated in its place in the second *Common Reader* in volume V. Again, in a bibliographical connection, every effort has been made, using manuscript reading notes, to trace references to sources in the editions Woolf used. A great deal is known on this subject thanks to the labours of Brenda Silver and of Elizabeth Steele but a number of mysteries remain. In a few cases it has been impossible to discover the work from which a quotation derives, let alone the relevant edition, and these failures are acknowledged in the notes.

Manuscript drafts of a number of articles survive. In the holograph of *To the Lighthouse* (Berg Collection, NYPL; transcribed in Susan Dick, ed. *To the Lighthouse: The original holograph draft*, Hogarth Press, 1983): 'Robinson Crusoe' (fos 41-2); 'How Should One Read a Book?' (fos 43-4, 282; see also Berg, Diary XIV, and see Appendix III below); 'Sterne's Ghost' ['The Ghost of Sterne'] (fos 156v, 157v); 'Impassioned Prose' (fo. 336) [misidentified in Dick]. See also 10 Notebooks, 1925-40, Berg Collection. Drafts of 'How Should One Read a Book?' (ts with holograph corrections) and of 'Street Haunting' (ts with holograph corrections; corrected galleys) are housed in the *Yale Review* Papers, Beinecke Rare Book and Manuscript Collection, Yale University Library. A manuscript draft of 'The Patron and the Crocus' ['The Patron'] is in the collection of Woolf papers in the William Allan Neilson Library, Smith College.

Acknowledgements

As with the previous volumes, I wish to acknowledge The Hogarth Press and Professor Quentin Bell and Angelica Garnett, administrators of Virginia Woolf's literary estate, for support and encouragement in the preparation of this volume. I am very grateful to the British Academy for a grant towards the cost of library visits, stationery, and the expense of photocopying. My greatest debt of gratitude is to Diana McNeillie, for her support, encouragement, and extensive reading through a considerable part of the contents of the London Library, and many sacrifices. Scarcely less, but of grammatical necessity so, must I thank Gail McNeillie and James McNeillie, for all manner of reasons. At The Hogarth Press I thank Alison Samuel and those of her desk-editorial and production colleagues who did so much to help with last-minute adjustments. Myrna Blumberg copy-edited with tact, expertise, and much-appreciated hospitality in the final throes of fine-tuning. My colleagues at Blackwell Publishers have been characteristically generous in their encouragement. I wish to thank them for turning a blind eye to my somewhat monumental 'Saturday job' and for the great stimulation of their company. (Among ex-colleagues too I must especially mention Jan Chamier.) My colleagues on the editorial board of The Shakespeare Head Press Edition of Virginia Woolf and those involved in preparing editions have helped extend my knowledge in innumerable directions and I cannot thank them too fully for this and for the great warmth of their friendship. They will excuse me if I single out S. P. Rosenbaum from their ranks for special mention in despatches. I want to thank Richard Schell for sending me a copy of his indispensable but unpublished bibliography of Leonard Woolf. I thank also Brownlee Kirkpatrick for so readily keeping me abreast of discoveries. Anne Olivier Bell, with whom I served my editorial apprenticeship, generously provided me with a transcript of the manuscript draft of 'How Should One Read a Book?' which forms Appendix III; I wish also to acknowledge the Berg Collection, NYPL, for permission to publish it. Michael Reynolds gave me invaluable information regarding Ernest Hemingway's reaction to 'An Essay in Criticism' (p. 449).

Elizabeth Inglis of Sussex University Library has provided me with all manner of information and material and I am very grateful to her for finding time to do so. Ruth Mortimer of the William Allan Neilson Library, Smith College, was similarly generous. At the Library of Congress, Karl Crosby of the Publications Division helped beyond the call of duty with invaluable guidance and materials. Olwen Terris at the National Film and Television Archive, British Film Institute, also provided a research service increasingly rare to find in our grey myopic age of cuts and under-funding. I must too thank Jane Griffiths for her patient labours in the British Library in pursuit of the Duchess of Newcastle and other fugitives.

I wish to acknowledge the resources of: The London Library, without which Carlylean anachronism progress with this volume would have been even slower than it has been; The British Library (both in Bloomsbury and at Colindale, but not yet at St Pancras . . .); The Bodleian Library; The English Faculty Library, University of Oxford; and the invaluable periodicals department at London University Library.

I owe direct and indirect thanks to many individuals not yet mentioned: Julia Briggs; Hugo Brunner; Frank J. Carroll; Melba Cuddy-Keane; Dominique Enright; Christine Froula; Peter Jacobs; Jeri Johnson; Sarah Kass; Hermione Lee; Jane Marcus; The Very Reverend Michael Mayne; Louis Menand; Catherine Nelson-McDermott; David Norbrook; Bernard O'Donoghue; Tanya Pollard; Elizabeth P. Richardson; Beth Rosenberg; Irene Schubert; John Spencer; Nicola Trott; Duncan Wu; Isabel Yandle. There are almost bound to be others I have forgotten, and to them, I apologise for my lapse of memory.

Abbreviations

B&P	*Books and Portraits*, ed. Mary Lyon (Hogarth Press, London, 1977; Harcourt Brace Jovanovich, New York, 1978
CDB	*The Captain's Death Bed and Other Essays*, ed. Leonard Woolf (Hogarth Press, London, 1950; Harcourt Brace Jovanovich, New York, 1950)
CE	*Collected Essays*, 4 vols ed. Leonard Woolf (vols 1–2, Hogarth Press, London, 1966, Harcourt Brace & World Inc., New York, 1967; vols 3–4, Hogarth Press, London, and Harcourt Brace & World Inc., New York, 1967)
CR	*The Common Reader*: 1st series (Hogarth Press, London, and Harcourt Brace & Co., New York, 1925; annotated edition, 1984), 2nd series (Hogarth Press, London, and Harcourt Brace & Co., New York, 1932; annotated edition, 1986)
CSF	*The Complete Shorter Fiction*, ed. Susan Dick (Hogarth Press, London, Harcourt Brace Jovanovich, New York, 1985)
DNB	*Dictionary of National Biography*
DoM	*The Death of the Moth and Other Essays*, ed. Leonard Woolf (Hogarth Press, London, and Harcourt Brace & Co., New York, 1942)
G&R	*Granite and Rainbow*, ed. Leonard Woolf (Hogarth Press, London, and Harcourt Brace & Co., New York, 1958)
Kp	B. J. Kirkpatrick, *A Bibliography of Virginia Woolf* (third ed., Oxford University Press, Oxford, 1980)

LM	*London Mercury*
LW	Leonard Woolf, *An Autobiography*, 2 vols (Oxford University Press, Oxford, 1980)
MHP	Monks House Papers, Sussex University Library
MoB	*Moments of Being*, ed. Jeanne Schulkind (2nd ed., Hogarth Press, London, 1985; Harcourt Brace Jovanovich, New York, 1985)
Mom	*The Moment and Other Essays*, ed. Leonard Woolf (Hogarth Press, London, 1947; Harcourt Brace & Co., New York, 1948)
N&A	*Nation & Athenaeum*
NPD	*Newspaper Press Directory*
NR	*New Republic*
NYHT	*New York Herald Tribune*
NYPL	New York Public Library
QB	Quentin Bell, *Virginia Woolf. A Biography. Volume One. Virginia Stephen, 1882–1912. Volume Two. Mrs Woolf, 1912–1941.* (Hogarth Press, London, and Harcourt Brace Jovanovich Inc., New York, 1972)
TLS	*Times Literary Supplement*
VW Diary	*The Diary of Virginia Woolf*, ed. Anne Olivier Bell (5 vols, Hogarth Press, London, and Harcourt Brace Jovanovich, New York, 1977–84)
VW Essays	*The Essays of Virginia Woolf*, 6 vols
VW Letters	*The Letters of Virginia Woolf*, ed. Nigel Nicolson and Joanne Trautmann (6 vols, Hogarth Press, London, and Harcourt Brace Jovanovich, New York, 1975–80)

The Essays

1925

Notes on an Elizabethan Play

VW's essay in the *TLS*, 5 March 1925, (Kp C259) was later revised for inclusion, under the same title, in *The Common Reader*, 1st series (1925). The reader is referred to p. 62 below, where the revised version, together with variants in the form of footnotes, is printed in its place as part of *The Common Reader*.

'Coming Back to London . . .'

Coming back to London after some weeks' absence, I was shocked by a sight for which the papers had not prepared me – a battered cottage, with jagged edges and broken windows, has replaced the stately and familiar masonry of Devonshire House. At the price of a penny fare, anyone can now sit on the top of an omnibus and see into the very saloons – in which the lovely Duchess received Fox and Burke and Sheridan.[2] Attics and bedrooms are all laid bare, and whatever his politics the spectator can scarcely help a spasm of pity as he pries into the innermost parts of that old house which, though never ornamental, had during the lives of all now living worn the same familiar air of respectability and inscrutable reserve. For close on two hundred years (Devonshire House was built when Berkeley House was burnt down in 1733) wits and beauties, statesmen and politicians, have met and feasted and argued and gambled where there are now ladders and cranes and heaps of old bricks. All the brilliant, all the fair, and many who were neither the one nor the other, have passed in procession up and down the marble stairs, which, for all we know, may already be halfway across the Atlantic. Now the March wind whistles through the ruins, and the ghosts of Duchess Georgiana and her friends must wrap their cloaks about them and toss their guineas for the last time.

1–A paragraph in the 'From Alpha to Omega' column in the *N&A*, 14 March 1925, (Kp C259.1). London residence of the Duke of Devonshire, built in 1665 and rebuilt in 1734–7, Devonshire House, which stood in Piccadilly, was sold to developers in 1919. Upon its demolition car showrooms and luxury flats were erected on the site.
2–Georgiana Cavendish, Duchess of Devonshire, *née* Spencer (1757–1806); Charles James Fox (1749–1806); Edmund Burke (1729–97); Richard Brinsley Sheridan (1751–1816).

Olive Schreiner

Olive Schreiner was neither a born letter-writer nor did she choose to make herself become one. She wrote carelessly, egotistically, of her health, of her sufferings, of her beliefs and desires, as if she were talking in the privacy of her room to a friend whom she trusted. This carelessness, while it has its charm, imposes some strain on the reader. If he is not to drop the book, dispirited by the jumble and muddle of odds and ends, plans and arrangements, bulletins of health and complaints of landladies – all of which are related as if Olive Schreiner were a figure of the highest importance – he must seek some point of view which imposes unity, some revelation in the light of which this rather distant and unfamiliar figure becomes of interest. He will find it perhaps in two sentences written in the same letter the year before she died. 'Nothing matters in life but love and a great pity for all our fellows,' she writes. That, indeed, was her teaching. A few lines lower down she adds, 'It's ten days ago since I've spoken to anyone except the girl who brings up my coals and water.'[2] That was her fate. The discrepancy between what she desired and what she achieved can be felt, jarring and confusing, throughout the book. Always she is striving for something which escapes her grasp. Always some fault or misfortune interferes with her success. She loves the world at large, but cannot endure any individual in particular. Such would seem to be an outline snapshot of her position. But it is difficult to say further where the fault or the misfortune lay. Early in life she won fame and popularity enough to gratify the most ambitious with her first book, *The Story of an African Farm*. She came to England,[3] and was at once the centre of an appreciative group of distinguished men. Her husband, as he told us last year in his biography, sacrificed a livelihood so that she might pursue her work under the most favourable conditions. She herself had a profound belief in her genius, and an overwhelming enthusiasm for her convictions. Nevertheless, all the strife and agony which ring through her letters – 'The hidden agony of my life no human being understands'; 'I am a fine genius, a celebrity, and tomorrow all these people would tread me under their feet'[4] – resulted in one remarkable novel and a few other fragmentary works which no admirer of *The Story of an African Farm* would care to place beside it. But that famous book itself provides some explanation of her failure to become, as she bade fair to become, the equal of our greatest novelists. In its brilliance and power it reminds us inevitably of the Brontë novels. In it, as in them, we feel ourselves in the presence of a powerful nature which can make us see what it saw, and feel what it felt with astounding vividness. But it has the limitations of those egotistical masterpieces without a full measure of their strength. The writer's interests are local, her passions personal, and we cannot help suspecting that she has neither the width nor the strength to enter with sympathy into the experiences of minds differing from her own, or to debate questions calmly and reasonably.

Unfortunately for her fame as a writer, it was into debate and politics, and not into thought and literature, that she was impelled, chiefly by her passionate interest in sex questions. She was driven to teach, to dream and prophesy. Questions affecting women, in particular the relations between the sexes, obsessed her. There is scarcely a letter in the present volume in which she does not discuss them with passion, insight, and force, but interminably, in season and out, while her gifts as a writer were bestowed upon a stupendous work upon woman, which, though it took up her time and thought for years, remained, unfortunately, an unfinished masterpiece.[5]

Her private life, disclosed very openly in the present book, seems

equally thwarted and disappointed. Driven by asthma to travel perpetually, unrest, dissatisfaction, and, in the end, a profound loneliness, seem to take possession of her. 'I am only a broken and
untried possibility,' she wrote. And again, '. . . the only feeling I
have about my life is that I have thrown it all away, done nothing
with it.'[6] Ironically enough, when she first came to London, her
landlady turned her out because she had too many gentlemen
visitors; in her last years she was expelled because she had a German name. It is impossible not to feel for her something of the pity
and respect which all martyrs inspire in us, and not least those martyrs who are not required to sacrifice their lives to a cause, but sacrifice, perhaps more disastrously, humour and sweetness and sense of
proportion. But there were compensations; the cause itself – the
emancipation of women – was of the highest importance, and it
would be frivolous to dismiss her as a mere crank, a piece of wreck-
age used and then thrown aside as the cause triumphed onwards.
She remains even now, when the vigour of her books is spent, and
her personal sway, evidently of the most powerful, is a memory
limited to those who knew her, too uncompromising a figure to be
so disposed of. Her obsessions and her egotism are perfectly
obvious in her letters; but so, too, are her convictions, her ruthless
sincerity, and the masterly sanity which so often contrasts on the
same page with childish outbursts of unreason. Olive Schreiner was
one half of a great writer; a diamond marred by a flaw.

1–A signed review in the NR, 18 March 1925, (Kp C260) of *The Letters of Olive Schreiner 1876–1920.* Ed. S. C. Cronwright-Schreiner (Fisher Unwin Ltd, 1924). Olive Emilie Albertina Schreiner (1855–1920), whose classic *The Story of an African Farm* (1883) was originally published under the pseudonym Ralph Iron. She married in 1894 Samuel Cron Cronwright, a South African politician, who took the name Cronwright-Schreiner. His *The Life of Olive Schreiner* was published in 1924. Reading Notes (MHP, B 2O).
2–For both quotations, Schreiner, to her husband, 26 January 1919, p. 361, adapted.
3–For the first time, in 1881.
4–For both quotations, *ibid.*, to Havelock Ellis, 18 March 1889, p. 158. The first begins: 'I have never moved without a motive;'.
5–This is presumably *Woman and Labour* (1911) which Schreiner, writing to Mrs Rhys Davids, 13 April 1913, p. 324, described as 'a broken fragment'.
6–For the first quotation, *ibid.*, to Havelock Ellis, 25 July 1899, p. 227, extracted from an extensive sentence; and for the second, *ibid.*, to Mrs Francis Smith, ?1915, p. 348.

'This for Remembrance'

It is strange to remember how many distinguished lawyers have the blood of the unpunctual and unpractical poet in their veins. Marks of their relationship are indeed to be traced. Gentle, formal, courteous, fond of nature, music, and poetry – the characteristics which Lord Coleridge discerns in his grandfather, Sir John Duke Coleridge, seem more fitted for the man of letters than the lawyer; and have descended, to judge by this modest and simple volume, to his grandson. Far from thrusting his personality upon us, as he accuses himself of doing, he is almost too reticent to win our full attention. He seems to prefer to speak of his grandfather rather than of himself; to eulogise the merits of the past rather than to make any definite claim for the present. The narrative, much of which is devoted to extracts from his grandfather's diaries, tends to shrink into a succession of little notes upon famous cases, anecdotes, and reflections, which allow the writer to steal away into congenial shades of his library and give us very little chance of seeing him face to face.

1–A notice in the *N&A*, 28 March 1925, (Kp C260.01) of *This for Remembrance* (Fisher Unwin Ltd, 1925) by Bernard John Seymour Coleridge, 2nd Baron Coleridge of Ottery St Mary (1851–1927), judge. Lord Coleridge was the *son* of John Duke Coleridge, Lord Chief Justice, 1st Baron, grandson of the judge Sir John Taylor, and great-grand-nephew of the poet.

The Two Samuel Butlers

Among the sumptuous volumes of the Shrewsbury edition of the works of Samuel Butler, two will probably be opened less often than the others. *The Life and Letters of Dr Samuel Butler* cannot compare for vivacity or interest with *The Way of All Flesh* or the 'Note-Books'.[2] The book is open to criticism from many points of view. It is too long; it is too dull; it is too shapeless; for chapters at a time it reads as if a skewer had been run through a bundle of old letters, and the printer had plodded his way doggedly through the file unaided. Though ostensibly devoted to the life of Dr Butler, the figure of the Bishop himself remains transparent; the very buildings of Shrewsbury School stand before us more plainly than the person of their Headmaster. But Samuel Butler the younger had certain qualities which, if they made it impossible for him to write a good biography, made it equally impossible for him to write a dull book. He had the virtues and vices of the crank; he was honest, angular, and egotistical; something of himself enters into whatever he did; whatever he touched, even with the tips of his fingers, he twisted a little this way or that. Hence though his life of his grandfather fails as a biography, as an autobiography it is full of amusement. Without intending any such thing, by his selections and omissions, his humour and his commentary, he has, in these two volumes, written a notable description of himself, added a valuable prelude to *The Way of All Flesh*.

The salient points of Samuel Butler the younger are his originality, his eye for queer angles, and his love for odd human situations. So we find him lighting upon the story of Dr Butler and Mr Jeudwine, who, being irrevocably bound together at Shrewsbury as headmaster and second master, were so incompatible by temperament, that 'for seven and thirty years [they] addressed each other by letter. They generally wrote in the third person, and presented their compliments to one another ... The two men were reconciled as Mr Jeudwine lay on his death-bed. I have been told, but cannot vouch for it, that they took the Sacrament together – a scene than which I can imagine nothing more full of pathos.'[3] But has not Butler invented the whole thing? we ask, and was it not his genius that christened Mr Jeudwine, and his imagination that made the two schoolmasters take the Sacrament in the end, after calling each other 'Dear Sir' for seven and thirty years? Such is the potency of style that it makes its own whatever it touches, and forbids its victims to live under any other conditions than those which it dictates. Next, stuck in between a sheaf of letters about Aeschylus (and we know Butler's private opinion of that great man), we come to a far more congenial topic – the disappearance of Owen Parfitt, the bedridden shepherd of Shepton Mallet. One evening 'between light and dark, when the mowing grass was about',[4] the old man vanished from his armchair at the cottage door and was never heard of again. The Bishop and the grandson were both profoundly interested in the mystery. The Bishop sent for some derelict bones to examine; but they proved to be those of a young woman. The grandson, long afterwards, went to Shepton Mallet to make inquiries on the spot, and was rewarded by an old woman's remark that she had heard the story, 'but whether it was true, or whether it was a miracle, that we shall never know'. 'I felt,' said Butler, 'as one who had stooped to pick up a piece of glass and has found a diamond.'[5] Again, the quizzical and caustic humour of Butler, after lying submissively dormant beneath heaps of school politics and scholars' dissertations, flickers round the figure of 'old Till', the fishing scholar and parson, that red-faced 'queer old rogue ... who never sees me without uttering imprecations on my head for defrauding him of a beefsteak which he says I have long promised him'.[6] It alights on Porson drinking deep and talking late, and telling an undergraduate the history of his life, and how in his poverty he 'used to lie awake through the whole night, and wish for a large pearl'.[7] It shows us the Bishop picking up a human rib on the field of Waterloo, and Dr Darwin suspecting that his son Charles has damp blankets on his bed; and Mrs Butler[8] engaging a cook, and an obscure schoolboy making tradesmen and business men believe that he was a millionaire – in short, whenever we are amused or interested, it is because we see the author of *The Way of All Flesh* grinning from behind his decorous disguise. We are told very little about the Bishop, but a great deal about his acute, uncompromising, opinionated grandson, that king of the cranks, Samuel Butler.

1 – A review in the *N&A*, 11 April 1925, (Kp C260.1) of *The Life and Letters of Dr Samuel Butler* [1774–1839], *headmaster of Shrewsbury School 1798–1836, and afterwards Bishop of Lichfield in so far as they illustrate the scholastic, religious and social life of England 1790–1840* by his grandson Samuel Butler [1835–1902] (1896; vols x–xi in the Shrewsbury Edition of *The Works of Samuel Butler*, ed. Henry Festing Jones and A. T. Bartholomew, 20 vols, Jonathan Cape, 1924). See also 'A Man with a View', *II VW Essays*; 'The Way of All Flesh', *III VW Essays*. The same issue of the *N&A* contained an article by Roger Fry on 'Chinese Art' (there was no 'World of Books' column by LW that week).

2 – Samuel Butler, *The Way of All Flesh* (1903); *The Note-Books of Samuel Butler* (1912).

3 – Butler, *Works*, vol. x, ch. iv, pp. 45–6, slightly adapted. J. Jeudwine, otherwise unidentified.

4 – *Ibid.*, ch. vii, p. 104.

5 – *Ibid.*

6 – For the first quotation, *ibid.*, ch. xvi, p. 309, and for the second, *ibid.*, ch. viii, p. 126, which has: 'He never sees'. Rev. S. Tillbrook (1784–1835), sometime tutor

and bursar of Peterhouse, Cambridge, and a friend to whom Dr Butler felt 'more cordially attached' (*ibid.*, p. 125) than to any other.

7—*Ibid.*, ch. v, p. 64. Professor Richard Porson (1759–1808), classicist, of Trinity College, Cambridge.

8—Harriet Butler, *née* Apthorp, who married Dr Butler in 1798. Charles Darwin (1809–82), son of Robert Waring Darwin (1766–1848), was a pupil at Shrewsbury School, 1818–25.

'Guests and Memories: Annals of a Seaside Villa'

The works of Henry Taylor are neither acted nor much read nowadays, nevertheless his name is almost bound to be mentioned whenever the Tennysons, or the Victorians, are discussed. He has taken his place permanently, though not prominently, as a member of a circle, and is thus assured of immortality. We are familiar with the knightly-looking old man, and his flowing beard and his flowing robes, who, without our knowing exactly why, is a person of eminence and distinction among the eminent and distinguished. In this affectionate book, an impression rather than a biography, his daughter tells us something more. He was a lonely boy, bred in the North, who, observing the world through a telescope from the roof, once saw a sister greet a brother on his return with joy. This telescope vision 'was the only phenomenon of human emotion which I had witnessed for three years',[2] he observed. Later at the Colonial Office, married, after a tempestuous wooing, to Alice Spring-Rice[3] – whose vivacity and spirit are refreshingly unusual in the wives of Victorian poets – he moved of course, among all the luminaries of his time. Mrs Norton, Stevenson, Tennyson, Mrs Cameron, Jowett, Carlyle[4] – that is the circle, and they centred round Bournemouth, which Taylor discovered, a lovely village, and lived to see what it is today.

1—A notice in the *N&A*, 11 April 1925, (Kp C260.2) of *Guests and Memories. Annals of a Seaside Villa* (OUP, 1924) by Una Taylor, daughter of Sir Henry Taylor (1800–86), verse dramatist. VW made some use of Taylor's account when writing 'Julia Margaret Cameron', see below.

2—Taylor, ch. ii, p. 41, which has: 'I think this was the only phenomenon'.

3 – Sir Henry Taylor served at the Colonial Office, 1824–72; he married Theodosia Alice Spring-Rice (d. 1891) in 1839.
4 – The Hon. Mrs (Caroline Elizabeth Sarah) Norton (1808–77), poet and novelist; Robert Louis Stevenson (1850–94); Alfred Lord Tennyson (1809–92); Julia Margaret Cameron (1815–79); Benjamin Jowett (1817–93); Thomas Carlyle (1795–1881).

'Mainly Victorian'

Mr Ellis is permeated through and through with Victorianism. Not since the great Queen died have we come across the delightful excuse for publishing a book that 'many friends have desired it'. Only a Victorian, too, could call the *London Mercury*[2] 'that super-organ of the youthfully clever'. Genuine admiration has done what time, rather cruelly, accomplished but imperfectly; for all that we can see, Mr Ellis might have been born in 1837 and died in 1901. To his thinking, 'Victorian' stands for everything stately and peaceful, good, solid, happy, and 'typical of English life at its best'. This theme he has illustrated by fifty-eight papers, mainly about minor Victorians – James Grant, Frank Smedley, and Mrs Antrobus are not famous – and one or two outlaws like Tutankhamen,[3] who, though they seem to have mistaken the proper time for being born, rather flagrantly have been forgiven. Mainly Victorian the book certainly is, and for those nimble enough to hop and skip and flit and swing upon the fifty-eight perches provided, entertaining enough. But we cannot commend Mr Ellis as a judge of poetry.

1 – A notice in the *N&A*, 11 April 1925, (Kp C260.3) of *Mainly Victorian*. With Sixteen Illustrations (Hutchinson and Co., 1924) by Stewart M. Ellis. The quotations are all from Ellis's preface. See also 'Small Talk About Meredith', *III VW Essays*.
2 – A monthly founded in 1919 by J. C. Squire, for an account of which see *III VW Essays*, Appendix IV.
3 – 'James Grant [1822–87, military novelist]', pp. 108–12; 'Frank Smedley [1818–64, popular novelist and poet]', pp. 113–28; 'Mrs C. L. Antrobus [Clara Louisa Antrobus, *née* Rogers, d. 1919, popular novelist]', pp. 382–6; 'Tutankhamen and Charles the First', pp. 360–2. (Ellis also has a chapter on 'Lytton Strachey', pp. 261–2.)

John Addington Symonds

Symonds's *History of the Italian Renaissance* is, of course, a classic. Despite its faults everybody has at some time or other to read it, but for the most part the image which its readers retain of the author is of a sad and troubled man who concentrated in his own person all the spiritual suffering of the age of Clough and Matthew Arnold,[2] to which, in his own case, was added the burden of a sickly body. Mrs Vaughan's book has the great merit of rolling up this dismal legend in the most authoritative way. She has not attempted another exhaustive inquiry into the state of her father's soul;[3] she has simply noted down from old letters, diaries, her note-books, and memory an impression of her father in private life. She thus brings to light a fascinating human being, who, delicate as he was, liked nothing better than driving at a hard gallop over an Alpine pass in a snowstorm; and joked with peasants and made friends with gondoliers at the same time that he was writing reams of dismal introspection to Henry Sidgwick and Jowett.[4] Despite ill-health his life was in many ways one of singular good fortune. He married a lady of noble presence and commanding character, who shared his enthusiasm for nature and flowers, and his hatred of convention and the middle classes. He had money enough to indulge his passion for travel, and to gratify the varied whims and caprices of an alert and pleasure-loving temperament. He loved, his daughter tells us, to buy new clothes and socks and silk pocket handkerchiefs and beads and Japanese match-boxes; owls fascinated him and it was one of his 'frequent wailing worries'[5] that he could not induce these birds to nest at Davos. More seriously, he was happy above all in being freed from the provincialities of English literary life, and able to spend most of his maturity unhampered by the conventions which he despised. The bourgeoisie was detestable to him. 'The individuals, when you know them, are magnificent, superb. It is only the way of living that I rail against – what I call the hedgerow scheme of existence.'[6] His own range of interests effectually freed him from such narrowness; with all his erudition, 'he was a very shrewd observer of character into the bargain ... old ladies consulted him about their wills, young ones about their love-affairs ... Clergymen invariably consulted him on every detail concerning the new English church.'[7] The peasants came to him in their difficulties; some he would persuade to marry; others, after careful consideration, he would start in life with a gift of a carthorse or a fishing boat. They would visit him in the evening and sing their songs in a study crammed with books, where masses of proof sheets and manuscripts were piled in craggy erections which he called 'precipices'.[8] Though Mrs Vaughan makes mention of these precipices, and has first-hand knowledge of their contents, she does not disturb their dust unduly, and it is as well. For her father was not a great writer; nor indeed was he primarily interested in literature. 'Nobody,' he wrote, 'except some very dry people, ever regarded their art except as a *pis aller*,' and the words explain his own comparative failure. 'Life,' he held, 'is more than literature';[9] so that Mrs Vaughan has done right to make us look past those dusty piles of old manuscripts to the peasants and the flowers and the eccentric and amusing and romantic people who came year after year to the house at Davos and made her own youth a season of unforgettable delight.

1—A review in the *N&A*, 18 April 1925, (Kp C261) reprinted in the *NR*, 3 June 1925, of *Out of the Past*. With an account of Janet Catherine Symonds by her daughter Mrs Walter Leaf (John Murray, 1925) by Margaret Symonds (Mrs W. W. Vaughan).

John Addington Symonds (1840–93), a graduate of Balliol College, Oxford, in 1863 suffered a collapse in health some six months after winning a fellowship at Magdalen College and retired to pursue a literary career. From 1878 he spent the greatest part of his life at Davos Platz in Switzerland. He married Janet Catherine North (d. 1913) in 1864. Symonds was a friend of Leslie Stephen and a valued contributor to the *Cornhill Magazine* during Stephen's editorship. His *History of the Renaissance in Italy* was published in 1875–86. Margaret Symonds (b. 1869), his third daughter, once the object of VW's most intense affections, married W. W. Vaughan, a cousin of the Stephen children, in 1898. She died in November 1925: 'Rustling among my emotions, I found nothing better than dead leaves. Her letters had eaten away the reality – the brilliancy, the warmth. Oh detestable time, that thus eats out the heart & lets the body go on. They buried a faggot of twigs at Highgate, as far as I am concerned' (*III VW Diary*, 27 November 1925). The same issue of the *N&A* contained LW's 'World of Books' column, on 'Modern Poetry' discussing work by John Drinkwater, Edith Sitwell, Edmund Blunden, F. R. Higgins and Harold Acton.

2—Arthur Hugh Clough (1819–61); Matthew Arnold (1822–88).

3—Symonds, Intro., p. viii, referring to Horatio F. Brown's *Life of John Addington Symonds* (1895).

4—Henry Sidgwick (1838–1900), fellow of Trinity College, Cambridge, 1859–69, professor of moral philosophy in the University of Cambridge, 1883–1900, and an

Apostle. Benjamin Jowett (1817–93), from 1838 fellow and from 1870 Master of Balliol.
5–Symonds, ch. iii, p. 194.
6–*Ibid.*, p. 197, Symonds writing to Margaret Symonds, no date.
7–*Ibid.*, p. 199, which does not have: 'into the bargain'.
8–*Ibid.*, p. 203.
9–For both quotations, *ibid.*, ch. vi, p. 263.

'Further Reminiscences, 1864–1894'

This further instalment of Mr Baring-Gould's autobiography is too largely composed of letters addressed to 'My dear G.', a Mr Gatrill, a clergyman with apparently an insatiable appetite for the details of Continental travel, to be altogether lively reading for those not so endowed. 'At St Peter's the service is performed in a side chapel behind glass doors. One may enter and stand against the door and listen to the squalling of the eunuchs, gross creatures. I do not, I cannot, appreciate St Peter's . . . I detest the church; every stone in it has cost a human soul . . . The beds are good, comfortable, and clean. The *pension* price is 8 francs a day; enough for what one gets.'[2] In England, especially at Lew Trenchard, his family home, Mr Baring-Gould becomes more succulent, for he had all that zeal for local antiquities, old customs, village characters, and parish gossip which so often distinguishes our English clergy and makes their note-books excellent reading. There were witches in Devonshire in the year 1911. Burnt sacrifices were offered in the year 1879; and though 'it seems to me that we never get mutton nowadays as we did when I was young',[3] still the oldest names persist – Kneebone, Suckbitch – and the adventurous may still be bogged on Dartmoor.

1–A notice in the *N&A*, 18 April 1925, (Kp C261.1) of *Further Reminiscences, 1864–1894* (Bodley Head, 1925) by Sabine Baring-Gould (1834–1924), divine and author, whose *Early Reminiscences, 1834–1864* had been published in 1923.
2–For the matter up to the second ellipsis, Baring-Gould, ch. xvi, to Rev. J. M. Gatrill, 13 March 1889, p. 223; and for the remainder, *ibid.*, to the same, 28 February 1889, p. 222, which has 'comfortable and'.
3–*Ibid.*, ch. xi, p. 128.

'The Letters of Mary Russell Mitford'

This handy little selection from the many volumes of Miss Mitford's letters is done with skill enough to revive our interest in that cultivated old maid, who won a lottery ticket and supported an incompetent father, and wrote excellent prose and knew all the literary gentlemen of her time, and possessed the now extinct art of writing letters which can go straight to the printer without the erasion of a single word. The art of letter-writing is of all arts the most dependent upon circumstances. Had there been a telephone in the days of Cowper and Madame de Sévigné[2] we should have lost some of the most delightful volumes in the world. Nowadays, Miss Mitford's calm, long, well-considered letters would never have been written at all. The telephone would have received them or the telegraph form. As it was, Sir William Elford[3] received every few weeks long, full pages about the Elizabethan drama, Scott's novels, and the sunshine, and the flowers and the cats, and anything in short that filled the leisurely life and the well-stocked mind of his friend. She was careful to assure him that she took no pains with her writing, and held literary letters in contempt; but the apology is a little self-conscious. Delightful as they are and entertaining, one would like occasionally to feel that Miss Mitford was in a hurry, or in a temper, or had something very urgent to say. But the telephone never rang; on she wrote imperturbably.

1–A notice in the *N&A*, 18 April 1925, (Kp C261.2) of *The Letters of Mary Russell Mitford* [1787–1855], selected with an Introduction by R. Brimley Johnson (Bodley Head, 1925). See also 'Miss Mitford' in *CR 1* below; and see 'An Imperfect Lady', 'A Good Daughter' and 'The Wrong Way of Reading', *III VW Essays*.
2–William Cowper (1731–1800), upon whose correspondence VW was to write in 'Cowper and Lady Austen', in *CR 2* and *V VW Essays*. For VW on Madame de Sévigné (1626–96), see *VI VW Essays* and *DoM*.
3–Sir William Elford (1749–1837), banker, politician and accomplished amateur painter.

The
Common Reader

To Lytton Strachey

'The Common Reader'

There is a sentence in Dr Johnson's Life of Gray which might well be written up in all those rooms, too humble to be called libraries, yet full of books, where the pursuit of reading is carried on by private people. '. . . I rejoice to concur with the common reader; for by the common sense of readers, uncorrupted by literary prejudices, after all the refinements of subtilty and the dogmatism of learning, must be finally decided all claim to poetical honours.' It defines their qualities; it dignifies their aims; it bestows upon a pursuit which devours a great deal of time, and is yet apt to leave behind it nothing very substantial, the sanction of the great man's approval.

The common reader, as Dr Johnson implies, differs from the critic and the scholar. He is worse educated, and nature has not gifted him so generously. He reads for his own pleasure rather than to impart knowledge or correct the opinions of others. Above all, he is guided by an instinct to create for himself, out of whatever odds and ends he can come by, some kind of whole – a portrait of a man, a sketch of an age, a theory of the art of writing. He never ceases, as he reads, to run up some rickety and ramshackle fabric which shall give him the temporary satisfaction of looking sufficiently like the real object to allow of affection, laughter, and argument. Hasty, inaccurate, and superficial, snatching now this poem, now that scrap of old furniture, without caring where he finds it or of what nature it may be so long as it serves his purpose and rounds his structure, his deficiencies as a critic are too obvious to be pointed out; but if he has, as Dr Johnson maintained, some say in the final distribution of poetical honours, then, perhaps, it may be worth while to write down a few of the ideas and opinions which, insignificant in themselves, yet contribute to so mighty a result.

1–Samuel Johnson, *Lives of the English Poets* (1779–81), 'Gray', opening of the final paragraph, which begins: 'In the character of his *Elegy* [*Written in a Country Churchyard*, 1751] I rejoice . . .' The passage is quoted in VW's Reading Notes (MHP, B 2d).

The Pastons and Chaucer

The Tower of Caister Castle still rises ninety feet into the air, and the arch still stands from which Sir John Fastolf's barges sailed out to fetch stone for the building of the great castle.[2] But now jackdaws nest on the tower, and of the castle, which once covered six acres of ground, only ruined walls remain, pierced by loop-holes and surmounted by battlements, though there are neither archers within nor cannon without. As for the 'seven religious men' and the 'seven poor folk'[3] who should, at this very moment, be praying for the souls of Sir John and his parents, there is no sign of them nor sound of their prayers. The place is a ruin. Antiquaries speculate and differ.

Not so very far off lie more ruins – the ruins of Bromholm Priory, where John Paston[4] was buried, naturally enough, since his house was only a mile or so away, lying on low ground by the sea, twenty miles north of Norwich. The coast is dangerous, and the land, even in our time, inaccessible. Nevertheless, the little bit of wood at Bromholm, the fragment of the true Cross, brought pilgrims incessantly to the Priory, and sent them away with eyes opened and limbs straightened. But some of them with their newly opened eyes saw a sight which shocked them – the grave of John Paston in Bromholm Priory without a tombstone. The news spread over the country-side. The Pastons had fallen; they that had been so powerful could no longer afford a stone to put above John Paston's head. Margaret, his widow, could not pay her debts; the eldest son, Sir John, wasted his property upon women and tournaments, while the younger, John also, though a man of greater parts, thought more of his hawks than of his harvests.[5]

The pilgrims of course were liars, as people whose eyes have just been opened by a piece of the true Cross have every right to be; but their news, none the less, was welcome. The Pastons had risen in the world. People said even that they had been bondmen not so very long ago. At any rate, men still living could remember John's grandfather Clement tilling his own land, a hard-working peasant;[6] and William, Clement's son, becoming a judge and buying land; and John, William's son, marrying well and buying more land and quite lately inheriting the vast new castle at Caister, and all Sir John's lands in Norfolk and Suffolk. People said that he had forged the old knight's will. What wonder, then, that he lacked a tombstone? But, if we consider the character of Sir John Paston, John's eldest son, and his upbringing and his surroundings, and the relations between himself and his father as the family letters reveal them, we shall see how difficult it was, and how likely to be neglected – this business of making his father's tombstone.

For let us imagine, in the most desolate part of England known to us at the present moment, a raw, new-built house, without telephone, bathroom or drains, armchairs or newspapers, and one shelf perhaps of books, unwieldy to hold, expensive to come by. The windows look out upon a few cultivated fields and a dozen hovels, and beyond them there is the sea on one side, on the other a vast fen. A single road crosses the fen, but there is a hole in it, which, one of the farm hands reports, is big enough to swallow a carriage. And, the man adds, Tom Topcroft, the mad bricklayer, has broken loose again and ranges the country half-naked, threatening to kill anyone who approaches him. That is what they talk about at dinner in the desolate house, while the chimney smokes horribly, and the draught lifts the carpets on the floor. Orders are given to lock all gates at sunset, and, when the long dismal evening has worn itself away, simply and solemnly, girt about the dangers as they are, these isolated men and women fall upon their knees in prayer.

In the fifteenth century, however, the wild landscape was broken suddenly and very strangely by vast piles of brand-new masonry. There rose out of the sand-hills and heaths of the Norfolk coast a huge bulk of stone, like a modern hotel in a watering-place; but there was no parade, no lodging-houses, and no pier at Yarmouth then, and this gigantic building on the outskirts of the town was built to house one solitary old gentleman without any children – Sir John Fastolf, who had fought at Agincourt and acquired great wealth. He had fought at Agincourt and got but little reward. No one took his advice. Men spoke ill of him behind his back. He was well aware of it; his temper was none the sweeter for it. He was a hot-tempered old man, powerful, embittered by a sense of grievance. But whether on the battlefield or at court he thought perpetually of Caister, and how, when his duties allowed, he would settle down on his father's land and live in a great house of his own building.

The gigantic structure of Caister Castle was in progress not so many miles away when the little Pastons were children. John Paston, the father, had charge of some part of the business, and the children listened, as soon as they could listen at all, to talk of stone and building, of barges gone to London and not yet returned, of the twenty-six private chambers, of the hall and chapel; of foundations, measurements, and rascally work-people. Later, in 1454, when the work was finished and Sir John had come to spend his last years at Caister, they may have seen for themselves the mass of treasure that was stored there; the tables laden with gold and silver plate; the wardrobes stuffed with gowns of velvet and satin and cloth of gold, with hoods and tippets and beaver hats and leather jackets and velvet doublets; and how the very pillow-cases on the beds were of green and purple silk. There were tapestries everywhere. The beds were laid and the bedrooms hung with tapestries representing sieges, hunting and hawking, men fishing, archers shooting, ladies playing on their harps, dallying with ducks, or a giant 'bearing the leg of a bear in his hand'.[7] Such were the fruits of a well-spent life. To buy land, to build great houses, to stuff these houses full of gold and silver plate (though the privy might well be in the bedroom), was the proper aim of mankind. Mr and Mrs Paston spent the greater part of their energies in the same exhausting occupation. For since the passion to acquire was universal, one could never rest secure in one's possessions for long. The outlying parts of one's property were in perpetual jeopardy. The Duke of Norfolk might covet this manor, the Duke of Suffolk that. Some trumped-up excuse, as for instance that the Pastons were bondmen, gave them the right to seize the house and batter down the lodges in the owner's absence. And how could the owner of Paston and Mauteby and Drayton and Gresham be in five or six places at once, especially now that Caister Castle was his, and he must be in London trying to get his rights recognised by the King? The King was mad too, they said; did not know his own child, they said; or the King was in flight; or there was civil war in the land. Norfolk was always the most distressed of counties and its country gentlemen the most quarrelsome of mankind. Indeed, had Mrs Paston chosen, she could have told her children how when she was a young woman a thousand men with bows and arrows and pans of burning fire had marched upon Gresham and broken the gates and mined the walls of the room where she sat alone. But much worse things than that had happened to women. She neither bewailed her lot nor thought herself a heroine. The long, long letters which she wrote so laboriously in her clear cramped hand to her husband, who was (as usual) away, make no mention of herself. The sheep had wasted the hay. Heyden's and Tuddenham's men were out. A dyke had been broken and a bullock stolen. They needed treacle badly, and really she must have stuff for a dress.

But Mrs Paston did not talk about herself.

Thus the little Pastons would see their mother writing or dictating page after page, hour after hour, long long letters, but to interrupt a parent who writes so laboriously of such important matters would have been a sin. The prattle of children, the lore of the nursery or schoolroom, did not find its way into these elaborate communications. For the most part her letters are the letters of an honest bailiff to his master, explaining, asking advice, giving news, rendering accounts. There was robbery and manslaughter; it was difficult to get in the rents; Richard Calle had gathered but little money; and what with one thing and another Margaret had not had time to make out, as she should have done, the inventory of the goods which her husband desired. Well might old Agnes, surveying her son's affairs rather grimly from a distance, counsel him to contrive it so that 'ye may have less to do in the world; your father said, In little business lieth much rest. This world is but a thoroughfare, and full of woe; and when we depart therefrom, right nought bear with us but our good deeds and ill.'[8]

The thought of death would thus come upon them in a clap. Old Fastolf, cumbered with wealth and property, had his vision at the end of Hell fire, and shrieked aloud to his executors to distribute alms, and see that prayers were said 'in perpetuum', so that his soul might escape the agonies of purgatory. William Paston, the judge, was urgent too that the monks of Norwich should be retained to pray for his soul 'for ever'.[9] The soul was no wisp of air, but a solid body capable of eternal suffering, and the fire that destroyed it was as fierce as any that burnt on mortal grates. For ever there would be monks and the town of Norwich, and for ever the Chapel of Our Lady in the town of Norwich. There was something matter-of-fact, positive, and enduring in their conception both of life and of death.

With the plan of existence so vigorously marked out, children of course were well beaten, and boys and girls taught to know their places. They must acquire land; but they must obey their parents. A mother would clout her daughter's head three times a week and break the skin if she did not conform to the laws of behaviour. Agnes Paston, a lady of birth and breeding, beat her daughter Elizabeth. Margaret Paston, a softer-hearted woman, turned her daughter out of the house for loving the honest bailiff Richard Calle. Brothers would not suffer their sisters to marry beneath them, and 'sell candle and mustard in Framlingham'.[10] The fathers quarrelled with the sons, and the mothers, fonder of their boys than of their girls, yet bound by all law and custom to obey their husbands, were torn asunder in their efforts to keep the peace. With all her pains, Margaret failed to prevent rash acts on the part of her eldest son John, or the bitter words with which his father denounced him. He was a 'drone among bees', the father burst out, 'which labour for gathering honey in the fields, and the drone doth naught but taketh his part of it'.[11] He treated his parents with insolence, and yet was fit for no charge of responsibility abroad.

But the quarrel was ended, very shortly, by the death (22nd May 1466) of John Paston, the father, in London. The body was brought down to Bromholm to be buried. Twelve poor men trudged all the way bearing torches beside it. Alms were distributed; masses and dirges were said. Bells were rung. Great quantities of fowls, sheep, pigs, eggs, bread, and cream were devoured, ale and wine drunk, and candles burnt. Two panes were taken from the church windows to let out the reek of the torches. Black cloth was distributed, and a light set burning on the grave. But John Paston, the heir, delayed to make his father's tombstone.

He was a young man, something over twenty-four years of age. The discipline and the drudgery of a country life bored him. When he ran away from home, it was, apparently, to attempt to enter the King's household. Whatever doubts, indeed, might be cast by their enemies on the blood of the Pastons, Sir John was unmistakably a gentleman. He had inherited his lands; the honey was his that the bees had gathered with so much labour. He had the instincts of enjoyment rather than of acquisition, and with his mother's parsimony was strangely mixed something of his father's ambition. Yet his own indolent and luxurious temperament took the edge from both. He was attractive to women, liked society and tournaments, and court life and making bets, and sometimes, even, reading books. And so life now that John Paston was buried started afresh upon rather a different foundation. There could be little outward change indeed. Margaret still ruled the house. She still ordered the lives of the younger children as she had ordered the lives of the elder. The boys still needed to be beaten into book-learning by their tutors, the girls still loved the wrong men and must be married to the right. Rents had to be collected; the interminable lawsuit for the Fastolf property dragged on. Battles were fought; the roses of York and Lancaster alternately faded and flourished. Norfolk was full of poor people seeking redress for their grievances, and Margaret worked for her son as she had worked for her husband, with this significant change only, that now, instead of confiding in her husband, she took the advice of her priest.

But inwardly there was a change. It seems at last as if the hard outer shell had served its purpose and something sensitive, appreciative, and pleasure-loving had formed within. At any rate Sir John, writing to his brother John at home, strayed sometimes from the business on hand to crack a joke, to send a piece of gossip, or to instruct him, knowingly and even subtly, upon the conduct of a love affair. Be 'as lowly to the mother as ye list, but to the maid not too lowly, nor that ye be too glad to speed, nor too sorry to fail. And I shall always be your herald both here, if she come hither, and at home, when I come home, which I hope hastily within XI days at the furthest.'[12] And then a hawk was to be bought, a hat, or new silk laces sent down to John in Norfolk, prosecuting his suit, flying his hawks, and attending with considerable energy and not too nice a sense of honesty to the affairs of the Paston estates.

The lights had long since burnt out on John Paston's grave. But still Sir John delayed; no tomb replaced them. He had his excuses; what with the business of the lawsuit, and his duties at Court, and the disturbance of the civil wars, his time was occupied and his money spent. But perhaps something strange had happened to Sir John himself, and not only to Sir John dallying in London, but to his sister Margery falling in love with the bailiff, and to Walter making Latin verses at Eton,[13] and to John flying his hawks at Paston. Life was a little more various in its pleasures. They were not quite so sure as the elder generation had been of the rights of man and of the dues of God, of the horrors of death, and of the importance of tombstones. Poor Margaret Paston scented the change and sought uneasily, with the pen which had marched so stiffly through so many pages, to lay bare the root of her troubles. It was not that the lawsuit saddened her; she was ready to defend Caister with her own hands if need be, 'though I cannot well guide nor rule soldiers'[14] but there was something wrong with the family since the death of her husband and master. Perhaps her son had failed in his service to God; he had been too proud or too lavish in his expenditure; or perhaps he had shown too little mercy to the poor. Whatever the fault might be, she only knew that Sir John spent twice as much money as his father for less result; that they could scarcely pay their debts without selling land, wood, or household stuff ('It is a death to me to think of it');[15] while every day people spoke ill of them in the country because they left John Paston to lie without a tombstone. The money that might have bought it, or more land, and more goblets and more tapestry, was spent by Sir John on clocks and trinkets, and upon paying a clerk to copy out Treatises upon Knighthood and other such stuff. There they stood at Paston – eleven volumes, with the poems of Lydgate and Chaucer[16] among them, diffusing a strange air into the gaunt, comfortless house, inviting men to indolence and vanity, distracting their thoughts from business, and leading them not only to neglect their own profit but to think lightly of the sacred dues of the dead.

For sometimes, instead of riding off on his horse to inspect his crops or bargain with his tenants, Sir John would sit, in broad daylight, reading. There, on the hard chair in the comfortless room with the wind lifting the carpet and the smoke stinging his eyes, he would sit reading Chaucer, wasting his time, dreaming – or what strange intoxication was it that he drew from books? Life was rough, cheerless, and disappointing. A whole year of days would pass fruitlessly in dreary business, like dashes of rain on the window-pane. There was no reason in it as there had been for his father; no imperative need to establish a family and acquire an important position for children who were not born, of if born, had no right to bear their father's name. But Lydgate's poems or Chaucer's, like a mirror in which figures move brightly, silently, and compactly, showed him the very skies, fields, and people whom he knew, but rounded and complete. Instead of waiting listlessly for news from London or piecing out from his mother's gossip some country tragedy of love and jealousy, here, in a few pages, the whole story was laid before him. And then as he rode or sat at table he would remember some description or saying which bore upon the present moment and fixed it, or some string of words would charm him, and putting aside the pressure of the moment, he would hasten home to sit in his chair and learn the end of the story.

To learn the end of the story – Chaucer can still make us wish to do that. He has pre-eminently that story-teller's gift, which is almost the rarest gift among writers at the present day. Nothing happens to us as it did to our ancestors; events are seldom important; if we recount them, we do not really believe in them; we have perhaps things of greater interest to say, and for these reasons natural story-tellers like Mr Garnett, whom we must distinguish from self-conscious story-tellers like Mr Masefield, have become rare.[17] For the story-teller, besides his indescribable zest for facts, must tell his story craftily, without undue stress or excitement, or we shall swallow it whole and jumble the parts together; he must let us stop, give us time to think and look about us, yet always be persuading us to move on. Chaucer was helped to this to some extent by the time of his birth; and in addition he had another advantage over the moderns which will never come the way of English poets again. England was an unspoilt country. His eyes rested on a virgin land, all unbroken grass and wood except for the small towns and an occasional castle in the building. No villa roofs peered through Kentish tree-tops; no factory chimney smoked on the hill-side. The state of the country, considering how poets go to Nature, how they use her for their images and their contrasts even when they do not describe her directly, is a matter of some importance. Her cultivation or her savagery influences the poet far more profoundly than the prose writer. To the modern poet, with Birmingham, Manchester, and London the size they are, the country is the sanctuary of moral excellence in contrast with the town which is the sink of vice. It is a retreat, the haunt of modesty and virtue, where men go to hide and moralise. There is something morbid, as if shrinking from human contact, in the Nature worship of Wordsworth, still more in the microscopic devotion which Tennyson[18] lavished upon the petals of roses and the buds of lime trees. But these were great poets. In their hands, the country was no mere jeweller's shop, or museum of curious objects to be described, even more curiously, in words. Poets of smaller gift, since the view is so much spoilt, and the garden or the meadow must replace the barren heath and the precipitous mountain-side, are now confined to little landscapes, to birds' nests, to acorns with every wrinkle drawn to the life. The wider landscape is lost.

But to Chaucer the country was too large and too wild to be altogether agreeable. He turned instinctively, as if he had painful experience of their nature, from tempests and rocks to the bright May

day and the jocund landscape, from the harsh and mysterious to the
gay and definite. Without possessing a tithe of the virtuosity in
word-painting which is the modern inheritance, he could give, in a
few words, or even, when we come to look, without a single word
of direct description, the sense of the open air.

> And se the fresshe floures how they sprynge[19]

— that is enough.

Nature, uncompromising, untamed, was no looking-glass for
happy faces, or confessor of unhappy souls. She was herself; sometimes, therefore, disagreeable enough and plain, but always in
Chaucer's pages with the hardness and the freshness of an actual
presence. Soon, however, we notice something of greater importance than the gay and picturesque appearance of the mediaeval
world — the solidity which plumps it out, the conviction which
animates the characters. There is immense variety in the *Canterbury
Tales*, and yet, persisting underneath, one consistent type. Chaucer
has his world; he has his young men; he has his young women. If
one met them straying in Shakespeare's world one would know
them to be Chaucer's, not Shakespeare's. He wants to describe a
girl, and this is what she looks like;

> Ful semely hir wimpel pinched was,
> Hir nose tretys; hir eyen greye as glas;
> Hir mouth ful smal, and ther-to soft and reed;
> But sikerly she hadde a fair foreheed;
> It was almost a spanne brood, I trowe;
> For, hardily, she was nat undergrowe.[20]

Then he goes on to develop her; she was a girl, a virgin, cold in her
virginity:

> I am, thou woost, yet of thy companye,
> A mayde, and love hunting and venerye,
> And for to walken in the wodes wilde,
> And noght to been a wyf and be with childe.[21]

Next he bethinks him how

> Discreet she was in answering alway;
> And though she had been as wise as Pallas
> No countrefeted termes hadde she
> To seme wys; but after hir degree
> She spak, and alle hir wordes more and lesse
> Souninge in vertu and in gentillesse.[22]

Each of these quotations, in fact, comes from a different Tale, but they are parts, one feels, of the same personage, whom he had in mind, perhaps unconsciously, when he thought of a young girl, and for this reason, as she goes in and out of the *Canterbury Tales* bearing different names, she has a stability which is only to be found where the poet has made up his mind about young women, of course, but also about the world they live in, its end, its nature, and his own craft and technique, so that his mind is free to apply its force fully to its object. It does not occur to him that his Griselda might be improved or altered. There is no blur about her, no hesitation; she proves nothing; she is content to be herself. Upon her, therefore, the mind can rest with that unconscious ease which allows it, from hints and suggestions, to endow her with many more qualities than are actually referred to. Such is the power of conviction, a rare gift, a gift shared in our day by Joseph Conrad[23] in his earlier novels, and a gift of supreme importance, for upon it the whole weight of the building depends. Once believe in Chaucer's young men and women and we have no need of preaching or protest. We know what he finds good, what evil; the less said the better. Let him get on with his story, paint knights and squires, good women and bad, cooks, shipmen, priests, and we will supply the landscape, give his society its belief, its standing towards life and death, and make of the journey to Canterbury a spiritual pilgrimage.

This simple faithfulness to his own conceptions was easier then than now in one respect at least, for Chaucer could write frankly where we must either say nothing or say it slyly. He could sound every note in the language instead of finding a great many of the best gone dumb from disuse, and thus, when struck by daring fingers, giving off a loud discordant jangle out of keeping with the rest. Much of Chaucer – a few lines perhaps in each of the Tales – is improper and gives us as we read it the strange sensation of being naked to the air after being muffled in old clothing. And, as a certain kind of humour depends upon being able to speak without self-consciousness of the parts and functions of the body, so with the advent of decency literature lost the use of one of its limbs. It lost its power to create the Wife of Bath, Juliet's nurse, and their recognisable though already colourless relation, Moll Flanders. Sterne, from fear of coarseness, is forced into indecency. He must be witty, not humorous; he must hint instead of speaking outright. Nor can we believe, with Mr Joyce's *Ulysses* before us, that laughter of the old kind will ever be heard again.[24]

> But, lord Christ! When that it remembreth me
> Up-on my yowthe, and on my Iolitee,
> It tikleth me aboute myn herte rote.
> Unto this day it doth myn herte bote
> That I have had my world as in my tyme.[25]

The sound of that old woman's voice is still.

But there is another and more important reason for the surprising brightness, the still effective merriment of the *Canterbury Tales*. Chaucer was a poet; but he never flinched from the life that was being lived at the moment before his eyes. A farmyard, with its straw, its dung, its cocks and its hens, is not (we have come to think) a poetic subject; poets seem either to rule out the farmyard entirely or to require that it shall be a farmyard in Thessaly and its pigs of mythological origin. But Chaucer says outright:

> Three large sowes hadde she, and namo,
> Three kyn, and eek a sheep that highte Malle;[26]

or again,

> A yard she hadde, enclosed al aboute
> With stikkes, and a drye ditch with-oute.[27]

He is unabashed and unafraid. He will always get close up to his object — an old man's chin —

> With thikke bristles of his berde unsofte,
> Lyk to the skin of houndfish, sharp as brere;[28]

or an old man's neck —

> The slakke skin aboute his nekke shaketh
> Whyl that he sang;[29]

and he will tell you what his characters wore, how they looked, what they ate and drank, as if poetry could handle the common facts of this very moment of Tuesday, the sixteenth day of April, 1387, without dirtying her hands. If he withdraws to the time of the Greeks or the Romans, it is only that his story leads him there. He has no desire to wrap himself round in antiquity, to take refuge in age, or to shirk the associations of common grocer's English.

Therefore when we say that we know the end of the journey, it is hard to quote the particular lines from which we take our knowledge. Chaucer fixed his eyes upon the road before him, not upon the world to come. He was little given to abstract contemplation. He deprecated, with peculiar archness, any competition with the scholars and divines:

> The answere of this I lete to divynis,
> But wel I woot, that in this world grey pyne is.[30]

> What is this world? What asketh men to have?
> Now with his love, now in the colde grave
> Allone, withouten any companye,[31]

> O cruel goddes, that governe
> This world with binding of your worde eterne,
> And wryten in the table of athamaunt
> Your parlement, and your eterne graunt,
> What is mankinde more un-to yow holde
> Than is the sheepe, that rouketh in the folde?[32]

Questions press upon him; he asks questions, but he is too true a poet to answer them; he leaves them unsolved, uncramped by the solution of the moment, and thus fresh for the generations that come after him. In his life, too, it would be impossible to write him down a man of this party or of that, a democrat or an aristocrat. He was a staunch churchman, but he laughed at priests. He was an able public servant and a courtier, but his views upon sexual morality were extremely lax. He sympathised with poverty, but did nothing to improve the lot of the poor. It is safe to say that not a single law has been framed or one stone set upon another because of anything that Chaucer said or wrote; and yet, as we read him, we are absorbing morality at every pore. For among writers there are two kinds: there are the priests who take you by the hand and lead you straight up to the mystery; there are the laymen who imbed their doctrines in flesh and blood and make a complete model of the world without excluding the bad or laying stress upon the good. Wordsworth, Coleridge, and Shelley are among the priests; they give us text after text to be hung upon the wall, saying after saying to be laid upon the heart like an amulet against disaster –

> Farewell, farewell, the heart that lives alone[33]

> He prayeth best that loveth best
> All things both great and small[34]

— such lines of exhortation and command spring to memory instantly. But Chaucer lets us go our ways doing the ordinary things with the ordinary people. His morality lies in the way men and women behave to each other. We see them eating, drinking, laughing, and making love, and come to feel without a word being said what their standards are and so are steeped through and through with their morality. There can be no more forcible preaching than this where all actions and passions are represented, and instead of being solemnly exhorted we are left to stray and stare and make out a meaning for ourselves. It is the morality of ordinary intercourse, the morality of the novel, which parents and librarians rightly judge to be far more persuasive than the morality of poetry.

And so, when we shut Chaucer, we feel that without a word being said the criticism is complete; what we are saying, thinking, reading, doing, has been commented upon. Nor are we left merely with the sense, powerful though that is, of having been in good company and got used to the ways of good society. For as we have jogged through the real, the unadorned country-side, with first one good fellow cracking his joke or singing his song and then another, we know that though this world resembles, it is not in fact our daily world. It is the world of poetry. Everything happens here more quickly and more intensely, and with better order than in life or in prose; there is a formal elevated dullness which is part of the incantation of poetry; there are lines speaking half a second in advance what we were about to say, as if we read our thoughts before words cumbered them; and lines which we go back to read again with that heightened quality, that enchantment which keeps them glittering in the mind long afterwards. And the whole is held in its place, and its variety and divagations ordered by the power which is among the most impressive of all — the shaping power, the architect's power. It is the peculiarity of Chaucer, however, that though we feel at once this quickening, this enchantment, we cannot prove it by quotation. From most poets quotation is easy and obvious; some metaphor suddenly flowers; some passage breaks off from the rest. But Chaucer is very equal, very even-paced, very unmetaphorical. If we take six or seven lines in the hope that the quality will be contained in them it has escaped.

> My lord, ye woot that in my fadres place,
> Ye dede me strepe out of my povre wede,
> And richely me cladden, o your grace

To yow broghte I noght elles, out of drede,
But feyth and nakedness and maydenhede.[35]

In its place that seemed not only memorable and moving but fit to
set beside striking beauties. Cut out and taken separately it appears
ordinary and quiet. Chaucer, it seems, has some art by which the
most ordinary words and the simplest feelings when laid side by
side make each other shine; when separated, lose their lustre. Thus
the pleasure he gives us is different from the pleasure that other
poets give us, because it is more closely connected with what we
have ourselves felt or observed. Eating, drinking, and fine weather,
the May, cocks and hens, millers, old peasant women, flowers –
there is a special stimulus in seeing all these common things so
arranged that they affect us as poetry affects us, and are yet bright,
sober, precise as we see them out of doors. There is a pungency in
this unfigurative language; a stately and memorable beauty in the
undraped sentences which follow each other like women so slightly
veiled that you see the lines of their bodies as they go –

And she set down hir water pot anon
Biside the threshold in an oxe's stall.[36]

And then, as the procession takes its way, out from behind peeps
the face of Chaucer, in league with all foxes, donkeys, and hens, to
mock the pomps and ceremonies of life – witty, intellectual, French,
at the same time based upon a broad bottom of English humour.

So Sir John read his Chaucer in the comfortless room with the wind
blowing and the smoke stinging, and left his father's tombstone unmade. But no book, no tomb, had power to hold him long. He was
one of those ambiguous characters who haunt the boundary line
where one age merges in another and are not able to inherit either.
At one moment he was all for buying books cheap; next he was off
to France and told his mother, 'My mind is now not most upon
books.'[37] In his own house, where his mother Margaret was perpetually making out inventories or confiding in Gloys the priest, he
had no peace or comfort. There was always reason on her side; she
was a brave woman, for whose sake one must put up with the
priest's insolence and choke down one's rage when the grumbling
broke into open abuse, and 'Thou proud priest' and 'Thou proud
Squire'[38] were bandied angrily about the room. All this, with the
discomforts of life and the weakness of his own character, drove

him to loiter in pleasanter places, to put off coming, to put off writing, to put off, year after year, the making of his father's tombstone.

Yet John Paston had now lain for twelve years under the bare ground. The Prior of Bromholm sent word that the grave-cloth was in tatters, and he had tried to patch it himself. Worse still, for a proud woman like Margaret Paston, the country people murmured at the Pastons' lack of piety, and other families she heard, of no greater standing than theirs, spent money in pious restoration in the very church where her husband lay unremembered. At last, turning from tournaments and Chaucer and Mistress Anne Hault,[39] Sir John bethought him of a piece of cloth of gold which had been used to cover his father's hearse and might now be sold to defray the expenses of his tomb. Margaret had it in safe keeping; she had hoarded it and cared for it, and spent twenty marks on its repair. She grudged it; but there was no help for it. She sent it him, still distrusting his intentions or his power to put them into effect. 'If you sell it to any other use,' she wrote, 'by my troth I shall never trust you while I live.'[40]

But this final act, like so many that Sir John had undertaken in the course of his life, was left undone. A dispute with the Duke of Suffolk in the year 1479 made it necessary for him to visit London in spite of the epidemic of sickness that was abroad; and there, in dirty lodgings, alone, busy to the end with quarrels, clamorous to the end for money, Sir John died and was buried at Whitefriars in London. He left a natural daughter; he left a considerable number of books; but his father's tomb was still unmade.

The four thick volumes of the Paston letters, however, swallow up this frustrated man as the sea absorbs a raindrop. For, like all collections of letters, they seem to hint that we need not care overmuch for the fortunes of individuals. The family will go on, whether Sir John lives or dies. It is their method to heap up in mounds of insignificant and often dismal dust the innumerable trivialities of daily life, as it grinds itself out, year after year. And then suddenly they blaze up; the day shines out, complete, alive, before our eyes. It is early morning, and strange men have been whispering among the women as they milk. It is evening, and there in the church-yard Warne's wife bursts out against old Agnes Paston: 'All the devils of Hell draw her soul to Hell.'[41] Now it is the autumn in Norfolk, and Cecily Dawne comes whining to Sir John for clothing. 'Moreover, Sir, liketh it your mastership to understand that winter and cold weather draweth nigh and I have few clothes but of your gift.'[42] There is the ancient day, spread out before us, hour by hour.

But in all this there is no writing for writing's sake; no use of the pen to convey pleasure or amusement or any of the million shades of endearment and intimacy which have filled so many English letters since. Only occasionally, under stress of anger for the most part, does Margaret Paston quicken into some shrewd saw or solemn curse. 'Men cut large thongs here out of other men's leather ... We beat the bushes and other men have the birds ... Haste reweth ... which is to my heart a very spear.'[43] That is her eloquence and that her anguish. Her sons, it is true, bend their pens more easily to their will. They jest rather stiffly; they hint rather clumsily; they make a little scene like a rough puppet show of the old priest's anger and give a phrase or two directly as they were spoken in person. But when Chaucer lived he must have heard this very language, matter of fact, unmetaphorical, far better fitted for narrative than for analysis, capable of religious solemnity or of broad humour, but very stiff material to put on the lips of men and women accosting each other face to face. In short, it is easy to see, from the Paston letters, why Chaucer wrote not *Lear* or *Romeo and Juliet*, but the *Canterbury Tales*.

Sir John was buried; and John the younger brother succeeded in his turn. The Paston letters go on; life at Paston continues much the same as before. Over it all broods a sense of discomfort and nakedness; of unwashed limbs thrust into splendid clothing; of tapestry blowing on the draughty walls; of the bedroom with its privy; of winds sweeping straight over land unmitigated by hedge or town; of Caister Castle covering with solid stone six acres of ground, and of the plain-faced Pastons indefatigably accumulating wealth, treading out the roads of Norfolk, and persisting with an obstinate courage which does them infinite credit in furnishing the bareness of England.

1–This essay was written specifically for *CR1*. VW evidently proposed the topic at an early stage in the book's evolution. She mentions it, amid a catalogue of other work, in her diary entry for 15 November 1921: '... Then I must do Hardy; then I want to write a life of Newnes; then I shall have to furbish up Jacob; & one of these days, if only I could find energy to tackle the Paston letters, I must start Reading: directly I've started Reading I shall think of another novel, I daresay ...' Her reading – 'my evening with the Pastons' – finally began on 3 January 1922 but two nights later suffered 'a fortnight's lapse' (diary 22 January) caused by influenza.

The next we hear of her preparations is on 22 July when she notes: 'It takes me a week to recover from Lady Colefax ... Col-fox = black fox. This is from my Chaucer reading.' By 16 August she had begun deliberately to alternate essay-writing with fiction: 'For my own part I am laboriously dredging my mind for Mrs Dalloway & bringing up light buckets. I don't like the feeling I'm writing too quickly. I must press it together. I wrote 4 thousand words of reading in record time, 10 days; but then it was merely a quick sketch of Pastons, supplied by books. Now I break off, according to my quick change theory, to write Mrs D. (who ushers in a host of others, I begin to perceive) then I do Chaucer; & finish the first chapter early in September. By that time, I have my Greek beginning perhaps, in my head; & so the future is all pegged out ...' On 28 August she notes that she is 'beginning Greek again' and proposes finishing Chaucer on 22 September. 'The new plan of rotating my crops is working well so far:' she observes on 3 September, 'I am always in a fizz & a stew, either to get my views on Chaucer clear, or on the Odyssey, or to sketch my next chapter.' On 4 October she announces the completion of her Chaucer chapter, which, it seems from her diary entry for 28 July 1923, she yet revised still further: 'I'm working variously & with intention. I've pulled through my Chaucer ... & written ahead at The Hours ...'

VW worked from two editions by James Gairdner: *The Paston Letters A.D. 1422–1509* ... with an introduction (6 vols, Chatto and Windus, James G. Commin, 1904), which is the one cited here, and: *The Paston Letters. 1422–1509 A.D.* New ed. (3 vols, Edward Arber, 1872–5. Annotated Reprints). She also used H. S. Bennett, *The Pastons and their England. Studies in an Age of Transition* (CUP, 1922), and J. R. Green, *A Short History of the English People* (new ed., Macmillan, 1888). Her reading notes on Chaucer similarly derive from two editions: Walter W. Skeat, *The Canterbury Tales*, vol. iv in *The Complete Works* (7 vols, Clarendon Press, 1894–7), and Alfred W. Pollard, *Works* ... (Macmillan, 1898), known as the Globe Edition. She also read: G. G. Coulton, *Chaucer and his England* (Methuen, 1908); Matthew Arnold, 'General Introduction', *The English Poets*, ed. Thomas Humphry Ward, vol. i (Macmillan, 1880); and James Russell Lowell, 'Chaucer', *My Study Windows* (Osgood, 1871). See also 'The Journal of Mistress Joan Martyn', *CSF*. Reading Notes (MHP, B 2d, o, q). Reprinted *CE*.

2–Sir John Fastolf (1378–1459), soldier in the French wars and landowner, son of John Fastolf and of a daughter, otherwise unidentified, of Nicholas Park. He had begun work on the castle before 1446 and building still continued in 1453.

3–The original source of these references has not been traced but the *DNB* entry on Fastolf has: 'seven priests and seven poor folk'.

4–John Paston (1421–66) was the eldest son of William Paston (1378–1444), judge, and his wife Agnes, *née* Berry (d. 1479). His wife Margaret Mauteby is described in the *DNB* as a Norfolk heiress and a cousin of Sir John Fastolf.

5–Sir John Paston (1442–79), courtier and letter writer; Sir John the younger (d. 1503), soldier, father of Sir William, lawyer and courtier.

6–Clement Paston (d. 1419); for his son William see note 4 above.

7–Gairdner, vol. iii, inventory of 'Sir John Fastolf's wardrobe', p. 178: 'Item, j. clothe for the nether hall, of arras, with a geyaunt in the myddell, berying a legge of a bere in his honde.'

8–*Ibid.*, letter no. 363, Agnes Paston to John Paston, undated: 'Be my conseyle dypose zoureselfe as myche as ze may to have lesse to do in the worlde; zoure fadye sayde: In lityl bysnes lyeth much reste. This world is but a thorough fare, and ful of woo; and whan we departe therefro, rizth nouzght bere with us but oure good dedys and ylle. And ther knoweth no man how son God will clepe hym, and therfor it is good for every creature to be redy. Qhom God vysyteth him he lovyth.'

9 – These references to Fastolf and to William Paston have not been traced. But the entry on the latter in the *DNB* records that his son endowed a priest to pray for his soul 'for ninety years'.

10 – Gairdner, vol. v, letter no. 710, John Paston to Sir John Paston, May 1469, p. 21.

11 – *Ibid.*, vol. iv, letter no. 575, John Paston to Margaret Paston and others, 15 January 1465, p. 122.

12 – *Ibid.*, letter no. 662, Sir John Paston to John Paston, March 1467, p. 271.

13 – Walter Paston died in 1479, a few weeks after graduating at Oxford. Margery Paston married Richard Calle in 1469.

14 – Gairdner, vol. iv, letter no. 671, Margaret Paston to Sir John Paston, 11 July 1467, p. 283, which has: 'Be whos power, or favour, or supportacion that he will do this, I knowe not; but ye wote wele that I have ben affrayd ther befor this tyme, whan that I had other comfort than I have now, and I can not wele gide ner rewle sodyours, and also thei set not be a woman as thei shuld set be a man.'

15 – *Ibid.*, vol. v, letter no. 791, Margaret Paston to John Paston, 29 November 1471, p. 124: 'Yt is a deth to me to thynk up on yt.' (VW's text originally had: 'think if it' which has been emended.)

16 – John Lydgate (1370?–1451?); Geoffrey Chaucer (1340?–1400).

17 – David Garnett (1892–1981), one of the younger generation in Bloomsbury, had by 1925 published two novels in his own name: *Lady into Fox* (1922) and *A Man in the Zoo* (1924). John Masefield (1878–1967): his famous narrative poem *Reynard the Fox* was published in 1919.

18 – William Wordsworth (1770–1850); Alfred, Lord Tennyson (1809–92).

19 – Globe Edition, 'Nun's Priest's Tale', p. 137, line 4392.

20 – Skeat, vol. iv, 'The Prologue', p. 5, lines 151–6.

21 – *Ibid.*, 'The Knight's Tale', p. 66, lines 2307–10.

22 – *Ibid.*, 'Physician's Tale', p. 291, lines 48–54, which has:

> 'Discreet she was in answering alway;
> Though she were wys as Pallas, dar I seyn,
> Hir facound eek ful wommanly and pleyn,
> No countrefeted termes hadde she ...'

23 – Joseph Conrad (1857–1924), for VW on whom see 'Joseph Conrad' below.

24 – For VW on Daniel Defoe (1660?–1731), see 'Defoe' and 'Robinson Crusoe' below (*Moll Flanders*, 1722); Laurence Sterne (1713–68), see 'Sterne', *I VW Essays*, and 'The "Sentimental Journey"', *CR2* and *V VW Essays*; James Joyce (1882–1941) and *Ulysses* (1922), see also 'Modern Fiction' below.

25 – Skeat, vol. iv, 'Wife of Bath's Prologue', p. 333, lines 469–73.

26 – *Ibid.*, 'Nun's Priest's Tale', p. 271, lines 4020–1, which has: 'malle'.

27 – *Ibid.*, p. 272, lines 4037–8, which has: 'A yerd'.

28 – *Ibid.*, 'Merchant's Tale', p. 443, lines 1824–5, which has: 'brere'.

29 – *Ibid.*, p. 444, lines 1849–50, which continues: 'so chaunteth he and craketh'.

30 – *Ibid.*, 'Knight's Tale', p. 39, lines 1323–4.

31–*Ibid.*, p. 79, lines 2777–9, which has: 'what asketh' and 'with-outen'.

32–*Ibid.*, p. 38, lines 1303–8.

33–First line, penultimate stanza, of Wordsworth's 'Elegiac Stanzas Suggested by a Picture of Peele Castle ... 1805'. (Percy Bysshe Shelley, 1792–1822.)

34–S. T. Coleridge, *The Ancient Mariner* (1798), lines 647–8.

35–Skeat, 'Clerk's Tale', p. 415, lines 862–6.

36–*Ibid.*, p. 398, lines 290–1, which has: 'And she sette doun hir water-pot anoon/ Bisyde the threshfold, in an oxes stalle,'.

37–Gairdner, vol. v, letter no. 865, Sir John Paston to Margaret Paston, 22 February 1475, p. 225.

38–No source for these quotations has been traced.

39–According to the *DNB*, Sir John, who never married, was 'plighted' to Anne Haute, a niece of the 1st Earl Rivers and a cousin of Edward IV's queen.

40–Gairdner, vol. v, letter no. 933, Margaret Paston to Sir John Paston, p. 323.

41–*Ibid.*, vol. ii, letter no. 207, Agnes Paston to John Paston, November 1451, p. 256.

42–*Ibid.*, vol. iv, letter no. 679, Cecily Dawne to Sir John Paston, 3 November 1463, p. 291: 'Moreover, Sir, like it your maistership to undirstand that wynter and colde weders draweth negh, and I have but fewe clothez but of your gift, God thanke you.'

43–For the quotation up to the first ellipsis, *ibid.*, letter no. 604, Margaret Paston to John Paston, 18 August 1465, p. 179; for the next quotation, *ibid.*, vol. v, letter no. 803, p. 142: 'We bette the busschysse and have the losse and the disworschuppe and ether men have the byrds.' 'Haste reweth' remains untraced. For the last quotation, *ibid.*, vol. v, letter no. 787, Margaret Paston to John Paston, 5 November 1471, p. 118: 'And it is not kepte cloos, ther be many persones now knowyn it, which me seemeth a great rebuke ... and whan I remember it, it is to myn hart a very spere, considering that he never gave comforte therein, ner of all the money that hath be reseyvyd wull never make shyft therfor.'

On Not Knowing Greek

For it is vain and foolish to talk of knowing Greek, since in our ignorance we should be at the bottom of any class of schoolboys, since we do not know how the words sounded, or where precisely we ought to laugh, or how the actors acted, and between this foreign people and ourselves there is not only difference of race and tongue but a tremendous breach of tradition. All the more strange, then, is it that we should wish to know Greek, try to know Greek, feel for ever drawn back to Greek, and be for ever making up some notion of the meaning of Greek, though from what incongruous odds and ends, with what slight resemblance to the real meaning of Greek, who shall say?

It is obvious in the first place that Greek literature is the impersonal literature. Those few hundred years that separate John Paston[2] from Plato, Norwich from Athens, make a chasm which the vast tide of European chatter can never succeed in crossing. When we read Chaucer, we are floated up to him insensibly on the current of our ancestors' lives, and later, as records increase and memories lengthen, there is scarcely a figure which has not its nimbus of association, its life and letters, its wife and family, its house, its character, its happy or dismal catastrophe. But the Greeks remain in a fastness of their own. Fate has been kind there too. She has preserved them from vulgarity. Euripides was eaten by dogs; Aeschylus killed by a stone; Sappho leapt from a cliff.[3] We know no more of them than that. We have their poetry, and that is all.

But that is not, and perhaps never can be, wholly true. Pick up any play by Sophocles, read —

Son of him who led our hosts at Troy of old, son of Agamemnon,[4]

and at once the mind begins to fashion itself surroundings. It makes some background, even of the most provisional sort, for Sophocles; it imagines some village, in a remote part of the country, near the sea. Even nowadays such villages are to be found in the wilder parts of England, and as we enter them we can scarcely help feeling that here, in this cluster of cottages, cut off from rail or city, are all the elements of a perfect existence. Here is the Rectory; here the Manor house, the farm and the cottages; the church for worship, the club for meeting, the cricket field for play. Here life is simply sorted out into its main elements. Each man and woman has his work; each works for the health or happiness of others. And here, in this little community, characters become part of the common stock; the eccentricities of the clergyman are known; the great ladies' defects of temper; the blacksmith's feud with the milkman, and the loves and matings of the boys and girls. Here life has cut the same grooves for centuries; customs have arisen; legends have attached themselves to hill-tops and solitary trees, and the village has its history, its festivals, and its rivalries.

It is the climate that is impossible. If we try to think of Sophocles here, we must annihilate the smoke and the damp and the thick wet mists. We must sharpen the lines of the hills. We must imagine a beauty of stone and earth rather than of woods and greenery. With warmth and sunshine and months of brilliant, fine weather, life of course is instantly changed; it is transacted out of doors, with the result, known to all who visit Italy, that small incidents are debated in the street, not in the sitting-room, and become dramatic; make people voluble; inspire in them that sneering, laughing, nimbleness of wit and tongue peculiar to the Southern races, which has nothing in common with the slow reserve, the low half-tones, the brooding introspective melancholy of people accustomed to live more than half the year indoors.

That is the quality that first strikes us in Greek literature, the lightning-quick, sneering, out-of-doors manner. It is apparent in the most august as well as in the most trivial places. Queens and Princesses in this very tragedy by Sophocles stand at the door bandying words like village women, with a tendency, as one might expect, to rejoice in language, to split phrases into slices, to be intent on verbal victory. The humour of the people was not good-natured like that of our postmen and cab-drivers. The taunts of men lounging at the street corners had something cruel in them as well as witty. There is a cruelty in Greek tragedy which is quite unlike our English brutality. Is not Pentheus, for example, that highly respectable man, made ridiculous in the *Bacchae*[5] before he is destroyed? In fact, of course, these Queens and Princesses were out of doors, with the bees buzzing past them, shadows crossing them, and the wind taking their draperies. They were speaking to an enormous audience rayed round them on one of those brilliant southern days when the sun is so hot and yet the air so exciting. The poet, therefore, had to bethink him, not of some theme which could be read for hours by people in privacy, but of something emphatic, familiar, brief, that would carry, instantly and directly, to an audience of seventeen thousand people perhaps, with ears and eyes eager and attentive, with bodies whose muscles would grow stiff if they sat too long without diversion. Music and dancing he would need, and naturally would choose one of those legends, like our Tristram and Iseult, which are known to every one in outline, so that a great fund of emotion is ready prepared, but can be stressed in a new place by each new poet.

Sophocles would take the old story of Electra, for instance, but would at once impose his stamp upon it. Of that, in spite of our weakness and distortion, what remains visible to us? That his genius was of the extreme kind in the first place; that he chose a design which, if it failed, would show its failure in gashes and ruin, not in the gentle blurring of some insignificant detail; which, if it succeeded, would cut each stroke to the bone, would stamp each finger-print in marble. His Electra stands before us like a figure so tightly bound that she can only move an inch this way, an inch that. But each movement must tell to the utmost, or, bound as she is, denied the relief of all hints, repetitions, suggestions, she will be nothing but a dummy, tightly bound. Her words in crisis are, as a matter of fact, bare; mere cries of despair, joy, hate

οἲ 'γὼ τάλαιν', ὅλωλα τῆδ' ἐν ἡμέα.
παῖσον, εἰ σθένεις, διπλῆν.[6]

But these cries give angle and outline to the play. It is thus, with a thousand differences of degree, that in English literature Jane Austen shapes a novel. There comes a moment – 'I will dance with you,'[7] says Emma – which rises higher than the rest, which, though not eloquent in itself, or violent, or made striking by beauty of language, has the whole weight of the book behind it. In Jane Austen, too, we have the same sense, though the ligatures are much less tight, that her figures are bound, and restricted to a few definite movements. She, too, in her modest everyday prose, chose the dangerous art where one slip means death.

But it is not so easy to decide what it is that gives these cries of Electra in her anguish their power to cut and wound and excite. It is partly that we know her, that we have picked up from little turns and twists of the dialogue hints of her character, of her appearance, which, characteristically, she neglected; of something suffering in her, outraged and stimulated to its utmost stretch of capacity, yet, as she herself knows ('my behaviour is unseemly and becomes me ill'),[8] blunted and debased by the horror of her position, an unwed girl made to witness her mother's vileness and denounce it in loud, almost vulgar, clamour to the world at large. It is partly, too, that we know in the same way that Clytemnestra is no unmitigated villainess. 'δεινὸν τὸ τίκτειν ἐστίν,' she says – 'there is a strange power in motherhood'.[9] It is no murderess, violent and unredeemed, whom Orestes kills within the house, and Electra bids him utterly destroy – 'Strike again.'[10] No; the men and women standing out in the sunlight before the audience on the hill-side were alive enough, subtle enough, not mere figures, or plaster casts of human beings.

Yet it is not because we can analyse them into feelings that they impress us. In six pages of Proust we can find more complicated and varied emotions than in the whole of the *Electra*. But in the *Electra* or in the *Antigone*[11] we are impressed by something different, by something perhaps more impressive – by heroism itself, by fidelity itself. In spite of the labour and the difficulty it is this that draws us back and back to the Greeks; the stable, the permanent, the original human being is to be found there. Violent emotions are needed to rouse him into action, but when thus stirred by death, by betrayal, by some other primitive calamity, Antigone and Ajax and Electra behave in the way in which we should behave thus struck down; the way in which everybody has always behaved; and thus we understand them more easily and more directly than we understand the characters in the *Canterbury Tales*. These are the originals, Chaucer's the varieties of the human species.

It is true, of course, that these types of the original man or woman, these heroic Kings, these faithful daughters, these tragic Queens who stalk through the ages always planting their feet in the same places, twitching their robes with the same gestures, from habit not from impulse, are among the greatest bores and the most demoralising companions in the world. The plays of Addison, Voltaire,[12] and a host of others are there to prove it. But encounter them in Greek. Even in Sophocles, whose reputation for restraint and mastery has filtered down to us from the scholars, they are decided, ruthless, direct. A fragment of their speech broken off would, we feel, colour oceans and oceans of the respectable drama. Here we meet them before their emotions have been worn into uniformity. Here we listen to the nightingale whose song echoes through English literature singing in her own Greek tongue. For the first time Orpheus with his lute makes men and beasts follow him. Their voices ring out clear and sharp; we see the hairy, tawny bodies at play in the sunlight among the olive trees, not posed gracefully on granite plinths in the pale corridors of the British Museum. And then suddenly, in the midst of all this sharpness and compression, Electra, as if she swept her veil over her face and forbade us to think of her any more, speaks of that very nightingale: 'that bird distraught with grief, the messenger of Zeus. Ah, queen of sorrow, Niobe, thee I deem divine – thee; who evermore weepest in thy rocky tomb.'[13]

And as she silences her own complaint, she perplexes us again with the insoluble question of poetry and its nature, and why, as she speaks thus, her words put on the assurance of immortality. For they are Greek; we cannot tell how they sounded; they ignore the obvious sources of excitement; they owe nothing of their effect to any extravagance of expression, and certainly they throw no light upon the speaker's character or the writer's. But they remain, something that has been stated and must eternally endure.

Yet in a play how dangerous this poetry, this lapse from the particular to the general must of necessity be, with the actors standing there in person, with their bodies and their faces passively waiting to be made use of! For this reason the later plays of Shakespeare, where there is more of poetry than of action, are better read than seen, better understood by leaving out the actual body than by having the body, with all its associations and movements, visible to the eye. The intolerable restrictions of the drama could be loosened, however, if a means could be found by which what was general and poetic, comment, not action, could be freed without interrupting the movement of the whole. It is this that the choruses supply; the old men or women who take no active part in the drama, the undifferentiated voices who sing like birds in the pauses of the wind; who can comment, or sum up, or allow the poet to speak himself or supply, by contrast, another side to his conception. Always in imaginative literature, where characters speak for themselves and the author has no part, the need of that voice is making itself felt. For though Shakespeare (unless we consider that his fools and madmen supply the part) dispensed with the chorus, novelists are always devising some substitute – Thackeray speaking in his own person. Fielding coming out and addressing the world before his curtain rises.[14] So to grasp the meaning of the play the chorus is of the utmost importance. One must be able to pass easily into those ecstasies, those wild and apparently irrelevant utterances, those sometimes obvious and commonplace statements, to decide their relevance or irrelevance, and give them their relation to the play as a whole.

We must 'be able to pass easily'; but that of course is exactly what we cannot do. For the most part the choruses, with all their obscurities, must be spelt out and their symmetry mauled. But we can guess that Sophocles used them not to express something outside the action of the play, but to sing the praises of some virtue, or the beauties of some place mentioned in it. He selects what he wishes to emphasise and sings of white Colonus and its nightingale, or of love unconquered in fight. Lovely, lofty, and serene, his choruses grow naturally out of his situations, and change, not the point of view, but the mood. In Euripides, however, the situations are not contained within themselves; they give off an atmosphere of doubt, of suggestion, of questioning; but if we look to the choruses to make this plain we are often baffled rather than instructed. At once in the *Bacchae* we are in the world of psychology and doubt; the world where the mind twists facts and changes them and makes the familiar aspects of life appear new and questionable. What is Bacchus, and who are the Gods, and what is man's duty to them, and what the rights of his subtle brain? To these questions the chorus makes no reply, or replies mockingly, or speaks darkly as if the straitness of the dramatic form had tempted Euripides to violate it, in order to relieve his mind of its weight. Time is so short and I have so much to say, that unless you will allow me to place together two apparently unrelated statements and trust to you to pull them together, you must be content with a mere skeleton of the play I might have given you. Such is the argument. Euripides therefore suffers less than Sophocles and less than Aeschylus from being read privately in a room, and not seen on a hill-side in the sunshine. He can be acted in the mind; he can comment upon the questions of the moment; more than the others he will vary in popularity from age to age.

If then in Sophocles the play is concentrated in the figures themselves, and in Euripides is to be retrieved from flashes of poetry and questions far flung and unanswered, Aeschylus makes these little dramas (the *Agamemnon* has 1663 lines; *Lear* about 2600) tremendous by stretching every phrase to the utmost, by sending them floating forth in metaphors, by bidding them rise up and stalk eyeless and majestic through the scene. To understand him it is not so necessary to understand Greek as to understand poetry. It is necessary to take that dangerous leap through the air without the support of words which Shakespeare also asks of us. For words, when opposed to such a blast of meaning, must give out, must be blown astray, and only by collecting in companies convey the meaning which each one separately is too weak to express. Connecting them in a rapid flight of the mind we know instantly and instinctively what they mean, but could not decant that meaning afresh into any other words. There is an ambiguity which is the mark of the highest

poetry; we cannot know exactly what it means. Take this from the
Agamemnon for instance –

ὀμμάτων δ' ἐν ἀχηνίαις ἔρρει πᾶσ' Ἀφροδίτα.[15]

The meaning is just on the far side of language. It is the meaning
which in moments of astonishing excitement and stress we perceive
in our minds without words; it is the meaning that Dostoevsky
(hampered as he was by prose and as we are by translation)[16] leads
us to by some astonishing run up the scale of emotions and points at
but cannot indicate; the meaning that Shakespeare succeeds in snar-
ing.

Aeschylus thus will not give, as Sophocles gives, the very words
that people might have spoken, only so arranged that they have in
some mysterious way a general force, a symbolic power, nor like
Euripides will he combine incongruities and thus enlarge his little
space, as a small room is enlarged by mirrors in odd corners. By the
bold and running use of metaphor he will amplify and give us, not
the thing itself, but the reverberation and reflection which, taken
into his mind, the thing has made; close enough to the original to
illustrate it, remote enough to heighten, enlarge, and make splendid.

For none of these dramatists had the licence which belongs to the
novelist, and, in some degree, to all writers of printed books, of
modelling their meaning with an infinity of slight touches which can
only be properly applied by reading quietly, carefully, and sometimes two or three times over. Every sentence had to explode on
striking the ear, however slowly and beautifully the words might
then descend, and however enigmatic might their final purport be.
No splendour or richness of metaphor could have saved the *Agamemnon* if either images or allusions of the subtlest or most dec-
orative had got between us and the naked cry

ὀτοτοτοῖ πόποι δᾶ. ὤ 'πολλον, ὤ 'πολλον.[17]

Dramatic they had to be at whatever cost.

But winter fell on these villages, darkness and extreme cold descended on the hill-side. There must have been some place indoors
where men could retire, both in the depths of winter and in the summer heats, where they could sit and drink, where they could lie
stretched at their ease, where they could talk. It is Plato, of course,
who reveals the life indoors, and describes how, when a party of
friends met and had eaten not at all luxuriously and drunk a little

wine, some handsome boy ventured a question, or quoted an opinion, and Socrates took it up, fingered it, turned it round, looked at it this way and that, swiftly stripped it of its inconsistencies and falsities and brought the whole company by degrees to gaze with him at the truth. It is an exhausting process; to contract painfully upon the exact meaning of words; to judge what each admission involves; to follow intently, yet critically, the dwindling and changing of opinion as it hardens and intensifies into truth. Are pleasure and good the same? Can virtue be taught? Is virtue knowledge? The tired or feeble mind may easily lapse as the remorseless questioning proceeds; but no one, however weak, can fail, even if he does not learn more from Plato, to love knowledge better. For as the argument mounts from step to step, Protagoras yielding, Socrates pushing on, what matters is not so much the end we reach as our manner of reaching it. That all can feel – the indomitable honesty, the courage, the love of truth which draw Socrates and us in his wake to the summit where, if we too may stand for a moment, it is to enjoy the greatest felicity of which we are capable.[18]

Yet such an expression seems ill fitted to describe the state of mind of a student to whom, after painful argument, the truth has been revealed. But truth is various; truth comes to us in different disguises; it is not with the intellect alone that we perceive it. It is a winter's night; the tables are spread at Agathon's house; the girl is playing the flute; Socrates has washed himself and put on sandals; he has stopped in the hall; he refuses to move when they send for him. Now Socrates has done; he is bantering Alcibiades; Alcibiades takes a fillet and binds it round 'this wonderful fellow's head'.[19] He praises Socrates. 'For he cares not for mere beauty, but despises more than any one can imagine all external possessions, whether it be beauty or wealth or glory, or any other thing for which the multitude felicitates the possessor. He esteems these things and us who honour them, as nothing, and lives among men, making all the objects of their admiration the playthings of his irony. But I know not if any one of you has ever seen the divine images which are within, when he has been opened and is serious. I have seen them, and they are so supremely beautiful, so golden, divine, and wonderful, that everything which Socrates commands surely ought to be obeyed even like the voice of a God.'[20] All this flows over the arguments of Plato – laughter and movement; people getting up and going out; the hour changing; tempers being lost; jokes cracked; the dawn rising. Truth, it seems, is various, Truth is to be pursued with all our faculties. Are we to rule out the amusements, the tendernesses, the frivolities of friendship because we love truth? Will truth be quicker found because we stop our ears to music and drink no wine, and sleep instead of talking through the long winter's night? It is not to the cloistered disciplinarian mortifying himself in solitude that we are to turn, but to the well-sunned nature, the man who practises the art of living to the best advantage, so that nothing is stunted but some things are permanently more valuable than others.

So in these dialogues we are made to seek truth with every part of us. For Plato, of course, had the dramatic genius. It is by means of that, by an art which conveys in a sentence or two the setting and the atmosphere, and then with perfect adroitness insinuates itself into the coils of the argument without losing its liveliness and grace, and then contracts to bare statement, and then, mounting, expands and soars in that higher air which is generally reached only by the more extreme measures of poetry – it is this art which plays upon us in so many ways at once and brings us to an exultation of mind which can only be reached when all the powers are called upon to contribute their energy to the whole.

But we must beware. Socrates did not care for 'mere beauty', by which he meant, perhaps, beauty as ornament. A people who judged as much as the Athenians did by ear, sitting out-of-doors at the play or listening to argument in the market-place, were far less apt than we are to break off sentences and appreciate them apart from the context. For them there were no Beauties of Hardy, Beauties of Meredith, Sayings from George Eliot. The writer had to think more of the whole and less of the detail. Naturally, living in the open, it was not the lip or the eye that struck them, but the carriage of the body and the proportions of its parts. Thus when we quote and extract we do the Greeks more damage than we do the English. There is a bareness and abruptness in their literature which grates upon a taste accustomed to the intricacy and finish of printed books. We have to stretch our minds to grasp a whole devoid of the prettiness of detail or the emphasis of eloquence. Accustomed to look directly and largely rather than minutely and aslant, it was safe for them to step into the thick of emotions which blind and bewilder an age like our own. In the vast catastrophe of the European war our emotions had to be broken up for us, and put at an angle from us, before we could allow ourselves to feel them in poetry or fiction. The only poets who spoke to the purpose spoke in the side-long, satiric manner of Wilfrid Owen and Siegfried Sassoon.[21] It was not possible for them to be direct without being clumsy; or to speak simply of emotion without being sentimental. But the Greeks could say, as if for the first time, 'Yet being dead they have not died'.[22] They could say, 'If to die nobly is the chief part of ex-cellence, to us out of all men Fortune gave this lot; for hastening to set a crown of freedom on Greece we lie possessed of praise that grows not old'.[23] They could march straight up, with their eyes open; and thus fearlessly approached, emotions stand still and suffer themselves to be looked at.

But again (the question comes back and back), Are we reading Greek as it was written when we say this? When we read these few words cut on a tombstone, a stanza in a chorus, the end or the open-ing of a dialogue of Plato's, a fragment of Sappho, when we bruise our minds upon some tremendous metaphor in the *Agamemnon* in-stead of stripping the branch of its flowers instantly as we do in reading *Lear* – are we not reading wrongly? losing our sharp sight in the haze of associations? reading into Greek poetry not what they have but what we lack? Does not the whole of Greece heap itself behind every line of its literature? They admit us to a vision of the earth unravaged, the sea unpolluted, the maturity, tried but un-broken, of mankind. Every word is reinforced by a vigour which pours out of olive-tree and temple and the bodies of the young. The nightingale has only to be named by Sophocles and she sings; the grove has only to be called ἄβατον, 'untrodden',[24] and we imagine the twisted branches and the purple violets. Back and back we are drawn to steep ourselves in what, perhaps, is only an image of the reality, not the reality itself, a summer's day imagined in the heart of a northern winter. Chief among these sources of glamour and per-haps misunderstanding is the language. We can never hope to get the whole fling of a sentence in Greek as we do in English. We can-not hear it, now dissonant, now harmonious, tossing sound from line to line across a page. We cannot pick up infallibly one by one all those minute signals by which a phrase is made to hint, to turn, to live. Nevertheless, it is the language that has us most in bondage; the desire for that which perpetually lures us back. First there is the compactness of the expression. Shelley takes twenty-one words in English to translate thirteen words of Greek – πᾶς γοῦν ποιητὴς γίγνεται, κἂν ἄμουσος ᾖ τὸ πρίν, οὗ ἂν Ἔρως ἅψηται ('. . . for everyone, even if before he were ever so undisciplined, becomes a poet as soon as he is touched by love').[25]

3Every ounce of fat has been pared off, leaving the flesh firm. Then, spare and bare as it is, no language can move more quickly, dancing, shaking, all alive, but controlled. Then there are the words themselves which, in so many instances, we have made expressive to us of our own emotions, θάλασσα, θάνατος, ἄνθος, ἀστήρ, σελήνη[26] – to take the first that come to hand; so clear, so hard, so intense, that to speak plainly yet fittingly without blurring the outline or clouding the depths, Greek is the only expression. It is useless, then, to read Greek in translations. Translators can but offer us a vague equivalent; their language is necessarily full of echoes and associations. Professor Mackail says 'wan', and the age of Burne-Jones and Morris is at once evoked.[27] Nor can the subtler stress, the flight and the fall of the words, be kept even by the most skilful of scholars –

> . . . thee, who evermore weepest in thy rocky tomb

is not

> ἅτ' ἐν τάφῳ πετραίῳ
> αἰεί δακρύεις.[28]

Further, in reckoning the doubts and difficulties there is this important problem – Where are we to laugh in reading Greek? There is a passage in the *Odyssey* where laughter begins to steal upon us, but if Homer were looking we should probably think it better to control our merriment. To laugh instantly it is almost necessary (though Aristophanes[29] may supply us with an exception) to laugh in English. Humour, after all, is closely bound up with a sense of the body. When we laugh at the humour of Wycherley,[30] we are laughing with the body of that burly rustic who was our common ancestor on the village green. The French, the Italians, the Americans, who derive physically from so different a stock, pause, as we pause in reading Homer, to make sure that they are laughing in the right place, and the pause is fatal. Thus humour is the first of the gifts to perish in a foreign tongue, and when we turn from Greek to English literature it seems, after a long silence, as if our great age were ushered in by a burst of laughter.

These are all difficulties, sources of misunderstanding, of distorted and romantic, of servile and snobbish passion. Yet even for the un-learned some certainties remain. Greek is the impersonal literature; it is also the literature of masterpieces. There are no schools; no forerunners; no heirs. We cannot trace a gradual process working in many men imperfectly until it expresses itself adequately at last in one. Again, there is always about Greek literature that air of vigour which permeates an 'age', whether it is the age of Aeschylus, or Racine,[31] or Shakespeare. One generation at least in that fortunate time is blown on to be writers to the extreme; to attain that uncon-sciousness which means that the consciousness is stimulated to the highest extent; to surpass the limits of small triumphs and tentative experiments. Thus we have Sappho with her constellations of adjec-tives; Plato daring extravagant flights of poetry in the midst of prose; Thucydides,[32] constricted and contracted; Sophocles gliding like a shoal of trout smoothly and quietly, apparently motionless, and then, with a flicker of fins, off and away; while in the *Odyssey* we have what remains the triumph of narrative, the clearest and at the same time the most romantic story of the fortunes of men and women.

The *Odyssey* is merely a story of adventure, the instinctive story-telling of a sea-faring race. So we may begin it, reading quickly in the spirit of children wanting amusement to find out what happens next. But here is nothing immature; here are full-grown people, crafty, subtle, and passionate. Nor is the world itself a small one, since the sea which separates island from island has to be crossed by little hand-made boats and is measured by the flight of the sea-gulls. It is true that the islands are not thickly populated, and the people, though everything is made by hands, are not closely kept at work. They have had time to develop a very dignified, a very stately society, with an ancient tradition of manners behind it, which makes every relation at once orderly, natural, and full of reserve. Penelope crosses the room; Telemachus goes to bed; Nausicaa washes her linen; and their actions seem laden with beauty because they do not know that they are beautiful, have been born to their possessions, are no more self-conscious than children, and yet, all those thousands of years ago, in their little islands, know all that is to be known. With the sound of the sea in their ears, vines, meadows, rivulets about them, they are even more aware than we are of a ruthless fate. There is a sadness at the back of life which they do not attempt to mitigate. Entirely aware of their own standing in the shadow, and yet alive to every tremor and gleam of existence, there they endure, and it is to the Greeks that we turn when we are sick of the vagueness, of the confusion, of the Christianity and its consolations, of our own age.

1—An essay written specifically for *CR1* for which VW began reading in the winter of 1922. 'I need not say that my wild duck stank like old sea weed & had to be buried,' she wrote in her diary on 27 November. 'But I cannot dally over this incident, which in tamer days might have provided some fun, because I have such a congeries of affairs to relate, & have to steal time from the Agamemnon.' On 1 December she announced in a letter to Gerald Brenan: 'I am now going to read Greek' (*III VW Letters*, no. 1433). Two days later, in her diary, she remarked: 'I should be at Aeschylus, for I am making a complete edition, text, translation, & notes of my own — mostly copied from Verrall; but carefully gone into by me.' (The manuscript of this edition is in the Berg Collection, NYPL.) Almost a year later, on 16 November, we read in her diary: 'I'm back from lunch Lady Colefax, meet Anrep at the Tate, tea Marjorie, discuss Ralph; Leonard back from Rodmell: & in rather a fritter, too much so to read Euripides ... I'm now writing my Greek chapter in alternate bursts of hot & cold. It seems so superficial & not worth foisting off upon a world provided with so much knowledge already. Yet I really must write a book about facts once in a way. And I cant keep grinding at fiction, which however goes easier this last lap than before.' On 5 April 1924, she noted: 'As for work, I have done the Dr chapter in my novel: & am furbishing up the Greeks; the usual depressions assail me. My criticism seems to me pretty flimsy sometimes. But there is no principle, except to follow this whimsical brain implicitly, pare away the ill fitting, till I have the shape exact, & if thats no good, it is the fault of God, after all. It is He that made us, not we ourselves. I like that text.'
  For her inquiries to Saxon Sydney-Turner (a classicist of formidable erudition) and to Janet Case (who succeeded Clara Pater as VW's Greek teacher; see *I QB*, p. 68), regarding their reactions to her essay, see *III VW Letters*, nos 1557 and 1563 respectively. See also 'The Perfect Language', *II VW Essays*, and see *Jacob's Room* (1922) *passim*. Reading Notes (Berg, XIX, XXV; MHP, B 20, B 2q). Reprinted *CE*.
2—John Paston (1421–66), see 'The Pastons and Chaucer', note 4.
3—Euripides (c. 485–406 BC), according to scholarly opinion, was probably not torn to pieces by the royal hounds as the old story of his death maintains. Aeschylus (525/4–456 BC) died at Gela; according to legend he was killed when an eagle, mistaking his bald head for a stone, dropped a tortoise on it. Sappho (b. c. 612 BC), neither the date nor circumstances of whose death are known; a story survived, as evidenced here, that she jumped from a cliff out of her love for Phaon.
4—Sophocles, *Electra* (CUP), 1894), trans. Richard C. Jebb, 1–2.
5—Euripides, *The Bacchae*.
6—Sophocles, *Electra*, 674: 'Oh, miserable that I am ! I am lost this day!'
7—Jane Austen, *Emma* (1816; Penguin, 1966, ch. 38, pp. 327–8): '"Whom are you going to dance with?" asked Mr Knightley./She hesitated a moment and then replied, "With you, if you will ask me."' See also 'George Eliot' note 25, below.
8—*Electra*, 618.

9—*Ibid.*, 770.

10—*Ibid.*, 1415.

11—Sophocles, *Antigone*.

12—Joseph Addison (1672–1719), for VW on whom see below. Voltaire (1694–1778).

13—*Electra*, 149–52.

14—W. M. Thackeray (1811–63); Henry Fielding (1707–54).

15—Aeschylus, *The Agamemnon of Aeschylus* with an introduction, commentary, and translation by A. W. Verrall (Macmillan and Co., 1889), 427–8. Verrall annotates 427: ὀμμάτων ἐν ἀχηνίαις *in the want of the eyes*: 'The question is raised whether the "eyes" are those of the husband, or of the lost wife, or of the blankly-gazing statues, a question which cannot and must not be answered. The eyes of the husband seek, but no longer find, the eyes that were wont to answer, and, for lack of response, love is for him no more. It is the advantage of the language here that it is ambiguous between "absence of eyes" and "hunger of eyes".'

16—For VW on Fyodor Dostoevsky (1821–81) see 'The Russian Point of View' below.

17—Aeschylus, *Agamemnon*, 1056–7. Verrall annotates 1056: 'Cassandra leaves the chariot and comes forward, away from the palace. The prophetic frenzy is upon her and she sees both the past and the future of the bloody house – (ὁποῖ δᾶ. The origin and original meaning of these exclamations is uncertain . . .'

18—Compare with this account of the Socratic method VW's description of discussions at 46 Gordon Square, in 'Old Bloomsbury', *Moments of Being* (Hogarth Press, 1985), pp. 189–90.

19—Percy Bysshe Shelley, *Essays, Letters from Abroad, Translations and Fragments*, ed. Mrs Shelley (2 vols, Edward Moxon, 1852), vol. i, 'The Banquet. Translated from Plato', p. 124, which has: 'the wonderful head of this fellow'.

20—*Ibid.*, p. 129, which has: 'wealth, or glory' and 'so divine'.

21—Wilfred Owen (1893–1918); Siegfried Sassoon (1886–1967), for VW on whom see 'Mr Sassoon's Poems' and 'Two Soldier-Poets', *II VW Essays*.

22—J. W. Mackail, *Select Epigrams from the Greek Anthology* (Longman's Green and Co., 1908), III, Epitaphs, ii, 'On the Lacedaemonian Dead at Plataea', Simonides, p. 45, which in full reads: 'These men having set a crown of imperishable glory on their own land were folded in the dark cloud of death; yet being dead they have not died, since from on high their excellence raises them gloriously out of the house of Hades.'

23—*Ibid.*, i, 'On the Athenian Dead at Plataea', Simonides, p. 45, which has: 'for hastening to set a crown of freedom on Hellas, we lie possessed of praise that grows not old'.

24—Sophocles, *Oedipus Coloneus* (CUP, 1885), trans. Jebb, 670–7, which has: 'Colonus, where the nightingale, a constant guest, trills her clear note in the covert of green glades, dwelling amid the wine-dark ivy and the god's inviolate bowers, rich in berries and fruit, unvisited by sun, unvexed by wind of any storm.' ἄβατον does mean 'untrodden', or rather 'not to be trodden'.

25—Shelley, 'The Banquet', p. 97, Agathon's discourse.

26—The words are: sea, death, flower, star, moon.

27—John William Mackail (1859–1945), classicist, Professor of Poetry at Oxford, biographer of William Morris and husband of Burne-Jones's daughter Margaret.

28—Sophocles, *Electra*, 151–2; Jebb's translation cannot strictly be faulted.
29—Aristophanes (d. c. 385 BC), whose works include *The Birds* and *The Frogs*.
30—William Wycherley (1641–1715).
31—Jean Racine (1639–99).
32—Thucydides (c. 460–c. 395 BC), Athenian historian.

The Elizabethan Lumber Room

These magnificent volumes are not often, perhaps, read through. Part of their charm consists in the fact that Hakluyt is not so much a book as a great bundle of commodities loosely tied together, an emporium, a lumber room strewn with ancient sacks, obsolete nautical instruments, huge bales of wool, and little bags of rubies and emeralds. One is for ever untying this packet here, sampling that heap over there, wiping the dust off some vast map of the world, and sitting down in semi-darkness to snuff the strange smells of silks and leathers and ambergris, while outside tumble the huge waves of the uncharted Elizabethan sea.

For this jumble of seeds, silks, unicorns' horns, elephants' teeth, wool, common stones, turbans, and bars of gold, these odds and ends of priceless value and complete worthlessness, were the fruit of innumerable voyages, traffics, and discoveries to unknown lands in the reign of Queen Elizabeth. The expeditions were manned by 'apt young men'[2] from the West country, and financed in part by the great Queen herself. The ships, says Froude, were no bigger than modern yachts.[3] There in the river by Greenwich the fleet lay gathered, close to the Palace. 'The Privy council looked out of the windows of the court ... the ships thereupon discharge their ordnance ... and the mariners they shouted in such sort that the sky rang again with the noise thereof.'[4] Then, as the ships swung down the tide, one sailor after another walked the hatches, climbed the shrouds, stood upon the mainyards to wave his friends a last farewell. Many would come back no more. For directly England and the coast of France were beneath the horizon, the ships sailed into the unfamiliar; the air had its voices, the sea its lions and serpents, its evaporations of fire and tumultuous whirlpools. But God too was very close; the clouds but sparely hid the divinity Himself; the limbs of Satan were almost visible. Familiarly the English sailors pitted their God against the God of the Turks, who 'can speake never a word of dulnes, much lesse can he helpe them in such an extremitie ... But howsoever their God behaved himself, our God showed himself a God indeed...'[5] God was as near by sea as by land, said Sir Humfrey Gilbert, riding through the storm. Suddenly one light disappeared; Sir Humfrey Gilbert had gone beneath the waves; when morning came, they sought his ship in vain. Sir Hugh Willoughby sailed to discover the North-West Passage and made no return. The Earl of Cumberland's men, hung up by adverse winds off the coast of Cornwall for a fortnight, licked the muddy water off the deck in agony.[6] And sometimes a ragged and worn-out man came knocking at the door of an English country house and claimed to be the boy who had left it years ago to sail the seas. 'Sir William his father, and my lady his mother knew him not to be their son, until they found a secret mark, which was a wart upon one of his knees.'[7] But he had with him a black stone, veined with gold, or an ivory tusk, or a silver ingot, and urged on the village youth with talk of gold strewn over the land as stones are strewn in the fields of England. One expedition might fail, but what if the passage to the fabled land of uncounted riches lay only a little farther up the coast? What if the known world was only the prelude to some more splendid panorama? When, after the long voyage, the ships dropped anchor in the great river of the Plate and the men went exploring through the undulating lands, startling grazing herds of deer, seeing the limbs of savages between the trees, they filled their pockets with pebbles that might be emeralds or sand that might be gold; or sometimes, rounding a headland, they saw, far off, a string of savages slowly descending to the beach bearing on their heads and linking their shoulders together with heavy burdens for the Spanish King.

These are the fine stories used effectively all through the West country to decoy 'the apt young men' lounging by the harbour-side to leave their nets and fish for gold. But the voyagers were sober merchants into the bargain, citizens with the good of English trade and the welfare of English work-people at heart. The captains are reminded how necessary it is to find a market abroad for English wool; to discover the herb from which blue dyes are made; above all to make inquiry as to the methods of producing oil, since all attempts to make it from radish seed have failed. They are reminded of the misery of the English poor, whose crimes, brought about by poverty, make them 'daily consumed by the gallows'.[8] They are reminded how the soil of England had been enriched by the discoveries of travellers in the past; how Dr Linaker brought seeds of the damask rose and tulipas, and how beasts and plants and herbs, 'without which our life were to be said barbarous',[9] have all come to England gradually from abroad. In search of markets and of goods, of the immortal fame success would bring them, the apt young men set sail for the North, and were left, a little company of isolated Englishmen surrounded by snow and the huts of savages, to make what bargains they could and pick up what knowledge they might before the ships returned in the summer to fetch them home again. There they endured, an isolated company, burning on the rim of the dark. One of them, carrying a charter from his company in London, went inland as far as Moscow, and there saw the Emperor 'sitting in his chair of estate with his crown on his head, and a staff of goldsmiths' work in his left hand'.[10] All the ceremony that he saw is carefully written out, and the sight upon which the English merchant first set eyes has the brilliancy of a Roman vase dug up and stood for a moment in the sun, until, exposed to the air, seen by millions of eyes, it dulls and crumbles away. There, all these centuries, on the outskirts of the world, the glories of Moscow, the glories of Constantinople have flowered unseen. The Englishman was bravely dressed for the occasion, led 'three fair mastiffs in coats of red cloth', and carried a letter from Elizabeth 'the paper whereof did smell most fragrantly of camphor and ambergris, and the ink of perfect musk'.[11] And sometimes, since trophies from the amazing new world were eagerly awaited at home, together with unicorns' horns and lumps of ambergris and the fine stories of the engendering of whales and 'debates' of elephants and dragons whose blood, mixed, congealed into vermilion, a living sample would be sent, a live savage caught somewhere off the coast of Labrador, taken to England, and shown about like a wild beast. Next year they brought him back, and took a woman savage on board to keep him company. When they saw each other they blushed; they blushed profoundly, but the sailors, though they noted it, knew not why. Later the two savages set up house together on board ship, she attending to his wants, he nursing her in sickness. But, as the sailors noted again, the savages lived together in perfect chastity.

All this, the new words, the new ideas, the waves, the savages, the adventures, found their way naturally into the plays which were being acted on the banks of the Thames. There was an audience quick to seize upon the coloured and the high-sounding; to associate those

> frigates bottom'd with rich Sethin planks,
> Topt with the lofty firs of Lebanon,[12]

with the adventures of their own sons and brothers abroad. The Verneys, for example, had a wild boy who had gone as pirate, turned Turk, and died out there, sending back to Claydon to be kept as relics of him some silk, a turban, and a pilgrim's staff.[13] A gulf lay between the spartan domestic housecraft of the Paston women and the refined tastes of the Elizabethan Court ladies, who, grown old, says Harrison, spent their time reading histories, or 'writing volumes of their own, or translating of other men's into our English and Latin tongue',[14] while the younger ladies played the lute and the citharne and spent their leisure in the enjoyment of music. Thus, with singing and with music, springs into existence the characteristic Elizabethan extravagance; the dolphins and lavoltas of Greene; the hyperbole, more surprising in a writer so terse and muscular, of Ben Jonson.[15] Thus we find the whole of Elizabethan literature strewn with gold and silver; with talk of Guiana's rarities, and references to that America – 'O my America! my new-found-land'[16] – which was not merely a land on the map, but symbolised the unknown territories of the soul. So, over the water, the imagination of Montaigne[17] brooded in fascination upon savages, cannibals, society, and government.

But the mention of Montaigne suggests that though the influence of the sea and the voyages, of the lumber room crammed with sea beasts and horns and ivory and old maps and nautical instruments, helped to inspire the greatest age of English poetry, its effects were by no means so beneficial upon English prose. Rhyme and metre helped the poets to keep the tumult of their perceptions in order. But the prose writer, without these restrictions, accumulated clauses, petered out in interminable catalogues, tripped and stumbled over the convolutions of his own rich draperies. How little Elizabethan prose was fit for its office, how exquisitely French prose was already adapted, can be seen by comparing a passage from Sidney's *Defense of Poesie* with one from Montaigne's *Essays*.

He beginneth not with obscure definitions, which must blur the margent with interpretations, and load the memory with doubtfulness: but he cometh to you with words set in delightful proportion, either accompanied with, or prepared for the well enchanting Skill of Music, and with a.tale (forsooth) he cometh unto you, with a tale which holdeth children from play, and old men from the Chimney corner; and pretending no more, doth intend the winning of the mind from wickedness to virtue; even as the child is often brought to take most wholesome things by hiding them in such other as have a pleasant taste: which if one should begin to tell them the nature of the *Aloës* or *Rhubarbarum* they should receive, would sooner take their physic at their ears than at their mouth, so is it in men (most of which are childish in the best things, till they be cradled in their graves) glad they will be to hear the tales of Hercules . . .[18]

And so it runs on for seventy-six words more. Sidney's prose in an uninterrupted monologue, with sudden flashes of felicity and splendid phrases, which lends itself to lamentations and moralities, to long accumulations and catalogues, but is never quick, never colloquial, unable to grasp a thought closely and firmly, or to adapt itself flexibly and exactly to the chops and changes of the mind. Compared with this, Montaigne is master of an instrument which knows its own powers and limitations, and is capable of insinuating itself into crannies and crevices which poetry can never reach; capable of cadences different but no less beautiful; of subtleties and intensities which Elizabethan prose entirely ignores. He is considering the way in which certain of the ancients met death:

. . . ils l'ont faicte couler et glisser parmy la lascheté de leurs occupations accoustumées entre des garses et bons compaignons; nul propos de consolation, nulle mention de testament, nulle affectation ambitieuse de constance, nul discours de leur condition future; mais entre les jeux, les festins, facecies, entretiens communs et populaires, et la musique, et des vers amoureux.[19]

An age seems to separate Sidney from Montaigne. The English compared with the French are as boys compared with men.

But the Elizabethan prose writers, if they have the formlessness of youth, have, too, its freshness and audacity. In the same essay Sidney shapes language, masterfully and easily, to his liking; freely and naturally reaches his hand for a metaphor. To bring this prose to perfection (and Dryden's[20] prose is very near perfection) only the discipline of the stage was necessary and the growth of self-consciousness. It is in the plays, and especially in the comic passages of the plays, that the finest Elizabethan prose is to be found. The stage was the nursery where prose learnt to find its feet. For on the stage people had to meet, to quip and crank, to suffer interruptions, to talk of ordinary things.

Cler. A pox of her autumnal face, her pieced beauty! there's no man can be admitted till she be ready now-a-days, till she has painted, and perfumed, and washed, and scoured, but the boy here; and him she wipes her oiled lips upon, like a sponge. I have made a song (I pray thee hear it) on the subject.

[Page *sings*.]

Still to be neat, still to be drest, &c.

True. And I am clearly on the other side: I love a good dressing before any beauty o' the world. O, a woman is then like a delicate garden; nor is there one kind of it; she may vary every hour; take often counsel of her glass, and choose the best. If she have good ears, show them; good hair, lay it out; good legs, wear short clothes; a good hand, discover it often: practise any art to mend breath, cleanse teeth, repair eyebrows; paint and profess it.[21]

So the talk runs in Ben Jonson's *Silent Woman,* knocked into shape by interruptions, sharpened by collisions, and never allowed to settle into stagnancy or swell into turbidity. But the publicity of the stage and the perpetual presence of a second person were hostile to that growing consciousness of one's self, that brooding in solitude over the mysteries of the soul, which, as the years went by, sought expression and found a champion in the sublime genius of Sir Thomas Browne.[22] His immense egotism has paved the way for all psychological novelists, autobiographers, confession-mongers, and dealers in the curious shades of our private life. He it was who first turned from the contacts of men with men to their lonely life within. 'The world that I regard is myself; it is the microcosm of my own frame that I cast mine eye on; for the other I use it but like my globe, and turn it round sometimes for my recreation.'[23] All was mystery and darkness as the first explorer walked the catacombs swinging his lanthorn. 'I feel sometimes a hell within myself; Lucifer keeps his court in my breast; Legion is revived in me.'[24] In these solitudes there were no guides and no companions. 'I am in the dark to all the world, and my nearest friends behold me but in a cloud.'[25] The strangest thoughts and imaginings have play with him as he goes about his work, outwardly the most sober of mankind and esteemed the greatest physician in Norwich. He has wished for death. He has doubted all things. What if we are asleep in this world and the conceits of life are as mere dreams? The tavern music, the Ave Mary bell, the broken pot that the workman has dug out of the field – at the sight and sound of them he stops dead, as if transfixed by the astonishing vista that opens before his imagination. 'We carry with us the wonders we seek without us; there is all Africa and her prodigies in us.'[26] A halo of wonder encircles everything that he sees; he turns his light gradually upon the flowers and insects and grasses at his feet so as to disturb nothing in the mysterious processes of their existence. With the same awe, mixed with a sublime complacency, he records the discovery of his own qualities and attainments. He was charitable and brave and averse from nothing. He was full of feeling for others and merciless upon himself. 'For my conversation, it is like the sun's, with all men, and with a friendly aspect to good and bad.'[27] He knows six languages, the laws, the customs and policies of several states, the names of all the constellations and most of the plants of his country, and yet, so sweeping is his imagination, so large the horizon in which he sees this little figure walking that 'methinks I do not know so many as when I did but know a hundred, and had scarcely ever simpled further than Cheapside'.[28]

He is the first of the autobiographers. Swooping and soaring at the highest altitudes, he stoops suddenly with loving particularity upon the details of his own body. His height was moderate, he tells us, his eyes large and luminous; his skin dark but constantly suffused with blushes. He dressed very plainly. He seldom laughed. He collected coins, kept maggots in boxes, dissected the lungs of frogs, braved the stench of the spermaceti whale, tolerated Jews, had a good word for the deformity of the toad, and combined a scientific and sceptical attitude towards most things with an unfortunate belief in witches. In short, as we say when we cannot help laughing at the oddities of people we admire most, he was a character, and the first to make us feel that the most sublime speculations of the human imagination are issued from a particular man, whom we can love. In the midst of the solemnities of the Urn Burial we smile when he remarks that afflictions induce callosities.[29] The smile broadens to laughter as we mouth out the splendid pomposities, the astonishing conjectures of the *Religio Medici*. Whatever he writes is stamped with his own idiosyncrasy, and we first become conscious of impurities which hereafter stain literature with so many freakish colours that, however hard we try, make it difficult to be certain whether we are looking at a man or his writing. Now we are in the presence of sublime imagination; now rambling through one of the finest lumber rooms in the world – a chamber stuffed from floor to ceiling with ivory, old iron, broken pots, urns, unicorns' horns, and magic glasses full of emerald lights and blue mystery.

1–An essay written specifically for *CR1* concerning which VW was conspicuously silent in her diary and her letters, making few and scattered references to reading which, although 'Elizabethan' in character, cannot be related directly to her essay. The volumes referred to in the opening sentence are *Hakluyt's Collection of the Early Voyages, Travels and Discoveries of the English Nation*. A new edition with additions (5 vols, R. H. Evans, 1809–12), to which references are traced here. VW also owned and made notes from the eight-volume Everyman edition of Hakluyt (J. M. Dent, E. P. Dutton, 1907–8). Richard Hakluyt (1552?–1616), geographer, educated at Christ Church, Oxford, 1570–4, actively promoted English discovery and colonisation and became a member of the London or South Virginian Company. A one-volume version of *The Principal Navigations . . .* first appeared in 1589, and a three-volume edition in 1598–1600. See also: 'Traffics and Discoveries', *I VW Essays*; 'Sir Walter Raleigh', 'Traffics and Discoveries', *II VW Essays*; 'Reading', 'Sir Thomas Browne' (upon both of which VW drew particularly closely in writing the present essay) and '*Richard Hakluyt*', *III VW Essays*; 'Notes on an Elizabethan Play' below; 'The Strange Elizabethans', *CR2* and *V VW Essays*. Reading Notes (Berg, XIX), (MHP, B 2d).

2–The source of this quotation has not been traced. Elizabeth I (1533–1603).

3–James Anthony Froude (1818–94), historian and man of letters, whose *English Seamen in the Sixteenth Century* (Longmans, Green and Co., 1895), which VW uses here, consists of lectures originally given at Oxford, where, in 1892, he was appointed regius professor of modern history.

4–Hakluyt, vol. i, 'The booke of the great and mighty Emperor of Russia, and Duke of Muscovia, and of the dominions, orders and commodities thereunto belonging; drawn by Richard Chancelour', p. 272.

5–*Ibid.*, vol. ii, 'The woorthy enterprise of John Foxe an Englishman in delvering 266. Christians out of captivity of the Turks at Alexandria, the 3. of Januarie 1577', p. 250.

6–Sir Humfrey Gilbert (1539?–83), Sir Hugh Willoughby (d. 1554), George Clifford, 3rd Earl of Cumberland (1558–1605).

7–Hakluyt, vol. iii, 'The voyage of M. Hore and divers other gentlemen, to Newfoundland, and Cape Briton, in the yeere 1536 and in the 28 yere of king Henry the 8', p. 169.

8–*Ibid.*, 'A discourse written by Sir Humphrey Gilbert Knight, to prove a passage by the Northwest to Cathaia, and the East Indies' 'What commodities would ensue, this passage once discovered', '4', p. 45: 'Also we might inhabite some part of those contreyes, and settle there such needy people of our countrey, which now trouble the common wealth, and through want here at home are inforced to commit outragious offences, whereby they are dayly consumed with the gallowes.'

9–*Ibid.*, vol. ii, 'Other some things to be remembered', p. 284. Dr Thomas Linacre (1460?–1524), English humanist and physician, founder of the Royal College of Physicians.

10–*Ibid.*, vol. i, 'The Voyage, wherein Osep Napea the Moscovite Ambassador returned home into his countrey, with his entertainment at his arrivall at Colmogro: and a large description of the manners of the Countrey,' p. 352.

11–For the three mastiffs, *ibid.*, vol. ii, 'The voyage of the Susan of London . . .', p. 291; and for the fragrant letter, *ibid.*, 'A letter written by the most high and mighty

Empresse the wife of the Grand Signior Sultan Murad Can to the Queenes Majesty of England, in the yeere of our Lord, 1594,' p. 453.

12—Robert Greene (1560?–92), *Friar Bacon and Friar Bungay* (acted in 1594; *Dramatic and Poetical Works of Robert Greene and George Peele* . . ., Routledge, 1883), viii, 53–4.

13—Concerning the Verney family of Claydon in Buckinghamshire VW read *Memoirs of the Verney Family During the Seventeenth Century* (1892, 1899).

14—William Harrison, *Description of England in Shakespeare's Youth*, ed. Frederick J. Furnivall, 1877, ch. xv, p. 272. The full context of the passage reads: 'Beside these things, I could in like sort set down the ways and means, whereby our ancient ladies of the court do shun and avoid idleness, some of them exercising their fingers with the needle, others in caul work, diverse in spinning of silk, some in continuall reading either of the holie scriptures, or histories of our own or forren nations about us, and diverse in writing volumes of their own, or translating other mens into our English and Latin tongue.'

15—Ben Jonson (1572–1637).

16—John Donne (1572–1631), Elegy 19, 'To his Mistress Going to Bed' (c. 1593–8), line 27. For VW on Donne see 'Donne After Three Centuries', in *CR2* and *V VW Essays*.

17—Michel Eyquem de Montaigne (1533–92), for VW on whom see 'Montaigne' below.

18—Sir Philip Sidney (1554–86), *Defense of Poesie* or *The Apologie for Poetrie* (1595), which VW read in the tenth edition of Sidney's *The Countess of Pembroke's Arcadia* (William DuGard, 1655), pp. 550–1, spelling modernised. (The passage continues as VW remarks for exactly 76 words more.)

19—*Les Essais de Montaigne*. Publiés d'après l'édition de 1588 avec les variantes de 1595 et une notice, des notes, un glossaire et un index par H. Motheau et D. Jouaust (Paris. Libraire des Bibliophiles, 1886–9), Tome Sixième, Livre Troisiesme, ch. ix, 'De la Vanité', pp. 185–6.

20—John Dryden (1631–1700).

21—Ben Jonson, *Epicoene, or the Silent Woman* (first acted in 1609), Clerimont and Truewit, I.i.

22—Sir Thomas Browne (1605–82).

23—Browne, *Religio Medici* [1642], pt ii, sect. xi (*The Works of Sir Thomas Browne*, ed. Simon Wilkin, 4 vols, Henry G. Bohn, 1846; vol. ii, p. 110).

24—*Ibid.*, vol. ii, pt i, sect. li, p. 75, which begins: 'The heart of man is the place the devils dwell in;'.

25—*Ibid.*, pt ii, sect. iv, p. 95, which begins: 'This I perceive in myself; for'.

26—*Religio Medici* (Golden Cockerel Press, 1923), ch. i, p. 20: ';we are that bold and adventurous piece of nature which he that studies wisely learns in a compendium what others labour at in a divided piece and endless volume.'

27—*Religio Medici* (Henry G. Bohn, 1846), vol. ii, pt ii, sect. x, p. 109.

28—*Ibid.*, p. 11, sect. viii, p. 104.

29—Browne, *Urn Burial: or a discourse of the sepulchral urns lately found in Norfolk* [1658], (Golden Cockerel Press, 1923), ch. v, p. 45: 'Afflictions induce callosities; miseries are slippery, or fall like snow upon us, which notwithstanding is no unhappy stupidity.'

Notes on an Elizabethan Play

There are, it must be admitted, some highly formidable tracts in English literature, and chief among them that jungle, forest, and wilderness which is the Elizabethan drama. For many reasons, not here to be examined, Shakespeare stands out, Shakespeare who has had the light on him from his day to ours, Shakespeare who towers highest when looked at from the level of his own contemporaries. But the plays of the lesser Elizabethans — Greene, Dekker, Peele, Chapman, Beaumont and Fletcher,[2] — to adventure into that wilderness is for the ordinary reader an ordeal, an upsetting experience which plies him with questions, harries him with doubts, alternately delights and vexes him with pleasures and pains. For we are apt to forget, reading, as we tend to do, only the masterpieces of a bygone age, how great a power the body of a literature possesses to impose itself: how it will not suffer itself to be read passively, but takes us and reads us;* flouts our preconceptions; questions principles which we had got into the habit of taking for granted, and, in fact, splits us into two parts as we read, making us, even as we enjoy, yield our ground or stick to our guns.

At the outset in reading an Elizabethan play we are overcome by the extraordinary discrepancy between the Elizabethan view of reality and our own. The reality to which we have grown accustomed is, speaking roughly, based upon the life and death of some knight called Smith, who succeeded his father in the family business of pitwood importers, timber merchants and coal exporters, was well known in political, temperance, and church circles, did much for the poor of Liverpool, and died last Wednesday of pneumonia while on a visit to his son at Muswell Hill. That is the world we know. That is the reality which our poets and novelists have to expound and illuminate. Then we open the first Elizabethan play that comes to hand and read how

> I once did see
> In my young travels through Armenia
> An angry unicorn in his full career
> Charge with too swift a foot a jeweller
> That watch'd him for the treasure of his brow,
> And ere he could get shelter of a tree
> Nail him with his rich antlers to the earth.[3]

Where is Smith, we ask, where is Liverpool? And the groves of Elizabethan drama echo 'Where?' Exquisite is the delight, sublime the relief of being set free to wander in the land of the unicorn and the jeweller among dukes and grandees, Gonzaloes and Bellimperias, who spend their lives in murder and intrigue, dress up as men if they are women, as women if they are men, see ghosts, run mad, and die in the greatest profusion on the slightest provocation, uttering as they fall imprecations of superb vigour or elegies of the wildest despair. But soon the low, the relentless voice, which if we wish to identify it we must suppose typical of a reader fed on modern English literature, and French and Russian, asks why, then, with all this to stimulate and enchant, these old plays are for long stretches of time so intolerably dull? Is it not that literature, if it is to keep us on the alert through five acts or thirty-two chapters, must somehow be based on Smith, have one toe touching Liverpool, take off into whatever heights it pleases from reality? We are not so purblind as to suppose that a man because his name is Smith and he lives at Liverpool is therefore 'real'. We know indeed that this reality is a chameleon quality, the fantastic becoming as we grow used to it often the closest to the truth, the sober the furthest from it, and nothing proving a writer's greatness more than his capacity to consolidate his scene by the use of what, until he touched them, seemed wisps of cloud and threads of gossamer. Our contention merely is that there is a station, somewhere in mid-air, whence Smith and Liverpool can be seen to the best advantage; that the great artist is the man who knows where to place himself above the shifting scenery; that while he never loses sight of Liverpool he never sees it in the wrong perspective. The Elizabethans bore us, then, because their Smiths are all changed to dukes, their Liverpools to fabulous islands and palaces in Genoa. Instead of keeping a proper poise above life they soar miles into the empyrean, where nothing is visible for long hours at a time but clouds at their revelry, and a cloud landscape is not ultimately satisfactory to human eyes. The Elizabethans bore us because they suffocate our imaginations rather than set them to work.

Still, though potent enough, the boredom of an Elizabethan play is of a different quality altogether from the boredom which a nineteenth-century play, a Tennyson or a Henry Taylor play, inflicts.[4] The riot of images, the violent volubility of language, all that cloys and satiates in the Elizabethans yet appears† to be drawn up with a roar as a feeble fire is sucked up by a newspaper. There is, even in the worst, an intermittent bawling vigour which gives us the sense in our quiet armchairs of ostlers and orange-girls catching up the lines, flinging them back, hissing or stamping applause. But the deliberate drama of the Victorian age is evidently written in a study. It has for audience ticking clocks and rows of classics bound in half-morocco. There is no stamping, no applause. It does not, as, with all its faults, the Elizabethan audience did, leaven the mass with fire. Rhetorical and bombastic, the lines are flung‡ and hurried into existence and reach the same impromptu felicities, have the same lip-moulded profusion and unexpectedness, which speech sometimes achieves, but seldom in our day the deliberate, solitary pen. Indeed, half the work of the dramatists, one feels, was done in the Elizabethan age by the public.

Against that, however, is to be set the fact that the influence of the public was in many respects detestable. To its door we must lay the greatest infliction that Elizabethan drama puts upon us – the plot; the incessant, improbable, almost unintelligible convolutions which presumably gratified the spirit of an excitable and unlettered public actually in the playhouse, but only confuse and fatigue a reader with the book before him. Undoubtedly something must happen; undoubtedly a play where nothing happens is an impossibility. But we have a right to demand (since the Greeks have proved that it is perfectly possible) that what happens shall have an end in view. It shall agitate great emotions; bring into existence memorable scenes; stir the actors so say what could not be said without this stimulus. Nobody can fail to remember the plot of the *Antigone*,[5] because what happens is so closely bound up with the emotions of the actors that we remember the people and the plot at one and the same time. But who can tell us what happens in the *White Devil*, or the *Maid's Tragedy*,[6] except by remembering the story apart from the emotions which it has aroused? As for the lesser Elizabethans, like Greene and Kyd,[7] the complexities of their plots are so great, and the violence which those plots demand so terrific, that the actors themselves are obliterated and emotions which, according to our convention at least, deserve the most careful investigation, the most delicate analysis, are clean sponged off the slate. And the result is inevitable. Outside Shakespeare and perhaps Ben Jonson,[8] there are no characters in Elizabethan drama, only violences whom we know so little that we can scarcely care what becomes of them. Take any hero or heroine in those early plays – Bellimperia in the *Spanish Tragedy*[9] will serve as well as another – and can we honestly say that we care a jot for the unfortunate lady who runs the whole gamut of human misery to kill herself in the end? No more than for an animated broomstick, we must reply, and in a work dealing with men and women the prevalence of broomsticks is a drawback. But the *Spanish Tragedy* is admittedly a crude forerunner, chiefly valuable because such primitive efforts lay bare the formidable framework which greater dramatists could modify, but had to use. Ford, it is claimed, is of the school of Stendhal and of Flaubert; Ford is a psychologist. Ford is an analyst. 'This man', says Mr Havelock Ellis, 'writes of women not as a dramatist nor as a lover, but as one who has searched intimately and felt with instinctive sympathy the fibres of their hearts.'[10]

The play – *'Tis pity she's a Whore*[11] – upon which this judgement is chiefly based shows us the whole nature of Annabella spun from pole to pole in a series of tremendous vicissitudes. First, her brother tells her that he loves her; next she confesses her love for him; next finds herself with child by him; next forces herself to marry Soranzo; next is discovered; next repents; finally is killed, and it is her lover and brother who kills her. To trace the trail of feelings which such crises and calamities might be expected to breed in a woman of ordinary sensibility might have filled volumes. A dramatist, of course, has no volumes to fill. He is forced to contract. Even so, he can illumine; he can reveal enough for us to guess the rest. But what is it that we know without using microscopes and splitting hairs about the character of Annabella? Gropingly we make out that she is a spirited girl, with her defiance of her husband when he abuses her, her snatches of Italian song, her ready wit, her simple glad love-making. But of character as we understand the word there is no trace. We do not know how she reaches her conclusions, only that she has reached them. Nobody describes her. She is always at the height of her passion, never at its approach. Compare her with Anna Karenina.[12] The Russian woman is flesh and blood, nerves and temperament, has heart, brain, body and mind where the English girl is flat and crude as a face painted on a playing card; she is without depth, without range, without intricacy. But as we say this we know that we have missed something. We have let the meaning of the play slip through our hands. We have ignored the emotion which has been accumulating because it has accumulated

in places where we have not expected to find it. We have been comparing the play with prose, and the play, after all, is poetry.

The play is poetry, we say, and the novel prose. Let us attempt to
obliterate detail, and place the two before us side by side, feeling, so
far as we can, the angles and edges of each, recalling each, so far as
we are able, as a whole. Then, at once, the prime differences
emerge; the long leisurely accumulated novel; the little contracted
play; the emotion all split up, dissipated and then woven together,
slowly and gradually massed into a whole, in the novel; the emotion
concentrated, generalised, heightened in the play. What moments of
intensity, what phrases of astonishing beauty the play shot at us!

> O, my lords,
> I but deceived your eyes with antic gesture,
> When one news straight came huddling on another
> Of death! and death! and death! still I danced forward.[13]

or

> You have oft for these two lips
> Neglected cassia or the natural sweets
> Of the spring-violet: they are not yet much wither'd.[14]

With all her reality, Anna Karenina could never say

> 'You have oft for these two lips
> Neglected cassia'.

Some of the most profound of human emotions are therefore
beyond her reach. The extremes of passion are not for the novelist;
the perfect marriages of sense and sound are not for him; he must
tame his swiftness to sluggardry; keep his eyes on the ground, not
on the sky: suggest by description, not reveal by illumination. Instead of singing

> Lay a garland on my hearse
> Of the dismal yew;
> Maidens, willow branches bear;
> Say I died true,[15]

he must enumerate the chrysanthemums fading on the grave and the
undertakers' men snuffling past in their four-wheelers. How then
can we compare this lumbering and lagging art with poetry?
Granted all the little dexterities by which the novelist makes us
know the individual and recognise the real, the dramatist goes
beyond the single and the separate, shows us not Annabella in love,

but love itself; not Anna Karenina throwing herself under the train, but ruin and death and the

> ... soul, like a ship in a black storm,
> ... driven, I know not whither.[16]

So with pardonable impatience we might exclaim as we shut our Elizabethan play. But what then is the exclamation with which we close *War and Peace*?[17] Not one of disappointment; we are not left lamenting the superficiality, upbraiding the triviality of the novelist's art. Rather we are made more than ever aware of the inexhaustible richness of human sensibility. Here, in the play, we recognise the general; here, in the novel, the particular. Here we gather all our energies into a bunch and spring. Here we extend and expand and let come slowly in from all quarters deliberate impressions, accumulated messages. The mind is so saturated with sensibility, language so inadequate to its experience, that, far from ruling off one form of literature or decreeing its inferiority to others, we complain that they are still unable to keep pace with the wealth of material, and wait impatiently the creation of what may yet be devised to liberate us of the enormous burden of the unexpressed.

Thus, in spite of dullness, bombast, rhetoric, and confusion, we still read the lesser Elizabethans, still find ourselves adventuring in the land of the jeweller and the unicorn. The familiar factories of Liverpool fade into thin air and we scarcely recognise any likeness between the knight who imported timber and died of pneumonia at Muswell Hill and the Armenian Duke who fell like a Roman on his sword while the owl shrieked in the ivy and the Duchess gave birth to a stillborn babe 'mongst women howling. To join those territories and recognise the same man in different disguises we have to adjust and revise. But make the necessary alterations in perspective, draw in those filaments of sensibility which the moderns have so marvellously developed, use instead the ear and the eye which the moderns have so basely starved, hear words as they are laughed and shouted, not as they are printed in black letters on the page, see before your eyes the changing faces and living bodies of men and women – put yourself, in short, into a different but not more elementary stage of your reading development and then the true merits of Elizabethan drama will assert themselves. The power of the whole is undeniable. Theirs, too, is the word-coining genius, as if thought plunged into a sea of words and came up dripping. Theirs is that broad humour based upon the nakedness of the body, which, however arduously the public-spirited may try, is impossible since the body is draped.[5] Then at the back of this, imposing not unity but some sort of stability, is what we may briefly call a sense of the presence of the Gods. He would be a bold critic who should attempt to impose any creed upon the swarm and variety of the Elizabethan dramatists, and yet it implies some timidity if we take it for granted that a whole literature with common characteristics is a mere evaporation of high spirits, a money-making enterprise, a fluke of the mind which, owing to favourable circumstances, came off successfully. Even in the jungle and the wilderness the compass still points.

> 'Lord, Lord, that I were dead!'[18]

they are for ever crying.

> O thou soft natural death that art joint-twin
> To sweetest slumber – [19]

The pageant of the world is marvellous, but the pageant of the world is vanity.

> glories
> Of human greatness are but pleasing dreams
> And shadows soon decaying: on the stage
> Of my mortality my youth hath acted
> Some scenes of vanity – [20]

To die and be quit of it all is their desire; the bell that tolls throughout the drama is death and disenchantment.

> All life is but a wandering to find home,
> When we're gone, we're there.[21]

Ruin, weariness, death, perpetually death, stand grimly to confront the other presence of Elizabethan drama which is life: life compact of frigates, fir trees and ivory, of dolphins and the juice of July flowers, of the milk of unicorns and panthers' breath, of ropes of pearl, brains of peacocks and Cretan wine. To this, life at its most reckless and abundant, they reply

> Man is a tree that hath no top in cares,
> No root in comforts; all his power to live
> Is given to no end but t'have power to grieve.[22]

It is this echo flung back and back from the other side of the play which, if it has not the name, still has the effect of the presence of the Gods. So we ramble through the jungle, forest, and wilderness of Elizabethan drama. So we consort with Emperors and clowns, jewellers and unicorns, and laugh and exult and marvel at the splendour and humour and fantasy of it all. A noble rage consumes us when the curtain falls; we are bored too, and nauseated by the wearisome old tricks and florid bombast. A dozen deaths of full-grown men and women move us less than the suffering of one of Tolstoy's flies. Wandering in the maze of the impossible and tedious story‖ suddenly some passionate intensity seizes us; some sublimity exalts, or some melodious snatch of song enchants. It is a world full of tedium and delight, pleasure and curiosity, of extravagant laughter, poetry, and splendour. But gradually it comes over us, what then are we being denied? What is it that we are coming to want so persistently, that unless we get it instantly we must seek elsewhere? It is solitude. There is no privacy here. Always the door opens and some one comes in. All is shared, made visible, audible, dramatic. Meanwhile, as if tired with company, the mind steals off to muse in solitude; to think, not to act; to comment, not to share; to explore its own darkness, not the bright lit-up surfaces of others. It turns to Donne, to Montaigne, to Sir Thomas Browne, to the keepers of the keys of solitude.[23]¶

* – *TLS*: 'rends us'.

† – *TLS*: 'nevertheless appears'.

‡ – *TLS*: 'with all its faults – its patriotism, rhetoric and bombast – the Elizabethan audience leavened the mass with fire. The lines are flung'.

§ – *TLS*: 'Theirs is the broad humour which was possible when the body was naked; impossible, however arduously the public-spirited may try, since the body is draped.'

‖ – *TLS*: 'wandering almost suffocated in the maze of the impossible and tedious story,'.

¶ – *TLS*: ' – all keepers of the keys of solitude.'

1–Originally published in the *TLS*, 5 March 1925, (Kp C259) this essay was revised for inclusion in *CR1*. 'What do I read?' VW asked Jacques Raverat on 4 September 1924 (*III VW Letters*, no. 1496), 'On my table are ... a good many Elizabethan plays which I'm going to write about...' In her diary entry for 6 January 1925 she remarked: 'I spent this morning writing a note on an Ethan play – for which I have been reading plays all this year.' See Editorial Note, p. xxv. See also 'The Elizabethan Lumber Room' and note 1 to that essay. Reading Notes (Berg, XIX). Reprinted *CE*.

2–William Shakespeare (1564–1616); Robert Greene (1558–92), a model for Nick Greene in VW's *Orlando* (1928); Thomas Dekker (?1570–1632); George Peele

(1556–96); George Chapman (?1559–1634); Francis Beaumont (1584–1616); John Fletcher (1579–1625).

3–Chapman, *Bussy D'Ambois* (1607), II, i, spoken by Nuntius (in *The Works of George Chapman*, ed. R. H. Shepherd, Chatto and Windus, 1875, p. 148).

4–Alfred, Lord Tennyson (1809–92), whose several dramas include *Queen Mary* (1875), *Harold* (1876) and *Becket* (1884); Sir Henry Taylor (1800–86), author of *Philip von Artevelde* (1834).

5–By Sophocles. See also 'On Not Knowing Greek' above.

6–John Webster (c. 1578–c. 1632), *The White Devil* (1612); Beaumont and Fletcher, *The Maid's Tragedy* (?1610–11).

7–Thomas Kyd (1558–94).

8–Ben Jonson (1572/3–1637).

9–Kyd, *The Spanish Tragedy* (1592).

10–Havelock Ellis (1859–1939), pioneering sexologist, edited and introduced the works of John Ford (1586–after 1639) in The Mermaid Series of 'The Best Plays of the Old Dramatists' (Vizetelly, 1888); see *ibid.*, 'Introduction', p. xvii, which continues: 'He was an analyst; he strained the limits of his art to the utmost; he foreboded new ways of expression. Thus he is less nearly related to the men who wrote *Othello*, and *A Woman Killed With Kindness*, and *Valentinian*, than to those poets and artists of the naked human soul, the writer of *Le Rouge et Le Noir* [Stendhal, 1785–1842], and the yet greater writer of *Madame Bovary* [Flaubert, 1821–80].'

11–Ford, *'Tis Pity She's a Whore*, printed 1633.

12–Eponymous heroine of Tolstoy's novel of 1873–7.

13–Ford, *The Broken Heart* (printed 1633), V, iii, spoken by Calantha (Ellis, p. 279).

14–Webster, *The White Devil*, V, i, spoken by Isabella (in *The Works of John Webster*, ed. Rev. Alexander Dyce, Routledge and Sons, 1857, p. 14).

15–Beaumont and Fletcher, *The Maid's Tragedy*, II, i, Aspatia's song (in *The Works of Beaumont and Fletcher*, ed. George Darley, 2 vols, Edward Moxon, 1840, vol. i, p. 6).

16–Webster, *The White Devil*, V, vi, spoken by Vittoria (Dyce, p. 50).

17–L. N. Tolstoy, *War and Peace* (1863–9).

18–Webster, *The White Devil*, III, ii, spoken by Giovanni (Dyce, p. 24).

19–*Ibid.*, V, iii, spoken by Brachiano (*ibid.*, p. 40).

20–Ford, *The Broken Heart* (printed 1633), III, v, spoken by Penthea (Ellis, pp. 240–1).

21–Dekker, Ford and William Rowley (?1585–1626), *The Witch of Edmonton* (performed ?1621), IV, ii, spoken by Frank (ed. Ernest Rhys, Mermaid Series, 1887, p. 453).

22–Chapman, *Bussy D'Ambois*, V, iii, spoken by Tamyra (Shepherd, p. 174).

23–For VW on: John Donne (1572–1631), see 'Donne After Three Centuries' in *CR*2 and *V VW Essays*; Michel Eyquem de Montaigne (1533–92), see below; Sir Thomas Browne (1605–82), see 'The Elizabethan Lumber Room' above, and 'Sir Thomas Browne' *III VW Essays*.

Montaigne

Once at Bar-le-Duc Montaigne saw a portrait which René, King of Sicily, had painted of himself, and asked, 'Why is it not, in like manner, lawful for every one to draw himself with a pen, as he did with a crayon?'[2] Offhand one might reply, Not only is it lawful, but nothing could be easier. Other people may evade us, but our own features are almost too familiar. Let us begin. And then, when we attempt the task, the pen falls from our fingers; it is a matter of profound, mysterious, and overwhelming difficulty.

After all, in the whole of literature, how many people have succeeded in drawing themselves with a pen? Only Montaigne and Pepys and Rousseau[3] perhaps. The *Religio Medici*[4] is a coloured glass through which darkly one sees racing stars and a strange and turbulent soul. A bright polished mirror reflects the face of Boswell[5] peeping between other people's shoulders in the famous biography. But this talking of oneself, following one's own vagaries, giving the whole map, weight, colour, and circumference of the soul in its confusion, its variety, its imperfection – this art belonged to one man only: to Montaigne. As the centuries go by, there is always a crowd before that picture, gazing into its depths, seeing their own faces reflected in it, seeing more the longer they look, never being able to say quite what it is that they see. New editions testify to the perennial fascination. Here is the Navarre Society in England reprinting in five fine volumes Cotton's translation; while in France the firm of Louis Conard is issuing the complete works of Montaigne with the various readings in an edition to which Dr Armaingaud has devoted a long lifetime of research.[6]

To tell the truth about oneself, to discover oneself near at hand, is not easy.

We hear of but two or three of the ancients who have beaten this road [said Montaigne]. No one since has followed the track; 'tis a rugged road, more so than it seems, to follow a pace so rambling and uncertain, as that of the soul; to penetrate the dark profundities of its intricate internal windings; to choose and lay hold of so many little nimble motions; 'tis a new and extraordinary undertaking, and that withdraws us from the common and most recommended employments of the world.[7]

There is, in the first place, the difficulty of expression. We all indulge in the strange, pleasant process called thinking, but when it comes to saying, even to some one opposite, what we think, then how little we are able to convey! The phantom is through the mind and out of the window before we can lay salt on its tail, or slowly sinking and returning to the profound darkness which it has lit up momentarily with a wandering light. Face, voice, and accent eke out our words and impress their feebleness with character in speech. But the pen is a rigid instrument; it can say very little; it has all kinds of habits and ceremonies of its own. It is dictatorial too: it is always making ordinary men into prophets, and changing the natural stumbling trip of human speech into the solemn and stately march of pens. It is for this reason that Montaigne stands out from the legions of the dead with such irrepressible vivacity. We can never doubt for an instant that his book was himself. He refused to teach; he refused to preach; he kept on saying that he was just like other people. All his effort was to write himself down, to communicate, to tell the truth, and that is a 'rugged road, more than it seems'.

For beyond the difficulty of communicating oneself, there is the supreme difficulty of being oneself. This soul, or life within us, by no means agrees with the life outside us. If one has the courage to ask her what she thinks, she is always saying the very opposite to what other people say. Other people, for instance, long ago made up their minds that old invalidish gentlemen ought to stay at home and edify the rest of us by the spectacle of their connubial fidelity. The soul of Montaigne said, on the contrary, that it is in old age that one ought to travel, and marriage, which, rightly, is very seldom founded on love, is apt to become, towards the end of life, a formal tie better broken up. Again with politics, statesmen are always praising the greatness of Empire, and preaching the moral duty of civilising the savage. But look at the Spanish in Mexico, cried Montaigne in a burst of rage. 'So many cities levelled with the ground, so many nations exterminated . . . and the richest and most beautiful part of the world turned upside down for the traffic of pearl and pepper! Mechanic victories!'[8] And then when the peasants came and told him that they had found a man dying of wounds and deserted him for fear lest justice might incriminate them, Montaigne asked:

What could I have said to these people? 'Tis certain that this office of humanity would have brought them into trouble ... There is nothing so much, nor so grossly, nor so ordinarily faulty as the laws.[9]

Here the soul, getting restive, is lashing out at the more palpable forms of Montaigne's great bugbears, convention and ceremony. But watch her as she broods over the fire in the inner room of that tower which, though detached from the main building, has so wide a view over the estate. Really she is the strangest creature in the world, far from heroic, variable as a weathercock, 'bashful, insolent; chaste, lustful; prating, silent; laborious, delicate; ingenious, heavy; melancholic, pleasant; lying, true; knowing, ignorant; liberal, covetous, and prodigal'[10] – in short, so complex, so indefinite, corresponding so little to the version which does duty for her in public, that a man might spend his life merely in trying to run her to earth. The pleasure of the pursuit more than rewards one for any damage that it may inflict upon one's worldly prospects. The man who is aware of himself is henceforward independent; and he is never bored, and life is only too short, and he is steeped through and through with a profound yet temperate happiness. He alone lives, while other people, slaves of ceremony, let life slip past them in a kind of dream. Once conform, once do what other people do because they do it, and a lethargy steals over all the finer nerves and faculties of the soul. She becomes all outer show and inward emptiness; dull, callous, and indifferent.

Surely then, if we ask this great master of the art of life to tell us his secret, he will advise us to withdraw to the inner room of our tower and there turn the pages of books, pursue fancy after fancy as they chase each other up the chimney, and leave the government of the world to others. Retirement and contemplation – these must be the main elements of his prescription. But no; Montaigne is by no means explicit. It is impossible to extract a plain answer from that subtle, half smiling, half melancholy man, with the heavy-lidded eyes and the dreamy, quizzical expression. The truth is that life in the country, with one's books and vegetables and flowers, is often extremely dull. He could never see that his own green peas were so much better than other people's. Paris was the place he loved best in the whole world – 'jusques à ses verrues et à ses taches'.[11] As for reading, he could seldom read any book for more than an hour at a time, and his memory was so bad that he forgot what was in his mind as he walked from one room to another. Book learning is nothing to be proud of, and as for the achievements of science, what do they amount to? He had always mixed with clever men, and his father had a positive veneration for them, but he had observed that, though they have their fine moments, their rhapsodies, their visions, the cleverest tremble on the verge of folly. Observe yourself: one moment you are exalted; the next a broken glass puts your nerves on edge. All extremes are dangerous. It is best to keep in the middle of the road, in the common ruts, however muddy. In writing choose the common words; avoid rhapsody and eloquence – yet, it is true, poetry is delicious; the best prose is that which is most full of poetry.

It appears, then, that we are to aim at a democratic simplicity. We may enjoy our room in the tower, with the painted walls and the commodious bookcases, but down in the garden there is a man digging who buried his father this morning, and it is he and his like who live the real life and speak the real language. There is certainly an element of truth in that. Things are said very finely at the lower end of the table. There are perhaps more of the qualities that matter among the ignorant than among the learned. But again, what a vile thing the rabble is! 'the mother of ignorance, injustice, and inconstancy. Is it reasonable that the life of a wise man should depend upon the judgement of fools?'[12] Their minds are weak, soft and without power of resistance. They must be told what it is expedient for them to know. It is not for them to face facts as they are. The truth can only be known by the well-born soul – 'l'âme bien née'.[13] Who, then, are these well-born souls, whom we would imitate if only Montaigne would enlighten us more precisely?

But no. 'Je n'enseigne poinct; je raconte.'[14] After all, how could he explain other people's souls when he could say nothing 'entirely simply and solidly, without confusion or mixture, in one word',[15] about his own, when indeed it became daily more and more in the dark to him? One quality or principle there is perhaps – that one must not lay down rules. The souls whom one would wish to resemble, like Étienne de La Boétie,[16] for example, are always the supplest. 'C'est estre, mais ce n'est pas vivre, que de se tenir attaché et obligé par necessité a un seul train.'[17] The laws are mere conventions, utterly unable to keep touch with the vast variety and turmoil of human impulses; habits and customs are a convenience devised for the support of timid natures who dare not allow their souls free play. But we, who have a private life and hold it infinitely the dearest of our possessions, suspect nothing so much as an attitude.

Directly we begin to protest, to attitudinise, to lay down laws, we perish. We are living for others, not for ourselves. We must respect those who sacrifice themselves in the public service, load them with honours, and pity them for allowing, as they must, the inevitable compromise; but for ourselves let us fly fame, honour, and all offices that put us under an obligation to others. Let us simmer over our incalculable cauldron, our enthralling confusion, our hotch-potch of impulses, our perpetual miracle – for the soul throws up wonders every second. Movement and change are the essence of our being; rigidity is death; conformity is death: let us say what comes into our heads, repeat ourselves, contradict ourselves, fling out the wildest nonsense, and follow the most fantastic fancies without caring what the world does or thinks or says. For nothing matters except life; and, of course, order.

This freedom, then, which is the essence of our being, has to be controlled. But it is difficult to see what power we are to invoke to help us, since every restraint of private opinion or public law has been derided, and Montaigne never ceases to pour scorn upon the misery, the weakness, the vanity of human nature. Perhaps, then, it will be well to turn to religion to guide us? 'Perhaps' is one of his favourite expressions; 'perhaps' and 'I think' and all those words which qualify the rash assumptions of human ignorance. Such words help one to muffle up opinions which it would be highly impolitic to speak outright. For one does not say everything; there are some things which at present it is advisable only to hint. One writes for a very few people, who understand. Certainly, seek the Divine guidance by all means, but meanwhile there is, for those who live a private life, another monitor, an invisible censor within, 'un patron au dedans',[18] whose blame is much more to be dreaded than any other because he knows the truth; nor is there anything sweeter than the chime of his approval. This is the judge to whom we must submit; this is the censor who will help us to achieve that order which is the grace of a well-born soul. For 'C'est une vie exquise, celle qui se maintient en ordre jusques en son privé'.[19] But he will act by his own light; by some internal balance will achieve that precarious and everchanging poise which, while it controls, in no way impedes the soul's freedom to explore and experiment. Without other guide, and without precedent, undoubtedly it is far more difficult to live well the private life than the public. It is an art which each must learn separately, though there are, perhaps, two or three men, like Homer, Alexander the Great, and Epaminondas[20] among the ancients, and Etienne de La Boétie among the moderns, whose example may help us. But it is an art; and the very material in which it works is variable and complex and infinitely mysterious – human nature. To human nature we must keep close. '. . . il faut vivre entre les vivants'.[21] We must dread any eccentricity or refinement which cuts us off from our fellow-beings. Blessed are those who chat easily with their neighbours about their sport or their buildings or their quarrels, and honestly enjoy the talk of carpenters and gardeners. To communicate is our chief business; society and friendship our chief delights; and reading, not to acquire knowledge, not to earn a living, but to extend our intercourse beyond our own time and province. Such wonders there are in the world; halcyons and undiscovered lands, men with dogs' heads and eyes in their chests, and laws and customs, it may well be, far superior to our own. Possibly we are asleep in this world; possibly there is some other which is apparent to beings with a sense which we now lack.

Here then, in spite of all contradictions and all qualifications, is something definite. These essays are an attempt to communicate a soul. On this point at least he is explicit. It is not fame that he wants; it is not that men shall quote him in years to come; he is setting up no statue in the market-place; he wishes only to communicate his soul. Communication is health; communication is truth; communication is happiness. To share is our duty; to go down boldly and bring to light those hidden thoughts which are the most diseased; to conceal nothing; to pretend nothing; if we are ignorant to say so; if we love our friends to let them know it.

. . . car, comme je scay par une trop certaine expérience, il n'est aucune si douce consolation en la perte de nos amis que celle que nous aporte la science de n'avoir rien oublié a leur dire et d'avoir eu avec eux une parfaite et entière communication.[22]

There are people who, when they travel, wrap themselves up, 'se défendans de la contagion d'un air incogneu'[23] in silence and suspicion. When they dine they must have the same food they get at home. Every sight and custom is bad unless it resembles those of their own village. They travel only to return. That is entirely the wrong way to set about it. We should start without any fixed idea where we are going to spend the night, or when we propose to come back; the journey is everything.[24] Most necessary of all, but rarest good fortune, we should try to find before we start some man of our own sort who will go with us and to whom we can say the first thing that comes into our heads. For pleasure has no relish unless we share it. As for the risks – that we may catch cold or get a headache – it is always worth while to risk a little illness for the sake of pleasure. 'Le plaisir est des principales espèces du profit.'[25] Besides if we do what we like, we always do what is good for us. Doctors and wise men may object, but let us leave doctors and wise men to their own dismal philosophy. For ourselves, who are ordinary men and women, let us return thanks to Nature for her bounty by using every one of the senses she has given us; vary our state as much as possible; turn now this side, now that, to the warmth, and relish to the full before the sun goes down the kisses of youth and the echoes of a beautiful voice singing Catullus.[26] Every season is likeable, and wet days and fine, red wine and white, company and solitude. Even sleep, that deplorable curtailment of the joy of life, can be full of dreams; and the most common actions – a walk, a talk, solitude in one's own orchard – can be enhanced and lit up by the association of the mind. Beauty is everywhere, and beauty is only two finger's-breadth from goodness. So, in the name of health and sanity, let us not dwell on the end of the journey. Let death come upon us planting our cabbages, or on horseback, or let us steal away to some cottage and there let strangers close our eyes, for a servant sobbing or the touch of a hand would break us down. Best of all, let death find us at our usual occupations, among girls and good fellows who make no protests, no lamentations; let him find us 'parmy les jeux, les festins, faceties, entretiens communs et populaires, et la musique, et des vers amoureux'.[27] But enough of death; it is life that matters.[28]

It is life that emerges more and more clearly as these essays reach not their end, but their suspension in full career. It is life that becomes more and more absorbing as death draws near, one's self, one's soul, every fact of existence: that one wears silk stockings summer and winter; puts water in one's wine; has one's hair cut after dinner; must have glass to drink from; has never worn spectacles; has a loud voice; carries a switch in one's hand; bites one's tongue; fidgets with one's feet; is apt to scratch one's ears; likes meat to be high; rubs one's teeth with a napkin (thank God, they are good!); must have curtains to one's bed; and, what is rather curious, began by liking radishes, then disliked them, and now likes them again. No fact is too little to let it slip through one's fingers, and besides the interest of facts themselves there is the strange power we have of changing facts by the force of the imagination.[†] Observe how the soul is always casting her own lights and shadows; makes the substantial hollow and the frail substantial; fills broad daylight with dreams; is as much excited by phantoms as by reality; and in the moment of death sports with a trifle. Observe, too, her duplicity, her complexity. She hears of a friend's loss and sympathises, and yet has a bitter-sweet malicious pleasure in the sorrows of others. She believes; at the same time she does not believe. Observe her extraordinary susceptibility to impressions, especially in youth. A rich man steals because his father kept him short of money as a boy. This wall one builds not for oneself, but because one's father loved building. In short, the soul is all laced about with nerves and sympathies which affect her every action, and yet, even now in 1580, no one has any clear knowledge – such cowards we are, such lovers of the smooth conventional ways – how she works or what she is except that of all things she is the most mysterious, and one's self the greatest monster and miracle in the world. '... plus je me hante et connois, plus ma difformité m'estonne, moins je m'entens en moy.'[29] Observe, observe perpetually, and, so long as ink and paper exist, 'sans cesse et sans travail'[30] Montaigne will write.

But there remains one final question which, if we could make him look up from his enthralling occupation, we should like to put to this great master of the art of life. In these extraordinary volumes of short and broken, long and learned, logical and contradictory statements, we have heard the very pulse and rhythm of the soul, beating day after day, year after year, through a veil which, as time goes on, fines itself almost to transparency.[‡] Here is some one who succeeded in the hazardous enterprise of living; who served his country and lived retired; was landlord, husband, father; entertained kings, loved women, and mused for hours alone over old books. By means of perpetual experiment and observation of the subtlest he achieved at last a miraculous adjustment of all these wayward parts that constitute the human soul. He laid hold of the beauty of the world with all his fingers. He achieved happiness. If he had had to live again, he said, he would have lived the same life over. But, as we watch with absorbed interest the enthralling spectacle of a soul living openly beneath our eyes, the question frames itself, Is pleasure the end of all? Whence this overwhelming interest in the nature of the soul? Why this overmastering desire to communicate with others? Is the beauty of this world enough, or is there, elsewhere, some explanation of the mystery? To this what answer can there be? There is none. There is only one more question: 'Que scais-je?'[31]§

*– *TLS*: 'Really, she is the strangest creature to watch,'
† – *TLS*: 'No fact is too little to let it slip through one's fingers and examine it; and, besides, there is the strange power we have in changing facts by the force of the imagination.'
‡ – *TLS*: 'fines itself almost to nothing.'
§ – *TLS*: 'mystery? But to this there is no answer only one more question – "Que scais-je?"'

1–An essay in the *TLS*, 31 January 1924, (Kp C243) based on *Essays of Montaigne*, translated by Charles Cotton, edited by William Carew Hazlitt (5 vols, Privately Printed for the Navarre Society, 1923), revised as shown for inclusion in *CR1*. See Editorial Note, p. xxv.

VW included 'Montaigne' as a candidate for *CR* treatment in the draft contents list which she made in her diary on 17 August 1923. But then on 11 September Bruce Richmond wrote suggesting a 'Montaigne' leader for the *TLS* (see MHP; in another, undated, letter he offers her as much time as she would like to complete her essay). By 19 December, in an end-of-year catalogue of activities, we find her, in her diary: 'doing Hardy & Montaigne & the Greeks & the Hours'. On 3 January 1924 she writes: 'Now it is sex, my boundary, & I must read Montaigne, & cut short those other reflections about, I think, reading & writing which were to fill up the page. I ought to describe the walk from Charleston too; but can't defraud Montaigne any longer. He gets better & better, & so I cant scamp him, & rush into writing, & earn my 20 guineas as I hope.' She was still working at her essay, amid numerous distractions, six days later: 'Am I more excited by buying Tavistock Sqre, or by buying my new fountain pen? – which reflection reminds me that I have volume 7 [sic] of Montaigne to polish off, & Saxon dining here. So in spite of a clouded brain, upstairs, fetch the books, & begin. First, though, one gaze into the fire – & oh dear, I've forgotten my ultimatum to the domestics. Both to go . . .' On 12 January she reflected: 'But the truth is – no, I dont think I know the truth. Undoubtedly my chief prop is my writing, which cant fail me here or in London. But according to Montaigne, one is various. I cant lay down a law for my own feelings.' Eight days later we find her complaining: 'Now, I must tackle my Montaigne quotations, since that's demanded by some Cockney in charge of the Supt.' She sent her essay off on 23 January, '& back again tomorrow to The Hours, which I was looking at disconsolately – oh the cold raw edges of one's relinquished pages . . .' For a compliment upon her essay from Logan Pearsall Smith see *III VW Diary*, 3 February 1924, and for VW's response see *III VW Letters*, no. 1442, 3 February 1924, and no. 1447, 25 February, a postscript: 'I am in your debt forever over Montaigne – altogether a different thing in French.' Reprinted *CE*.

2—Montaigne, vol. iii, bk ii, ch. xvii, 'Of Presumption', p. 352. Michel Eyquem de Montaigne (1533–92) was at Bar-le-Duc with the court of Francis II in 1559.

3—Samuel Pepys (1633–1703), Jean-Jacques Rousseau (1712–78).

4—Sir Thomas Browne (1605–82), *Religio Medici* (1643). For VW on Browne, see 'The Elizabethan Lumber Room' above, and 'Sir Thomas Browne', *III VW Essays*.

5—James Boswell (1740–95).

6—*Oeuvres complètes de Michel de Montaigne* . . . ed. Dr Arthur Armaingaud (L. Conard, Paris, 1924–).

7—Montaigne, vol. ii, bk ii, ch. vi, 'Of Exercitation', p. 299, which has: 'We hear but two or three of the ancients, who have beaten this path, and yet I cannot say if it was after this manner, knowing no more of them but their names. No one since . . .'

8—*Ibid.*, vol. v, bk iii, ch. vi, 'Of Coaches', p. 21, which has: 'for the traffic of pearl and pepper?'; the ellipsis marks the omission of: ', so many millions of people fallen by the edge of the sword,'.

9—For the matter up to the ellipsis, *ibid.*, ch. xiii, 'Of Experience', p. 257; for the remaining sentence, *ibid.*, p. 260, which has 'so ordinarily faulty, as'.

10—*Ibid.*, vol. ii, bk ii, ch. i, 'Of the Inconstancy of Our Actions', p. 241.

11—*Les Essais de Montaigne*. Publiés d'après l'édition de 1588 avec les variantes de 1595 et une notice, des notes, un glossaire et un index par H. Motheau et D. Jouaust (Paris. Libraire des Bibliophiles, 1886–9), Tome Sixième, Livre Trosiesme, ch. ix, 'De la Vanité', p. 164: 'Je ne veux pas oublier cecy, que je ne me mutine jamais tant contre la France que je ne regarde Paris de bon oeil . . . Je l'ayme par elle mesme, et plus en son propre estre que rechargée de pompe estrangiere; je l'ayme tendrement jusques à ses verrues et à ses taches.'

12—Montaigne, vol. iii, bk ii, ch. xvi, 'Of Glory', pp. 308–9.

13—Motheau/Jouaust, Tome Cinquième, Livre Troisiesme, ch. iii, 'De Trois Commerces', p. 222: 'Une ame bien née et exercée à la practique des hommes se rend plainement aggreable d'elle mesme.' Also: *ibid.*, Tome Sixième, Livre Troisiesme, ch. viii, 'De l'Art de conferer', p. 91: 'C'est chose de qualité à peu prés indifferente; tres-utile accessoire à une ame bien née, pernicieux à une autre ame et dommageable; ou plustost chose de tres-noble et tres-pretieux usage, qui ne se laisse pas posseder à vil pris: en quelque main, c'est un sceptre; en quelque autre, une marotte.'

14—*Ibid.*, ch. ii, 'Du Repentir', p. 192 and fn.

15—Montaigne, vol. ii, bk ii, ch. i, 'Of the Inconstancy of Our Actions', p. 241, which has: 'I have nothing to say of myself entirely, simply, and solidly without mixture and confusion.'

16—Étienne de la Boétie (1530–63), humanist writer, intimate friend of Montaigne.

17—Motheau/Jouaust, Tome Cinquième, Livre Troisiesme, ch. iii, 'De Trois Commerces', p. 212.

18—*Ibid.*, ch. ii, 'Du Repentir', p. 194: 'Nous autres principalement, qui vivons une vie privée qui n'est en montre qu'à nous, devons avoir estably un patron au dedans, auquel toucher nos actions, et, selon iceluy, nous caresser tantost, tantost nous chastier.'

19—*Ibid.*, p. 195.

20—Epaminondas (c. 418–362 BC), Theban general and statesman, frequently referred to in the essays.

21—Motheau/Jouaust, Tome Sixième, Livre Troisisme, ch. viii, 'De l'Art de Conferer', p. 93, fn. 3.

22 – *Ibid.*, Tome Troisième, Livre Second, ch. viii, p. 99, which has 'entiere'.

23 – *Ibid.*, Tome Sixième, Livre Troisiesme, ch. ix, 'de la Vanité', p. 188.

24 – Cf. the title to Leonard Woolf's final volume of autobiography: *The Journey Not the Arrival Matters* (1969).

25 – Motheau/Jouaust, Tome Septième, Livre Troisiesme, ch. xiii, 'De l'Experience', p. 43, fn. 6.

26 – *Ibid.*, Tome Troisiesme, Livre Second, ch. xii, 'Apologie de Raimond Sebond', pp. 146–7: 'Quant à moy, je ne m'estime point assez fort pour ouyr en sens rassis des vers d'Horace et de Catulle, chantez d'une voix suffisante par une belle et jeune bouche.'

27 – *Ibid.*, Tome Sixième, Livre Troisiesme, ch. ix, 'De la Vanité', pp. 185–6, which has: 'mais entre les jeux'.

28 – See *III VW Diary*, 8 April 1925: 'More & more do I repeat my own version of Montaigne "Its life that matters".'

29 – Motheau/Jouaust, Tome Sixième, Livre Troisiesme, ch. xi, 'Des Boyteux', pp. 256–7, which has: 'me connois'.

30 – *Ibid.*, ch. ix, 'De la Vanité', p. 119.

31 – *Ibid.*, Tome Quatrième, Livre Second, ch. xii, 'Apologie de Raimond Sebond', p. 31: 'Cette fantasie est plus seurement conceuë par interrogation: QUE SÇAY-JE? voyla comme je la porte à la devise d'une balance.'

The Duchess of Newcastle

'. . . All I desire is fame',[2] wrote Margaret Cavendish, Duchess of Newcastle. And while she lived her wish was granted. Garish in her dress, eccentric in her habits, chaste in her conduct, coarse in her speech, she succeeded during her lifetime in drawing upon herself the ridicule of the great and the applause of the learned. But the last echoes of that clamour have now all died away; she lives only in the few splendid phrases that Lamb scattered upon her tomb;[3] her poems, her plays, her philosophies, her orations, her discourses – all those folios and quartos in which, she protested, her real life was shrined – moulder in the gloom of public libraries, or are decanted into tiny thimbles which hold six drops of their profusion. Even the curious student, inspired by the words of Lamb, quails before the mass of her mausoleum, peers in, looks about him, and hurries out again, shutting the door.

But that hasty glance has shown him the outlines of a memorable figure. Born (it is conjectured) in 1624, Margaret was the youngest child of a Thomas Lucas, who died when she was an infant, and her upbringing was due to her mother, a lady of remarkable character, of majestic grandeur and beauty 'beyond the ruin of time'. 'She was very skilful in leases, and setting of lands and court keeping, ordering of stewards, and the like affairs.'[4] The wealth which thus accrued she spent, not on marriage portions, but on generous and delightful pleasures, 'out of an opinion that if she bred us with needy necessity it might chance to create in us sharking qualities'.[5] Her eight sons and daughters were never beaten, but reasoned with, finely and gaily dressed, and allowed no conversation with servants, not because they are servants but because servants 'are for the most part ill-bred as well as meanly born'.[6] The daughters were taught the usual accomplishments 'rather for formality than for benefit', it being their mother's opinion that character, happiness, and honesty were of greater value to a woman than fiddling and singing, or 'the prating of several languages'.[7]

Already Margaret was eager to take advantage of such indulgence to gratify certain tastes. Already she liked reading better than needlework, dressing and 'inventing fashions'[8] better than reading, and writing best of all. Sixteen paper books of no title, written in straggling letters, for the impetuosity of her thought always outdid the pace of her fingers, testify to the use she made of her mother's liberality. The happiness of their home life had other results as well. They were a devoted family. Long after they were married, Margaret noted, these handsome brothers and sisters, with their well-proportioned bodies, their clear complexions, brown hair, sound teeth, 'tunable voices', and plain way of speaking, kept themselves 'in a flock together'.[9] The presence of strangers silenced them. But when they were alone, whether they walked in Spring Gardens or Hyde Park, or had music, or supped in barges upon the water, their tongues were loosed and they made 'very merry amongst themselves, . . . judging, condemning, approving, commending, as they thought good'.[10]

The happy family life had its effect upon Margaret's character. As a child, she would walk for hours alone, musing and contemplating and reasoning with herself of 'everything her senses did present'.[11] She took no pleasure in activity of any kind. Toys did not amuse her, and she could neither learn foreign languages nor dress as other people did. Her great pleasure was to invent dresses for herself, which nobody else was to copy, 'for', she remarks, 'I always took delight in a singularity, even in accoutrements of habits'.[12]

Such a training, at once so cloistered and so free, should have

bred a lettered old maid, glad of her seclusion, and the writer perhaps of some volume of letters or translations from the classics,
which we should still quote as proof of the cultivation of our ances-
tresses. But there was a wild streak in Margaret, a love of finery and
extravagance and fame, which was forever upsetting the orderly
arrangements of Nature. When she heard that the Queen, since the
outbreak of the Civil War, had fewer maids-of-honour than usual
she had 'a great desire'[13] to become one of them. Her mother let her
go against the judgement of the rest of the family, who, knowing
that she had never left home and had scarcely been beyond their
sight, justly thought that she might behave at Court to her disadvantage. 'Which indeed I did,' Margaret confessed; 'for I was so
bashful when I was out of my mother's, brothers', and sisters' sight
that . . . I durst neither look up with my eyes, no speak, nor be any
way sociable, insomuch as I was thought a natural fool.'[14] The cour-
tiers laughed at her; and she retaliated in the obvious way. People
were censorious; men were jealous of brains in a woman; women
suspected intellect in their own sex; and what other lady, she might
justly ask, pondered as she walked on the nature of matter and
whether snails have teeth? But the laughter galled her, and she
begged her mother to let her come home. This being refused, wisely
as the event turned out, she stayed on for two years (1643–45),
finally going with the Queen to Paris, and there, among the exiles
who came to pay their respects to the Court, was the Marquis of
Newcastle. To the general amazement, the princely nobleman, who
had led the King's forces to disaster with indomitable courage but
little skill, fell in love with the shy, silent, strangely dressed maid-of-
honour. It was not 'amorous love, but honest, honourable love',[15]
according to Margaret. She was no brilliant match; she had gained
a reputation for prudery and eccentricity. What, then, could have
made so great a nobleman fall at her feet? The onlookers were full
of derision, disparagement, and slander. 'I fear,' Margaret wrote to
the Marquis, 'others foresee we shall be unfortunate, though we see
it not ourselves, or else there would not be such pains to untie the
knot of our affections.' Again, 'Saint Germains is a place of much
slander, and thinks I send too often to you.' 'Pray consider,' she
warned him, 'that I have enemies.'[16] But the match was evidently
perfect. The Duke, with his love of poetry and music and play-
writing, his interest in philosophy, his belief 'that nobody knew or
could know the cause of anything',[17] his romantic and generous

temperament, was naturally drawn to a woman who wrote poetry herself, was also a philosopher of the same way of thinking, and lavished upon him not only the admiration of a fellow-artist, but the gratitude of a sensitive creature who had been shielded and succoured by his extraordinary magnanimity. 'He did approve,' she wrote, 'of those bashful fears which many condemned, . . . and though I did dread marriage and shunned men's company as much as I could, yet I . . . had not the power to refuse him.'[18] She kept him company during the long years of exile; she entered with sympathy, if not with understanding, into the conduct and acquirements of those horses which he trained to such perfection that the Spaniards crossed themselves and cried 'Miraculo!' as they witnessed their corvets, voltoes, and pirouettes; she believed that the horses even made a 'trampling action'[19] for joy when he came into the stables; she pleaded his cause in England during the Protectorate; and, when the Restoration made it possible for them to return to England, they lived together in the depths of the country in the greatest seclusion and perfect contentment, scribbling plays, poems, philosophies, greeting each other's works with raptures of delight, and confabulating, doubtless, upon such marvels of the natural world as chance threw their way. They were laughed at by their contemporaries; Horace Walpole sneered at them.[20] But there can be no doubt that they were perfectly happy.

For now Margaret could apply herself uninterruptedly to her writing. She could devise fashions for herself and her servants. She could scribble more and more furiously with fingers that became less and less able to form legible letters. She could even achieve the miracle of getting her plays acted in London and her philosophies humbly perused by men of learning. There they stand, in the British Museum, volume after volume, swarming with a diffused, uneasy, contorted vitality. Order, continuity, the logical development of her argument are all unknown to her. No fears impede her. She has the irresponsibility of a child and the arrogance of a Duchess. The wildest fancies come to her, and she canters away on their backs. We seem to hear her, as the thoughts boil and bubble, calling to John, who sat with a pen in his hand next door, to come quick, 'John, John, I conceive!'[21] And down it goes – whatever it may be; sense or nonsense; some thought on women's education – 'Women live like Bats or Owls, labour like Beasts, and die like Worms, . . . the best-bred women are those whose minds are civilest';[22] some speculation that had struck her, perhaps, walking that afternoon alone – why 'hogs have the measles', why 'dogs that rejoice swing their tails',[23] or what the stars are made of, or what this chrysalis is that her mind has brought her, and she keeps warm in a corner of her room. On and on, from subject to subject she flies, never stopping to correct, 'for there is more pleasure in making than in mending',[24] talking aloud to herself of all those matters that filled her brain to her perpetual diversion – of wars, and boarding-schools, and cutting down trees, of grammar and morals, of monsters and the British, whether opium in small quantities is good for lunatics, why it is that musicians are mad. Looking upwards, she speculates still more ambitiously upon the nature of the moon, and if the stars are blazing jellies; looking downwards she wonders if the fishes know that the sea is salt; opines that our heads are full of fairies, 'dear to God as we are'; muses whether there are not other worlds than ours, and reflects that the next ship may bring us word of a new one. In short, 'we are in utter darkness'.[25] Meanwhile, what a rapture is thought!

As the vast books appeared from the stately retreat at Welbeck the usual censors made the usual objections, and had to be answered, despised, or argued with, as her mood varied, in the preface to every work. They said, among other things, that her books were not her own, because she used learned terms, and 'wrote of many matters outside her ken'.[26] She flew to her husband for help, and he answered, characteristically, that the Duchess 'had never conversed with any professed scholar in learning except her brother and myself'. The Duke's scholarship, moreover, was of a peculiar nature. 'I have lived in the great world a great while, and have thought of what has been brought to me by the senses, more than was put into me by learned discourse; for I do not love to be led by the nose, by authority, and old authors; ipse dixit will not serve my turn.'[27] And then she takes up the pen and proceeds, with the importunity and indiscretion of a child, to assure the world that her ignorance is of the finest quality imaginable. She has only seen Des Cartes and Hobbes, not questioned them; she did indeed ask Mr Hobbes to dinner, but he could not come; she often does not listen to a word that is said to her; she does not know any French, though she lived abroad for five years; she has only read the old philosophers in Mr Stanley's account of them; of Des Cartes she has read but half of his work on Passion; and of Hobbes only 'the little book called De Cive',[28] all of which is infinitely to the credit of her native wit, so abundant that outside succour pained it, so honest that it would not accept help from others. It was from the plain of complete ignorance, the untilled field of her own consciousness, that she proposed to erect a philosophic system that was to oust all others. The results were not altogether happy. Under the pressure of such vast structures, her natural gift, the fresh and delicate fancy which had led her to her first volume to write charmingly of Queen Mab and fairyland, was crushed out of existence.

> The palace of the Queen wherein she dwells,
> Its fabric's built all of hodmandod shells;
> The hangings of a Rainbow made that's thin,
> Shew wondrous fine, when one first enters in;
> The chambers made of Amber that is clear,
> Do give a fine sweet smell, if fire be near;
> Her bed a cherry stone, is carved throughout,
> And with a butterfly's wing hung about;
> Her sheets are of the skin of Dove's eyes made
> Where on a violet bud her pillow's laid.[29]

So she could write when she was young. But her fairies, if they survived at all, grew up into hippopotami. Too generously her prayer was granted:

> Give me the free and noble style,
> Which seems uncurb'd, though it be wild.[30]

She became capable of involutions, and contortions and conceits of which the following is among the shortest, but not the most terrific:

> The human head may be likened to a town:
> The mouth when full, begun
> Is market day, when empty, market's done;
> The city conduct, where the water flows,
> Is with two spouts, the nostrils and the nose.[31]

She similised, energetically, incongruously, eternally; the sea became a meadow, the sailors shepherds, the mast a maypole. The fly was the bird of summer, trees were senators, houses ships, and even the fairies, whom she loved better than any earthly thing, except the Duke, are changed into blunt atoms and sharp atoms, and take part in some of those horrible manoeuvres in which she delighted to marshal the universe. Truly, 'my Lady Sanspareille hath a strange spreading wit'.[32] Worse still, without an atom of dramatic power, she turned to play-writing. It was a simple process. The unwieldly thoughts which turned and tumbled within her were christened Sir Golden Riches, Moll Meanbred, Sir Puppy Dogman,[33] and the rest, and sent revolving in tedious debate upon the parts of the soul, or whether virtue is better than riches, round a wise and learned lady who answered their questions and corrected their fallacies at considerable length in tones which we seem to have heard before.

Sometimes, however, the Duchess walked abroad. She would issue out in her own proper person, dressed in a thousand gems and furbelows, to visit the houses of the neighbouring gentry. Her pen made instant report of these excursions. She recorded how Lady C. R. 'did beat her husband in a public assembly'; Sir F. O. 'I am sorry to hear hath undervalued himself so much below his birth and wealth as to marry his kitchen-maid'; 'Miss P. I. has become a sanctified soul, a spiritual sister, she has left curling her hair, black patches are become abominable to her, laced shoes and Galoshoes are steps to pride – she asked me what posture I thought was the best to be used in prayer'.[34] Her answer was probably unacceptable. 'I shall not rashly go there again,' she says of one such 'gossip-making'.[35] She was not, we may hazard, a welcome guest or an altogether hospitable hostess. She had a way of 'bragging of myself'[36] which frightened visitors so that they left, nor was she sorry to see them go. Indeed, Welbeck was the best place for her, and her own company the most congenial, with the amiable Duke wandering in and out, with his plays and his speculations, always ready to answer a question or refute a slander. Perhaps it was this solitude that led her, chaste as she was in conduct, to use language which in time to come much perturbed Sir Egerton Brydges. She used, he complained, 'expressions and images of extraordinary coarseness as flowing from a female of high rank brought up in courts'.[37] He forgot that this particular female had long ceased to frequent the Court; she consorted chiefly with fairies; and her friends were among the dead. Naturally, then, her language was coarse. Nevertheless, though her philosophies are futile, and her plays intolerable, and her verses mainly dull, the vast bulk of the Duchess is leavened by a vein of authentic fire. One cannot help following the lure of her erratic and lovable personality as it meanders and twinkles through page after page. There is something noble and Quixotic and high-spirited, as well as crack-brained and bird-witted, about her. Her simplicity is so open; her intelligence so active; her sympathy with fairies and animals so true and tender. She has the freakishness of an elf, the irresponsibility of some non-human creature, its heart-lessness, and its charm. And although 'they', those terrible critics who had sneered and jeered at her ever since, as a shy girl, she had not dared look her tormentors in the face at Court, continued to mock, few of her critics, after all, had the wit to trouble about the nature of the universe, or cared a straw for the sufferings of the hunted hare, or longed, as she did, to talk to some one 'of Shake-speare's fools'.[38] Now, at any rate, the laugh is not all on their side.

But laugh they did. When the rumour spread that the crazy Duchess was coming up from Welbeck to pay her respects at Court, people crowded the streets to look at her, and the curiosity of Mr Pepys twice brought him to wait in the Park to see her pass. But the pressure of the crowd about her coach was too great. He could only catch a glimpse of her in her silver coach with her footmen all in vel-vet, a velvet cap on her head, and her hair about her ears. He could only see for a moment between the white curtains the face of 'a very comely woman',[39] and on she drove through the crowd of staring Cockneys, all pressing to catch a glimpse of that romantic lady, who stands, in the picture at Welbeck, with large melancholy eyes, and something fastidious and fantastic in her bearing, touching a table with the tips of long pointed fingers, in the calm assurance of im-mortal fame.

1—An essay written specifically for *CR1*. In her diary entry for 19 January 1915, VW had listed the Duchess of Newcastle as a candidate for a possible 'book of "Eccentrics"' but there are no references contemporary with the writing of this essay to Margaret Cavendish, *née* Lucas, Duchess of Newcastle (1624?–74) in either diary or letters. A footnote to the title in the original edition of *CR1* lists VW's reading thus: *The Life of William Cavendish, Duke of Newcastle, Etc.*, edited by C. H. Firth; *Poems and Fancies*, by the Duchess of Newcastle; *The World's Olio, Orations of Divers Sorts Accommodated to Divers Places; Female Orations; Plays; Philosophical Letters*, etc., etc. See also *A Room of One's Own* (1929), ch. 4, and see 'The Duke and Duchess of Newcastle-upon-Tyne', *I VW Essays*. See Editorial Note, p. xxv. Reprinted *CE*.
2—Margaret, Duchess of Newcastle, *The Life of William Cavendish, Duke of Newcastle* [1592–1676]. To which is added 'The True Relation of My Birth, Breed-ing, and Life' (1667; ed. C. H. Firth, John C. Nimmo, 1886), Preface, p. xl: "'It will satisfy me," she says, "if my writing please the readers, though not the learned; for I had rather be praised, in this, by the most, although not the best; for all I desire is fame, and fame is nothing but a great noise, and noise lives most in a multitude."'
3—Charles Lamb (1775–1834) makes several references to Margaret Cavendish, notably in *Elia*, 1823: in 'A Complaint of the Decay of Beggars in the Metropolis', where he speaks of 'Dear Margaret Newcastle'; in 'Mackery End, in Hertfordshire' where he calls her 'a dear favourite of mine'; and in 'The Two Races of Man',

where she is 'that princely woman, the thrice noble Margaret Newcastle'. She is also mentioned in 'Detached Thoughts on Books and Reading' (*Elia*, 1828).

4 – For the first quotation, Newcastle, 'The True Relation of My Birth, Breeding, and Life', p. 291, and for the second, p. 294, which has 'lands, and'.

5 – *Ibid.*, p. 278.

6 – *Ibid.*, p. 279, which has 'Not because they were servants were we so reserved; for many noble persons are forced to serve through necessity; but by reason the vulgar sort of servants are as ill bred as meanly born, giving children ill examples and worse counsel.'

7 – *Ibid.*, p. 280.

8 – *Ibid.*, p. 312: '. . . I took great delight in attiring, fine dressing, and fashions, especially such fashions as I did invent myself, not taking that pleasure in such fashions as was [sic] invented by others.'

9 – For the first quotation, *ibid.*, p. 292, and for the second, p. 285.

10 – *Ibid.*, pp. 311–12.

11 – *Ibid.*, p. 310, adapted.

12 – *Ibid.*, p. 312.

13 – *Ibid.*, p. 286.

14 – For the matter up to the ellipsis, *ibid.*, p. 286, and for the remainder, p. 287.

15 – *Ibid.*, p. 288, adapted.

16 – For the first quotation, T. Longueville, *The First Duke and Duchess of Newcastle-upon-Tyne* (Longmans, Green and Co., 1910), ch. xv, November 1645, p. 180, which has: 'such pains taken' and 'affection'; for the second and third quotations respectively, pp. 182 and 185.

17 – Newcastle, Preface, p. xxxvi.

18 – *Ibid.*, 'A True Relation of My Birth, Breeding and Life', p. 288, adapted.

19 – For the Spaniards, *ibid.*, Preface, p. xxvi, and for the joyful horses, 'The Life of the Most Illustrious Prince, William, Duke of Newcastle', bk ii, p. 101.

20 – Horace Walpole in *A Catalogue of the Royal and Noble Authors of England*, vol. ii (1758), makes several scathing comments about the Newcastles, e.g.: 'What a picture of foolish nobility was this stately poetic couple, retired to their little domain, and intoxicating each other with circumstantial flattery on what was of consequence to no mortal but themselves!'

21 – The source of this quotation has not been discovered.

22 – For the matter up to the ellipsis, Newcastle, *Orations of Divers Sorts Accommodated to Divers Places* (London: 1662), Park XI, 'Female Orations', p. 226, which has: '. . . we live like Bats'. For the remainder, which VW also quotes in *A Room of One's Own*, Newcastle, *CCXI Sociable Letters* (London, 1644), no. XXVI, p. 51, which has: '. . . wherefore those Women are best bred, whose Minds are Civilest . . .'

23 – The origin of the first quotation remains undiscovered; for the second, Newcastle, *Philosophical Letters, or Modest Reflections Upon Some Opinions in Natural Philosophy, Maintained by Several Famous and Learned Authors of this Age, Expressed by Way of Letters* (London: 1664), Letter XVII (section IV), p. 485: '(Why) A Dog that Rejoyces swings its tail'.

24 – The source of this quotation has not been traced.

25 – The origin of the first quotation remains undiscovered; for the second, Newcastle, *The World's Olio* (1655), 'Of Chymistry', p. 177.

26—This quotation remains untraced.

27—Newcastle, *Philosophical and Physical Opinions* (London: 1655), 'An Epistle to justify the Lady Newcastle, and Truth against falsehood, laying those false and malicious aspersions of her, that she was not Author of her Books; the *Philosophical and Physical Opinions* written by her Excellency, the Lady Marchioness of Newcastle', page unnumbered, which has 'Authority', 'old Authors' and 'then' for 'than'.

28—Newcastle, *Philosophical and Physical Opinions*, 'An Epilogue to My Philosophical Opinions', pages unnumbered. Thomas Stanley (1625–78), author of a three-volume study of Greek philosophy, *History of Philosophy* (1655–62). René Descartes (1591–1650), *Traité des passions de l'âme* (1649); Thomas Hobbes (1588–1679), *De Cive* (1642). The Duke of Newcastle was a patron of Descartes and of Hobbes, both of whom are reputed to have dined with him during his stay in Paris (see *The Life of William Cavendish*, p. 197n.).

29—It is not clear what source VW used for her extracts from Newcastle's poems but the version here of 'The Palace of the Fairy-Queen', although modernised in spelling and different in punctuation, comes closer to that in *Poems, or Several Fancies in Verse. With the Animal Parliament, in Prose* (3rd edition, London: 1668), Part IV, p. 259, than that for example in *Poems, and Fancies* (London: 1653), p. 155.

30—*Poems, and Fancies*, 'The Claspe', p. 110: 'Give *Mee* the *Free*, and *Noble Stile/* Which seems *uncurb'd*, though it be *wild*.' (1668, p. 158, has: 'Give me a Free and Noble Style, that goes/In an Uncurbed Strain, though Wild it shows:'.)

31—The first line here has echoes in Newcastle (e.g. 'The City is the Brain, incompast in/Double walls', 1653) but it is possible that it is a mistransposed line of VW's, originally intended to introduce the text, for which see *Poems, and Fancies* (London: 1653), 'The City of the Fairies', p. 168:

> 'The *Market-place* the *Mouth*, when full, begun
> Is *Market-day*, when empty, Markets done.
> The City *Conduit* where the water flowes,
> In through two *Spouts*, the *nostrils* of the *Nose*.'

32—Newcastle, *Playes* (London: 1662), 'The Second Part of Youths Glory, and Deaths Banquet', Act I, scene iii, p 158.

33—For Sir Golden Riches and Moll (Mall) Meanbred, *ibid.*, 'The Lady Contemplation', p. 181; for Sir Puppy Dogman, Newcastle, *Plays, Never Before Printed* (London: 1668), 'A Piece of a Play', end of volume.

34—For Lady C. R., *CCXI Sociable Letters*, no. XXVI, pp. 48–9, adapted; for Sir F. O., *ibid.*, no. LI, p. 103, which has: 'Miss P. I. has become an Altered Woman, as being a sanctified soul'.

35—*Ibid.*, no. CIII, p. 208, which has: '. . . and it hath so Frighted me, as I shall not hastily go to a gossiping meeting again'.

36—*Ibid.*, no. CXXII, pp. 243–4, apparently an adaptation.

37—*Select Poems of Margaret Cavendish, Duchess of Newcastle*, ed. Sir Egerton Brydges (Privately printed, 1813), Advertisement, dated 24 August 1813, which has: 'coarseness, and more extraordinary as flowing from a female of high rank'.

38—This appears possibly to be VW's invention from *CCXI Sociable Letters*, no. CXXIII, pp. 244–8, all about Shakespeare and especially in praise of his fools.

39—Newcastle, *The Life of William Cavendish*, p. 312 n.1, quoting from the entry for 26 April 1667 in the diary of Samuel Pepys (1633–1703).

Rambling Round Evelyn

Should you wish to make sure that your birthday will be celebrated three hundred years hence, your best course is undoubtedly to keep a diary. Only first be certain that you have the courage to lock your genius in a private book and the humour to gloat over a fame that will be yours only in the grave. For the good diarist writes either for himself alone or for a posterity so distant that it can safely hear every secret and justly weigh every motive. For such an audience there is need neither of affectation nor of restraint. Sincerity is what they ask, detail, volume; skill with the pen comes in conveniently, but brilliance is not necessary; genius is a hindrance even; and should you know your business and do it manfully, posterity will let you off mixing with great men, reporting famous affairs, or having lain with the first ladies in the land.

The diary, for whose sake we are remembering the three hundredth anniversary of the birth of John Evelyn, is a case in point. It is sometimes composed like a memoir, sometimes jotted down like a calendar; but he never used its pages to reveal the secrets of his heart, and all that he wrote might have been read aloud in the evening with a calm conscience to his children. If we wonder, then, why we still trouble to read what we must consider the uninspired work of a good man we have to confess, first that diaries are always diaries, books, that is, that we read in convalescence, on horseback, in the grip of death; second, that this reading, about which so many fine things have been said, is for the most part mere dreaming and idling; lying in a chair with a book; watching the butterflies on the dahlias; a profitless occupation which no critic has taken the trouble to investigate, and on whose behalf only the moralist can find a good word to say. For he will allow it to be an innocent employment; and happiness, he will add, though derived from trivial sources, has probably done more to prevent human beings from changing their religions and killing their kings than either philosophy or the pulpit.

It may be well, indeed, before reading much further in Evelyn's book, to decide where it is that our modern view of happiness differs from his. Ignorance, surely, ignorance is at the bottom of it; his ignorance and our comparative erudition. No one can read the story of Evelyn's foreign travels without envying in the first place his simplicity of mind, in the second his activity. To take a simple example of the difference between us – that butterfly will sit motionless on the dahlia while the gardener trundles his barrow past it, but let him flick the wings with the shadow of a rake, and off it flies, up it goes, instantly on the alert. So, we may reflect, a butterfly sees but does not hear; and here no doubt we are much on a par with Evelyn. But as for going into the house to fetch a knife and with that knife dissecting a Red Admiral's head, as Evelyn would have done, no sane person in the twentieth century would entertain such a project for a second. Individually we may know as little as Evelyn, but collectively we know so much that there is little incentive to venture on private discoveries. We seek the encyclopaedia, not the scissors; and know in two minutes not only more than was known to Evelyn in his lifetime, but that the mass of knowledge is so vast that it is scarcely worth while to possess a single crumb. Ignorant, yet justly confident that with his own hands he might advance not merely his private knowledge but the knowledge of mankind, Evelyn dabbled in all the arts and sciences, ran about the Continent for ten years, gazed with unflagging gusto upon hairy women and rational dogs, and drew inferences and framed speculations which are now only to be matched by listening to the talk of old women round the village pump. The moon, they say, is so much larger than usual this autumn that no mushrooms will grow, and the carpenter's wife will be brought to bed of twins. So Evelyn, Fellow of the Royal Society, a gentleman of the highest culture and intelligence, carefully noted all comets and portents, and thought it a sinister omen when a whale came up the Thames. In 1658, too, a whale had been seen. 'That year died Cromwell.'[2] Nature, it seems, was determined to stimulate the devotion of her seventeenth-century admirers by displays of violence and eccentricity from which she now refrains. There were storms, floods, and droughts; the Thames frozen hard; comets flaring in the sky. If a cat so much as kittened in Evelyn's bed the kitten was inevitably gifted with eight legs, six ears, two bodies, and two tails.

But to return to happiness. It sometimes appears that if there is an insoluble difference between our ancestors and ourselves it is that we draw our happiness from different sources. We rate the same things at different values. Something of this we may ascribe to their ignorance and our knowledge. But are we to suppose that ignorance alters the nerves and the affections? Are we to believe that it would have been an intolerable penance for us to live familiarly with the Elizabethans? Should we have found it necessary to leave the room because of Shakespeare's habits, and to have refused Queen Elizabeth's invitation to dinner? Perhaps so. For Evelyn was a sober man of unusual refinement, and yet he pressed into a torture chamber as we crowd to see the lions fed.

. . . they first bound his wrists with a strong rope or small cable, and one end of it to an iron ring made fast to the wall about four feet from the floor, and then his feet with another cable, fastened about five feet farther than his utmost length to another ring on the floor of the room. Thus suspended, and yet lying but aslant, they slid a horse of wood under the rope which bound his feet, which so exceedingly stiffened it, as severed the fellow's joints in miserable sort, drawing him out at length in an extraordinary manner, he having only a pair of linen drawers upon his naked body . . .[3]

And so on. Evelyn watched this to the end, and then remarked that 'the spectacle was so uncomfortable that I was not able to stay the sight of another',[4] as we might say that the lions growl so loud and the sight of raw meat is so unpleasant that we will now visit the penguins. Allowing for his discomfort, there is enough discrepancy between his view of pain and ours to make us wonder whether we see any fact with the same eyes, marry any women from the same motives, or judge any conduct by the same standards. To sit passive when muscles tore and bones cracked, not to flinch when the wooden horse was raised higher and the executioner fetched a horn and poured two buckets of water down the man's throat, to suffer this iniquity on a suspicion of robbery which the man denied – all this seems to put Evelyn in one of those cages where we still mentally seclude the riff-raff of Whitechapel. Only it is obvious that we have somehow got it wrong. If we could maintain that our susceptibility to suffering and love of justice were proof that all our humane instincts were as highly developed as these, then we could say that the world improves, and we with it. But let us get on with the diary.

In 1652, when it seemed that things had settled down unhappily enough, 'all being entirely in the rebels' hands', Evelyn returned to England with his wife, his Tables of Veins and Arteries,[5] his Venetian glass and the rest of his curiosities, to lead the life of a country gentleman of strong Royalist sympathies at Deptford. What with going to church and going to town, settling his accounts and planting his garden – 'I planted the orchard at Sayes Court; new moon, wind west'[6] – his time was spent much as ours is. But there was one difference which it is difficult to illustrate by a single quotation, because the evidence is scattered all about in little insignificant phrases. The general effect of them is that he used his eyes. The visible world was always close to him. The visible world has receded so far from us that to hear all this talk of buildings and gardens, statues and carving, as if the look of things assailed one out of doors as well as in, and were not confined to a few small canvases hung upon the wall, seems strange. No doubt there are a thousand excuses for us; but hitherto we have been finding excuses for him. Wherever there was a picture to be seen by Julio Romano, Polydore, Guido, Raphael, or Tintoretto,[7] a finely built house, a prospect, or a garden nobly designed, Evelyn stopped his coach to look at it, and opened his diary to record his opinion. On August 27, Evelyn, with Dr Wren and others, was in St Paul's surveying 'the general decay of that ancient and venerable church'; held with Dr Wren another judgement from the rest; and had a mind to build it with 'a noble cupola, a form of church building not as yet known in England but of wonderful grace', in which Dr Wren concurred. Six days later the Fire of London altered their plans.[8] It was Evelyn again who, walking by himself, chanced to look in at the window of 'a poor solitary thatched house in a field in our parish', there saw a young man carving at a crucifix, was overcome with an enthusiasm which does him the utmost credit, and carried Grinling Gibbons and his carving to Court.[9]

Indeed it is all very well to be scrupulous about the sufferings of worms and sensitive to the dues of servant girls, but how pleasant also if, with shut eyes, one could call up street after street of beautiful houses. A flower is red; the apples rosy-gilt in the afternoon sun; a picture has charm, especially as it displays the character of a grandfather and dignifies a family descended from such a scowl; but these are scattered fragments – little relics of beauty in the world that has grown indescribably drab. To our charge of cruelty Evelyn might well reply by pointing to Bayswater and the purlieus of Clapham; and if he should assert that nothing now has character or conviction, that no farmer in England sleeps with an open coffin at his bedside to remind him of death, we could not retort effectually offhand. True, we like the country. Evelyn never looked at the sky.

But to return. After the Restoration Evelyn emerged in full possession of a variety of accomplishments which in our time of speci-
alists seems remarkable enough. He was employed on public
business; he was Secretary to the Royal Society;[10] he wrote plays
and poems; he was the first authority upon trees and gardens in
England; he submitted a design for the rebuilding of London; he
went into the question of smoke and its abatement – the lime trees
in St James's Park being, it is said, the result of his cogitations; he
was commissioned to write a history of the Dutch war – in short, he
completely outdid the Squire of 'The Princess', whom in many respects he anticipated –

> A lord of fat prize-oxen and of sheep,
> A raiser of huge melons and of pine,
> A patron of some thirty charities,
> A pamphleteer on guano and on grain,
> A quarter-sessions chairman abler none.[11]

All that he was, and shared with Sir Walter another characteristic
which Tennyson does not mention. He was, we cannot help suspecting, something of a bore, a little censorious, a little patronising,
a little too sure of his own merits, and a little obtuse to those of
other people. Or what is the quality, or absence of quality, that
checks our sympathies? Partly, perhaps, it is due to some incon-
sistency which it would be harsh to call by so strong a name as
hypocrisy. Though he deplored the vices of his age he could never
keep away from the centre of them. 'The luxurious dallying and
profaneness' of the Court, the sight of 'Mrs Nelly' looking over her
garden wall and holding 'very familiar discourse' with King
Charles[12] on the green walk below, caused him acute disgust; yet he
could never decide to break with the Court and retire to 'my poor
but quiet villa',[13] which was of course the apple of his eye and one
of the show-places in England. Then, though he loved his daughter
Mary, his grief at her death did not prevent him from counting the
number of empty coaches drawn by six horses apiece that attended
her funeral. His women friends combined virtue with beauty to
such an extent that we can hardly credit them with wit into the bargain. Poor Mrs Godolphin at least, whom he celebrated in a sincere
and touching biography, 'loved to be at funerals' and chose, habitually 'the dryest and and leanest morsels of meat',[14] which may be the
habits of an angel but do not present her friendship with Evelyn in
an alluring light. But it is Pepys who sums up our case against Evelyn; Pepys who said of him after a long morning's entertainment:

'In fine a most excellent person he is and must be allowed a little for a little conceitedness; but he may well be so, being a man so much above others.'[15] The words exactly hit the mark, 'A most excellent person he was'; but a little conceited.

Pepys it is who prompts us to another reflection, inevitable, unnecessary, perhaps unkind. Evelyn was no genius. His writing is opaque rather than transparent; we see no depths through it, nor any very secret movements of mind or heart. He can neither make us hate a regicide nor love Mrs Godolphin beyond reason. But he writes a diary; and he writes it supremely well. Even as we drowse, somehow or other the bygone gentleman sets up, through three centuries, a perceptible tingle of communication, so that without laying stress on anything in particular, stopping to dream, stopping to laugh, stopping merely to look, we are yet taking notice all the time. His garden, for example – how delightful is his disparagement of it, and how acid his criticism of the gardens of others. Then, we may be sure, the hens at Sayes Court laid the very best eggs in England, and when the Tsar drove a wheelbarrow through his hedge, what a catastrophe it was,[16] and we can guess how Mrs Evelyn dusted and polished, and how Evelyn himself grumbled, and how punctilious and efficient and trustworthy he was, how ready to give advice, how ready to read his own works aloud, and how affectionate, withal, lamenting bitterly, but not effusively, for the man with the long-drawn sensitive face was never that, the death of the little prodigy Richard, and recording how 'after evening prayers was my child buried near the rest of his brothers – my very dear children'.[17] He was not an artist; no phrases linger in the mind; no paragraphs build themselves up in memory; but as an artistic method this of going on with the day's story circumstantially, bringing in people who will never be mentioned again, leading up to crises which never take place, introducing Sir Thomas Browne[18] but never letting him speak has its fascination. All through his pages good men, bad men, celebrities, nonentities are coming into the room and going out again. The greater number we scarcely notice; the door shuts upon them and they disappear. But now and again the sight of a vanishing coat-tail suggests more than a whole figure sitting still in a full light. Perhaps it is that we catch them unawares. Little they think that for three hundred years and more they will be looked at in the act of jumping a gate, or observing, like the old Marquis of Argyle, that the turtle doves in the aviary are owls.[19] Our eyes wander from one to the other; our affections settle here or there – on hot-tempered Captain Wray, for instance, who was choleric, had a dog that killed a goat, was for shooting the goat's owner, was for shooting his horse when it fell down a precipice; on M. Saladine; on M. Saladine's daughter; on Captain Wray lingering at Geneva to make love to M. Saladine's daughter;[20] on Evelyn himself most of all, grown old, walking in his garden at Wotton, his sorrows smoothed out, his grandson doing him credit, the Latin quotations falling pat from his lips, his trees flourishing, and the butterflies flying and flaunting on his dahlias too.

1–Originally published in the *TLS*, 28 October 1920, (Kp C208) under the title 'John Evelyn' (see *III VW Essays*), this essay was significantly revised for inclusion in *CR1*. It is based on a reading of *The Diary of John Evelyn* [1620–1706] (1818), probably in the 2-vol. edition published by J. M. Dent in 1911. The original version also reviewed *The Early Life and Education of John Evelyn 1620–1641*. With a commentary by H. Maynard Smith (OUP, 1920). (For Smith's complaints at VW's review and her riposte see *III VW Essays*, pp. 267–8.)

2–Diary, 26 March 1699 (J. M. Dent, 1911, vol. ii, p. 353). Oliver Cromwell (1599–1658).

3–*Ibid.*, 11 March 1651, vol. i, pp. 264–5. This was in Paris, at the Grand Châtelet, seat of the city's criminal and civil judiciary.

4–*Ibid.*

5–For the quotation, *ibid.*, 9 March 1652, vol. i, p. 276. Evelyn attended anatomy lectures at Padua and there obtained his tables, *ibid.*, 16 January 1646, vol. i, p. 214. On his way home he visited Paris where he met and on 27 June 1647 married Mary Browne (c. 1635–1709), daughter of the King's Ambassador.

6–*Ibid.*, 19 February 1653, vol. i, p. 285. Evelyn lived at Sayes Court, Deptford, from 1652 until 1694, when he removed to Wotton House in the parish of Wotton or Blackheath, Surrey.

7–Giulio Romano (c. 1492–1546); Polidoro Caldara da Caravaggio (c. 1500–43); Guido Reni (1575–1642); Raphael (1483–1520); Tintoretto (1518–94).

8–For both quotations, Diary, 27 August 1666, vol. ii, pp. 9–10. The thirteenth-century cathedral restored by Inigo Jones in the mid-seventeenth century was almost destroyed by the great fire, 2–7 September 1666. Sir Christopher Wren (1632–1723) was commissioned to design and build the new cathedral in 1668.

9–*Ibid.*, 18 January 1671, vol. ii, p. 56. Grinling Gibbons (1648–1721).

10–Evelyn, who became a Fellow of the Royal Society in 1661, was three times its Secretary: 1672–3, 1682, 1691.

11–Tennyson, *The Princess* (1847), 'Conclusion', ll. 86–90.

12–For the Court, Diary, 25 January 1685, vol. ii, p. 207; and for Nell Gwyn (1650–87), who bore Charles II (1630–85) two sons, *ibid.*, 1 March 1671, vol. ii, p. 60.

13–*Ibid.*, 4 October 1683, vol. ii, p. 192.

14–For the first quotation, Evelyn, *The Life of Margaret Godolphin* [1652–78], ed. Bishop Wilberforce (William Pickering, 1847), p. 14, and for the second, *ibid.*, p. 175, which does not have 'of meat'.

15 – *The Diary of Samuel Pepys*, 5 November 1665 (ed. Latham and Matthews, G. Bell, 1972, pp. 289–90).

16 – Evelyn let Sayes Court and in the summer of 1698 it was sub-let to Peter the Great (1672–1725).

17 – *Diary*, 29 March 1664, vol. i, p. 386. This was Richard (b. and d. 1664), not the prodigy Richard (1652–8).

18 – For Evelyn's visit to Sir Thomas Browne (1605–82), *ibid.*, 17 October 1671, vol. ii, pp. 69–70.

19 – For Archibald Campbell (c. 1607–61), Marquis of Argyll, and the owl-like doves, *ibid.*, 28 June 1656, vol. i, p. 318.

20 – Sir William Wray (c. 1625–69), believed to have been the Captain Wray who was Governor of Beaumaris Castle during the Protectorate. M. Saladine, unidentified.

Defoe

The fear which attacks the recorder of centenaries lest he should find himself measuring a diminishing spectre and forced to foretell its approaching dissolution is not only absent in the case of *Robinson Crusoe* but the mere thought of it is ridiculous. It may be true that *Robinson Crusoe* is two hundred years of age upon the twenty-fifth of April 1919[2] but far from raising the familiar speculations as to whether people now read it and will continue to read it, the effect of the bi-centenary is to make us marvel that *Robinson Crusoe*, the perennial and immortal, should have been in existence so short a time as that. The book resembles one of the anonymous productions of the race rather than the effort of a single mind; and as for celebrating its centenary we should as soon think of celebrating the centenaries of Stonehenge itself. Something of this we may attribute to the fact that we have all had *Robinson Crusoe* read aloud to us as children, and were thus much in the same state of mind towards Defoe and his story that the Greeks were in towards Homer. It never occurred to us that there was such a person as Defoe, and to have been told that *Robinson Crusoe* was the work of a man* with a pen in his hand would either have disturbed us unpleasantly or meant nothing at all. The impressions of childhood are those that last longest and cut deepest.† It still seems that the name of Daniel

Defoe has no right to appear upon the title-page of *Robinson Crusoe*, and if we celebrate the bi-centenary of the book we are making a slightly unnecessary allusion to the fact that, like Stonehenge, it is still in existence.

The great fame of the book has done its author some injustice; for while it has given him a kind of anonymous glory it has obscured the fact that he was a writer of other works which, it is safe to assert, were not read aloud to us as children. Thus when the editor of the *Christian World* in the year 1870 appealed to 'the boys and girls of England'[3] to erect a monument upon the grave of Defoe, which a stroke of lightning had mutilated, the marble was inscribed to the memory of the author of *Robinson Crusoe*. No mention was made of *Moll Flanders*. Considering the topics which are dealt with in that book, and in *Roxana, Captain Singleton, Colonel Jack* and the rest, we need not be surprised, though we may be indignant, at the omission. We may agree with Mr Wright, the biographer of Defoe, that these 'are not works for the drawing-room table'.[4] But unless we consent to make that useful piece of furniture the final arbiter of taste, we must deplore the fact that their superficial coarseness, or the universal celebrity of *Robinson Crusoe*, has led them to be far less widely famed than they deserve. On any monument worthy of the name of monument the names of *Moll Flanders* and *Roxana*, at least, should be carved as deeply as the name of Defoe. They stand among the few English novels which we can call indisputably great. The occasion of the bi-centenary of their more famous companion may well lead us to consider in what their greatness, which has so much in common with his, may be found to consist.

Defoe was an elderly man when he turned novelist, many years the predecessor of Richardson and Fielding,[5] and one of the first indeed to shape the novel and launch it on its way. But it is unnecessary to labour the fact of his precedence, except that he came to his novel-writing with certain conceptions about the art which he derived partly from being himself one of the first to practise it. The novel had to justify its existence by telling a true story and preaching a sound moral. 'This supplying a story by invention is certainly a most scandalous crime,' he wrote; 'it is a sort of lying that makes a great hole in the heart, in which by degrees a habit of lying enters in.'[6] Either in the preface or in the text of each of his works, therefore, he takes pains to insist that he has not used his invention at all but has depended upon facts, and that his purpose has been the highly moral desire to convert the vicious or to warn the innocent. Happily these were principles that tallied very well with his natural disposition and endowments. Facts had been drilled into him by sixty years of varying fortunes before he turned his experience to account in fiction. 'I have some time ago summed up the Scenes of my life in this distich,' he wrote:

> No man has tasted differing fortunes more,
> And thirteen times I have been rich and poor.[7]

He had spent eighteen months in Newgate and talked with thieves, pirates, highwaymen, and coiners before he wrote the history of Moll Flanders. But to have facts thrust upon you by dint of living and accident is one thing; to swallow them voraciously and retain the imprint of them indelibly, is another.[‡] It is not merely that Defoe knew the stress of poverty and had talked with the victims of it, but that the unsheltered life, exposed to circumstances and forced to shift for itself, appealed to him imaginatively as the right matter for his art. In the first pages of each of his great novels he reduces his hero or heroine to such a state of unfriended misery that their existence must be a continued struggle, and their survival at all the result of luck and their own exertions. Moll Flanders was born in Newgate of a criminal mother; Captain Singleton was stolen as a child and sold to the gipsies; Colonel Jack, though 'born a gentleman, was put 'prentice to a pickpocket';[8] Roxana starts under better auspices, but, having married at fifteen, she sees her husband go bankrupt and is left with five children in 'a condition the most deplorable that words can express'.[9]

Thus each of these boys and girls has the world to begin and the battle to fight for himself. The situation thus created was entirely to Defoe's liking. From her very birth or with half a year's respite at most, Moll Flanders, the most notable of them, is goaded by 'that worst of devils, poverty',[10] forced to earn her living as soon as she can sew, driven from place to place, making no demands upon her creator for the subtle domestic atmosphere which he was unable to supply, but drawing upon him for all he knew of strange people and customs. From the outset the burden of proving her right to exist is laid upon her. She has to depend entirely upon her own wits and judgement, and to deal with each emergency as it arises by a rule-of-thumb morality which she has forged in her own head. The briskness of the story is due partly to the fact that having transgressed the accepted laws at a very early age she has henceforth the freedom of the outcast. The one impossible event is that she should settle down in comfort and security. But from the first the peculiar genius of the author asserts itself, and avoids the obvious danger of the novel of adventure. He makes us understand that Moll Flanders was a woman on her own account and not only material for a succession of adventures. In proof of this she begins, as Roxana also begins, by falling passionately, if unfortunately, in love. That she must rouse herself and marry some one else and look very closely to her settlements and prospects is no slight upon her passion, but to be laid to the charge of her birth; and, like all Defoe's women, she is a person of robust understanding. Since she makes no scruple of telling lies when they serve her purpose, there is something undeniable about her truth when she speaks it. She has no time to waste upon the refinements of personal affection; one tear is dropped, one moment of despair allowed, and then 'on with the story'. She has a spirit that loves to breast the storm. She delights in the exercise of her own powers. When she discovers that the man she has married in Virginia is her own brother she is violently disgusted; she insists upon leaving him; but as soon as she sets foot in Bristol, 'I took the diversion of going to Bath, for as I was still far from being old so my humour, which was always gay, continued so to an extreme.'[11] Heartless she is not, nor can any one charge her with levity; but life delights her, and a heroine who lives has us all in tow. Moreover, her ambition has that slight strain of imagination in it which puts it in the category of the noble passions. Shrewd and practical of necessity, she is yet haunted by a desire for romance and for the quality which to her perception makes a man a gentleman. 'It was really a true gallant spirit he was of, and it was more grievous to me. 'Tis something of relief even to be undone by a man of honour rather than by a scoundrel,'[12] she writes when she had misled a highwayman as to the extent of her fortune. It is in keeping with this temper that she should be proud of her final partner because he refuses to work when they reach the plantations but prefers hunting, and that she should take pleasure in buying him wigs and silver-hilted swords 'to make him appear, as he really was, a very fine gentleman'.[13] Her very love of hot weather is in keeping, and the passion with which she kissed the ground that her son had trod on, and her noble tolerance of every kind of fault so long as it is not 'complete baseness of spirit, imperious, cruel, and relentless when uppermost, abject and low-spirited when down'.[14] For the rest of the world she has nothing but goodwill.

Since the list of the qualities and graces of this seasoned old sinner is by no means exhausted we can well understand how it was that Borrow's apple-woman on London Bridge called her 'blessed Mary' and valued her book above all the apples on her stall;[15] and that Borrow, taking the book deep into the booth, read till his eyes ached. But we dwell upon such signs of character only by way of proof that the creator of Moll Flanders was not, as he has been accused of being, a mere journalist and literal recorder of facts with no conception of the nature of psychology. It is true that his characters take shape and substance of their own accord, as if in despite of the author and not altogether to his liking. He never lingers or stresses any point of subtlety or pathos, but presses on imperturbably as if they came there without his knowledge. A touch of imagination, such as that when the Prince sits by his son's cradle and Roxana observes how 'he loved to look at it when it was asleep',[16] seems to mean much more to us than to him. After the curiously modern dissertation upon the need of communicating matters of importance to a second person lest, like the thief in Newgate, we should talk of it in our sleep, he apologises for his digression. He seems to have taken his characters so deeply into his mind that he lived them without exactly knowing how; and, like all unconscious artists, he leaves more gold in his work than his own generation was able to bring to the surface.

The interpretation that we put on his characters might therefore well have puzzled him. We find for ourselves meanings which he was careful to disguise even from his own eye.[5] Thus it comes about that we admire Moll Flanders far more than we blame her. Nor can we believe that Defoe had made up his mind as to the precise degree of her guilt, or was unaware that in considering the lives of the abandoned he raised many deep questions and hinted, if he did not state, answers quite at variance with his professions of belief. From the evidence supplied by his essay upon the 'Education of Women' we know that he had thought deeply and much in advance of his age upon the capacities of women, which he rated very high, and the injustice done to them, which he rated very harsh.

I have often thought of it as one of the most barbarous customs in the world, considering us as a civilised and a Christian country, that we deny the advantages of learning to women. We reproach the sex every day with folly and impertinence;

which I am confident, had they the advantages of education equal to us, they would be guilty of less than ourselves.[17]

The advocates of women's rights would hardly care, perhaps, to claim Moll Flanders and Roxana among their patron saints; and yet it is clear that Defoe not only intended them to speak some very modern doctrines upon the subject, but placed them in circumstances where their peculiar hardships are displayed in such a way as to elicit our sympathy. Courage, said Moll Flanders, was what women needed, and the power to 'stand their ground';[18] and at once gave practical demonstration of the benefits that would result. Roxana, a lady of the same profession, argues more subtly against the slavery of marriage. She 'had started a new thing in the world' the merchant told her; 'it was a way of arguing contrary to the general practise'.[19] But Defoe is the last writer to be guilty of bald preaching. Roxana keeps our attention‖ because she is blessedly unconscious that she is in any good sense an example to her sex and is thus at liberty to own that part of her argument is 'of an elevated strain which was really not in my thoughts at first, at all'.[20] The knowledge of her own frailties and the honest questioning of her own motives, which that knowledge begets, have the happy result of keeping her fresh and human when the martyrs and pioneers of so many problem novels have shrunken and shrivelled to the pegs and props of their respective creeds.

But the claim of Defoe upon our admiration does not rest upon the fact that he can be shown to have anticipated some of the views of Meredith, or to have written scenes which (the odd suggestion occurs)¶ might have been turned into plays by Ibsen.[21] Whatever his ideas upon the position of women, they are an incidental result of his chief virtue, which is that he deals with the important and lasting side of things and not with the passing and trivial. He is often dull. He can imitate the matter-of-fact precision of a scientific traveller until we wonder that his pen could trace or his brain conceive what has not even the excuse of truth to soften its dryness. He leaves out the whole of vegetable nature, and a large part of human nature.** All this we may admit, though we have to admit defects as grave in many writers whom we call great. But that does not impair the peculiar merit of what remains. Having at the outset limited his scope and confined his ambitions he achieves a truth of insight†† which is far rarer and more enduring than the truth of fact which he professed to make his aim. Moll Flanders and her friends recommended themselves to him not because they were, as we should say, 'picturesque'; nor, as he affirmed, because they were examples of evil living by which the public might profit. It was their natural veracity, bred in them by a life of hardship, that excited his interest. For them there were no excuses; no kindly shelter obscured their motives. Poverty was their taskmaster. Defoe did not pronounce more than a judgement of the lips upon their failings. But their courage and resource and tenacity delighted him. He found their society full of good talk, and pleasant stories, and faith in each other, and morality of a home-made kind. Their fortunes had that infinite variety which he praised and relished and beheld with wonder in his own life. These men and women, above all, were free to talk openly of the passions and desires which have moved men and women since the beginning of time, and thus even now they keep their vitality undiminished. There is a dignity in everything that is looked at openly.‡‡ Even the sordid subject of money, which plays so large a part in their histories, becomes not sordid but tragic when it stands not for ease and consequence§§ but for honour, honesty, and life itself. You may object that Defoe is humdrum, but never that he is engrossed with petty things.

He belongs, indeed, to the school of the great plain writers, whose work is founded upon a knowledge of what is most persistent, though not most seductive, in human nature. The view of London from Hungerford Bridge, grey, serious, massive, and full of the subdued stir of traffic and business, prosaic if it were not for the masts of the ships and the towers and domes of the city, brings him to mind.[22] The tattered girls with violets in their hands at the street corners, and the old weather-beaten women patiently displaying their matches and bootlaces beneath the shelter of arches, seem like characters from his books. He is of the school of Crabbe and of Gissing,[23]‖‖ and not merely a fellow-pupil in the same stern place of learning, but its founder and master.

---

* – *TLS*: 'an individual'.
† – *TLS*: 'longest and are most unyielding.'
‡ – *TLS*: 'indelibly, as if they had a particular significance, is another.'
§ – *TLS*: does not give the two preceding sentences and begins: 'Admitting that Defoe would have been the first to deny any more elaborate philosophy than his explicit desire to convert and to warn, we cannot lay aside *Moll Flanders* or *Roxana* without suspecting that the matter is far more complex than he allowed. Turning novelist at the age of sixty, having, as he said, "seen the rough side of the world

as well as the smooth", and acted a bold part in practical affairs, Defoe could not paint a flat unshaded picture of human life with the colours of good and evil unmixed and distinct, however sincerely he attempted it.'

‖ – *TLS*: '. . . that would result. But Roxana supplies a subtler illustration of the difficult position in which a woman might find herself, and what new thoughts might be bred in her of the crisis. She is of the same profession as Moll Flanders, but in a more exalted sphere; she does not need to mend her fortunes by stealing. Among her entanglements is one with a merchant of Paris who proposes to marry her. She refuses on the ground that she would then become his slave, whereas at present she keeps her freedom. But if we love each other, he asks, how can there be a question of slavery? "Ay," she cried. "The pretence of affection takes from a woman everything that can be called herself"; and she treats him to a vehement disquisition upon the case of the wife who has surrendered everything on this plea "to be engulphed in misery and beggary". He then implores her to marry him for the sake of their unborn child. She returns that "if the woman marries the man afterwards she bears the reproach of it to the last hour". It is better to part; "there is an end of the crime, and an end of the clamour." After considering this argument the merchant replies "that I had started a new thing in the world . . . it was a way of arguing contrary to the general practice." Roxana indeed excites our sympathy more than some of her successors, because she is . . .'

¶ – *TLS*: does not give the matter in parenthesis.

˙˙ – *TLS*: '; he leaves out the whole of nature and a large part of humanity.'

†† – *TLS*: 'achieves a kind of truth which'.

‡‡ – *TLS*: does not give this sentence.

§§ – *TLS*: 'ease and social dignity, but'.

‖‖ – *TLS*: 'school of Borrow and of Crabbe'.

1–Originally published in the *TLS*, 24 April 1919, (Kp C148) under the title 'The Novels of Defoe', this essay was revised for inclusion in *CR1*. Bruce Richmond had written to VW on 14 February 1919 to say that he would manufacture an excuse for a front page article on Daniel Defoe (1660–1731) whenever she liked (MHP). By 10 April we discover in her diary that she has been 'submerged in Defoe; & only steal 10 minutes from Roxana to write this' and that she has 'to read one book a day in order to start on Saturday – such is the life of a hack.' On 12 April she exclaims in the same pages: 'A great writer – & Forster has never read his books! I was beckoned by Forster from the Library as I approached. We shook hands very cordially; & yet I always feel him shrinking sensitively from me, as a woman, a clever woman, an up to date woman. Feeling this I commanded him to read Defoe, & left him, & went & got some more Defoe, having bought one volume at Bickers on the way.' Bruce Richmond called in person to collect the essay on 19 April and next day in her diary she reflected: 'In the idleness which succeeds any long article, & Defoe is the 2nd leader this month, I got out this diary & read as one always does read one's own writing, with a kind of guilty intensity.' See Editorial Note, p. xxv. See also 'Robinson Crusoe' below. Reading Notes (Berg, III).

2–*The Life and Strange Surprising Adventures of Robinson Crusoe, of York, Mariner*, was entered in the Stationer's Register by the printer William Taylor on 23 April 1719 and was indeed published as VW states, two days later.

3—Thomas Wright, *The Life of Daniel Defoe* (Cassell and Company Ltd, 1894), ch. xiv, p. 386. (Wright is VW's chief biographical source for her article but she also made notes from Leslie Stephen's entry on Defoe in the *DNB*.)

4—*Ibid.*, ch. xii, pp. 277: 'And if Defoe is not to be castigated for thinking fit to write the lives of thieves and harlots, neither is it fair to charge him with being coarse. "Moll Flanders", "Colonel Jack", and "Roxana" are not books for the drawing-room table, but neither are "Hamlet", "Gulliver's Travels" (unexpurgated), "Tom Jones", "Joseph Andrews", or "Tristram Shandy". Defoe belonged to an age when a spade was called a spade. Had he lived at the present day, he would doubtless have used a decent periphrasis.' *Moll Flanders* (1722), *Roxana* (1724), *Captain Singleton* (1720), *Colonel Jack* (1722).

5—Samuel Richardson (1689–1761), Henry Fielding (1707–54).

6—Wright, ch. xii, p. 287, quoting Defoe's *Serious Reflections of Robinson Crusoe* (1720).

7—*Ibid.* ch. vii, p. 163.

8—From the title page to the original edition of *Colonel Jack*.

9—*Roxana; or the Fortunate Mistress* (*Works*, Bohn's British Classics, 1854–6, vol. iv), p. 8.

10—*Moll Flanders* (Works, Bohn, 1854–6, vol. iii), p. 152.

11—*Ibid.*, p. 82.

12—*Ibid.*, p. 120.

13—*Ibid.*, p. 280.

14—*Ibid.*, p. 206–7.

15—George Borrow (1803–81), *Lavengro* (1851; J. M. Dent, 1906, ch. xxxi, p. 190): '"So you think there is no harm in stealing?"/"No harm in the world, dear! Do you think my own child would have been transported for it, if there had been any harm in it? and what's more, would the blessed woman in the book here have written her life as she has done, and given it to the world, if there had been any harm in the thing? . . . . . . /Her name, blessed Mary Flanders."'

16—*Roxana*, p. 68. In the preceding sentence the original had 'as they if', now emended.

17—*An English Garner: Later Stuart Tracts* with an introduction by George A. Aitken (Constable and Co. Ltd, 1903), 'Daniel Defoe. The Education of Women', p. 281, which has 'while I am confident'.

18—*Moll Flanders*, p. 55: 'Thus I convinced her, that if the men made their advantage of our sex in the affair of marriage, upon the supposition of there being such a choice to be had, and of the woman being so easy, it was only owing to this, that the women wanted courage to maintain their ground . . .'

19—*Roxana*, pp. 133–4.

20—*Ibid.*, p. 128, which has 'strain, which'.

21—Henrik Ibsen (1828–1906). George Meredith (1828–1909), for VW on whom see below.

22—See *I VW Diary*, 12 April 1919: 'These ten minutes are stolen from Moll Flanders, which I failed to finish yesterday in accordance with my time sheet, yielding to a desire to stop reading & go up to London. But I saw London, in particular the view of white city churches & palaces from Hungerford Bridge through the eyes of Defoe. I saw the old women selling matches through his eyes; & the draggled girl skirting round the pavement of St. James' Square seemed to me out of Roxana or Moll Flanders. Yes, a great writer surely to be thus imposing himself upon me after 200 years.' Hungerford footbridge crosses the Thames between Waterloo and Charing Cross. VW used it regularly on her way up to town from Richmond.

23 – George Crabbe (1754–1832), for VW on whom see *VI VW Essays* and *CDB*. George Gissing (1857–1903), for VW on whom see 'The Private Papers of Henry Ryecroft', 'The Novels of George Gissing', *I VW Essays*; 'An Impression of George Gissing', *III VW Essays*; and *'George Gissing'*, V *VW Essays* and *CR2*.

Addison

In July, 1843, Lord Macaulay pronounced the opinion that Joseph Addison had enriched our literature with compositions 'that will live as long as the English language'.[2] But when Lord Macaulay pronounced an opinion it was not merely an opinion. Even now, at a distance of seventy-six years, the words seem to issue from the mouth of the chosen representative of the people. There is an authority about them, a sonority,* a sense of responsibility, which puts us in mind of a Prime Minister making a proclamation on behalf of a great empire rather than of a journalist writing about a deceased man of letters for a magazine. The article upon Addison is, indeed, one of the most vigorous of the famous essays. Florid, and at the same time extremely solid, the phrases seem to build up a monument, at once square and lavishly festooned with ornament, which should serve Addison for shelter so long as one stone of Westminster Abbey stands upon another. Yet, though we may have read and admired this particular essay times out of number (as we say when we have read anything three times over), it has never occurred to us, strangely enough, to believe that it is true. That is apt to happen to the admiring reader of Macaulay's essays. While delighting in their richness, force, and variety, and finding every judgement, however emphatic, proper in its place, it seldom occurs to us to connect these sweeping assertions and undeniable convictions with anything so minute as a human being. So it is with Addison. 'If we wish,' Macaulay writes, 'to find anything more vivid than Addison's best portraits, we must go either to Shakespeare or to Cervantes.' 'We have not the least doubt that if Addison had written a novel on an extensive plan it would have been superior to any that we possess.' His essays, again, 'fully entitle him to the rank of a great poet'; and, to complete the edifice, we have

Voltaire proclaimed 'the prince of buffoons',[3] and together with Swift forced to stoop so low that Addison takes rank above them both as a humorist.

Examined separately, such flourishes of ornament look grotesque enough, but in their place – such is the persuasive power of design – they are part of the decoration; they complete the monument. Whether Addison or another is interred within, it is a very fine tomb. But now that two centuries have passed since the real body of Addison was laid by night under the Abbey floor, we are, through no merit of our own, partially qualified to test the first of the flourishes on that fictitious tombstone to which, though it may be empty, we have done homage, in a formal kind of way, these sixty-seven years. The compositions of Addison will live as long as the English language. Since every moment brings proof that our mother tongue is more lusty and lively than sorts with complete sedateness or chastity, we need only concern ourselves with the vitality of Addison. Neither lusty nor lively is the adjective we should apply to the present condition of the *Tatler* and the *Spectator*.[4] To take a rough test, it is possible to discover how many people in the course of a year borrow Addison's works from the public library, and a particular instance affords us the not very encouraging information that during nine years two people yearly take out the first volume of the *Spectator*. The second volume is less in request than the first. The inquiry is not a cheerful one. From certain marginal comments and pencil marks it seems that these rare devotees seek out only the famous passages and, as their habit is, score what we are bold enough to consider the least admirable phrases. No; if Addison lives at all, it is not in the public libraries. It is in libraries that are markedly private, secluded, shaded by lilac trees and brown with folios, that he still draws his faint, regular breath. If any man or woman is going to solace himself or herself with a page of Addison before the June sun is out of the sky today, it is in some such pleasant retreat as this.

Yet all over England at intervals, perhaps wide ones, we may be sure that there are people engaged in reading Addison, whatever the year or season. For Addison is very well worth reading. The temptation to read Pope on Addison, Macaulay on Addison, Thackeray on Addison, Johnson on Addison[5] rather than Addison himself is to be resisted, for you will find, if you study the *Tatler* and the *Spectator*, glance at *Cato*,[6] and run through the remainder of the six moderate-sized volumes,[7] that Addison is neither Pope's Addison nor anybody else's Addison, but a separate, independent individual still capable of casting a clear-cut shape of himself upon the consciousness, turbulent and distracted as it is, of nineteen hundred and nineteen. It is true that the fate[†] of the lesser shades is always a little precarious. They are so easily obscured or distorted. It seems so often scarcely worth while to go through the cherishing and humanising process which is necessary to get into touch with a writer of the second class who may, after all, have little to give us. The earth is crusted over them; their features are obliterated, and perhaps it is not a head of the best period that we rub clean in the end, but only the chip of an old pot. The chief difficulty with the lesser writers, however, is not only the effort. It is that our standards have changed. The things that they like are not the things that we like; and as the charm of their writing depends much more upon taste than upon conviction, a change of manners is often quite enough to put us out of touch altogether. That is one of the most troublesome barriers between ourselves and Addison.[‡] He attached great importance to certain qualities. He had a very precise notion of what we are used to call 'niceness' in man or woman. He was extremely fond of saying that men ought not to be atheists, and that women ought not to wear large petticoats. This directly inspires in us not so much a sense of distaste as a sense of difference. Dutifully, if at all, we strain our imaginations to conceive the kind of audience to whom these precepts were addressed. The *Tatler* was published in 1709; the *Spectator* a year or two later. What was the state of England at that particular moment? Why was Addison so anxious to insist upon the necessity of a decent and cheerful religious belief? Why did he so constantly, and in the main kindly, lay stress upon the foibles of women and their reform? Why was he so deeply impressed with the evils of party government? Any historian will explain; but it is always a misfortune to have to call in the services of any historian. A writer should give us direct certainty; explanations are so much water poured into the wine. As it is, we can only feel that[§] these counsels are addressed to ladies in hoops and gentlemen in wigs – a vanished audience which has learnt its lesson and gone its way and the preacher with it. We can only smile and marvel and perhaps admire the clothes.

And that is not the way to read. To be thinking that dead people deserved these censures and admired this morality, judged the eloquence, which we find so frigid, sublime, and philosophy to us so superficial, profound, to take a collector's joy in such signs of antiquity, is to treat literature as if it were a broken jar of undeniable age but doubtful beauty, to be stood in a cabinet behind glass doors. The charm which still makes *Cato* very readable is much of this nature. When Syphax exclaims,

> So, where our wide Numidian wastes extend,
> Sudden, th'impetuous hurricanes descend,
> Wheel through the air, in circling eddies play,
> Tear up the sands, and sweep whole plains away.
> The helpless traveller, with wild surprise,
> Sees the dry desert all around him rise,
> And smother'd in the dusty whirlwind dies,[8]

we cannot help imagining the thrill in the crowded theatre, the feathers nodding emphatically on the ladies' heads, the gentlemen leaning forward to tap their canes, and every one exclaiming to his neighbour how vastly fine it is and crying 'Bravo!' But how can *we* be excited? And so with Bishop Hurd and his notes – his 'finely observed', his 'wonderfully exact, both in the sentiment and expression', his serene confidence that when 'the present humour of idolising Shakespeare is over', the time will come when *Cato* is 'supremely admired by all candid and judicious critics'.[9] This is all very amusing and productive of pleasant fancies, both as to the faded frippery of our ancestors' minds and the bold opulence of our own. But it is not the intercourse of equals, let alone that other kind of intercourse, which as it makes us contemporary with the author, persuades us that his object is our own.[||] Occasionally in *Cato* one may pick up a few lines that are not obsolete; but for the most part the tragedy which Dr Johnson thought 'unquestionably the noblest production of Addison's genius'[10] has become collector's literature.

Perhaps most readers approach the essays also with some suspicion as to the need of condescension in their minds. The question to be asked is whether Addison, attached as he was to certain standards of gentility, morality, and taste, has not become one of those people of exemplary character and charming urbanity who must never be talked to about anything more exciting than the weather. We have some slight suspicion that the *Spectator* and the *Tatler* are nothing but talk, couched in perfect English, about the number of fine days this year compared with the number of wet the year before. The difficulty of getting on to equal terms with him is shown by the little fable which he introduces into one of the early numbers of the *Tatler*, of 'a young gentleman, of moderate understanding, but great vivacity, who ... had got a little smattering of knowledge, just enough to make an atheist or a freethinker, but not a philosopher, or a man of sense'.[11] This young gentleman visits his father in the country, and proceeds 'to enlarge the narrowness of the country notions; in which he succeeded so well, that he had seduced the butler by his table-talk, and staggered his eldest sister ... 'Till one day, talking of his setting dog ... said "he did not question but Tray was as immortal as any one of the family"; and in the heat of the argument told his father, that for his own part, "he expected to die like a dog". Upon which, the old man, starting up in a very great passion, cried out, "Then, sirrah, you shall live like one"; and taking his cane in his hand, cudgelled him out of his system. This had so good an effect upon him, that he took up from that day, fell to reading good books, and is now a bencher in the Middle-Temple.'[12] There is a good deal of Addison in that story: his dislike of 'dark and uncomfortable prospects'; his respect for 'principles which are the support, happiness and glory of all public societies, as well as private persons';[13] his solicitude for the butler; and his conviction that to read good books and become a bencher in the Middle Temple is the proper end for a very vivacious young gentleman. This Mr Addison married a Countess, 'gave his little senate laws',[14] and, sending for young Lord Warwick, made that famous remark about seeing how a Christian can die which has fallen upon such evil days that our sympathies are with the foolish, and perhaps fuddled, young peer rather than with the frigid gentleman, not too far gone for a last spasm of self-complacency, upon the bed.[15]

Let us rub off such incrustations, so far as they are due to the corrosion of Pope's wit or the deposit of mid-Victorian lachrymosity, and see what, for us in our time, remains. In the first place, there remains the not despicable virtue, after two centuries of existence, of being readable. Addison can fairly lay claim to that; and then, slipped in on the tide of the smooth, well-turned prose, are little eddies, diminutive waterfalls, agreeably diversifying the polished surface. We begin to take note of whims, fancies, peculiarities on the part of the essayist which light up the prim, impeccable countenance of the moralist and convince us that, however tightly he may have pursed his lips, his eyes are very bright and not so shallow after all. He is alert to his fingertips. Little muffs, silver garters, fringed gloves draw his attention; he observes with a keen, quick glance, not unkindly, and full rather of amusement than of censure. To be sure, the age was rich in follies. Here were coffee-houses packed with politicians talking of Kings and Emperors and letting their own small affairs go to ruin. Crowds applauded the Italian opera every night without understanding a word of it. Critics discoursed of the unities. Men gave a thousand pounds for a handful of tulip roots. As for women – or 'the fair sex', as Addison liked to call them – their follies were past counting. He did his best to count them, with a loving particularity which roused the ill-humour of Swift.[1] But he did it very charmingly, with a natural relish for the task, as the following passage shows:

I consider woman as a beautiful romantic animal, that may be adorned with furs and feathers, pearls and diamonds, ores and silks. The lynx shall cast its skin at her feet to make her a tippet; the peacock, parrot, and swan, shall pay contributions to her muff; the sea shall be searched for shells, and the rocks for gems; and every part of nature furnish out its share towards the embellishment of a creature that is the most consummate work of it. All this I shall indulge them in; but as for the petticoat I have been speaking of, I neither can nor will allow it.[16]

In all these matters Addison was on the side of sense and taste and civilisation. Of that little fraternity, often so obscure and yet so indispensable, who in every age keep themselves alive to the importance of art and letters and music, watching, discriminating, denouncing and delighting, Addison was one – distinguished and strangely contemporary with ourselves. It would have been, so one imagines, a great pleasure to take him a manuscript; a great enlightenment, as well as a great honour, to have his opinion. In spite of Pope, one fancies that his would have been criticism of the best order, open-minded and generous to novelty, and yet, in the final resort, unfaltering in its standards. The boldness which is a proof of vigour is shown by his defence of 'Chevy Chase'. He had so clear a notion of what he meant by the 'very spirit and soul of fine writing'[17] as to track it down in an old barbarous ballad or rediscover it in 'that divine work' Paradise Lost.[18] Moreover, far from being a connoisseur only of the still, settled beauties of the dead, he was aware of the present; a severe critic of its 'Gothic taste',[19] vigilant in protecting the rights and honours of the language, and all in favour of simplicity and quiet. Here we have the Addison of Will's and Button's, who, sitting late into the night and drinking more than was good for him, gradually overcame his taciturnity and began to talk. Then he 'chained the attention of every one to him'. 'Addison's conversation,' said Pope, 'had something in it more charming than I have found in any other man.'[20] One can well believe it, for his essays at their best preserve the very cadence** of easy yet exquisitely modulated conversation – the smile checked before it has broadened into laughter, the thought lightly turned from frivolity or abstraction, the ideas springing, bright, new, various, with the utmost spontaneity. He seems to speak what comes into his head, and is never at the trouble of raising his voice. But he has described himself in the character of the lute better than any one can do it for him.

The lute is a character directly opposite to the drum, that sounds very finely by itself, or in a very small concert. Its notes are exquisitely sweet, and very low, easily drowned in a multitude of instruments, and even lost among a few, unless you give a particular attention to it. A lute is seldom heard in a company of more than five, whereas a drum will show itself to advantage in an assembly of 500. The lutanists, therefore, are men of a fine genius, uncommon reflection, great affability, and esteemed chiefly by persons of a good taste, who are the only proper judges of so delightful and soft a melody.[21]

Addison was a lutanist. No praise, indeed, could be less appropriate than Lord Macaulay's. To call Addison on the strength of his essays a great poet, or to prophesy that if he had written a novel on an extensive plan it would have been 'superior to any that we possess', is to confuse him with the drums and trumpets; it is not merely to overpraise her merits, but to overlook them. Dr Johnson superbly, and, as his manner is, once and for all has summed up the quality of Addison's poetic genius:

His poetry is first to be considered; of which it must be confessed that it has not often those felicities of diction which give lustre to sentiments, or that vigour of sentiment that animates diction; there is little of ardour, vehemence, or transport; there is very rarely the awfulness of grandeur, and not very often the splendour of elegance. He thinks justly; but he thinks faintly.[22]

The Sir Roger de Coverley papers[23] are those which have the most resemblance, on the surface, to a novel. But their merit consists in the fact that they do not adumbrate, or initiate, or anticipate anything; they exist, perfect, complete, entire in themselves. To read them as if they were a first hesitating experiment containing the seed of greatness to come is to miss the peculiar point of them. They are studies done from the outside by a quiet spectator. When read together they compose a portrait of the Squire and his circle all in characteristic positions – one with his rod, another with his hounds

– but each can be detached from the rest without damage to the design or harm to himself. In a novel, where each chapter gains from the one before it or adds to the one that follows it, such separations would be intolerable. The speed, the intricacy, the design, would be mutilated. These particular qualities are perhaps lacking, but nevertheless Addison's method has great advantages. Each of these essays is very highly finished. The characters are defined by a succession of extremely neat, clean strokes. Inevitably, where the sphere is so narrow – an essay is only three or four pages in length – there is not room for great depth or intricate subtlety.[tt] Here, from the *Spectator*, is a good example of the witty and decisive manner in which Addison strikes out a portrait to fill the little frame:

Sombrius is one of these sons of sorrow. He thinks himself obliged in duty to be sad and disconsolate. He looks on a sudden fit of laughter as a breach of his baptismal vow. An innocent jest startles him like blasphemy. Tell him of one who is advanced to a title of honour, he lifts up his hands and eyes; describe a public ceremony, he shakes his head; shew him a gay equipage, he blesses himself. All the little ornaments of life are pomps and vanities. Mirth is wanton, and wit profane. He is scandalised at youth for being lively, and at childhood for being playful. He sits at a christening, or at a marriage-feast, as at a funeral; sighs at the conclusion of a merry story, and grows devout when the rest of the company grow pleasant. After all Sombrius is a religious man, and would have behaved himself very properly, had he lived when Christianity was under a general persecution.[24]

The novel is not a development from that model, for the good reason that no development along these lines is possible. Of its kind such a portrait is perfect; and when we find, scattered up and down the *Spectator* and the *Tatler*, numbers of such little masterpieces with fancies and anecdotes in the same style, some doubt as to the narrowness of such a sphere becomes inevitable. The form of the essay admits of its own particular perfection; and if anything is perfect the exact dimensions of its perfection become immaterial. One can scarcely settle whether, on the whole, one prefers a raindrop to the River Thames. When we have said all that we can say against them – that many are dull, others superficial, the allegories faded, the piety conventional, the morality trite – there still remains the fact that the essays of Addison are perfect essays. Always at the highest point of any art there comes a moment when everything seems in a conspiracy to help the artist, and his achievement becomes a natural felicity on his part of which he seems, to a later age, half-unconscious. So Addison, writing day after day, essay after essay, knew instinctively and exactly how to do it. Whether it was a high thing, or whether it was a low thing, whether an epic is more profound or a lyric more passionate, undoubtedly[‡‡] it is due to Addison that prose is now prosaic – the medium which makes it possible for people of ordinary intelligence to communicate their ideas to the world. Addison is the respectable ancestor of an innumerable progeny. Pick up the first weekly journal and the article upon the 'Delights of Summer' or the 'Approach of Age' will show his influence. But it will also show, unless the name of Mr Max Beerbohm,[25] our solitary essayist, is attached to it, that we have lost the art of writing essays. What with our views and our virtues, our passions and profundities, the shapely silver drop, that held the sky in it and so many bright little visions of human life, is now nothing but a hold-all knobbed with luggage packed in a hurry. Even so the essayist will make an effort, perhaps without knowing it, to write like Addison.

In his temperate and reasonable way Addison more than once amused himself with speculations as to the fate of his writings. He had a just idea of their nature and value. 'I have new-pointed all the batteries of ridicule,'[26] he wrote. Yet, because so many of his darts had been directed against ephemeral follies, 'absurd fashions, ridiculous customs, and affected forms of speech', the time would come, in a hundred years, perhaps, when his essays, he thought, would be 'like so many pieces of old plate, where the weight will be regarded, but the fashion lost'.[27] Two hundred years have passed; the plate is worn smooth; the pattern almost rubbed out; but the metal is pure silver.

---

[*] – TLS: 'them, a roundness, a sonority'.

[†] – TLS: 'It is true, to digress for a moment, that the case'.

[‡] – TLS: 'The chief difficulty with the lesser writers is, perhaps, that our standards have changed; the things that they like are not the things that we like. That is one of the most troublesome impediments between us and Addison.'

[§] – TLS: 'Any historian of the eighteenth century will explain. Meanwhile we feel that'.

[‖] – TLS: 'intercourse, which, as we read Urn Burial or the Religio Medici, or Christian Morals, makes us contemporary with the author, and, as it expands our range of delights, persuades us that the whole business of life is better worth while.'

[¶] – TLS: 'which annoyed Swift.'

[**] – TLS: 'decadence'.

[††] – TLS: 'depth or subtlety.'

[‡‡] – TLS: 'how to do it. Was it a high thing that he set himself to do? Was it not

only that he perfected a method of talking to people, without raising his voice about trifles? Undoubtedly ...'

1–Originally published in the *TLS*, 19 June 1919, (Kp C155) under the title 'Joseph Addison', this essay was revised as shown for inclusion in *CR1*. Two days after Lytton Strachey had come to tea at Hogarth House, Richmond, VW noted in her diary, on 25 May 1919: 'Lytton ... half maliciously assured me that my industry amazed him. My industry & my competence, for he thinks me the best reviewer alive, & the inventor of a new prose style, & the creator of a new version of the sentence. People's compliments generally manage to reserve the particular praise they wish to have themselves ... But then money – he must make money – he cant write reviews – & I've to do Addison, & other books, & protested that all the same I'm not a hack, & he runs the risk of becoming a Logan [Pearsall Smith], a superior dilettante. To which he agreed, & then we talked about Addison, & read scraps of Johnson's lives; & so enjoyed ourselves.' Writing next day to Strachey, she mentioned that 'Addison improves a little – if one likes that sort of thing. I mean he's very much better than Robert Lynd or Jack Squire' (*II VW Letters*, no. 1051). On 30 May she wrote, now from Asheham House in Sussex, to another Bloomsbury friend: 'And now, Saxon [Sydney-Turner], what is your opinion of Addison's writings? That is the problem of my life. But owing to my lethargy, I can't endure to open the Spectator; in a sort of coma I've glided through Sir Roger de Coverley, who seems a very pleasant old gentleman, but not the sort who much interests me. The propriety is so fearful, and the kindliness; and his death leaves me – Well I'm ashamed to say I began my great task of weeding the terrace, and then Duncan came – however I know its one of the masterpieces of English prose – Can I say, on your authority, that he's a complete humbug? The worst of it is that he's not' (*ibid.*, no. 1052). See also 'The Modern Essay' below. Reading Notes (Berg 11), where, in addition to works cited below, notes are also made from Leslie Stephen's entry on Addison in the *DNB*. See Editorial Note, p. xxv. Reprinted *CE*.

2–Thomas Babington Macaulay, 'The Life and Writings of Addison', originally published in the *Edinburgh Review*, July 1843; in *Critical and Historical Essays* (Everyman, 2 vols, J. M. Dent and E. P. Dutton, 1907), vol. ii, p. 488: 'As yet his fame rested on performances which, though highly respectable, were not built for duration ... The time had come when he was to prove himself a man of genius, and to enrich our literature with compositions which will live as long as the English language.' Joseph Addison (1672–1719).

3–For the first quotation, *ibid.*, p. 490, and for the second, p. 498, which has: 'plan, it', and continues: 'As it is he is entitled to be considered, not only as the greatest of the English essayists, but as the forerunner of the greatest English novelists.' For the third quotation, *ibid.*, p. 490: 'The numerous fictions, generally original, often wild and grotesque, but always singularly graceful and happy, which are found in his essays, fully entitle him to the rank of a great poet, a rank to which his metrical compositions give him no claim.' For the fourth quotation, *ibid.*, p. 491: 'Voltaire is the prince of buffoons. His merriment is without disguise or restraint. He gambols; he grins; he shakes his sides; he points the finger; he turns up the nose; he shoots out the tongue.' Miguel de Cervantes Saavedra (1547–1616), William Shakespeare (1564–1616), Voltaire (1694–1778), Jonathan Swift (1667–1795).

4 – The *Tatler* first appeared on 12 April 1709 and was published thrice-weekly until 2 January 1711; Addison's first contribution was to no. 81 (15 October 1709). The *Spectator* was first issued on 1 March 1711 and appeared daily, until no. 555 (6 December 1712). Addison and Richard Steele (1672-1729) were its principal contributors.

5 – Alexander Pope (1688–1744), 'Atticus', written c. 1715, first published in 1722, revised and incorporated in the *Epistle to Dr Arbuthnot* (1735); see also Pope's correspondence, fraudulently slanted to discredit Addison. W. M. Thackeray (1811–63), *The English Humourists of the Eighteenth Century* (1853), ch. ii, 'Congreve and Addison' (and see 'The Famous Mr Joseph Addison', ch. xi, in *The History of Henry Esmond*, 1852). Samuel Johnson (1709–84), 'Addison', *The Lives of the English Poets* (1779–81).

6 – Addison's tragedy *Cato* was produced to enormous success in 1713.

7 – *The Works of the Right Honourable Joseph Addison*, ed. Richard Hurd (6 vols, T. Cadell and W. Davies, 1811; also Bohn British Classics, 1856). VW made notes from both editions but drew chiefly upon that for 1811, in which references are cited here.

8 – *Works* (1811), vol. i, *Cato*, II, vi, end of act, p. 256.

9 – For the first quotation, *ibid.*, I, ii, p. 219, fn. a, annotating the phrase 'cold youth', spoken by Sempronius on seeing Portius. For the second: *ibid.*, p. 220, fn. a, annotating the third line here from Portius's speech: 'Alas! Sempronius, wouldst thou talk of Love / To Marcia, whilst her father's life's in danger? / Thou might'st as well court the pale trembling vestal, / When she beholds the holy flame expiring.' For the third and fourth: *ibid.*, p. 217, fn. a, which has: 'While the present humour of idolising Shakespeare continues, no quarter will be given to this poem . . .'

10 – Johnson, 'Addison', *The Lives of the English Poets* (ed. G. B. Hill, 3 vols, OUP, 1945, vol. ii, p. 132).

11 – *Works* (1811), vol. ii, *Tatler*, no. 108 (Saturday, 17 December 1709), p. 265.

12 – *Ibid.*, which has 'their country notions'.

13 – For both quotations, *ibid.*, p. 266.

14 – *Ibid.*, vol. i, '"Prologue" by Mr [Alexander] Pope, Spoken by Mr Wilks' (1713), lines 23–4: 'While Cato gives his little senate laws, / What bosom beats not in his Country's cause?' Addison married in 1716, Charlotte, Dowager Countess of Warwick (d. 1731).

15 – Edward Rich, 7th Earl of Warwick; the remark is quoted by Samuel Johnson.

16 – *Works* (1811), vol. ii, *Tatler*, no. 116 (Thursday, 5 January 1710), pp. 284–5.

17 – For the quotation, *ibid.*, vol. iv, *Spectator*, no. 409, Thursday, 19 June 1712, p. 334. For Addison's defence of 'Chevy Chase' see *ibid.*, vol. iii, *Spectator*, nos. 70 and 74, 21 and 25 May 1710, pp. 173–9, 186–91.

18 – Addison wrote a series of *Spectators* (between nos 267 and 369 inclusive) on Milton's *Paradise Lost* (1667). For the phrase 'that divine work', *Works* (1811), vol. iv, *Spectator*, no. 409, 19 June 1811, p. 335.

19 – Cf. *ibid.*, vol. iii, *Spectator*, no. 70, 21 May 1710, pp. 173–4: 'Molière, as we are told by Monsieur Boileau, used to read all his comedies to an old woman who was his housekeeper . . . and could foretell the success of his play in the theatre from the reception it met with at his fire-side . . . I know nothing which shows the essential and inherent perfection of simplicity of thought, above that which I call the Gothic manner of writing, than this; the first pleases all kinds of palates, and the latter only such as have formed to themselves a wrong artificial taste upon little fanciful authors and writers of epigram.'

20—Rev. Joseph Spence, *Observations, Anecdotes and Characters of Books and Men Collected from Conversation* (1820; ed. James M. Osborn, 2 vols, OUP, 1966, Anecdote no. 148, 13 December 1730, p. 62): 'Addison was perfect good company with intimates, and had something more charming in his conversation that I ever knew in any other man. But with any mixture of strangers, and sometimes with only one [or with any man he was too jealous of], he seemed to preserve his dignity much, with a stiff sort of silence.'
21—*Works* (1811), vol. ii, *Tatler*, no. 153, Saturday, 1 April 1710, p. 342.
22—Johnson, 'Addison', p. 127.
23—Sir Roger de Coverley is most fully portrayed in fifteen issues of the *Spectator* in July 1711 but appears between nos 2 and 553, 2 March 1711–4 December 1712.
24—*Works* (1811), vol. v, *Spectator*, no. 494, Friday, 26 September 1711, p. 15.
25—Max Beerbohm (1872–1956), for VW on whom see 'The Modern Essay' below.
26—*Works* (1811), vol. iv, *Spectator*, no. 445, Thursday, 31 July 1712, p. 400.
27—*Ibid.*, no. 435, Saturday, 19 July 1712, p. 384, which has 'as so many pieces'.

The Lives of the Obscure

Five shillings, perhaps, will secure a life subscription to this faded, out-of-date, obsolete library, which, with a little help from the rates, is chiefly subsidised from the shelves of clergymen's widows, and country gentlemen inheriting more books than their wives like to dust. In the middle of the wide airy room, with windows that look to the sea and let in the shouts of men crying pilchards for sale on the cobbled street below, a row of vases stands, in which specimens of the local flowers droop, each with its name inscribed beneath. The elderly, the marooned, the bored, drift from newspaper to newspaper, or sit holding their heads over back numbers of *The Illustrated London News* and the *Wesleyan Chronicle*.[1] No one has spoken aloud here since the room was opened in 1854. The obscure sleep on the walls, slouching against each other as if they were too drowsy to stand upright. Their backs are flaking off; their titles often vanished. Why disturb their sleep? Why reopen those peaceful graves, the librarian seems to ask, peering over his spectacles, and resenting the duty, which indeed has become laborious, of retrieving from among those nameless tombstones Nos 1763, 1080, and 606.*

I

Taylors and Edgeworths

For one likes romantically to feel oneself a deliverer advancing with lights across the waste of years to the rescue of some stranded ghost – a Mrs Pilkington, a Rev. Henry Elman, a Mrs Ann Gilbert[2] – waiting, appealing, forgotten, in the growing gloom. Possibly they hear one coming. They shuffle, they preen, they bridle. Old secrets well up to their lips. The divine relief of communication will soon again be theirs. The dust shifts and Mrs Gilbert – but the contact with life is instantly salutary. Whatever Mrs Gilbert may be doing, she is not thinking about us. Far from it. Colchester, about the year 1800, was for the young Taylors, as Kensington had been for their mothers, 'a very Elysium'.[3] There were the Strutts, the Hills, the Stapletons; there was poetry, philosophy, engraving. For the young Taylors were brought up to work hard, and if, after a long day's toil upon their father's pictures, they slipped round to dine with the Strutts, they had a right to their pleasure. Already they had won prizes in Darton and Harvey's pocket-book. One of the Strutts knew James Montgomery,[4] and there was talk, at those gay parties, with the Moorish decorations and all the cats – for old Ben Strutt was a bit of a character: did not communicate; would not let his daughters eat meat, so no wonder they died of consumption – there was talk of printing a joint volume to be called *The Associate Minstrels*, to which James, if not Robert[5] himself, might contribute. The Stapletons were poetical, too. Moira and Bithia would wander over the old town wall at Balkerne Hill reading poetry by moonlight. Perhaps there was a little too much poetry in Colchester in 1800. Looking back in the middle of a prosperous and vigorous life, Ann had to lament many broken careers, much unfulfilled promise. The Stapletons died young, perverted, miserable; Jacob, with his 'dark, scorn-speaking countenance', who had vowed that he would spend the night looking for Ann's lost bracelet in the street, disappeared, 'and I last heard of him vegetating among the ruins of Rome – himself too much a ruin';[6] as for the Hills, their fate was worst of all. To submit to public baptism was flighty, but to marry Captain M.! Anybody could have warned pretty Fanny Hill against Captain M. Yet off she drove with him in his fine phaeton. For years nothing more was heard of her. Then one night, when the Taylors had moved to Ongar and old Mr and Mrs Taylor were sitting over the fire, thinking how, as it was nine o'clock, and the moon was full, they ought, according to their promise, to look at it and think of their absent children, there came a knock at the door. Mrs Taylor went down to open it. But who was this sad, shabby-looking woman outside? 'Oh, don't you remember the Strutts and the Stapletons, and how you warned me against Captain M.?' cried Fanny Hill,[7] for it was Fanny Hill – poor Fanny Hill, all worn and sunk; poor Fanny Hill, that used to be so sprightly. She was living in a lone house not far from the Taylors, forced to drudge for her husband's mistress, for Captain M. had wasted all her fortune, ruined all her life.

Ann married Mr G., of course – of course. The words toll persistently through these obscure volumes. For in the vast world to which the memoir writers admit us there is a solemn sense of something unescapable, of a wave gathering beneath the frail flotilla and carrying it on. One thinks of Colchester in 1800. Scribbling verses, reading Montgomery– so they begin; the Hills, the Stapletons, the Strutts disperse and disappear as one knew they would; but here, after long years, is Ann still scribbling, and at last here is the poet Montgomery himself in her very house, and she begging him to consecrate her child to poetry by just holding him in his arms, and he refusing (for he is a bachelor), but taking her for a walk, and they hear the thunder, and she thinks it the artillery, and he says in a voice which she will never, never forget: 'Yes! The artillery of Heaven!'[8] It is one of the attractions of the unknown, their multitude, their vastness; for, instead of keeping their identity separate, as remarkable people do, they seem to merge into one another, their very boards and title-pages and frontispieces dissolving, and their innumerable pages melting into continuous years so that we can lie back and look up into the fine mist-like substance of countless lives, and pass unhindered from century to century, from life to life. Scenes detach themselves. We watch groups. Here is young Mr Elman talking to Miss Biffen at Brighton. She has neither arms nor legs; a footman carries her in and out. She teaches miniature painting to his sister. Then he is in the stage coach on the road to Oxford with Newman.[9] Newman says nothing. Elman nevertheless reflects that he has known all the great men of his time. And so back and so forwards, he paces eternally the fields of Sussex until, grown to an extreme old age, there he sits in his Rectory thinking of Newman, thinking of Miss Biffen, and making — it is his great consolation — string bags for missionaries. And then? Go on looking. Nothing much happens. But the dim light is exquisitely refreshing to the eyes. Let us watch little Miss Frend trotting along the Strand with her father. They meet a man with very bright eyes. 'Mr Blake,' says Mr Frend.[10] It is Mrs Dyer who pours out tea for them in Clifford's Inn. Mr Charles Lamb has just left the room.[11*] Mrs Dyer says she married George because his washerwoman cheated him so. What do you think George paid for his shirts, she asks? Gently, beautifully, like the clouds of a balmy evening, obscurity once more traverses the sky, an obscurity which is not empty but thick with the star dust of innumerable lives. And suddenly there is a rift in it, and we see a wretched little packet-boat pitching off the Irish coast in the middle of the nineteenth century. There is an unmistakable air of 1840 about the tarpaulins and the hairy monsters in sou'westers lurching and spitting over the sloping decks, yet treating the solitary young woman who stands in shawl and poke bonnet gazing, gazing, not without kindness. No. no, no! She will not leave the deck. She will stand there till it is quite dark, thank you! 'Her great love of the sea ... drew this exemplary wife and mother every now and then irresistibly away from home. No one but her husband knew where she had gone, and her children learnt only later in life that on these occasions, when suddenly she disappeared for a few days, she was taking short sea voyages ...'[12] a crime which she expiated by months of work among the Midland poor. Then the craving would come upon her, would be confessed in private to her husband, and off she stole again — the mother of Sir George Newnes.[13]

One would conclude that human beings were happy, endowed with such blindness to fate, so indefatigable an interest in their own activities, were it not for those sudden and astonishing apparitions staring in at us, all taut and pale in their determination never to be forgotten, men who have just missed fame, men who have passionately desired redress — men like Haydon, and Mark Pattison, and the Rev. Blanco White.[14] And in the whole world there is probably but one person who looks up for a moment and tries to interpret the menacing face, the furious beckoning fist, before, in the multitude of human affairs, fragments of face, echoes of voices, flying coat-tails, and bonnet strings disappearing down the shrubbery walks, one's attention is distracted for ever. What is that enormous wheel, for example, careering downhill in Berkshire in the eighteenth century? It runs faster and faster; suddenly a youth jumps out from within; next moment it leaps over the edge of a chalk pit and is dashed to smithereens. This is Edgeworth's doing – Richard Lovell Edgeworth,[15] we mean, the portentous bore.

For that is the way he has come down to us in his two volumes of memoirs – Byron's bore, Day's friend,[16] Maria's father, the man who almost invented the telegraph, and did, in fact, invent machines for cutting turnips, climbing walls, contracting on narrow bridges and lifting their wheels over obstacles – a man meritorious, industrious, advanced, but still, as we investigate his memoirs, mainly a bore. Nature endowed him with irrepressible energy. The blood coursed through his veins at least twenty times faster than the normal rate. His face was red, round, vivacious. His brain raced. His tongue never stopped talking. He had married four wives and had nineteen children, including the novelist Maria. Moreover, he had known every one and done everything. His energy burst open the most secret doors and penetrated to the most private apartments. His wife's grandmother, for instance, disappeared mysteriously every day. Edgeworth blundered in upon her and found her, with her white locks flowing and her eyes streaming, in prayer before a crucifix. She was a Roman Catholic then, but why a penitent? He found out somehow that her husband had been killed in a duel, and she had married the man who killed him. 'The consolations of religion are fully equal to its terrors,'[17] Dick Edgeworth reflected as he stumbled out again. Then there was the beautiful young woman in the castle among the forests of Dauphiny. Half-paralysed, unable to speak above a whisper, there she lay when Edgeworth broke in and found her reading. Tapestries flapped on the castle walls; fifty thousand bats – 'odious animals whose stench is uncommonly noisome'[18] – hung in clusters in the caves beneath. None of the inhabitants understood a word she said. But to the Englishman she talked for hour after hour about books and politics and religion. He listened; no doubt he talked. He sat dumbfounded. But what could one do for her? Alas, one must leave her lying among the tusks, and the old men, and the cross-bows, reading, reading, reading. For Edgeworth was employed in turning the Rhone from its course. He must get back to his job. One reflection he would make. 'I determined on steadily persevering in the cultivation of my understanding.'[19]

He was impervious to the romance of the situations in which he found himself. Every experience served only to fortify his character.

He reflected, he observed, he improved himself daily. You can improve, Mr Edgeworth used to tell his children, every day of your life. 'He used to say that with this power of improving they might in time be anything, and without it in time they would be nothing.'[20] Imperturbable, indefatigable, daily increasing in sturdy self-assurance, he has the gift of the egoist. He brings out, as he bustles and bangs on his way, the diffident, shrinking figures who would otherwise be drowned in darkness. The aged lady, whose private penance he disturbed, is only one of a series of figures who start up on either side of his progress, mute, astonished, showing us in a way that is even now unmistakable, their amazement at this well-meaning man who bursts in upon them at their studies and interrupts their prayers. We see him through their eyes; we see him as he does not dream of being seen. What a tyrant he was to his first wife! How intolerably she suffered! But she never utters a word. It is Dick Edgeworth who tells her story in complete ignorance that he is doing anything of the kind. 'It was a singular trait of character in my wife,' he observes, 'who had never shown any uneasiness at my intimacy with Sir Francis Delaval, that she should take a strong dislike to Mr Day. A more dangerous and seductive companion than the one, or a more moral and improving companion than the other, could not be found in England.'[21] It was, indeed, very singular.

For the first Mrs Edgeworth was a penniless girl, the daughter of a ruined country gentleman, who sat over his fire picking cinders from the hearth and throwing them into the grate, while from time to time he ejaculated. 'Hein! Heing!'[22] as yet another scheme for making his fortune came into his head. She had had no education. An itinerant writing-master had taught her to form a few words. When Dick Edgeworth was an undergraduate and rode over from Oxford she fell in love with him and married him in order to escape the poverty and the mystery and the dirt, and to have a husband and children like other women. But with what result? Gigantic wheels ran downhill with the bricklayer's son inside them. Sailing carriages took flight and almost wrecked four stage coaches. Machines did cut turnips, but not very efficiently. Her little boy was allowed to roam the country like a poor man's son, bare-legged, untaught. And Mr Day, coming to breakfast and staying to dinner, argued incessantly about scientific principles and the laws of Nature.

But here we encounter one of the pitfalls of this nocturnal rambling among forgotten worthies. It is so difficult to keep, as we must with highly authenticated people, strictly to the facts. It is so difficult to refrain from making scenes which, if the past could be recalled, might perhaps be found lacking in accuracy. With a character like Thomas Day, in particular, whose history surpasses the bounds of the credible, we find ourselves oozing amazement, like a sponge which has absorbed so much that it can retain no more but fairly drips. Certain scenes have the fascination which belongs rather to the abundance of fiction than to the sobriety of fact. For instance, we conjure up all the drama of poor Mrs Edgeworth's daily life; her bewilderment, her loneliness, her despair, how she must have wondered whether any one really wanted machines to climb walls, and assured the gentlemen that turnips were better cut simply with a knife, and so blundered and floundered and been snubbed that she dreaded the almost daily arrival of the tall young man, with his pompous, melancholy face, marked by the smallpox, his profusion of uncombed black hair, and his finical cleanliness of hands and person. He talked fast, fluently, incessantly, for hours at a time about philosophy and nature, and M. Rousseau.[23] Yet it was her house; she had to see to his meals, and, though he ate as though he were half asleep, his appetite was enormous. But it was no use complaining to her husband. Edgeworth said, 'She lamented about trifles.' He went on to say: 'The lamenting of a female with whom we live does not render home delightful.'[24] And then, with his obtuse open-mindedness he asked her what she had to complain of. Did he ever leave her alone? In the five or six years of their married life he had slept from home not more than five or six times. Mr Day could corroborate that. Mr Day corroborated everything that Mr Edgeworth said. He egged him on with his experiments. He told him to leave his son without education. He did not care a rap what the people of Henley said. In short, he was at the bottom of all the absurdities and extravagances which made Mrs Edgeworth's life a burden to her.

Yet let us choose another scene – one of the last that poor Mrs Edgeworth was to behold. She was returning from Lyons, and Mr Day was her escort. A more singular figure, as he stood on the deck of the packet which took them to Dover, very tall, very upright, one finger in the breast of his coat, letting the wind blow his hair out, dressed absurdly, though in the height of fashion, wild, romantic, yet at the same time authoritative and pompous, could scarcely be imagined; and this strange creature, who loathed women, was in charge of a lady who was about to become a mother, had adopted two orphan girls, and had set himself to win the hand of Miss Elizabeth Sneyd[25] by standing between boards for six hours daily in order to learn to dance. Now and again he pointed his toe with rigid precision; then, waking from the congenial dream into which the dark clouds, the flying waters, and the shadow of England upon the horizon had thrown him, he rapped out an order in the smart, affected tones of a man of the world. The sailors stared, but they obeyed. There was something sincere about him, something proudly indifferent to what you thought; yes, something comforting and humane, too, so that Mrs Edgeworth for her part was determined never to laugh at him again. But men were strange; life was difficult, and with a sigh of bewilderment, perhaps of relief, poor Mrs Edgeworth landed at Dover, was brought to bed of a daughter, and died.

Day meanwhile proceeded to Lichfield. Elizabeth Sneyd, of course, refused him – gave a great cry, people said; exclaimed that she had loved Day the blackguard, but hated Day the gentleman, and rushed from the room. And then, they said, a terrible thing happened. Mr Day, in his rage, bethought him of the orphan, Sabrina Sydney, whom he had bred to be his wife; visited her at Sutton Coldfield; flew into a passion at the sight of her; fired a pistol at her skirts, poured melted sealing-wax over her arms, and boxed her ears. 'No; I could never have done that,'[26] Mr Edgeworth used to say, when people described the scene. And whenever, to the end of his life, he thought of Thomas Day, he fell silent. So great, so passionate, so inconsistent – his life had been a tragedy, and in thinking of his friend, the best friend he had ever had, Richard Edgeworth fell silent.

It is almost the only occasion upon which silence is recorded of him. To muse, to repent, to contemplate were foreign to his nature. His wife and friends and children are silhouetted with extreme vividness upon a broad disc of interminable chatter. Upon no other background could we realise so clearly the sharp fragment of his first wife, or the shades and depths which make up the character, at once humane and brutal, advanced and hidebound, of the inconsistent philosopher, Thomas Day. But his power is not limited to people; landscapes, groups, societies seem, even as he describes them, to split off from him, to be projected away, so that we are able to run just ahead of him and anticipate his coming. They are brought out all the more vividly by the extreme incongruity which so often marks his comment and stamps his presence; they live with a peculiar beauty, fantastic, solemn, mysterious, in contrast with Edgeworth, who is none of these things. In particular, he brings before us a garden in Cheshire, the garden of a parsonage, an ancient but commodious parsonage.

One pushed through a white gate and found oneself in a grass court, small but well kept, with roses growing in the hedges and grapes hanging from the walls. But what, in the name of wonder, were those objects in the middle of the grass plot? Through the dusk of an autumn evening there shone out an enormous white globe. Round it at various distances were others of different sizes – the planets and their satellites, it seemed. But who could have placed them there, and why? The house was silent; the windows shut; nobody was stirring. Then, furtively peeping from behind a curtain, appeared for a second the face of an elderly man, handsome, dishevelled, distraught. It vanished.

In some mysterious way, human beings inflict their own vagaries upon nature. Moths and birds must have flitted more silently through the little garden; over everything must have brooded the same fantastic peace. Then, red-faced, garrulous, inquisitive, in burst Richard Lovell Edgeworth. He looked at the globes; he satisfied himself that they were of 'accurate design and workmanlike construction'.[27] He knocked at the door. He knocked and knocked. No one came. At length, as his impatience was overcoming him, slowly the latch was undone, gradually the door was opened; a clergyman, neglected, unkempt, but still a gentleman, stood before him. Edgeworth named himself, and they retired to a parlour littered with books and papers and valuable furniture now fallen to decay. At last, unable to control his curiosity any longer, Edgeworth asked what were the globes in the garden? Instantly the clergyman displayed extreme agitation. It was his son who had made them, he exclaimed; a boy of genius, a boy of the greatest industry, and of virtue and acquirements far beyond his age. But he had died. His wife had died. Edgeworth tried to turn the conversation, but in vain. The poor man rushed on passionately, incoherently about his son, his genius, his death. 'It struck me that his grief had injured his understanding,'[28] said Edgeworth, and he was becoming more and more uncomfortable, when the door opened and a girl of fourteen or fifteen entering with a tea-tray in her hand, suddenly changed the course of his host's conversation. Indeed, she was beautiful; dressed in white; her nose a shade too prominent, perhaps – but no, her proportions were exquisitely right. 'She is a scholar and an artist!'[29] the clergyman exclaimed as she left the room. But why did she leave the room? If she was his daughter why did she not preside at the tea-table? Was she his mistress? Who was she? And why was the house in this state of litter and decay? Why was the front door locked? Why was the clergyman apparently a prisoner, and what was his secret story? Questions began to crowd into Edgeworth's head as he sat drinking his tea; but he could only shake his head and make one last reflection, 'I feared that something was not right,'[30] as he shut the white wicket gate behind him, and left alone for ever in the un-tidy house among the planets and their satellites, the mad clergy-man and the lovely girl.

II

Laetitia Pilkington

Let us bother the librarian once again. Let us ask him to reach down, dust, and hand over to us that little brown book over there, *The Memoirs of Mrs Pilkington*, three volumes bound in one, printed by Peter Hoey in Dublin, MDCCLXXVI. The deepest obscur-ity shades her retreat; the dust lies heavy on her tomb – one board is loose, that is to say, and nobody has read her since early in the last century when a reader, presumably a lady, whether disgusted by her obscenity or striken by the hand of death, left off in the middle and marked her place with a faded list of goods and groceries. If ever a woman wanted a champion, it is obviously Laetitia Pilkington. Who then was she?[*]

Can you imagine a very extraordinary cross between Moll Flanders and Lady Ritchie,[2] between a rolling and rollicking woman of the town and a lady of breeding and refinement? Laetitia Pilkington (1712–1759)[3] was something of the sort – shady, shifty, adventurous, and yet, like Thackeray's daughter, like Miss Mitford, like Madame de Sévigné and Jane Austen and Maria Edgeworth,[4] so imbued with the old traditions of her sex that she wrote, as ladies talk, to give pleasure. Throughout her *Memoirs*,[†] we can never for-get that it is her wish to entertain, her unhappy fate to sob. Dabbing her eyes and controlling her anguish, she begs us to forgive an odious breach of manners which only the suffering of a lifetime, the

intolerable persecutions of Mr P——n, the malignant, she must say
the h——h, spite of Lady C——t can excuse. For who should
know better than the Earl of Killmallock's great-granddaughter that
it is the part of a lady to hide her sufferings?[5] Thus Laetitia is in the
great tradition of English women of letters. It is her duty to entertain; it is her instinct to conceal. Still, though her room near the
Royal Exchange is threadbare, and the table is spread with old play-
bills instead of a cloth, and the butter is served in a shoe, and Mr
Worsdale has used the teapot to fetch small beer that very morning,
still she presides, still she entertains. Her language is a trifle coarse,
perhaps. But who taught her English? The great Doctor Swift.[6]

In all her wanderings, which were many, and in her failings,
which were great, she looked back to those early Irish days when
Swift had pinched her into propriety of speech. He had beaten her
for fumbling at a drawer: he had daubed her cheeks with burnt cork
to try her temper; he had bade her pull off her shoes and stockings
and stand against the wainscot and let him measure her. At first she
had refused; then she had yielded. 'Why,' said the Dean, 'I suspected you had either broken Stockings or foul toes, and in either
case should have delighted to expose you.'[7] Three feet two inches
was all she measured, he declared, though, as Laetitia complained,
the weight of Swift's hand on her head had made her shrink to half
her size. But she was foolish to complain. Probably she owed her intimacy to that very fact – she was only three feet two. Swift had
lived a lifetime among the giants; now there was a charm in dwarfs.
He took the little creature into his library. '"Well," said he, "I have
brought you here to show you all the Money I got when I was in the
Ministry, but don't steal any of it." "I won't, indeed, Sir," said I; so
he opened a Cabinet, and showed me a whole parcel of empty
drawers. "Bless me," says he, "the Money is flown."'[8] There was a
charm in her surprise; there was a charm in her humility. He could
beat her and bully her, make her shout when he was deaf, force her
husband to drink the lees of the wine, pay their cab fares, stuff
guineas into a piece of gingerbread, and relent surprisingly, as if
there were something grimly pleasing to him in the thought of so
foolish a midget setting up to have a life and a mind of her own. For
with Swift she was herself; it was the effect of his genius. She had to
pull off the stockings if he told her to. So, though his satire terrified
her, and she found it highly unpleasant to dine at the Deanery and
see him watching, in the great glass which hung before him for that

purpose, the butler stealing beer at the sideboard, she knew that it was a privilege to walk with him in his garden; to hear him talk of Mr Pope and quote Hudibras;[9] and then be hustled back in the rain to save coach hire, and then to sit chatting in the parlour with Mrs Brent, the housekeeper, about the Dean's oddity and charity, and how the sixpence he saved on the coach he gave to the lame old man who sold gingerbread at the corner, while the Dean dashed up the front stairs and down the back so violently that she was afraid he would fall and hurt himself.

But memories of great men are no infallible specific. They fall upon the race of life like beams from a lighthouse. They flash, they shock, they reveal, they vanish. To remember Swift was of little avail to Laetitia when the troubles of life came thick about her. Mr Pilkington left her for Widow W—rr—n. Her father – her dear father – died. The sheriff's officers insulted her. She was deserted in an empty house with two children to provide for. The tea chest was secured, the garden gate locked, and the bills left unpaid. And still she was young and attractive and gay, with an inordinate passion for scribbling verses and an incredible hunger for reading books. It was this that was her undoing. The book was fascinating and the hour late. The gentleman would not lend it, but would stay till she had finished. They sat in her bedroom. It was highly indiscreet, she owned. Suddenly twelve watchmen broke through the kitchen window, and Mr Pilkington appeared with a cambric handkerchief tied about his neck. Swords were drawn and heads broken. As for her excuse, how could one expect Mr Pilkington and the twelve watchmen to believe this? Only reading! Only sitting up late to finish a new book! Mr Pilkington and the watchmen interpreted the situation as such men would. But lovers of learning, she is persuaded, will understand her passion and deplore its consequences.

And now what was she to do? Reading had played her false, but still she could write. Ever since she could form her letters, indeed, she had written with incredible speed and considerable grace, odes, addresses, apostrophes to Miss Hoadley, to the Recorder of Dublin, to Dr Delville's place in the country. 'Hail, happy Delville, blissful seat!' 'Is there a man whose fixed and steady gaze – ' the verses flowed without the slightest difficulty on the slightest occasion.[10] Now, therefore, crossing to England, she set up, as her advertisement had it, to write letters upon any subject, except the law, for twelve pence ready money, and no trust given. She lodged opposite

White's Chocolate House, and there, in the evening, as she watered her flowers on the leads the noble gentlemen in the window across the road drank her health, sent her over a bottle of burgundy; and later she heard old Colonel —— crying, 'Poke after me, my lord, poke after me,'[11] as he shepherded the D—— of M—lb—gh up her dark stairs. That lovely gentleman, who honoured his title by wearing it, kissed her, complimented her, opened his pocket-book, and left her with a bank-note for fifty pounds upon Sir Francis Child.[12] Such tributes stimulated her pen to astonishing outbursts of impromptu gratitude. If, on the other hand, a gentleman refused to buy or a lady hinted impropriety, this same flowery pen writhed and twisted in agonies of hate and vituperation. 'Had I said that your F——r died Blaspheming the Almighty,' one of her accusations begins, but the end is unprintable.[13] Great ladies were accused of every depravity, and the clergy, unless their taste in poetry was above reproach, suffered an incessant castigation. Mr Pilkington, she never forgot, was a clergyman.

Slowly but surely the Earl of Killmallock's great-granddaughter descended in the social scale. From St James's Street and its noble benefactors she migrated to Green Street to lodge with Lord Stair's *valet de chambre* and his wife, who washed for persons of distinction. She, who had dallied with dukes, was glad for company's sake to take a hand at quadrille with footmen and laundresses and Grub Street writers, who, as they drank porter, sipped green tea, and smoked tobacco, told stories of the utmost scurrility about their masters and mistresses. The spiciness of their conversation made amends for the vulgarity of their manners. From them Laetitia picked up those anecdotes of the great which sprinkled her pages with dashes and served her purpose when subscribers failed and landladies grew insolent. Indeed, it was a hard life – to trudge to Chelsea in the snow wearing nothing but a chintz gown and be put off with a beggarly half-crown by Sir Hans Sloane;[14] next to tramp to Ormond Street and extract two guineas from the odious Dr Meade, which, in her glee, she tossed in the air and lost in a crack of the floor; to be insulted by footmen; to sit down to a dish of boiling water because her landlady must not guess that a pinch of tea was beyond her means. Twice on moonlight nights, with the lime trees in flower, she wandered in St James's Park and contemplated suicide in Rosamond's Pond. Once, musing among the tombs in

Westminster Abbey, the door was locked on her, and she had to spend the night in the pulpit wrapped in a carpet from the Communion Table to protect herself from the assaults of rats. 'I long to listen to the young-ey'd cherubims!' she exclaimed.[15] But a very different fate was in store for her. In spite of Mr Colley Cibber, and Mr Richardson,[16] who supplied her first with gilt-edged notepaper and then with baby linen, those harpies, her landladies, after drinking her ale, devouring her lobsters, and failing often for years at a time to comb their hair, succeeded in driving Swift's friend, and the Earl's great-granddaughter, to be imprisoned with common debtors in the Marshalsea.

Bitterly she cursed her husband, who had made her a lady of adventure instead of what nature intended, 'a harmless household dove'.[17] More and more wildly she ransacked her brains for anecdotes, memories, scandals, views about the bottomless nature of the sea, the inflammable character of the earth – anything that would fill a page and earn her a guinea. She remembered that she had eaten plovers' eggs with Swift. 'Here, Hussey,' said he, 'is a Plover's egg. King William used to give crowns apiece for them . . .'[18] Swift never laughed, she remembered. He used to suck in his cheeks instead of laughing. And what else could she remember? A great many gentlemen, a great many landladies; how the window was thrown up when her father died, and her sister came downstairs, with the sugar-basin, laughing. All had been bitterness and struggle, except that she had loved Shakespeare, known Swift, and kept through all the shifts and shades of an adventurous career a gay spirit, something of a lady's breeding, and the gallantry which, at the end of her short life, led her to crack her joke and enjoy her duck with death at her heart and duns at her pillow.

III

Miss Ormerod

The trees stood massively in all their summer foliage spotted and grouped upon a meadow which sloped gently down from the big white house. There were unmistakable signs of the year 1835 both in the trees and in the sky, for modern trees are not nearly so voluminous as these ones, and the sky of those days had a kind of pale diffusion in its texture which was different from the more concentrated tone of the skies we know.

Mr George Ormerod stepped from the drawing-room window of Sedbury House, Gloucestershire, wearing a tall furry hat and white trousers strapped under his instep; he was closely, though deferentially, followed by a lady wearing a yellow-spotted dress over a crinoline, and behind her, singly and arm in arm, came nine children in nankeen jackets and long white drawers. They were going to see the water let out of a pond.

The youngest child, Eleanor,[2] a little girl with a pale face, rather elongated features, and black hair, was left by herself in the drawing-room, a large sallow apartment with pillars, two chandeliers for some reason enclosed in holland bags, and several octagonal tables, some of inlaid wood and others of greenish malachite. At one of these little Eleanor Ormerod was seated in a high chair.

'Now Eleanor,' said her mother, as the party assembled for the expedition to the pond, 'here are some pretty beetles. Don't touch the glass. Don't get down from your chair, and when we come back little George will tell you all about it.'[3]

So saying, Mrs Ormerod placed a tumbler of water containing about half a dozen great water grubs in the middle of the malachite table, at a safe distance from the child, and followed her husband down the slope of old-fashioned turf towards a cluster of extremely old-fashioned sheep; opening, directly she stepped on to the terrace, a tiny parasol of bottle green silk with a bottle green fringe, though the sky was like nothing so much as a flock bed covered with a counterpane of white dimity.

The plump pale grubs gyrated slowly round and round in the tumbler. So simple an entertainment must surely soon have ceased to satisfy. Surely Eleanor would shake the tumbler, upset the grubs, and scramble down from her chair. Why, even a grown person can hardly watch those grubs crawling down the glass wall, then floating to the surface, without a sense of boredom not untinged with disgust. But the child sat perfectly still. Was it her custom, then, to be entertained by the gyrations of grubs? Her eyes were reflective, even critical. But they shone with increasing excitement. She beat one hand upon the edge of the table. What was the reason? One of the grubs had ceased to float: he lay at the bottom; the rest, descending, proceeded to tear him to pieces.

'And how has little Eleanor enjoyed herself?' asked Mr Ormerod, in rather a deep voice, stepping into the room and with a slight air of heat and of fatigue upon his face.

'Papa,' said Eleanor almost interrupting her father in her eagerness to impart her observations, 'I saw one of the grubs fall down and the rest came and ate him!'

'Nonsense, Eleanor,' said Mr Ormerod. 'You are not telling the truth.' He looked severely at the tumbler in which the beetles were still gyrating as before.

'Papa, it was true!'

'Eleanor, little girls are not allowed to contradict their fathers,' said Mrs Ormerod, coming in through the window, and closing her green parasol with a snap.

'Let this be a lesson,' Mr Ormerod began, signing to the other children to approach, when the door opened, and the servant announced,

'Captain Fenton.'

Captain Fenton 'was at times thought to be tedious in his recurrence to the charge of the Scots Greys in which he had served at the battle of Waterloo'.[4]

But what is this crowd gathered round the door of the George Hotel in Chepstow? A faint cheer rises from the bottom of the hill. Up comes the mail coach, horses steaming, panels mud-splashed. 'Make way! Make way!' cries the ostler and the vehicle dashed into the courtyard, pulls up sharp before the door. Down jumps the coachman, the horses are led off, and a fine team of spanking greys is harnessed with incredible speed in their stead. Upon all this – coachman, horses, coach, and passengers – the crowd looked with gaping admiration every Wednesday evening all through the year. But today, the twelfth of March, 1852, as the coachman settled his rug, and stretched his hands for the reins, he observed that instead of being fixed upon him, the eyes of the people of Chepstow darted this way and that. Heads were jerked. Arms flung out. Here a hat swooped in a semi-circle. Off drove the coach almost unnoticed. As it turned the corner all the outside passengers craned their necks, and one gentleman rose to his feet and shouted, 'There! there! there!' before he was bowled into eternity. It was an insect – a redwinged insect. Out the people of Chepstow poured into the high road; down the hill they ran; always the insect flew in front of them; at length by Chepstow Bridge a young man, throwing his bandanna over the blade of an oar, captured it alive and presented it to a highly respectable elderly gentleman who now came puffing upon the scene – Samuel Budge, doctor, of Chepstow. By Samuel Budge it was presented to Miss Ormerod; by her sent to a professor at Oxford. And he, declaring it 'a fine specimen of the rose under-winged locust' added the gratifying information that it 'was the first of the kind to be captured so far west.'[5]

And so, at the age of twenty-four Miss Eleanor Ormerod was thought the proper person to receive the gift of a locust.

When Eleanor Ormerod appeared at archery meetings and croquet tournaments young men pulled their whiskers and young ladies looked grave. It was so difficult to make friends with a girl who could talk of nothing but black beetles and earwigs – 'Yes, that's what she likes, isn't it queer? – Why, the other day Ellen, Mama's maid, heard from Jane, who's under-kitchenmaid at Sedbury House, that Eleanor tried to boil a beetle in the kitchen saucepan and he wouldn't die, and swam round and round, and she got into a terrible state and sent the groom all the way to Gloucester to fetch chloroform – all for an insect my dear! – and she gives the cottagers shillings to collect beetles for her – and she spends hours in her bedroom cutting them up – and she climbs trees like a boy to find wasps' nests – oh, you can't think what they don't say about her in the village – for she does look so odd, dressed anyhow, with that great big nose and those bright little eyes, so like a caterpillar herself, I always think – but of course she's wonderfully clever and very good, too, both of them. Georgiana has a lending library for the cottagers, and Eleanor never misses a service – but there she is – that short pale girl in the large bonnet. Do go and talk to her, for I'm sure I'm too stupid, but you'd find plenty to say –' But neither Fred nor Arthur, Henry nor William found anything to say – '. . . probably the lecturer would have been equally well pleased had none of her own sex put in an appearance.'

This comment upon a lecture delivered in the year 1889 throws some light, perhaps, upon archery meetings in the 'fifties.[6]

It being nine o'clock on a February night some time about 1862 all the Ormerods were in the library; Mr Ormerod making architectural designs at a table; Mrs Ormerod lying on a sofa making pencil drawings upon grey paper; Eleanor making a model of a snake to serve as a paper weight; Georgiana making a copy of the font in Tidenham Church; some of the others examining books with beautiful illustrations; while at intervals someone rose, unlocked the wire book case, took down a volume for instruction or entertainment, and perused it beneath the chandelier.

Mr Ormerod required complete silence for his studies. His word was law, even to the dogs, who, in the absence of their master, instinctively obeyed the eldest male person in the room. Some whispered colloquy there might be between Mrs Ormerod and her daughters –

'The draught under the pew was really worse than ever this morning, Mama – '

'And we could only unfasten the latch in the chancel because Eleanor happened to have her ruler with her – '

'–hm–m–m. Dr Armstrong –Hm–m–m– '

' – Anyhow things aren't as bad with us as they are at Kinghampton. They say Mrs Briscoe's Newfoundland dog follows her right up to the chancel rails when she takes the sacrament – '

'And the turkey is still sitting on its eggs in the pulpit.'

– 'The period of incubation for a turkey is between three and four weeks' –[7] said Eleanor thoughtfully looking up from her cast of the snake and forgetting, in the interest of her subject, to speak in a whisper.

'Am I to be allowed no peace in my own house?'[8] Mr Ormerod exclaimed angrily, rapping with his ruler on the table, upon which Mrs Ormerod half shut one eye and squeezed a little blob of Chinese white on to her high light, and they remained silent until the servants came in, when everyone, with the exception of Mrs Ormerod, fell on their knees. For she, poor lady, suffered from a chronic complaint and left the family party for ever a year or two later, when the green sofa was moved into the corner, and the drawings given to her nieces in memory of her. But Mr Ormerod went on making architectural drawings at nine p.m. every night (save on Sundays when he read a sermon) until he too lay upon the green sofa, which had not been used since Mrs Ormerod lay there, but still looked much the same. 'We deeply felt the happiness of ministering to his welfare,' Miss Ormerod wrote, 'for he would not hear of our leaving him for even twenty-four hours and he objected to visits from my brothers excepting occasionally for a short time. They, not being used to the gentle ways necessary for an aged invalid, worried him ... the Thursday following, the 9th October, 1873, he passed gently away at the mature age of eighty-seven years.'[9] Oh, graves in country churchyards – respectable burials –

mature old gentlemen – D.C.L., L.L.D., F.R.S., F.S.A. – lots of letters come after your names, but lots of women are buried with you!

There remained the Hessian Fly and the Bot – mysterious insects! Not, one would have thought, among God's most triumphant creations, and yet – if you see them under a microscope! – the Bot, obese, globular, obscene; the Hessian, booted, spurred, whiskered, cadaverous. Next slip under the glass an innocent grain; behold it pock-marked and livid; or take this strip of hide, and note those odious pullulating lumps – well, what does the landscape look like then?

The only palatable object for the eye to rest on in acres of England is a lump of Paris Green. But English people won't use microscopes; you can't make them use Paris Green either – or if they do, they let it drip. Dr Ritzema Bos[10] is a great stand-by. For they won't take a woman's word. And indeed, though for the sake of the Ox Warble one must stretch a point, there are matters, questions of stock infestation, things one has to go into – things a lady doesn't even like to see, much less discuss in print – 'these, I say, I intend to leave entirely to the Veterinary surgeons. My brother – oh, he's dead now – a very good man – for whom I collected wasps' nests – lived at Brighton and wrote about wasps – he, I say, wouldn't let me learn anatomy, never liked me to do more than take sections of teeth.'[11]

Ah, but Eleanor, the Bot and the Hessian have more power over you than Mr Edward Ormerod himself.[12] Under the microscope you clearly perceive that these insects have organs, orifices, excrement; they do, most emphatically, copulate. Escorted on the one side by the Bot or Warble, on the other by the Hessian Fly, Miss Ormerod advanced statelily, if slowly, into the open. Never did her features show more sublime than when lit up by the candour of her avowal. 'This is excrement; these, though Ritzema Bos is positive to the contrary, are the generative organs of the male. I've proved it.'[13] Upon her head the hood of Edinburgh most fitly descended; pioneer of purity even more than of Paris Green.

'If you're sure I'm not in your way,' said Miss Lipscomb unstrapping her paint box and planting her tripod firmly in the path, '– I'll try to get a picture of those lovely hydrangeas against the sky – What flowers you have in Penzance!'

The market gardener crossed his hands on his hoe, slowly twined a piece of bass round his finger, looked at the sky, said something about the sun, also about the prevalence of lady artists, and then, with a nod of his head, observed sententiously that it was to a lady that he owed everything he had.

'Ah?' said Miss Lipscomb, flattered, but already much occupied with her composition.

'A lady with a queer sounding name,' said Mr Pascoe, 'but that's the lady I've called my little girl after – I don't think there's such another in christendom.'[14]

Of course it was Miss Ormerod, equally of course Miss Lipscomb was the sister of Miss Ormerod's family doctor; and so she did no sketching that morning, but left with a handsome bunch of grapes instead – for every flower had drooped, ruin had stared him in the face – he had written, not believing one bit what they told him – to the lady with the queer name, back there came a book In-ju-ri-ous In-sects,[15] with the page turned down, perhaps by her very hand, also a letter which he kept at home under the clock, but he knew every word by heart, since it was due to what she said there that he wasn't a ruined man – and the tears ran down his face and Miss Lipscomb, clearing a space on the lodging-house table, wrote the whole story to her brother.

'The prejudice against Paris Green certainly seems to be dying down,' said Miss Ormerod when she read it. – 'But now,' she sighed rather heavily being no longer young and much afflicted with the gout, 'now it's the sparrows.'[16]

One might have thought that *they* would have left her alone – innocent dirt-grey birds, taking more than their share of the breakfast crumbs, otherwise inoffensive. But once you look through a microscope – once you see the Hessian and the Bot as they really are – there's no peace for an elderly lady pacing her terrace on a fine May morning. For example, why, when there are crumbs enough for all, do only the sparrows get them? Why not swallows or martins? Why – oh, here come the servants for prayers –

'It does no good to keep people waiting for an answer,' sighed Miss Ormerod, 'though I don't feel as able as I did since that unlucky accident at Waterloo. And no one realises what the strain of the work is – often I'm the only lady in the room, and the gentlemen so learned, though I've always found them most helpful, most generous in every way. But I'm growing old, Miss Hartwell, that's what it is. That's what led me to be thinking of this difficult matter of flour infestation in the middle of the road so that I didn't see the horse until he had poked his nose into my ear . . . Then there's this nonsense about a pension. What could possess Mr Barron to think of such a thing? I should feel inexpressibly lowered if I accepted a pension. Why, I don't altogether like writing LL.D. after my name, though Georgie would have liked it. All I ask is to be let go on in my own quiet way. Now where is Messrs Langridge's sample? We must take that first. "Gentlemen, I have examined your sample and find . . ."'[17]

'If any one deserves a thorough good rest it's you, Miss Ormerod,' said Dr Lipscomb, who had grown a little white over the ears. 'I should say the farmers of England ought to set up a statue to you, bring offerings of corn and wine – make you a kind of Goddess, eh – what was her name?'

'Not a very shapely figure for a Goddess,' said Miss Ormerod with a little laugh. 'I should enjoy the wine though. You're not going to cut me off my one glass of port surely?'

'You must remember,' said Dr Lipscomb, shaking his head, 'how much your life means to others.'

'Well, I don't know about that,' said Miss Ormerod, pondering a little. 'To be sure, I've chosen my epitaph. "She introduced Paris Green into England,"[18] and there might be a word or two about the Hessian fly – that, I do believe, was a good piece of work.'

'No need to think about epitaphs yet,' said Dr Lipscomb.

'Our lives are in the hands of the Lord,' said Miss Ormerod simply.

Dr Lipscomb bent his head and looked out of the window. Miss Ormerod remained silent.

'English entomologists care little or nothing for objects of practical importance,' she exclaimed suddenly. 'Take this question of flour infestation – I can't say how many grey hairs that hasn't grown me.'

'Figuratively speaking, Miss Ormerod,' said Dr Lipscomb, for her hair was still raven black.

'Well, I do believe all good work is done in concert,' Miss Ormerod continued. 'It is often a great comfort to me to think that.'

'It's beginning to rain,' said Dr Lipscomb. 'How will your enemies like that, Miss Ormerod?'

'Hot or cold, wet or dry, insects always flourish!' cried Miss Ormerod energetically sitting up in bed.

'Old Miss Ormerod is dead,' said Mr Drummond, opening *The Times* on Saturday, July 20th, 1901.[19]

'Old Miss Ormerod?' asked Mrs Drummond.

'Forgive us our trespasses as we forgive them that trespass against us ... For thine is the Kingdom and the power and the glory, for ever and ever. Amen –'

'*The Times* ma'am –'

'Thank you, Dixon ... The Queen's birthday! We must drink her Majesty's health in the old white port, Dixon. Home Rule – tut – tut – tut. All that madman Gladstone. My father would have thought the world was coming to an end, and I'm not at all sure that it isn't. I must talk to Dr Lipscomb –'

Yet all the time in the tail of her eye she saw myriads of sparrows, and retiring to the study proclaimed in a pamphlet of which 36,000 copies were gratuitously distributed that the sparrow is a pest.

'When he eats an insect,' she said to her sister Georgiana, 'which isn't often, it's one of the few insects that one wants to keep – one of the very few,' she added with a touch of acidity natural to one whose investigations have all tended to the discredit of the insect race.

'But there'll be some very unpleasant consequences to face,' she concluded – 'Very unpleasant indeed.'

Happily the port was now brought in, the servants assembled; and Miss Ormerod, rising to her feet, gave the toast 'Her Blessed Majesty.' She was extremely loyal, and moreover she liked nothing better than a glass of her father's old white port. She kept his pigtail, too, in a box.

Such being her disposition it went hard with her to analyse the sparrow's crop, for the sparrow she felt, symbolises something of the homely virtue of English domestic life, and to proclaim it stuffed with deceit was disloyal to much that she and her fathers before her, held dear. Sure enough the clergy – the Rev. J. E. Walker – denounced her for her brutality; 'God Save the Sparrow!' exclaimed the Animal's Friend; and Miss Carrington, of the Humanitarian League, replied in a leaflet described by Miss Ormerod as 'spirity, discourteous, and inaccurate'.[20]

'Well,' said Miss Ormerod to her sister, 'it did me no harm before to be threatened to be shot at, also hanged in effigy, and other little attentions.'

'Still it was very disagreeable, Eleanor — more disagreeable, I believe, to me than to you,' said Georgiana.[21] Soon Georgiana died. She had however finished the beautiful series of insect diagrams at which she worked every morning in the dining-room and they were presented to Edinburgh University. But Eleanor was never the same woman after that.

Dear forest fly — flour moths — weevils — grouse and cheese flies — beetles — foreign correspondents — eel worms — ladybirds — wheat midges — resignation from the Royal Agricultural Society — gall mites — boot beetles — Announcement of honorary degree to be conferred — feelings of appreciation and anxiety — paper on wasps — last annual report — warning of serious illness — proposed pension — gradual loss of strength — Finally Death.

That is life, so they say.

Lives of the Obscure

* — LM and Dial, (NY), do not give this paragraph but are introduced by the following paragraphs:

Little is now known of Laetitia Pilkington, and not all that is known is certainly true. Moreover, if one looks along the shelves upon which her three small volumes stand — The Memoirs of Mrs Laetitia Pilkington, wife to the Rev. Mr Matt. Pilkington, written by herself, Dublin M.DCC.LXX.VI. — there are other books of much greater importance than hers without going beyond the letter P — Pope, Peacock, possibly Pindar, to seek no further. Yet what a debt of gratitude we owe to her and her sort! — Not for what they did or for what they said, but for being themselves; for persisting, in spite of their invincible mediocrity, in writing their memoirs; for providing precisely that background, atmosphere, and standing of common earth which nourish people of greater importance and prevent them from shrivelling to dry sticks or congealing to splendid pinnacles of inaccessible ice. For imagine a literature composed entirely of good books; imagine having nothing to read but the plays of Shakespeare, the poems of Milton, the essays of Bacon, the letters of Madame de Sévigné, and the biography of Johnson. Starvation would soon ensue. No one would read at all. The difficult art, practised by a few heroic spirits whose singular genius withdrew them more and more into learned societies and the backwaters of college life, would become extinct; and writing would follow suit.

The great literatures of Greece and Rome, so much admired, but so seldom read, prove how difficult it is for good books to survive unless they are liberally supported by bad ones. The isolation is too great. There is nothing handy and personal to pull oneself up by. There are no gradations of merit, but we are faced directly by the sublime and precipitous — by Aeschylus, Sophocles, Lucretius, Plato, Virgil, Aristotle. There is no W. E. Norris;[†] no Creevey; no Indiscretions of a Countess;

no Mrs Pilkington. But such trivial ephemeral books do not merely break the ascent and encourage us to mightier efforts. They have a more important office. They are the dressing-rooms, the workshops, the wings, the sculleries, the bubbling cauldrons, where life seethes and steams and is for ever on the boil. By sousing ourselves in memoirs we keep our minds supple, and so when at last we tackle the finished product – Hamlet for example – we bring to the understanding of him fertile minds imbued with ideas, at once creative and receptive. So we can never approach Ajax and Electra; and in consequence they are never taken into the depths of our beings, but remain always a little craggy, a little indissoluble, an inch or two beyond our grasp. For literature did undoubtedly once lie down with life, and all her progeny, being the result of that misalliance, are more or less impure. To understand them we must live. And then, since we are seeking excuses, who can say where life ends and literature begins? And then who can guide us? And then how delicious to ramble and explore!†

† – LM: 'There is no Fanny Burney, no Creevey, no indiscretions'.

‡ – Ibid.: And then how pleasant to lead expeditions, to ramble, to explore'.

I Taylors and Edgeworths

* – LM and Dial, N.Y.: 'room, but there is a peculiar feeling about rooms which Charles Lamb has just left.'

II Laetitia Pilkington

* – N&A does not give this paragraph.

† – N&A: 'Memoirs, three little volumes, printed by Peter Hoey, in Dublin, MDCCLXXVI.'

Lives of the Obscure

1–Established in 1842, the Illustrated London News described itself as a non-political news periodical, famous, among other things, for its illustrations of the most recent events in exploration, science and archaeology. The Wesleyan Chronicle was first published on 5 May 1843 and ceased publication on 27 December 1844, after which it was incorporated in the Wesleyan and Christian Record.

I Taylors and Edgeworths

1–Originally entitled 'The Lives of the Obscure' and first published in LM, January 1924, (Kp C244) this essay was revised as shown for inclusion in CR1 (published: 23 April 1925) and reprinted in Dial (NY), May 1925. It is chiefly based on: Autobiography and Other Memorials of Mrs Gilbert (formerly Ann Taylor). With portrait and illustrations. Edited by Josiah Gilbert (2 vols, London, 1874); and on: Memoirs of Richard Lovell Edgeworth Esq. Begun by Himself and Concluded by His Daughter Maria Edgeworth (2 vols, London, 1820). 'Shall I then dash off an article for Squire upon memoirs?' VW had asked herself in her diary on 7 January 1923. 'And then?' she wrote again on 17 March, 'As to the soul, I've been snubbed by Squire. I sent him my memoir article, asking terms: he accepted offering £13; £15 I said, or my ms back; & got it back by return. And now I accept £13 – which perhaps I shan't get after all. Yet I dont much mind. & only think that poverty & the shifts it puts one to is unbecoming, as I've said.' For the significance of the idea of 'obscure lives' for VW see Introduction. See also Editorial Note p. xxv. Reprinted *CE*.

2 – Ann Gilbert, *née* Taylor (1782–1866), writer – often in collaboration with her sister Jane – of poetry for children. She was the eldest child of Isaac Taylor of Ongar, an engraver who became a Nonconformist minister in Colchester. In 1813 she married, as his second wife, the Rev. Joseph Gilbert. For another account of her life and of her husband see the *DNB*. By the Rev. Henry Elman VW appears to have intended Edward Ellman, author of *Recollections of a Sussex Parson* (1912). For Laetitia Pilkington see below.

3 – Cf. Gilbert, vol. i, ch. i, p. 14, which has: 'Yet her attachment to Kensington was extreme, and she regarded it as an Elysium to her life's end.'

4 – James Montgomery (1771–1854), poet of Scottish origin, 'something less than a genius and something more than a mediocrity' (*DNB*), much revered in religious circles. Darton and Harvey, publishers of the 'Minor's Pocket Book'.

5 – Robert Montgomery (1807–55), poetaster, famously condemned by Macaulay, author of poems on religious subjects.

6 – For both quotations, Gilbert, vol. i, ch. iv, p. 144, which has 'dark scorn-speaking'.

7 – *Ibid.*, ch. iii, p. 113, which has Fanny Hills; the matter attributed to whom is apparently VW's invention.

8 – *Ibid.*, ch. vi, p. 203, which has no exclamation mark.

9 – For John Henry Newman (1801–90), created cardinal in 1879, see Ellman, ch. xxiv, p. 120. For Sarah Biffen or Beffin (1784–1850), miniature painter, see *ibid.*, ch. xiii, p. 69; born without limbs, Miss Biffin contrived 'by means of her mouth, to use the pen, the pencil, the paint-brush, and even the scissors and needle' (*DNB*).

10 – For this episode, see *Threescore Years and Ten. Reminiscences of the late Sophia Elizabeth De Morgan* edited by her daughter Mary A. De Morgan (E. Bentley, 1895), ch. ii, pp. 67–8. Sophia Elizabeth Frend, eldest daughter of the Unitarian and Whig reformer William Frend (1757–1841), vigorous opponent at Cambridge of the Thirty-nine Articles. William Blake (1757–1827).

11 – Mrs Dyer, formerly a Mrs Mather, married George Dyer (1755–1841), author and friend of Charles Lamb (1775–1834), out of pity at, according to Leslie Stephen in the *DNB*, 'the slovenly state of his abode' in Clifford's Inn.

12 – Hulda Friedrichs, *The Life of Sir George Newnes Bart* (Hodder and Stoughton, 1911), ch. i, p. 7, adapted.

13 – Sir George Newnes (1851–1910), founder of *Tit-Bits*, was the son of Sarah Urquhart (d. 1885) and the Rev. Thomas Mold Newnes (d. 1883).

14 – Benjamin Robert Haydon (1786–1846), possessed a genius for offending the Royal Academy, if not for painting, a matter he took considerably to heart. For VW on Haydon see 'Genius' below. Mark Pattison (1813–84) was permanently embittered by the failure of his fellow dons to elect him Rector of Lincoln College, Oxford, in 1851, though the fact was rectified in 1861. The Rev. Joseph Blanco White (1775–1841), Spanish-born convert to Protestantism, driven from Oxford by the raillery of the fellows of Oriel College.

15 – Richard Lovell Edgeworth (1744–1817), Irish author, father of the novelist Maria Edgeworth (1767–1849), with whom he wrote, under the influence of Rousseau, *Practical Education* (1798). See also his life in the *DNB*, contributed by Leslie Stephen.

16–Thomas Day (1748–89), author of *The History of Sandford and Merton* (1783–9); see the entry on Day in the *DNB*, again by Leslie Stephen. For George Gordon, Lord Byron (1788–1824), on Edgeworth as a bore, see his letter to John Murray, 4 November 1820, in the *The Works of Lord Byron* (John Murray, 1837).

17–Edgeworth, vol. i, ch. iv, p. 90, slightly adapted.

18–*Ibid.*, ch. xi, p. 287, slightly adapted.

19–*Ibid.*, p. 295, slightly adapted.

20–*Ibid.*, vol. ii, ch. xx, p. 415, which has 'to say, that'.

21–*Ibid.*, vol. i, ch. vii, pp. 183–4. The first Mrs Edgeworth was Anna Maria Elers (d. 1773), with whom he had eloped in 1763. Sir Francis Blake Delaval, man of fashion, shared Edgeworth's interest in 'conjuring tricks and mechanical contrivances' (*DNB*).

22–*Ibid.*, ch. v, p. 114. Mrs Edgeworth's father was Paul Elers of Black Bourton, near Oxford.

23–Jean-Jacques Rousseau (1712–78).

24–Edgeworth, vol. i, ch. vii, p. 184, slightly adapted.

25–Sister of Edgeworth's second wife Honora Sneyd (d. April 1780) who in December 1780 became the third Mrs Edgeworth.

26–Cf., Edgeworth, vol. i, ch. xiv, p. 219: 'Mr Day's reasons for breaking off this attachment proved to my understanding, that, with his peculiarities, he judged well for his own happiness; but I felt, that, in the same situation, I could not have acted as he had done.'

27–Cf., *ibid.*, ch. xvi, p. 386: 'I examined this apparatus leisurely before I went further, and was satisfied of its accuracy, and of the workmanlike manner in which it had been performed.'

28–*Ibid.*, p. 388, part of a more extensive sentence.

29–*Ibid.*, p. 390, which has: '"She is a scholar, and an artist, and is neither proud nor vain of any of her mental or personal accomplishments."'

30–*Ibid.*, p. 391: 'I scarcely ventured to make any farther inquiries about this gentleman: I feared that something was not right. But from what little I did hear, the fact seemed to be, that the mother of his favourite son had not always been his wife; and that his pecuniary difficulties arose from his being entangled in the meshes of the law by a nefarious attorney, who confined him to his house by writs, which were not legally obtained. This attorney had impoverished him by the most vexatious litigation, and had vowed that his life should finish in a jail.'

II Laetitia Pilkington

1–First published in the *N&A*, 30 June 1923, (Kp C237) this essay was revised as shown for inclusion in *CR1*. It is based on *Memoirs of Mrs Laetitia Pilkington, wife to the Rev. Matthew Pilkington, written by herself. Wherein are occasionally interspersed all her Poems, with Anecdotes of several eminent persons living and dead*: first produced in 2 vols in 1748; there was a second edition in 1749, and a third in 1751; vol. iii first appeared in 1754. No edition as cited by VW has been traced. 'Then do the Greek chapter . . .' she ruminated in her diary on 7 January 1923, '. . . This puts off writing till rather late in the day; but I want to make myself a certain amount of money regularly, if only for pocket money. Now, therefore, I must finish Pilkington . . .'

2–Anne Isabella Thackeray Ritchie (1837–1919), daughter of W. M. Thackeray, wife of Sir Richmond Ritchie. Her sister Harriet Marian ('Minnie') was Leslie

Stephen's first wife. For VW on her aunt's great gifts as a memoirist see 'Lady Ritchie', *III VW Essays*; see also *'Blackstick Papers'*, *I VW Essays*; 'The Enchanted Organ', *III VW Essays*.

3 – Pilkington's dates are given in the *DNB* as 1712–1750.

4 – For VW on Miss Mitford and on Maria Edgeworth see 'Outlines' below; for 'Jane Austen' see below; and for VW's essay on Madame de Sévigné (1626–96) see *VI VW Essays*.

5 – Laetitia Pilkington was the daughter of Dr Van Lewen, a Dutch 'man midwife', who settled in Dublin c. 1710; she married in 1729 Matthew Pilkington (fl. 1773), parson and poet. Her great-grandmother was a daughter of the Earl of Kilmallock.

6 – Jonathan Swift (1667–1745), for VW on whom see 'Swift's Journal to Stella' below.

7 – Pilkington (London. Printed for R. Griffiths at the Dunciad in Paternoster Row, 1754), vol. iii, p. 148.

8 – Pilkington (Dublin Printed: London Reprinted: and sold by R. Griffiths, at the Dunciad in Ludgate Street, 1749), vol. i, p. 54, which has: '"Well," says he', 'do not steal' and 'I will not, indeed'.

9 – Alexander Pope (1688–1744); *Hudibras* (1663–78) by Samuel Butler (1612–80).

10 – The poems referred to are: 'Flavia's Birthday, May the 16th/To Miss Hoadley'; 'Delville, the seat of the Rev. Dr Delany/1685?–1768' from which VW quotes the first line (Pilkington, vol. i, p. 47); and 'Advice to the People of Dublin in their Choice of a Recorder', which has 'fixed and steady soul' (*ibid.*, p. 142).

11 – Pilkington, vol. ii (Dublin Printed: London Reprinted . . . 1749), p. 28.

12 – Sir Francis Child, the younger (1684?–1740), banker and politician.

13 – For the accusation, Pilkington, vol. iii, p. 13, which has: 'Why, Madam, had I said that your Fa——r died blaspheming the Almighty, and of the foul Disease; had I said that he refus'd to see his Wife's Cubbs, as he call'd your Sisters, at the Hour of his Death; had I said, that you hid Lady D—— behind the Arras, to see —— Nothing – which you said, your little Tom Titmouse of a Husband had, you cou'd not have used me worse.'

14 – Sir Hans Sloane (1660–1753), physician.

15 – Pilkington, vol. iii, p. 86.

16 – Colley Cibber (1671–1757); Samuel Richardson (1689–1761).

17 – Pilkington, vol. ii, p. 252.

18 – *Ibid.*, vol. iii, p. 63, which has 'egg; King' and 'Crowns'.

III 'Miss Ormerod'

1 – An essay originally published in the *Dial* (NY), December 1924, (Kp C257) and included in the first American edition of *CR1* (see Editorial Note p. xxv), in both of which publications it was described in a footnote as being: 'Founded upon the Life of Eleanor Ormerod, by Robert Wallace Murray, 1904'. VW in fact improvises her account from *Eleanor Ormerod, LL.D. Economic Entomologist. Autobiography and Correspondence*. Edited by Robert Wallace, Professor of Agriculture and Rural Economy in the University of Edinburgh. With Portrait and Illustrations (John Murray, 1904). Her 'quotations' are seldom verbatim. Indeed, they are often inventions only indirectly derived from Ormerod. For this reason the following annotations are only apparently unsystematic.

2–In the *DNB*, that most patriarchal of institutions, Eleanor Anne Ormerod (1828–1901) is described under the entry for her father, George Ormerod (1785–1873), historian of Cheshire, as 'a distinguished entomologist'. Her mother was Sarah Latham (1784–1860).

3–Cf., Ormerod, ch. i, p. 2, for this and for subsequent references to Ormerod's 'first step in Entomology'. George Wareing Ormerod (1810–91), Eleanor's brother, became a geologist.

4–Cf., *ibid.*, ch. iv, p. 32. Captain Fenton otherwise unidentified.

5–Cf., *ibid.*, ch. viii, p. 53: 'The date was some time before coaches were discontinued, and the usual gathering of people in those days had collected at the door of the George Hotel in Chepstow to see the coach change horses when, to the astonishment of all, a fine rose-underwinged locust appeared amongst them. Chepstow is on a steep hill, and the "George" about half a mile from the bridge (pl. xvii). Down the hill set off the locust, pursued by a party from the George, until it was captured at the bridge, and our family doctor conveyed it alive and uninjured to me. On my father sending it to Professor Daubeney as a probable curiosity, he identified it as being the first of the kind which had been taken so far west. If he gave us the name, I have forgotten it.'

6–*Ibid.*, ch. xii, pp. 86–7.

7–For the origins of the foregoing 'colloquy', parts of which appear to be pure invention, see *ibid.* ch. iv, pp. 24–9.

8–This exclamation is apparently fictional.

9–*Ibid.*, ch. viii, pp. 56–7, punctuation slightly adapted.

10–Professor J. Ritzema Bos of Amsterdam, with whom Ormerod regularly corresponded. Paris Green was an insecticide – 'indispensable . . . in orchard-growing', ch. xix, p. 203 – the use of which Ormerod pioneered and promoted.

11–Improvised from Ormerod, ch. iii, p. 17 and ch. ix, p. 61.

12–Dr Edward Latham Ormerod (1819–73), physician.

13–Undiscovered in Ormerod.

14–For the origins of Miss Lipscomb – otherwise unidentified sister of Dr Eustace Lipscomb, Ormerod's medical attendant – and her Penzance painting, see Ormerod, ch. xi, p. 75, where the market gardener concerned is not named. (VW had something of a penchant for the name Pascoe, which occurs in *Jacob's Room*, 1922, and may be traced to the Pascoes of St Ives with whom the Stephen family were acquainted, see Woolf, *A Passionate Apprentice. The Early Journals* (Hogarth Press, 1990).)

15–*Ibid.*, p. 75, where the words 'Injurious Insects' are not broken with hyphens. Eleanor Ormerod, *Manual of Injurious Insects. With Methods of Prevention and Remedy* (1881).

16–For the origins of which see *ibid.*, ch. xix, p. 208.

17–This passage and the remainder of the essay is improvised freely from disparate points in Ormerod.

18–Ormerod, ch. xix, p. 207, has: 'SHE INTRODUCED PARIS GREEN INTO ENGLAND'.

19–*Ibid.*, ch. xxvi, pp. 325–6, which quotes from this obituary notice.

20–*Ibid.*, ch. xvi, pp. 163, 165, adapted.

21–*Ibid.*, p. 160, adapted from a letter to W. B. Tegetmeier, FZS, MBOU, 3 July 1897.

Jane Austen

It is probable that if Miss Cassandra Austen had had her way we should have had nothing of Jane Austen's except her novels.[2] To her elder sister alone did she write freely; to her alone she confided her hopes and, if rumour is true, the one great disappointment of her life; but when Miss Cassandra Austen grew old, and the growth of her sister's fame made her suspect that a time might come when strangers would pry and scholars speculate, she burnt, at great cost to herself, every letter that could gratify their curiosity, and spared only what she judged too trivial to be of interest.

Hence our knowledge of Jane Austen is derived from a little gossip, a few letters, and her books. As for the gossip, gossip which has survived its day is never despicable; with a little rearrangement it suits our purpose admirably. For example, Jane 'is not at all pretty and very prim, unlike a girl of twelve ... Jane is whimsical and affected,'[3] says little Philadelphia Austen of her cousin. Then we have Mrs Mitford, who knew the Austens as girls and thought Jane 'the prettiest, silliest, most affected husband-hunting butterfly she ever remembers'.[4] Next, there is Miss Mitford's anonymous friend who visits her now [and] says that she has stiffened into the most perpendicular, precise, taciturn piece of 'single blessedness' that ever existed, and that, until *Pride and Prejudice* showed what a precious gem was hidden in that unbending case, she was no more regarded in society than a poker or firescreen ... The case is very different now', the good lady goes on; 'she is still a poker – but a poker of whom everybody is afraid ... A wit, a delineator of character, who does not talk is terrific indeed!'[5] On the other side, of course, there are the Austens, a race little given to panegyric of themselves, but nevertheless, they say, her brothers 'were very fond and very proud of her. They were attached to her by her talents, her virtues, and her engaging manners, and each loved afterwards to fancy a resemblance in some niece or daughter of his own to the dear sister Jane, whose perfect equal they yet never expected to see.'[6] Charming but perpendicular, loved at home but feared by strangers, biting of tongue but tender of heart – these contrasts are by no means incompatible, and when we turn to the novels we shall find ourselves stumbling there too over the same complexities in the writer.

To begin with, that prim little girl whom Philadelphia found so unlike a child of twelve, whimsical and affected, was soon to be the authoress of an astonishing and unchildish story, *Love and Freindship*,[7] which, incredible though it appears, was written at the age of fifteen. It was written, apparently, to amuse the schoolroom; one of the stories in the same book is dedicated with mock solemnity to her brother; another is neatly illustrated with water-colour heads by her sister. There are jokes which, one feels, were family property; thrusts of satire, which went home because all little Austens made mock in common of fine ladies who 'sighed and fainted on the sofa'.[8]

Brothers and sisters must have laughed when Jane read out loud her last hit at the vices which they all abhorred. 'I die a martyr to my grief for the loss of Augustus. One fatal swoon has cost me my life. Beware of Swoons, Dear Laura . . . Run mad as often as you chuse, but do not faint . . .'[9] And on she rushed, as fast as she could write and quicker than she could spell, to tell the incredible adventures of Laura and Sophia, of Philander and Gustavus, of the gentleman who drove a coach between Edinburgh and Stirling every other day, of the theft of the fortune that was kept in the table drawer, of the starving mothers and the sons who acted Macbeth. Undoubtedly, the story must have roused the schoolroom to uproarious laughter. And yet, nothing is more obvious than that this girl of fifteen, sitting in her private corner of the common parlour, was writing not to draw a laugh from brother and sisters, and not for home consumption. She was writing for everybody, for nobody, for our age, for her own; in other words, even at that early age Jane Austen was writing. One hears it in the rhythm and shapeliness and severity of the sentences. 'She was nothing more than a mere good-tempered, civil, and obliging young woman; as such we could scarcely dislike her – she was only an object of contempt.'[10] Such a sentence is meant to outlast the Christmas holidays. Spirited, easy, full of fun, verging with freedom upon sheer nonsense, – *Love and Freindship* is all that; but what is this note which never merges in the rest, which sounds distinctly and penetratingly all through the volume? It is the sound of laughter. The girl of fifteen is laughing, in her corner, at the world.

Girls of fifteen are always laughing. They laugh when Mr Binney helps himself to salt instead of sugar. They almost die of laughing when old Mrs Tomkins sits down upon the cat. But they are crying the moment after. They have no fixed abode from which they see that there is something eternally laughable in human nature, some quality in men and women that for ever excites our satire. They do not know that Lady Greville who snubs, and poor Maria who is snubbed, are permanent features of every ballroom. But Jane Austen knew it from her birth upwards. One of those fairies who perch upon cradles must have taken her a flight through the world directly she was born. When she was laid in the cradle again she knew not only what the world looked like, but had already chosen her kingdom. She had agreed that if she might rule over that territory, she would covet no other. Thus at fifteen she had few illusions about other people and none about herself. Whatever she writes is finished and turned and set in its relation, not to the parsonage, but to the universe. She is impersonal; she is inscrutable. When the writer, Jane Austen, wrote down in the most remarkable sketch in the book a little of Lady Greville's conversation,[11] there is no trace of anger at the snub which the clergyman's daughter, Jane Austen, once received. Her gaze passes straight to the mark, and we know precisely where, upon the map of human nature, that mark is. We know because Jane Austen kept to her compact; she never trespassed beyond her boundaries. Never, even at the emotional age of fifteen, did she round upon herself in shame, obliterate a sarcasm in a spasm of compassion, or blur an outline in a mist of rhapsody. Spasms and rhapsodies, she seems to have said, pointing with her stick, end *there*; and the boundary line is perfectly distinct. But she does not deny that moons and mountains and castles exist – on the other side. She has even one romance of her own. It is for the Queen of Scots. She really admired her very much. 'One of the first characters in the world,' she called her, 'a bewitching Princess whose only friend was then the Duke of Norfolk, and whose only ones now Mr Whitaker, Mrs Lefroy, Mrs Knight and myself.'[12] With these words her passion is neatly circumscribed, and rounded with a laugh. It is amusing to remember in what terms the young Brontës wrote, not very much later, in their northern parsonage, about the Duke of Wellington.[13]

The prim little girl grew up. She became 'the prettiest, silliest, most affected husband-hunting butterfly'[14] Mrs Mitford ever remembered, and, incidentally, the authoress of a novel called *Pride and Prejudice*, which, written stealthily under cover of a creaking door, lay for many years unpublished. A little later, it is thought, she began another story, *The Watsons*,[15] and being for some reason dissatisfied with it, left it unfinished. The second-rate works of a great writer are worth reading because they offer the best criticism of his masterpieces. Here her difficulties are more apparent, and the method she took to overcome them less artfully concealed. To begin with, the stiffness and the bareness of the first chapters prove that she was one of those writers who lay their facts out rather baldly in the first version and then go back and back and back and cover them with flesh and atmosphere. How it would have been done we cannot say – by what suppressions and insertions and artful devices. But the miracle would have been accomplished; the dull history of fourteen years of family life would have been converted into another of those exquisite and apparently effortless introductions; and we should never have guessed what pages of preliminary drudgery Jane Austen forced her pen to go through. Here we perceive that she was no conjuror after all. Like other writers, she had to create the atmosphere in which her own peculiar genius could bear fruit. Here she fumbles; here she keeps us waiting. Suddenly she has done it; now things can happen as she likes things to happen. The Edwardses are going to the ball. The Tomlinsons' carriage is passing; she can tell us that Charles is 'being provided with his gloves and told to keep them on';[16] Tom Musgrave retreats to a remote corner with a barrel of oysters and is famously snug. Her genius is freed and active. At once our senses quicken; we are possessed with the peculiar intensity which she alone can impart. But of what is it all composed? Of a ball in a country town; a few couples meeting and taking hands in an assembly room; a little eating and drinking; and for catastrophe, a boy being snubbed by one young lady and kindly treated by another. There is no tragedy and no heroism. Yet for some reason the little scene is moving out of all proportion to its surface solemnity. We have been made to see that if Emma acted so in the ball-room, how considerate, how tender, inspired by what sincerity of feeling she would have shown herself in those graver crises of life which, as we watch her, come inevitably before our eyes. Jane Austen is thus a mistress of much deeper emotion than appears upon the surface. She stimulates us to supply what is not there. What she offers is, apparently, a trifle, yet is composed of something that expands in the reader's mind and endows with the most enduring form of life scenes which are outwardly trivial. Always the stress is laid upon character. How, we are made to wonder, will Emma behave when Lord Osborne and Tom Musgrave make their call at five minutes before three, just as Mary is bringing in the tray and the knife-case? It is an extremely awkward situation. The young men are accustomed to much greater refinement. Emma may prove herself ill-bred, vulgar, a nonentity. The turns and twists of the dialogue keep us on the tenterhooks of suspense. Our attention is half upon the present moment, half upon the future. And when in the end, Emma behaves in such a way as to vindicate our highest hopes of her, we are moved as if we had been made witnesses of a matter of the highest importance. Here, indeed, in this unfinished and in the main inferior story, are all the elements of Jane Austen's greatness. It has the permanent quality of literature. Think away the surface animation, the likeness to life, and there remains, to provide a deeper pleasure, an exquisite discrimination of human values. Dismiss this too from the mind and one can dwell with extreme satisfaction upon the more abstract art which, in the ball-room scene, so varies the emotions and proportions the parts that it is possible to enjoy it, as one enjoys poetry, for itself, and not as a link which carries the story this way and that.

But the gossip says of Jane Austen that she was perpendicular, precise, and taciturn — 'a poker of whom everybody is afraid'. Of this too there are traces; she could be merciless enough; she is one of the most consistent satirists in the whole of literature. Those first angular chapters of *The Watsons* prove that hers was not a prolific genius; she had not, like Emily Brontë,[17] merely to open the door to make herself felt. Humbly and gaily she collected the twigs and straws out of which the nest was to be made and placed them neatly together. The twigs and straws were a little dry and a little dusty in themselves. There was the big house and the little house; a tea party, a dinner party, and an occasional picnic; life was hedged in by valuable connections and adequate incomes; by muddy roads, wet feet, and a tendency on the part of the ladies to get tired; a little principle supported it, a little consequence, and the education commonly enjoyed by upper middle-class families living in the country. Vice, adventure, passion were left outside. But of all this prosiness, of all this littleness, she evades nothing, and nothing is slurred over. Patiently and precisely she tells us how they 'made no stop anywhere till they reached Newbury, where a comfortable meal, uniting dinner and supper wound up the enjoyments and fatigues of the day'.[18] Nor does she pay to conventions merely the tribute of lip homage; she believes in them besides accepting them. When she is

describing a clergyman, like Edmund Bertram,[19] or a sailor, in particular, she appears debarred by the sanctity of his office from the free
use of her chief tool, the comic genius, and is apt therefore to lapse
into decorous panegyric or matter-of-fact description. But there are
exceptions; for the most part her attitude recalls the anonymous
lady's ejaculation – 'A wit, a delineator of character, who does not
talk is terrific indeed!' She wishes neither to reform nor to annihilate; she is silent; and that is terrific indeed. One after another she
creates her fools, her prigs, her worldlings, her Mr Collinses, her Sir
Walter Elliotts, her Mrs Bennetts.[20] She encircles them with the lash
of a whip-like phrase which, as it runs round them, cuts out their
silhouettes for ever. But there they remain; no excuse is found for
them and no mercy shown them. Nothing remains of Julia and
Maria Bertram when she has done with them; Lady Bertram is left
'sitting and calling to Pug and trying to keep him from the flower-
beds'[21] eternally. A divine justice is meted out; Dr Grant, who
begins by liking his goose tender, ends by bringing on 'apoplexy and
death, by three great institutionary dinners in one week'.[22] Sometimes it seems as if her creatures were born merely to give Jane Austen the supreme delight of slicing their heads off. She is satisfied; she
is content; she would not alter a hair on anybody's head, or move
one brick or one blade of grass in a world which provides her with
such exquisite delight.

Nor, indeed, would we. For even if the pangs of outraged vanity,
or the heat of moral wrath, urged us to improve away a world so
full of spite, pettiness, and folly, the task is beyond our powers.
People are like that – the girl of fifteen knew it; the mature woman
proves it. At this very moment some Lady Bertram is trying to keep
Pug from the flower beds; she sends Chapman to help Miss Fanny a
little late.[23] The discrimination is so perfect, the satire so just, that,
consistent though it is, it almost escapes our notice. No touch of
pettiness, no hint of spite, rouse us from our contemplation. Delight
strangely mingles with our amusement. Beauty illumines these
fools.

That elusive quality is, indeed, often made up of very different
parts, which it needs a peculiar genius to bring together. The wit of
Jane Austen has for partner the perfection of her taste. Her fool is a
fool, her snob is a snob, because he departs from the model of sanity
and sense which she has in mind, and conveys to us unmistakably
even while she makes us laugh. Never did any novelist make more

use of an impeccable sense of human values. It is against the disc of an unerring heart, an unfailing good taste, an almost stern morality, that she shows up those deviations from kindness, truth, and sincerity which are among the most delightful things in English literature. She depicts a Mary Crawford in her mixture of good and bad entirely by this means. She lets her rattle on against the clergy, or in favour of a baronetage and ten thousand a year, with all the ease and spirit possible; but now and again she strikes one note of her own, very quietly, but in perfect tune, and at once all Mary Crawford's chatter, though it continues to amuse, rings flat. Hence the depth, the beauty, the complexity of her scenes. From such contrasts there comes a beauty, a solemnity even, which are not only as remarkable as her wit, but an inseparable part of it. In *The Watsons* she gives us a foretaste of this power; she makes us wonder why an ordinary act of kindness, as she describes it, becomes so full of meaning. In her masterpieces, the same gift is brought to perfection. Here is nothing out of the way; it is midday in Northamptonshire; a dull young man is talking to rather a weakly young woman on the stairs as they go up to dress for dinner, with housemaids passing. But, from triviality, from commonplace, their words become suddenly full of meaning, and the moment for both one of the most memorable in their lives. It fills itself; it shines; it glows; it hangs before us, deep, trembling, serene for a second; next, the housemaid passes, and this drop, in which all the happiness of life has collected, gently subsides again to become part of the ebb and flow of ordinary existence.

What more natural, then, with this insight into their profundity, than that Jane Austen should have chosen to write of the trivialities of day-to-day existence, of parties, picnics, and country dances? No 'suggestions to alter her style of writing'[24] from the Prince Regent or Mr Clarke could tempt her; no romance, no adventure, no politics or intrigue could hold a candle to life on a country-house staircase as she saw it. Indeed, the Prince Regent and his librarian had run their heads against a very formidable obstacle; they were trying to tamper with an incorruptible conscience, to disturb an infallible discretion. The child who formed her sentences so finely when she was fifteen never ceased to form them, and never wrote for the Prince Regent or his Librarian, but for the world at large. She knew exactly what her powers were, and what material they were fitted to deal with as material should be dealt with by a writer whose standard of

finality was high. There were impressions that lay outside her province; emotions that by no stretch or artifice could be properly
coated and covered by her own resources. For example, she could
not make a girl talk enthusiastically of banners and chapels. She
could not throw herself whole-heartedly into a romantic moment.
She had all sorts of devices for evading scenes of passion. Nature
and its beauties she approached in a sidelong way of her own. She
describes a beautiful night without once mentioning the moon.
Nevertheless, as we read the few formal phrases about 'the brilliancy of an unclouded night and the contrast of the deep shade of
the woods', the night is at once as 'solemn, and soothing, and
lovely'[25] as she tells us, quite simply, that it was.

The balance of her gifts was singularly perfect. Among her
finished novels there are no failures, and among her many chapters
few that sink markedly below the level of the others. But, after all,
she died at the age of forty-two. She died at the height of her
powers. She was still subject to those changes which often make the
final period of a writer's career the most interesting of all. Vivacious, irrepressible, gifted with an invention of great vitality, there
can be no doubt that she would have written more, had she lived,
and it is tempting to consider whether she would not have written
differently. The boundaries were marked; moons, mountains, and
castles lay on the other side. But was she not sometimes tempted to
trespass for a minute? Was she not beginning, in her own gay and
brilliant manner, to contemplate a little voyage of discovery?

Let us take *Persuasion*, the last completed novel, and look by its
light at the books she might have written had she lived.* There is a
peculiar beauty and a peculiar dullness in *Persuasion*. The dullness
is that which so often marks the transition stage between two different periods. The writer is a little bored. She has grown too familiar with the ways of her world; she no longer notes them freshly.
There is an asperity in her comedy with suggests that she has almost
ceased to be amused by the vanities of a Sir Walter or the snobbery
of a Miss Elliott. The satire is harsh, and the comedy crude. She is
no longer so freshly aware of the amusements of daily life. Her
mind is not altogether on her object. But, while we feel that Jane
Austen has done this before, and done it better, we also feel that she
is trying to do something which she has never yet attempted. There
is a new element in *Persuasion*, the quality, perhaps, that made Dr
Whewell fire up and insist that it was 'the most beautiful of her

works'.[26] She is beginning to discover that the world is larger, more mysterious, and more romantic than she had supposed. We feel it to be true of herself when she says of Anne: 'She had been forced into prudence in her youth, she learned romance as she grew older – the natural sequel of an unnatural beginning'.[27] She dwells frequently upon the beauty and the melancholy of nature, upon the autumn where she had been wont to dwell upon the spring.† She talks of the 'influence so sweet and so sad of autumnal months in the country'.[28] She marks 'the tawny leaves and withered hedges'.[29] 'One does not love a place the less because one has suffered in it,'[30] she observes. But it is not only in a new sensibility to nature that we detect the change. Her attitude to life itself is altered. She is seeing it, for the greater part of the book, through the eyes of a woman who, unhappy herself, has a special sympathy for the happiness and unhappiness of others, which, until the very end, she is forced to comment upon in silence. Therefore the observation is less of facts and more of feelings than is usual. There is an expressed emotion in the scene at the concert and in the famous talk about woman's constancy which proves not merely the biographical fact that Jane Austen had loved, but the aesthetic fact that she was no longer afraid to say so. Experience, when it was of a serious kind, had to sink very deep, and to be thoroughly disinfected by the passage of time, before she allowed herself to deal with it in fiction. But now, in 1817, she was ready. Outwardly, too, in her circumstances, a change was imminent. Her fame had grown very slowly. 'I doubt,' wrote Mr Austen Leigh, 'whether it would be possible to mention any other author of note whose personal obscurity was so complete.'[31] Had she lived a few more years only, all that would have been altered. She would have stayed in London, dined out, lunched out, met famous people, made new friends, read, travelled, and carried back to the quiet country cottage a hoard of observations to feast upon at leisure.

And what effect would all this have had upon the six novels that Jane Austen did not write? She would not have written of crime, of passion, or of adventure. She would not have been rushed by the importunity of publishers or the flattery of friends into slovenliness or insincerity. But she would have known more. Her sense of security would have been shaken. Her comedy would have suffered. She would have trusted less (this is already perceptible in *Persuasion*) to dialogue and more to reflection to give us a knowledge of her characters. Those marvellous little speeches which sum up, in a few minutes' chatter, all that we need in order to know an Admiral Croft or a Mrs Musgrove[32] for ever, that shorthand, hit-or-miss method which contains chapters of analysis and psychology, would have become too crude to hold all that she now perceived of the complexity of human nature. She would have devised a method, clear and composed as ever, but deeper and more suggestive, for conveying not only what people say, but what they leave unsaid; not only what they are, but what life is.[†] She would have stood farther away from her characters, and seen them more as a group, less as individuals. Her satire, while it played less incessantly, would have been more stringent and severe. She would have been the forerunner of Henry James and of Proust[33] – but enough. Vain are these speculations: the most perfect artist among women, the writer whose books are immortal, died 'just as she was beginning to feel confidence in her own success'.[34][§]

---

[*] – *N&A*: 'Jane Austen at Sixty' opens with the following two paragraphs: 'Anybody who has had the temerity to write about Jane Austen is aware of two facts: first, that of all great writers she is the most difficult to catch in the act of greatness; second, that there are twenty-five elderly gentlemen living in the neighbourhood of London who resent any slight upon her genius as if it were an insult offered to the chastity of their Aunts. It would be interesting, indeed, to inquire how much of her present celebrity Jane Austen owes to masculine sensibility; to the fact that her dress was becoming, her eyes bright, and her age the antithesis in all matters of female charm to our own. A companion inquiry might investigate the problem of George Eliot's nose; and decide how long it will be before the equine profile is once again in favour, and the Clarendon Press celebrates the genius of the author of *Middlemarch* in an edition as splendid, as authoritative, and as exquisitely illustrated as this.

'But it is not mere cowardice that prompts us to say nothing of the six famous novels, which in their new edition will shortly be celebrated in these columns by another hand. It is impossible to say too much about the novels that Jane Austen did write; but enough attention perhaps has never yet been paid to the novels that Jane Austen did not write. Owing to the peculiar finish and perfection of her art, we tend to forget that she died at forty-two, at the height of her powers, still subject to all those changes which often make the final period of a writer's career the most interesting of them all. Let us take *Persuasion*, the last completed book, and look by its light at the novels that she might have written had she lived to be sixty. We do not grudge it him, but her brother the Admiral lived to be ninety-one.'

It continues with a third paragraph opening, as follows in the text here: 'There is a peculiar beauty and a peculiar dullness in *Persuasion*' etc.

[†] – *N&A* does not give: 'upon the autumn . . . upon the spring.'

‡ – *N&A*: 'but (if we may be pardoned the vagueness of the expression) what life is.'

§ – *N&A*: 'Vain are these speculations: she died "just as she was beginning to feel confidence in her own success".'

1 – First published in *CR1*, this essay incorporates, with variants as shown, 'Jane Austen at Sixty', *N&A*, 15 December 1923, reprinted *NR*, 30 January 1924, (Kp C241), a signed review of *The Novels of Jane Austen*, ed. R. W. Chapman (5 vols, Clarendon Press, 1923) and draws upon 'Jane Austen', *II VW Essays*. See also 'Jane Austen and the Geese', 'Jane Austen Practising', *III VW Essays*. Reading Notes (MHP, B 2q). Reprinted *CE*.

2 – Jane Austen (1775–1817) and her only sister Cassandra (1772–1845).

3 – William Austen-Leigh, *Jane Austen. Her Life and Letters* (Smith, Elder and Co., 1913), ch. iv, p. 58, Philadelphia Walter writing to her brother James, July 1788.

4 – *Ibid.*, ch. vi, p. 84, Mary Russell Mitford (1787–1855), writing to Sir William Elford, 3 April 1815.

5 – *Ibid.*, which has: 'a poker of whom everybody is afraid', and 'But a wit'. *Pride and Prejudice* (1813).

6 – J. E. Austen-Leigh, *A Memoir of Jane Austen* (1870; in *Persuasion. With a Memoir* . . . , Penguin, 1965, p. 388).

7 – See *Love and Freindship and Other Early Works* (Chatto and Windus, 1922), which VW reviewed in 'Jane Austen Practising'.

8 – Austen, *Love and Freindship*, Letter 9th, Laura to Marianne, p. 18: 'Ah! what could we do but what we did! We sighed and fainted on the sofa.'

9 – *Ibid.*, 'Letter the 14th', Laura to Marianne, p. 34, which has ellipses after 'Augustus' and 'Life', and: 'chuse; but'.

10 – *Ibid.*, 'Love and Freindship', pp. 32–3, which has: 'Object of Contempt'.

11 – *Ibid.*, 'A Collection of Letters', 'Letter the Third, from a Young Lady in distressed Circumstances to her freind', pp. 109–14.

12 – For the first quotation, *ibid.*, 'The History of England', 'Henry the 7th', p. 88, slightly adapted; and for the second, *ibid.*, 'Elizabeth', p. 92, which has: 'this bewitching Princess'.

13 – For the Brontës and the 1st Duke of Wellington (1769–1852), see for example the Rev. Patrick Brontë in Elizabeth Gaskell, *The Life of Charlotte Brontë* (1857; Penguin, 1975, pp. 93–4).

14 – Austen-Leigh, *Jane Austen. Life and Letters*, ch. vi, p. 84, Mary Russell Mitford writing to Sir William Elford, 3 April 1815.

15 – *Pride and Prejudice* was written 1796–7. *The Watsons* (1871) was begun c. 1804.

16 – Austen, *The Watsons*, in *Lady Susan/The Watsons/Sanditon* (Penguin, 1974, p. 122, which has: 'charged to keep them on').

17 – Emily Brontë (1818–48), for VW on whom see '"Jane Eyre" and "Wuthering Heights"' below.

18 – Austen, *Mansfield Park* (1814; Chapman, vol. 3, ch. vii, p. 376, which has: 'any where').

19 – In *Mansfield Park*.

20 – Mr Collins and Mrs Bennett appear in *Pride and Prejudice*; Sir Walter Elliot is a character in *Persuasion*.

21 – *Mansfield Park* (Chapman, vol. 1, ch. vii, p. 74: 'Sitting and calling to Pug, and trying to keep him from the flower-beds, was almost too much for me.').

22 – *Ibid.*, vol. 3, ch. xvii, p. 469.

23 – For Lady Bertram sending her maid Mrs Chapman ('too late of course to be any use') to help Fanny Price, *ibid.*, vol. 2, ch. ix, p. 271.

24 – J. E. Austen-Leigh, *A Memoir* . . ., pp. 350–9. J. S. Clarke, librarian at Carlton House.

25 – For both quotations, *ibid.*, ch. xi, p. 139, punctuation adapted.

26 – J. E. Austen-Leigh, p. 369. Dr William Whewell (1794–1866), Master of Trinity College, Cambridge.

27 – Austen, *Persuasion* (Chapman, vol. 3, ch. iv, p. 30).

28 – *Ibid.*, ch. v, p. 33, which has: 'the autumnal'.

29 – *Ibid.*, ch. x, p. 84.

30 – *Ibid.*, vol. 4, ch. viii, p. 184, which has: 'less for having suffered in it'.

31 – J. E. Austen-Leigh, p. 348.

32 – Character in *Persuasion*.

33 – Henry James (1843–1916); Marcel Proust (1871–1922).

34 – J. E . Austen-Leigh, p. 387.

Modern Fiction

In making any survey, even the freest and loosest, of modern fiction, it is difficult not to take it for granted that the modern practice of the art is somehow an improvement upon the old. With their simple tools and primitive materials, it might be said, Fielding did well and Jane Austen[2] even better, but compare their opportunities with ours! Their masterpieces certainly have a strange air of simplicity. And yet the analogy between literature and the process, to choose an example, of making motor cars scarcely holds good beyond the first glance. It is doubtful whether in the course of the centuries, though we have learnt much about making machines, we have learnt anything about making literature. We do not come to write better; all that we can be said to do is to keep moving, now a little in this direction, now in that, but with a circular tendency should the whole course of the track be viewed from a sufficiently lofty pinnacle. It need scarcely be said that we make no claim to stand, even momentarily, upon that vantage ground. On the flat, in the crowd, half-blind with dust, we look back with envy to those happier warriors, whose battle is won and whose achievements wear so serene an air of accomplishment that we can scarcely refrain from whispering that the fight was not so fierce for them as for us. It is for the historian of literature to decide; for him to say if we are now beginning or ending or standing in the middle of a great period of prose fiction, for down in the plain little is visible. We only know that certain gratitudes and hostilities inspire us; that certain paths seem to lead to fertile land, others to the dust and the desert; and of this perhaps it may be worth while to attempt some account.

Our quarrel, then, is not with the classics, and if we speak of quarrelling with Mr Wells, Mr Bennett, and Mr Galsworthy,[3] it is partly that by the mere fact of their existence in the flesh their work has a living, breathing, everyday imperfection which bids us take what liberties with it we choose. But it is also true that, while we thank them for a thousand gifts, we reserve our unconditional gratitude for Mr Hardy, for Mr Conrad, and in a much lesser degree for the Mr Hudson of *The Purple Land, Green Mansions*, and *Far Away and Long Ago*.[4] Mr Wells, Mr Bennett, and Mr Galsworthy have excited so many hopes and disappointed them so persistently that our gratitude largely takes the form of thanking them for having shown us what they might have done but have not done; what we certainly could not do, but as certainly, perhaps, do not wish to do. No single phrase will sum up the charge or grievance which we have to bring against a mass of work so large in its volume and embodying so many qualities, both admirable and the reverse. If we tried to formulate our meaning in one word we should say that these three writers are materialists. It is because they are concerned not with the spirit but with the body that they have disappointed us, and left us with the feeling that the sooner English fiction turns its back upon them, as politely as may be, and marches, if only into the desert, the better for its soul. Naturally, no single word reaches the centre of three separate targets. In the case of Mr Wells it falls notably wide of the mark. And yet even with him it indicates to our thinking the fatal alloy in his genius, the great clod of clay that has got itself mixed up with the purity of his inspiration. But Mr Bennett is perhaps the worst culprit of the three, inasmuch as he is by far the best workman. He can make a book so well constructed and solid in its craftsmanship that it is difficult for the most exacting of critics to see through what chink or crevice decay can creep in. There is not so much as a draught between the frames of the windows, or a crack in the boards. And yet – if life should refuse to live

there? That is a risk which the creator of *The Old Wives' Tale*,
George Cannon, Edwin Clayhanger,[5] and hosts of other figures,
may well claim to have surmounted. His characters live abundantly,
even unexpectedly, but it remains to ask how do they live, and what
do they live for? More and more they seem to us, deserting even the
well-built villa in the Five Towns, to spend their time in some softly
padded first-class railway carriage, pressing bells and buttons innumerable; and the density to which they travel so luxuriously
becomes more and more unquestionably an eternity of bliss spent in
the very best hotel in Brighton. It can scarcely be said of Mr Wells
that he is a materialist in the sense that he takes too much delight in
the solidity of his fabric. His mind is too generous in its sympathies
to allow him to spend much time in making things shipshape and
substantial. He is a materialist from sheer goodness of heart, taking
upon his shoulders the work that ought to have been discharged by
Government officials, and in the plethora of his ideas and facts
scarcely having leisure to realise, or forgetting to think important,
the crudity and coarseness of his human beings. Yet what more
damaging criticism can there be both of his earth and of his Heaven
than that they are to be inhabited here and hereafter by his Joans
and his Peters?[6] Does not the inferiority of their natures tarnish
whatever institutions and ideals may be provided for them by the
generosity of their creator? Nor, profoundly though we respect the
integrity and humanity of Mr Galsworthy, shall we find what we
seek in his pages.

If we fasten, then, one label on all these books, on which is one
word materialists, we mean by it that they write of unimportant
things; that they spend immense skill and immense industry making
the trivial and the transitory appear the true and the enduring.

We have to admit that we are exacting, and, further, that we find
it difficult to justify our discontent by explaining what it is that we
exact. We frame our question differently at different times. But it re-
appears most persistently as we drop the finished novel on the crest
of a sigh – Is it worth while? What is the point of it all? Can it be
that, owing to one of those little deviations which the human spirit
seems to make from time to time, Mr Bennett has come down with
his magnificent apparatus for catching life just an inch or two on the
wrong side? Life escapes; and perhaps without life nothing else is
worth while. It is a confession of vagueness to have to make use of
such a figure as this, but we scarcely better the matter by speaking,

as critics are prone to do, of reality. Admitting the vagueness which afflicts all criticism of novels, let us hazard the opinion that for us at this moment the form of fiction most in vogue more often misses than secures the thing we seek. Whether we call it life or spirit, truth or reality, this, the essential thing, has moved off, or on, and refuses to be contained any longer in such ill-fitting vestments as we provide. Nevertheless, we go on perseveringly, conscientiously, constructing our two and thirty chapters after a design which more and more ceases to resemble the vision in our minds. So much of the enormous labour of proving the solidity, the likeness to life, of the story is not merely labour thrown away but labour misplaced to the extent of obscuring and blotting out the light of the conception. The writer seems constrained, not by his own free will but by some powerful and unscrupulous tyrant who has him in thrall, to provide a plot, to provide comedy, tragedy, love interest, and an air of probability embalming the whole so impeccable that if all his figures were to come to life they would find themselves dressed down to the last button of their coats in the fashion of the hour. The tyrant is obeyed; the novel is done to a turn. But sometimes, more and more often as time goes by, we suspect a momentary doubt, a spasm of rebellion, as the pages fill themselves in the customary way. Is life like this? Must novels be like this?

Look within and life, it seems, is very far from being 'like this'. Examine for a moment an ordinary mind on an ordinary day. The mind receives a myriad impressions – trivial, fantastic, evanescent, or engraved with the sharpness of steel. From all sides they come, an incessant shower of innumerable atoms; and as they fall, as they shape themselves into the life of Monday or Tuesday,[7] the accent falls differently from of old; the moment of importance came not here but there; so that, if a writer were a free man and not a slave, if he could write what he chose, not what he must, if he could base his work upon his own feeling and not upon convention, there would be no plot, no comedy, no tragedy, no love interest or catastrophe in the accepted style, and perhaps not a single button sewn on as the Bond Street tailors would have it. Life is not a series of gig lamps symmetrically arranged; life is a luminous halo, a semi-transparent envelope surrounding us from the beginning of consciousness to the end. Is it not the task of the novelist to convey this varying, this unknown and uncircumscribed spirit, whatever aberration or complexity it may display, with as little mixture of the alien and external as possible? We are not pleading merely for courage and sincerity; we are suggesting that the proper stuff of fiction is a little other than custom would have us believe it.

It is, at any rate, in some such fashion as this that we seek to define the quality which distinguishes the work of several young writers, among whom Mr James Joyce[8] is the most notable, from that of their predecessors. They attempt to come closer to life, and to preserve more sincerely and exactly what interests and moves them, even if to do so they must discard most of the conventions which are commonly observed by the novelist. Let us record the atoms as they fall upon the mind in the order in which they fall, let us trace the pattern, however disconnected and incoherent in appearance, which each sight or incident scores upon the consciousness. Let us not take it for granted that life exists more fully in what is commonly thought big than in what is commonly thought small. Any one who has read *The Portrait of the Artist as a Young Man* or, what promises to be a far more interesting work, *Ulysses*, now appearing in the *Little Review*, will have hazarded some theory of this nature as to Mr Joyce's intention.[9] On our part, with such a fragment before us, it is hazarded rather than affirmed; but whatever the intention of the whole, there can be no question but that it is of the utmost sincerity and that the result, difficult or unpleasant as we may judge it, is undeniably important. In contrast with those whom we have called materialists, Mr Joyce is spiritual; he is concerned at all costs to reveal the flickerings of that innermost flame which flashes its messages through the brain, and in order to preserve it he disregards with complete courage whatever seems to him adventitious, whether it be probability, or coherence, or any other of these signposts which for generations have served to support the imagination of a reader when called upon to imagine what he can neither touch nor see. The scene in the cemetery, for instance, with its brilliancy, its sordidity, its incoherence, its sudden lightning flashes of significance, does undoubtedly come so close to the quick of the mind that, on a first reading at any rate, it is difficult not to acclaim a masterpiece. If we want life itself, here surely we have it. Indeed, we find ourselves fumbling rather awkwardly if we try to say what else we wish, and for what reason a work of such originality yet fails to compare, for we must take high examples, with *Youth* or *The Mayor of Casterbridge*.[10] It fails because of the comparative poverty of the writer's mind, we might say simply and have done with it. But it is possible to press a little further and wonder whether we may not refer our sense of being in a bright yet narrow room, confined and shut in, rather than enlarged and set free, to some limitation imposed by the method as well as by the mind. Is it the method that inhibits the creative power? Is it due to the method that we feel neither jovial nor magnanimous, but centred in a self which, in spite of its tremor of susceptibility, never embraces or creates what is outside itself and beyond? Does the emphasis laid, perhaps didactically, upon indecency, contribute to the effect of something angular and isolated? Or is it merely that in any effort of such originality it is much easier, for contemporaries especially, to feel what it lacks than to name what it gives? In any case it is a mistake to stand outside examining 'methods'. Any method is right, every method is right, that expresses what we wish to express, if we are writers; that brings us closer to the novelist's intention if we are readers. This method has the merit of bringing us closer to what we were prepared to call life itself; did not the reading of *Ulysses* suggest how much of life is excluded or ignored, and did it not come with a shock to open *Tristram Shandy* or even *Pendennis*[11] and be by them convinced that there are not only other aspects of life, but more important ones into the bargain.

However this may be, the problem before the novelist at present, as we suppose it to have been in the past, is to contrive means of being free to set down what he chooses. He has to have the courage to say that what interests him is no longer 'this' but 'that': out of 'that' alone must he construct his work. For the moderns 'that', the point of interest, lies very likely in the dark places of psychology. At once, therefore, the accent falls a little differently; the emphasis is upon something hitherto ignored; at once a different outline of form becomes necessary, difficult for us to grasp, incomprehensible to our predecessors. No one but a modern, no one perhaps but a Russian, would have felt the interest of the situation which Tchehov has made into the short story which he calls 'Gusev'.[12] Some Russian soldiers lie ill on board a ship which is taking them back to Russia. We are given a few scraps of their talk and some of their thoughts; then one of them dies and is carried away; the talk goes on among the others for a time, until Gusev himself dies, and looking 'like a carrot or a radish'[13] is thrown overboard. The emphasis is laid upon such unexpected places that at first it seems as if there were no emphasis at all; and then, as the eyes accustom themselves to twilight and discern the shapes of things in a room we see how complete the story is, how profound, and how truly in obedience to his vision Tchehov has chosen this, that, and the other, and placed them together to compose something new. But it is impossible to say 'this is comic', or 'that is tragic', nor are we certain, since short stories, we have been taught, should be brief and conclusive, whether this, which is vague and inconclusive, should be called a short story at all.

The most elementary remarks upon modern English fiction can hardly avoid some mention of the Russian influence, and if the Russians are mentioned one runs the risk of feeling that to write of any fiction save theirs is waste of time. If we want understanding of the soul and heart where else shall we find it of comparable profundity? It we are sick of our own materialism the least considerable of their novelists has by right of birth a natural reverence for the human spirit. 'Learn to make yourself akin to people . . . But let this sympathy be not with the mind — for it is easy with the mind — but with the heart, with love towards them.'[14] In every great Russian writer we seem to discern the features of a saint, if sympathy for the sufferings of others, love towards them, endeavour to reach some goal worthy of the most exacting demands of the spirit constitute saintliness. It is the saint in them which confounds us with a feeling of our own irreligious triviality, and turns so many of our famous novels to tinsel and trickery. The conclusions of the Russian mind, thus comprehensive and compassionate, are inevitably, perhaps, of the utmost sadness. More accurately indeed we might speak of the inconclusiveness of the Russian mind. It is the sense that there is no answer, that if honestly examined life presents question after question which must be left to sound on and on after the story is over in hopeless interrogation that fills us with a deep, and finally it may be with a resentful, despair. They are right perhaps; unquestionably they see further than we do and without our gross impediments of vision. But perhaps we see something that escapes them, or why should this voice of protest mix itself with our gloom? The voice of protest is the voice of another and an ancient civilisation which seems to have bred in us the instinct to enjoy and fight rather than to suffer and understand. English fiction from Sterne to Meredith[15] bears witness to our natural delight in humour and comedy, in the beauty of earth, in the activities of the intellect, and in the splendour of the body. But any deductions that we may draw from the comparison of two fictions so immeasurably far apart are futile save indeed as they flood us with a view of the infinite possibilities of the art and remind us that there is no limit to the horizon, and that nothing – no 'method', no experiment, even of the wildest – is forbidden, but only falsity and pretence. 'The proper stuff of fiction' does not exist; everything is the proper stuff of fiction, every feeling, every thought; every quality of brain and spirit is drawn upon; no perception comes amiss. And if we can imagine the art of fiction come alive and standing in our midst, she would undoubtedly bid us break her and bully her, as well as honour and love her, for so her youth is renewed and her sovereignty assured.

1–Originally published in the *TLS*, 10 April 1919, (Kp C147) under the title 'Modern Novels' (see *III VW Essays*), this essay was revised for inclusion in *CR1*. See also 'On Re-reading Novels', 'Mr Bennett and Mrs Brown' and 'Character in Fiction', *III VW Essays*. Reading Notes (Berg, XXXI).
2–Henry Fielding (1707–54); Jane Austen (1775–1817), for VW on whom see 'Jane Austen' above.
3–H. G. Wells (1866–1946), on whose *Joan and Peter* (1918) VW wrote in 'The Rights of Youth', *II VW Essays*; Arnold Bennett (1867–1931), for VW on whom see 'Mr Bennett and Mrs Brown' and 'Character in Fiction', *III VW Essays*; John Galsworthy (1867–1933), on whose *Beyond* (1917) VW wrote in 'Mr Galsworthy's Novel', *II VW Essays*.
4–Thomas Hardy (1840–1928), for VW on whom see 'Thomas Hardy's Novels' and 'Half of Thomas Hardy' below; Joseph Conrad (1857–1924), for VW on whom see 'Joseph Conrad' below; W. H. Hudson (1841–1922), *The Purple Land* (1885), *Green Mansions* (1904), and *Far Away and Long Ago* (1918), for VW's review of which see 'Mr Hudson's Childhood' in *II VW Essays*.
5–*The Old Wives' Tale* (1908); George Cannon appears in the 'Clayhanger' trilogy (*Clayhanger*, 1910, *Hilda Lessways*, 1911, *These Twain*, 1916).
6–See note 3 above.
7–See VW's eponymous story in the collection *Monday or Tuesday* (1921). (CSF, p. 137.)
8–James Joyce (1882–1941).
9–*A Portrait of the Artist as a Young Man* (1916–17), *Ulysses* (1922). As early as April 1918 Harriet Weaver had approached the Woolfs in the hope that The Hogarth Press might publish the whole of *Ulysses* (of which the first thirteen episodes, and part of the fourteenth, had started appearing in the *Little Review* the previous month, continuing until December 1920), but for several reasons, legal and practical, this proved impossible. However, VW made notes on those episodes that appeared in the *Little Review* March–October 1918. Reading Notes (Berg, XXXI.)
10–'Youth' (1902); for VW's views upon it see 'Mr Conrad's *Youth*', *II VW Essays*. Thomas Hardy, *The Mayor of Casterbridge* (1886). For the cemetery scene in *Ulysses* see II Odyssey, 6 Hades (ed. Jeri Johnson, OUP, 1993, pp 84–111).
11–*The Life and Opinions of Tristram Shandy* (1759–67) by Laurence Sterne, for

VW on whom see 'Sterne', I VW Essays, 'Sterne's Ghost' below, and 'The "Sentimental Journey"', V VW Essays and CR2. The History of Pendennis (1848–50) by
W. M. Thackeray.
12—For this story see The Witch and Other Stories by Anton Chekov (1860–1904),
trans. Constance Garnett (Chatto and Windus, 1918), a volume discussed by VW
in 'Tchehov's Questions', II VW Essays.
13—The Witch and Other Stories, 'Gusev', p. 166: 'Sewn up in the sail cloth he
looked like a carrot or a radish: broad at the head and narrow at the feet . . .'
14—Elena Militsina and Mikhail Saltikov, The Village Priest and Other Stories;
trans. from the Russian by Beatrix L. Tollemache, with an intro. by C. Hagberg
Wright (T. Fisher Unwin, 1918), the title story (by Militsina), p. 34; the ellipsis
marks the omission of: 'I would even like to add: make yourself indispensable to
them'. The full passage is quoted in 'The Russian View', II VW Essays; see also
'The Russian Point of View', below.
15—George Meredith (1828–1909), for VW on whom see 'The Novels of George
Meredith' below.

'Jane Eyre' and 'Wuthering Heights'

Of the hundred years that have passed since Charlotte Brontë was
born,[2] she, the centre now of so much legend, devotion, and literature, lived but thirty-nine. It is strange to reflect how different those
legends might have been had her life reached the ordinary human
span. She might have become, like some of her famous contemporaries, a figure familiarly met with in London and elsewhere, the subject of pictures and anecdotes innumerable, the writer of many
novels, of memoirs possibly, removed from us well within the
memory of the middle-aged in all the splendour of established fame.
She might have been wealthy, she might have been prosperous. But
it is not so. When we think of her we have to imagine some one who
had no lot in our modern world; we have to cast our minds back to
the 'fifties of the last century, to a remote parsonage upon the wild
Yorkshire moors. In that parsonage, and on those moors, unhappy
and lonely, in her poverty and her exaltation, she remains for ever.

These circumstances, as they affected her character, may have left
their traces on her work. A novelist, we reflect, is bound to build up
his structure with much very perishable material which begins by
lending it reality and ends by cumbering it with rubbish. As we open
Jane Eyre once more we cannot stifle the suspicion that we shall find

her world of imagination as antiquated, mid-Victorian, and out of date as the parsonage on the moor, a place only to be visited by the curious, only preserved by the pious. So we open *Jane Eyre*; and in two pages every doubt is swept clean from our minds.

> Folds of scarlet drapery shut in my view to the right hand; to the left were the clear panes of glass, protecting, but not separating me from the drear November day. At intervals, while turning over the leaves of my book, I studied the aspect of that winter afternoon. Afar, it offered a pale blank of mist and cloud; near, a scene of wet lawn and storm-beat shrub, with ceaseless rain sweeping away wildly before a long and lamentable blast.[3]

There is nothing there more perishable than the moor itself, or more subject to the sway of fashion than the 'long and lamentable blast'. Nor is this exhilaration short-lived. It rushes us through the entire volume, without giving us time to think, without letting us lift our eyes from the page. So intense is our absorption that if some one moves in the room the movement seems to take place not there but up in Yorkshire. The writer has us by the hand, forces us along her road, makes us see what she sees, never leaves us for a moment or allows us to forget her. At the end we are steeped through and through with the genius, the vehemence, the indignation of Charlotte Brontë. Remarkable faces, figures of strong outline and gnarled feature have flashed upon us in passing; but it is through her eyes that we have seen them. Once she is gone, we seek for them in vain. Think of Rochester and we have to think of Jane Eyre. Think of the moor, and again there is Jane Eyre. Think of the drawing-room,* even, those 'white carpets on which seemed laid brilliant garlands of flowers', that 'pale Parian mantelpiece' with its Bohemia glass of 'ruby red' and the 'general blending of snow and fire' — what is all that except Jane Eyre?

The drawbacks of being Jane Eyre are not far to seek. Always to be a governess and always to be in love is a serious limitation in a world which is full, after all, of people who are neither one nor the

---

* VW's fn: Charlotte and Emily Brontë had much the same sense of colour. '. . . we saw – ah! it was beautiful! – a splendid place carpeted with crimson, and crimson-covered chairs and tables, and a pure white ceiling bordered by gold, a shower of glass drops hanging in silver chains from the centre, and shimmering with little soft tapers' (*Wuthering Heights*). 'Yet it was merely a very pretty drawing-room, and within it a boudoir, both spread with white carpets, on which seemed laid brilliant garlands of flowers; both ceiled with snowy mouldings of white grapes and vine leaves, beneath which glowed in rich contrast crimson couches and ottomans; while the ornaments on the pale Parian mantelpiece were of sparkling Bohemia glass, ruby red; and between the windows large mirrors repeated the general blending of snow and fire' (*Jane Eyre*).[4]

other. The characters of a Jane Austen or of a Tolstoy[5] have a million facets compared with these. They live and are complex by means of their effect upon many different people who serve to mirror them in the round. They move hither and thither whether their creators watch them or not, and the world in which they live seems to us an independent world which we can visit, now that they have created it, by ourselves. Thomas Hardy is more akin to Charlotte Brontë in the power of his personality and the narrowness of his vision. But the differences are vast. As we read *Jude the Obscure*[6] we are not rushed to a finish; we brood and ponder and drift away from the text in plethoric trains of thought which build up round the characters an atmosphere of question and suggestion of which they are themselves, as often as not, unconscious. Simple peasants as they are, we are forced to confront them with destinies and questionings of the hugest import, so that often it seems as if the most important characters in a Hardy novel are those which have no names. Of this power, of this speculative curiosity, Charlotte Brontë has no trace. She does not attempt to solve the problems of human life; she is even unaware that such problems exist; all her force, and it is the more tremendous for being constricted, goes into the assertion, 'I love', 'I hate', 'I suffer'.

For the self-centred and self-limited writers have a power denied the more catholic and broad-minded. Their impressions are close packed and strongly stamped between their narrow walls. Nothing issues from their minds which has not been marked with their own impress. They learn little from other writers, and what they adopt they cannot assimilate. Both Hardy and Charlotte Brontë appear to have founded their styles upon a stiff and decorous journalism. The staple of their prose is awkward and unyielding. But both with labour and the most obstinate integrity, by thinking every thought until it has subdued words to itself, have forged for themselves a prose which takes the mould of their minds entire; which has, into the bargain, a beauty, a power, a swiftness of its own. Charlotte Brontë, at least, owed nothing to the reading of many books. She never learnt the smoothness of the professional writer, or acquired his ability to stuff and sway his language as he chooses. 'I could never rest in communication with strong, discreet, and refined minds, whether male or female,' she writes, as any leader-writer in a provincial journal might have written; but gathering fire and speed goes on in her own authentic voice 'till I had passed the outworks of conventional reserve and crossed the threshold of confidence, and won a place by their hearts' very hearthstone.'[7] It is there that she takes her seat; it is the red and fitful glow of the heart's fire which illumines her page. In other words, we read Charlotte Brontë not for exquisite observation of character – her characters are vigorous and elementary; not for comedy – hers is grim and crude; not for a philosophic view of life – hers is that of a country parson's daughter; but for her poetry. Probably that is so with all writers who have, as she has, an overpowering personality, so that, as we say in real life, they have only to open the door to make themselves felt. There is in them some untamed ferocity perpetually at war with the accepted order of things which makes them desire to create instantly rather than to observe patiently. This very ardour, rejecting half shades and other minor impediments, wings its way past the daily conduct of ordinary people and allies itself with their more inarticulate passions. It makes them poets, or, if they choose to write in prose, intolerant of its restrictions. Hence it is that both Emily and Charlotte are always invoking the help of Nature. They both feel the need of some more powerful symbol of the vast and slumbering passions in human nature than words or actions can convey. It is with a description of a storm that Charlotte ends her finest novel *Villette*. 'The skies hang full and dark – a wrack sails from the west; the clouds cast themselves into strange forms.'[8] So she calls in Nature to describe a state of mind which could not otherwise be expressed. But neither of the sisters observed nature accurately as Dorothy Wordsworth observed it, or painted it minutely as Tennyson painted it.[9] They seized those aspects of the earth which were most akin to what they themselves felt or imputed to their characters, and so their storms, their moors, their lovely spaces of summer weather are not ornaments applied to decorate a dull page or display the writer's powers of observation – they carry on the emotion and light up the meaning of the book.

The meaning of a book, which lies so often apart from what happens and what is said and consists rather in some connection which things in themselves different have had for the writer, is necessarily hard to grasp. Especially this is so when, like the Brontës, the writer is poetic, and his meaning inseparable from his language, and itself rather a mood than a particular observation. *Wuthering Heights* is a more difficult book to understand than *Jane Eyre*, because Emily was a greater poet than Charlotte. When Charlotte wrote she said with eloquence and splendour and passion 'I love', 'I hate', 'I suffer'. Her experience, though more intense, is on a level with our own. But there is no 'I' in *Wuthering Heights*. There are no governesses. There are no employers. There is love, but it is not the love of men and women. Emily was inspired by some more general conception. The impulse which urged her to create was not her own suffering or her own injuries. She looked out upon a world cleft into gigantic disorder and felt within her the power to unite it in a book. That gigantic ambition is to be felt throughout the novel – a struggle, half-thwarted but of superb conviction, to say something through the mouths of her characters which is not merely 'I love' or 'I hate', but 'we, the whole human race' and 'you, the eternal powers . . .' the sentence remains unfinished. It is not strange that it should be so; rather it is astonishing that she can make us feel what she had it in her to say at all. It surges up in the half-articulate words of Catherine Earnshaw, 'If all else perished and *he* remained, I should still continue to be; and if all else remained and he were annihilated, the universe would turn to a mighty stranger; I should not seem part of it.'[10] It breaks out again in the presence of the dead. 'I see a repose that neither earth nor hell can break, and I feel an assurance of the endless and shadowless hereafter – the eternity they have entered – where life is boundless in its duration, and love in its sympathy and joy in its fulness.'[11] It is this suggestion of power underlying the apparitions of human nature and lifting them up into the presence of greatness that gives the book its huge stature among other novels. But it was not enough for Emily Brontë to write a few lyrics, to utter a cry, to express a creed. In her poems she did this once and for all, and her poems will perhaps outlast her novel. But she was novelist as well as poet. She must take upon herself a more laborious and a more ungrateful task. She must face the fact of other existences, grapple with the mechanism of external things, build up, in recognisable shape, farms and houses and report the speeches of men and women who existed independently of herself. And so we reach these summits of emotion not by rant or rhapsody but by hearing a girl sing old songs to herself as she rocks in the branches of a tree; by watching the moor sheep crop the turf; by listening to the soft wind breathing through the grass. The life at the farm with all its absurdities and its improbability is laid open to us. We are given every opportunity of comparing *Wuthering Heights* with a real farm and Heathcliff with a real man. How, we are allowed to ask, can there be truth or insight or the finer shades of emotion in men and women who so little resemble what we have seen ourselves? But even as we ask it we see in Heathcliff the brother that a sister of genius might have seen; he is impossible we say, but nevertheless no boy in literature has a more vivid existence than his. So it is with the two Catherines; never could women feel as they do or act in their manner, we say. All the same, they are the most lovable women in English fiction. It it as if she could tear up all that we know human beings by, and fill these unrecognisable transparences with such a gust of life that they transcend reality. Hers, then, is the rarest of all powers. She could free life from its dependence on facts; with a few touches indicate the spirit of a face so that it needs no body; by speaking of the moor make the wind blow and the thunder roar.

1 – Written specifically for *CR1*, this essay incorporates in part 'Charlotte Brontë' (Kp C52) *II VW Essays*. See also 'Haworth, November, 1904', 'Mrs Gaskell', *I VW Essays*; and 'Charlotte Brontë' (Kp C93) *II VW Essays*.
2 – Charlotte Brontë (d. 1855) was born on 21 April 1816.
3 – *Jane Eyre* (1847; The Haworth Edition: *The Life and Works of Charlotte Brontë and Her Sisters* (7 vols, Smith, Elder, and Co., 1899 –; vol. i, *Jane Eyre*, ch. i, p. 2).
4 – For the first quotation from Emily Brontë (1818–48), *Wuthering Heights* (1847; The Haworth Edition, vol. v, ch. vi, p. 47); for that from *Jane Eyre*: ch. xi, p. 122, which has 'Bohemian glass'.
5 – For VW on Jane Austen (1775–1817) see above; L. N. Tolstoy (1828–1910).
6 – For VW on Thomas Hardy (1840–1928) see below; *Jude the Obscure* (1895).
7 – *Jane Eyre*, ch. xxxii, p. 457, which has 'their heart's'.
8 – *Villette* (The Haworth Edition, vol. iii, ch. xlii, p. 593).
9 – For VW on Dorothy Wordsworth (1771–1855) see *CR2* and *V VW Essays*. Alfred, Lord Tennyson (1809–92).
10 – *Wuthering Heights*, ch. ix, p. 84, which has 'stranger:'.
11 – *Ibid.*, ch. xvi, p. 172, which has 'Eternity' and 'sympathy,'.

George Eliot

To read George Eliot attentively is to become aware how little one knows about her. It is also to become aware of the credulity, not very creditable to one's insight, with which, half-consciously and partly maliciously, one had accepted the late Victorian version of a deluded woman who held phantom sway over subjects even more deluded than herself. At what moment and by what means her spell was broken it is difficult to ascertain. Some people attribute it to the publication of her *Life*.[2] Perhaps George Meredith, with his phrase about the 'mercurial little showman' and the 'errant woman'[3] on the daïs, gave point and poison to the arrows of thousands incapable of aiming them so accurately, but delighted to let fly. She became one of the butts for youth to laugh at, the convenient symbol of a group of serious people who were all guilty of the same idolatry and could be dismissed with the same scorn. Lord Acton had said that she was greater than Dante;[4] Herbert Spencer exempted her novels, as if they were not novels, when he banned all fiction from the London Library.[5] She was the pride and paragon of her sex. Moreover, her private record was not more alluring than her public. Asked to describe an afternoon at the Priory, the storyteller always intimated that the memory of those serious Sunday afternoons had come to tickle his sense of humour. He had been so much alarmed by the grave lady in her low chair; he had been so anxious to say the intelligent thing. Certainly, the talk had been very serious, as a note in the fine clear hand of the great novelist bore witness. It was dated on the Monday morning, and she accused herself of having spoken without due forethought of Marivaux when she meant another; but no doubt, she said, her listener had already supplied the correction.[6] Still, the memory of talking about Marivaux to George Eliot on a Sunday afternoon was not a romantic memory. It had faded with the passage of the years. It had not become picturesque.

Indeed, one cannot escape the conviction that the long, heavy face with its expression of serious and sullen and almost equine power has stamped itself depressingly upon the minds of people who remember George Eliot, so that it looks out upon them from her pages. Mr Gosse has lately described her as he saw her driving through London in a victoria:

a large, thick-set sybil, dreamy and immobile, whose massive features, somewhat grim when seen in profile, were incongruously bordered by a hat, always in the height of Paris fashion, which in those days commonly included an immense ostrich feather.[7]

Lady Ritchie, with equal skill, has left a more intimate indoor portrait:

She sat by the fire in a beautiful black satin gown, with a green shaded lamp on the table beside her, where I saw German books lying and pamphlets and ivory paper-cutters. She was very quiet and noble, with two steady little eyes and a sweet voice. As I looked I felt her to be a friend, not exactly a personal friend, but a good and benevolent impulse.[8]

A scrap of her talk is preserved. 'We ought to respect our influence,' she said. 'We know by our own experience how very much others affect our lives, and we must remember that we in turn must have the same effect upon others.'[9] Jealously treasured, committed to memory, one can imagine recalling the scene, repeating the words, thirty years later and suddenly, for the first time, bursting into laughter.

In all these records one feels that the recorder, even when he was in the actual presence, kept his distance and kept his head, and never read the novels in later years with the light of a vivid, or puzzling, or beautiful personality dazzling in his eyes. In fiction, where so much of personality is revealed, the absence of charm is a great lack; and her critics, who have been, of course, mostly of the opposite sex, have resented, half consciously perhaps, her deficiency in a quality which is held to be supremely desirable in women. George Eliot was not charming; she was not strongly feminine; she had none of those eccentricities and inequalities of temper which give to so many artists the endearing simplicity of children. One feels that to most people, as to Lady Ritchie, she was 'not exactly a personal friend, but a good and benevolent impulse'.[10] But if we consider these portraits more closely we shall find that they are all the portraits of an elderly celebrated woman, dressed in black satin, driving in her victoria, a woman who has been through her struggle and issued from it with a profound desire to be of use to others, but with no wish for intimacy, save with the little circle who had known her in the days of her youth. We know very little about the days of her youth; but we do know that the culture, the philosophy, the fame, and the influence were all built upon a very humble foundation – she was the granddaughter of a carpenter.

The first volume of her life is a singularly depressing record. In it we see her raising herself with groans and struggles from the intolerable boredom of petty provincial society (her father had risen in the world and become more middle class, but less picturesque) to be the assistant editor of a highly intellectual London review,[11] and the esteemed companion of Herbert Spencer. The stages are painful as she reveals them in the sad soliloquy in which Mr Cross condemned her to tell the story of her life. Marked in early youth as one 'sure to get something up very soon in the way of a clothing club',[12] she proceeded to raise funds for restoring a church by making a chart of ecclesiastical history; and that was followed by a loss of faith which so disturbed her father that he refused to live with her. Next came the struggle with the translation of Strauss, which, dismal and 'soul-stupefying'[13] in itself, can scarcely have been made less so by the usual feminine tasks of ordering a household and nursing a dying father, and the distressing conviction, to one so dependent upon affection, that by becoming a blue-stocking she was forfeiting her brother's respect. 'I used to go about like an owl,' she said, 'to the great disgust of my brother.'[14] 'Poor thing,' wrote a friend who saw her toiling through Strauss with a statue of the risen Christ in front of her, 'I do pity her sometimes, with her pale sickly face and dreadful headaches, and anxiety, too, about her father.'[15] Yet, though we cannot read the story without a strong desire that the stages of her pilgrimage might have been made, if not more easy, at least more beautiful, there is a dogged determination in her advance upon the citadel of culture which raises it above our pity. Her development was very slow and very awkward, but it had the irresistible impetus behind it of a deep-seated and noble ambition. Every obstacle at length was thrust from her path. She knew every one. She read everything. Her astonishing intellectual vitality had triumphed. Youth was over, but youth had been full of suffering. Then, at the age of thirty-five, at the height of her powers, and in the fulness of her freedom, she made the decision which was of such profound moment to her and still matters even to us, and went to Weimar, alone with George Henry Lewes.[16]

The books which followed so soon after her union testify in the fullest manner to the great liberation which had come to her with personal happiness. In themselves they provide us with a plentiful feast. Yet at the threshold of her literary career one may find in some of the circumstances of her life influences that turned her mind to the past, to the country village, to the quiet and beauty and simplicity of childish memories and away from herself and the present. We understand how it was that her first book was *Scenes of Clerical Life*, and not *Middlemarch*.[17] Her union with Lewes had surrounded her with affection, but in view of the circumstances and of the conventions it had also isolated her. 'I wish it to be understood,' she wrote in 1857, 'that I should never invite any one to come and see me who did not ask for the invitation.'[18] She had been 'cut off from what is called the world',[19] she said later, but she did not regret it. By becoming thus marked, first by circumstances and later, inevitably, by her fame, she lost the power to move on equal terms unnoted among her kind; and the loss for a novelist was serious. Still, basking in the light and sunshine of *Scenes of Clerical Life*, feeling the large mature mind spreading itself with a luxurious sense of freedom in the world of her 'remotest past',[20] to speak of loss seems inappropriate. Everything to such a mind was gain. All experience filtered down through layer after layer of perception and reflection, enriching and nourishing. The utmost we can say, in qualifying her attitude towards fiction by what little we know of her life, is that she had taken to heart certain lessons not usually learnt early, if learnt at all, among which, perhaps, the most branded upon her was the melancholy virtue of tolerance; her sympathies are with the everyday lot, and play most happily in dwelling upon the home-spun of ordinary joys and sorrows. She has none of that romantic intensity which is connected with a sense of one's own individuality, unsated and unsubdued, cutting its shape sharply upon the back-ground of the world. What were the loves and sorrows of a snuffly old clergyman, dreaming over his whisky, to the fiery egotism of Jane Eyre? The beauty of those first books, *Scenes of Clerical Life, Adam Bede, The Mill on the Floss*, is very great.[21] It is impossible to estimate the merit of the Poysers, the Dodsons, the Gilfils, the Bartons,[22] and the rest with all their surroundings and dependencies, because they have put on flesh and blood and we move among them, now bored, now sympathetic, but always with that un-questioning acceptance of all that they say and do, which we accord to the great originals only. The flood of memory and humour which she pours so spontaneously into one figure, one scene after another, until the whole fabric of ancient rural England is revived, has so much in common with a natural process that it leaves us with little consciousness that there is anything to criticise. We accept;* we feel the delicious warmth and release of spirit which the great creative writers alone procure for us. As one comes back to the books after years of absence they pour out, even against our expectation, the same store of energy and heat, so that we want more than anything to idle in the warmth as in the sun beating down from the red orchard wall. If there is an element of unthinking abandonment in thus submitting to the humours of Midland farmers and their wives, that, too, is right in the circumstances. We scarcely wish to analyse what we feel to be so large and deeply human. And when we consider how distant in time the world of Shepperton and Hayslope is, and how remote the minds of farmer and agricultural labourers from those of most of George Eliot's readers, we can only attribute the ease and pleasure with which we ramble from house to smithy, from cottage parlour to rectory garden, to the fact that George Eliot makes us share their lives, not in a spirit of condescension or of curiosity, but in a spirit of sympathy. She is no satirist. The movement of her mind was too slow and cumbersome to lend itself to comedy. But she gathers in her large grasp a great bunch of the main elements of human nature and groups them loosely together with a tolerant and wholesome understanding which, as one finds upon re-reading, has not only kept her figures fresh and free, but has given them an unexpected hold upon our laughter and tears. There is the famous Mrs Poyser. It would have been easy to work her idiosyncrasies to death, and, as it is, perhaps, George Eliot gets her laugh in the same place a little too often. But memory, after the book is shut, brings out, as sometimes in real life, the details and subtleties which some more salient characteristic has prevented us from noticing at the time. We recollect that her health was not good. There were occasions upon which she said nothing at all. She was patience itself with a sick child. She doted upon Totty. Thus one can muse and speculate about the greater number of George Eliot's characters and find, even in the least important, a roominess and margin where those qualities lurk which she has no call to bring from their obscurity.

But in the midst of all this tolerance and sympathy there are, even in the early books, moments of greater stress. Her humour has shown itself broad enough to cover a wide range of fools and failures, mothers and children, dogs and flourishing midland fields, farmers, sagacious or fuddled over their ale, horse-dealers, inn-keepers, curates, and carpenters. Over them all broods a certain romance, the only romance that George Eliot allowed herself – the romance of the past. The books are astonishingly readable and have no trace of pomposity or pretence. But to the reader who holds a large stretch of her early work in view it will become obvious that the mist of recollection gradually withdraws. It is not that her power diminishes, for, to our thinking, it is at its highest in the mature *Middlemarch*, the magnificent book which with all its imperfections is one of the few English novels written for grown-up people.[†] But the world of fields and farms no longer contents her. In real life she had sought her fortunes elsewhere; and though to look back into the past was calming and consoling, there are, even in the early works, traces of that troubled spirit, that exacting and questioning and baffled presence who was George Eliot herself. In *Adam Bede* there is a hint of her in Dinah. She shows herself far more openly and completely in Maggie in *The Mill on the Floss*. She is Janet in *Janet's Repentance*, and Romola, and Dorothea seeking wisdom and finding one scarcely knows what in marriage with Ladislaw.[23] Those who fall foul of George Eliot do so, we incline to think, on account of her heroines; and with good reason; for there is no doubt that they bring out the worst of her, lead her into difficult places, make her self-conscious, didactic, and occasionally vulgar. Yet if you could delete the whole sisterhood you would leave a much smaller and a much inferior world, albeit a world of greater artistic perfection and far superior jollity and comfort. In accounting for her failure, in so far as it was a failure, one recollects that she never wrote a story until she was thirty-seven, and that by the time she was thirty-seven she had come to think of herself with a mixture of pain and something like resentment. For long she preferred not to think of herself at all. Then, when the first flush of creative energy was exhausted and self-confidence had come to her, she wrote more and more from the personal standpoint, but she did so without the unhesitating abandonment of the young. Her self-consciousness is always marked when her heroines say what she herself would have said. She disguised them in every possible way. She granted them beauty and wealth into the bargain; she invented, more improbably, a taste for brandy. But the disconcerting and stimulating fact remained that she was compelled by the very power of her genius to step forth in person upon the quiet bucolic scene.

The noble and beautiful girl who insisted upon being born into the Mill on the Floss is the most obvious example of the ruin which a heroine can strew about her. Humour controls her and keeps her lovable so long as she is small and can be satisfied by eloping with the gipsies or hammering nails into her doll; but she develops; and before George Eliot knows what has happened she has a full-grown woman on her hands demanding what neither gipsies, nor dolls, nor St Ogg's itself is capable of giving her. First Philip Wakem is produced, and later Stephen Guest. The weakness of the one and the coarseness of the other have often been pointed out; but both, in their weakness and coarseness, illustrate not so much George Eliot's inability to draw the portrait of a man, as the uncertainty, the infirmity, and the fumbling which shook her hand when she had to conceive a fit mate for a heroine. She is in the first place driven beyond the home world she knew and loved, and forced to set foot in middle-class drawing-rooms where young men sing all the summer morning and young women sit embroidering smoking-caps for bazaars. She feels herself out of her element, as her clumsy satire of what she calls 'good society' proves.

Good society has its claret and its velvet carpets, its dinner engagements six weeks deep, its opera, and its faëry ball rooms . . . gets its science done by Faraday and its religion by the superior clergy who are to be met in the best houses; how should it have need of belief and emphasis?[24]

There is no trace of humour or insight there, but only the vindictiveness of a grudge which we feel to be personal in its origin. But terrible as the complexity of our social system is in its demands upon the sympathy and discernment of a novelist straying across the boundaries, Maggie Tulliver did worse than drag George Eliot from her natural surroundings. She insisted upon the introduction of the great emotional scene. She must love; she must despair; she must be drowned clasping her brother in her arms. The more one examines the great emotional scenes the more nervously one anticipates the brewing and gathering and thickening of the cloud which will burst upon our heads at the moment of crisis in a shower of disillusionment and verbosity. It is partly that her hold upon dialogue, when it is not dialect, is slack; and partly that she seems to shrink with an elderly dread of fatigue from the effort of emotional concentration. She allows her heroines to talk too much. She has little verbal felicity. She lacks the unerring taste which chooses one sentence and compresses the heart of the scene within that. 'Whom are you going to dance with?' asked Mr Knightley, at the Westons' ball. 'With you, if you will ask me,' said Emma;[25] and she has said enough. Mrs Casaubon would have talked for an hour and we should have looked out of the window.

Yet, dismiss the heroines without sympathy, confine George Eliot to the agricultural world of her 'remotest past', and you not only diminish her greatness but lose her true flavour. That greatness is here we can have no doubt. The width of the prospect, the large strong outlines of the principal features, the ruddy light of the early books, the searching power and reflective richness of the later tempt us to linger and expatiate beyond our limits. But it is upon the heroines that we would cast a final glance. 'I have always been finding out my religion since I was a little girl,' says Dorothea Casaubon. 'I used to pray so much – now I hardly ever pray. I try not to have desires merely for myself . . .'[26] She is speaking for them all. That is their problem. They cannot live without religion, and they start out on the search for one when they are little girls. Each has the deep feminine passion for goodness, which makes the place where she stands in aspiration and agony the heart of the book – still and cloistered like a place of worship, but that she no longer knows to whom to pray. In learning they seek their goal; in the ordinary tasks of womanhood; in the wider service of their kind. They do not find what they seek, and we cannot wonder. The ancient consciousness of woman, charged with suffering and sensibility, and for so many ages dumb, seems in them to have brimmed and overflowed and uttered a demand for something – they scarcely know what – for something that is perhaps incompatible with the facts of human existence. George Eliot had far too strong an intelligence to tamper with those facts, and too broad a humour to mitigate the truth because it was a stern one.[†] Save for the supreme courage of their endeavour, the struggle ends, for her heroines, in tragedy, or in a compromise that is even more melancholy. But their story is the incomplete version of the story of George Eliot herself. For her, too, the burden and the complexity of womanhood were not enough; she must reach beyond the sanctuary and pluck for herself the strange bright fruits of art and knowledge. Clasping them as few women have ever clasped them, she would not renounce her own inheritance – the difference of view, the difference of standard – nor accept an inappropriate reward. Thus we behold her, a memorable figure, inordinately praised and shrinking from her fame, despondent, reserved, shuddering back into the arms of love as if there alone were satisfaction and, it might be, justification, at the same time reaching out with 'a fastidious yet hungry ambition'[27] for all that life could offer the free and inquiring mind and confronting her feminine aspirations with the real world of men. Triumphant was the issue for her, whatever it may have been for her creations, and as we recollect all that she dared and achieved, how with every obstacle against her – sex and health and convention – she sought more knowledge and more freedom till the body, weighted with its double burden, sank worn out, we must lay upon her grave whatever we have it in our power to bestow of laurel and rose.⁵

* – *TLS*: 'We accept; we expand; we feel'.
† – *TLS* does not give: 'the magnificent . . . grown-up people.'
‡ – *TLS*: 'tamper with those facts, or to mitigate the truth because it was a stern one.'
⁵ – *TLS*: 'achieved, how, crushed by sorrow, she mastered even that desolation and sought more knowledge and more understanding till the body, weighted with its double burden, sank and died worn out, we must lay upon her grave whatever we have it in our power to bestow of laurel and rose.'

1 – Originally published in the *TLS*, 20 November 1919, (Kp C175) this essay was written at the request of Bruce Richmond (letter dated 14 February 1919, MHP) to mark the centenary of George Eliot's birth, on 22 November, and subsequently included in CR1 revised as shown. 'But oh, dear, what a lot I've got to read!,' VW exclaimed in her diary of 5 March 1919, 'The entire works of Mr James Joyce, Wyndham Lewis, Ezra Pound, so as to compare them with the entire works of Dickens & Mrs Gaskell; besides that George Eliot; & finally Hardy.' A letter to Lady Robert Cecil (*II VW Letters*, no. 1010, dated by the editors 'Sunday [26 January? 1919]' but evidently written later, given the date of Richmond's request for a commemorative essay) expatiates enthusiastically on her task: 'I am reading through the whole of George Eliot, in order to sum her up, once and for all, upon her anniversary, which happily is still months ahead. So far, I have only made way with her life, which is a book of the greatest fascination, and I can see already that no one else has ever known her as I know her. However, I always think this whatever I read – don't you? I think she is a highly feminine and attractive character – most impulsive and ill-balanced (Mrs Prothero once told me that she – George Eliot that is – had a child by a Professor in Edinburgh – she knew it for a fact – indeed the child is a well known Professor somewhere else –) and I only wish she had lived nowadays, and so been saved all that nonsense. I mean, being so serious, and digging up fossils, and all the rest of it. Perhaps too she would have written, not exactly better, but less facetiously. It was an unfortunate thing to be the first woman of the age. But she comes very well out of it so far, better anyhow than Herbert Spencer, and George Frederick Watts, – but I haven't begun her novels.'
     On 17 August we find her writing to Margaret Llewelyn-Davies (*ibid.*, no. 1075): 'I've got to read the whole of George Eliot, the whole of Thomas Hardy, and a good deal of Henry James in order to write articles about them. Its rather humiliating, reading other peoples novels. George Eliot fascinates me. Did your father know her? or was she too much under a cloud? Nobody called on her, so she says; and yet her virtue seems to me excessive . . .' She wrote to Lytton Strachey on 14 September suggesting that he had never read Eliot but wishing he had 'because then perhaps you would explain the whole puzzle' (*ibid.*, no. 1082); and to Katherine Arnold-Forster on 9 October: '. . . Whatever one may say about the Victorians, there's no doubt they had twice our – not exactly brains – perhaps hearts. I don't

know quite what it is; but I'm a good deal impressed.' Her days as November approached were 'crammed' with George Eliot (19 October 1919, *I VW Diary*). 'Shall I ever again get time for writing here? Never have I been so pressed with reviewing, for theres George Eliot to fill up all crannies left by other books ... November descends. Squire's new monthly out; and now – Middlemarch!' (*ibid.*, 1 November). In a postscript to her endeavours she explains, to Lady Robert Cecil (*II VW Letters*, no. 1096, late November): 'I didn't write on G. E. in the Times; but in the Suppt, and I was so much struck by her goodness that I hope it wasn't my article that you thought hard. She is as easy to read as Tit Bits: and it was a surprise to me; magnificent in many ways.'

See also 'George Eliot (1819–1880)', *III VW Essays*, and 'George Eliot' below. Reading Notes (MHP, B 2i). See Editorial Note, p. xxv. Reprinted *CE*.

2–J. W. Cross, *George Eliot's Life as Related in her Letters and Journals* (3 vols, W. Blackwood, 1885); this edition is cited by Silver and by Steele but the page references in the reading notes show that in preparing her essay VW used the 1886 'Cabinet Edition', in which the pagination differs from that in the edition of 1885.

3–*Letters of George Meredith*, ed. W. M. Meredith (2 vols, Constable and Co., 1912), vol. ii, to Leslie Stephen, 18 August 1902, p. 540: 'In the *George Eliot* [by Leslie Stephen, English Men of Letters, 1902] I could not have refrained from touches on the comic scenes of the Priory – with the dais, and the mercurial little showman, and the Bishop about the feet of an errant woman worshipped as a literary idol and light of philosophy.'

4–*Letters of Lord Acton* [1834–1902] *to Mary, Daughter of The Right Hon. W. E. Gladstone*, ed. Herbert Paul (George Allen, 1904), 27 December 1880, p. 57: 'If Sophocles or Cervantes had lived in the light of our culture, if Dante had prospered like Manzoni, George Eliot might have had a rival.'

5–Herbert Spencer (1820–1903) served on the London Library Committee and opposed the acquisition of modern novels. He was an intimate friend of George Eliot, but he did not, and was not empowered to, ban fiction from the Library.

6–See *The Letters of George Eliot*, ed. Gordon S. Haight (ix vols, OUP, 1954–78), vol. vii, p. 3, for Eliot's previously unpublished letter to Leslie Stephen, dated 7 January 1878, concerning her confusion regarding the authorship of an anonymous article in the *Cornhill Magazine* (then under Stephen's editorship) on the French playwright and novelist Pierre de Marivaux (1688–1763).

7–Edmund Gosse (1849–1928), 'George Eliot', *London Mercury*, November 1919, p. 34, which continues: '; this was George Eliot'.

8–Anne Thackeray-Ritchie, *From the Porch* (Smith, Elder and Co., 1913), 'A Discourse on Modern Sibyls', p. 11.

9–*Ibid.*, pp. 11–12.

10–*Ibid.*, p. 11.

11–George Eliot's father, Robert Evans, a builder and carpenter's son, became an agent on estates in Derbyshire and Warwickshire. Mary Ann Evans was assistant editor of the *Westminster Review*, 1851–3, under John Chapman.

12–Cross (1886), vol. i, 'Introductory Sketch of Childhood, 1819 to 1838', p. 22.

13–*Ibid.*, ch. ii, 'Coventry – Translation of Strauss', letter to Sara Hennell, end June ?1845, p. 105. Mary Ann Evans had in 1844 succeeded a Miss Brabant as translator of David Friedrich Strauss's *The Life of Jesus* (1846), originally published in 1835–6.

14—*Ibid.*, ch. iii, 'Life in Coventry till Mr Evans's death', p. 127, quoting Mary Cash, *née* Sibree, regarding Mary Ann Evans's attitude to evangelical religion.

15—*Ibid.*, ch. ii, 'Coventry – Translation of Strauss', Caroline Bray to Sara Hennell, 14 February 1846, p. 112.

16—George Henry Lewes (1817–78), writer and editor, author of a *Biographical History of Philosophy* (1845, 1846) and of *Comte's Philosophy of Sciences* (1853), had married in 1840; he first met George Eliot in 1851, by which date his marriage had effectively foundered, and, from 1854, although there was no legal divorce, she and Lewes lived together as man and wife.

17—*Scenes of Clerical Life* (1857), *Middlemarch* (1871–2).

18—Cross, vol. i, ch. vii, 'Richmond – "Scenes of Clerical Life"', George Eliot to Caroline Bray, 5 June 1857, p. 368.

19—*Ibid.*, vol. ii, ch. xi, '"Silas Marner" – "Romola" begun', George Eliot to Mrs Peter Taylor, 1 April 1861, p. 250.

20—*Ibid.*, ch. ix, '"The Mill on the Floss"', George Eliot to Madame Bodichon, 11 August 1859, p. 103.

21—*Adam Bede* (1859), *The Mill on the Floss* (1860). (For VW on Jane Eyre, see '"Jane Eyre" and "Wuthering Heights"' above.)

22—For the Poysers, see *Adam Bede*; for the Gilfils and Bartons, *Scenes of Clerical Life*.

23—'Janet's Repentance', an episode in *Scenes of Clerical Life*; the historical novel *Romola* was published in 1863; for Dorothea Brooke and Will Ladislaw, see *Middlemarch*.

24—*The Mill on the Floss* (3 vols, William Blackwood and Sons, 1860), vol. ii, 'Book Fourth', ch. iii, 'A Voice from the Past', p. 188, which has: 'But then, good society has . . .' and 'houses: how should it have time or need for belief and emphasis?'

25—Jane Austen, *Emma* (1816; Penguin, 1966, ch. 38, pp. 327–8). See also 'On Not Knowing Greek', n. 7, above.

26—*Middlemarch. A Study of Provincial Life* (4 vols, William Blackwood and Sons, 1871–2), vol. ii, bk iv, ch. xxxix, pp. 308–9, which continues: ', because they may not be good for others, and I have too much already.'

27—Cross, vol. iii, ch. xvi, 'Poems – "Middlemarch"', George Eliot to Mrs Richard Congreve, 2 December 1870, p. 106.

The Russian Point of View

Doubtful as we frequently are whether either the French or the Americans, who have so much in common with us, can yet understand English literature, we must admit graver doubts whether, for all their enthusiasm, the English can understand Russian literature. Debate might protract itself indefinitely as to what we mean by 'understand'. Instances will occur to everybody of American writers in particular who have written with the highest discrimination of our literature and of ourselves; who have lived a lifetime among us, and finally have taken legal steps to become subjects of King George. For all that, have they understood us, have they not remained to the end of their days foreigners? Could any one believe that the novels of Henry James were written by a man who had grown up in the society which he describes, or that his criticism of English writers was written by a man who had read Shakespeare without any sense of the Atlantic Ocean and two or three hundred years on the far side of it separating his civilisation from ours?[2] A special acuteness and detachment, a sharp angle of vision the foreigner will often achieve; but not that absence of self-consciousness, that ease and fellowship and sense of common values which make for intimacy, and sanity, and the quick give and take of familiar intercourse.

Not only have we all this to separate us from Russian literature, but a much more serious barrier — the difference of language. Of all those who feasted upon Tolstoy, Dostoevsky, and Tchehov[3] during the past twenty years, not more than one or two perhaps have been able to read them in Russian. Our estimate of their qualities has been formed by critics who have never read a word of Russian, or seen Russia, or even heard the language spoken by natives; who have had to depend, blindly and implicitly, upon the work of translators.

What we are saying amounts to this, then, that we have judged a whole literature stripped of its style. When you have changed every word in a sentence from Russian to English, have thereby altered the sense a little, the sound, weight, and accent of the words in relation to each other completely, nothing remains except a crude and coarsened version of the sense. Thus treated, the great Russian writers are like men deprived by an earthquake or a railway accident not only of all their clothes, but also of something subtler and more important — their manners, the idiosyncrasies of their characters. What remains is, as the English have proved by the fanaticism of their admiration, something very powerful and very impressive, but it is difficult to feel sure, in view of these mutilations, how far we can trust ourselves not to impute, to distort, to read into them an emphasis which is false.

They have lost their clothes, we say, in some terrible catastrophe, for some such figure as that describes the simplicity, the humanity, startled out of all effort to hide and disguise its instincts, which Russian literature, whether it is due to translation or to some more profound cause, makes upon us. We find these qualities steeping it through, as obvious in the lesser writers as in the greater. 'Learn to make yourselves akin to people. I would even like to add: make yourself indispensable to them. But let this sympathy be not with the mind – for it is easy with the mind – but with the heart, with love towards them.'[4] 'From the Russian', one would say instantly, wherever one chanced on that quotation. The simplicity, the absence of effort, the assumption that in a world bursting with misery the chief call upon us is to understand our fellow-sufferers, 'and not with the mind – for it is easy with the mind – but with the heart' – this is the cloud which broods above the whole of Russian literature, which lures us from our own parched brilliancy and scorched thoroughfares to expand in its shade – and of course with disastrous results. We become awkward and self-conscious; denying our own qualities, we write with an affectation of goodness and simplicity which is nauseating in the extreme. We cannot say 'Brother' with simple conviction. There is a story by Mr Galsworthy in which one of the characters so addresses another (they are both in the depths of misfortune).[5] Immediately everything becomes strained and affected. The English equivalent for 'Brother' is 'Mate' – a very different word, with something sardonic in it, an indefinable suggestion of humour. Met though they are in the depths of misfortune the two Englishmen who thus accost each other will, we are sure, find a job, make their fortunes, spend the last years of their lives in luxury, and leave a sum of money to prevent poor devils from calling each other 'Brother' on the Embankment. But it is common suffering, rather than common happiness, effort, or desire that produces the sense of brotherhood. It is the 'deep sadness'[6] which Dr Hagberg Wright finds typical of the Russian people that creates their literature.

A generalisation of this kind will, of course, even if it has some degree of truth when applied to the body of literature, be changed profoundly when a writer of genius sets to work on it. At once other questions arise. It is seen that an 'attitude' is not simple; it is highly complex. Men reft of their coats and their manners, stunned by a railway accident, say hard things, harsh things, unpleasant things, difficult things, even if they say them with the abandonment and simplicity which catastrophe has bred in them. Our first impressions of Tchehov are not of simplicity but of bewilderment. What is the point of it, and why does he make a story out of this? we ask as we read story after story. A man falls in love with a married woman, and they part and meet, and in the end are left talking about their position and by what means they can be free from 'this intolerable bondage'.

'"How? How?" he asked, clutching his head . . . And it seemed as though in a little while the solution would be found and then a new and splendid life would begin.'[7] That is the end. A postman drives a student to the station and all the way the student tries to make the postman talk, but he remains silent. Suddenly the postman says unexpectedly, 'It's against the regulations to take anyone with the post.'[8] And he walks up and down the platform with a look of anger on his face. 'With whom was he angry? Was it with people, with poverty, with the autumn nights?'[9] Again, that story ends.

But is it the end, we ask? We have rather the feeling that we have overrun our signals; or it is as if a tune had stopped short without the expected chords to close it. These stories are inconclusive, we say, and proceed to frame a criticism based upon the assumption that stories ought to conclude in a way that we recognise. In so doing, we raise the question of our own fitness as readers. Where the tune is familiar and the end emphatic – lovers united, villains discomfited, intrigues exposed – as it is in most Victorian fiction, we can scarcely go wrong, but where the tune is unfamiliar and the end a note of interrogation or merely the information that they went on talking, as it is in Tchehov, we need a very daring and alert sense of literature to make us hear the tune, and in particular those last notes which complete the harmony. Probably we have to read a great many stories before we feel, and the feeling is essential to our satisfaction, that we hold the parts together, and that Tchehov was not merely rambling disconnectedly, but struck now this note, now that with intention, in order to complete his meaning.

We have to cast about in order to discover where the emphasis in these strange stories rightly comes. Tchehov's own words give us a lead in the right direction. '. . . such a conversation as this between us,' he says, 'would have been unthinkable for our parents. At night they did not talk, but slept sound; we, our generation, sleep badly, are restless, but talk a great deal, and are always trying to settle whether we are right or not.'[10] Our literature of social satire and psychological finesse both sprang from that restless sleep, that incessant talking; but after all, there is an enormous difference between Tchehov and Henry James, between Tchehov and Bernard

Shaw.[11] Obviously – but where does it arise? Tchehov, too, is aware of the evils and injustices of the social state; the condition of the peasants appals him, but the reformer's zeal is not his – that is not the signal for us to stop. The mind interests him enormously; he is a most subtle and delicate analyst of human relations. But again, no; the end is not there. Is it that he is primarily interested not in the soul's relation with other souls, but with the soul's relation to health – with the soul's relation to goodness? These stories are always showing us some affectation, pose, insincerity. Some woman has got into a false relation; some man has been perverted by the inhumanity of his circumstances. The soul is ill; the soul is cured; the soul is not cured. Those are the emphatic points in his stories.

Once the eye is used to these shades, half the 'conclusions' of fiction fade into thin air; they show like transparences with a light behind them – gaudy, glaring, superficial. The general tidying up of the last chapter, the marriage, the death, the statement of values so sonorously trumpeted forth, so heavily underlined, become of the most rudimentary kind. Nothing is solved, we feel; nothing is rightly held together. On the other hand, the method which at first seemed so casual, inconclusive, and occupied with trifles, now appears the result of an exquisitely original and fastidious taste, choosing boldly, arranging infallibly, and controlled by an honesty for which we can find no match save among the Russians themselves. There may be no answer to these questions, but at the same time let us never manipulate the evidence so as to produce something fitting, decorous, agreeable to our vanity. This may not be the way to catch the ear of the public; after all, they are used to louder music, fiercer measures; but as the tune sounded so he has written it. In consequence, as we read these little stories about nothing at all, the horizon widens; the soul gains an astonishing sense of freedom.

In reading Tchehov we find ourselves repeating the word 'soul' again and again. It sprinkles his pages. Old drunkards use it freely; '... you are high up in the service, beyond all reach, but haven't real soul, my dear boy ... there's no strength in it.'[12] Indeed, it is the soul that is the chief character in Russian fiction. Delicate and subtle in Tchehov, subject to an infinite number of humours and distempers, it is of greater depth and volume in Dostoevsky, liable to violent diseases and raging fevers, but still the prominent concern. Perhaps that is why it needs so great an effort on the part of an

English reader to read *The Brothers Karamazov* or *The Possessed* a second time.[13] The 'soul' is alien to him. It is even antipathetic. It has little sense of humour and no sense of comedy. It is formless. It has slight connection with the intellect. It is confused, diffuse, tumultuous, incapable, it seems, of submitting to the control of logic or the discipline of poetry. The novels of Dostoevsky are seething whirlpools, gyrating sandstorms, waterspouts which hiss and boil and suck us in. They are composed purely and wholly of the stuff of the soul. Against our wills we are drawn in, whirled round, blinded, suffocated, and at the same time filled with a giddy rapture. Out of Shakespeare there is no more exciting reading. We open the door and find ourselves in a room full of Russian generals, the tutors of Russian generals, their step-daughters and cousins, and crowds of miscellaneous people who are all talking at the tops of their voices about their most private affairs. But where are we? Surely it is the part of a novelist to inform us whether we are in an hotel, a flat, or hired lodging. Nobody thinks of explaining. We are souls, tortured, unhappy souls, whose only business it is to talk, to reveal, to confess, to draw up at whatever rending of flesh and nerve those crabbed sins which crawl on the sand at the bottom of us. But, as we listen, our confusion slowly settles. A rope is flung to us; we catch hold of a soliloquy; holding on by the skin of our teeth, we are rushed through the water; feverishly, wildly, we rush on and on, now submerged, now in a moment of vision understanding more than we have ever understood before, and receiving such revelations as we are wont to get only from the press of life at its fullest. As we fly we pick it all up – the names of the people, their relationships, that they are staying in an hotel at Roulettenburg, that Polina is involved in an intrigue with the Marquis de Grieux[14] – but what unimportant matters these are compared with the soul! It is the soul that matters, its passion, its tumult, its astonishing medley of beauty and vileness. And if our voices suddenly rise into shrieks of laughter, or if we are shaken by the most violent sobbing, what more natural? – it hardly calls for remark. The pace at which we are living is so tremendous that sparks must rush off our wheels as we fly. Moreover, when the speed is thus increased and the elements of the soul are seen, not separately in scenes of humour or scenes of passion as our slower English minds conceive them, but streaked, involved, inextricably confused, a new panorama of the human mind is revealed. The old divisions melt into each other. Men are at the same time villains and saints; their acts are at once beautiful and despicable. We love and we hate at the same time. There is none of that precise division between good and bad to which we are used. Often those for whom we feel most affection are the greatest criminals, and the most abject sinners move us to the strongest admiration as well as love.

Dashed to the crest of the waves, bumped and battered on the stones at the bottom, it is difficult for an English reader to feel at ease. The process to which he is accustomed in his own literature is reversed. If we wished to tell the story of a General's love affair (and we should find it very difficult in the first place not to laugh at a General), we should begin with his house; we should solidify his surroundings. Only when all was ready should we attempt to deal with the General himself. Moreover, it is not the samovar but the teapot that rules in England; time is limited; space crowded; the influence of other points of view, of other books, even of other ages, makes itself felt. Society is sorted out into lower, middle, and upper classes, each with its own traditions, its own manners, and, to some extent, its own language. Whether he wishes it or not, there is a constant pressure upon an English novelist to recognise these barriers, and, in consequence, order is imposed on him and some kind of form; he is inclined to satire rather than to compassion, to scrutiny of society rather than understanding of individuals themselves.

No such restraints were laid on Dostoevsky. It is all the same to him whether you are noble or simple, a tramp or a great lady. Whoever you are, you are the vessel of this perplexed liquid, this cloudy, yeasty, precious stuff, the soul. The soul is not restrained by barriers. It overflows, it floods, it mingles with the souls of others. The simple story of a bank clerk who could not pay for a bottle of wine spreads, before we know what is happening, into the lives of his father-in-law and the five mistresses whom his father-in-law treated abominably, and the postman's life, and the charwoman's, and the Princesses' who lodged in the same block of flats; for nothing is outside Dostoevsky's province; and when he is tired, he does not stop, he goes on. He cannot restrain himself. Out it tumbles upon us, hot, scalding, mixed, marvellous, terrible, oppressive – the human soul.

There remains the greatest of all novelists – for what else can we call the author of *War and Peace*?[15] Shall we find Tolstoy, too, alien, difficult, a foreigner? Is there some oddity in his angle of vision which, at any rate until we have become disciples and so lost our bearings, keeps us at arm's length in suspicion and bewilderment? From his first words we can be sure of one thing at any rate – here is a man who sees what we see, who proceeds, too, as we are accustomed to proceed, not from the inside outwards, but from the outside inwards. Here is a world in which the postman's knock is heard at eight o'clock, and people go to bed between ten and eleven. Here is a man, too, who is no savage, no child of nature; he is educated; he has had every sort of experience. He is one of those born aristocrats who have used their privileges to the full. He is metropolitan, not suburban. His senses, his intellect, are acute, powerful, and well nourished. There is something proud and superb in the attack of such a mind and such a body upon life. Nothing seems to escape him. Nothing glances off him unrecorded. Nobody, therefore, can so convey the excitement of sport, the beauty of horses, and all the fierce desirability of the world to the senses of a strong young man. Every twig, every feather sticks to his magnet. He notices the blue or red of a child's frock; the way a horse shifts its tail; the sound of a cough; the action of a man trying to put his hands into pockets that have been sewn up. And what his infallible eye reports of a cough or a trick of the hands his infallible brain refers to something hidden in the character, so that we know his people, not only by the way they love and their views on politics and the immortality of the soul, but also by the way they sneeze and choke. Even in a translation we feel that we have been set on a mountain-top and had a telescope put into our hands. Everything is astonishingly clear and absolutely sharp. Then, suddenly, just as we are exulting, breathing deep, feeling at once braced and purified, some detail – perhaps the head of a man – comes at us out of the picture in an alarming way, as if extruded by the very intensity of its life. 'Suddenly a strange thing happened to me: first I ceased to see what was around me; then his face seemed to vanish till only the eyes were left, shining over against mine; next the eyes seemed to be in my own head, and then all became confused – I could see nothing and was forced to shut my eyes, in order to break loose from the feeling of pleasure and fear which his gaze was producing in me . . .'[16] Again and again we share Masha's feelings in *Family Happiness*. One shuts one's eyes to escape the feeling of pleasure and fear. Often it is pleasure that is uppermost. In this very story there are two descriptions, one of a girl walking in a garden at night with her lover, one of a newly married couple prancing down their drawing-room, which so convey the feeling of intense happiness that we shut the book to feel it better. But always there is an element of fear which makes us, like Masha, wish to escape from the gaze which Tolstoy fixes on us. Is it the sense, which in real life might harass us, that such happiness as he describes is too intense to last, that we are on the edge of disaster? Or is it not that the very intensity of our pleasure is somehow questionable and forces us to ask, with Pozdnyshev in the *Kreutzer Sonata*, 'But why live?'[17] Life dominates Tolstoy as the soul dominates Dostoevsky. There is always at the centre of all the brilliant and flashing petals of the flower this scorpion, 'Why live?' There is always at the centre of the book some Olenin, or Pierre, or Levin[18] who gathers into himself all experience, turns the world round between his fingers, and never ceases to ask, even as he enjoys it, what is the meaning of it, and what should be our aims. It is not the priest who shatters our desires most effectively; it is the man who has known them, and loved them himself. When he derides them, the world indeed turns to dust and ashes beneath our feet. Thus fear mingles with our pleasure, and of the three great Russian writers, it is Tolstoy who most enthralls us and most repels.

But the mind takes its bias from the place of its birth, and no doubt, when it strikes upon a literature so alien as the Russian, flies off at a tangent far from the truth.

1 – Written specifically for *CR1*, this essay draws considerably upon 'The Russian View', and upon 'Tchehov's Questions', *II VW Essays*. Reprinted *CE*.
2 – Henry James (1843–1916) became a naturalised British subject in 1915.
3 – L. N. Tolstoy (1828–1910), for VW on whom see 'Tolstoy's "The Cossacks"', *II VW Essays*. Fyodor Dostoevsky (1821–81), for VW on whom see 'More Dostoevsky', 'A Minor Dostoevsky' *II VW Essays*, and 'Dostoevsky in Cranford', 'Dostoevsky the Father', *III VW Essays*. Anton Chekhov (1860–1904), for VW on whom see 'Tchehov's Questions', *II VW Essays*, and 'The Cherry Orchard', *III VW Essays*.
4 – Elena Militsina and Mikhail Saltikov, *The Village Priest and Other Stories*, trans. Beatrix L. Tollemache, with an intro. by C. Hagberg Wright (T. Fisher Unwin Ltd, 1918), 'The Village Priest' (by Militsina), p. 34.
5 – John Galsworthy (1867–1933), 'The First and Last', in the collection *Five Tales* (Heinemann, 1918), p. 18: 'A surge of feeling came up in Laurence for this creature, more unfortunate than himself . . . "Well, brother," he said, "*you* don't look too prosperous".'
6 – Militsina and Saltikov, 'Introduction', p. xii: 'They [Saltikov's sketches] reveal his love of humanity and his greatness of heart, while giving us a typical picture of the Russian people, their deep sadness, their inherent simplicity and kindliness. They should help us to realise that a change in the government of Russia was inevitable.' Sir Charles Hagberg Wright (1862–1940) was from 1893 until his death secretary and librarian of the London Library.

7–Chekhov, *The Lady with the Dog and Other Stories*, trans. Constance Garnett (Chatto and Windus, 1917), title story, which concludes: '. . . a new splendid life would begin; and it was clear to both of them that they had still a long way to go, and that the most complicated and difficult part of it was only just beginning.'

8–Chekhov, *The Witch and Other Stories*, trans. by Constance Garnett (Chatto and Windus, 1918), 'The Post', p. 57.

9–*Ibid.*, p. 58.

10–The source of this illuminating quotation has tantalisingly resisted repeated efforts at discovery.

11–George Bernard Shaw (1856–1950).

12–Chekhov, *The Wife and Other Stories*, trans. by Constance Garnett (Chatto and Windus, 1918).

13–Dostoevsky, *The Brothers Karamazov* (1880), *The Possessed* (1871).

14–The allusion is to Dostoevsky's 'The Gambler' (1866) which VW writes about in 'A Minor Dostoevsky'.

15–Tolstoy, *War and Peace* (1865–72).

16–Tolstoy, 'Family Happiness' (1859), trans. J. D. Duff in *The Kreutzer Sonata and Other Stories*, ed. Aylmer Maude (OUP, 1924), p. 57.

17–'The Kreutzer Sonata' (1889), trans. Louise and Aylmer Maude, in *ibid.*, XI, p. 254: 'But why live? If life has no aim, if life is given us for life's sake, there is no reason for living . . . But if life has an aim, it is clear that it ought to come to an end when that aim is reached.'

18–Dimitri Olenin, character in Tolstoy's *The Cossacks* (1863); Pierre Bezrakhov and Konstantin Levin in *Anna Karenina* (1873–7).

Outlines

I

Miss Mitford

Speaking truthfully, *Mary Russell Mitford and her Surroundings* is not a good book. It neither enlarges the mind nor purifies the heart. There is nothing in it about Prime Ministers and not very much about Miss Mitford. Yet, as one is setting out to speak the truth, one must own that there are certain books which can be read without the mind and without the heart, but still with considerable enjoyment. To come to the point, the great merit of these scrapbooks, for they can scarcely be called biographies, is that they license mendacity. One cannot believe what Miss Hill says about Miss Mitford, and thus one is free to invent Miss Mitford for oneself. Not for a second do we accuse Miss Hill of telling lies. That infirmity is entirely ours. For example: 'Alresford was the birthplace of one who loved nature as few have loved her, and whose writings "breathe the air of the hayfields and the scent of the hawthorn boughs", and seem to waft to us "the sweet breezes that blow over ripened corn-fields and daisied meadows".'[2] It is perfectly true that Miss Mitford was born at Alresford, and yet, when it is put like that, we doubt whether she was ever born at all. Indeed she was, says Miss Hill; she was born 'on the 16th December, 1787. "A pleasant house in truth it was," Miss Mitford writes. "The breakfast-room . . . was a lofty and spacious apartment."'[3] So Miss Mitford was born in the breakfast-room about eight-thirty on a snowy morning between the Doctor's second and third cups of tea. 'Pardon me,' said Mrs Mitford,[4] turning a little pale, but not omitting to add the right quantity of cream to her husband's tea, 'I feel . . .' That is the way in which Mendacity begins. There is something plausible and even ingenious in her approaches. The touch about the cream, for instance, might be called historical, for it is well known that when Mary won £20,000 in the Irish lottery, the Doctor spent it all upon Wedgwood china, the winning number being stamped upon the soup plates in the middle of an Irish harp, the whole being surmounted by the Mitford arms, and encircled by the motto of Sir John Bertram, one of William the Conqueror's knights, from whom the Mitfords claimed descent. 'Observe,' says Mendacity, 'with what an air the Doctor drinks his tea, and how she, poor lady, contrives to curtsey as she leaves the room.' Tea? I inquire, for the Doctor, though a fine figure of a man, is already purple and profuse, and foams like a crimson cock over the frill of his fine laced shirt. 'Since the ladies have left the room,' Mendacity begins, and goes on to make up a pack of lies with the sole object of proving that Dr Mitford kept a mistress in the purlieus of Reading and paid her money on the pretence that he was investing it in a new method of lighting and heating houses invented by the Marquis de Chavannes.[5] It came to the same thing in the end – to the King's Bench Prison, that is to say; but instead of allowing us to recall the literary and historical associations of the place, Mendacity wanders off to the window and distracts us again by the platitudinous remark that it is still snowing. There is something very charming in an ancient snowstorm. The weather has varied almost as much in the course of generations as mankind.

The snow of those days was more formally shaped and a good deal softer than the snow of ours, just as an eighteenth-century cow was no more like our cows than she was like the florid and fiery cows of Elizabethan pastures. Sufficient attention has scarcely been paid to this aspect of literature, which, it cannot be denied, has its importance.

Our brilliant young men might do worse, when in search of a subject, than devote a year or two to cows in literature, snow in literature, the daisy in Chaucer and in Coventry Patmore.[6] At any rate, the snow falls heavily. The Portsmouth mail-coach has already lost its way; several ships have foundered, and Margate pier has been totally destroyed. At Hatfield Peveral twenty sheep have been buried, and though one supports itself by gnawing wurzels which it has found near it, there is grave reason to fear that the French king's coach has been blocked on the road to Colchester. It is now the 16th of February 1808.

Poor Mrs Mitford! Twenty-one years ago she left the breakfast-room, and no news has yet been received of her child. Even Mendacity is a little ashamed of itself, and, picking up *Mary Russell Mitford and her Surroundings*, assures us that everything will come right if we possess ourselves in patience. The French king's coach was on its way to Bocking; at Bocking lived Lord and Lady Charles Murray-Aynsley; and Lord Charles was shy. Lord Charles had always been shy. Once when Mary Mitford was five years old – sixteen years, that is, before the sheep were lost and the French king went to Bocking – Mary 'threw him into an agony of blushing by running up to his chair in mistake for that of my papa'. He had indeed to leave the room. Miss Hill, who, somewhat strangely, finds the society of Lord and Lady Charles pleasant, does not wish to quit it without 'introducing an incident in connection with them which took place in the month of February 1808'.[7] But is Miss Mitford concerned in it? we ask, for there must be an end of trifling. To some extent, that is to say, Lady Charles was a cousin of the Mitfords, and Lord Charles was shy. Mendacity is quite ready to deal with 'the incident' even on these terms; but, we repeat, we have had enough of trifling. Miss Mitford may not be a great woman; for all we know she was not even a good one; but we have certain responsibilities as a reviewer which we are not going to evade.

There is, to begin with, English literature. A sense of the beauty of Nature has never been altogether absent, however much the cow may change from age to age, from English poetry. Nevertheless, the difference between Pope and Wordsworth in this respect is very considerable. *Lyrical Ballads* was published in 1798; *Our Village* in 1824.[8] One being in verse and the other in prose, it is not necessary to labour a comparison which contains, however, not only the elements of justice, but the seeds of many volumes. Like her great predecessor, Miss Mitford much preferred the country to the town; and thus, perhaps, it may not be inopportune to dwell for a moment upon the King of Saxony, Mary Anning, and the ichthyosaurus. Let alone the fact that Mary Anning and Mary Mitford had a Christian name in common, they are further connected by what can scarcely be called a fact, but may, without hazard, be called a probability. Miss Mitford was looking for fossils at Lyme Regis only fifteen years before Mary Anning found one. The King of Saxony visited Lyme in 1844, and seeing the head of an ichthyosaurus in Mary Anning's window, asked her to drive to Pinny and explore the rocks. While they were looking for fossils, an old woman seated herself in the King's coach – was she Mary Mitford? Truth compels us to say that she was not;[9] but there is no doubt, and we are not trifling when we say it, that Mary Mitford often expressed a wish that she had known Mary Anning, and it is singularly unfortunate to have to state that she never did. For we have reached the year 1844; Mary Mitford is fifty-seven years of age, and so far, thanks to Mendacity and its trifling ways, all we know of her is that she did not know Mary Anning, had not found an ichthyosaurus, had not been out in a snowstorm, and had not seen the King of France.

It is time to wring the creature's neck, and begin again at the very beginning.

What considerations, then, had weight with Miss Hill when she decided to write *Mary Russell Mitford and her Surroundings?* Three emerge from the rest, and may be held of paramount importance. In the first place, Miss Mitford was a lady; in the second, she was born in the year 1787; and in the third, the stock of female characters who lend themselves to biographic treatment by their own sex is, for one reason or another, running short. For instance, little is known of Sappho, and that little is not wholly to her credit. Lady Jane Grey has merit, but is undeniably obscure. Of George Sand, the more we know the less we approve. George Eliot was led into evil ways which not all her philosophy can excuse. The Brontës, however highly we rate their genius, lacked that indefinable something which marks the lady; Harriet Martineau was an atheist; Mrs

Browning was a married woman; Jane Austen, Fanny Burney, and
Maria Edgeworth have been done already;[10] so that, what with one
thing and another, Mary Russell Mitford is the only woman left.

There is no need to labour the extreme importance of the date
when we see the word 'surroundings' on the back of a book. Surroundings, as they are called, are invariably eighteenth-century surroundings. When we come, as of course we do, to that phrase which
relates how 'as we looked upon the steps leading down from the
upper room, we fancied we saw the tiny figure jumping from step to
step',[11] it would be the grossest outrage upon our sensibilities to be
told that those steps were Athenian, Elizabethan, or Parisian. They
were, of course, eighteenth-century steps, leading down from the
old panelled room into the shady garden, where, tradition has it,
William Pitt played marbles,[12] or, if we like to be bold, where on
still summer days we can almost fancy that we hear the drums of
Bonaparte on the coast of France. Bonaparte is the limit of the imagination on one side, as Monmouth[13] is on the other; it would be
fatal if the imagination took to toying with Prince Albert or sport-
ing with King John. But fancy knows her place, and there is no need
to labour the point that her place is the eighteenth century. The
other point is more obscure. One must be a lady. Yet what that
means, and whether we like what it means, may both be doubtful. If
we say that Jane Austen was a lady and that Charlotte Brontë was
not one, we do as much as need be done in the way of definition,
and commit ourselves to neither side.

It is undoubtedly because of their reticence that Miss Hill is on
the side of the ladies. They sigh things off and they smile things off,
but they never seize the silver table by the legs or dash the teacups
on the floor. It is in many ways a great convenience to have a subject
who can be trusted to live a long life without once raising her voice.
Sixteen years is a considerable stretch of time, but of a lady it is
enough to say, 'Here Mary Mitford passed sixteen years of her life
and here she got to know and love not only their own beautiful
grounds but also every turn of the surrounding shady lanes.'[14] Her
loves were vegetable, and her lanes were shady. Then, of course, she
was educated at the school where Jane Austen and Mrs Sherwood[15]
had been educated. She visited Lyme Regis, and there is mention of
the Cobb. She saw London from the top of St Paul's, and London
was much smaller then than it is now. She changed from one charming house to another, and several distinguished literary gentlemen

paid her compliments and came to tea. When the dining-room ceiling fell down it did not fall on her head, and when she took a ticket in a lottery she did win the prize. If in the foregoing sentences there are any words of more than two syllables, it is our fault and not Miss Hill's; and to do that writer justice, there are not many whole sentences in the book which are neither quoted from Miss Mitford nor supported by the authority of Mr Crissy.[16]

But how dangerous a thing is life! Can one be sure that anything not wholly made of mahogany will to the very end stand empty in the sun? Even cupboards have their secret springs, and when, inadvertently we are sure, Miss Hill touches this one, out, terrible to relate, topples a stout old gentleman. In plain English, Miss Mitford had a father. There is nothing actually improper in that. Many women have had fathers. But Miss Mitford's father was kept in a cupboard; that is to say, he was not a nice father. Miss Hill even goes so far as to conjecture that when 'an imposing procession of neighbours and friends' followed him to the grave, 'we cannot help thinking that this was more to show sympathy and respect for Miss Mitford than from special respect for him'.[17] Severe as the judgement is, the gluttonous, bibulous, amorous old man did something to deserve it. The less said about him the better. Only, if from your earliest childhood your father has gambled and speculated, first with your mother's fortune, then with your own, spent your earnings, driven you to earn more, and spent that too; if in old age he has lain upon a sofa and insisted that fresh air is bad for daughters; if, dying at length, he has left debts that can only be paid by selling everything you have or sponging upon the charity of friends – then even a lady sometimes raises her voice. Miss Mitford herself spoke out once. 'It was grief to go; there I had toiled and striven and tasted as deeply of bitter anxiety, of fear, and of hope as often falls to the lot of woman.'[18] What language for a lady to use! for a lady, too, who owns a teapot. There is a drawing of the teapot at the bottom of the page. But it is now of no avail; Miss Mitford has smashed it to smithereens. That is the worst of writing about ladies; they have fathers as well as teapots. On the other hand, some pieces of Dr Mitford's Wedgwood dinner service are still in existence, and a copy of Adam's Geography, which Mary won as a prize at school, is 'in our temporary possession'.[19] If there is nothing improper in the suggestion, might not the next book be devoted entirely to them?

II

Dr Bentley

As we saunter through those famous courts where Dr Bentley once reigned supreme we sometimes catch sight of a figure hurrying on its way to Chapel or Hall which, as it disappears, draws our thoughts enthusiastically after it. For that man, we are told, has the whole of Sophocles at his finger-ends; knows Homer by heart; reads Pindar as we read *The Times*; and spends his life, save for these short excursions to eat and pray, wholly in the company of the Greeks. It is true that the infirmities of our education prevent us from appreciating his emendations as they deserve; his life's work is a sealed book to us; none the less, we treasure up the last flicker of his black gown, and feel as if a bird of Paradise had flashed by us, so bright is his spirit's raiment, and in the murk of a November evening we had been privileged to see it winging its way to roost in fields of amaranth and beds of moly. Of all men, great scholars are the most mysterious, the most august. Since it is unlikely that we shall ever be admitted to their intimacy, or see much more of them than a black gown crossing a court at dusk, the best we can do is to read their lives – for example, the *Life of Dr Bentley* by Bishop Monk.

There we shall find much that is odd and little that is reassuring. The greatest of our scholars, the man who read Greek as the most expert of us read English not merely with an accurate sense of meaning and grammar but with a sensibility so subtle and widespread that he perceived relations and suggestions of language which enabled him to fetch up from oblivion lost lines and inspire new life into the little fragments that remained, the man who should have been steeped in beauty (if what they say of the Classics is true) as a honey-pot is ingrained with sweetness was, on the contrary, the most quarrelsome of mankind.

'I presume that there are not many examples of an individual who has been a party in six distinct suits before the Court of King's Bench within the space of three years',[2] his biographer remarks; and adds that Bentley won them all. It is difficult to deny his conclusion that though Dr Bentley might have been a first-rate lawyer or a great soldier 'such a display suited any character rather than that of a learned and dignified clergyman'.[3] Not all these disputes, however, sprung from his love of literature. The charges against which he had to defend himself were directed against him as Master of

Trinity College, Cambridge. He was habitually absent from chapel; his expenditure upon building and upon his household was excessive; he used the college seal at meetings which did not consist of the statutable number of sixteen, and so on. In short, the career of the Master of Trinity was one continuous series of acts of aggression and defiance, in which Dr Bentley treated the Society of Trinity College as a grown man might treat an importunate rabble of street boys. Did they dare to hint that the staircase at the Lodge which admitted four persons abreast was quite wide enough? – did they refuse to sanction his expenditure upon a new one? Meeting them in the Great Court one evening after chapel he proceeded urbanely to question them. They refused to budge. Whereupon, with a sudden alteration of colour and voice, Bentley demanded whether 'they had forgotten his rusty sword?' Mr Michael Hutchinson[4] and some others, upon whose backs the weight of that weapon would have first descended, brought pressure upon their seniors. The bill for £350 was paid and their preferment secured. But Bentley did not wait for this act of submission to finish his staircase.

So it went on, year after year. Nor was the arrogance of his behaviour always justified by the splendour or utility of the objects he had in view – the creation of the Backs, the erection of an observatory, the foundation of a laboratory. More trivial desires were gratified with the same tyranny. Sometimes he wanted coal; sometimes bread and ale; and then Madame Bentley, sending her servant with a snuff-box in token of authority, got from the butteries at the expense of the college a great deal more of these commodities than the college thought that Dr Bentley ought to require. Again, when he had four pupils to lodge with him who paid him handsomely for their board, it was drawn from the College, at the command of the snuff-box, for nothing. The principles of 'delicacy and good feeling'[5] which the Master might have been expected to observe (great scholar as he was, steeped in the wine of the Classics) went for nothing. His argument that the 'few College loaves'[6] upon which the four young patricians were nourished were amply repaid by the three sash windows which he had put into their rooms at his own expense failed to convince the Fellows. And when, on Trinity Sunday 1719, the Fellows found the famous College ale not to their liking, they were scarcely satisfied when the butler told them that it had been brewed by the Master's orders, from the Master's malt, which was stored in the Master's granary, and though damaged by 'an insect called the weevil'[7] had been paid for at the very high rates which the Master demanded.

Still these battles over bread and beer are trifles and domestic trifles at that. His conduct in his profession will throw more light upon our inquiry. For, released from brick and building, bread and beer, patricians and their windows, it may be found that he expanded in the atmosphere of Homer, Horace, and Manilius, and proved in his study the benign nature of those influences which have been wafted down to us through the ages. But there the evidence is even less to the credit of the dead languages. He acquitted himself magnificently, all agree, in the great controversy about the letters of Phalaris.[8] His temper was excellent and his learning prodigious. But that triumph was succeeded by a series of disputes which force upon us the extraordinary spectacle of men of learning and genius, of authority and divinity, brawling about Greek and Latin texts, and calling each other names for all the world like bookies on a racecourse or washerwomen in a back street. For this vehemence of temper and virulence of language were not confined to Bentley alone; they appear unhappily characteristic of the profession as a whole. Early in life, in the year 1691, a quarrel was fastened upon him by his brother chaplain Hody for writing Malelas, not as Hody preferred, Malela. A controversy in which Bentley displayed learning and wit, and Hody accumulated endless pages of bitter argument against the letter s ensued. Hody was worsted, and 'there is too much reason to believe, that the offence given by this trivial cause was never afterwards healed'.[9] Indeed, to mend a line was to break a friendship. James Gronovius of Leyden – 'homunculus eruditione mediocri, ingenio nullo',[10] as Bentley called him – attacked Bentley for ten years because Bentley had succeeded in correcting a fragment of Callimachus where he had failed.

But Gronovius was by no means the only scholar who resented the success of a rival with a rancour that grey hairs and forty years spent in editing the Classics failed to subdue. In all the chief towns of Europe lived men like the notorious de Pauw of Utrecht, 'a person who has justly been considered the pest and disgrace of letters', who, when a new theory or new edition appeared, banded themselves together to deride and humiliate the scholar. '. . . all his writings,' Bishop Monk remarks of de Pauw, 'prove him to be devoid of candour, good faith, good manners, and every gentlemanly feeling: and while he unites all the defects and bad qualities that were ever found in a critic or commentator, he adds one peculiar to himself, an incessant propensity to indecent allusions.[11] With such tempers and such habits it is not strange that the scholars of those days sometimes ended lives made intolerable by bitterness, poverty, and neglect by their own hands, like Johnson, who after a lifetime spent in the detection of minute errors of construction, went mad and drowned himself in the meadows near Nottingham.[12] On May 20, 1712, Trinity College was shocked to find that the professor of Hebrew, Dr Sike, had hanged himself 'some time this evening, before candlelight, in his sash'.[13] When Kuster died, it was reported that he, too, had killed himself. And so, in a sense, he had. For when his body was opened 'there was found a cake of sand along the lower region of his belly. This, I take it, was occasioned by his sitting nearly double, and writing on a very low table, surrounded with three or four circles of books placed on the ground, which was the situation we usually found him in.'[14] The minds of poor schoolmasters like John Ker of the dissenting Academy,[15] who had had the high gratification of dining with Dr Bentley at the Lodge, when the talk fell upon the use of the word *equidem*, were so distorted by a lifetime of neglect and study that they went home, collected all uses of the word *equidem* which contradicted the Doctor's opinion, returned to the Lodge, anticipating in their simplicity a warm welcome, met the Doctor issuing to dine with the Archbishop of Canterbury, followed him down the street in spite of his indifference and annoyance and, being refused even a word of farewell, went home to brood over their injuries and wait the day of revenge.

But the bickerings and animosities of the smaller fry were magnified, not obliterated, by the Doctor himself in the conduct of his own affairs. The courtesy and good temper which he had shown in his early controversies had worn away. '. . . a course of violent animosities and the indulgence of unrestrained indignation for many years had impaired both his taste and judgement in controversy', and he condescended, though the subject in dispute was the Greek Testament, to call his antagonist 'maggot', 'vermin', 'gnawing rat', and 'cabbage head',[16] to refer to the darkness of his complexion, and to insinuate that his wits were crazed, which charge he supported by dwelling on the fact that his brother, a clergyman, wore a beard to his girdle.

Violent, pugnacious, and unscrupulous, Dr Bentley survived these storms and agitations, and remained, though suspended from his degrees and deprived of his mastership, seated at the Lodge imperturbably. Wearing a broad-brimmed hat indoors to protect his eyes, smoking his pipe, enjoying his port, and expounding to his friends his doctrine of the digamma, Bentley lived those eighty years which, he said, were long enough 'to read everything which was worth reading', 'Et tunc', he added, in his peculiar manner,

Et tunc magna mei sub terris ibit imago.[17]

A small square stone marked his grave in Trinity College, but the Fellows refused to record upon it the fact that he had been their Master.

But the strangest sentence in this strange story has yet to be written, and Bishop Monk writes it as if it were a commonplace requiring no comment. 'For a person who was neither a poet, nor possessed of poetical taste to venture upon such a task was no common presumption.' The task was to detect every slip of language in *Paradise Lost*,[18] and all instances of bad taste and incorrect imagery. The result was notoriously lamentable. Yet in what, we may ask, did it differ from those in which Bentley was held to have acquitted himself magnificently? And if Bentley was incapable of appreciating the poetry of Milton, how can we accept his verdict upon Horace and Homer? And if we cannot trust implicitly to scholars, and if the study of Greek is supposed to refine the manners and purify the soul – but enough. Our scholar has returned from Hall; his lamp is lit; his studies are resumed; and it is time that our profane speculations should have an end. Besides, all this happened many, many years ago.

III

Lady Dorothy Nevill

She had stayed, in a humble capacity, for a week in the ducal household. She had seen the troops of highly decorated human beings descending in couples to eat, and ascending in couples to bed. She had, surreptitiously, from a gallery, observed the Duke himself dusting the miniatures in the glass cases, while the Duchess let her crochet fall from her hands as if in utter disbelief that the world had need of crochet. From an upper window she had seen, as far as eye could reach, gravel paths swerving round isles of greenery and losing themselves in little woods designed to shed the shade without the severity of forests; she had watched the ducal carriage bowling in and out of the prospect, and returning a different way from the way it went. And what was her verdict? 'A lunatic asylum.'[2]

It is true that she was a lady's-maid, and that Lady Dorothy Nevill, had she encountered her on the stairs, would have made an opportunity to point out that that is a very different thing from being a lady.

My mother never failed to point out the folly of work-women, shop-girls, and the like calling each other 'Ladies'. All this sort of thing seemed to her to be mere vulgar humbug, and she did not fail to say so.[3]

What can we point out to Lady Dorothy Nevill? that with all her advantages she had never learned to spell? that she could not write a grammatical sentence? that she lived for eighty-seven years and did nothing but put food into her mouth and slip gold through her fingers? But delightful though it is to indulge in righteous indignation, it is misplaced if we agree with the lady's-maid that high birth is a form of congenital insanity, that the sufferer merely inherits the diseases of his ancestors, and endures them, for the most part very stoically, in one of those comfortably padded lunatic asylums which are known, euphemistically, as the stately homes of England.

Moreover, the Walpoles are not ducal. Horace Walpole's mother was a Miss Shorter; there is no mention of Lady Dorothy's mother in the present volume, but her great-grandmother was Mrs Oldfield the actress, and, to her credit, Lady Dorothy was 'exceedingly proud' of the fact.[4] Thus she was not an extreme case of aristocracy; she was confined rather to a bird-cage than to an asylum; through the bars she saw people walking at large, and once or twice she made a surprising little flight into the open air. A gayer, brighter, more vivacious specimen of the caged tribe can seldom have existed; so that one is forced at times to ask whether what we call living in a cage is not the fate that wise people, condemned to a single sojourn upon earth, would choose. To be at large is, after all, to be shut out; to waste most of life in accumulating the money to buy and the time to enjoy what the Lady Dorothys find clustering and glowing about their cradles when their eyes first open – as hers opened in the year 1826 at number eleven Berkeley Square. Horace Walpole had lived there. Her father, Lord Orford, gambled it away in one night's play the year after she was born. But Wolterton Hall, in Norfolk, was full of carving and mantelpieces, and there were rare trees in the garden, and a large and famous lawn. No novelist could wish a more charming and even romantic environment in which to set the story of two little girls, growing up, wild yet secluded, reading Bossuet[5] with their governess, and riding out on their ponies at the head of the tenantry on polling day. Nor can one deny that to have had the author of the following letter among one's ancestors would have been a source of inordinate pride. It is addressed to the Norwich Bible Society, which had invited Lord Orford to become its president:

I have long been addicted to the Gaming Table. I have lately taken to the Turf. I fear I frequently blaspheme. But I have never distributed religious tracts. All this was known to you and your Society. Notwithstanding which you think me a fit person to be your president. God forgive your hypocrisy.[6]

It was not Lord Orford who was in the cage on that occasion. But, alas! Lord Orford owned another country house, Ilsington Hall, in Dorsetshire, and there Lady Dorothy came in contact first with the mulberry tree, and later with Mr Thomas Hardy;[7] and we get our first glimpse of the bars. We do not pretend to the ghost of an enthusiasm for Sailors' Homes in general; no doubt mulberry trees are much nicer to look at; but when it comes to calling people 'vandals' who cut them down to build houses, and to having footstools made from the wood, and to carving upon those footstools inscriptions which testify that 'often and often has King George III taken his tea' under this very footstool, then we want to protest – 'Surely you must mean Shakespeare?' But as her subsequent remarks upon Mr Hardy tend to prove, Lady Dorothy does not mean Shakespeare. She 'warmly appreciated' the works of Mr Hardy, and used to complain 'that the county families were too stupid to appreciate his genius at its proper worth'.[8] George the Third drinking his tea; the county families failing to appreciate Mr Hardy: Lady Dorothy is undoubtedly behind the bars.

Yet no story more aptly illustrates the barrier which we perceive hereafter between Lady Dorothy and the outer world* than the story of Charles Darwin and the blankets. Among her recreations Lady Dorothy made a hobby of growing orchids, and thus got into touch with 'the great naturalist'.[9] Mrs Darwin, inviting her to stay with them, remarked with apparent simplicity that she had heard that people who moved much in London society were fond of being tossed in blankets. 'I am afraid,' her letter ended, 'we should hardly be able to offer you anything of that sort.'[10] Whether in fact the necessity of tossing Lady Dorothy in a blanket had been seriously debated at Down, or whether Mrs Darwin obscurely hinted her sense of some incongruity between her husband and the lady of the orchids, we do not know. But we have a sense of two worlds in collision; and it is not the Darwin world that emerges in fragments. More and more do we see Lady Dorothy hopping from perch to perch, picking at groundsel here, and at hempseed there, indulging in exquisite trills and roulades, and sharpening her beak against a lump of sugar in a large, airy, magnificently equipped bird-cage. The cage was full of charming diversions. Now she illuminated leaves which had been macerated to skeletons; now she interested herself in improving the breed of donkeys; next she took up the cause of silkworms, almost threatened Australia with a plague of them, and 'actually succeeded in obtaining enough silk to make a dress';[11] again she was the first to discover that wood, gone green with decay, can be made, at some expense, into little boxes; she went into the question of funguses and established the virtues of the neglected English truffle; she imported rare fish; spent a great deal of energy in vainly trying to induce storks and Cornish choughs to breed in Sussex; painted on china; emblazoned heraldic arms, and, attaching whistles to the tails of pigeons, produced wonderful effects 'as of an aerial orchestra'[12] when they flew through the air. To the Duchess of Somerset belongs the credit of investigating the proper way of cooking guinea-pigs; but Lady Dorothy was one of the first to serve up a dish of these little creatures at luncheon in Charles Street.

But all the time the door of the cage was ajar. Raids were made into what Mr Nevill calls 'Upper Bohemia'; from which Lady Dorothy returned with 'authors, journalists, actors, actresses, or other agreeable and amusing people'.[13] Lady Dorothy's judgement is proved by the fact that they seldom misbehaved, and some indeed became quite domesticated, and wrote her 'very gracefully turned letters'.[14] But once or twice, she made a flight beyond the cage herself. 'These horrors,' she said, alluding to the middle class, 'are so clever and we are so stupid; but then look how well they are educated, while our children learn nothing but how to spend their parents' money!'[15] She brooded over the fact. Something was going wrong. She was too shrewd and too honest not to lay the blame partly at least upon her own class. 'I suppose she can just about read?' she said of one lady calling herself cultured; and of another, 'She is indeed curious and well adapted to open bazaars.'[16] But to our thinking her most remarkable flight took place a year or two before her death, in the Victoria and Albert Museum:

I do so agree with you, [she wrote] – though I ought not to say so – that the upper class are very – I don't know what to say – but they seem to take no interest in any-thing – but golfing, etc. One day I was at the Victoria and Albert Museum, just a few sprinkles of legs, for I am sure they looked too frivolous to have bodies and souls attached to them – but what softened the sight to my eyes were 2 little Japs poring over each article with a handbook . . . our bodies, of course, giggling and looking at nothing. Still worse, not one soul of the higher class visible: in fact I never heard of any one of them knowing of the place, and for this we are spending millions – it is all too painful.[17]

It was all too painful, and the guillotine, she felt, loomed ahead. That catastrophe she was spared, for who could wish to cut off the head of a pigeon with a whistle attached to its tail? But if the whole bird-cage had been overturned and the aerial orchestra sent scream-ing and fluttering through the air, we can be sure, as Mr Joseph Chamberlain told her, that her conduct would have been 'a credit to the British aristocracy'.[18]

IV

Archbishop Thomson

The origin of Archbishop Thomson was obscure. His great-uncle 'may reasonably be supposed' to have been 'an ornament to the middle classes'.[2] His aunt married a gentleman who was present at the murder of Gustavus III of Sweden;[3] and his father met his death at the age of eighty-seven by treading on a cat in the early hours of the morning. The physical vigour which this anecdote implies was combined in the Archbishop with powers of intellect which promised success in whatever profession he adopted. At Oxford it seemed likely that he would devote himself to philosophy or science. While reading for his degree he found time to write the *Outlines of the Laws of Thought*, which 'immediately became a recognised text-book for Oxford classes'.[4] But though poetry, philosophy, medicine, and the law held out their temptations he put such thoughts aside, or never entertained them, having made up his mind from the first to dedicate himself to Divine service. The measure of his success in the more exalted sphere is attested by the following facts: ordained deacon in 1842 at the age of twenty-three, he became Dean and Bursar of Queen's College, Oxford, in 1845; Provost in 1855, Bishop of Gloucester and Bristol in 1861, and Archbishop of York in 1862. Thus at the early age of forty-three he stood next in rank to the Archbishop of Canterbury himself; and it was commonly though erroneously expected that he would in the end attain to that dignity also.

It is a matter of temperament and belief whether you read this list with respect or with boredom; whether you look upon an archbishop's hat as a crown or as an extinguisher. If, like the present reviewer, you are ready to hold the simple faith that the outer order corresponds to the inner – that a vicar is a good man, a canon a better man, and an archbishop the best man of all – you will find the study of the Archbishop's life one of extreme fascination. He has turned aside from poetry and philosophy and law, and specialised in virtue. He has dedicated himself to the service of the Divine. His spiritual proficiency has been such that he has developed from deacon to dean, from dean to bishop, and from bishop to archbishop in the short space of twenty years. As there are only two archbishops in the whole of England the inference seems to be that he is the second best man in England; his hat is the proof of it. Even in a material sense his hat was one of the largest; it was larger than Mr Gladstone's; larger than Thackeray's; larger than Dickens's; it was in fact, so his hatter told him and we are inclined to agree, an 'eight full'.[5] Yet he began much as other men begin. He struck an undergraduate in a fit of temper and was rusticated; he wrote a textbook of logic and rowed a very good oar. But after he was ordained his diary shows that the specialising process had begun. He thought a great deal about the state of his soul; about 'the monstrous tumour of Simony';[6] about Church reform; and about the meaning of Christianity. 'Self-renunciation,' he came to the conclusion, 'is the foundation of Christian Religion and Christian Morals ... The highest wisdom is that which can enforce and cultivate this self-renunciation. Hence (against Cousin) I hold that religion is higher far than philosophy.[7] There is one mention of chemists and capillarity, but science and philosophy were, even at this early stage, in danger of being crowded out. Soon the diary takes a different tone. 'He seems,' says his biographer, 'to have had no time for committing his thoughts to paper';[8] he records his engagements only, and he dines out almost every night. Sir Henry Taylor, whom he met at one of these parties, described him as 'simple, solid, good, capable, and pleasing'.[9] Perhaps it was his solidity combined with his 'eminently scientific'[10] turn of mind, his blandness as well as his bulk, that impressed some of these great people with the confidence that in him the Church had found a very necessary champion. His 'brawny logic'[11] and massive frame seemed to fit him to grapple with a task that taxed the strongest – how, that is, to reconcile the scientific discoveries of the age with religion, and even prove them 'some of the strongest witnesses for the truth'.[12] If any one could do this Thomson could; his practical ability, unhampered by any mystical or dreaming tendency, had already proved itself in the conduct of the business affairs of his College. From Bishop he became almost instantly Archbishop; and in becoming Archbishop he became Primate of England, Governor of the Charterhouse and King's College, London, patron of one hundred and twenty livings, with the Archdeaconries of York, Cleveland, and the East Riding in his gift, and the Canonries and Prebends in York Minster. Bishopthorpe itself was an enormous palace; he was immediately faced by the 'knotty question' of whether to buy all the furniture – 'much of it only poor stuff' –[13] or to furnish the house anew, which would cost a fortune. Moreover there were seven cows in the park; but these, perhaps, were counterbalanced by nine children in the nursery. Then the Prince and Princess of Wales came to stay, and the Archbishop took upon himself the task of furnishing the Princess's apartments. He went up to London and bought eight Moderator lamps, two Spanish figures holding candles, and reminded himself of the necessity of buying 'soap for Princess'.[14] But meanwhile far more serious matters claimed every ounce of his strength. Already he had been exhorted to 'wield the sure lance of your brawny logic against the sophistries'[15] of the authors of *Essays and Reviews*, and had responded in a work called *Aids to Faith*.[16] Near at hand the town of Sheffield, with its large population of imperfectly educated working men, was a breeding ground of scepticism and discontent. The Archbishop made it his special charge. He was fond of watching the rolling of armour plate, and constantly addressed meetings of working men. 'Now what are these Nihilisms, and Socialisms, and Communisms, and Fenianisms, and Secret Societies – what do they all mean?' he asked. 'Selfishness,' he replied, and 'assertion of one class against the rest is at the bottom of them all'.[17] There was a law of nature, he said, by which wages went up and wages went down. 'You must accept the declivity as well as the ascent . . . If we could only get people to learn that, then things would go on a great deal better and smoother.'[18] And the working men of Sheffield responded by giving him five hundred pieces of cutlery mounted in sterling silver. But presumably there were a certain number of knives among the spoons and the forks.

Bishop Colenso,[19] however, was far more troublesome than the working men of Sheffield; and the Ritualists vexed him so persistently that even his vast strength felt the strain. The questions which were referred to him for decision were peculiarly fitted to tease and annoy even a man of his bulk and his blandness. Shall a drunkard found dead in a ditch, or a burglar who has fallen through a skylight, be given the benefit of the Burial Service? he was asked. The question of lighted candles was 'most difficult';[20] the wearing of coloured stoles and the administration of the mixed chalice taxed him considerably; and finally there was the Rev. John Purchas, who, dressed in cope, alb, biretta and stole 'cross-wise', lit candles and extinguished them 'for no special reason'; filled a vessel with black powder and rubbed it into the foreheads of his congregation; and hung over the Holy Table 'a figure, image, or stuffed skin of a dove, in a flying attitude'.[21] The Archbishop's temper, usually so positive and imperturbable, was gravely ruffled, 'Will there ever come a time when it will be thought a crime to have striven to keep the Church of England as representing the common sense of the Nation? he asked. 'I suppose it may, but I shall not see it. I have gone through a good deal, but I do not repent of having done my best.'[22] If, for a moment, the Archbishop himself could ask such a question, we must confess to a state of complete bewilderment. What has become of our superlatively good man? He is harassed and cumbered; spends his time settling questions about stuffed pigeons and coloured petticoats; writes over eighty letters before breakfast sometimes; scarcely has time to run over to Paris and buy his daughter a bonnet; and in the end has to ask himself whether one of these days his conduct will not be considered a crime.

Was it a crime? And if so, was it his fault? Did he not start out in the belief that Christianity had something to do with renunciation and was not entirely a matter of common sense? If honours and obligations, pomps and possessions, accumulated and encrusted him, how, being an Archbishop, could he refuse to accept them? Princesses[†] must have their soap; palaces must have their furniture;

children must have their cows. And, pathetic though it seems, he never completely lost his interest in science. He wore a pedometer; he was one of the first to use a camera; he believed in the future of the typewriter;[‡] and in his last years he tried to mend a broken clock. He was a delightful father too; he wrote witty, terse, sensible letters; his good stories were much to the point; and he died in harness. Certainly he was a very able man, but if we insist upon goodness – is it easy, is it possible, for a good man to be an Archbishop?

III Lady Dorothy Nevill

[*] – *Athenaeum*: 'Lady Dorothy and ourselves than the story'.

IV Archbishop Thomson

[*] – *Athenaeum*: 'Moderator lamps, and the Spanish figures holding candles, among other things,'.
[†] – *Athenaeum:* 'Princesses, after all, must'.
[‡] – *Athenaeum:* 'use a camera and to believe in a typewriter;'.

I 'Miss Mitford'

1 – This essay is based on 'The Wrong Way of Reading' (*Athenaeum*, 28 May 1920; see *III VW Essays*) and on 'An Imperfect Lady' (*TLS*, 6 May 1920; see *ibid.*), two of three reviews by VW of *Mary Russell Mitford* [1787–1855] *and Her Surroundings. With illustrations by Ellen G. Hill and reproductions of portraits* (John Lane, 1920) by Constance Hill. See also *'The Letters of Mary Russell Mitford'* above and 'A Good Daughter', *III VW Essays*.
2 – Hill, ch. i, pp. 1–2; the source of the matter quoted by Hill has not been traced.
3 – For the first quotation, *ibid.*, p. 2; and for the remainder, *ibid.*, p. 3.
4 – Dr George Mitford (d. 1842) and his wife Mary, *née* Russell (d. 1830).
5 – For Dr Mitford and the Marquis, a French refugee, in whose scheme the doctor invested and lost £5,000, plus the cost of a subsequent, protracted lawsuit, Hill, ch. xvii, pp. 140–1.
6 – Coventry Patmore (1823–96).
7 – Louis XVIII (1755–1824), reigned from 1814–15. Lord Charles Murray Aynsley, Dean of Bocking, was a son of John Murray, 3rd Duke of Athol (1729–74) and Lady Charlotte; his wife was a first cousin of Dr Mitford. For the first quotation, *ibid.*, ch. iv, p. 28, and for the second, *ibid.*, ch. xix, p. 110, which has: 'We should like to introduce'.
8 – Alexander Pope (1688–1744); William Wordsworth (1770–1850). Mitford's *Our Village* (1824–32) was originally serialised in the *Lady's Magazine* from 1819.
9 – Cf. Hill, ch. iv, pp. 44–6.
10 – Sappho (born c. 612 BC); Lady Jane Grey (1637–54), daughter of the Earl of Dorset and Frances Brandon, a niece of Henry VIII, was nominally and reluctantly

for nine days queen of England. George Sand (1804–76), George Eliot (1819–80); Charlotte (1816–55), Emily (1818–48) and Anne Brontë (1820–49); Harriet Martineau (1802–76), Elizabeth Barrett Browning (1806–61), Jane Austen (1775–1817), Fanny Burney (1752–1840), Maria Edgeworth (1767–1849).

11–Hill, ch. v, p. 37.

12–*Ibid.*, p. 30: 'This old porch has its special historical association, for here William Pitt [1759–1806] as a child used to play marbles when his father the great Lord Chatham [1708–78] rented the Great House [at Lyme Regis].'

13–*Ibid.*, p. 33: 'The Great House is full of traditions of past history, and its gloomy vaults and passages below ground must have witnessed many a tragic scene at the time of the Monmouth Rebellion [1685]' etc. etc.

14–*Ibid.*, ch. xii, pp. 99–100, which continues: 'where the first violets and primroses were to be found, and delighted in the wide expanse of it neighbouring common gay with gorse and broom.'

15–*Ibid.*, ch. viii, p. 64, concerning the Abbey School 'for young ladies' at Reading, which in 1798 removed to London where it was attended by Miss Mitford. Mrs Mary Martha Sherwood, *née* Butt (1775–1851), author of popular books for the young.

16–J. Crissy published *The Works of M. R. Mitford, Prose and Verse* (1840).

17–Hill, ch. xxxvi, pp. 341–2, which has 'We cannot'. Dr George Mitford (d. 1842) – 'clever, selfish, unprincipled, and extravagant, with an unhappy love of speculation and whist' (*DNB*) – who married an heiress, is estimated to have frittered away some £70,000 before finally becoming totally dependent upon his literary daughter.

18–*Ibid.*, ch. xxxvii, p. 358, slightly adapted.

19–*Ibid.*, ch. ix, p. 72. Alexander Adam, *A Summary of Geography and History Both Ancient and Modern* (1794).

II Dr Bentley

1–An essay based on *The Life of Richard Bentley* [1662–1742] *DD Master of Trinity College* (1830; 2nd ed., revised and corrected, 2 vols, London, 1833) by James Henry Monk (1784–1856) D. D., Lord Bishop of Gloucester, first published in *CR1*. VW included Monk's account of Bentley in her reading list for 'On Not Knowing Greek', above; see *II VW Diary*, 28 August 1922, and see the entry for 14 October 1922: '. . . making rather a hasty end of Bentley, who is not really much to my purpose'. See also 'The Perfect Language', *II VW Essays*. Reading Notes (Berg, xxv; MHP, B 2q).

2–Monk, vol. ii, ch. xvii, p. 209, from a more extensive sentence, which has 'Bench, within'.

3–*Ibid.*, vol. i, ch. xx, p. 386.

4–For the quotation, *ibid.*, vol. ii, ch. vii, p. 177. Michael Hutchinson, Fellow of Trinity College, otherwise unidentified, had been offered a Stall in Lichfield Cathedral, eligibility for which was dependent upon his being appointed college preacher at Trinity.

5–*Ibid.*, vol. i, ch. viii, p. 201.

6–*Ibid.*

7–*Ibid.*, vol. ii, ch. xiii, p. 24.

8 – For Bentley's decisive role in the *Epistles of Phalaris* controversy, see Monk, vol. i, ch. vii, pp. 178–9.

9 – *Ibid.*, ch. ii, p. 30. Humphrey Hody (1659–1707), author of the 'Prolegomena' to the Greek Chronicle of John Malela (Iohannes Malalas (c. 491–578), rhetorician and historian).

10 – *Ibid.*, ch. viii, p. 226. Jakob Gronovius (1645–1716), professor of Greek at Leyden. Callimachus (c. 305–240), Alexandrian poet.

11 – For the first quotation, *ibid.*, ch. ix, p. 277, and for the second, p. 278. John Cornelius de Pauw, otherwise unidentified.

12 – Richard Johnson (d. 1721), grammarian, fellow student of Bentley at St John's College, Cambridge, attacked Bentley in *Aristarchus Anti-Bentleianus ...* (1717).

13 – Monk, vol. i, ch. xi, p. 329, n. 3. Henry Sike of Bremen, eminent orientalist, brought to Trinity by Bentley.

14 – *Ibid.*, ch. xii, p. 404, n. 17. Ludolph Kuster, editor of Aristophanes.

15 – Otherwise unidentified.

16 – For the quotation, Monk, vol. ii, ch. xv, pp. 133–4, which has 'years, had', and for the catalogue of abuse, p. 136.

17 – *Ibid.*, ch. xx, p. 412. The line quoted is from Virgil, *Aeneid*, iv, 1. 654, Dido's speech from her funeral pile ('tunc' should be 'nunc'): 'And now my great ghost will go under the earth.'

18 – For the quotation, *ibid.*, ch. xix, p. 310, which has 'taste, to venture'. According to the *DNB*, Bentley's edition of *Paradise Lost*, published in 1732, 'has the faults of [his] classical criticisms in senile form, while it can have none of their merits.'

III   Lady Dorothy Nevill

1 – This essay, originally published as 'Behind the Bars' (*Athenaeum*, 12 December 1919), (Kp C179)a review of *The Life and Letters of Lady Dorothy Nevill* [1826–1913] (Methuen and Co. Ltd, 1919) by Ralph Nevill, was revised as shown for inclusion in CR1. 'As for Lady Dorothy Nevill,' VW wrote to Violet Dickinson, 27 November 1919 (*II VW Letters*, no. 1098), 'she made me laugh so with her pigeons, guinea pigs, funguses and the rest I couldn't hurt a hair on her head.' On 6 December she recorded in her diary Elizabeth Bibesco's observation, while discussing Lady Dorothy, that '"Memory comes to take the place of character in the old".' See also 'The Memoirs of Lady Dorothy Nevill', *I VW Essays*. See Editorial Note, p. xxv.

2 – No source for this intriguing reference has been traced.

3 – Nevill, ch. iii, p. 61.

4 – For the quotation, *ibid.*, ch. iv, p. 79, which has 'great-great-grandmother'. Ann Oldfield (1683–1730), the celebrated actress, whose clarity of diction was famously praised by Voltaire; her illegitimate son by General Charles Churchill married Lady Mary Walpole. Lady Dorothy was the daughter of the 3rd Earl of Orford. Horace Walpole (1717–97) was the fourth son of Sir Robert Walpole, 1st Earl of Orford, by his first wife, Catherine Shorter.

5 – Jacques-Benigne Bossuet (1627–1704), French divine, famous for his sermons and funeral orations.

6 – Nevill, ch. i, p. 18.

7–Thomas Hardy (1840–1928).

8–For the four preceding quotations, Nevill, ch. i, p. 9.

9–*Ibid.*, ch. iii, p. 56: 'She was able to furnish the great naturalist with many specimens which she liked to think were of use to him in his wonderful researches.' Charles Darwin (1809–82).

10–*Ibid.*, p. 57. Emma Darwin, *née* Wedgwood.

11–*Ibid.*, ch. iii, p. 68.

12–*Ibid.*, p. 69: 'She dearly loved all quaint devices, and being sent some pigeon whistles from China by Sir Harry Parkes, organised an aerial orchestra. These whistles ... produced a very pleasant effect, resembling that of Aeolian harps.'

13–*Ibid.*, ch. v, p. 108.

14–*Ibid.*, 115.

15–*Ibid.*, ch. xi, p. 300, which has '"Those horrors" (meaning the Radicals) ...'

16–For both quotations, *ibid.*, slightly adapted.

17–*Ibid.*, pp. 300–1. The ellipsis omitted by VW and here inserted in square brackets marks the omission of: 'It makes me quite sad when I go to any of the museums to see not a soul hardly there, and the few that are there only giggling, etc.'

18–*Ibid.*, ch. v, p. 119, quoting a letter from Joseph Chamberlain (1836–1914), dated 19 August 1892: 'We sympathise with you in your fears for the future, although I feel sure that when you go to the guillotine (or will it be the Dynamo in the present enlightened age?) your conduct will be ...'

IV   Archbishop Thomson

1–This essay, originally published as 'The Soul of an Archbishop' (*Athenaeum*, 9 May 1919), a review of *The Life and Letters of William Thomson, Archbishop of York* [1819–90] (John Lane, 1919) by Ethel H. Thomson, was revised as shown for inclusion in *CR1*. See Editorial Note, p. xxv.

2–Thomson, ch. i, p. 3. The archbishop's great-uncle Walter Thomson was a businessman of Whitehaven in the north of England.

3–Gustavus III (1746–92), king of Sweden, 1771–92, was assassinated by members of the Swedish nobility.

4–Thomson, ch. i, p. 6. Thomson's *Outlines of the Laws of Thought* was published in 1842.

5–*Ibid.*, ch. xi, p. 319, fn. 1, where the following hat sizes are given: Dickens 7⅛, Gladstone 7⅛, and Thackeray 7⅞.

6–*Ibid.*, ch. i, p. 17, from Thomson's diary, 28 December 1843.

7–*Ibid.*, pp. 21–2, diary 19 April 1845. 'Religion' and 'Morals' are not capitalised in the original.

8–*Ibid.*, ch. ii, p. 40.

9–*Ibid.*, p. 42. Sir Henry Taylor (1800–86), verse dramatist.

10–*Ibid.*, p. 38.

11–*Ibid.*, ch. iv, p. 117, quoting Canon Thorold, writing to Thomson, 10 January 1861; see note 15 below.

12–*Ibid.*, ch. ii, p. 38.

13–For the first quotation, *ibid.*, ch. iii, p. 62, Thomson writing to Mrs Thomson, 15 November 1862; and for the second, *ibid.*, p. 63, adapted.

14–*Ibid.*, ch. iii, p. 73, letter to Mrs Thomson, July 1866.

15–*Ibid.*, ch. iv, p. 117.

16–*Essays and Reviews* (1860) by the Rev. Henry Bristow Wilson and seven collaborators, including Benjamin Jowett; in answer to the unorthodoxies of which Thomson edited, and contributed to, *Aids to Faith* (1861).

17–Thomson, ch. v, p. 167, which has: 'Therefore there is this one common ground amongst them all – that selfishness – self-assertion of one class as against the rest is at the bottom of them all.'

18–*Ibid.*, p. 172, adapted.

19–John William Colenso (1814–83), the controversial Bishop of Natal.

20–Thomson, ch. vi, p. 191.

21–For the three preceding quotations, *ibid.*, p. 196. John Purchas (1823–72).

22–*Ibid.*, ch. vi, p. 211, Thomson writing to the Bishop of Manchester, 29 April 1883.

The Patron and the Crocus

Young men and women beginning to write are generally given the plausible but utterly impracticable advice to write what they have to write as shortly as possible, as clearly as possible, and without other thought in their minds except to say exactly what is in them. Nobody ever adds on these occasions the one thing needful: 'And be sure you choose your patron wisely', though that is the gist of the whole matter. For a book is always written for somebody to read, and, since the patron is not merely the paymaster, but also in a very subtle and insidious way the instigator and inspirer of what is written, it is of the utmost importance that he should be a desirable man.

But who, then, is the desirable man – the patron who will cajole the best out of the writer's brain and bring to birth the most varied and vigorous progeny of which he is capable? Different ages have answered the question differently. The Elizabethans, to speak roughly, chose the aristocracy to write for and the playhouse public. The eighteenth-century patron was a combination of coffee-house wit and Grub Street bookseller. In the nineteenth century the great writers wrote for the half-crown magazines and the leisured classes. And looking back and applauding the splendid results of these different alliances, it all seems enviably simple, and plain as a pikestaff compared with our own predicament – for whom should we write? For the present supply of patrons is of unexampled and bewildering variety. There is the daily Press, the weekly Press, the monthly Press; the English public and the American public; the best-seller public and the worst-seller public; the highbrow public and the red-blood public; all now organised self-conscious entities capable through their various mouthpieces of making their needs known and their approval or displeasure felt. Thus the writer who has been moved by the sight of the first crocus in Kensington Gardens has, before he sets pen to paper, to choose from a crowd of competitors the particular patron who suits him best. It is futile to say, 'Dismiss them all; think only of your crocus', because writing is a method of communication; and the crocus is an imperfect crocus until it has been shared. The first man or the last may write for himself alone, but he is an exception and an unenviable one at that, and the gulls are welcome to his works if the gulls can read them.

Granted, then, that every writer has some public or other at the end of his pen, the high-minded will say that it should be a submissive public, accepting obediently whatever he likes to give it. Plausible as the theory sounds, great risks are attached to it. For in that case the writer remains conscious of his public, yet is superior to it – an uncomfortable and unfortunate combination, as the works of Samuel Butler, George Meredith, and Henry James[2] may be taken to prove. Each despised the public; each desired a public; each failed to attain a public; and each wreaked his failure upon the public by a succession, gradually increasing in intensity, of angularities, obscurities, and affectations which no writer whose patron was his equal and friend would have thought it necessary to inflict. Their crocuses, in consequence, are tortured plants, beautiful and bright, but with something wry-necked about them, malformed, shrivelled on the one side, overblown on the other. A touch of the sun would have done them a world of good. Shall we then rush to the opposite extreme and accept (if in fancy alone) the flattering proposals which the editors of *The Times* and the *Daily News* may be supposed to make us – 'Twenty pounds down for your crocus in precisely fifteen hundred words, which shall blossom upon every breakfast table from John O'Groats to the Land's End before nine o'clock tomorrow morning with the writer's name attached'?

But will one crocus be enough, and must it not be a very brilliant yellow to shine so far, to cost so much, and to have one's name attached to it? The Press is undoubtedly a great multiplier of crocuses. But if we look at some of these plants, we shall find that they are only very distantly related to the original little yellow or purple flower which pokes up through the grass in Kensington Gardens early in March every year. The newspaper crocus is an amazing but still a very different plant. It fills precisely the space allotted to it. It radiates a golden glow. It is genial, affable, warm-hearted. It is beautifully finished, too, for let nobody think that the art of 'our dramatic critic' of The Times or of Mr Lynd of the Daily News is an easy one.[3] It is no despicable feat to start a million brains running at nine o'clock in the morning, to give two million eyes something bright and brisk and amusing to look at. But the night comes and these flowers fade. So little bits of glass lose their lustre if you take them out of the sea; great prima donnas howl like hyenas if you shut them up in telephone boxes; and the most brilliant of articles when removed from its element is dust and sand and the husks of straw. Journalism embalmed in a book is unreadable.

The patron we want, then, is one who will help us to preserve our flowers from decay. But as his qualities change from age to age, and it needs considerable integrity and conviction not to be dazzled by the pretensions or bamboozled by the persuasions of the competing crowd, this business of patron-finding is one of the tests and trials of authorship. To know whom to write for is to know how to write. Some of the modern patron's qualities are, however, fairly plain. The writer will require at this moment, it is obvious, a patron with the book-reading habit rather than the play-going habit. Nowadays, too, he must be instructed in the literature of other times and races. But there are other qualities which our special weaknesses and tendencies demand in him. There is the question of indecency, for instance, which plagues us and puzzles us much more than it did the Elizabethans. The twentieth-century patron must be immune from shock. He must distinguish infallibly between the little clod of manure which sticks to the crocus of necessity, and that which is plastered to it out of bravado. He must be a judge, too, of those social influences* which inevitably play so large a part in modern literature, and able to say which matures and fortifies, which inhibits and makes sterile. Further, there is emotion for him to pronounce on, and in no department can he do more useful work than in bracing a writer against sentimentality on the one hand and a craven fear of expressing his feeling on the other. It is worse, he will say, and perhaps more common, to be afraid of feeling than to feel too much. He will add, perhaps, something about language, and point out how many words Shakespeare used and how much grammar Shakespeare violated, while we, though we keep our fingers so demurely to the black notes on the piano, have not appreciably improved upon *Antony and Cleopatra*. And if you can forget your sex altogether, he will say, so much the better; a writer has none.[†] But all this is by the way – elementary and disputable. The patron's prime quality is something different, only to be expressed perhaps by the use of that convenient word which cloaks so much – atmosphere. It is necessary that the patron should shed and envelop the crocus in an atmosphere which makes it appear a plant of the very highest importance, so that to misrepresent it is the one outrage not to be forgiven this side of the grave. He must make us feel that a single crocus, if it be a real crocus, is enough for him; that he does not want to be lectured, elevated, instructed, or improved; that he is sorry that he bullied Carlyle into vociferation, Tennyson into idyllics, and Ruskin into insanity;[4] that he is now ready to efface himself or assert himself as his writers require; that he is bound to them by a more than maternal tie; that they are twins indeed, one dying if the other dies, one flourishing if the other flourishes; that the fate of literature depends upon their happy alliance – all of which proves, as we began by saying, that the choice of a patron is of the highest importance. But how to choose rightly? How to write well? Those are the questions.

* – *N&A*: 'those influences'.

† – *N&A* does not give the preceding sentence.

1 – This essay, first published in *N&A*, 12 April 1924, and reprinted in *NR*, 7 May, (Kp C246) was revised as shown for inclusion in *CR1*. See Editorial Note, p. xxv. Reprinted *CE*.

2 – Samuel Butler (1835–1902), George Meredith (1828–1909), Henry James (1843–1916).

3 – Robert Wilson Lynd (1879–1949), essayist, literary editor of the *Daily News* from 1912. The dramatic critic on *The Times* at this time was Arthur Bingham Walkley (1855–1926), who once accused VW of sentimentalism (see *II VW Diary*, 15 April 1920).

4 – Thomas Carlyle (1795–1881), Alfred, Lord Tennyson (1809–92); for VW on John Ruskin (1819–1900) see 'Ruskin Looks Back on Life' below.

The Modern Essay

As Mr Rhys truly says, it is unnecessary to go profoundly into the history and origin of the essay – whether it derives from Socrates or Siranney the Persian – since, like all living things, its present is more important than its past. Moreover, the family is widely spread; and while some of its representatives have risen in the world and wear their coronets with the best, others pick up a precarious living in the gutter near Fleet Street. The form, too, admits variety. The essay can be short or long, serious or trifling, about God and Spinoza, or about turtles and Cheapside.[2] But as we turn over the pages of these five little volumes, containing essays written between 1870 and 1920, certain principles appear to control the chaos, and we detect in the short period under review something like the progress of history.

Of all forms of literature, however, the essay is the one which least calls for the use of long words. The principle which controls it is simply that it should give pleasure; the desire which impels us when we take it from the shelf is simply to receive pleasure. Everything in an essay must be subdued to that end. It should lay us under a spell with its first word, and we should only wake, refreshed, with its last. In the interval we may pass through the most various experiences of amusement, surprise, interest, indignation; we may soar to the heights of fantasy with Lamb or plunge to the depths of wisdom with Bacon,[3] but we must never be roused. The essay must lap us about and draw its curtain across the world.

So great a feat is seldom accomplished, though the fault may well be as much on the reader's side as on the writer's. Habit and lethargy have dulled his palate. A novel has a story, a poem rhyme; but what art can the essayist use in these short lengths of prose to sting us wide awake and fix us in a trance which is not sleep but rather an intensification of life – a basking, with every faculty alert, in the sun of pleasure? He must know – that is the first essential – how to write. His learning may be as profound as Mark Pattison's, but in an essay it must be so fused by the magic of writing that not a fact juts out, not a dogma tears the surface of the texture. Macaulay in one way, Froude in another, did this superbly over and over again.[4] They have blown more knowledge into us in the course of one essay than the innumerable chapters of a hundred text-books. But when Mark Pattison has to tell us, in the space of thirty-five little pages, about Montaigne, we feel that he had not previously assimilated M. Grün.[5] M. Grün was a gentleman who once wrote a bad book. M. Grün and his book should have been embalmed for our perpetual delight in amber. But the process is fatiguing; it requires more time and perhaps more temper than Pattison had at his command. He served M. Grün up raw, and he remains a crude berry among the cooked meats, upon which our teeth must grate for ever. Something of the sort applies to Matthew Arnold and a certain translator of Spinoza.[6] Literal truth-telling and finding fault with a culprit for his good are out of place in an essay, where everything should be for our good and rather for eternity than for the March number of the *Fortnightly Review*.[7] But if the voice of the scold should never be heard in this narrow plot, there is another voice which is as a plague of locusts – the voice of a man stumbling drowsily among loose words, clutching aimlessly at vague ideas, the voice, for example, of Mr Hutton in the following passage:

Add to this that his married life was very brief, only seven years and a half, being unexpectedly cut short, and that his passionate reverence for his wife's memory and genius – in his own words, 'a religion' – was one which, as he must have been perfectly sensible, he could not make to appear otherwise than extravagant, not to say an hallucination, in the eyes of the rest of mankind, and yet that he was possessed by an irresistible yearning to attempt to embody it in all the tender and enthusiastic hyperbole of which it is so pathetic to find a man who gained his fame by his 'dry-light' a master, and it is impossible not to feel that the human incidents in Mr Mill's career are very sad.[8]

A book could take that blow, but it sinks an essay. A biography in two volumes is indeed the proper depository; for there, where the licence is so much wider, and hints and glimpses of outside things make part of the feast (we refer to the old type of Victorian volume), these yawns and stretches hardly matter, and have indeed some positive value of their own. But that value, which is contributed by the reader, perhaps illicitly, in his desire to get as much into the book from all possible sources as he can, must be ruled out here.

There is no room for the impurities of literature in an essay. Somehow or other, by dint of labour or bounty of nature, or both combined, the essay must be pure – pure like water or pure like wine, but pure from dullness, deadness, and deposits of extraneous matter. Of all writers in the first volume, Walter Pater best achieves this arduous task, because before setting out to write his essay ('Notes on Leonardo da Vinci')[9] he has somehow contrived to get his material fused. He is a learned man, but it is not knowledge of Leonardo that remains with us, but a vision, such as we get in a good novel where everything contributes to bring the writer's conception as a whole before us. Only here, in the essay, where the bounds are so strict and facts have to be used in their nakedness, the true writer like Walter Pater makes these limitations yield their own quality. Truth will give it authority; from its narrow limits he will get shape and intensity; and then there is no more fitting place for some of those ornaments which the old writers loved and we, by calling them ornaments, presumably despise. Nowadays nobody would have the courage to embark on the once famous description of Leonardo's lady who has

learned the secrets of the grave; and has been a diver in deep seas and keeps their fallen day about her; and trafficked for strange webs with Eastern merchants; and, as Leda, was the mother of Helen of Troy, and, as Saint Anne, the mother of Mary . . .[10]

The passage is too thumb-marked to slip naturally into the context. But when we come unexpectedly upon 'the smiling of women and the motion of great waters', or upon 'full of refinement of the dead in sad, earth-coloured raiment, set with pale stones',[11] we suddenly remember that we have ears and we have eyes, and that the English language fills a long array of stout volumes with innumerable words, many of which are of more than one syllable. The only living Englishman who ever looks into these volumes is, of course, a gentleman of Polish extraction.[12] But doubtless our abstention saves us much gush, much rhetoric, much high-stepping and cloud-prancing, and for the sake of the prevailing sobriety and hard-headedness we should be willing to barter the splendour of Sir Thomas Browne and the vigour of Swift.[13]

Yet, if the essay admits more properly than biography or fiction of sudden boldness and metaphor, and can be polished till every atom of its surface shines, there are dangers in that too. We are soon in sight of ornament. Soon the current, which is the life-blood of literature, runs slow; and instead of sparkling and flashing or moving with a quieter impulse which has a deeper excitement, words coagulate together in frozen sprays which, like the grapes on a

Christmas-tree, glitter for a single night, but are dusty and garish the day after. The temptation to decorate is great where the theme may be of the slightest. What is there to interest another in the fact that one has enjoyed a walking tour, or has amused oneself by rambling down Cheapside and looking at the turtles in Mr Sweeting's shop window? Stevenson[14] and Samuel Butler chose very different methods of exciting our interest in these domestic themes. Stevenson, of course, trimmed and polished and set out his matter in the traditional eighteenth-century form. It is admirably done, but we cannot help feeling anxious, as the essay proceeds, lest the material may give out under the craftsman's fingers. The ingot is so small, the manipulation so incessant. And perhaps that is why the peroration –

To sit still and contemplate – to remember the faces of women without desire, to be pleased by the great deeds of men without envy, to be everything and everywhere in sympathy and yet content to remain where and what you are –[15]

has the sort of insubstantiality which suggests that by the time he got to the end he had left himself nothing solid to work with. Butler adopted the very opposite method. Think your own thoughts, he seems to say, and speak them as plainly as you can. These turtles in the shop window which appear to leak out of their shells through heads and feet suggest a fatal faithfulness to a fixed idea. And so, striding unconcernedly from one idea to the next, we traverse a large stretch of ground; observe that a wound in the solicitor is a very serious thing; that Mary Queen of Scots wears surgical boots and is subject to fits near the Horse Shoe in Tottenham Court Road; take it for granted that no one really cares about Aeschylus; and so, with many amusing anecdotes and some profound reflections, reach the peroration, which is that, as he had been told not to see more in Cheapside than he could get into twelve pages of the *Universal Review*,[16] he had better stop. And yet obviously Butler is at least as careful of our pleasure as Stevenson; and to write like oneself and call it not writing is a much harder exercise in style than to write like Addison[17] and call it writing well.

But, however much they differ individually, the Victorian essayists yet had something in common. They wrote at greater length than is now usual, and they wrote for a public which had not only time to sit down to its magazine seriously, but a high, if peculiarly Victorian, standard of culture by which to judge it. It was worth while to speak out upon serious matters in an essay; and there was nothing absurd in writing as well as one possibly could when, in a month or two, the same public which had welcomed the essay in a magazine would carefully read it once more in a book. But a change came from a small audience of cultivated people to a larger audience of people who were not quite so cultivated. The change was not altogether for the worse. In volume iii we find Mr Birrell and Mr Beerbohm.[18] It might even be said that there was a reversion to the classic type, and that the essay by losing its size and something of its sonority was approaching more nearly the essay of Addison and Lamb. At any rate, there is a great gulf between Mr Birrell on Carlyle[19] and the essay which one may suppose that Carlyle would have written upon Mr Birrell. There is little similarity between *A Cloud of Pinafores*, by Max Beerbohm, and *A Cynic's Apology*, by Leslie Stephen.[20] But the essay is alive; there is no reason to despair. As the conditions change so the essayist, most sensitive of all plants to public opinion, adapts himself, and if he is good makes the best of the change, and if he is bad the worst. Mr Birrell is certainly good; and so we find that, though he has dropped a considerable amount of weight, his attack is much more direct and his movement more supple. But what did Mr Beerbohm give to the essay and what did he take from it? That is a much more complicated question, for here we have an essayist who has concentrated on* the work and is without doubt the prince of his profession.

What Mr Beerbohm gave was, of course, himself. This presence, which has haunted the essay fitfully from the time of Montaigne, had been in exile since the death of Charles Lamb. Matthew Arnold was never to his readers Matt, nor Walter Pater affectionately abbreviated in a thousand homes to Wat. They gave us much, but that they did not give. Thus, some time in the nineties, it must have surprised readers accustomed to exhortation, information, and denunciation to find themselves familiarly addressed by a voice which seemed to belong to a man no larger than themselves. He was affected by private joys and sorrows, and had no gospel to preach and no learning to impart. He was himself, simply and directly, and himself he has remained. Once again we have an essayist capable of using the essayist's most proper but most dangerous and delicate tool. He has brought personality into literature, not unconsciously and impurely, but so consciously and purely that we do not know whether there is any relation between Max the essayist and Mr Beerbohm the man. We only know that the spirit of personality permeates every word that he writes. The triumph is the triumph of style. For it is only by knowing how to write that you can make use in literature of your self; that self which, while it is essential to literature, is also its most dangerous antagonist. Never to be yourself and yet always – that is the problem. Some of the essayists in Mr Rhys's collection, to be frank, have not altogether succeeded in solving it. We are nauseated by the sight of trivial personalities decomposing in the eternity of print. As talk, no doubt it was charming, and certainly the writer is a good fellow to meet over a bottle of beer.[†] But literature is stern; it is no use being charming, virtuous, or even learned and brilliant into the bargain, unless, she seems to reiterate, you fulfil her first condition – to know how to write.

This art is possessed to perfection by Mr Beerbohm. But he has not searched the dictionary for polysyllables. He has not moulded firm periods or seduced our ears with intricate cadences and strange melodies. Some of his companions – Henley[21] and Stevenson, for example – are momentarily more impressive. But *A Cloud of Pinafores* had in it that indescribable inequality, stir, and final expressiveness which belong to life and to life alone. You have not finished with it because you have read it, any more than friendship is ended because it is time to part. Life wells up and alters and adds. Even things in a book-case change if they are alive; we find ourselves wanting to meet them again; we find them altered. So we look back upon essay after essay by Mr Beerbohm, knowing that, come September or May, we shall sit down with them and talk.[‡] Yet it is true that the essayist is the most sensitive of all writers to public opinion. The drawing-room is the place where a great deal of reading is done nowadays, and the essays of Mr Beerbohm lie, with an exquisite appreciation of all that the position exacts, upon the drawing-room table. There is no gin about; no strong tobacco; no puns, drunkenness, or insanity. Ladies and gentlemen talk together, and some things, of course, are not said.

But if it would be foolish to attempt to confine Mr Beerbohm to one room, it would be still more foolish, unhappily, to make him, the artist, the man who gives us only his best, the representative of our age. There are no essays by Mr Beerbohm in the fourth or fifth volumes of the present collection. His age seems already a little distant, and the drawing-room table, as it recedes, begins to look rather like an altar where, once upon a time, people deposited offerings – fruit from their own orchards, gifts carved with their own hands. Now once more the conditions have changed. The public needs essays as much as ever, and perhaps even more. The demand for the light middle not exceeding fifteen hundred words, or in special cases seventeen hundred and fifty, much exceeds the supply. Where Lamb wrote one essay and Max perhaps writes two, Mr Belloc[22] at a rough computation produces three hundred and sixty-five. They are very short, it is true. Yet with what dexterity the practised essayist will utilise his space – beginning as close to the top of the sheet as possible, judging precisely how far to go, when to turn, and how, without sacrificing a hair's-breadth of paper, to wheel about and alight accurately upon the last word his editor allows! As a feat of skill it is well worth watching. But the personality upon which Mr Belloc, like Mr Beerbohm, depends suffers in the process. It comes to us not with the natural richness of the speaking voice, but strained and thin and full of mannerisms and affectations, like the voice of a man shouting through a megaphone to a crowd on a windy day. 'Little friends, my readers', he says in the essay called 'An Unknown Country', and he goes on to tell us how –

There was a shepherd the other day at Findon Fair who had come from the east by Lewes with sheep, and who had in his eyes that reminiscence of horizons which makes the eyes of shepherds and of mountaineers different from the eyes of other men . . . I went with him to hear what he had to say, for shepherds talk quite differently from other men.[23]

Happily this shepherd had little to say, even under the stimulus of the inevitable mug of beer,[5] about the Unknown Country, for the only remark that he did makes proves him either a minor poet, unfit for the care of sheep, or Mr Belloc himself masquerading with a fountain pen. That is the penalty which the habitual essayist must now be prepared to face. He must masquerade. He cannot afford the time either to be himself or to be other people. He must skim the surface of thought and dilute the strength of personality. He must give us a worn weekly halfpenny instead of a solid sovereign once a year.

But it is not Mr Belloc only who has suffered from the prevailing conditions. The essays which bring the collection to the year 1920 may not be the best of their authors' work, but if we except writers like Mr Conrad and Mr Hudson,[24] who have strayed into essay writing accidentally, and concentrate upon those who write essays habitually, we shall find them a good deal affected by the change in their circumstances. To write weekly, to write daily, to write shortly, to write for busy people catching trains in the morning or for tired people coming home in the evening, is a heart-breaking task for men who know good writing from bad. They do it, but instinctively draw out of harm's way anything precious that might be damaged by contact with the public, or anything sharp that might irritate its skin.‖ And so, if one reads Mr Lucas, Mr Lynd, or Mr Squire[25] in the bulk, one feels that a common greyness silvers everything. They are as far removed from the extravagant beauty of Walter Pater as they are from the intemperate candour of Leslie Stephen. Beauty and courage are dangerous spirits to bottle in a column and a half; and thought, like a brown paper parcel in a waistcoat pocket, has a way of spoiling¶ the symmetry of an article. It is a kind, tired, apathetic world for which they write, and the marvel is that they never cease to attempt, at least, to write well.

But there is no need to pity Mr Clutton Brock[26] for this change in the essayist's conditions. He has clearly made the best of his circumstances and not the worst. One hesitates even to say that he has had to make any conscious effort in the matter, so naturally has he effected the transition from the private essayist to the public, from the drawing-room to the Albert Hall. Paradoxically enough, the shrinkage in size has brought about a corresponding expansion of individuality. We have no longer the 'I' of Max and of Lamb, but the 'we' of public bodies and other sublime personages. It is 'we' who go to hear the *Magic Flute*; 'we' who ought to profit by it; 'we', in some mysterious way, who, in our corporate capacity, once upon a time actually wrote it. For music and literature and art must submit to the same generalisation or they will not carry to the farthest recesses of the Albert Hall. That the voice of Mr Clutton Brock, so sincere and so disinterested, carries such a distance and reaches so many without pandering to the weakness of the mass or its passions must be a matter of legitimate satisfaction to us all. But while 'we' are gratified, 'I', that unruly partner in the human fellowship, is reduced to despair. 'I' must always think things for himself, and feel things for himself. To share them in a diluted form with the majority of well-educated and well-intentioned men and women is for him sheer agony; and while the rest of us listen intently and profit profoundly, 'I' slips off to the woods and the fields and rejoices in a single blade of grass or a solitary potato.

In the fifth volume of modern essays, it seems, we have got some way from pleasure and the art of writing. But in justice to the essayists of 1920 we must be sure that we are not praising the famous because they have been praised already and the dead because we shall never meet them wearing spats in Piccadilly. We must know what we mean when we say that they can write and give us pleasure. We must compare them; we must bring out the quality. We must point to this and say it is good because it is exact, truthful, and imaginative:**

Nay, retire men cannot when they would; neither will they, when it were Reason; but are impatient of Privateness, even in age and sickness, which require the shadow: like old Townsmen: that will still be sitting at their street door, though therby they offer Age to Scorn . . .[27]

and to this, and say it is bad because it is loose, plausible, and commonplace:[++]

With courteous and precise cynicism on his lips, he thought of quiet virginal chambers, of waters singing under the moon, of terraces where taintless music sobbed into the open night, of pure maternal mistresses with protecting arms and vigilant eyes, of fields slumbering in the sunlight, of leagues of ocean heaving under warm tremulous heavens, of hot ports, gorgeous and perfumed . . .[28]

It goes on, but already we are bemused with sound and neither feel nor hear. The comparison makes us suspect that the art of writing has for backbone[++] some fierce attachment to an idea. It is on the back of an idea, something believed in with conviction or seen with precision and thus compelling words to its shape, that the diverse company which includes Lamb and Bacon, and Mr Beerbohm and Hudson, and Vernon Lee[29] and Mr Conrad, and Leslie Stephen and Butler and Walter Pater reaches the farther shore. Very various talents have helped or hindered the passage of the idea into words. Some scrape through painfully; others fly with every wind favouring. But Mr Belloc and Mr Lucas and Mr Squire are not fiercely attached to anything in itself. They share the contemporary dilemma – that lack of an obstinate conviction which lifts ephemeral sounds through the misty sphere of anybody's language to the land where there is a perpetual marriage, a perpetual union. Vague as all definitions are, a good essay must have this permanent quality about it; it must draw its curtain round us, but it must be a curtain that shuts us in, not out.[§§]

* – *TLS*: 'has given himself wholly to'.

† – *TLS*: 'eternity of print; yet it was charming as it was spoken, and the writer is a good fellow in private, we feel sure.'

‡ – *TLS*: 'alive. So we look back upon essay after essay by Mr Beerbohm, knowing that we shall return and start again as with people who have been living all the time.'

§ – *TLS*: 'stimulus of a mug of beer'.

‖ – *TLS*: 'that might inflict pain upon it.'

¶ – *TLS*: 'pocket, destroys the symmetry'.

** – *TLS*: 'We must point to this and say it is good:'.

†† – *TLS* gives instead: 'It is good because it is exact, truthful, and imaginative. And what follows is bad because it is the opposite:'.

‡‡ – *TLS*: 'writing consists in some'.

§§ – 'a perpetual life. Vague as all definitions are, a good essay must have this permanent quality about it: it must draw its curtain across the world, but it must be a curtain which shuts us in, not out.'

1–Written for the *TLS*, 30 November 1922, (Kp C229) and published under the title 'Modern Essays', a review of *Modern English Essays 1870 to 1920* (5 vols, J. M. Dent, 1922), ed. Ernest Rhys (1850–1946), man of letters, founding editor of the Everyman Library, this essay was revised as shown for inclusion in *CR1*. 'So evidently my plan of the two books running side by side is practicable, & certainly I enjoy my reading with a purpose,' VW noted in her diary on 4 October 1922, 'I am committed to only one Supt. article – on Essays – & that at my own time; so I am free. I shall read Greek now steadily & begin "The Prime Minister" on Friday morning.' Ten days later she declared: '. . . I must be ready to start my Essay article for the Times: say on the 23rd. That will take say till 2nd Nov.' In fact it appears to have taken until the 8th, if we can judge from a letter of that date to Dora Carrington: 'Please excuse illiteracy; I have had to scribble all day to finish an article and this leaves one very much out of language' (*II VW Letters*, no. 1316). See also: 'Montaigne', 'Addison', above; 'Impassioned Prose', below; and see: 'The Decay of Essay-Writing', 'The Sentimental Traveller', 'The English Mail Coach', *I VW Essays*; 'Mr Symons's Essays', 'Melodious Meditations', 'Imitative Essays', 'A Book of Essays', 'Bad Writers', *II VW Essays*; 'Within the Rim', 'A Flying Lesson', 'Henley's Criticism', 'Patmore's Criticism', *III VW Essays*; 'Augustine Birrell', 'Lockhart's Criticism', 'De Quincey's Autobiography', 'William Hazlitt', *V VW Essays*. Reading Notes (MHP, B 2q). See Editorial Note, p. xxv. Reprinted *CE*.

2–The essays referred to here are: Matthew Arnold (1822–88), 'A Word About Spinoza', and Samuel Butler (1835–1902), 'Ramblings in Cheapside', in Rhys, vols i and ii respectively.

3–Charles Lamb (1775–1834), Francis Bacon (1561–1626).

4–Mark Pattison (1813–84), Thomas Babington Macaulay (1800–59), James Anthony Froude (1818–94).

5–Pattison, in his essay 'Montaigne', Rhys vol. i, discusses *La vie publique de Michel Montaigne* (1855) by Alphonse Grün.

6–Arnold's essay originally appeared in *Macmillan's Magazine*, December 1863, as 'A Word More About Spinoza' and was reprinted in the first edition of *Essays in*

Criticism (1865), as 'Spinoza'. The translator (of Spinoza's *Tractatus Theologico-Politicus*), not identified by Arnold, was Robert Willis.

7—Founded in 1865 the *Fortnightly* had very shortly afterwards become a monthly.

8—Rhys, vol. i, Richard Holt Hutton (1826–97), 'John Stuart Mill's "Autobiography"', pp. 124–5, which has: 'he could not possibly make to appear otherwise'. Hutton had been joint editor and part proprietor of the *Spectator*.

9—Walter Pater (1839–94) whose 'Notes on Leonardo Da Vinci', Rhys, vol. i, was first published in 1869 and forms a chapter in his *The Renaissance* (1873).

10—Rhys, vol. i, 'Notes on Leonardo Da Vinci', p. 185.

11—For the first quotation, *ibid.*, p. 166, and for the second, p. 173.

12—Joseph Conrad (1857–1924) is represented in Rhys, vol. iv, by 'Tales of the Sea'.

13—For VW on the splendours of Sir Thomas Browne (1605–82), see 'The Elizabethan Lumber Room' above; and for the vigorous Jonathan Swift (1667–1745), see 'Swift's Journal to Stella' below.

14—Robert Louis Stevenson (1850–94).

15—Rhys, vol. ii, Robert Louis Stevenson, 'Walking Tours', p. 191.

16—Butler's essay first appeared in 1890 in the *Universal Review*.

17—Joseph Addison (1672–1719).

18—Augustine Birrell (1850–1933), Max Beerbohm (1872–1956).

19—Rhys, vol. ii, Augustine Birrell, 'Carlyle'. (Birrell on 'The Essays of Elia' appears in *ibid.*, vol. iii).

20—*Ibid.*, vol. iii, Max Beerbohm, 'A Cloud of Pinafores'; *ibid.*, vol. ii, Leslie Stephen (1832–1904), 'A Cynic's Apology'.

21—W. E. Henley (1849–1903), a man of letters, sometime friend of Stevenson and inspiration for Long John Silver. See Rhys, vol. iii, 'William Hazlitt'.

22—Hilaire Belloc (1870–1953). See Rhys, vol. iv, 'On An Unknown Country'.

23—*Ibid.*, p. 59, which has 'up at Findon Fair', and continues: 'And when we came on to the shoulder of Chanctonbury and looked down upon the Weald, which stretched out like the Plains of Heaven, he said to me: "I never come here but it seems like a different place down below, and as though it were not the place where I have gone afoot with sheep under the hills. It seems quite different when you are looking down at it." He added that he had never known why. Then I knew that he, like myself, was perpetually in perception of the Unknown Country, and I was very pleased.'

24—W. H. Hudson (1841–1922) is represented in Rhys, vol. v, by 'The Samphire Gatherer'. For VW on Hudson, see 'Mr Hudson's Childhood', *II VW Essays*.

25—E. V. Lucas (1868–1938), man of letters, represented in Rhys, vol. iv, by 'A Philosopher that Failed'. Robert Lynd (1879–1949), journalist, on whom VW wrote in 'A Book of Essays' (see note 1), represented in Rhys, vol. v, by 'Hawthorne'. J. C. Squire (1884–1958), founder and editor of the *London Mercury*, represented in Rhys, vol. v, by 'A Dead Man' and 'The Lonely Author'. For VW on Squire see 'Imitative Essays' (see note 1).

26—Arthur Clutton Brock (1868–1924), art critic on *The Times* from 1908, and a friend of Clive Bell, represented in Rhys, vol. v, by 'The Magic Flute'.

27—Francis Bacon, 'Of Great Place', Essay XI, *Essays* (Everyman, 1972), p. 31.

28—Rhys, vol. v, J. C. Squire, 'A Dead Man', p. 79.

29—Vernon Lee (pseudonym of Violet Paget, 1856–1935), represented in Rhys, vol. ii, by 'Genius Loci'. For VW on Lee see 'The Sentimental Traveller' (see note 1 above) and also 'Art and Life', *I VW Essays*.

Joseph Conrad

Suddenly, without giving us time to arrange our thoughts or prepare our phrases, our guest˙ has left us; and his withdrawal without farewell or ceremony is in keeping with his mysterious arrival, long years ago, to take up his lodging in this country. For there was always an air of mystery about him. It was partly his Polish birth, partly his memorable appearance, partly his preference for living in the depths of the country, out of ear-shot of gossips, beyond reach of hostesses, so that for news of him one had to depend upon the evidence of simple visitors with a habit of ringing door-bells who reported of their unknown host that he had the most perfect manners, the brightest eyes, and spoke English with a strong foreign accent.

Still, though it is the habit of death to quicken and focus our memories, there clings to the genius of Conrad something essentially, and not accidentally, difficult to approach. His reputation of later years was, with one obvious exception, undoubtedly the highest in England; yet he was not popular. He was read with passionate delight by some; others he left cold and lustreless. Among his readers were people of the most opposite ages and sympathies. Schoolboys of fourteen, driving their way through Marryat, Scott, Henty, and Dickens,[2] swallowed him down with the rest; while the seasoned and the fastidious, who in process of time have eaten their way to the heart of literature and there turn over and over a few precious crumbs, set Conrad scrupulously upon their banqueting table. One source of difficulty and disagreement is, of course, to be found where men have at all times found it, in his beauty. One opens his pages and feels as Helen must have felt when she looked in her glass and realised that, do what she would, she could never in any circumstances pass for a plain woman. So Conrad had been gifted, so he had schooled himself, and such was his obligation to a strange language wooed characteristically for its Latin qualities rather than its Saxon that it seemed impossible for him to make an ugly or insignificant movement of the pen. His mistress, his style, is a little somnolent sometimes in repose. But let somebody speak to her, and then how magnificently she bears down upon us, with what colour, triumph, and majesty! Yet it is arguable that Conrad would have gained both in credit and in popularity if he had written what he had to write without this incessant care for appearances. They block and impede and distract, his critics say, pointing to those famous passages which it is becoming the habit to lift from their context and exhibit among other cut flowers of English prose. He was self-conscious and stiff and ornate, they complain, and the sound of his own voice was dearer to him than the voice of humanity in its anguish. The criticism is familiar, and as difficult to refute as the remarks of deaf people when *Figaro* is played. They see the orchestra; far off they hear a dismal scrape of sound; their own remarks are interrupted, and, very naturally, they conclude that the ends of life would be better served if instead of scraping Mozart those fifty fiddlers broke stones upon the road. That beauty teaches, that beauty is a disciplinarian, how are we to convince them, since her teaching is inseparable from the sound of her voice and to that they are deaf? But read Conrad, not in birthday books but in the bulk, and he must be lost indeed to the meaning of words who does not hear in that rather stiff and sombre music, with its reserve, its pride, its vast and implacable integrity, how it is better to be good than bad, how loyalty is good and honesty and courage, though ostensibly Conrad is concerned merely to show us the beauty of a night at sea. But it is ill work dragging such intimations from their element. Dried in our little saucers, without the magic and mystery of language, they lose their power to excite and goad; they lose the drastic power which is a constant quality of Conrad's prose.

For it was by virtue of something drastic in him, the qualities of a leader and captain, that Conrad kept his hold over boys and young people. Until *Nostromo*[3] was written his characters, as the young were quick to perceive, were fundamentally simple and heroic, however subtle the mind and indirect the method of their creator. They were seafarers, used to solitude and silence. They were in conflict with Nature, but at peace with man. Nature was their antagonist; she it was who drew forth honour, magnanimity, loyalty, the qualities proper to man; she who in sheltered bays reared to womanhood beautiful girls unfathomable and austere. Above all, it was Nature who turned out such gnarled and tested characters as Captain Whalley and old Singleton,[4] obscure but glorious in their obscurity, who were to Conrad the pick of our race, the men whose praises he was never tired of celebrating:

They had been strong as those are strong who know neither doubts nor hopes. They had been impatient and enduring, turbulent and devoted, unruly and faithful. Well-meaning people had tried to represent these men as whining over every mouthful of their food, as going about their work in fear of their lives. But in truth they had been men who knew toil, privation, violence, debauchery – but knew not fear, and had no desire of spite in their hearts. Men hard to manage, but easy to inspire; voiceless men – but men enough to scorn in their hearts the sentimental voices that bewailed the hardness of their fate. It was a fate unique and their own; the capacity to bear it appeared to them the privilege of the chosen! Their generation lived inarticulate and indispensable, without knowing the sweetness of affections or the refuge of a home – and died free from the dark menace of a narrow grave. They were the everlasting children of the mysterious sea.[5]

Such were the characters of the early books – *Lord Jim, Typhoon, The Nigger of the 'Narcissus', Youth*;[6] and these books, in spite of the changes and fashions, are surely secure of their place among our classics. But they reach this height by means of qualities which the simple story of adventure, as Marryat told it, or Fenimore Cooper,[7] has no claim to possess. For it is clear that to admire and celebrate such men and such deeds, romantically, whole-heartedly and with the fervour of a lover, one must be possessed of the double vision; one must be at once inside and out. To praise their silence one must possess a voice. To appreciate their endurance one must be sensitive to fatigue. One must be able to live on equal terms with the Whalleys and the Singletons and yet hide from their suspicious eyes the very qualities which enable one to understand them. Conrad alone was able to live that double life, for Conrad was compound of two men; together with the sea captain dwelt that subtle, refined, and fastidious analyst whom he called Marlow. 'A most discreet, understanding man', he said of Marlow.[8]

Marlow was one of those born observers who are happiest in retirement. Marlow liked nothing better than to sit on deck, in some obscure creek of the Thames, smoking and recollecting; smoking and speculating;[†] sending after his smoke beautiful rings of words until all the summer's night became a little clouded with tobacco smoke. Marlow, too, had a profound respect for the men with whom he had sailed; but he saw the humour of them. He nosed out and described in masterly fashion those livid creatures who prey successfully upon the clumsy veterans. He had a flair for human deformity; his humour was sardonic. Nor did Marlow live entirely wreathed in the smoke of his own cigars. He had a habit of opening his eyes suddenly and looking – at a rubbish heap, at a port, at a shop counter – and then complete in its burning ring of light that thing is flashed bright upon the mysterious background. Introspective and analytical, Marlow was aware of this peculiarity. He said the power came to him suddenly. He might, for instance, overhear a French officer murmur 'Mon Dieu, how the time passes!'

Nothing [he comments] could have been more commonplace than this remark; but its utterance coincided for me with a moment of vision. It's extraordinary how we go through life with eyes half shut, with dull ears, with dormant thoughts ... Nevertheless, there can be but few of us who had never known one of these rare moments of awakening, when we see, hear, understand, ever so much – everything – in a flash, before we fall back again into our agreeable somnolence. I raised my eyes when he spoke, and I saw him as though I had never seen him before.[9]

Picture after picture he painted thus upon that dark background; ships first and foremost, ships at anchor, ships flying before the storm, ships in harbour; he painted sunsets and dawns; he painted the night; he painted the sea in every aspect; he painted the gaudy brilliancy of Eastern ports, and men and women, their houses and their attitudes. He was an accurate and unflinching observer, schooled to that 'absolute loyalty towards his feelings and sensations', which, Conrad wrote, 'an author should keep hold of in his most exalted moments of creation'.[10] And very quietly and compassionately Marlow sometimes lets fall a few words of epitaph which remind us, with all that beauty and brilliancy before our eyes, of the darkness of the background.

Thus a rough-and-ready distinction would make us say that it is Marlow who comments, Conrad who creates. It would lead us, aware that we are on dangerous ground, to account for that change which, Conrad tells us, took place when he had finished the last story in the *Typhoon* volume – 'a subtle change in the nature of the inspiration' – by some alteration in the relationship of the two old friends. '. . . it seemed somehow that there was nothing more in the world to write about.'[11] It was Conrad, let us suppose, Conrad the creator, who said that, looking back with sorrowful satisfaction upon the stories he had told; feeling as he well might that he could never better the storm in *The Nigger of the 'Narcissus'*, or render more faithful tribute to the qualities of British seamen than he had done already in *Youth* and *Lord Jim*. It was then that Marlow, the commentator, reminded him how, in the course of nature, one must grow old, sit smoking on deck, and give up seafaring. But, he reminded him, those strenuous years had deposited their memories; and he even went so far perhaps as to hint that, though the last word might have been said about Captain Whalley and his relation to the universe, there remained on shore a number of men and women whose relationships, though of a more personal kind, might be worth looking into. If we further suppose that there was a volume of Henry James on board and that Marlow gave his friend the book to take to bed with him, we may seek support in the fact that it was in 1905 that Conrad wrote a very fine essay upon that master.[12]

For some years, then, it was Marlow who was the dominant partner. *Nostromo, Chance, The Arrow of Gold*[13] represent that stage of the alliance which some will continue to find the richest of all. The human heart is more intricate than the forest, they will say; it has its storms; it has its creatures of the night; and if as novelist you wish to test man in all his relationships, the proper antagonist is man; his ordeal is in society, not solitude. For them there will always be a peculiar fascination in the books where the light of those brilliant eyes falls not only upon the waste of waters[14] but upon the heart in its perplexity. But it must be admitted that, if Marlow thus advised Conrad to shift his angle of vision, the advice was bold. For the vision of a novelist is both complex and specialised; complex, because behind his characters and apart from them must stand something stable to which he relates them; specialised because since he is a single person with one sensibility the aspects of life in which he can believe with conviction are strictly limited. So delicate a balance is easily disturbed. After the middle period Conrad never again was able to bring his figures into perfect relation with their background. He never believed in his later and more highly sophisticated characters as he had believed in his early seamen. When he had to indicate their relation to that other unseen world of novelists, the world of values and convictions, he was far less sure what those values were. Then, over and over again, a single phrase, 'He steered with care,'[15] coming at the end of a storm, carried in it a whole morality. But in this more crowded and complicated world such terse phrases became less and less appropriate. Complex men and women of many interests and relations would not submit to so summary a judgement; or, if they did, much that was important in them escaped the verdict. And yet it was very necessary to Conrad's genius, with its luxuriant and romantic power, to have some law by which its creations could be tried. Essentially – such remained his creed – this world of civilised and self-conscious people is based upon 'a few very simple ideas';[16] but where, in the world of thoughts and personal relations, are we to find them? There are no masts in drawing-rooms; the typhoon does not test the worth of politicians and business men. Seeking and not finding such supports, the world of Conrad's later period has about it an involuntary obscurity, an inconclusiveness, almost a disillusionment which baffles and fatigues. We lay hold in the dusk only of the old nobilities and sonorities: fidelity, compassion, honour, service – beautiful always, but now a little wearily reiterated, as if times had changed. Perhaps it was Marlow who was at fault. His habit of mind was a trifle sedentary. He had sat upon deck too long; splendid in soliloquy, he was less apt in the give and take of conversation; and those 'moments of vision'[17] flashing and fading, do not serve as well as steady lamplight to illumine the ripple of life and its long, gradual years. Above all, perhaps, he did not take into account how, if Conrad was to create, it was essential first that he should believe.

Therefore, though we shall make expeditions into the later books and bring back wonderful trophies, large tracts of them will remain by most of us untrodden. It is the earlier books – *Youth, Lord Jim, Typhoon, The Nigger of the 'Narcissus'* – that we shall read in their entirety. For when the question is asked, what of Conrad will survive and where in the ranks of novelists we are to place him, these books, with their air of telling us something very old and perfectly true, which had lain hidden but is now revealed, will come to mind and make such questions and comparisons seem a little futile. Complete and still, very chaste and very beautiful, they rise in the memory as, on these hot summer nights, in their slow and stately way first one star comes out and then another.

* – *TLS*: 'our remarkable guest'.
† – *TLS*: 'smoking and recollecting;'.

1–Written for the *TLS*, 14 August 1924, (Kp C252) upon the death, on 3 August 1924, of Joseph Conrad (b. 1857), this essay was revised as shown for inclusion in *CR1*.

On 15 August, VW noted in her diary: 'Into all these calculations [towards completing *Mrs Dalloway* and making 'a systematic beginning' to the writing to *CR1*], broke the death of Conrad, followed by a wire from the Lit. Sup. earnestly asking me kindly to do a leader on him, which flattered & loyal, but grudgingly, I did; & its out; & that number of the Lit. Sup. corrupted for me (for I cant, & never shall be able to, read my own writings . . .)' See also: 'Lord Jim', 'Mr Conrad's "Youth"', 'Mr Conrad's Crisis', *II VW Essays*; 'A Disillusioned Romantic', 'A Prince of Prose', 'Mr Conrad: A Conversation', *III VW Essays*. Reading Notes (MHP, B 20). See Editorial Notes, p. xxv. Reprinted *CE*.

2–Frederick Marryat (1792–1848), for VW on whom see 'The Captain's Death Bed', *VI VW Essays*; Sir Walter Scott (1771–1832); George Alfred Henty (1832–1902); Charles Dickens (1812–70).

3–*Nostromo – A Tale of the Seaboard* (1904).

4–For Captain Whalley see Conrad's *The End of the Tether* (1902) and for Old Singleton, *The Nigger of the 'Narcissus'* (1897).

5–Conrad, *The Nigger of the 'Narcissus'. A Tale of the Sea* (1897; William Heinemann, 1910), ch. i, pp. 34–5, which has 'strong, as' and 'flood; as'.

6–*Lord Jim – A Tale* (1900), *Typhoon, and Other Stories* (1903), *Youth: A Narrative; and Two Other Stories* (1902).

7–James Fenimore Cooper (1789–1851), whose works include *The Pilot* (1823) and *The Red Rover* (1828), two tales of the sea, as well as the more famous 'Leatherstocking Tales'.

8–Conrad, *Youth* (J. M. Dent, 1918), author's note, p. viii; Charles Marlow, character in *Lord Jim* (1900), *Heart of Darkness* (1902) and *Chance* (1913).

9–Conrad, *Lord Jim* (J. M. Dent and Sons Ltd, 1917), ch. xiii, p. 142, which has 'awakening when' and '– in a flash –'.

10–Conrad, *Notes on Life and Letters* (1921; J. M. Dent, 1970), 'Books', p. 9.

11–Conrad, *Typhoon* (J. M. Dent, 1918), Author's Note, p. vii.

12–Conrad, 'Henry James. An Appreciation', *The North American Review*, January 1905. Henry James (1843–1916).

13–*The Arrow of Gold – A Story Between Two Notes* (1919).

14–A phrase echoed in *The Waves* (Hogarth Press, 1931), p. 206, and recorded by the arch phrase-maker Bernard: 'I note under F., therefore, "Fin in a waste of waters". I, who am perpetually making notes in the margin of my mind for some final statement, make this mark, waiting for some winter's evening.'

15–Conrad, *The Nigger of the "Narcissus"*, conclusion of chapter 3.

16–Conrad, *Some Reminiscences* (Eveleigh Nash, 1912), 'A Familiar Preface', p. 26.

17–See note 9 above.

How It Strikes a Contemporary

In the first place a contemporary can scarcely fail to be struck by the fact that two critics at the same table at the same moment will pronounce completely different opinions about the same book. Here, on the right, it is declared a masterpiece of English prose; on the left, simultaneously, a mere mass of waste-paper which, if the fire could survive it, should be thrown upon the flames. Yet both critics are in agreement about Milton and about Keats.[2] They display an exquisite sensibility and have undoubtedly a genuine enthusiasm. It is only when they discuss the work of contemporary writers that they inevitably come to blows. The book in question, which is at once a lasting contribution to English literature and a mere farrago of pretentious mediocrity, was published about two months ago. That is the explanation; that is why they differ.

The explanation is a strange one. It is equally disconcerting to the reader who wishes to take his bearings in the chaos of contemporary literature and to the writer who has a natural desire to know whether his own work, produced with infinite pains and in almost utter darkness, is likely to burn for ever among the fixed luminaries of English letters or, on the contrary, to put out the fire. But if we identify ourselves with the reader and explore his dilemma first, our bewilderment is short-lived enough. The same thing has happened so often before. We have heard the doctors disagreeing about the new and agreeing about the old twice a year on the average, in spring and autumn, ever since Robert Elsmere, or was it Stephen Phillips,[3] somehow pervaded the atmosphere, and there was the same disagreement among grown-up people about these books too. It would be much more marvellous, and indeed much more upsetting if, for a wonder, both gentleman agreed, pronounced Blank's book an undoubted masterpiece, and thus faced us with the necessity of deciding whether we should back their judgement to the extent of ten and sixpence. Both are critics of reputation; the opinions tumbled out so spontaneously here will be starched and stiffened into columns of sober prose which will uphold the dignity of letters in England and America.

It must be some innate cynicism, then, some ungenerous distrust of contemporary genius, which determines us automatically as the talk goes on that, were they to agree — which they show no signs of doing — half a guinea is altogether too large a sum to squander upon contemporary enthusiasms, and the case will be met quite adequately by a card to the library. Still the question remains, and let us put it boldly to the critics themselves. Is there no guidance nowadays for a reader who yields to none in reverence for the dead, but is tormented by the suspicion that reverence for the dead is vitally connected with understanding of the living? After a rapid survey both critics are agreed that there is unfortunately no such person. For what is their own judgement worth where new books are concerned? Certainly not ten and sixpence. And from the stores of their experience they proceed to bring forth terrible examples of past blunders; crimes of criticism which, if they had been committed against the dead and not against the living, would have lost them their jobs and imperilled their reputations. The only advice they can offer is to respect one's own instincts, to follow them fearlessly and, rather than submit them to the control of any critic or reviewer alive, to check them by reading and reading again the masterpieces of the past.

Thanking them humbly, we cannot help reflecting that it was not always so. Once upon a time, we must believe, there was a rule, a discipline, which controlled the great republic of readers in a way which is now unknown. That is not to say that the great critic – the Dryden, the Johnson, the Coleridge, the Arnold[4] – was an impeccable judge of contemporary work, whose verdicts stamped the book indelibly and saved the reader the trouble of reckoning the value for himself. The mistakes of these great men about their own contemporaries are too notorious to be worth recording. But the mere fact of their existence had a centralising influence. That alone, it is not fantastic to suppose, would have controlled the disagreements of the dinner-table and given to random chatter about some book just out an authority now entirely to seek. The diverse schools would have debated as hotly as ever, but at the back of every reader's mind would have been the consciousness that there was at least one man who kept the main principles of literature closely in view: who, if you had taken to him some eccentricity of the moment, would have brought it into touch with permanence and tethered it by his own authority in the contrary blasts of praise and blame.* But when it comes to the making of a critic, Nature must be generous and society ripe. The scattered dinner-tables of the modern world, the chase and eddy of the various currents which compose the society of our time, could only be dominated by a giant

---

* How violent these are two quotations will show. 'It [*Told by an Idiot*] should be read as the *Tempest* should be read, and as *Gulliver's Travels* should be read, for if Miss Macaulay's poetic gift happens to be less sublime than those of the author of the *Tempest*, and if her irony happens to be less tremendous than that of the author of *Gulliver's Travels*, her justice and wisdom are no less noble than theirs.' – *The Daily News*.

The next day we read: 'For the rest one can only say that if Mr Eliot had been pleased to write in demotic English *The Waste Land* might not have been, as it just is to all but anthropologists, and literati, so much waste-paper.' – *The Manchester Guardian.*[5]

of fabulous dimensions. And where is even the very tall man whom we have the right to expect? Reviewers we have but no critic; a million competent and incorruptible policemen but no judge. Men of taste and learning and ability are for ever lecturing the young and celebrating the dead. But the too frequent result of their able and industrious pens is a desiccation of the living tissues of literature into a network of little bones. Nowhere shall we find the downright vigour of a Dryden, or Keats with his fine and natural bearing, his profound insight and sanity, or Flaubert[6] and the tremendous power of his fanaticism, or Coleridge, above all, brewing in his head the whole of poetry and letting issue now and then one of those profound general statements which are caught up by the mind when hot with the friction of reading as if they were of the soul of the book itself.

And to all this, too, the critics generously agree. A great critic, they say, is the rarest of beings. But should one miraculously appear, how should we maintain him, on what should we feed him? Great critics, if they are not themselves great poets, are bred from the profusion of the age. There is some great man to be vindicated, some school to be founded or destroyed. But our age is meagre to the verge of destitution. There is no name which dominates the rest. There is no master in whose workshop the young are proud to serve apprenticeship. Mr Hardy has long since withdrawn from the arena, and there is something exotic about the genius of Mr Conrad[7] which makes him not so much an influence as an idol, honoured and admired, but aloof and apart. As for the rest, though they are many and vigorous and in the full flood of creative activity, there is none whose influence can seriously affect his contemporaries, or penetrate beyond our day to that not very distant future which it pleases us to call immortality. If we make a century our test, and ask how much of the work produced in these days in England will be in existence then, we shall have to answer not merely that we cannot agree upon the same book, but that we are more than doubtful whether such a book there is. It is an age of fragments. A few stanzas, a few pages, a chapter here and there, the beginning of this novel, the end of that, are equal to the best of any age or author. But can we go to posterity with a sheaf of loose pages, or ask the readers of those days, with the whole of literature before them, to sift our enormous rubbish heaps for our tiny pearls? Such are the questions which the critics might lawfully put to their companions at table, the novelists and poets.

At first the weight of pessimism seems sufficient to bear down all opposition. Yes, it is a lean age, we repeat, with much to justify its poverty; but, frankly, if we pit one century against another the comparison seems overwhelmingly against us. *Waverley, The Excursion, Kubla Khan, Don Juan, Hazlitt's Essays, Pride and Prejudice, Hyperion,* and *Prometheus Unbound* were all published between 1800 and 1821.[8] Our century has not lacked industry; but if we ask for masterpieces it appears on the face of it that the pessimists are right. It seems as if an age of genius must be succeeded by an age of endeavour; riot and extravagance by cleanliness and hard work. All honour, of course, to those who have sacrificed their immortality to set the house in order. But if we ask for masterpieces, where are we to look? A little poetry, we may feel sure, will survive; a few poems by Mr Yeats, by Mr Davies, by Mr De la Mare. Mr Lawrence, of course, has moments of greatness, but hours of something very different. Mr Beerbohm, in his way, is perfect, but it is not a big way. Passages in *Far Away and Long Ago* will undoubtedly go to posterity entire. *Ulysses*[9] was a memorable catastrophe – immense in daring, terrific in disaster. And so, picking and choosing, we select now this, now that, hold it up for display, hear it defended or derided, and finally have to meet the objection that even so we are only agreeing with the critics that it is an age incapable of sustained effort, littered with fragments, and not seriously to be compared with the age that went before.

But it is just when opinions universally prevail and we have added lip service to their authority that we become sometimes most keenly conscious that we do not believe a word that we are saying. It is a barren and exhausted age, we repeat; we must look back with envy to the past. Meanwhile it is one of the first fine days of spring. Life is not altogether lacking in colour. The telephone, which interrupts the most serious conversations and cuts short the most weighty observations, has a romance of its own. And the random talk of people who have no chance of immortality and thus can speak their minds out has a setting, often, of lights, streets, houses, human beings, beautiful or grotesque, which will weave itself into the moment for ever. But this is life; the talk is about literature. We must try to disentangle the two, and justify the rash revolt of optimism against the superior plausibility, the finer distinction, of pessimism.

Our optimism, then, is largely instinctive. It springs from the fine day and the wine and the talk; it springs from the fact that when life throws up such treasures daily, daily suggests more than the most voluble can express, much though we admire the dead, we prefer life as it is. There is something about the present which we would not exchange, though we were offered a choice of all past ages to live in. And modern literature, with all its imperfections, has the same hold on us and the same fascination. It is like a relation whom we snub and scarify daily, but, after all, cannot do without. It has the same endearing quality of being that which we are, that which we have made, that in which we live, instead of being something, however august, alien to ourselves and beheld from the outside. Nor has any generation more need than ours to cherish its contemporaries. We are sharply cut off from our predecessors. A shift in the scale – the war, the sudden slip of masses held in position for ages – has shaken the fabric from top to bottom, alienated us from the past and made us perhaps too vividly conscious of the present. Every day we find ourselves doing, saying, or thinking things that would have been impossible to our fathers. And we feel the differences which have not been noted far more keenly than the resemblances which have been very perfectly expressed. New books lure us to read them partly in the hope that they will reflect this rearrangement of our attitude – these scenes, thoughts, and apparently fortuitous groupings of incongruous things which impinge upon us with so keen a sense of novelty – and, as literature does, give it back into our keeping, whole and comprehended. Here indeed there is every reason for optimism. No age can have been more rich than ours in writers determined to give expression to the differences which separate them from the past and not to the resemblances which connect them with it. It would be invidious to mention names, but the most casual reader dipping into poetry, into fiction, into biography can hardly fail to be impressed by the courage, the sincerity, in a word, by the widespread originality of our time. But our exhilaration is strangely curtailed. Book after book leaves us with the same sense of promise unachieved, of intellectual poverty, of brilliance which has been snatched from life but not transmuted into literature. Much of what is best in contemporary work has the appearance of being noted under pressure, taken down in a bleak shorthand which preserves with astonishing brilliance the movements and expressions of the figures as they pass across the screen. But the flash is soon over, and there remains with

us a profound dissatisfaction. The irritation is as acute as the pleasure was intense.

After all, then, we are back at the beginning, vacillating from extreme to extreme, at one moment enthusiastic, at the next pessimis-
tic, unable to come to any conclusion about our contemporaries.
We have asked the critics to help us, but they have deprecated the
task. Now, then, is the time to accept their advice and correct these
extremes by consulting the masterpieces of the past. We feel ourselves indeed driven to them, impelled not by calm judgement but
by some imperious need to anchor our instability upon their
security. But, honestly, the shock of the comparison between past
and present is at first disconcerting. Undoubtedly there is a dullness
in great books. There is an unabashed tranquillity in page after page
of Wordsworth and Scott and Miss Austen which is sedative to the
verge of somnolence. Opportunities occur and they neglect them.
Shades and subtleties accumulate and they ignore them. They seem
deliberately to refuse to gratify those senses which are stimulated so
briskly by the moderns; the senses of sight, of sound, of touch —
above all, the sense of the human being, his depth and the variety of
his perceptions, his complexity, his confusion, his self, in short.
There is little of all this in the works of Wordsworth and Scott and
Jane Austen. From what, then, arises that sense of security which
gradually, delightfully, and completely overcomes us? It is the
power of their belief — their conviction, that imposes itself upon us.
In Wordsworth, the philosophic poet, this is obvious enough. But it
is equally true of the careless Scott, who scribbled masterpieces to
build castles before breakfast, and of the modest maiden lady who
wrote furtively and quietly simply to give pleasure. In both there is
the same natural conviction that life is of a certain quality. They
have their judgement of conduct. They know the relations of human
beings towards each other and towards the universe. Neither of
them probably has a word to say about the matter outright, but
everything depends on it. Only believe, we find ourselves saying,
and all the rest will come of itself. Only believe, to take a very
simple instance which the recent publication of *The Watsons*[10]
brings to mind, that a nice girl will instinctively try to soothe the
feelings of a boy who has been snubbed at a dance, and then, if you
believe it implicitly and unquestioningly, you will not only make
people a hundred years later feel the same thing, but you will make
them feel it as literature. For certainty of that kind is the condition

which makes it possible to write. To believe that your impressions hold good for others is to be released from the cramp and confinement of personality. It is to be free, as Scott was free, to explore with a vigour which still holds us spell-bound the whole world of adventure and romance. It is also the first step in that mysterious process in which Jane Austen was so great an adept. The little grain of experience once selected, believed in, and set outside herself, could be put precisely in its place, and she was then free to make of it, by a process which never yields its secrets to the analyst, into that complete statement which is literature.

So then our contemporaries afflict us because they have ceased to believe. The most sincere of them will only tell us what it is that happens to himself. They cannot make a world, because they are not free of other human beings. They cannot tell stories because they do not believe that stories are true. They cannot generalise. They depend on their senses and emotions, whose testimony is truthworthy, rather than on their intellects whose message is obscure. And they have perforce to deny themselves the use of some of the most powerful and some of the most exquisite of the weapons of their craft. With the whole wealth of the English language at the back of them, they timidly pass about from hand to hand and book to book only the meanest copper coins. Set down at a fresh angle of the eternal prospect they can only whip out their note-books and record with agonised intensity the flying gleams, which light on what? and the transitory splendours, which may, perhaps, compose nothing whatever. But here the critics interpose, and with some show of justice.

If this description holds good, they say, and is not, as it may well be, entirely dependent upon our position at the table and certain purely personal relationships to mustard pots and flower vases, then the risks of judging contemporary work are greater than ever before. There is every excuse for them if they are wide of the mark; and no doubt it would be better to retreat, as Matthew Arnold advised, from the burning ground of the present to the safe tranquillity of the past. 'We enter on burning ground,' wrote Matthew Arnold, 'as we approach the poetry of times so near to us, poetry like that of Byron, Shelley, and Wordsworth, of which the estimates are so often not only personal, but personal with passion,'[11] and this, they remind us, was written in the year 1880. Beware, they say, of putting under the microscope one inch of a ribbon which runs many miles; things sort themselves out if you wait; moderation, and a study of the classics are to be recommended. Moreover, life is short; the Byron centenary is at hand; and the burning question of the moment is, did he, or did he not, marry his sister? To sum up, then – if indeed any conclusion is possible when everybody is talking at once and it is time to be going – it seems that it would be wise for the writers of the present to renounce the hope of creating masterpieces. Their poems, plays, biographies, novels are not books but note-books, and Time, like a good schoolmaster, will take them in his hands, point to their blots and scrawls and erasions, and tear them across; but he will not throw them into the waste-paper basket. He will keep them because other students will find them very useful. It is from note-books of the present that the masterpieces of the future are made. Literature, as the critics were saying just now, has lasted long, has undergone many changes, and it is only a short sight and a parochial mind that will exaggerate the importance of these squalls, however they may agitate the little boats now tossing out at sea. The storm and the drenching are on the surface; continuity and calm are in the depths.

As for the critics whose task it is to pass judgement upon the books of the moment, whose work, let us admit, is difficult, dangerous, and often distasteful, let us ask them to be generous of encouragement, but sparing of those wreaths and coronets which are so apt to get awry, and fade, and make the wearers, in six months time, look a little ridiculous. Let them take a wider, a less personal view of modern literature, and look indeed upon the writers as if they were engaged upon some vast building, which being built by common effort, the separate workmen may well remain anonymous. Let them slam the door upon the cosy company where sugar is cheap and butter plentiful, give over, for a time at least, the discussion of that fascinating topic – whether Byron married his sister – and, withdrawing, perhaps, a handsbreadth from the table where we sit chattering, say something interesting about literature. Let us buttonhole them as they leave, and recall to their memory that gaunt aristocrat, Lady Hester Stanhope,[12] who kept a milk-white horse in her stable in readiness for the Messiah and was for ever scanning the mountain tops, impatiently but with confidence, for signs of his approach, and ask them to follow her example; scan the horizon; see the past in relation to the future; and so prepare the way for masterpieces to come.

1—Written for the *TLS*, 5 April 1923 (see *III VW Essays*), this essay was slightly revised for inclusion in *CR1*. The essay's title derives from that of Browning's poem in *Men and Women* (1855). Some years later, on reading through *CR1*, VW noted in her diary, 23 June 1929: '. . . this is very important — I must learn to write more succinctly. Especially in the general idea essays like the last, How It Strikes a Contemporary, I am horrified at my own looseness. This is partly that I dont think things out first; partly that I stretch my style to take in crumbs of meaning. But the result is a wobble & diffusity & breathlessness which I detest. See Editorial Note p. xxv. Reading Notes (Berg XIX). Reprinted *CE*.

2—John Milton (1608–74), John Keats (1795–1821).

3—Mrs Humphry Ward, *Robert Elsmere* (1888), an immensely popular bestseller, promulgating its author's view 'that Christianity could be revitalised by discarding its miraculous element and emphasising its social mission' (*DNB*); Stephen Phillips (1864–1915), dramatic poet, who, upon the performance of his *Paolo and Francesca* (1900) in 1902 was 'greeted as the successor of Sophocles and Shakespeare' (*ibid.*).

4—John Dryden (1631–1700), Samuel Johnson (1709–84), S. T. Coleridge (1772–1834), Matthew Arnold (1822–88).

5—The quotations VW cites in her footnote are from a review by Sylvia Lynd of Rose Macaulay's *Told by an Idiot* (1923), *Daily News*, 1 November 1923; and from a review signed 'C.P.' in the *Manchester Guardian*, 31 October 1923.

6—Gustave Flaubert (1821–80).

7—Thomas Hardy (1840–1928), Joseph Conrad (1857–1924).

8—Sir Walter Scott, *Waverley* (1814); William Wordsworth *The Excursion* (1814); S. T. Coleridge, 'Kubla Khan' (1816); George Gordon, Lord Byron, *Don Juan* (1819–24); William Hazlitt's career as an essayist reached its peak in the period 1817–25 — it began in 1805 with the publication of *On the Principles of Human Action*; Jane Austen, *Pride and Prejudice* (1813); John Keats, 'Hyperion' (1820); Percy Bysshe Shelley, *Prometheus Unbound* (1820).

9—W. B. Yeats (1865–1939), for VW on whom see 'Mr Yeats' below; W. H. Davies (1871–1940); Walter de la Mare (1873–1956); D. H. Lawrence (1885–1930), for VW on whom see 'Postscript or Prelude?', *III VW Essays*; Max Beerbohm (1872–1956), for VW on whom see 'The Modern Essay' above; W. H. Hudson (1841–1922), for VW on *Far Away and Long Ago* (1918), see *II VW Essays*; James Joyce (1882–1941), for VW on *Ulysses* (1922), see 'Modern Fiction' above.

10—Jane Austen, *The Watsons* (1871), republished with an introduction by A. B. Walkley (Leonard Parsons, 1923), for VW on which see 'Jane Austen' above.

11—T. H. Ward, ed., *The English Poets* (OUP, 1880), vol. i, Matthew Arnold, 'General Introduction', p. xlvi: 'But we enter on burning ground as we approach the poetry of times so near us, poetry like that of Byron, Shelley, and Wordsworth, of which . . .'

12—Lady Hester Lucy Stanhope (1776–1839), indefatigable eccentric, upon whom VW wrote in 'Lady Hester Stanhope', *I VW Essays*; see also 'The Eccentrics', *III VW Essays*.

Pictures

Probably some Professor has written a book on the subject, but it has not come our way. 'The Loves of the Arts' – that is more or less the title it would bear, and it would be concerned with the flirtations between music, letters, sculpture, and architecture, and the effects that the arts have had upon each other throughout the ages. Pending his inquiry, it would seem on the face of it that literature has always been the most sociable and the most impressionable of them all; that sculpture influenced Greek literature, music Elizabethan, architecture the English of the eighteenth century, and now, undoubtedly, we are under the dominion of painting. Were all modern paintings to be destroyed, a critic of the twenty-fifth century would be able to deduce from the works of Proust alone the existence of Matisse, Cézanne, Derain, and Picasso;[2] he would be able to say with those books before him that painters of the highest originality and power must be covering canvas after canvas, squeezing tube after tube, in the room next door.

Yet it is extremely difficult to put one's finger on the precise spot where paint makes itself felt in the work of so complete a writer. In the partial and incomplete writers it is much easier to detect. The world is full of cripples at the moment, victims of the art of painting, who paint apples, roses, china, pomegranates, tamarinds, and glass jars as well as words can paint them, which is, of course, not very well. We can say for certain that a writer whose writing appeals mainly to the eye is a bad writer; that if, in describing, say, a meeting in a garden, he describes roses, lilies, carnations, and shadows on the grass, so that we can see them, but allows to be inferred from them ideas, motives, impulses, and emotions, it is that he is incapable of using his medium for the purposes for which it was created, and is, as a writer, a man without legs.

But it is impossible to bring that charge against Proust, Hardy, Flaubert, or Conrad.[3] They are using their eyes without in the least impeding their pens, and they are using them as novelists have never used them before. Moors and woods, tropical seas, ships, harbours, streets, drawing-rooms, flowers, clothes, attitudes, effects of light and shade – all this they have given us with an accuracy and a subtlety that make us exclaim that now at last writers have begun to use their eyes. Not, indeed, that any of these great writers stops for a moment to describe a crystal jar as if that were an end in itself; the jars on their mantelpieces are always seen through the eyes of women in the room. The whole scene, however solidly and pictorially built up, is always dominated by an emotion which has nothing to do with the eye. But it is the eye that has fertilised their thought; it is the eye, in Proust above all, that has come to the help of the other senses, combined with them, and produced effects of extreme beauty and of a subtlety hitherto unknown. Here is a scene in a theatre, for example. We have to understand the emotions of a young man for a lady in a box below. With an abundance of images and comparisons we are made to appreciate the forms, the colours, the very fibre and texture of the plush seats and the ladies' dresses and the dullness or glow, sparkle or colour, of the light. At the same time that our senses drink in all this our minds are tunnelling, logically and intellectually, into the obscurity of the young man's emotions which, as they ramify and modulate and stretch further and further, at last penetrate so far, peter out into such a shred of meaning, that we can scarcely follow any more, were it not that suddenly, in flash after flash, metaphor after metaphor, the eye lights up that cave of darkness, and we are shown the hard, tangible, material shapes of bodiless thoughts hanging like bats in the primeval darkness where light has never visited them before.

A writer thus has need of a third eye whose function it is to help out the other senses when they flag. But it is extremely doubtful whether he learns anything directly from painting. Indeed, it would seem to be true that writers are of all critics of painting the worst — the most prejudiced, the most distorted in their judgements; if we accost them in picture galleries, disarm their suspicions, and get them to tell us honestly what it is that pleases them in pictures, they will confess that it is not the art of painting in the least. They are not there to understand the problems of the painter's art. They are after something that may be helpful to themselves. It is only thus that they can turn these long galleries from torture chambers of boredom and despair into smiling avenues, pleasant places filled with birds, sanctuaries where silence reigns supreme. Free to go their own way, to pick and choose at their will, they find modern pictures, they say, very helpful, very stimulating. Cézanne, for example — no painter is more provocative to the literary sense, because his pictures are so audaciously and provocatively content to be paint and not words that the very pigment, they say, seems to challenge us, to press on some nerve, to stimulate, to excite. That picture, for example, they explain (standing before a rocky landscape, all cleft in ridges of opal colour as if by a giant's hammer, silent, solid, serene), stirs words in us where we had not thought words to exist; suggests forms where we had never seen anything but thin air. As we gaze, words begin to raise their feeble limbs in the pale border land of no man's language, to sink down again in despair. We fling them like nets upon a rocky and inhospitable shore; they fade and disappear. It is vain, it is futile; but we can never resist the temptation. The silent painters, Cézanne and Mr Sickert,[4] make fools of us as often as they choose.

But painters lose their power directly they attempt to speak. They must say what they have to say by shading greens into blues, posing block upon block. They must weave their spells like mackerel behind the glass at the aquarium, mutely, mysteriously. Once let them raise the glass and begin to speak and the spell is broken. A story-telling picture is as pathetic and ludicrous as a trick played by a dog, and we applaud it only because we know that it is as hard for a painter to tell a story with his brush as it is for a sheep dog to balance a biscuit on its nose. Dr Johnson at the Mitre is much better told by Boswell; in paint Keats's nightingale is dumb; with half a sheet of notepaper we can tell all the stories of all the pictures in the world.

Nevertheless, they admit, moving round the gallery, even when they do not tempt us to the heroic efforts which have produced so many abortive monsters, pictures are very pleasant things. There is a great deal to be learnt from them. That picture of a wet marsh on a blowing day shows us much more clearly than we could see for ourselves the greens and silvers, and sliding streams, the gusty willows shivering in the wind, and sets us trying to find phrases for them, suggests even a figure lying there among the bulrushes, or coming out at the farmyard gate in top boots and mackintosh. That still life, they proceed, pointing to a jar of red-hot pokers, is to us what a beefsteak is to an invalid – an orgy of blood and nourishment, so starved we are on our diet of thin black print. We nestle into its colour, feed and fill ourselves with yellow and red and gold, till we drop off, nourished and content. Our sense of colour seems miraculously sharpened. We carry those roses and red-hot pokers about with us for days, working them over again in words. From a portrait, too, we get almost always something worth having – somebody's room, nose, or hands, some little effect of character or circumstance, some knick-knack to put in our pockets and take away. But again, the portrait painter must not attempt to speak; he must not say, 'This is maternity; that intellect'; the utmost he must do is to tap on the wall of the room, or the glass of the aquarium; he must come very close, but something must always separate us from him.

There are artists, indeed, who are born tappers; no sooner do we see a picture of a dancer tying up her shoe by Degas[5] than we exclaim, 'How witty!' exactly as if we had read a speech by Congreve. Degas detaches a scene and comments upon it exactly as a great comic writer detaches and comments, but silently, without for a moment infringing the reticence of paint. We laugh, but not with the muscles that laugh in reading. Mlle Lessore[6] has the same rare and curious power. How witty her circus horses are, or her groups standing with field-glasses gazing, or her fiddlers in the pit of the orchestra! How she quickens our sense of the point and gaiety of life by tapping on the other side of the wall! Matisse taps; Derain taps; Mr Grant taps; Picasso, Sickert, Mrs Bell,[7] on the other hand, are all mute as mackerel.

But the writers have said enough. Their consciences are uneasy. No one knows better than they do, they murmur, that this is not the way to look at pictures; that they are irresponsible dragon-flies, mere insects, children wantonly destroying works of art by pulling petal from petal. In short, they had better be off, for here, oaring his way through the waters, mooning, abstract, contemplative, comes a painter, and, stuffing their pilferings into their pockets, out they bolt, lest they should be caught at their mischief and made to suffer the most extreme of penalties, the most exquisite of tortures – to be made to look at pictures with a painter.

1–An essay in the *N&A*, 25 April 1925, (Kp C262) also published in *NR*, 13 May 1925. The same issue of the *N&A* contained: LW's 'World of Books' column, on 'The Religion of a ——', discussing Bertrand Russell's *What I Believe* (1925), Sir Arthur Keith's *The Religion of a Darwinist* (1925) and J. Arthur Thomson's *Science and Religion* (1925); and an article by Edwin Muir, on 'Lytton Strachey'.
2–Marcel Proust (1871–1922); Henri Matisse (1869–1954); Paul Cézanne (1839–1906); André Derain (1880–1954); Pablo Picasso (1881–1973).
3–Thomas Hardy (1840–1928); Gustave Flaubert (1821–80); Joseph Conrad (1857–1924).

4–Walter Sickert (1860–1942).
5–Edgar Degas (1834–1917).
6–Thérèse Lessore (1884–1944), who married Sickert in 1926.
7–Duncan Grant (1885–1978); Vanessa Bell (1879–1961).

'What the Bloods of the 'Nineties Used to Say . . .'

What the bloods of the 'nineties used to say in mockery is now a commonplace of the staid and prosaic – that, if you wish to enjoy your evening and at the same time sample British acting at its best, you must go not to the playhouses, but to the Music Halls. In that free atmosphere of short turns and individual humours the English genius seems to flower most spontaneously, and to appreciate its own flowers most genuinely. At the Coliseum last week,[2] Joe Jackson, the tramp cyclist, rocked a whole house into good humour by hitching up his trousers and scratching his head – that is to say, by something so personal and private to himself that no ordinary farce could fail to extinguish it utterly. The statuesque Flemings looked as noble as marble busts, and proved themselves as supple as eels. In its brazen and lawless way Mr Birmingham's brass band blared and crashed towards some object – we are not sure what – far off in the future of music; while no one could sit under the torrent of Spanish vociferated to the click of castanets by Spanish dancers in crimson and silver without feeling the Southern sun hot on his cheeks. But the most notable triumph was that of Madame Lopokova and M. Idzikowski in 'The Postman'. They have danced in more ambitious pieces, but in none that has so drawn out the marrow of their charm. Credit is due, of course, to Beethoven, to Mr Grant, and to Mr Williams.[3] But our heaviest debt is to Madame Lopokova who, as she weaves round the pillar-box all the drama of the letter that was posted, regretted, and retrieved, bewitched the audience almost as much by her dramatic power as by her dancing – if, indeed, dramatic is the word to apply to a performance as effortless and as gay as the tossing of a bunch of spring flowers from the stage to the stalls. Dressed as a bright green postman riding a red bicycle, M.

Idzikowski has never coruscated and corkscrewed with greater brilliance or with an appearance of more consummate ease.

1–A note in the column 'From Alpha to Omega', N&A, 25 April 1925, (Kp C262.1).
2–In *The Times*, 18 April 1925, was announced the following bill at the Coliseum, Charing Cross, twice daily at 2.30 and 7.45: '"Women and Flowers of Spain", A Choreographic and Lyrical Fantasy by Casimir Jiralt and Jose Vinas. / Joe Jackson. The Original Comedy Tramp Cyclist. / Lydia Lopokova with Stanislav Idzikowski in a Ballet Comedy "The Postman". / Mr and Mrs Moffat in the Scottish Playlet "Till the Bells Ring". / John Birmingham and his Band: "The Big Twelve"'. There is no mention of the 'statuesque Flemings'.
3–Lydia Lopokova (1891–1981), the Russian ballerina, was the following August to marry Maynard Keynes. Stanislav Idzikowski (1894–1972), Polish dancer. Duncan Grant (1885–1978). Mr Williams, unidentified.

'A Player Under Three Reigns'

One of the first actors of our time, it is surprising to learn, gave up his profession with joy, and filled up all his leisure moments painting pictures. 'Rarely, very rarely,' writes Sir Johnston Forbes-Robertson, 'have I enjoyed myself in acting . . . I am persuaded, as I look back upon my career, that I was not temperamentally suited to my calling.'[2] Indeed, throughout his modest and charming book he speaks with far more relish of the painters and writers he has known than of his dramatic friends; there is a glamour over his Bohemian days, when he met Rossetti and Swinburne and Millais,[3] which dissolves in the limelight. He lingers over his youth, and recalls with joy that sturdy art student at Heatherly's who could never get into the Academy and worshipped Handel and Shakespeare, and one day thrust *Erewhon* into his hand, and the delight with which he was able to tell Butler, 'Sam, my people say you are a great writer!'[4] Later we meet Mr Walter Sickert[5] as a lifeboatman volunteering to rescue a distressed ship, but more intent upon the look of the waves than upon his oar. And then the usual tours and triumphs begin, but over all the writer passes quietly and composedly as though he would much rather have painted a picture that looked so like the real thing that the birds pecked his fruit (his standards are not sophisticated), than have been the greatest Hamlet of his time.

1–A notice in the *N&A*, 25 April 1925, (Kp C262.2) of *A Player Under Three Reigns* (Fisher Unwin Ltd, 1925) by Sir Johnston Forbes-Robertson (1853–1937) who studied painting at the Royal Academy Schools but for financial reasons turned to acting. He made his reputation relatively early, as Hamlet, at the Lyceum Theatre in 1897, and retired from the stage in 1913.
2–Forbes-Robertson, ch. xv, p. 288.
3–D. G. Rossetti (1828–82); A. C. Swinburne (1837–1909); J. E. Millais (1829–96).
4–For the quotation, Forbes-Robertson, ch. iv, p. 54. Samuel Butler (1835–1902), *Erewhon* (1872).
5–Walter Sickert (1860–1942).

'The Tragic Life of Vincent Van Gogh'

Since the standard life of van Gogh by Meier-Graefe is beyond most pockets, the present translation of M. Piérard's more modest biography is welcome. Several reproductions of pictures are given, but M. Piérard refrains purposely from aesthetic criticism. He has been able indeed to throw new light upon some obscure places, and the life is strange enough and tragic enough to be worth reading, were there no question of the genius of the artist. For here we have the astonishing spectacle of an entirely uncompromising man. Van Gogh believed what Christ said, and, therefore, he cut up his clothes and gave them to the poor. He thought that picture-dealing was robbery, and, therefore, though he was employed by the firm, he stood up in the middle of Messrs Goupil's shop and told them so.[2] He gave up being a schoolmaster to preach religion among the working men of London. His expenditure upon Bibles was so great that his father, a Dutch Minister, had to put a stop to it. Whatever he did, 'his excess of zeal bordered on scandal'.[3] When late in life he settled down to paint pictures, where, perhaps, zeal was less reprehensible, he painted with such intensity that he finished them with incredible quickness and the paint was so thick 'that it ran off the canvas on to the polished floor'.[4] Again, the authorities were horrified. Soon symptoms of madness showed themselves. He cut off his own ear, and is said to have threatened to kill Gauguin.[5] The peasants of Arles made mock of him, and, at length, having spent his life in 'a frantic desire for the absolute', he ended it with his own hands, remarking: 'Ah, well, my work – I risked my life for it, and my reason has almost foundered.'[6]

1–A notice in the *N&A*, 9 May 1925, (Kp C262.3) of *The Tragic Life of Vincent Van Gogh* [1853–90] (John Castle, 1925) by Louis Piérard, trans. Herbert Garland. The standard life referred to in VW's opening sentence is: Julius Meier-Graefe, *Vincent* (1912; Eng. trans. *Vincent Van Gogh*, 1922).
2–Piérard, ch. i, p. 17. Goupil Brothers, international firm of art dealers, for whom Van Gogh worked, at The Hague, in London and in Paris, 1869–76.
3–*Ibid.*, ch. vi, p. 51.
4–*Ibid.*, ch. xv, p. 92.
5–Paul Gauguin (1848–1903).
6–For the first quotation, Piérard, Intro., p. 2, and for the second, *ibid.*, ch. xviii, p. 117.

Gipsy or Governess?

There can be no doubt that the same fate awaits Mrs Asquith (if we may still use the familiar name) that has already befallen so many of her sisters in the past. Every age boasts a few of these dominating figures, like Madame du Deffand, the Duchess of Devonshire, Lady Hester Stanhope,[2] who survive not in their works but perhaps more immortally in their charm, their wit, or in some strange combination of opposite qualities which fascinates us against our expectation and out of all proportion to our sense of fitness. That Mrs Asquith's reign was long and her empire vast is indisputable. Open any memoir of Victorian worthies, the lives of Tennyson, Jowett, Gladstone, Symonds;[3] by all these men Mrs Asquith was lectured, praised, blamed, and petted. Open any volume of social reminiscence; there is Mrs Asquith again, brilliant, outrageous, adored. To all these people she meant something vital, individual; she was unlike anybody else in the world. Nor are we, though of a later generation and kept at arm's length by the printed page, impervious to the vibration of this extraordinary personality. As we turn the pages

of her latest book we find ourselves at the old game of trying to
determine of what parts this composite power is composed.

'A mixture of city clerk or post office woman and a wandering
circus girl' – that is her own contribution to the problem. With a
gipsy's love of the open air and bright colours and 'making love in
the sun',[4] she has a stringent business woman's dislike of dirt,
discomfort, and unpunctuality. There is truth in this, for Mrs
Asquith is singularly truthful, but one word could with advantage
be changed; Mrs Asquith has more of the governess in her than of
the clerk. As we hear her scolding and praising and laying down the
law, we feel that we are all once more in the nursery and Mrs
Asquith is sending some into the corner, giving others marks for
good behaviour, and holding forth, with all the conviction and
asperity of a governess whose schoolroom is her world, upon the
sins of greed, untidiness, upsetting the inkpot, and being late for
prayers. Here is a lecture upon *If Winter Comes*: 'If we cared
enough . . . we all have it in us to develop some of Sabre's qualities,
but we must be equally independent of public opinion, equally
tolerant, and, above all, equally selfless and loving.'[5] Or here are a
few maxims to be written out five hundred times between tea and
bedtime: 'To stick to an opinion is the privilege of fools . . . To pursue war after conquest is to invite contempt . . . There are many
signs of the Cross, could we but see them.'[6] It is with a start that we
remember that these are not schoolroom commonplaces, but the
opinions and reflections of a woman who has seen as much of the
world and known as much of mankind as any woman of her time.
But the governess, we must remember is mixed with the gipsy. One
may change the quality of a glass of cold water completely by dropping into it one small white pellet. Drop a tabloid of gipsy into a
pint of governess and the result is the most exhilarating of potions.
Great men drink and are intoxicated, though it is probable that if
Jowett had had a lesson in Plato, or Gladstone in politics, or Tennyson in poetry from the governess pure and simple, he would have
crushed his hat over his eyes and fled in the opposite direction. But
when the governess rode like a bird, dressed like an angel, and had
the courage of a hero, the shallowness of her philosophy and the
crudity of her criticism could be forgiven.

Vitality of the utmost elasticity and toughness Mrs Asquith undoubtedly possesses. And if she has the defects of that quality – its
impatience, its self-assurance, its inability to stop and think, so that

of all the characters she has described there is none that is known to us intimately – she has too its courage, its recklessness, its ecstasy in the mere fact of living, which is infectious even in print. 'I think you have more social courage than anyone I ever saw in my life,'[7] said her mother. And indeed it needed something more than courage to be Miss Margot Tennant in the year 1891 – to dance with her casta-nets on the deck of a Nile steamer; to gallop over the desert with her skirt pinned up, but 'showing more ankle than the safety pin had guaranteed'; to have tea with Lord Athlumney in his room; to let Major Lewis kiss your hand and say 'I was the most wonderful per-son he had ever met – gay, kind and true, and a delight to be with';[8] to have a mind of your own on art, religion, politics; to correspond with Mr Asquith, Oscar Wilde, Mr Rodd, Mr Algernon West;[9] to be bitingly frank about your parents and yet remain on the best of terms with them; to burst into the most sacred enclosures of English society with a nose that 'will always be more of a limb than a feature'[10] and no ancestors to speak of; to be, in short, as much of a pioneer of woman's freedom as any educationist or suffragist, and with it all to enjoy life to the core. Irreticent to a degree which makes her irreticence sublime, childishly convinced that the world is interested in all the sayings and doings of her aunts and grand-children, marching indomitably up to St Peter's, or Michael Angelo, or Mr Hutchinson, and delivering her verdict, pugnacious, un-daunted, irrepressible, Mrs Asquith remains, indeed, as she says of the Tennants, of 'a race apart'. But the last word is with the gipsies and not with the governesses: 'They said I would always be young enough to make love and inspire it, and that I was unmercenary and of a kindly disposition.'[11]

1–A review in the N&A, 16 May 1925, (Kp C262.4) of *Places & Persons* (Thorn-ton Butterworth Ltd, 1925) by Margot Asquith. Emma Alice Margaret, Countess of Oxford and Asquith, *née* Tennant (1864–1945), daughter of Charles and Emma Tennant, and a member of the group known as the 'Souls'. In 1894 she married the Liberal statesman and prime minister Herbert Henry Asquith (1852–1928), as his second wife. *The Autobiography of Margot Asquith* was published in two volumes, in 1920 and 1922.

'No, I can't fire it off; Mrs Asquith sticks in my gullet,' VW wrote in her diary on Monday, 4 May 1925, 'I shall read [George] Moore till dinner, & a paper then again till Leonard comes in.' For descriptions of Margot Asquith, whom VW met and who had known VW's parents, see *II VW Diary*, 4 June 1923, and *IV VW Diary*, 9 March 1931. See also 'The Governess of Downing Street' below.

The same issue of the *N&A* contained: LW's 'World of Books' column, on 'Mr Belloc', discussing Hilaire Belloc's *The Cruise of the Nona*.

2–Madame du Deffand (1697–1780); Georgiana, Duchess of Devonshire (1757–1806); Lady Hester Stanhope (1776–1839), for VW on whom see *I VW Essays*.

3–Alfred, Lord Tennyson (1809–92); Benjamin Jowett (1817–93); W. E. Gladstone (1809–98); John Addington Symonds (1840–93), for VW on whom see above.

4–For both quotations, Asquith, 'A Little Journey to Egypt, 1891', ch. iii, p. 38, which has: 'make love in the sun'.

5–*Ibid.*, 'Impressions of America, 1922', ch. vii, p. 110. A. S. M. Hutchinson, *If Winter Comes* (1921).

6–*Ibid.*, 'My Visit to Italy in 1924', ch. iii, p. 240, which has no comma after 'Cross'.

7–*Ibid.*, 'A Little Journey to Egypt, 1891', ch. v, p. 73.

8–For the first quotation, *ibid.*, ch. iv, p. 55, and for the second, *ibid.*, p. 56. Lord Athlumney and Major Lewis, otherwise unidentified, were both British officers stationed at Assouan in Egypt.

9–Oscar Wilde (1856–1900); James Rennell Rodd, later first Baron Rennell (1858–1941), diplomatist and scholar, and a friend of Wilde; Sir Algernon Edward West (1832–1921), civil servant.

10–Asquith, 'Impressions of America, 1922', ch. iii, p. 85.

11–For the first quotation, *ibid.*, p. 92, and for the second, *ibid.*, p. 93.

'Celebrities of Our Times'

For fifteen years Mr Bernstein has been in the habit of putting pistol-shots at the heads of great men – What do you think of the future of America? What is your opinion of the Jews? What are the qualities of a work of art? – and the great men have obligingly shouted their answers to these questions through the megaphone of Mr Bernstein's brain. The present volume is the result. We hear Tolstoy saying that Russia should at once put into practice the views of Henry George; declaring that his artistic works are insignificant; prophesying that Darwinism will be laughed at in two or three hundred years; lamenting that almost all modern writers are 'full of enormous self-conceit'.[2] Next, Mr Shaw, pressing on Tolstoy's heels, remarks that *What is Art?* is a 'very silly little book ... Tolstoy was a prodigious genius ... but he was devoid of any humour or fun. That's why he could not understand me.' As for America, 'there is nothing there that can interest me ... When America will be a real American nation ... when the American's skin turns red and his forehead recedes, then it will be interesting to go to America.'[3] Rodin takes up the story. 'Genius is order personified ... Sculpture and architecture belong together ... It seems to be a peculiarity of our time to put works of sculpture in the wrong place.'[4] So they go on, these thirty-two famous men, capping and contradicting each other till we feel that we must seek shelter from the storm of dogma in any simple shelter, if only that of the evening paper.

1–A notice in the *N&A*, 16 May 1925, (Kp C262.5) of *Celebrities of Our Times* (Hutchinson and Co., 1925) by Herman Bernstein.
2–Bernstein, 'Leo Tolstoy', p. 14. Leo Tolstoy (1828–1920); Henry George (1839–97), American political economist, author of *Progress and Poverty* (1879) and *The Land Question* (1883).
3–For George Bernard Shaw (1856–1950) on Tolstoy's *What Is Art?* (1898), and on America, see Bernstein, 'Bernard Shaw', pp. 102 and 103, respectively. The ellipsis between 'me' and 'When' does not represent a lacuna in the text, which is at this point continuous.
4–For Auguste Rodin (1840–1917) on genius, *ibid.*, 'Auguste Rodin', p. 122, and for the remainder, p. 114.

Harriette Wilson

Across the broad continent of a woman's life falls the shadow of a sword. On one side all is correct, definite, orderly; the paths are strait, the trees regular, the sun shaded; escorted by gentlemen, protected by policemen, wedded and buried by clergymen, she has only to walk demurely from cradle to grave and no one will touch a hair of her head. But on the other side all is confusion. Nothing follows a regular course. The paths wind between bogs and precipices. The trees roar and rock and fall in ruin. There, too, what strange company is to be met – in what bewildering variety! Stone-masons hobnob with Dukes of the blood royal – Mr Blore treads on the heels of His Grace the Duke of Argyll. Byron rambles through, the Duke of Wellington[2] marches in with all his orders on him. For in that strange land gentlemen are immune; any being of the male sex can cross from sun to shade with perfect safety. In that strange land money is poured out lavishly; bank-notes drop on to breakfast plates; pearl rings are found beneath pillows; champagne flows in fountains; but over it all broods the fever of a nightmare and the transiency of a dream. The brilliant fade; the great mysteriously disappear; the diamonds turn to cinders, and the Queens are left sitting on three-legged stools shivering in the cold. That great Princess, Harriette Wilson, with her box at the Opera and the Peerage at her feet, found herself before she was fifty reduced to solitude, to poverty, to life in foreign parts, to marriage with a Colonel,[3] to scribbling for cash whatever she could remember or invent of her past.

Nevertheless it would be a grave mistake to think that Harriette repented her ways or would have chosen another career had she had the chance. She was a girl of fifteen when she stepped across the sword and became, for reasons which she will not specify, the mistress of the Earl of Craven.[4] A few facts leak out later. She was educated at a convent and shocked the nuns. Her parents had fifteen children; their home was 'truly uncomfortable';[5] her father was a Swiss with a passion for mathematics, always on the point of solving a problem, and furious if interrupted; while the unhappiness of her parents' married life had decided Harriette before she was ten 'to live free as air from any restraint but that of my own conscience'.[6] So she stepped across. And at once, the instant her foot touched those shifting sands, everything wobbled; her character, her principles, the world itself – all suffered a sea change. For ever after (it is one of the curiosities of her memoirs – one of the obstacles to any certain knowledge of her character) she is outside the pale of ordinary values and must protest till she is black in the face, and run up a whole fabric of lies into the bargain, before she can make good her claim to a share in the emotions of human kind. Could an abandoned woman love a sister, could a mere prostitute grieve genuinely for a mother's death? Mr Thomas Seccombe, in the *Dictionary of National Biography*, had his doubts. Harriette Wilson, he said, described her sister's death 'with an appearance of feeling', whereas to Mr Seccombe Lord Hertford's kindness in soothing the same creature's last hours was indisputably genuine.[7]

Outcast as she was, her position had another and an incongruous result. She was impelled, though nothing was further from her liking than serious thought, to speculate a little curiously about the law of society, to consult, with odd results, the verdict of 'my own conscience'. For example, the marriage-law – was that as impeccably moral as people made out? 'I cannot for the life of me divest myself of the idea that if all were alike honourable and true, as I wish to be, it would be unnecessary to bind men and women together by law, since two persons who may have chosen each other from affection, possessing heart and honour, could not part, and where there is neither the one nor the other, even marriage does not bind. My idea may be wicked or erroneous,'[8] she adds hastily, for what could be more absurd than that Harriette Wilson should set herself up as a judge of morality – Harry, as the gentlemen called her, whose only rule of conduct was 'One wants a little variety in life',[9] who left one man because he bored her, and another because he drew pictures of cocoa-trees on vellum paper, and seduced poor young Lord Worcester, and went off to Melton Mowbray with Mr Meyler,[10] and, in short, was the mistress of any man who had money and rank and a person that took her fancy? No, Harriette was not moral, nor refined, nor, it appears, very beautiful, but merely a bustling bouncing vivacious creature with good eyes and dark hair and 'the manners of a wild schoolboy', said Sir Walter Scott,[11] who had dined in her presence. But it cannot be doubted – otherwise her triumph is inexplicable – that gifts she had, gifts of dash and go and enthusiasm, which still stir among the dead leaves of her memoirs and impart even to their rambling verbosity and archness and vulgarity some thrill of that old impetuosity, some flash of those fine dark eyes, some fling of those wild schoolboy manners which, when furbished up in plumes and red plush and diamonds, held our ancestors enthralled.

She was, of course, always falling in love. She saw a stranger riding with a Newfoundland dog in Knightsbridge and lost her heart to his 'pale expressive beauty' at once. She venerated his door-knocker even, and when Lord Ponsonby – [12] for Lord Ponsonby it was – deserted her, she flung herself sobbing on a doorstep in Half Moon Street and was carried, raving and almost dying, back to bed. Large and voluptuous herself, she loved for the most part little men with small hands and feet, and, like Mr Meyler, skins of remarkable transparency, 'churchyard skins', foreboding perhaps an early death; 'yet it would be hard to die, in the bloom of youth and beauty, beloved by everybody, and with thirty thousand a year'.[13] She loved, too, the Apollo Belvedere, and sat entranced at the Louvre, exclaiming in ecstasy at the 'quivering lips – the throat!', till it seemed as if she must share the fate of another lady who sat by the Apollo, 'whom she could not warm, till she went raving mad, and in that state died'.[14] But it is not her loves that distinguish her; her passions tend to become perfunctory; her young men with fine skins and large fortunes innumerable; her rhapsodies and recriminations monotonous. It is when off duty, released from the necessity of painting the usual picture in the usual way, that she becomes capable of drawing one of those pictures which only seem to await some final stroke to become a page in *Vanity Fair* or a sketch by Hogarth.[15] All the materials of comedy seem heaped in disorder before us as she, the most notorious woman in London, retires to Charmouth to await the return of her lover, Lord Worcester, from the Spanish wars, trots to church on the arm of the curate's aged father, or peeps from her window at the rustic beauties of Lyme Regis tripping down to the sixpenny Assembly Rooms with 'turbans or artificial flowers twined around the wigs'[16] to dance at five in the evening on the shores of the innocent sea. So a famous prima donna, hidden behind a curtain in strict incognito, might listen to country girls singing a rustic ballad with contempt and amusement, and a dash of envy too, for how simply the good people accepted her. Harriette could not help reflecting how kindly they sympathised with her anxiety about her husband at the wars, and sat up with her to watch for the light of the postwoman's lanthorn as she came late at night over the hill from Lyme Regis with letters from Mr Wilson in Spain! All she could do to show her gratitude was to pay twice what they asked her, to shower clothes upon ragged children, to mend a poor countrywoman's roof, and then, tired of the role of Lady Bountiful, she was off to join Lord Worcester in Spain.

Now, for a moment, before the old story is resumed, sketched with a stump of rapid charcoal, springs into existence, to fade for ever after, the figure of Miss Martha Edmonds, her landlady's sister. 'I am old enough,' exclaimed the gallant old maid, 'and thank God I am no beauty ... I have never yet been ten miles from my native place, and I want to see the world.'[17] She declared her intention of escorting Mrs Wilson to Falmouth; she had her ancient habit made up for the purpose. Off they started, the old maid and the famous courtesan, to starve and freeze in an upper room of a crowded Falmouth inn, the winds being adverse, until in some mysterious way Mrs Wilson got into touch first with the Consul and then with the Captain, who were so hospitable, so generous, so kind, that Aunt

Martha bought a red rose for her cap, drank champagne, took a hand at cards, and was taught to waltz by Mr Brown.[18] Their gaieties were cut short, however; a letter demanded Mrs Wilson's instant presence in London, and Aunt Martha, deposited in Charmouth, could only regret that she had not seen something of life a little sooner, and declare that there 'was a boldness and grandeur about the views in Cornwall which far exceeded anything she had seen in Devonshire'.[19]

Involved once more with Meylers, Lornes, Lambtons, Berkeleys, Leicesters,[20] gossiping as usual in her box at the Opera about this lady and that gentleman, letting young noblemen pull her hair, tapping late at night at Lord Hertford's[21] little private gate in Park Lane, Harriette's life wound in and out among the bogs and precipices of the shadowy underworld which lies on the far side of the sword. Occasionally the jingling and junketing was interrupted by a military figure; the great Duke himself, very like a ratcatcher in his red ribbon, marched in; asked questions; left money; said he remembered her; had dreamed of her in Spain. 'I dreamed you came out on my staff,'[22] he said. Or there was Lord Byron sitting entirely alone, dressed in brown flowing robes at a masquerade, 'bright, severe, beautiful', demanding 'in a tone of wild and thrilling despondency "Who shall console us for acute bodily anguish?"'[23] Or again the spangled curtain goes up and we see those famous entertainers the sisters Wilson sitting at home at their ease, sparring and squabbling and joking about their lovers; Amy, who adored black puddings; good-natured Fanny, who doted upon donkey-riding; foolish Sophie, who was made a Peeress by Lord Berwick and dropped her sisters; Moll Raffles, Julia, niece to Lord Carysfort[24] and daughter to a maid of honour with the finest legs in Europe – there they sit gossiping profanely and larding their chatter with quotations from Shakespeare and Sterne. Some died prematurely; some married and turned virtuous; some became villains, sorceresses, serpents, and had best be forgotten; while as for Harriette herself, she was scandalously treated by the Beauforts,[25] had to retire to France with her Colonel, would continue to tell the truth about her fine friends so long as they treated her as they did, and grew, we cannot doubt, into a fat good-humoured disreputable old woman who never doubted the goodness of God or denied that the world had treated her well, or regretted, even when the darkness of obscurity and poverty blotted her entirely from view, that she had lived her life on the shady side of the sword.

1—A signed essay in the *N&A*, 13 June 1925, (Kp C263), reprinted with very slight, chiefly punctuational alterations, as: 'On the Wrong Side of the Sword', *NR*, 24 June 1925, and based on *The Memoirs of Harriette Wilson* [1789–1846] *Written by Herself* (2 vols, Navarre Society Ltd, 1924). VW later used James Laver's edition of the *Memoirs* (Peter Davies, 1929), to research her essay 'Beau Brummell', *N&A*, 28 September 1929; see *V VW Essays*. The same issue of the *N&A* contained: LW's 'World of Books' column on 'Canning', discussing *The Foreign Policy of Canning 1822–1827* by Harold Temperley; an article by Bertrand Russell, on 'The Dogmas of Naturalism'; and Thomas Hardy's poem, 'Coming Up Oxford Street: Evening'. See Editorial Note, p. xxv. Reprinted: *Mom*, *CE*.

2—Mr Blore, stonemason of Piccadilly, brought an action against Harriette Wilson, who claimed he had made her a proposal of marriage (see Wilson, vol. i, ch. xvii, p. 334), upon the original publication of her *Memoirs* in 1825, and was awarded £300 damages. George William Campbell, 6th Duke of Argyll (1766–1839). Lord Byron (1788–1824). Arthur Wellesley, Duke of Wellington (1769–1852).

3—Wilson, vol. i, prefatory note, p. 3, states that after 1825 'very little is known . . . beyond the fact that she lived abroad and married a Colonel Rochfort, with whom she resided for a time at 111 Rue du Faubourg, St Honoré, Paris.'

4—Wilson opens her memoirs, *ibid.*, ch. i, p. 5: 'I shall not say why and how I became at the age of fifteen, the mistress of the Earl of Craven.' William Craven, 7th Baron, cr. Earl 1801 (1770–1825).

5—*Ibid.*, ch. viii, p. 146.

6—*Ibid.*, ch. ii, p. 25, which has: 'my conscience'.

7—The relevant passage in the *DNB* entry by Thomas Seccombe (1866–1923) reads: 'Among the sisters . . . may be mentioned Fanny, who lived for many years as Mrs Parker, but whose last hours (described by Harriette with an appearance of feeling) were soothed by Lord Hertford (Thackeray's "Marquis of Steyne") . . .'

8—Wilson, vol. ii, ch. xxix, from an undated letter to Richard Meyler, p. 490, which has: 'and, where'.

9—*Ibid.*, ch. xxviii, p. 472.

10—Henry Somerset, Marquis of Worcester, subsequently 7th Duke of Beaufort (1792–1853), aide-de-camp to the Duke of Wellington, 1812–14, MP for Monmouth, 1813–32. Richard William Meyler: 'a young Hampshire gentleman, in the possession of a very large West India property' (Wilson, vol. ii, ch. xxv, p. 442).

11—Wilson, vol. i, prefatory note, p. 3, quoting Sir Walter Scott's journal, 9 December 1825. (The description is also quoted by Seccombe in the *DNB*.)

12—For the quotation, *ibid.*, ch. iv, p. 65. John, Viscount Ponsonby (1770–1855), diplomat.

13—*Ibid.*, vol. ii, ch. xxix, p. 496, which has: 'It is, in fact, a churchyard skin, like my own I think', and: 'for it would be hard to die'.

14—For both quotations, *ibid.*, ch. xxxii, p. 553, which has 'Apollo Belvidere'. Wilson's enthusiasm for the Apollo, at least, was not singular; the figure enjoyed an enormous cult in the 18th and 19th centuries, as the epitome of classic beauty.

15—W. M. Thackeray, *Vanity Fair* (1847–8); William Hogarth (1697–1764).

16—Wilson, vol. ii, ch. xxviii, p. 483. The subsequent epithet 'innocent' is, as we might expect, VW's. Wilson has: 'They were very pleasantly situated near the sea . . .'

17–*Ibid.*, ch. xxx, p. 510.

18–Dominic Brown, 'a great, big, stupid Irishman' (*ibid.*, vol. i, ch. xv, p. 290).

19–*Ibid.*, vol. ii, ch. xxx, p. 512.

20–The Marquis of Lorne, i.e. the Duke of Argyll, see note 2. Mr Lambton, 'the little curly-headed Opposition man, second son of Lady Ann Wyndham' (*ibid.*, vol. i, ch. xi, p. 214). Colonel Berkeley and his brother Augustus, otherwise unidentified. No member of the Leicester family has been traced in Wilson; VW may have intended Leinster, Augustus Frederick, 3rd Duke, who figured considerably in Wilson's affairs.

21–Francis Charles Seymour-Conway, 3rd Marquis of Hertfort (1777–1842), see also note 7.

22–Wilson, vol. i, ch. ix, p. 163.

23–For the first quotation concerning Byron, *ibid.*, vol. ii, ch. xxxviii, p. 616, which has: 'His whole countenance so bright, severe, and beautiful, that I should have been afraid to have loved him'; and for the second, *ibid.*, p. 622, adapted.

24–Of Wilson's sisters: Amy, having been mistress to Count Palmella, the Portuguese ambassador, married Robert Nicolas Charles Bochsa, described in the *DNB* as a 'disreputable musician'; Fanny, lived for some years as Mrs Parker with one Colonel Parker, but latterly enjoyed the support of Lord Hertford (see note 7). Sophia married, in 1812, Thomas Noel Hill, 2nd Baron Berwick (1770–1832).

Moll Raffles, otherwise unidentified; Julia Storer, niece of John Proby, 1st Baron Carysfort (1720–72), was a lifelong friend of Wilson.

25–Laurence Sterne (1713–68). The Beauforts, parents of the Marquis of Worcester, opposed their son's liaison with Wilson and tried by various means to separate them, including granting her an annuity. Finally she was brought before the King's Bench, to swear that she had honestly listed all the Marquis's letters to her, had retained none of them, nor delivered any to a third person.

George Moore

The only criticism worth having at present is that which is spoken, not written – spoken over wine glasses and coffee cups late at night, flashed out on the spur of the moment by people passing who have not time to finish their sentences, let alone consider the dues of editors or the feelings of friends. Above living writers these talkers (it is one of their most engaging peculiarities) are always in violent disagreement. Take George Moore, for example. George Moore is the best living novelist – and the worst; writes the most beautiful prose of his time – and the feeblest; has a passion for literature which none of those dismal pundits, his contemporaries, shares; but how whimsical his judgements are, how ill-balanced, childish and egotistical, into the bargain! So they hammer the horseshoe out; so the sparks fly; and the worth of the criticism lies not so much in the accuracy of each blow as in the heat it engenders, the sense it kindles that the matter of George Moore and his works is of the highest importance, which, without waiting another instant, we must settle for ourselves.

Perhaps it is not accident only, but a vague recollection of dipping and dallying in *Esther Waters, Evelyn Innes, The Lake*,[2] which makes us take down in its new and stately form *Hail and Farewell* (Heinemann) – the two large volumes which George Moore has written openly and directly about himself. For all his novels are written, covertly and obliquely, about himself, so at least memory would persuade us, and it may help us to understand them if we steep ourselves in the pure waters which are elsewhere tinged with fictitious flavours. But are not all novels about the writer's self, we might ask? It is only as he sees people that we can see them; his fortunes colour and his oddities shape his vision until what we see is not the thing itself, but the thing seen and the seer inextricably mixed. There are degrees, however. The great novelist feels, sees, believes with such intensity of conviction that he hurls his belief outside himself and it flies off and lives an independent life of its own, becomes Natasha, Pierre, Levin, and is no longer Tolstoy.[3] When, however, Mr Moore creates a Natasha she may be charming, foolish, lovely, but her beauty, her folly, her charm are not hers but Mr Moore's. All her qualities refer to him. In other words, Mr Moore is completely lacking in dramatic power. On the face of it, *Esther Waters* has all the appearance of a great novel; it has sincerity, shapeliness, style; it has surpassing seriousness and integrity; but because Mr Moore has not the strength to project Esther from himself its virtues collapse and fall about it like a tent with a broken pole. There it lies, this novel without a heroine, and what remains of it is George Moore himself, a ruin of lovely language and some exquisite descriptions of the Sussex downs. For the novelist who has no dramatic power, no fire of conviction within, leans upon nature for support; she lifts him up and enhances his mood without destroying it.

But the defects of a novelist may well be the glories of his brother the autobiographer, and we find, to our delight, that the very qualities which weaken Mr Moore's novels are the making of his

memoirs. This complex character, at once diffident and self-assertive, this sportsman who goes out shooting in ladies' high-heeled
boots, this amateur jockey who loves literature beyond the apple of
his eye, this amorist who is so innocent, this sensualist who is so
ascetic, this complex and uneasy character, in short, with its lack of
starch and pomp and humbug, its pliability and malice and shrewdness and incompetence, is made of too many incompatible elements
to concentrate into the diamond of a great artist, and is better occupied in exploring its own vagaries than in explaining those of other
people. For one thing, Mr Moore is without that robust belief in
himself which leads men to prophesy and create. Nobody was ever
more diffident. As a little boy they told him that only an ugly old
woman would marry him, and he has never got over it. 'For it is difficult for me to believe any good of myself. Within the oftentimes
bombastic and truculent appearance that I present to the world
trembles a heart shy as a wren in the hedgerow or a mouse along the
wainscotting.'⁴ The least noise startles him, and the ordinary pro-
ceedings of mankind fill him with wonder and alarm. Their streets
have so many names: their coats have so many buttons; the ordinary business of life is altogether beyond him. But with the timidity
of the mouse he has also its gigantic boldness. This meek grey innocent creature runs right over the lion's paws. There is nothing
that Mr Moore will not say; by his own confession he ought to be
excluded from every drawing-room in South Kensington. If his
friends forgive him it is only because to Mr Moore all things are forgiven. Once when he was a child, 'inspired by an uncontrollable
desire to break the monotony of infancy,' he threw all his clothes
into a hawthorn tree and 'ran naked in front of my nurse or governess screaming with delight at the embarrassment I was causing
her.'⁵ The habit has remained with him. He loves to take off his
clothes and run screaming with delight at the fuss and blush and
embarrassment which he is causing that dear old governess, the
British Public. But the antics of Mr Moore, though impish and impudent, are, after all, so amusing and so graceful that the governess,
it is said, sometimes hides behind a tree to watch. That scream of
his, that garrulous chuckle as of small birds chattering in a nest, is a
merry sound; and then how melodiously he draws out his long
notes when dusk descends and the stars rise! Always you will find
him haunting the evening, when the downs are fading into waves of
silver and the grey Irish fields are melting into the grey Irish hills.

The storm never breaks over his head, the thunder never roars in his ears, the rain never drenches him. No; the worst that befalls him is that Teresa has not filled the Moderator lamp sufficiently full, so that the company which is dining in the garden under the apple tree must adjourn to the dining-room, where Mr Osborne, Mr Hughes, Mr Longworth, Mr Seumas O'Sullivan, Mr Atkinson and Mr Yeats are awaiting them.[6]

And then in the dining-room, Mr Moore sitting down and offering a cigar to his friends, takes up again the thread of that interminable discourse, which, if it lapses into the gulfs of reverie for a moment, begins anew wherever he finds a bench or chair to sit on or can link his arm in a friend's, or can find even some discreet sympathetic animal who will only occasionally lift a paw in silence. He talks incessantly about books and politics; of the vision that came to him in the Chelsea road; how Mr Colville[7] bred Belgian hares on the Sussex downs; about the death of his cat; the Roman Catholic religion; how dogma is the death of literature; how the names of poets determine their poetry; how Mr Yeats is like a crow, and he himself has been forced to sit on the window sill in his pyjamas. One thing follows another; out of the present flowers the past; it is as easy, inconsequent, melodious as the smoke of those fragrant cigars. But as one listens more attentively one perceives that while each topic floats up as easily as cigar smoke into the air, the blue wreaths have a strange fixity; they do not disperse, they unite; they build up the airy chambers of a lifetime, and as we listen in the Temple Gardens, in Ebury Street, in Paris, in Dublin to Mr Moore talking we explore from start to finish, from those earliest days in Ireland to these latest in London, the habitation of his soul.

But let us apply Mr Moore's own test to Mr Moore's own work. What interests him, he says, is not the three or four beautiful poems that a man may have written, but the mind that he brings into the world; and 'by a mind I mean a new way of feeling and seeing.'[8] When the fierce tide of talk once more washes the battlements of Mr Moore's achievements let us throw into mid-stream these remarks; not one of his novels is a masterpiece; they are silken tents which have no poles; but he has brought a new mind into the world; he has given us a new way of feeling and seeing; he has devised – very painfully, for he is above all things painstaking, eking out a delicate gift laboriously – a means of liquidating the capricious and volatile essence of himself and decanting it in these memoirs; and that, whatever the degree, is triumph, achievement, immortality. If, further, we try to establish the degree we shall go on to say that no one so inveterately literary is among the great writers; literature has wound itself about him like a veil, forbidding him the free use of his limbs; the phrase comes to him before the emotion; but we must add that he is nevertheless a born writer, a man who detests meals, servants, ease, respectability or anything that gets between him and his art; who has kept his freedom when most of his contemporaries have long ago lost theirs; who is ashamed of nothing but of being ashamed; who says whatever he has it in his mind to say, and has taught himself an accent, a cadence, indeed a language, for saying it in which, though they are not English, but Irish, will give him his place among the lesser immortals of our tongue.

1 – A signed review in *Vogue*, early June 1925, (Kp C263.1) of *Hail and Farewell!* (2 vols, William Heinemann Ltd, 1925) by George Moore (1852–1933), whose autobiography, here collected in two volumes, was originally published as *Ave* (1911), *Salve* (1912) and *Vale* (1914). The review carried a sub-heading: '"Hail and Farewell" Contains the Volatile Essence of a/Complex Character and an Inveterately Literary Man'. For thumbnail sketches of Moore see VW's diary entries for 9 March 1926 and 15 May 1929. See also 'Winged Phrases' and 'A Born Writer', *III VW Essays*. Reprinted *DoM*, *CE*.
2 – *Esther Waters* (1894), subject of VW's review 'A Born Writer'; *Evelyn Innes* (1898); *The Lake* (1905).
3 – Natasha Rostov and Pierre Bezuhov, characters in *War and Peace* (1865–72), and Konstantin Levin, character in *Anna Karenina* (1875–6), by L. N. Tolstoy (1828–1910).
4 – Moore, vol. i, 'Ave', II, p. 71, which has: 'World, trembles'.
5 – *Ibid.*, p. 92, which has: 'governess, screaming'.
6 – Walter Osborne (1859–1903), painter; John Hughes (1864–d. ?), taught at the Dublin School of Art up until 1902 and died in impoverished obscurity in Paris; E. V. Longworth, a Dublin barrister; Seumas O'Sullivan, pseudonym of Dr James Sullivan Starkey (1879–1958), poet; F. MacCurdy Atkinson, an associate of Longworth, otherwise unidentified; W. B. Yeats (1865–1939).
7 – Otherwise unidentified.
8 – Moore, vol. ii, 'Salve', xv, p. 43.

'The Tale of Genji'

Our readers will scarcely need to be reminded that it was about the year 991 that Aelfric composed his Homilies, that his treatises upon the Old and New Testament were slightly later in date, and that both works precede that profound, if obscure, convulsion which set Swegen of Denmark upon the throne of England.[2] Perpetually fighting, now men, now swine, now thickets and swamps, it was with fists swollen with toil, minds contracted by danger, eyes stung with smoke and feet that were cold among the rushes that our ancestors applied themselves to the pen, transcribed, translated and chronicled, or burst rudely, and hoarsely into crude spasms of song.

> Sumer is icumen in,
> Lhude sing cuccu[3]

– such is their sudden harsh cry. Meanwhile, at the same moment, on the other side of the globe the Lady Murasaki was looking out into her garden, and noticing how 'among the leaves were white flowers with petals half unfolded like the lips of people smiling at their own thoughts'.[4]

While the Aelfrics and the Aelfreds croaked and coughed in England, this court lady, about whom we know nothing, for Mr Waley artfully withholds all information until the six volumes of her novel are before us, was sitting down in her silk dress and trousers with pictures before her and the sound of poetry in her ears, with flowers in her garden and nightingales in the trees, with all day to talk in and all night to dance in – she was sitting down about the year 1000 to tell the story of the life and adventures of Prince Genji.[5] But we must hasten to correct the impression that the Lady Murasaki was in any sense a chronicler. Since her book was read aloud, we may imagine an audience; but her listeners must have been astute, subtle minded, sophisticated men and women. They were grown-up people, who needed no feats of strength to rivet their attention; no catastrophe to surprise them. They were absorbed, on the contrary, in the contemplation of man's nature; how passionately he desires things that are denied; how his longing for a life of tender intimacy is always thwarted; how the grotesque and the fantastic excite him beyond the simple and straightforward; how beautiful the falling snow is, and how, as he watches it, he longs more than ever for someone to share his solitary joy.

The Lady Murasaki lived, indeed, in one of those seasons which are most propitious for the artist, and, in particular, for an artist of her own sex. The accent of life did not fall upon war; the interests of men did not centre upon politics. Relieved from the violent pressure of these two forces, life expressed itself chiefly in the intricacies of

behaviour, in what men said and what women did not quite say, in
poems that break the surface of silence with silver fins, in dance and
painting, and in that love of the wildness of nature which only
comes when people feel themselves perfectly secure. In such an age
as this Lady Murasaki, with her hatred of bombast, her humour,
her common sense, her passion for the contrasts and curiosities of
human nature, for old houses mouldering away among the weeds
and the winds, and wild landscapes, and the sound of water falling,
and mallets beating, and wild geese screaming, and the red noses of
princesses, for beauty indeed, and that incongruity which makes
beauty still more beautiful, could bring all her powers into play
spontaneously. It was one of those moments (how they were
reached in Japan and how destroyed we must wait for Mr Waley to
explain) when it was natural for a writer to write of ordinary things
beautifully, and to say openly to her public. 'It is the common that is
wonderful, and if you let yourselves be put off by extravagance and
rant and what is surprising and momentarily impressive you will be
cheated of the most profound of pleasure.'[6] For there are two kinds
of artists, said Murasaki: one who makes trifles to fit the fancy of
the passing day, the other who 'strives to give real beauty to the
things which men actually use, and to give to them the shapes which
tradition has ordained.' How easy it is, she said, to impress and surprise; 'to paint a raging sea monster riding a storm'[7] – any toy
maker can do that, and be praised to the skies. 'But ordinary hills
and rivers, just as they are, houses such as you may see anywhere,
with all their real beauty and harmony of form – quietly to draw
such scenes as this, or to show what lies behind some intimate hedge
that is folded away far from the world, and thick trees upon some
unheroic hill, and all this with befitting care for composition, proportion, and the like – such works demand the highest master's
utmost skill and must needs draw the common craftsman into a
thousand blunders.'[8]

Something of her charm for us is doubtless accidental. It lies in
the fact that when she speaks of 'houses such as you may see anywhere' we at once conjure up something graceful, fantastic,
decorated with cranes and chrysanthemums, a thousand miles removed from Surbiton and the Albert Memorial. We give her, and
luxuriate in giving her, all those advantages of background and
atmosphere which we are forced to do without in England today.
But we should wrong her deeply if, thus seduced, we prettified and

sentimentalised an art which, exquisite as it is, is without a touch of decadence, which, for all its sensibility, is fresh and childlike and without a trace of the exaggeration or languor of an outworn civilisation. But the essence of her charm lies deeper far than cranes and chrysanthemums. It lies in the belief which she held so simply – and was, we feel, supported in holding by Emperors and waiting maids, by the air she breathed and the flowers she saw – that the true artist 'strives to give real beauty to the things which men actually use and to give to them the shapes which tradition has ordained'. On she went, therefore, without hesitation or self-consciousness, effort or agony, to tell the story of the enchanting boy – the Prince who danced 'The Waves of the Blue Sea'[9], so beautifully that all the princes and great gentlemen wept aloud; who loved those whom he could not possess; whose libertinage was tempered by the most perfect courtesy; who played enchantingly with children, and preferred, as his women friends knew, that the song should stop before he had heard the end. To light up the many facets of his mind, Lady Murasaki, being herself a woman, naturally chose the medium of other women's minds. Aoi, Asagao, Fujitsubo, Murasaki, Yugao, Suyetsumuhana,[10] the beautiful, the red-nosed, the cold, the passionate – one after another they turn their clear or freakish light upon the gay young man at the centre, who flies, who pursues, who laughs, who sorrows, but is always filled with the rush and bubble and chuckle of life.

Unhasting, unresting, with unabated fertility, story after story flows from the brush of Murasaki. Without this gift of invention we might well fear that the tale of Genji would run dry before the six volumes are filled. With it, we need have no such foreboding. We can take our station and watch, through Mr Waley's beautiful telescope, the new star rise in perfect confidence that it is going to be large and luminous and serene – but not, nevertheless, a star of the first magnitude. No; the lady Murasaki is not going to prove herself the peer of Tolstoy and Cervantes[11] or those other great story-tellers of the Western world whose ancestors were fighting or squatting in their huts while she gazed from her lattice window at flowers which unfold themselves 'like the lips of people smiling at their own thoughts'. Some element of horror, of terror, or sordidity, some root of experience has been removed from the Eastern world so that crudeness is impossible and coarseness out of the question, but with it too has gone some vigour, some richness, some maturity of the human spirit, failing which the gold is silvered and the wine mixed with water. All comparisons between Murasaki and the great Western writers serve but to bring out her perfection and their force. But it is a beautiful world; the quiet lady with all her breeding, her insight and her fun, is a perfect artist; and for years to come we shall be haunting her groves, watching her moons rise and her snow fall, hearing her wild geese cry and her flutes and lutes and flageolets tinkling and chiming, while the Prince tastes and tries all the queer savours of life and dances so exquisitely that men weep, but never passes the bounds of decorum, or relaxes his search for something different, something finer, something withheld.

1 – A signed review in *Vogue*, late July 1925, (Kp C264) of *The Tale of the Genji by Lady Murasaki*, translated from the Japanese by Arthur Waley [1889–1966] (vol. i, George Allen and Unwin Ltd, 1925). VW had met Waley, an acquaintance of Bloomsbury, at a recent dinner party, and found him 'a little demure and discreet' (*III VW Letters*, no. 1553 to Desmond MacCarthy, 17 May 1925). On 14 June she noted in her diary that she '. . . must answer Gerald Brenan, & read the Genji, for tomorrow I make a second £20 from Vogue;' and wrote that day to Brenan, urging him to: 'Put this letter where it deserves to be, in Mrs Levey's earth closet; I would not send it, if I could write a better, but it is not possible, not in this perfectly divine heat. I'm reading Waley's Japanese novel and David Copperfield' (*III VW Letters*, no. 1560).
2 – Aelfric, called Gramaticus (d. c. 1020), 'Homilies' (990–2), 'A Treatise on the Old and New Testaments' (1005–12). Aelfred (849–901), king of the West Saxons (871–901). Swegen or Svein or Sweyn (c. 960–1014), king of Denmark, 986–1014, son of Harold Bluetooth, father of Canute, became king of England in 1013 upon the capitulation of Aethelred the Unready but died before he could be crowned.
3 – Anonymous lyric of the earlier part of the 13th century, the second line quoted here being generally given as: 'Lhude sing! cuccu.'
4 – Waley, vol. i, p. 93. Lady Shikibu Murasaki (c. 978–?1031).
5 – According to Waley (Appendix I, p. 297) Book I of Murasaki's tale was read to the Emperor in 1008.
6 – This passage does not occur in Waley and has not been discovered elsewhere.
7 – For both quotations, Waley, ch. ii, 'The Broom-Tree', p. 49, which has 'striving to give', 'actually use and to give' and: 'One paints the Mountain of Hōrai; another a raging sea-monster riding a storm; another, ferocious animals from the land beyond the sea, or faces of imaginary demons. Letting their fancy run wildly riot they have no thought of beauty, but only of how best they may astonish the beholder's eye.'
8 – *Ibid.*, p. 50, which has: 'like, – such work,'.
9 – For the account of this episode, *ibid.*, ch. vii, 'The Festival of the Red Leaves', p. 211.
10 – Princess Aoi was Genji's first wife. Princess Asagao resisted his attempts to court her. Fujitsubo was the Emperor's consort and an aunt of Murasaki. Yūgao

became a mistress of Genji. Princess Suyetsumuhana was, according to Waley (p. 12) 'A timid and eccentric lady'.

11–L. N. Tolstoy (1828–1910); Miguel Cervantes Saavedra (1547–1616).

American Fiction

Excursions into the literature of a foreign country much resemble our travels abroad. Sights that are taken for granted by the inhabitants seem to us astonishing; however well we seemed to know the language at home, it sounds differently on the lips of those who have spoken it from birth; and above all, in our desire to get at the heart of the country we seek out whatever it may be that is most unlike what we are used to, and declaring this to be the very essence of the French or American genius proceed to lavish upon it a credulous devotion, to build up upon it a structure of theory which may well amuse, annoy, or even momentarily enlighten those who are French or American by birth.

The English tourist in American literature wants above all things something different from what he has at home. For this reason the one American writer whom the English whole-heartedly admire is Walt Whitman. There, you will hear them say, is the real American undisguised. In the whole of English literature there is no figure which resembles his – among all our poetry none in the least comparable to *Leaves of Grass*.[2] This very unlikeness becomes a merit, and leads us, as we steep ourselves in the refreshing unfamiliarity, to become less and less able to appreciate Emerson, Lowell, Hawthorne,[3] who have had their counterparts among us and drew their culture from our books. The obsession, whether well or ill founded, fair or unfair in its results, persists at the present moment. To dismiss such distinguished names as those of Henry James, Mr Hergesheimer, and Mrs Wharton[4] would be impossible; but their praises are qualified with the reservation – they are not Americans; they do not give us anything that we have not got already.

Thus having qualified the tourist's attitude, in its crudity and one-sidedness, let us begin our excursion into modern American fiction by asking what are the sights we ought to see. Here our bewilderment begins; for the names of so many authors, the titles of so many

books, rise at once to the lips. Mr Dreiser, Mr Cabell, Miss Canfield, Mr Sherwood Anderson, Miss Hurst, Mr Sinclair Lewis, Miss
Willa Cather, Mr Ring Lardner[5] – all have done work which, if time
allowed, we should do well to examine carefully, and, if we must
concentrate upon two or three at most, it is because, travellers and
tourists as we are, it seems best to sketch a theory of the tendency of
American fiction from the inspection of a few important books
rather than to examine each writer separately by himself. Of all
American novelists the most discussed and read in England at the
present moment are probably Mr Sherwood Anderson and Mr Sinclair Lewis. And among all their fiction we find one volume, *A Story
Teller's Story*,[6] which, being fact rather than fiction, may serve as
interpreter, may help us to guess the nature of American writers'
problems before we see them tussled with or solved. Peering over
Mr Sherwood Anderson's shoulder, we may get a preliminary view
of the world as it looks to the novelist before it is disguised and
arranged for the reception of his characters. Indeed, if we look over
Mr Anderson's shoulder, America appears a very strange place.
What is it that we see here? A vast continent, scattered here and
there with brand-new villages which Nature has not absorbed into
herself with ivy and moss, summer and winter, as in England, but
man has built recently, hastily, economically, so that the village is
like the suburb of a town. The slow English wagons are turned into
Ford cars; the primrose banks have become heaps of old tins; the
barns, sheds of corrugated iron. It is cheap, it is new, it is ugly, it is
made of odds and ends, hurriedly flung together, loosely tied in temporary cohesion – that is the burden of Mr Anderson's complaint.
And, he proceeds to ask, how can the imagination of an artist take
root here, where the soil is stony and the imagination stubs itself
upon the rocks? There is one solution and one only – by being re-
solutely and defiantly American. Explicitly and implicitly that is the
conclusion he reaches; that is the note which turns the discord to
harmony. Mr Anderson is forever repeating over and over like a
patient hypnotising himself, 'I am the American man.'[7] The words
rise in his mind with the persistency of a submerged but fundamental desire. Yes, he is the American man; it is a terrible misfortune; it is an enormous opportunity; but for good or for bad, he
is the American man. 'Behold in me the American man striving to
become an artist, to become conscious of himself, filled with wonder concerning himself and others, trying to have a good time and

not fake a good time. I am not English, Italian, Jew, German, Frenchman, Russian. What am I?'[8] Yes, we may be excused for repeating, what is he? One thing is certain – whatever the American man may be he is not English; whatever he may become, he will not become an Englishman.

For that is the first step in the process of being American – to be not English. The first step in the education of an American writer is to dismiss the whole army of English words which have marched so long under the command of dead English generals. He must tame and compel to his service the 'little American words;'[9] he must forget all that he learnt in the school of Fielding and Thackeray;[10] he must learn to write as he talks to men in Chicago barrooms, to men in the factories of Indiana. That is the first step; but the next step is far more difficult. For having decided what he is not, he must proceed to discover what he is. This is the beginning of a stage of acute self-consciousness which manifests itself in writers otherwise poles asunder. Nothing, indeed, surprises the English tourist more than the prevalence of this self-consciousness and the bitterness, for the most part against England, with which it is accompanied. One is reminded constantly of the attitude of another race, till lately subject and still galled by the memory of its chains. Women writers have to meet many of the same problems that beset Americans. They too are conscious of their own pecularities as a sex; apt to suspect insolence, quick to avenge grievances, eager to shape an art of their own. In both cases all kinds of consciousness – consciousness of self, of race, of sex, of civilisation – which have nothing to do with art, have got between them and the paper, with results that are, on the surface at least, unfortunate. It is easy enough to see that Mr Anderson, for example, would be a much more perfect artist if he could forget that he is an American; he would write better prose if he could use all words impartially, new or old, English or American, classical or slang.

Nevertheless as we turn from his autobiography to his fiction we are forced to own (as some women writers also make us own) that to come fresh to the world, to turn a new angle to the light, it is so great an achievement that for its sake we can pardon the bitterness, the self-consciousness, the angularity which inevitably go with it. In *The Triumph of the Egg*[11] there is some rearrangement of the old elements of art which makes us rub our eyes. The feeling recalls that with which we read Tchehov[12] for the first time. There are no familiar handles to lay hold of in *The Triumph of the Egg*. The stories baffle our efforts, slip through our fingers and leave us feeling, not that it is Mr Anderson, who has failed us, but that we as readers have muffed our work and must go back, like chastened school-children, and spell the lesson over again in the attempt to lay hold of the meaning.

Mr Anderson has bored into that deeper and warmer layer of human nature which it would be frivolous to ticket new or old, American or European. In his determination to be 'true to the essence of things'[13] he has fumbled his way into something genuine, persistent, of universal significance, in proof of which he has done what, after all, very few writers succeed in doing – he has made a world of his own. It is a world in which the senses flourish; it is dominated by instincts rather than by ideas; race horses make the hearts of little boys beat high; cornfields flow around the cheap towns like golden seas, illimitable and profound; everywhere boys and girls are dreaming of voyages and adventures, and this world of sensuality and instinctive desire is clothed in a warm cloudy atmos-phere, wrapped about in a soft caressing envelope, which always seems a little too loose to fit the shape. Pointing to the formlessness of Mr Anderson's work, the vagueness of his language, his tendency to land his stories softly in a bog, the English tourist would say that all this confirms him in his theory of what is to be expected of an American writer of insight and sincerity. The softness, the shell-lessness of Mr Anderson are inevitable since he has scooped out from the heart of America matter which has never been confined to a shell before. He is too much enamoured of this precious stuff to squeeze it into any of those old and intricate poems which the art and industry of Europe have secreted. Rather he will leave what he has found exposed, defenceless, naked to scorn and laughter.

But if this theory holds good of the work of American novelists, how then are we to account for the novels of Mr Sinclair Lewis? Does it not explode at the first touch of *Babbit* and *Main Street* and *Our Mr Wrenn*[14] like a soap bubble dashed against the edge of a hard mahogany wardrobe? For it is precisely by its hardness, its effi-ciency, its compactness that Mr Lewis's work excels. Yet he also is an American; he also has devoted book after book to the descrip-tion and elucidation of America. Far from being shell-less, however, his books, one is inclined to say, are all shell; the only doubt is whether he has left any room for the snail. At any rate Babbitt com-pletely refutes the theory that an American writer, writing about

America, must necessarily lack the finish, the technique, the power to model and control his material which one might suppose to be the bequest of an old civilisation to its artists. In all these respects, *Babbitt* is the equal of any novel written in English in the present century. The tourist therefore must make his choice between two alternatives. Either there is no profound difference between English and American writers, and their experience is so similar that it can be housed in the same form; or Mr Lewis has modelled himself so closely upon the English – H. G. Wells[15] is a very obvious master – that he has sacrificed his American characteristics in the process. But the art of reading would be simpler and less adventurous than it is if writers could be parcelled out in strips of green and blue. Study of Mr Lewis more and more convinces us that the surface appearance of downright decision is deceptive; the outer composure hardly holds together the warring elements within; the colours have run.

For though Babbitt would appear as solid and authentic a portrait of the American business man as can well be painted, certain doubts run across us and shake our conviction. But, we may ask, where all is so masterly, self-assured and confident, what foothold can there be for doubt to lodge upon? To begin with we doubt Mr Lewis himself: we doubt that is to say that he is nearly as sure of himself or of his subject as he would have us believe. For he, too, though in a way very different from Mr Anderson's way, is writing with one eye on Europe, a division of attention which the reader is quick to feel and resent. He too has the American self-consciousness though it is masterfully suppressed, and allowed only to utter itself once or twice in a sharp cry of bitterness ('Babbitt was as much amused by the antiquated provincialism as any proper Englishman by any American.'[16]). But the uneasiness is there. He has not identified himself with America; rather he has constituted himself the guide and interpreter between the Americans and the English, and, as he conducts his party of Europeans over the typical American city (of which he is a native) and shows them the typical American citizen (to whom he is related) he is equally divided between shame at what he has to show and anger at the Europeans for laughing at it. Zenith is a despicable place, but the English are even more despicable for despising it.

In such an atmosphere intimacy is impossible. All that a writer of Mr Lewis's powers can do is to be unflinchingly accurate and more and more on his guard against giving himself away. Accordingly, never was so complete a model of a city made before. We turn on the taps and the water runs; we press a button and cigars are lit and beds warmed. But this glorification of machinery; this lust for 'toothpastes, socks, tires, cameras, instantaneous hot water bottles ... at first the signs, then the substitutes for joy and passion and wisdom'[17] is only a device for putting off the evil day which Mr Lewis sees looming ahead. However he may dread what people will think of him, he must give himself away. Babbitt must be proved to possess some share in truth and beauty, some character, some emotion of his own, or Babbitt will be nothing but an improved device for running motor cars, a convenient surface for the display of mechanical ingenuity. To make us care for Babbitt – that was his problem. With this end in view Mr Lewis shamefacedly assures us that Babbitt has his dreams. Stout though he is, this elderly business man dreams of a fairy child waiting at a gate. 'Her dear and tranquil hand caressed his cheek. He was gallant and wise and well-beloved; warm ivory were her arms; and beyond perilous moors the brave sea glittered.'[18] But that is not a dream; that is simply the protest of a man who has never dreamed in his life but is determined to prove that dreaming is as easy as shelling peas. What are dreams made of – the most expensive dreams? Seas, fairies, moors? Well, he will have a little of each, and if this is not a dream, he seems to demand, jumping out of bed in a fury, what then is it? With sex relations and family affection he is much more at ease. Indeed it would be impossible to deny that if we put our ears to his shell, the foremost citizen in Zenith can be heard moving cumbrously but unmistakably within. One has moments of affection for him, moments of sympathy and even of desire that some miracle may happen, the rock be cleft asunder, and the living creature, with his capacity for fun, suffering, and happiness be set at liberty. But no; his movements are too sluggish; Babbitt will never escape; he will die in his prison bequeathing only the chance of escape to his son.

In some such way as this, then, the English tourist makes his theory embrace both Mr Anderson and Mr Sinclair Lewis. Both suffer as novelists from being American; Mr Anderson because he must protest his pride; Mr Lewis, because he must conceal his bitterness. Mr Anderson's way is the less injurious to him as an artist, and his imagination is the more vigorous of the two. He has gained more than he has lost by being the spokesman of a new country, the worker in fresh clay. Mr Lewis it would seem was meant by nature to take his place with Mr Wells and Mr Bennett,[19] and had he been born in England would undoubtedly have proved himself the equal of these two famous men. Denied however the richness of an old civilisation – the swarm of ideas upon which the art of Mr Wells has battened, the solidity of custom which has nourished the art of Mr Bennett – he has been forced to criticise rather than to explore, and the object of his criticism – the civilisation of Zenith – was unfortunately too meagre to sustain him. Yet a little reflection, and a comparison between Mr Anderson and Mr Lewis, put a different colour on our conclusion. Look at Americans as an American, see Mrs Opal Emerson Mudge as she is herself, not as a type and symbol of America displayed for the amusement of the condescending Britisher, and then, we dimly suspect, Mrs Mudge is no type, no scarecrow, no abstraction. Mrs Mudge is – but it is not for an English writer to say what. He can only peep and peer between the chinks of the barrier and hazard the opinion that Mrs Mudge and the Americans generally are, somehow, human beings into the bargain.

That suspicion suddenly becomes a certainty as we read the first pages of Mr Ring Lardner's *You Know Me, Al*,[20] and the change is bewildering. Hitherto we have been kept at arms' length, reminded constantly of our superiority, of our inferiority, of the fact, anyhow, that we are alien blood and bone. But Mr Lardner is not merely unaware that we differ; he is unaware that we exist. When a crack player is in the middle of an exciting game of baseball he does not stop to wonder whether the audience likes the colour of his hair. All his mind is on the game. So Mr Lardner does not waste a moment when he writes in thinking whether he is using American slang or Shakespeare's English; whether he is remembering Fielding or forgetting Fielding; whether he is proud of being American or ashamed of not being Japanese; all his mind is on the story. Hence all our minds are on the story. Hence, incidentally, he writes the best prose that has come our way. Hence we feel at last freely admitted to the society of our fellows.

That this should be true of *You Know Me, Al*, a story about baseball, a game which is not played in England, a story written often in a language which is not English, gives us pause. To what does he owe his success? Besides his unconsciousness and the additional power which he is thus free to devote to his art, Mr Lardner has

talents of a remarkable order. With extraordinary ease and aptitude, with the quickest strokes, the surest touch, the sharpest insight
he lets Jack Keefe the baseball player cut out his own outline, fill in
his own depths, until the figure of the foolish, boastful, innocent
athlete lives before us. As he babbles out his mind on paper there
rise up friends, sweethearts, the scenery, town, and country – all
surround him and make him up in his completeness. We gaze into
the depths of a society which goes its ways intent on its own con-
cerns. There, perhaps, is one of the elements of Mr Lardner's success. He is not merely himself intent on his own game, but his
characters are equally intent on theirs. It is no coincidence that the
best of Mr Lardner's stories are about games, for one may guess
that Mr Lardner's interest in games has solved one of the most difficult problems of the American writer; it has given him a clue, a
centre, a meeting place for the divers activities of people whom a
vast continent isolates, whom no tradition controls. Games give
him what society gives his English brother. Whatever the precise
reason, Mr Lardner at any rate provides something unique in its
kind, something indigenous to the soil, which the traveller may
carry off as a trophy to prove to the incredulous that he has actually
been to America and found it a foreign land. But the time has come
when the tourist must reckon up his expenses and experiences, and
attempt to cast up his account of the tour as a whole.

At the outset let us admit that our impressions are highly mixed
and the opinions we have come to, if anything, less definite, less
assured than those with which we started. For when we consider the
mixed origin of the literature we are trying to understand, its youth,
its age, and all those currents which are blowing across the stream
of its natural development, we may well exclaim that French is
simpler, English is simpler, all modern literatures are simpler to sum
up and understand than this new American literature. A discord lies
at the root of it; the natural bent of the American is twisted at the
start. For the more sensitive he is, the more he must read English
literature; the more he reads English literature, the more alive he
must become to the puzzle and perplexity of this great art which
uses the language on his own lips to express an experience which is
not his and to mirror a civilisation which he has never known. The
choice has to be made – whether to yield or to rebel. The more sensitive, or at least the more sophisticated, the Henry Jameses, the
Hergesheimers, the Edith Whartons, decide in favour of England

and pay the penalty by exaggerating the English culture, the traditional English good manners, and stressing too heavily or in the wrong places those social differences which, though the first to strike the foreigner, are by no means the most profound. What their work gains in refinement it loses in that perpetual distortion of values, that obsession with surface distinctions – the age of old houses, the glamour of great names – which makes it necessary to remember that Henry James was a foreigner if we are not to call him a snob.

On the other hand, the simpler and cruder writers, like Walt Whitman, Mr Anderson, Mr Masters[21] – decide in favour of America, but truculently, self-consciously, protestingly, 'showing off' as the nurses would say, their newness, their independence, their individuality. Both influences are unfortunate and serve to obscure and delay the development of the real American literature itself. But, some critics would interpose, are we not making mountains out of molehills, conjuring up distinctions where none exist? The 'real American literature' in the time of Hawthorne, Emerson, and Lowell was much of a piece with contemporary English literature, and the present movement towards a national literature is confined to a few enthusiasts and extremists who will grow older and wiser and see the folly of their ways.

But the tourist can no longer accept this comfortable doctrine, flattering though it be to his pride of birth. Obviously there are American writers who do not care a straw for English opinion or for English culture, and write very vigorously none the less – witness Mr Lardner; there are Americans who have all the accomplishment of culture without a trace of its excess – witness Miss Willa Cather; there are Americans whose aim it is to write a book off their own bat and no one else's – witness Miss Fannie Hurst. But, the shortest tour, the most superficial inspection, must impress him with what is of far greater importance – the fact that where the land itself is so different, and the society so different, the literature must needs differ and differ more and more widely as time goes by from those of other countries.

American literature will be influenced, no doubt, like all others, and the English influence may well predominate. But clearly the English tradition is already unable to cope with this vast land, these prairies, these cornfields, these lonely little groups of men and women scattered at immense distances from each other, these vast industrial cities with their skyscrapers and their night signs and their perfect organisation of machinery. It cannot extract their meaning and interpret their beauty. How could it be otherwise? The English tradition is formed upon a little country; its centre is an old house with many rooms each crammed with objects and crowded with people who know each other intimately, whose manners, thoughts, and speech are ruled all the time, if unconsciously, by the spirit of the past. But in America there is baseball instead of society; instead of the old landscape which has moved men to emotion for endless summers and springs a new land, its tin cans, its prairies, its cornfields flung disorderly about like a mosaic of incongruous pieces waiting order at the artist's hands; while the people are equally diversified into fragments of many nationalities.

To describe, to unify, to make order out of all these severed parts, a new art is needed and the control of a new tradition. That both are in the process of birth the language itself gives us proof. For the Americans are doing what the Elizabethans did – they are coining new words. They are instinctively making the language adapt itself to their needs. In England, save for the impetus given by the war, the word coining power has lapsed; our writers vary the metres of their poetry, remodel the rhythms of prose, but one may search English fiction in vain for a single new word. It is significant that when we want to freshen our speech we borrow from America – poppycock, rambunctious, flipflop, booster, good-mixer – all the expressive ugly vigorous slang which creeps into use among us first in talk, later in writing, comes from across the Atlantic. Nor does it need much foresight to predict that when words are being made, a literature will be made out of them. Already we hear the first jars and dissonances, the strangled difficult music of the prelude. As we shut our books and look out again upon the English fields a strident note rings in our ears. We hear the first lovemaking and the first laughter of the child who was exposed by its parents three hundred years ago upon a rocky shore and survived solely by its own exertions and is a little sore and proud and diffident and self-assertive in consequence and is now on the threshold of man's estate.

1–A signed essay in the *Saturday Review of Literature*, 1 August 1925, (Kp C265). VW's choice of reading for her essay was influenced by Logan Pearsall Smith (1865–1946), the American-born man of letters, who came to tea at 52 Tavistock Square on 24 January 1925 and two days later sent her Sherwood Anderson's autobiography and a collection of his stories. In his accompanying letter (MHP), Smith also mentions Willa Cather, 'Miss' Thurber, and William Dubois. VW replied: 'It is very good of you to send me the books, and to bother to make enquiries. It will be a great help to me, as I am completely at sea about Modern American Literature.

'I am sorry your visit was so disagreeable to you – one ought to leave a tea party happier not more miserable' (*III VW Letters*, no. 1527, 28 January 1925). On 8 April she prompted herself in her diary: 'I must get my American books in order'; and on the 19th she reflected: 'It is now after dinner, our first summer time night, & the mood for writing has left me, only just brushed & left me. I have not achieved my sacred half hour yet. But think – in time to come I would rather read something here than reflect that I did polish off Mr Ring Lardner successfully. I'm out to make £300 this summer by writing . . . But, hush, hush – my books tremble on the verge of coming out, & my future is uncertain.' See also 'An Essay in Criticism' below, and see 'Emerson's Journals', *I VW Essays*, 'Thoreau', *II VW Essays*. Reprinted *Mom, CE*.

2 – Walt Whitman (1819–92), *Leaves of Grass* (1855). For VW on Whitman see 'Melodious Meditations', 'Visits to Walt Whitman', *II VW Essays*.

3 – Ralph Waldo Emerson (1803–82), for VW on whom see 'Emerson's Journals', *I VW Essays*; James Russell Lowell (1819–91), who was VW's 'godfather'; Nathaniel Hawthorne (1804–64).

4 – Henry James (1843–1916), for VW on whom see 'Mr Henry James's Latest Novel', *I VW Essays*; 'The Old Order', '*The Method of Henry James*', *II VW Essays*; 'Within the Rim', 'The Letters of Henry James', 'Henry James's Ghost Stories', *III VW Essays*. Joseph Hergesheimer (1880–1954), for VW on whom see '*The Three Black Pennys*', *II VW Essays*; '*Java Head*', '*Gold and Iron*', 'The Pursuit of Beauty' and 'Pleasant Stories', *III VW Essays*. Edith Wharton (1862–1937), for VW on whom see '*The House of Mirth*', *I VW Essays*.

5 – Theodore Dreiser (1871–1945), Thomas Branch Cabell (1879–1958), Dorothy Canfield (1879–1958), Sherwood Anderson (1876–1941), Fannie Hurst (1889–1968), Sinclair Lewis (1885–1951), Willa Cather (1876–1947), Ring Lardner (1885–1933).

6 – Sherwood Anderson, *A Story Teller's Story* (1924).

7 – Anderson, *A Story Teller's Story* (Jonathan Cape Ltd, 1925), Book III, Note II, p. 307.

8 – *Ibid.*

9 – *Ibid.*, Book IV, Note I, p. 360, which has: 'I had smiled to myself a little at the sudden realisation of how little native American words had been used by American story-writers. When most American writers wanted to be very American they went in for slang. Surely we American scribblers had paid long and hard for the English blood in our veins . . . Words as commonly used in our writing were in reality an army that marched in a certain array and the generals in command of the army were still English.'

10 – Henry Fielding (1707–54); W. M. Thackeray (1811–63).

11 – Sherwood Anderson, *The Triumph of the Egg, and other stories* (1921).

12 – Anton Chekhov (1860–1904).

13 – Anderson, *A Story Teller's Story*, Book I, Note VIII, p. 100.

14 – Sinclair Lewis, *Babbitt* (1922), *Main Street* (1920), *Our Mr Wrenn* (1914).

15 – H. G. Wells (1866–1946), to whom allusion is made in *Babbitt* (with an introduction by Hugh Walpole; Eveleigh Nash and Grayson Ltd, 1922), ch. 19, 3, p.

239: 'It was after the third drink that Sir Gerald proclaimed, "How do you Yankees get the notion that writing chaps like Bertrand [sic] Shaw and this Wells represent us? The real business England, we think those chaps are traitors."'
16—*Ibid.*, ch. 6, 1, p. 74: 'Whenever Thompson twanged "Put your John Hancock on that line," Babbitt was as much amused . . . He knew himself to be of a breeding altogether more aesthetic and sensitive than Thompson's.'
17—*Ibid.*, ch. 7, 3, p. 99, which has 'hot-water heaters'.
18—*Ibid.*, 6, p. 105.
19—Arnold Bennett (1867–1931), for VW on whom see 'Books and Persons', *II VW Essays*; 'Mr Bennett and Mrs Brown', 'Character in Fiction', *III VW Essays*.
20—Ring Lardner, *You Know Me, Al* (1916).
21—Edgar Lee Masters (1869–1950), for VW on whom see 'A Talker', *II VW Essays*.

'Pattledom'

One day in the early years of the nineteenth century a corpse burst the coffin in which it was contained on the deck of an East India-man and shot high into the air. The sailors, it is said, had drunk the embalming spirit dry; the widow, it is said, died of the shock. What remains of certainty is that the corpse was the corpse of James Pat-tle; that his widow was a French lady whose father had been page to Marie Antoinette and was exiled to India after the Revolution; that they left six daughters of surpassing beauty and one daughter of un-doubted genius; and that without James Pattle a great many ladies of beauty and charm and wit and character, including Lady Trou-bridge herself, would never have existed.[2] From how gifted, if eccentric, a stock Lady Troubridge is sprung we are made aware in the first and most amusing chapters of her recollections. For the seven daughters of that indomitable corpse ruled a Victorian empire, and to be a small child in the heart of Pattledom (as Sir Henry Taylor[3] christened the sisters' dominion) was a fascinating if bewildering experience. Half French, half English, they were all ex-citable, unconventional, extreme in one form or another, all of a distinguished presence, tall, impressive, and gifted with a curious mixture of shrewdness and romance. No domestic detail was too small for their attention, no flight too fantastic for their daring. In the fervour of hospitality – and they could scarcely spend a day without company – a new window would be thrown out in a dark room to cheer an invalid's fancy; in the fervour of religion a laundry would be set up to wash the surplices of choir and clergy. Now Tennyson would be contradicted at his own table; now chased into his tower by Mrs Cameron, who stood at the bottom of the steps vociferating 'Coward! Coward!'[4] until he slunk down and submitted himself to vaccination. Lady Troubridge, the daughter of a Gurney and a Prinsep, was brought up in the very heart of the sisterhood in the Prinseps' home at Little Holland House. From her childish angle she there beheld innumerable garden parties, and Watts and Tennyson and Meredith and Ellen Terry, until the rambling old house with its many gables and lawns was cut up into a street of villas, and the Prinseps and their troop of friends and relations departed for Freshwater.[5] It was then that photography added a new element of excitement to their lives. With the enthusiasm of her race, Mrs Cameron quickly became the best amateur photographer of her time, converted hen-houses into dark rooms, and parlourmaids into princesses. Setting sail in old age to visit her sons in Ceylon, she was last seen tipping porters with photographs in default of small change, while her coffin – for she was of opinion that the coffins of Ceylon were undependable – was borne before her stuffed with the family china. 'They seem to me now,' writes Lady Troubridge, 'like grown-up children, with their superabundant energy, their untempered enthusiasms, their strangle-hold on life, their passionate loves and hates.'[6] It is strange to think, she adds, that all this energy and beauty are forgotten; yet something of their vitality remains. For though in the later chapters she has to deal with stirring times and people of importance, they do not compare for fun and vitality with those early years which she spent in the company of the daughters of the indomitable corpse.

1–A review in the N&A, 1 August 1925, (Kp C265.1) of *Memories and Reflections* (Heinemann, 1925) by Lady Troubridge. See also 'Julia Margaret Cameron' below. The same issue of the N&A also contained: LW's 'World of Books' column on 'Every Man's One Good Book', reflections occasioned by *My Circus Life* by James Lloyd and *Fifty Years of Sport* by Lt Col. E. D. Miller; and an article by Clive Bell on 'Landmarks in Modern Art. VI. Syncretism'.
2–James Pattle (1775–1845) of the Bengal Civil Service, had married Adeline (1793–1945), daughter of Antoine, Chevalier de L'Étang and Thérèse Blin de Grincourt. Their seven daughters were: Adeline (Mackenzie, 1812–36); Julia Margaret (Cameron, 1815–79); Sarah (Prinsep, 1816–87), grandmother of Laura, Lady

Troubridge (who married Sir Thomas Troubridge, her first cousin); Maria (Jackson, 1818–92), grandmother of Virginia Woolf; Louisa (Bayley, 1821–73); Virginia (Somers, 1827–1910); and Sophia (Dalrymple, 1829–1911).
3 – Sir Henry Taylor (1800–86), whose relations with Pattledom may be discovered in his two-volume *Autobiography* (1885).
4 – Troubridge, ch. ii, p. 38: '"You are a coward, Alfred, a coward," she called to him, repeating the word "coward" at intervals until he gave way, when she made room for the doctor to pass her and the deed was done.' Alfred, Lord Tennyson (1809–92).
5 – Lady Troubridge's parents were Charles Gurney and Alice Prinsep, daughter of Henry Thoby Prinsep (1793–1878), who, at the age of eighty, when he could no longer attend the meetings of the East India Council, sold Little Holland House to developers, and, together with his wife Sarah and their friend George Frederic Watts (1817–1904), removed to The Briary, Freshwater, Isle of Wight. George Meredith (1828–1909); Ellen Terry (1847–1928).
6 – Troubridge, ch. ii, p. 38, which has: 'They seem to me now, these dear dead people, like grown-up children . . .'

'Unknown Essex'

The best way to know Essex is to have a yacht and a sketch-book. Your yacht will infallibly stick on a mudbank; you will have to wait many hours for the tide to float you off again; and then if you are Mr Maxwell you pull out your paints and paper and produce one of those charming pictures which, whatever their artistic merits, seem to prove that Essex is a country famous for the height of its mountains and the size of its lakes. It has also vast forests, romantic castles, and houses lately inhabited by famous authors. Getting at last on shore, Mr Maxwell leads us by easy stages in and out of Mucking Flats, to Horning-on-the-Hill and Hockley and Pleshey and Helions Bumpstead, so called after one Tihellus Brito, who held it at the Domesday Survey. Mr Maxwell, in short, without being an enthusiast, puts forward quite good reasons why, if you like marshes, flat country, very old houses, tumbledown castles, scenery which is plain but modest, fine sunsets, and extremely odd names, you should discover Essex. But take a sketch-book and Mr Maxwell with you; the yacht is bound to stick on the mudbank.

1 – A notice in the *N&A*, 8 August 1925, (Kp C265.2) of *Unknown Essex. Being a series of unmethodical Explorations of the County illustrated in line and colour by the Author*. (Bodley Head Ltd, 1925) by Donald Maxwell.

'In My Anecdotage'

Mr Elliot's book, as his title gives warning, belongs to that marked class of autobiography which scarcely mentions the writer's life or opinions save as they serve as pegs for innumerable stories. He does not know men and women: he knows anecdotes about them. He does not discuss the stage; he tells stories about actors. As his stories are almost wholly humorous, we bring away an impression that all his life has been gay and all his merriment unspoilt by a single touch of malice, satire, or ill-temper. 'I do not know any scandalous tales of a blackmailing kind about *my* friends,'[2] he says. And it is true. His friends – and he has known actors, painters, sportsmen, men of the world – have been given to practical jokes rather than to more sinister tricks. Sir Herbert Beerbohm Tree dressed up as Pierpont Morgan; Mr Grossmith impersonated one of the wax-works in Madame Tussaud's Chamber of Horrors; Mr Elliot himself pulled Mr Allan's[3] chair from under him – so it goes on, facetious, irrepressible, simple-minded. It is all very readable and laughable; but it does sometimes occur to the reader to wish that Mr Elliot were not so modest, and could believe that a few plain facts about himself would be a relief from this long, varied, sprightly process of good stories about other people.

1–A notice in the *N&A*, 8 August 1925, (Kp C265.3) of *In My Anecdotage* (Philip Allan & Co., 1925) by W. G. Elliot.
2–Elliot, ch. xii, p. 269.
3–Sir Herbert Beerbohm Tree (1853–1917), actor-manager; John Pierpont Morgan (1837–1913), banker, philanthropist and art collector; Weedon Grossmith (1852–1919), co-author of *The Diary of a Nobody* (1892) and author of several plays; Charles Allan, otherwise unidentified.

'Time, Taste, and Furniture'

A third of the ill-temper of the world, Mr Gloag believes, 'may be set down to unrestful surroundings'.[2] Now in England, with all its conflict of tradition, 'surroundings' are very likely to be unrestful. There is Sheraton[3] clashing with Stuart; there is the snob who wants

a bare outline, and the fleshly who want padded repose. In short, it
is extremely difficult even for the rich to furnish a room so that the
artistic and the practical desires are gratified. But Mr Gloag's
admirable book, with its photographs and drawings, should make
their lot easier. He is no mere antiquary. He remarks: 'It is as well to
remember that there has been both good and bad work in the past,
and that it matters very little if at all, so far as appearance is concerned, whether a piece of furniture is a genuine antique or a faithful reproduction of an old model. The *design* of the article is the
vital point.'[4] These beliefs lead him to devote much space and many
illustrations to twentieth-century furniture – to the work of men
who died yesterday or are still with us, so that perhaps for the first
time we can compare Gimson with Hepplewhite and Ambrose
Heal[5] with those nameless eighteenth-century designers who have
absorbed our sympathies, often to the detriment of the living. He
boldly states that 'during the first quarter of the twentieth century
we have had at work a group of original designers far more brilliantly inventive than any of the fashion-dominated furniture
makers of the long Georgian period'.[6] And accordingly the chapters
devoted to the moderns are the best in the book.

1 – A notice in the *N&A*, 15 August 1925, (Kp C265.4) of *Time, Taste and Furniture* (Grant Richards, 1925) by John Gloag, illustrated with drawings by E. J.
Warne and reproductions from photographs.
2 – Gloag, Part III, ch. ii, p. 265.
3 – Thomas Sheraton (1751–1806).
4 – Gloag, Introduction, p. 13, adapted.
5 – Ernest Gimson (1864–1919), George Heppelwhite (d. 1786), Sir Ambrose Heal
(1872–1959).
6 – Gloag, Part II, ch. iii, p. 225.

'David Copperfield'

Like the ripening of strawberries, the swelling of apples, and all
other natural processes, new editions of Dickens – cheap, pleasant-
looking, well printed – are born into the world and call for no more
notice than the season's plums and strawberries, save when by some
chance the emergence of one of these masterpieces in its fresh, green

binding, suggests an odd and overwhelming enterprise – that one should read *David Copperfield* for the second time. There is perhaps no person living who can remember reading *David Copperfield* for the first time. Like *Robinson Crusoe* and Grimm's *Fairy Tales* and the Waverley Novels, *Pickwick*² and *David Copperfield* are not books, but stories communicated by word of mouth in those tender years when fact and fiction merge, and thus belong to the memories and myths of life, and not to its aesthetic experience. When we lift it from this hazy atmosphere, when we consider it as a book, bound and printed and ordered by the rules of art, what impression does *David Copperfield* make upon us? As Peggotty and Barkis, the rooks and the workbox with the picture of St Paul's, Traddles who drew skeletons, the donkeys who would cross the green, Mr Dick and the Memorial, Betsey Trotwood and Jip and Dora and Agnes and the Heeps and the Micawbers once more come to life with all their appurtenances and peculiarities, are they still possessed of the old fascination, or have they in the interval been attacked by that parching wind which blows about books and, without our reading them, remodels them and changes their features while we sleep? The rumour about Dickens is to the effect that his sentiment is disgusting and his style commonplace; that in reading him every refinement must be hidden and every sensibility kept under glass; but that with these precautions and reservations, he is of course Shakespearean; like Scott a born creator; like Balzac prodigious in his fecundity;³ but, rumour adds, it is strange that while one reads Shakespeare and one reads Scott, the precise moment for reading Dickens seldom comes our way.

This last charge may be resolved into this – that he lacks charm and idiosyncrasy, is everybody's writer and no one's in particular, is an institution, a monument, a public thoroughfare trodden dusty by a million feet. It is based largely upon the fact that of all great writers Dickens is both the least personally charming and the least personally present in his books. No one has ever loved Dickens as he loves Shakespeare and Scott. Both in his life and in his work the impression that he makes is the same. He has to perfection the virtues conventionally ascribed to the male; he is self-assertive, self-reliant, self-assured; energetic in the extreme. His message, when he parts the veil of the story and steps forward in person, is plain and forcible; he preaches the value of 'plain hardworking qualities',⁴ of punctuality, order, diligence, of doing what lies before one with all one's might. Agitated as he was by the most violent passions, ablaze with indignation, teeming with queer characters, unable to keep the dreams out of his head at night, nobody appears, as we read him, more free from the foibles and eccentricities and charms of genius. He comes before us, as one of his biographers described him, 'like a prosperous sea captain',[5] stalwart, weather-beaten, self-reliant, with a great contempt for the finicky, the inefficient, or the effeminate. His sympathies indeed have strict limitations. Speaking roughly, they fail him whenever a man or woman has more than two thousand a year, has been to the university, or can count his ancestors back to the third generation. They fail him when he has to treat of the mature emotions – the seduction of Emily, for example, or the death of Dora, whenever it is no longer possible to keep moving and creating, but it is necessary to stand still and search into things and penetrate to the depths of what is there. Then, indeed, he fails grotesquely, and the pages in which he describes what, in our convention, are the peaks and pinnacles of human life, the explanation of Mrs Strong, the despair of Mrs Steerforth, or the anguish of Ham, are of an indescribable unreality – of that uncomfortable complexion which, if we heard Dickens talking so in real life, would either make us blush to the roots of our hair, or dash out of the room to conceal our laughter. '. . . tell him then,' says Emily, 'that when I hear the wind blowing at night, I feel as if it was passing angrily from seeing him and uncle, and was going up to God against me.'[6] Miss Dartle raves – about carrion and pollution and earthworms, and worthless spangles and broken toys, and how she will have Emily 'proclaimed on the common stair'.[7] The failure is akin to that other failure to think deeply, to describe beautifully. Of the many men who go to make up the perfect novelist and should live in amity under his hat, two – the poet and the philosopher – failed to come when Dickens called them.

But the greater the creator the more derelict the regions where his powers fail him; all about their fertile lands are deserts where not a blade of grass grows, swamps where the foot sinks deep in mud. Nevertheless, while we are under their spell these great geniuses make us see the world any shape they choose. We remodel our psychological geography when we read Dickens; we forget that we have ever felt the delights of solitude, or observed with wonder the intricate emotions of our friends, or luxuriated in the beauty of Nature. What we remember is the ardour, the excitement, the humour, the oddity of people's characters; the smell and savour and soot of London; the incredible coincidences which hook the most remote lives together; the city, the law courts; this man's nose, that man's limp; some scene under an archway or on the high road; and, above all, some gigantic and dominating figure, so stuffed and swollen with life that he does not exist singly and solitarily, but seems to need for his own realisation a host of others, to call into existence the severed parts that complete him, so that wherever he goes he is the centre of conviviality and merriment and punch-making; the room is full, the lights are bright; there are Mrs Micawber, the twins, Traddles, Betsey Trotwood – all in full swing.

This is the power which cannot fade or fail in its effect – the power not to analyse or to interpret, but to produce, apparently without thought or effort or calculation of the effect upon the story, characters who exist not in detail, not accurately or exactly, but abundantly in a cluster of wild and yet extraordinarily revealing remarks, bubble climbing on the top of bubble as the breath of the creator fills them. And the fecundity and apparent irreflectiveness have a strange effect. They make creators of us and not merely readers and spectators. As we listen to Micawber pouring himself forth and venturing perpetually some new flight of astonishing imagination, we see, unknown to Mr Micawber, into the depths of his soul. We say, as Dickens himself says while Micawber holds forth: 'How wonderfully like Mr Micawber that is!'[8] Why trouble, then, if the scenes where emotion and psychology are to be expected fail us completely? Subtlety and complexity are all there if we know where to look for them, if we can get over the surprise of finding them – as it seems to us, who have another convention in these matters – in the wrong places. As a creator of character his peculiarity is that he creates wherever his eyes rest – he has the visualising power in the extreme. His people are branded upon our eyeballs, before we hear them speak, by what he sees them doing, and it seems as if it were the sight that sets his thought in action. He saw Uriah Heep 'breathing into the pony's nostrils and immediately covering them with his hand';[9] he saw David Copperfield looking in the glass to see how red his eyes were after his mother's death; he saw oddities and blemishes, gestures and incidents, scars, eyebrows, everything that was in the room in a second. His eye brings in almost too rich a harvest for him to deal with, and gives him an aloofness and a hardness which freeze his sentimentalism and make it seem a concession to the public, a veil thrown over the penetrating glance, which, left to itself, pierced to the bone. With such a power at his command Dickens made his books blaze up not by tightening the plot or sharpening the wit, but by throwing another handful of people upon the fire. The interest flags, and he creates Miss Mowcher, completely alive, equipped in every detail as if she were to play a great part in the story, whereas, once the dull stretch of road is passed by her help, she disappears; she is needed no longer. Hence a Dickens novel is apt to become a bunch of separate characters loosely held together, often by the most arbitrary conventions, who tend to fly asunder and split our attention into so many different parts that we drop the book in despair. But that danger is surmounted in *David Copperfield*. There, though characters swarm and life flows into every creek and cranny, some common feeling – youth, gaiety, hope – envelops the tumult, brings the scattered parts together, and invests the most perfect of all the Dickens novels with an atmosphere of beauty.[10]

1–A signed essay in the *N&A*, 22 August 1925, (Kp C266) inspired by the publication of *The Uncommon Traveller* (1860; Thomas Nelson, 1925), *Reprinted Pieces*, with an introduction by G. K. Chesterton (1874–1936) (J. M. Dent, 1921), *Christmas Stories* (1871; Thomas Nelson, 1925) by Charles Dickens (1812–70), and based on *The Personal History of David Copperfield* (1849–50), for which VW used vols xv and xvi in the Library Edition of *The Works of Charles Dickens* (Chapman and Hall, 1859). 'Dickens next,' VW wrote to Margaret Llewelyn-Davies, on 9 February 1925, 'I used to think David Copperfield a masterpiece; but having read Hard Times lately, I was disgusted and disappointed. It seems to me mere sentiment and melodrama, and your boasted zest for life nothing but rant and rage. No doubt it is a bad one; and I shall try another. If you want a modern writer with zest, why not try Proust? He has as much of it as Dickens, and his life is (to me) of a far more interesting kind. Ten volumes however, difficult French; I've only read three' *III VW Letters*, no. 1536). These illuminating remarks are only indirectly related to the review in question, reading for which appears to have been progressing, somewhat unevenly, in June. 'I'm reading Waley's Japanese novel and David Copperfield,' she informed Gerald Brenan on the 14th (*III VW Letters*, no. 1560), while two days later in her diary she noted: '"Them's his words" – this reminds me I must get to D. Copperfield. There are moments when all the masterpieces do no more than strum upon broken strings. It is very rare – the right mood for reading – in its way as intense a delight as any; but for the most part pain.' The same issue of *N&A* contained LW's 'World of Books' column, on 'An Unfortunate Man', discussing *The Life of Thomas Holcroft* (1745–1809) by Elbridge Colby. Reading Notes (Berg v). Reprinted *Mom*, *CE*.

2–For VW on '*Robinson Crusoe*' by Daniel Defoe (1660?–1731) see below. Jacob Ludwig Carl (1785–1863) and Wilhelm Carl Grimm (1786–1859), whose fairy tales (1812–15) first appeared in English in a translation by George Cruikshank in 1823 (Mrs Ramsay reads Grimm's 'The Fisherman and his Wife' to her son James in *To the Lighthouse* (1927), see 'The Window', 10). The novels of Sir Walter Scott (1771–1832), the first of which to be published was *Waverley* (1814). Dickens's *The Pickwick Papers*, first published 1836–7.

3–Honoré de Balzac (1799–1850), published some 91 novels in the period 1829–48.

4–Dickens, *Works*, vol. xvi, ch. xiii, 'Mischief', p. 176, which has: 'plain, hard-working qualities'.

5–The source of this quotation has not been traced (it does not appear to occur in John Forster's 3-volume *Life of Dickens*, 1872, 1874). But Leslie Stephen in his *DNB* entry on Dickens remarks that he was 'frequently compared in later life to a bronzed sea captain'.

6–Dickens, *Works*, vol. xvi, ch. xi, 'The Wanderer', p. 156, which has: ' – tell him then (but not else) that when I hear . . .' and continues: 'Tell him that if I was to die to-morrow (and oh, if I was fit, I would be so glad to die!) I would bless him and uncle with my last words, and pray for his happy home with my last breath!'

7–*Ibid.*, ch. xxi, 'Mr Peggoty's Dream Comes True', p. 297.

8–*Ibid.*, ch. xxviii, 'The Emigrants', p. 387: 'I think, now, how odd it was, but how wonderfully like Mr Micawber, that, when he went from London to Canterbury, he should have talked as if he were going to the farthest limits of the earth; and, when he went from England to Australia, as if he were going a little trip across the channel.'

9–*Ibid.*, vol. xv, ch. xv, 'I Make Another Beginning', p. 225: '. . . I caught a glimpse, as I went in, of Uriah Heep breathing into the pony's nostrils, and immediately covering them with his hand, as if he were putting some spell upon him.'

10–'Kappa', a columnist in the *N&A*, remarked in the issue for 5 September upon VW's 'delightful essay' in terms which she countered the following week (12 September) with the following letter to the editor: 'Fear of a sudden death very naturally distracted Kappa's mind from my article on *David Copperfield*, or he would, I think, have taken my meaning. That nobody can remember reading *David Copperfield* for the first time is a proof, not as he infers, that the reading makes so little impression that it slips off the mind unremembered, but that *David Copperfield* takes such rank among our classics, and is a book of such astonishing vividness, that parents will read it aloud to their children before they can quite distinguish fact from fiction, and they will never in later life be able to recall the first time they read it. Grimm's *Fairy Tales* and *Robinson Crusoe* are for many people in the same case.

'Questions of affection are, of course, always disputable. I can only reiterate that while I would cheerfully become Shakespeare's cat, Scott's pig, or Keats's canary, if by so doing I could share the society of these great men, I would not cross the road (reasons of curiosity apart) to dine with Wordsworth, Byron, or Dickens. Yet I venerate their genius; and my tears would certainly help to swell the "unparalleled flow of popular grief" at their deaths. It only means that writers have characters apart from their books, which are sympathetic to some, antipathetic to others. And I maintain that if it could be put to the vote, Which do you prefer as man, Shakespeare, Scott, or Dickens? Shakespeare would be first, Scott second, and Dickens nowhere at all.'

'A Brilliant Englishwoman Writes to Me . . .'

A brilliant Englishwoman writes to me – Would it much affect us, we ask ourselves, if a sea monster erected his horrid head off the coast of Sussex and licked up the entire population of Peacehaven and then sank to the bottom of the sea? Should we mourn them, or wish for their resurrection? No; for none of the qualities for which we love our kind and respect its misfortunes are here revealed; all for which we despise it and suspect it are here displayed. All that is cheap and greedy and meretricious, that is to say, has here come to the surface, and lies like a sore, expressed in gimcrack red houses and raw roads and meaningless decorations and 'constant hot water' and 'inside sanitation' and 'superb views of the sea'. We did not know that we had so much evil in us. Here shown up against the background of nature we can weigh it to the last ounce. The road has been turned into a switchback; the cliff into a 'park' for motor-cars. Human beings bask inside them, dipping alternately into paper bags for peppermints and into newspapers for comic cuts, while the sea and the downs perform for them the same function that the band performs when they eat ices at Lyons's. Compared with this, Wembley is beautiful, and the Mile End Road respectable, while, when we cut loose at last and turn into open country, we feel inclined to worship the first flock of sheep that we meet and venerate the simplest of shepherds.

1–A note in the column by 'Kappa' in the *N&A*, 5 September 1925, (Kp C266.1). The modernity of Peacehaven (initially called Anzac Cove), built after the Great War on the coast road between Newhaven and Brighton, both shocked and, if we may judge from her diary entry of 5 September 1927, challenged VW: 'Now a really comprehensive magnificent statesmanlike mind would take stock of all this human activity & direct it & weld it together. I see this possibility by fits & starts: I see human beings as at the beginning of a vast enterprise, not merely with the usual writers care for aesthetic quality. This is a point of view which is more & more forced upon one by places like Peacehaven. All aesthetic quality is there destroyed. Only turning & tumbling energy is left. The mind is like a dog going round & round to make itself a bed. So, give me new & detestable ideas, I will somehow trample a bed out of them.' For his diatribe against Peacehaven, see Leonard Woolf, *Beginning Again* (1964; 2 vols, *Leonard Woolf. An Autobiography*, OUP, 1980, vol. ii, ch. 3, pp. 104–5) in which 'the civilisation of the sheep' is again extolled.

'In Any Family Save the Darwins...'

In any family save the Darwins Sir Francis Darwin would have
stood out as a very exceptional man. In that most consistently gifted
of English families, his rare scientific powers, his disinterestedness,
his devotion, might almost be taken for granted. No currency has
stood the test of time like the Darwin currency. But if the accumulated fame of the family inevitably overshadowed the individual
fame of the three remarkable brothers – George, Frank, and Horace
– the figure of Sir Francis remains, even to those who knew him
slightly, one of abiding and peculiar charm. There must have been
in him a large measure of that simplicity and candour of spirit
which drew men's affection, together with their reverence, towards
his father. He seemed a perfect type of the man of science whose
constant search for truth, without chilling his human sympathies,
permeates his whole being with cleanliness and integrity. No pre-
tension, no insincerity would take root in that soil. His researches
were necessarily remote from interests of ordinary people, but no
one could be in his presence without an increased respect for the
family whose record he upheld, and for science which breeds so
sound and wholesome a race of men.

1–A note in the 'Life and Politics' column in the *N&A*, 26 September 1925, (Kp
C267.1). Sir Francis Darwin (b. 1848), botanist, son of Charles Darwin, had died at
Cambridge on 18 September 1925. Sir George Howard Darwin (1845–1912) was a
mathematician and astronomer, Sir Horace (1851–1928), a civil engineer. The
Stephens and Darwins were acquainted. The George Darwins, and also Elizabeth
Darwin, daughter of Charles, invited the Stephen sisters to stay with them on a
prospective visit to Cambridge in 1902 (*I VW Letters*, no. 47).

Swift's Journal to Stella

In any highly sophisticated society, such as our own or Swift's, disguise plays so large a part, politeness is so essential, that to do as
one likes, to speak straight out, to throw off the ceremonies and

conventions and speak a 'little language'[2] for one or two to understand, is as much a necessity as a breath of air in a hot room. The reserved, the powerful, the admired have the most need of such a
refuge. Swift himself found it so. The proudest of men coming home
from the company of great men who praised him, of lovely women
who flattered him, from intrigue and politics, put all that aside,
settled himself comfortably in bed, pursed his severe lips into baby
language and prattled to his 'two monkies', his 'dear Sirrahs', his
'naughty rogues'[3] on the other side of the Irish Channel.

Well, let me see you now again. My wax candle's almost out, but however I'll
begin. Well then don't be so tedious, Mr. Presto; what can you say to MD's letter?
Make haste, have done with your preambles – why, I say, I am glad you are so
often abroad.[4]

So long as Swift wrote to Stella[5] in that strain, so long as he eased
his mind in her company when the day's business was over, she had
no need to be jealous. It was true that she was wearing away the
flower of her youth in Ireland with Rebecca Dingley, who wore
hinged spectacles, consumed large quantities of Brazil tobacco, and
stumbled over her petticoats as she walked. Further, the conditions
in which the two ladies lived, for ever in Swift's company when he
was at home, occupying his house when he was absent, gave rise to
gossip; so that, though Stella never saw him except in Mrs Dingley's
presence, she was one of those ambiguous women who live chiefly
in the society of the other sex. But surely it was well worth while.
The packets kept coming from England, each sheet written to the
rim in Swift's crabbed little hand, which she imitated to perfection,
full of nonsense words, and capital letters, and hints which no one
but Stella could understand, and secrets which Stella was to keep,
and little commissions which Stella was to execute. Tobacco came
for Dingley, and chocolate and silk aprons for Stella. Whatever
people might say, surely it was well worth while.

Of this Presto, who was so different from that formidable character 't'other I',[6] the world knew nothing. The world knew only that
Swift was over in England again, soliciting the new Tory Government on behalf of the Irish Church for those First Fruits which he
had begged the Whigs in vain to restore. The business was soon
accomplished; nothing indeed could exceed the cordiality and affection with which Harley and St John greeted him;[7] and now the
world saw what even in those days of small societies and individual

pre-eminence must have been a sight to startle and amaze – the 'mad parson',[8] who had marched up and down the coffee-houses in silence and unknown a few years ago, admitted to the inmost councils of State, the man who had begun life a mere secretary[9] without birth or money or influence dining with highest Ministers of the Crown, making dukes do his bidding, dispensing patronage, and so run after for his good offices that his servant's chief duty was to know how to keep people out. Addison[10] himself forced his way up only by pretending that he was a gentleman come to pay a bill. For the time being Swift was omnipotent. Nobody could buy his services; everybody feared his pen. He went to Court, and 'am so proud I make all the lords come up to me'.[11] The Queen wished to hear him preach; Harley and St John added their entreaties; but he refused. When Mr Secretary one night dared show his temper, Swift called upon him and warned him

never to appear cold to me, for I would not be treated like a schoolboy . . . He took all right; said I had reason . . . would have had me dine with him at Mrs Masham's brother, to make up matters; but I would not. I don't know, but I would not.[12]

He scribbled all this down to Stella without exultation or vanity. That he should command and dictate, prove himself the peer of great men and make rank abase itself before him, called for no comment on his part or hers. Had she not known him years ago at Moor Park and seen him lose his temper with Sir William Temple and predicted all this and guessed his greatness and heard from his own lips what he planned and hoped? Did she not know better than anyone how strangely good and bad were blent in him, and all his foibles and eccentricities of temper, and how he could be at once so coarse and so delicate, so cynical and yet cherish a depth of feeling which she had never met with in any other human being? They knew each other in and out, good and bad, so that without effort or concealment he could use those precious moments late at night or the first thing on waking to rattle off the whole story of his day: to tell her what he had spent on coal; how Patrick had been drunk again and bought a linnet to give Dingley;[13] where he had dined and what he had paid for his dinner; the latest gossip of the Court; how the lime trees in the Park were out and how he longed for Laracor and his willows; how Lady Berkeley stole his hat and stuck it on another lady's head;[14] how he had caught a cold, and thought he heard burglars in the night, and dined with his Brethren at the Society, and thought of Stella, who must be sure to walk every day and read good books – the whole story, in short, of his charities and meannesses, his affections, ambitions and despairs, was poured out on top of her as though he were thinking aloud.

With such proof of his affection, admitted to intimacy with this Presto whom no one else in the world knew, Stella had no cause to be jealous. It was perhaps the opposite that happened. As she read the crowded pages she could see him and hear him and imagine so exactly the impression he must be making on all these fine people who crowded about him in amazement and fear and admiration that she fell more deeply in love than ever, or, if that were impossible, admired him more. She could piece together the contradictory elements as they followed each other casually in the Journal so as to make a perfect picture of him. Here he was picking the coals off his fire, saving halfpence on coaches, scandalising the Lords with whom he dined by his stinginess, and yet by the help of these very economies practising the most considerate and secret of charities – giving poor Patty Rolt 'a pistole to help her a little forward against she goes to board in the country',[15] taking twenty guineas to a sick poet in a garret. She could follow step by step the story of 'young Harrison':[16] how he helped and protected him; thought well of him and then not so well; worried to find him ill and penniless, carried him off to Knightsbridge, took him a hundred pounds only to find that he was dead an hour before. 'Think what grief this is to me! . . . I could not dine with Lord-Treasurer, nor anywhere else; but got a bit of meat toward evening.'[17] And then, in his masterful way, grieving and grumbling, he must take all Harrison's affairs upon his shoulders, order the funeral as economically as possible, see the mother, keep the money out of her clutches. Everybody seemed to call upon him when they were in trouble. She could imagine the strange scene, that November morning, when the Duke of Hamilton was killed in Hyde Park and Swift went at once to the Duchess and sat with her for two hours and heard her rage and storm and rail, and took her affairs, too, on his shoulders as if it were his natural office, and none could dispute his place in the house of mourning. 'She has moved my very soul,' he said.[18] When young Lady Ashburnham died he burst out, 'I hate life when I think it exposed to such accidents; and to see so many thousand wretches burdening the earth, while such as her die, makes me think God did never intend life for a blessing.'[19] And then, with that instinct to rend and tear his own emotions which made him angry in the midst of his pity, he would round upon the mourners, even the mother and sister of the dead woman, and part them as they cried together and complain how 'people will pretend to grieve more than they really do, and that takes off from their true grief'.[20]

The gloom was there, smouldering; the unsparing blade was ready to leap forth; but to Stella both were veiled. To her he showed himself genial and benignant: the man whom Harley teased by calling him Dr Thomas Swift,[21] and Lady Berkeley romped with, the man who busied himself with all the little businesses and pleasures of life, buying books, enjoying wine, to Stella at least fatherly or brotherly, laughing at her spelling, scolding her about her health. If he had written only to Stella, Swift would have been very different from the Swift we know. For, like all good letter writers, Swift took colour from the person he was writing to. He was with her when he wrote to her, talking baby language in front of Mrs Dingley, letting Stella influence him this way and that, calling up all they had done and felt together, though he was in London and she over against St Mary's Church, near Capel-street, in Dublin. They had a fund of memories in common. They had spent many happy hours together. 'Do not you remember I used to come into your chamber, and turn Stella out of her chair, and rake up the fire in a cold morning, and cry *uth, uth, uth!*'[22] She was often in his mind; he wondered if she were out walking when he was; when Prior abused one of his puns it made him think of Stella and of her puns and their vileness.[23] Inevitably Swift's influence was everywhere on her life – on her mind, on her affections, on the books she read, on the hand she wrote and the 'very judicious abstracts'[24] she made, on the friends she knew and the suitors she rejected. Indeed, he was half-responsible for her being.

But the woman he had chosen was no insipid slave. She had a character of her own. She was capable of thinking for herself. She was reserved, aloof, a severe critic for all her grace and sympathy, a little formidable, perhaps, with her love of plain speaking and her fiery temper and her fearlessness in saying what she thought. But with all her gifts she was little known. With her slender means and feeble health her way of life was very modest; and the society which gathered round her came for the simple pleasure of talking to a woman who listened and understood and said very little herself, but in the most agreeable of voices and generally the best thing of the evening. For the rest, she was not, perhaps, very learned. Her health had prevented her from serious study, and, though she had run over a great variety of subjects and had a fine severe taste in letters, what she read did not stick in her mind. She had been extravagant as a girl and flung her money about until her good sense took control of her and she lived with the utmost frugality ('five nothings on five plates of delf'[25] made her supper), dressing very plainly, but contriving from the sums she laid by both to help the poor and to bestow upon her friends (it was an extravagance she could not resist) the 'most agreeable presents in the world'. Swift never knew her equal in that art, 'although it be an affair of as delicate a nature as most in the course of life'.[26] She had in addition that sincerity which Swift called 'honour',[27] something virile, a courage, a fire which inspired the delicacy of her body and lent her womanliness a sharper charm. Such, then, was the influence which worked on Swift as he wrote; such the memory which mingled with the thought of his fruit trees and the willows and the river with trout in it at Laracor, when he saw the trees budding in St James's Park and heard the politicians wrangle. Unknown to all of them he had his retreat; and if the Ministers again played him false and once more, after making his friends' fortunes, he went empty-handed away, then after all he could retire to Ireland and to Stella and have 'no shuddering at all'[28] at the thought.

But Stella was the last woman in the world to press her claims. None knew better than she that Swift loved power and the company of men; that though he had his moods of tenderness and his fierce spasms of disgust at society, still for the most part he infinitely preferred the dust and bustle of London to all the trout streams and cherry trees in the world. Above all, he hated interference. If anyone laid a finger upon his liberty or hinted the least threat to his independence, were they men or women, queens or kitchenmaids, he turned upon them with a ferocity which made a savage of him on the spot. Harley once dared offer him a bank-note; Miss Waring dared hint that the obstacles to their marriage were now removed.[29] Both were chastised, the woman brutally. But Stella knew better than to invite such treatment. Stella had learnt patience; Stella had learnt discretion. Even in a matter like this of staying in London or coming back to Ireland she allowed him every latitude, asking nothing for herself, and was rewarded. Swift was half-annoyed.

...your generosity makes me mad; I know you repine inwardly at Presto's absence; you think he has broken his word, of coming in three months, and that this is always his trick: and now Stella says, she does not see possibly how I can come away in haste, and that MD is satisfied, &c. An't you a rogue to overpower me thus?[30]

But it was 'thus' that she kept him. Again and again he burst into language of intense affection.

Farewell dear Sirrahs, dearest lives: there is peace and quiet with MD, and nowhere else . . . Farewell again, dearest rogues: I am never happy, but when I write or think of MD . . .[31] You are as welcome as my blood to every farthing I have in the world; and all that grieves me is, I am not richer, for MD's sake.[32]

One thing alone dashed the pleasure that such words gave her. It was always in the plural that he spoke of her; it was always 'dearest Sirrahs, dearest lives'; MD stood for Stella and Mrs Dingley together. Swift and Stella were never alone. Grant that this was for form's sake merely, grant that the presence of Mrs Dingley, busy with her keys and her lapdog and never listening to a word that was said to her, scarcely counted, was a form too, why should such forms be necessary? Why impose a strain that wasted her health and half spoilt her pleasure and kept 'perfect friends'[33] who were happy only in each other's company apart? Why indeed? There was a reason; a secret which Stella knew, a secret which Stella did not impart. Divided they had to be. Since then no bond bound them, since she was afraid to lay the least restriction upon her friend, all the more jealously must she have searched into his words and analysed his conduct to ascertain the temper of his mood and acquaint herself instantly with the least change in it. So long as he told her frankly of his 'favourites' and showed himself the bluff tyrant who required every woman to make advances to him and lectured fine ladies and let them tease him, nothing in the Journal roused her suspicions. Lady Berkeley might steal his hat; the Duchess of Hamilton might lay bare her agony; and Stella, who was kind to her sex, laughed with the one and sorrowed with the other.

But were there traces in the Journal of a different sort of influence? – something far more dangerous because more equal and more intimate? Imagine some one of Swift's own station in life, a girl such as Stella had been when Swift first knew her, dissatisfied with the ordinary ways of life, eager, as Stella put it, to know right from wrong, charming, witty, untaught – she, indeed, if she existed, might be a rival to be feared. But did she exist? If so, there would be no open mention of her in the Journal. Instead there would be hesitations, excuses, some uneasiness and embarrassment when, writing his heart out and never stopping to read it over, Swift was brought up by something that he could not say. Indeed, he had only been a month or two in England when some such silence roused Stella's suspicion. Who was it, she asked, that boarded near him, that he dined with now and then? 'I know no such person,' Swift replied; 'I do not dine with boarders. What the pox! You know whom I have dined with every day since I left you, better than I do. What do you mean, Sirrah?'[34] But he knew what she meant; she meant Mrs Vanhomrigh, the widow who lived near him; she meant her daughter Esther.[35] The name kept coming again and again after that in the Journal. Swift was too proud to conceal the truth, but he sought nine times out of ten to excuse it. When he was in Suffolk-street the Vanhomrighs were in St James's-street, and thus saved him a walk. When he was in Chelsea they were in London, and it was convenient to keep his best gown and periwig there. Sometimes the heat kept him there, sometimes the rain; now they were playing cards, and young Lady Ashburnham reminded him so much of Stella that he stayed on to help her. Sometimes he stayed out of listlessness; again because he was very busy and they were simple people who did not stand on ceremony. At the same time Stella had only to hint that these Vanhomrighs were people of no consequence for him to retort, 'Why, they keep as good female company as I do male ... I saw two lady Bettys there this afternoon.'[36] In short, to tell the truth, to write whatever came into his head, was not easy.

Nevertheless, it was his necessity. To be Presto and not 't'other I', to have some 'sluttery'[37] or private chamber where he could relax and talk a 'little language' to a woman who understood him, was the need of his nature, and surely not a base one. Surely it was for this girl's good, as it had been for Stella's, to know the great Swift; and if he taught Vanessa too, as she said he did, 'to distinguish', could she complain if also he 'left her miserable'?[38] But Vanessa was not Stella. She was younger, more vehement, less disciplined, less wise. She had no Mrs Dingley to restrain her, no memories or Journals to solace her. She pursued, she threatened, she forced the truth from him. And when she got it, and the full force of those bright blue eyes blazed upon her, she dwindled beneath their illumination;[39] of all her arbours and laurels, her talks, her entreaties, nothing remained. To Stella she was no more than an uneasy ghost, appearing, beckoning, vanishing, one of those shadows which must ever haunt the troubled background of her life, must always people her solitude with fears. At any rate, Vanessa died; Stella had the Journal; Presto was hers again. She lived on to practise always those sad arts by which she kept her friend at her side and enjoyed his confidence and his lovemaking, until worn out with the strain and the concealment, with Mrs Dingley and her chatter and her lapdogs, she died herself and left Swift to mourn and to rage, to recount her qualities while they buried her, to sit at length, year after year in silence, broken once by a whisper, 'I am what I am', which the servants caught up as they took a knife that was by him and put it away.[40]

1—An essay based on *The Journal to Stella 1710–1713* by Jonathan Swift (1667–1745), published in the *TLS*, 24 September 1925, (Kp C268), subsequently revised for inclusion in CR2. 'So when I wake early now,' VW wrote in her diary on 27 June 1925, 'I luxuriate most in a whole day alone; a day of easy natural poses, a little printing, slipping tranquilly off into the deep water of my own thoughts navigating the underworld; & then replenishing my cistern at night with Swift. I am going to write about Stella & Swift for Richmond, as a sign of grace, after sweeping guineas off the Vogue counter. The first fruit of the C.R. (a book too highly praised now) is a request to write for the Atlantic Monthly. So I am getting pushed into criticism. It is a great stand by – this power to make large sums by formulating views on Stendhal & Swift.' On 19 July she noted: 'By bringing this book down here to the Studio, I have rather stinted it I think as my mornings have all been spent writing – Swift or letters'; and on the following day: 'Here the door opened, & Morgan came in to ask us out to lunch with him at the Etoile, which we did, though we had a nice veal & ham pie at home (this is in the classic style of journalists). It comes of Swift perhaps, the last words of which I have just written, & so fill up time here.' Reading Notes (Berg v). Reprinted CE.

2—*Journal to Stella* (Bohn's Standard Library, *The Prose Work of Jonathan Swift*, ed. Temple Scott; vol. ii, ed. Frederick Ryland, George Bell and Sons, 1900), Letter xxii, 28 April 1711 (4 May), p. 170: 'Do you know that every syllable I write I hold my lips just for all the world as if I were talking in our own little language to MD. Faith, I am very silly; but I can't help it for my life.'

3—These expressions, in various formulations, are scattered throughout the *Journal*, e.g. Letter viii, 31 October 1710 (2 November), p. 44: 'Well, little monkies mine'; Letter xi, 9 December 1710 (23 December), p. 80: 'Good morrow, dear sirrahs'; Letter viii (3 November), p. 45: 'a certain naughty rogue called MD'.

4—*Ibid.*, Letter x, 25 November 1710 (30 November), p. 62, which continues: '; your mother thinks it is want of exercise hurts you, and so do I.'

5—Stella was Esther Johnson (d. 1728). She had moved to live in Ireland, with her companion Rebecca Dingley, in 1700/1.

6—*Journal*, Letter xxix, 25 August 1711, p. 231: 'But let me alone, sirrahs; for Presto is going to be very busy; not Presto, but t'other I.'

7—Robert Harley, 1st Earl of Oxford (1661–1724), chancellor of the exchequer, and Henry St John, 1st Viscount Bolingbroke (1678–1751), secretary of state.

8—Leslie Stephen, *Swift*. English Men of Letters (1882; Macmillan and Co. Ltd, 1909), ch. iv, p. 56: 'At one time, according to a story vague as to dates, he got the name of the "mad parson" from Addison and others, by his habit of taking half-an-hour's smart walk to and fro in the coffee-house, and then departing in silence.' (See also Stephen on Swift in the *DNB*.)

9—Swift was secretary to Sir William Temple (1628–99), during 1689–94 and 1696–99, in whose household at Moor Park he first met Esther Johnson.

10—Joseph Addison (1672–1719), for VW on whom see above.

11—*Journal*, Letter xxvii, 19 July 1711 (29 July), p. 215.

12—*Ibid.*, Letter xix, 24 March 1710–11 (3 April), p. 148.

13—For this incident, see *ibid.*, Letters xiii and xv.

14—For Lady Louisa Lennox, Countess of Berkeley and her prank with Swift's hat, see *ibid.*, Letter xxiv.

15—*Ibid.*, Letter xxvii, 19 July 1711 (27 July), p. 214; Patty Rolt, afterwards Mrs Lancelot, was a cousin of Swift.

16—William Harrison (1685–1713), poet, diplomatist and sometime 'Tatler', a protégé of Swift who generally refers to him in the *Journal* as 'little Harrison'.

17—*Journal*, Letter lix, 25 January 1712–13 (14 February), p. 428.

18—*Ibid.*, Letter lv, 15 November 1712, p. 393; James Douglas, 4th Duke of Hamilton (1658–1712) and Charles, 4th Baron Mohun (1675?–1712) died duelling on 15 November. The duke's (second) wife was Elizabeth, only daughter and heiress of Digby, Lord Gerard.

19—*Ibid.*, Letter lvii, 18 December 1712 (3 January 1712–13), p. 410; Lady Mary Butler, daughter of the Duke of Ormond, had married Lord Ashburnham in 1710.

20—*Ibid.*, Letter lviii, 4 January 1712–13 (14 January), p. 415.

21—Dr Thomas Swift, a cousin of Swift, who laid claim to a share in the authorship of *A Tale of a Tub* (1704).

22—*Journal*, Letter xiv, 16 January 1710–11 (22 January), p. 106, which has: 'Don't you remember' and concludes with an interrogation mark not an apostrophe.

23—*Ibid.*, Letter xxi, 14 April 1711 (23 April): 'After dinner we had coarse Doiley napkins, fringed at each end . . . I told him I was glad to see there was such a *Fringeship* [Friendship] between Mr Prior and his lordship. Prior swore it was the worst he ever heard: I said I thought so too; but at the same time I thought it was most like one of Stella's that I ever heard.' Matthew Prior (1664–1721).

24—Swift, *Works*, ed. Sir Walter Scott (1814, Constable and Co.; 2nd Edition, 1824, vol. ix), 'On the Death of Mrs Johnson [Stella]', p. 286: '. . . She understood the Platonic and Epicurean philosophy, and judged very well of the defects of the latter. She made very judicious abstracts of the best books she had read. She understood the nature of government, and could point out all the errors of Hobbes, both in that and religion.'

25—*Ibid.*, vol. xiv, 'Stella at Wood Park. / A House of Charles Ford, Esq. Near Dublin. 1723', p. 523:

> Howe'er, to keep her spirits up,
> She sent for company to sup:
> When all the while you might remark,
> She strove in vain to ape Wood Park.

Two bottles call'd for, (half her store,
The cupboard could contain but four:)
A supper worthy of herself,
Five nothings in five plates of delf.

26—*Ibid.*, vol. ix, 'On the Death of Mrs Johnson', p. 289: 'But she had another quality that much delighted her ... I mean that of making agreeable presents; wherein I never knew her equal, although it be an affair of as delicate a nature as most in the course of life.'

27—E.g., *ibid.*, p. 289: 'Honour, truth, liberality, good nature, and modesty, were the virtues she chiefly possessed, and most valued in her acquaintance.'

28—*Journal*, Letter xxxii, 9 October 1711 (22 October), p. 265.

29—For Harley's attempt to bribe Swift and its consequence, see Stephen, ch. v, p. 85; for the unfortunate Miss Waring, called 'Varina', see *ibid.*, ch. iv, p. 52: 'Poor Varina had resisted Swift's entreaties, on the ground of her own ill-health and Swift's want of fortune. She now, it seems, thought that the economical difficulty was removed by Swift's preferment, and wished the marriage to take place. Swift replied in a letter, which contains all our information: and to which I can only apply the epithet brutal.'

30—*Journal*, Letter xix, 24 March 1710–11 (5 April), p. 150.

31—*Ibid.*, Letter xxviii, 11 August 1711 (25 August), p. 230.

32—*Ibid.*, Letter xxiii, 12 May 1711 (23 May), p. 181.

33—The source of this quotation has resisted all efforts at discovery.

34—*Journal*, Letter viii, 31 October 1710 (8 November), p. 48.

35—Esther Vanhomrigh (d. 1723), whom Swift first met in 1708 and for whom he wrote the poem 'Cadenus and Vanessa' (1713).

36—*Journal*, Letter xvii, 24 February 1710–11 (26 February), p. 128, which has: 'You say they are of no consequence; why, they keep ...'

37—*Works*, vol. xix, Swift to Esther Vanhomrigh, n.d., pp. 318–19: 'I long to drink a dish of coffee in the sluttery, and hear you dun me for Secrete, and "Drink your coffee. – Why don't you drink your coffee?"'

38—*Ibid.*, Esther Vanhomrigh to Swift, Dublin 1714, p. 344.

39—Stephen, ch. vi, p. 136: 'He rode in a fury to Celbridge. His countenance, says Orrery, could be terribly expressive of the sterner passions. Prominent eyes – "azure as the heavens" (says Pope) ... Vanessa had spoken of the "something awful in his looks", and of his killing words. He now entered her room, silent with rage, threw down her letter on the table and rode off. He had struck Vanessa's death blow.'

40—*Ibid.*, ch. ix, p. 208: 'Another time he was heard to mutter, "I am what I am; I am what I am."'

Congreve

None of the Oxford Press reprints is more timely or necessary than this of Congreve's Comedies, to be followed by a second volume containing the 'Mourning Bride' and the Miscellanies.[2] Congreve is, perhaps, the only post-Shakespearean dramatist who still lives outside the walls of the British Museum, and, therefore, a small cheap edition for ordinary hands and ordinary purses (the Nonesuch Press edition was large in size and necessarily, though not correspondingly, large in price)[3] is needed. His vitality depends upon the union of several qualities elsewhere perhaps more highly developed, but nowhere so blended and proportioned. His plays move forward by the kiss and conjunction of beauty and wit. He lives also because, more than Wycherley's, Vanbrugh's, or Farquhar's, his world is our world.[4] There is no need for the modern reader to put himself into a strained attitude in reading him. He need be no more licentious, no more hearty, no more fond of oaths and horse-play than he is by nature. To appreciate Congreve one need not be much different from what one is – only better.

Mr Dobrée's introduction serves its purpose admirably, if we define it to be the purpose of an introduction to add substantially to our knowledge, to help us to sort out our own emotions when we have read the book, and to leave us convinced that our own reading is the true one.

Mr Dobrée is in wholesome reaction against those critics of the cuttlefish school who suffuse their pages with the many-coloured ink of their own impressions. He is a scientist rather than a cuttlefish, with a handy little hammer with which he taps the page and proves it hard. Thus he breaks up the most famous passages of The Way of the World, and shows us where the stresses fall; how the vowel sounds are disposed; how Congreve when he came to the more delicate passages 'nearly always closed upon a trochee'.[5] This is refreshingly matter of fact after the vapours of the other set, and Mr Dobrée is not wanting in ardour to point his dryness. But when it comes to analysing Lady Wishfort's imaginative volubility, to talking of the 'delicious modelling' of one phrase, and bidding us mark the sound contrasts between 'bird-cage' and 'starve',[6] then we begin to feel that in his laudable anxiety to cut things into little bits he has lost the power of seeing them whole. We are driven to read the play again in order to piece the parts together as Congreve wrote them. But that is another way of saying that the introduction has served its purpose.

1–A review in the N&A, 17 October 1925, (Kp C268.1) of Comedies by William

Congreve [1670–1729] ed., with introduction and notes, by Bonamy Dobrée (OUP, 1926). See also 'Congreve', 'Restoration Comedy', *III VW Essays*; 'Congreve's Comedies: Speed, Stillness and Meaning', *VI VW Essays*. Reading Notes (Berg, XVIII).

2–Congreve, *The Mourning Bride* [1697] *Poems, and Miscellanies,* ed. Bonamy Dobrée (OUP, 1928).

3–*The Complete Works of William Congreve*, ed. Montague Summers (4 vols, Nonesuch Press, 1923). The Nonesuch Press was founded in 1923 by Francis Meynell, Vera Mendel and David Garnett. It aimed to produce moderately priced books of high quality.

4–William Wycherley (1640–1716); Sir John Vanbrugh (1664–1726); George Farquhar (1678–1707).

5–Dobrée, p. xxv; *The Way of the World* (1700).

6–For Dobrée's minute critical analysis, ibid., p. xxvi.

'Twenty Years of My Life'

The pictures of Mrs Jopling-Rowe are, we may guess, out of fashion nowadays; but this book proves that the lovely ingenuous girls, the roses, the landscapes, the well-bred portraits of well-bred people in full evening-dress kept her successfully afloat through twenty years – 1867–1887 – which, hard inevitably for a woman artist, were particularly stormy for her. Lightly, jauntily, skipping from grave to gay, printing casually, it seems, the relics of her blotting-book, she skims many adventures and sorrows, and meets, of course, Oscar Wilde and the Prince of Wales.[2] She was almost untaught into the bargain. M. Chaplin, in whose studio she learnt the rudiments of painting in Paris, had just pronounced her (and from him it was the highest compliment) 'serious'[3] when family misfortunes drove her back to London, and the task fell upon her of educating her children and keeping a roof above their heads. Cash failed her even to buy brushes and paints, until Mr Shirley Brooks[4] gave her a five-pound note and enabled her to hire a nursemaid and buy materials sufficient at any rate to paint the portrait of a cook, with which she earned her first guineas. Again and again the sale of a picture just staved off distress. But Mrs Jopling-Rowe had one qualification which even M. Chaplin could not procure for her – a face, a figure, a personality which made her as welcome in the dining-room as in the studio. The fact cannot be concealed. Millais's portrait is there to prove it.[5] And who shall say that the fact is not important where English art patrons are concerned? The English, said M. Chaplin, 'comprennent absolument rien à l'art'.[6] In beauty, however, they are connoisseurs.

1–A notice in the *N&A*, 17 October 1925, (Kp C268.2) of *Twenty Years of My Life. 1867 to 1887* with twenty-eight illustrations (Bodley Head Ltd, 1925) by Louise Jopling (Mrs Jopling-Rowe).
2–Oscar Wilde (1854–1900); Edward, Prince of Wales (1841–1910).
3–Jopling, ch. i, p. 4: 'Ah! elle est sérieuse, cette petite, elle arrivera.' Monsieur Charles Chaplin ('whose Studio for women students was the fashion just then', p. 3), otherwise unidentified.
4–Shirley Brooks, editor of *Punch* (1870–4).
5–Jopling, Frontispiece: 'Louise Jopling. From the painting by Sir John Millais [1829–96] in the National Portrait Gallery'.
6–*Ibid.*, ch. xv, p. 133.

<hr>

Sterne's Ghost

That men have ghosts; that ghosts revisit the places where life ran quickest; that Sterne therefore haunts no churchyard, but the room where *Tristram Shandy* was written[2] – all this may be taken for granted; even if we find it no such easy matter to decide in what mood and with what motives the ghost of Sterne beat regularly at midnight upon the wall of Mrs Simpson's best bedroom in Stonegate, York.

Mrs Simpson made no secret of the matter, which perhaps was too notorious to be concealed. Owing to the ghost, she told the young Mathews, she would let the rooms, large as they were and convenient for the theatre, very cheap indeed, and, perceiving something in Mrs Mathews's aspect which made her think her, as indeed she was, 'a candidate for literary gains',[3] she added how it was in this room and at that table that a very famous book called *Tristram Shandy* was written, she believed, some forty years before. Even without its literary associations the cheapness of the lodging was enough to excuse the ghost, for the young Mathews were extremely poor – Charles acting at a salary of twenty-five shillings a week in Tate Wilkinson's[4] company, but Tate did not scruple to tell him that with his screwed-up face and threadpaper body he had better keep a shop than go upon the stage, while poor Eliza, the girl whom Charles had married, out of pity, the second Mrs Mathews said, without '*really* loving her',[5] had not a penny to her name, which happened to be Strong. And Strong she had need to be, said Charles's father,[6] strong in character, strong in health, strong in principles, strong in affections, if she became the wife of the misguided boy who so wantonly preferred the stage and all its evils to selling serious books to saintly personages in the Strand. But Eliza herself was conscious of one source of strength only (besides that she was very much in love with her husband), and that was her gift for writing – her passion for literature. When Mrs Simpson at one and the same moment lowered the rent and mentioned Sterne the bargain was struck and the rooms taken. The ghost must be endured.

That necessity arose indeed the very first night the Mathews went to bed. As York Minster struck the first chimes of midnight, three powerful blows resounded on the wall at the back of the young couple's bed. The same thing happened night after night. York Minster had only to begin striking twelve and the ghost struck three. Watch was set; experiments were made; but whether it was the ghost of Sterne or the malevolence of some ill-wisher, no cause could be discovered, and the young people could only move their bed, and shift their bedtime, which, as the playhouse hours were late, and Charles had a passion for reading or talking late at night, was a matter of not much difficulty. Such courage could hardly have been expected of so frail a woman. But unfortunately Eliza had a reason for tolerating ghosts if they reduced the rent which she dared not tell her husband. Every week, like the honest and affectionate creature he was, he poured his salary – twenty-five shillings – into her lap, and every week she assured him that twenty-five shillings was ample – all their bills were paid. But every week a certain number, an increasing number for all she could do to keep their expenses down, were slipped, unpaid, into Sterne's table drawer. Eliza perhaps had some inkling of the fact that her husband had married her impetuously in the goodness of his heart, from pity that the only child of the late Dr Strong should have to support herself by inculcating the principles of arithmetic into the daughters of the gentlemen of Swansea. At any rate, she was determined that he should never suffer for his generosity. Comforts he must have, and if twenty-five shillings a week were not enough to pay for them, she would pay for them herself out of her own earnings. She was confident that she could do it. She would write a novel, a novel like *Tristram Shandy* perhaps, save that her knowledge of life was unfortunately limited, which would set all London in a roar. And then she would come to her husband with the bills receipted and her deception confessed, and give him the proceeds of her famous novel to do what he liked with. But that day was still far distant – at present she must work. While Charles was acting and reading, while Charles, who loved talk and hated bedtime, was gossiping and chattering and taking off odd characters, so that he was famous in the green room whatever he might be upon the stage, Eliza wrote. She wrote every kind of piece – novels, sonnets, elegies, love songs. The publishers took them, the publishers printed them, but they never paid her a penny for them, and on she toiled, always carefully concealing her work from her husband, so that his surprise when the day of revelation came might be entire.

Meanwhile, the bills accumulated, and act as Charles might (and there were some young ladies in York who thought him the finest comic actor they had ever seen, and would stand a whole evening in the wings to hear him), his salary remained twenty-five shillings and no more. It was useless for the ghost to knock; useless for Eliza's back to ache; useless for her good brother-in-law William to implore her to write everything twice over, peruse the best works of the best authors, and find mottoes for all her chapters – she had no choice; write she must. Surely the novel she was now engaged on – *What Has Been* – promised better than the others, and with a little help from William, who knew Mr Wordsworth and could perhaps solicit the favours of reviewers, might, indeed must, bring her fame.[7] Sitting where Sterne had sat, writing where Sterne had written, the omens were auspicious.

There, at any rate, long after the ghost had knocked thrice and York Minster had tolled twelve times, she sat writing. She neglected to take exercise. She never allowed herself to stand in the wings a whole evening to see her Charles in his comic parts. At last signs of exhaustion became apparent. Alarmed by her wasted looks, Charles brought a doctor to see her. But one glance was enough. Nothing could now be done. Whatever the cause, lack of exercise or lack of food, or whether the nervous strain of hearing those three taps delivered nightly had hopelessly injured her constitution, consumption was far advanced; and all the doctor could do was to prescribe apothecaries' stuff, which, expensive as it was, Charles feared to be useless.

Eliza was now confined to bed. Her projects had totally failed. *What Has Been* appeared, but, even corrected and at least partially supplied with mottoes by the kindness of Mr William Mathews, failed like its predecessors, and she was at an end of her resources. Even so, the worst was still to come. The butcher or the baker stopped Charles in the street and demanded payment. The drawer and its bills had to be revealed. The whole of her miserable, innocent, overwhelming deception must be confessed. Charles took the blow like an angel, said not a word of complaint, though the bills were to hang about his neck for years to come. And now, for the first time, the ghost fell silent. York Minster struck midnight and there was no reply. But really the silence was worse than the sound! To lie and wait for the three stout strokes as York Minster struck twelve and then to hear nothing – that seemed to convey a more appalling message than the blow itself – as if the enemy had worked its will and gone its way. But this very silence inspired Eliza Mathews with a desperate courage. With the ghost quiescent, the novels unsold, the bills unpaid, Charles all day at the playhouse, often cast down by his failure and the thought of his father's displeasure – for the God-fearing bookseller in the Strand, where the whole house was hung with portraits of the Saints framed in ebony and canting humbugs bamboozled the simple old tradesman out of his livelihood, had been justified in his warnings – with all this that she had caused, or failed to prevent, to oppress her and the daily decline of her own health to appal, Eliza framed a terrible and desperate resolve. There was a girl at the playhouse for whom she had an affection, a singer who was friendless as Eliza herself had been, and timid and charming. For this young woman, Anne Jackson[8] by name, Eliza sent. She was better, Eliza claimed, as Anne came in, and indeed her looks confirmed it; much better, because of an idea that had come to her, which she counted on her friend's help to carry out. First, before her husband came back, she wished to be propped up in bed in order, she said mysteriously, 'to be able to look at you both while I reveal my project'.[9] Directly Charles Mathews appeared and exclaimed in his turn at her sparkle, her animation, she began. Sitting up, forced often to pause for breath, she said how she knew her fate; death was inevitable; how the thought of her husband's loneliness oppressed her – worse, the thought that he would marry again a woman who did not understand him. Here she paused exhausted, and Charles looked at Anne and Anne at Charles, as if to ask had she lost her reason? On she went again. It was even worse, she said, to think of Anne left in her youth and inexperience without such help as she, Eliza, might have given her. Thoughts of this kind embittered her last moments. Surely, then, they would grant the last request she would ever make? She took her husband's hand and kissed it; then took her friend's and kissed that too 'in a solemn manner, which I remember made me tremble all over',[10] and at last framed her terrible request. Would they, there and then, pledge themselves to marry each other when she was dead?

Both were flabbergasted. Anne burst into floods of tears. Never, she cried, never could she contemplate marriage with Mr Mathews! She esteemed him; she admired him; she thought him the first comic actor of the age; that was all. Charles himself fairly scolded the dying woman for putting them in such an awful predicament. He ran after the sobbing girl to implore her to believe that it was none of his doing – that his wife was raving and no longer knew what she said. And so Eliza died. For months a coldness, an awkwardness, existed between the widower and his wife's friend. They scarcely met. Then, at the same moment, on the same night, the same vision visited them, far apart as they were in their sleep. Eliza came imploring to the side of each. Well, said Anne, it must be destiny; Shakespeare said so; 'marriage comes of destiny'[11] he said, and she was disposed to agree with Shakespeare. Twelve months after she had sworn that she could never feel anything but esteem for Mr Mathews she was his wife.

But what conclusions are we led to draw from the behaviour of Sterne's ghost? Was it malicious or tender, did it come to warn or to mock, or merely to dip its handkerchief once more in the tears of lovers? Nobody could say. Charles Mathews told the story of the Stonegate ghost a hundred times in the green room at York but nobody came forward with an explanation. Again one night he was telling the story when an old actress, who had returned to the stage after a long absence, and had heard nothing of the ghost or of the Mathews, exclaimed in astonishment, 'Why, that was my dear Billy Leng!'[12] And then she told them how they lodged next door to Mrs Simpson's in Stonegate; how her dear Billy had been bedridden for many years; how, as his infirmities increased, so did his fear of robbers; how, being the most methodical of men and growing more so with age, he waited always for York Minster to chime midnight and then took his crutch-handled stick and beat forcibly on the calico at the back of his bed to warn any thief who might be concealed there. 'It was no ghost,' she cried. 'It was my dear Billy Leng!'[13]

Cleared of the imputation which the ghost of Sterne had cast upon them, Mrs Simpson now let her rooms for the ordinary sum.

1—A signed essay in the N&A, 7 November 1925, (Kp C269) based on *Memoirs of Charles Mathews* [1776–1835], *Comedian* (4 vols, Richard Bentley, 1838–9) by Mrs [Anne] Mathews (d. 1869). The same issue of the N&A contained LW's 'World of Books' column, on 'A Painful Mystery', discussing *My Friend Toto*, a book about a chimpanzee by Cherry Kearton, and *Lions 'n Tigers 'n Everything* by Courtney Ryley Cooper. See also 'Sterne', *I VW Essays*; 'Eliza and Sterne', *III VW Essays*; and *A Sentimental Journey CR2* and *V VW Essays*. See Editorial Note, p. xxv. Reading Notes (Berg XVIII), entitled 'Sterne's Room'. Reprinted: *Mom, CE*.
2—Laurence Sterne (1713–68) began writing *The Life and Opinions of Tristram Shandy* (1759–67) in 1759.
3—Mathews, vol. i, ch. xi, p. 214. Mathews and his first wife Eliza Kirkham Strong (d. 1802), author of a volume of poems and several unsuccessful novels, were married in 1797. Mrs Simpson's perception is VW's embellishment. The account of the haunted room occurs in *ibid.*, ch. xiii.
4—Tate Wilkinson (1739–1803), actor and theatre manager, upon whom VW writes in 'Jones and Wilkinson' below.
5—*Ibid.*, ch. x, p. 200, an adaptation, it appears, from: 'He had settled to marry . . . without what is called *being in love!*' and 'his second wife, (whom he *really* loved,)'.
6—James Mathews, bookseller and Wesleyan preacher.
7—Mathew's eldest brother William was a barrister and an intimate friend and former fellow student of William Wordsworth (1770–1850) at Cambridge. He died of yellow fever at Tobago in 1801, the year in which Eliza's novel *What Has Been* was published.
8—Anne Jackson (d. 1869), actress, married Charles Mathews in 1803.
9—Mathews, vol. i, ch. xvi, p. 333, adapted from a third person account.
10—*Ibid.*, p. 334.
11—*Ibid.*, p. 352, source [*All's Well That Ends Well*, I, iii, 63] not given.
12—*Ibid.*, ch. xiii, p. 254, which has: 'why that was'.
13—See previous note, adapted.

Saint Samuel of Fleet Street

If this were the age of faith, Dr Johnson would certainly be Saint Samuel, Fleet Street would be full of holy places where he preached his sermons and performed his miracles, and the Boswells, the Thrales, and the Hawkinses[2] would all be exalted to the rank of prophets. Our age has somehow lost the art of making haloes; but a man may fairly be said to be a Saint when cabmen, who can scarcely be said to secrete *Rasselas* in their pockets, quote Johnson's sayings or invent Johnson's sayings on a wet night in the Strand, as a writer in *The Times* has lately heard them doing.[3] Then, indeed, he has eaten his way into the fabric of life and performs all the functions of the gods, presiding over the fortunes of men, and inspiring, albeit he wears a wig, a snuff-coloured coat, rolls as he walks, and has a gluttonous appetite for dinner. There can be no doubt – these two new editions, this abridgement of the famous biography show it – that Dr Johnson has proved himself of the stuff that Saints are made of, and, if we were to hazard a guess at the reason, it would be that he is one of the very few human beings who love their kind. Every other good quality is to be had in profusion; this alone is rare, as can be proved by counting those who can unanimously be said to possess it. One might begin with Christ and Socrates; add Shakespeare and Montaigne; perhaps Sir Thomas Browne. Then, if we confine our search to the British Isles, whom do we find? Milton is hopelessly out of the running; so are Wycherley, Swift, Pope, Congreve. The names of statesmen and soldiers do not leap to the mind. Pepys, for all his defects, is a possible candidate; Lamb[4] stands as good a chance as any, but it is Dr Johnson, the coarse, moody, rough-tempered man, who possesses, by virtue perhaps of his coarseness and his moodiness, the peculiar sympathy, the majestic tolerance, the broad humour, which, when he has been in his grave a century and a half, still make the cabmen think of him on a wet night in the Strand.

That this myth-making quality springs from some personal ascendancy, and has little to do with intellect or art, is clear. People who have never read a word of Johnson's writings are inspired by this power in him to add to the myth from their own stores, by which means alone he is assured of immortality. His figure, at least, will never dry up and dwindle away; always somebody will be dabbing a fresh handful of clay on the surface. Whether the myth thus created will not, in process of time, altogether cease to resemble the actual man remains to be proved. The religion may entirely misinterpret the founder. But in Johnson's case the test is near at hand and easy to apply. There are his books – *The Rambler, The Vanity* of *Human Wishes*, the *Tour to the Hebrides*, the *Lives of the Poets*[5], and it cannot be denied that they fix and refine features which, under the influence of the myth-makers, tend to wobble and to spread. In the first place they make us revise that part of the legend which will have it, for the fun of exaggeration partly, that Johnson laboured always under what Canon Ainger called 'the Johnsonian incubus'.[6] He was pompous and sententious and Latin. It took all Lamb's genius to liberate English prose from the thrall. With this in mind we open the *Lives of the Poets*, and what do we find? A prose which, beside our daily diet of *Times* leaders and statesmen's letters, appears brief, pointed, almost elegant; which alights with all its feet neatly together for the most part and exactly upon its meaning; which indulges frequently in a thrust or lunge of phrase of the utmost vigour and vivacity. 'Among this lagging race of frosty grovellers he might still have risen into eminence,'[7] and so on. The words occur in that life of Milton which is more often quoted as an example of the perversity of the great critic's judgement than of the grace and elasticity of his style. And he goes on, warped by one of those prejudices which tend to twist his judgement from the straight, to comment a little censoriously upon 'a kind of respect, perhaps unconsciously paid to the great man by his biographers; every house in which he resided is historically mentioned, as if it were an injury to neglect naming any place which he honoured by his presence.'[8] That respect is now far more profusely lavished upon Johnson than upon Milton. Here, prefixed to Mr Glover's edition, is an article by Austin Dobson[9] carefully, precisely, methodically enumerating each of Johnson's dwelling-places throughout his life, while in the two large volumes edited by Mr Ingpen these same sacred precincts, together with Johnson in every attitude and Johnson's friends in all their variety, are illustrated so profusely that the biography becomes a rivulet of words flowing round a ceaseless procession of pictures. Both editions meet different needs. Mr Glover's, with the notes of Malone,[10] is the handier, the smaller, the more literary; Mr Ingpen's is a refreshment and stimulus for the eye when it has absorbed as much print as it can deal with. Holding its rather unwieldy volumes, the reader, transformed into a seer, foretells the day when the cinematograph will be the natural accompaniment of the *Life and Letters*.

Finally, there is the bold, the candid, the adventurous Mr Pritchard. 'Years are few,' he says, 'and books are many.'[11] Much of Boswell, he confesses, we can well spare. Johnson was a great skipper himself. So let us be frank with ourselves; and away he goes, cutting and slashing, until the whole of Boswell is reduced to a neat text-book for industrious scholars, who, when they have mugged up Boswell, can turn their cramming to account by doing a string of exercises thoughtfully provided at the end. Still, there has to be a beginning to all things, and who knows if the little boy who starts on Pritchard may not prove in years to come, the most hearty Boswellian of them all?

1–A review in the *N&A*, 14 November 1925, (Kp C269.1) of *The Life of Samuel Johnson. By James Boswell.* Edited with Notes by Arnold Glover. With an Introduction by Austin Dobson. Illustrated by Herbert Railton (3 vols, Dent, 1925); *The Life of Samuel Johnson. By James Boswell.* Newly edited with notes by Roger Ingpen (2 vols, George Bayntun, 1925); and *Boswell's Life of Johnson.* Abridged and edited by F. H. Pritchard (Harrap, 1925).

The same issue of the *N&A* contained: LW's 'World of Books' column, on 'Charlotte Brontë', discussing The *Twelve Adventures and Other Stories*, collected by Clement Shorter.

2–Samuel Johnson (1709–84); James Boswell (1740–95), whose life of Johnson first appeared in 1791; Hester Lynch Thrale (1741–1821), who published her *Anecdotes of the late Samuel Johnson* in 1786; Sir John Hawkins (1719–89), the famously 'unclubbable' author of the first full-length biography of Johnson, published in 1787.

3–See Ingpen, 'Preface to the New Edition', p. xiii, who takes the story of the cabman from John Cann Bailey, *Dr Johnson and His Circle* (1913). Samuel Johnson, *The History of Rasselas, Prince of Abissinia* (1759).

4–Sir Thomas Browne (1605–82), John Milton (1608–74), William Wycherley (1640–1716), Jonathan Swift (1667–1745), Alexander Pope (1688–1744), William Congreve (1670–1729), Samuel Pepys (1633–1703), Charles Lamb (1775–1834).

5–*The Rambler*, a periodical, 1750–2; *The Vanity of Human Wishes* (1749), *A Journey to the Western Islands of Scotland* (1775), *The Lives of the Most Eminent English Poets*, 1779–81.

6–The source of this expression by Canon Alfred Ainger (1837–1904), biographer and editor of Charles Lamb, has not been discovered.

7–Johnson, *Lives of the Most Eminent English Poets* ... With a sketch of the author's life by Sir Walter Scott (Chandos Library, Frederick Warne and Co., n.d.), 'Milton', p. 57: 'His submission to the seasons was at least more reasonable than his dread of decaying nature, or a frigid zone; for general causes must operate uniformly in a general abatement of mental power; if less could be performed by the writer, less likewise would content the judges of his work. Among this lagging race of frosty grovellers he might still have risen into eminence by producing something which they should not willingly let die. However inferior to the heroes who were born in better ages, he might still be great among his contemporaries, with hope of growing every day greater in the dwindle of posterity. He might still be the giant of the pigmies, the one-eyed monarch of the blind.'

9—Henry Austin Dobson (1840–1921), versifier, and biographer of several eighteenth-century writers, though not of Johnson.
10—Edward Malone (1741–1812), member of the Club, friend of Boswell and subsequently editor of his life of Johnson.
11—Pritchard, Preface, p. 5, adapted.

Melba

It would not be difficult to make Melba's life into a fairy-story — how there was a poor goose-girl who took a kitchen shovel in her hands and struck open a gold mine in the cabbage patch, and great kings paid her homage, and she lived in silks and finery happily ever afterwards. It is true that the facts are slightly less romantic — Melba's father was the son of a Scotch farmer, and came to Melbourne with a pound in his pocket and made a fortune. But it is also true that his daughter was so short of funds when she took lessons from Marchesi[2] in Paris that she had only one dress, which she wore week in, week out, in spite of Marchesi's protests. Then suddenly the mine was discovered — the bottomless gold mine in Melba's throat. In an incredibly short time she was appearing in Brussels, singing to an incredulous, silent, finally uproarious house, and waking next day to find herself, soberly and solidly, famous throughout Europe. Indeed, every door was open to a woman with that voice; every city in the world clamoured to hear it. But the golden voice was lodged, as such voices often are, in a shrewd, business-like body. She did not penetrate to strange places, nor sing strange songs. 'Home, Sweet Home' rang out almost incessantly in the palaces of kings and millionaires. But once at least the prosperous pilgrimage was interrupted, and she stooped over Sarah Bernhardt on her deathbed. The great actress whispered, 'Ah, Melba . . . my golden voice needs me no longer, for I am dying!'[3] and when Melba got out into the street her friend stared at her. Her face was daubed with the dying Bernhardt's rouge. Melba's own make-up was always extremely efficient. She brought her father's business temperament on to the stage. No sacrifice of time or food was too great in the cause of her work, and she prided herself upon singing exactly what the composer wrote. Only once, apparently, did she fail, when she sang Brunhilde in *Siegfried*. 'The music was too much for me . . . I had a sensation almost of suffocation, of battling with some immense monster'[4] – and she never sang Wagner again. But the crown was not without its thorns. She has been accused of having no roof to her mouth, of eating three raw eggs before each set of *La Bohème*, and finally half London believed that Melba had to give up singing because of her passion for eating mice.[5] The real culprit was a magpie; for birds and beasts, scents and ices have all been named after her; but even so, there are compensations.

1–A review in the *N&A*, 5 December 1925, (Kp C269.2) of *Memories and Melodies* (Thornton Butterworth Ltd, 1925) by Nellie Melba (1861–1931), prima donna, born Helen Porter Mitchell, daughter of David and Isabella Mitchell of Forfarshire, created DBE in 1918. The same issue of the *N&A* also contained: LW's 'World of Books' column, on '"Jug Jug" to Dirty Ears', discussing T. S. Eliot's *Poems 1909–1925*, Edmund Blunden's *English Poems* and Thomas Hardy's *Human Shows: Far Phantasies: Songs and Trifles*.
2–Mathilde Marchesi, *née* Grauman (1826–1913), German mezzo-soprano, a celebrated teacher at the Paris conservatory.
3–Melba, ch. iv, p. 65. Sarah Bernhardt (1844–1923), upon whom VW wrote in 'The Memoirs of Sarah Bernhardt', *I VW Essays*.
4–For the quotation, *ibid.*, ch. xiii, p. 159. Melba's unhappy performance in *Siegfried* (1871) by Richard Wagner (1813–83) took place at the Metropolitan Opera House, New York, in December 1896.
5–For the accusations, *ibid.*, ch. xviii, p. 211. Melba studied *La Bohème* (1896) under its composer, Giacomo Puccini (1858–1924).

'Some of the Smaller Manor Houses of Sussex'

Lady Wolseley is not possessed of a light pen, but she is possessed of method and conscience, and a dogged desire to tunnel her way into the heart of her subject. That subject is one of inexhaustible fascination. Scattered about Sussex are innumerable old houses of the lesser sort, small enough to be lived in and used, humble enough to die in harness as barns and pigsties, if fate so wills it, which is perhaps a better lot than to be preserved artificially, like some of our statelier homes, where life is now too costly to be possible. Massetts

Place, Wapsbourne, Laughton Place, Halland House, Colin God-man[2] – the names sound sweet in the ear, and recall, perhaps, even to idle tourists, glimpses of the charming old places themselves and envious thoughts, which Lady Wolseley's admirable photographs revive, cast in their direction. But Lady Wolseley has not been content with envious thoughts. She has got the owners' permission to make a thorough investigation, has gathered up the local traditions, has searched the parish registers, tramped the fields, examined locks, hinges, and trap-doors, and so built up an authentic history stretching back often for many centuries. The history of these lesser houses is often obscure. They have changed hands often, and the hands have been those of obscure men. Nevertheless, Lady Wolseley increases our sense of the close-knit antiquity of Sussex. The same names turn up again and again – now in a Tudor manuscript, now over a modern shop door. The reddest Socialist could scarcely lift a hand against a Dalyngrygge, a Lewknor, or a Keynes.

1–A notice in the *N&A*, 5 December 1925, (Kp C269.3) of *Some of the Smaller Manor Houses in Sussex* (The Medici Society, 1925) by Viscountess Wolseley, citizen and gardener of London.
2–Massetts Place, Lindfield; Wapsbourne – 'only three fields from Massetts'. Laughton Place, not far from either Glynde or Firle, and known to VW, was the home of the Pelham family, who subsequently moved to nearby Halland House. Colin Godman, near Sheffield Forest, was also known as 'the Smuggler's House'.

'From Hall-Boy to House-Steward'

By ability and economy Mr Lanceley, who began as a hall-boy on eight pounds a year, rose to be house-steward to the Duke of Connaught. But the good servant is the last person from whom to expect a racy description of a servant's life. He becomes the echo of his master; he becomes even more aristocratic than the aristocrat. 'There is a quotation among old servants,' he says, which runs:

> You may break, you may shatter the vase as you will,
> But the scent of the roses will cling to it still

and Mr Lanceley's book entirely bears out this praise of the rose. They feed you well, they house you well; in addition, they 'never pass a remark on a servant in the hearing of another', and so on.[2] Indeed, when Mr Lanceley went into service in the 'seventies, servants never asked for holidays, for the food and comfort they enjoyed at the great house were infinitely superior to what they got at home. They worshipped their master's goods. He has a story of a housemaid whose boast it was that she had washed the same dinner service for twenty-five years without so much as chipping a single piece. They stayed long in their places. They observed decorous rites as to chairs and benches. But Mr Lanceley was too much of a gentleman to eavesdrop, and so, though he handed a great many dishes to well-known people, he seldom heard a complete story fall from their lips, and, naturally, had no time to listen to Oscar Wilde,[3] though he often helped him off with his coat. His vivacity steadily diminishes as he climbs higher. When he began life the squire swore and drank and dropped the candle-grease about. Nowadays, gentlemen are as exemplary as their butlers. But on the whole, Mr Lanceley makes out a good case for the life of a servant, nor has successful serving by any means blinded him to the problems of the future. He himself keeps servants now, and, to his great credit, for the promoted servant is apt to be a tyrant, they stay with him for years.

1—A notice in the *N&A*, 26 December 1925, (Kp C269.4), of *From Hall-Boy to House-Steward*. With Portrait (Edward Arnold and Co., 1925) by William Lanceley.
2—For both quotations (the latter slightly adapted), Lanceley, ch. xi, p. 153.
3—While in the service of an unidentified Irish heiress, when 'G. A. Sala, Sir Henry Irving, Mr R. Browning, Mr Wiley, Oscar Wilde, Lady Morgan, Baroness Burdett-Coutts' were 'constant callers'.

1926

On Being Ill

Considering how common illness is, how tremendous the spiritual change that it brings, how astonishing, when the lights of health go down, the undiscovered countries that are then disclosed, what wastes and deserts of the soul a slight attack of influenza brings to light, what precipices and lawns sprinkled with bright flowers a little rise of temperature reveals, what ancient and obdurate oaks are uprooted in us in the act of sickness, how we go down into the pit of death and feel the waters of annihilation close above our heads and wake thinking to find ourselves in the presence of the angels and the harpers when we have a tooth out and come to the surface in the dentist's arm chair and confuse his 'Rinse the mouth – rinse the mouth' with the greeting of the Deity stooping from the floor of Heaven to welcome us[2] – when we think of this and infinitely more, as we are so frequently forced to think of it, it becomes strange indeed that illness has not taken its place with love, battle, and jealousy among the prime themes of literature. Novels, one would have thought, would have been devoted to influenza; epic poems to typhoid; odes to pneumonia, lyrics to toothache. But no; with a few exceptions – De Quincey attempted something of the sort in *The Opium Eater*; there must be a volume or two about disease scattered through the pages of Proust[3] – literature does its best to maintain that its concern is with the mind; that the body is a sheet of plain glass through which the soul looks straight and clear, and, save for one or two passions such as desire and greed, is null, negligible and non-existent. On the contrary, the very opposite is true. All day, all night the body intervenes; blunts or sharpens, colours or discolours, turns to wax in the warmth of June, hardens to tallow in the murk of February. The creature within can only gaze through the pane – smudged or rosy; it cannot separate off from the body like the sheath of a knife or the pod of a pea for a single instant; it must go through the whole unending procession of changes, heat and cold, comfort and discomfort, hunger and satisfaction, health and illness, until there comes the inevitable catastrophe; the body smashes itself to smithereens, and the soul (it is said) escapes. But of all this daily drama of the body there is no record. People write always about the doings of the mind; the thoughts that come to it; its noble plans; how it has civilised the universe. They show it ignoring the body in the philosopher's turret; or kicking the body, like an old leather football, across leagues of snow and desert in the pursuit of conquest or discovery. Those great wars which it wages by itself, with the mind a slave to it, in the solitude of the bedroom against the assault of fever or the oncome of melancholia, are neglected. Nor is the reason far to seek. To look these things squarely in the face would need the courage of a lion tamer; a robust philosophy; a reason rooted in the bowels of the earth. Short of these, this monster, the body, this miracle, its pain, will soon make us taper into mysticism, or rise, with rapid beats of the wings, into the raptures of transcendentalism. More practically speaking, the public would say that a novel devoted to influenza lacked plot; they would complain that there was no love in it – wrongly however, for illness often takes on the disguise of love, and plays the same old tricks, investing certain faces with divinity, setting us to wait, hour after hour, with pricked ears for the creaking of a stair, and wreathing the faces of the absent (plain enough in health, Heaven knows) with a new significance, while the mind concocts a thousand legends and romances about them for which it has neither time nor liberty in health. Finally, among the drawbacks of illness as matter for literature there is the poverty of the language. English, which can express the thoughts of Hamlet and the tragedy of Lear, has no words for the shiver and the headache. It has all grown one way. The merest schoolgirl, when she falls in love, has Shakespeare, Donne, Keats to speak her mind for her; but let a sufferer try to describe a pain in his head to a doctor and language at once runs dry. There is nothing ready made for him. He is forced to coin words himself, and, taking his pain in one hand, and a lump of pure sound in the other (as perhaps the inhabitants of Babel did in the beginning) so to crush them together that a brand new word in the end drops out. Probably it will be something laughable. For who of English birth can take liberties with the language? To us it is a sacred thing and therefore doomed to die, unless the Americans, whose genius is so much happier in the making of new words than in the disposition of the old, will come to our help and set the springs aflow. Yet it is not only a new language that we need, primitive, subtle, sensual, obscene, but a new hierarchy of the passions; love must be deposed in favour of a temperature of 104; jealousy give place to the pangs of sciatica; sleeplessness play the part of villain, and the hero become a white liquid with a sweet taste – that mighty Prince with the moths' eyes and the feathered feet, one of whose names is Chloral.

But to return to the invalid. 'I am in bed with influenza,' he says, and actually complains that he gets no sympathy. 'I am in bed with influenza' – but what does that convey of the great experience; how the world has changed its shape; the tools of business grown remote; the sounds of festival become romantic like a merry-go-round heard across far fields; the friends have changed, some putting on a strange beauty, others deformed to the squatness of toads, while the whole landscape of life lies remote and fair, like the shore seen from a ship far out at sea, and he is now exalted on a peak and needs no help from man or God, and now grovels supine on the floor glad of a kick from a housemaid – the experience cannot be imparted and, as is always the way with these dumb things, his own suffering serves but to wake memories in his friends' minds of *their* influenzas, *their* aches and pains which went unwept last February, and now cry out, desperately, clamorously, for the divine relief of sympathy.

But sympathy we cannot have. Wisest Fate says no. If her children, weighted as they already are with sorrow, were to take on them that burden too, adding in imagination other pains to their own, buildings would cease to rise, roads would peter out into grassy tracks; there would be an end of music and of painting; one great sigh alone would rise to Heaven, and the only attitudes for men and women would be those of horror and despair. As it is, there is always some little distraction – an organ grinder at the corner of the hospital, a shop with book or trinket to decoy one past the prison or the workhouse, some absurdity of cat or dog to prevent one from turning the old beggar's hieroglyphic of misery into volumes of sordid suffering, and the vast effort of sympathy which those barracks of pain and discipline, those dried symbols of sorrow, ask us to exert on their behalf, is uneasily shuffled off for another time. Sympathy nowadays is dispensed chiefly by the laggards and failures, women for the most part (in whom the obsolete exists so strangely side by side with anarchy and newness), who, having dropped out of the race, have time to spend upon fantastic and unprofitable excursions; C.L., for example, who sitting by the stable sickroom fire builds up with touches at once sober and imaginative, the nursery fender, the loaf, the lamp, barrel organs in the street, and all the simple old wives' tales of pinafores and escapades; A.R., the rash, the magnanimous, who if you fancied a giant tortoise to solace you, or a theorbo to cheer you would ransack the markets of London and procure them somehow, wrapped in paper, before the end of the day; the frivolous K.T., dressed in silks and feathers, painted and powdered (which takes time too) as if for a banquet of kings and queens, who spends her whole brightness in the gloom of the sick room, and makes the medicine bottles ring and the flames shoot up with her gossip and her mimicry.[4] But such follies have had their day; civilisation points to a different goal; if the cities of the Middle West are to blaze with electric light, Mr Insull 'must keep twenty or thirty engagements every day of his working months'[5] – and then, what place is there for the tortoise and the theorbo?

There is, let us confess it (and illness is the great confessional) a childish outspokenness in illness; things are said, truths blurted out, which the cautious respectability of health conceals. About sympathy for example; we can do without it. That illusion of a world so shaped that it echoes every groan, of human beings so tied together by common needs and fears that a twitch at one wrist jerks another, where however strange your experience other people have had it too, where however far you travel in your own mind someone has been there before you – is all an illusion. We do not know our own souls, let alone the souls of others. Human beings do not go hand in hand the whole stretch of the way. There is a virgin forest, tangled, pathless, in each; a snow field where even the print of birds' feet is unknown. Here we go alone, and like it better so. Always to have sympathy, always to be accompanied, always to be understood would be intolerable. But in health the genial pretence must be kept up and the effort renewed – to communicate, to civilise, to share, to cultivate the desert, educate the native, to work by day together and by night to sport. In illness this make-believe ceases. Directly the bed is called for, or, sunk deep among pillows in one chair, we raise our feet even an inch above the ground on another, we cease to be soldiers in the army of the upright; we become deserters. They march to battle. We float with the sticks on the stream; helter skelter with the dead leaves on the lawn, irresponsible and disinterested and able, perhaps for the first time for years, to look round, to look up – to look, for example, at the sky.

The first impression of that extraordinary spectacle is strangely overcoming. Ordinarily to look at the sky for any length of time is impossible. Pedestrians would be impeded and disconcerted by a public sky-gazer. What snatches we get of it are mutilated by chimneys and churches, serve as a background for man, signify wet weather or fine, daub windows gold, and, filling in the branches, complete the pathos of dishevelled autumnal plane trees in London squares. Now, become as the leaf or the daisy, lying recumbent, staring straight up, the sky is discovered to be something so different from this that really it is a little shocking. This then has been going on all the time without our knowing it! – this incessant making up of shapes and casting them down, this buffeting of clouds together, and drawing vast trains of ships and waggons from North to South, this incessant ringing up and down of curtains of light and shade, this interminable experiment with gold shafts and blue shadows, with veiling the sun and unveiling it, with making rock ramparts and wafting them away – this endless activity, with the waste of Heaven knows how many million horse power of energy, has been left to work its will year in year out. The fact seems to call for comment and indeed for censure. Some one should write to *The Times* about it. Use should be made of it. One should not let this gigantic cinema play perpetually to an empty house. But watch a little longer and another emotion drowns the stirrings of civic ardour. Divinely beautiful it is also divinely heartless. Immeasurable resources are used for some purpose which has nothing to do with human pleasure or human profit. If we were all laid prone, frozen, stiff, still the sky would be experimenting with its blues and golds. Perhaps then, looking down at something very small and close and familiar, we shall find sympathy. Let us examine the rose. We have seen it so often flowering in bowls, connected it so often with beauty in its prime, that we have forgotten how it stands, still and steady, throughout an entire afternoon in the earth. It preserves a demeanour of perfect dignity and self-possession. The suffusion of its petals is of inimitable rightness. Now perhaps one deliberately falls; now all the flowers, the voluptuous purple, the creamy, in whose waxen flesh a spoon has left a swirl of cherry juice; gladioli; dahlias; lilies, sacerdotal, ecclesiastical; flowers with prim cardboard collars tinged apricot and amber, all gently incline their heads to the breeze – all, with the exception of the heavy sunflower, who proudly acknowledges the sun at midday, and perhaps at midnight rebuffs the moon. There they stand; and it is of these, the stillest, the most self-sufficient of all things that human beings have made companions; these that symbolise their passions, decorate their festivals, and lie (as if they knew sorrow) upon the pillows of the dead! Wonderful to relate, poets have found religion in Nature; people live in the country to learn virtue from plants. It is in their indifference that they are comforting. That snowfield of the mind, where man has not trodden, is visited by the cloud, kissed by the falling petal, as, in another sphere, it is the great artists, the Miltons, the Popes, who console, not by their thought of us, but by their forgetfulness.

Meanwhile, with the heroism of the ant or the bee, however indifferent the sky or disdainful the flowers, the army of the upright marches to battle. Mrs Jones catches her train. Mr Smith mends his motor. The cows are driven home to be milked. Men thatch the roof. The dogs bark. The rooks, rising in a net, fall in a net upon the elm trees.[6] The wave of life flings itself out indefatigably. It is only the recumbent who know what, after all, Nature is at no pains to conceal – that she in the end will conquer; the heat will leave the world; stiff with frost we shall cease to drag our feet about the fields; ice will lie thick upon factory and engine; the sun will go out. Even so, when the whole earth is sheeted and slippery some undulation, some irregularity of surface will mark the boundary of an ancient garden, and there, thrusting its head up undaunted in the starlight, the rose will flower, the crocus will burn. But with the hook of life still in us still we must wriggle. We cannot stiffen peaceably into glassy mounds. Even the recumbent spring up at the mere imagination of frost about the toes and stretch out to avail themselves of the universal hope – Heaven, Immortality. Surely, since men have been wishing all these ages, they will have wished something into existence; there will be some green isle for the mind to rest on even if the foot cannot plant itself there. The co-operative imagination of mankind must have drawn some firm outline. But no. One opens the *Morning Post* and reads the Bishop of Lichfield on Heaven[7] – a vague discourse, weak, watery, inconclusive. One watches the church-goers file in to those gallant temples where, on the bleakest day, in the wettest fields, lamps will be burning, bells will be ringing, and however the autumn leaves may shuffle and the winds sigh outside, hopes and desires will be changed to beliefs and certainties within. Do they look serene? Are their eyes filled with the light of their sublime conviction? Would one of them dare leap straight into Heaven off Beachy Head? None but a simpleton would ask such questions; the little company of believers lags and drags and prys; the mother is worn; the father tired. The Bishops are tired too. Frequently we read in the same paper how the Diocese has presented its bishop with a motor-car; how at the presentation some leading citizen has remarked, with obvious truth, that the Bishop has more need of motor-cars than any of his flock. But this Heaven making needs no motor cars; it needs time and concentration. It needs the imagination of a poet. Left to ourselves we can but trifle with it – imagine Pepys in Heaven, adumbrate little interviews with celebrated people on tufts of thyme, soon fall into gossip about such of our friends as have stayed in Hell, or, worse still, revert again to earth and choose, since there is no harm in choosing, to live over and over, now as man, now as woman, as sea-captain, court lady, Emperor, farmer's wife, in splendid cities and on remote moors, in Teheran and Tunbridge Wells, at the time of Pericles or Arthur, Charlemagne, or George the Fourth – to live and live till we have lived out those embryo lives which attend about us in early youth and been consumed by that tyrannical 'I', who has conquered so far as this world is concerned but shall not, if wishing can alter it, usurp Heaven too, and condemn us, who have played our parts here as William or Amelia, to remain William or Amelia for ever. Left to ourselves we speculate thus carnally. We need the poets to imagine for us. The duty of Heaven-making should be attached to the office of Poet Laureate.

Indeed, it is to the poets that we turn. Illness makes us disinclined for the long campaigns that prose exacts. We cannot command all our faculties and keep our reason and our judgement and our memory at attention while chapter swings on top of chapter, and, as one settles into place, we must be on the watch for the coming of the next, until the whole structure – arches, towers, battlements – stands firm on its foundations. *The Decline and Fall of the Roman Empire* is not the book for influenza, nor *The Golden Bowl*, nor *Madame Bovary*.[8] On the other hand, with responsibility shelved and reason in abeyance – for who is going to exact criticism from an invalid or sound sense from the bed-ridden? – other tastes assert themselves; sudden, fitful, intense. We rifle the poets of their flowers. We break off a line or two and let them open in the depths of the mind, spread their bright wings, swim like coloured fish in green waters:

> and oft at eve
> Visits the herds along the twilight meadows[9]

> wandering in thick flocks along the mountains
> Shepherded by the slow, unwilling wind.[10]

Or there is a whole three volume novel to be mused over and spread out in a verse of Hardy's, or a sentence of La Bruyère's.[11] We dip in Lamb's *Letters* – some prose writers are to be read as poets – and find 'I am a sanguinary murderer of time, and would kill him inch-meal just now. But the snake is vital'[12] and who shall explain the delight of that? or open Rimbaud and read

> O saisons, ô châteaux
> Quelle âme est sans défauts?[13]

and who shall rationalise the charm? In illness words seem to possess a mystic quality. We grasp what is beyond their surface meaning, gather instinctively this, that, and the other – a sound, a colour, here a stress, there a pause – which the poet, knowing words to be meagre in comparison with ideas, has strewn about his page to evoke, when collected, a state of mind which neither words can express nor the reason explain. Incomprehensibility has an enormous power over us in illness, more legitimately perhaps than the upright will allow. In health meaning has encroached upon sound. Our intelligence domineers over our senses. But in illness, with the police off duty, we creep beneath some obscure poem by Mallarmé[14] or Donne, some phrase in Latin or Greek, and the words give out their scent, and ripple like leaves, and chequer us with light and shadow, and then, if at last we grasp the meaning, it is all the richer for having travelled slowly up with all the bloom upon its wings.

Foreigners, to whom the tongue is strange, have us at a disadvantage. The Chinese must know better the sound of *Antony and Cleopatra* than we do.

Rashness is one of the properties of illness – outlaws, that we are – and it is rashness that we chiefly need in reading Shakespeare. It is not that we should doff the intelligence in reading him, but that fully conscious and aware his fame intimidates us, and all the books of all the critics dull in us that thunder clap of conviction that nothing stands between us and him, which, if an illusion, is still so helpful an illusion, so prodigious a pleasure, so keen a stimulus in reading the great. Shakespeare is getting flyblown; a paternal government might well forbid writing about him, as they put his monument at Stratford beyond the reach of scribbling pencils. With all this buzz of criticism about, one may hazard one's conjectures privately, make one's notes in the margin; but knowing that some-one has said it before, or said it better, the zest is gone. Illness in its kingly sublimity sweeps all that aside, leaves nothing but Shakespeare and oneself, and what with his overweening power, our overweening arrogance, the barriers go down, the knots run smooth, the brain rings and resounds with *Lear* or *Macbeth*, and even Coleridge himself squeaks like a distant mouse. Of all the plays and even of the sonnets this is true; it is *Hamlet* that is the exception. *Hamlet* one reads once only in one's life, between the ages of twenty and twenty-five. Then one is Hamlet, one is youth; as, to make a clean breast of it, Hamlet is Shakespeare, is youth. And how can one explain what one is? One can but be it. Thus forced always to look back or sidelong at his own past the critic sees something moving and vanishing in *Hamlet*, as in a glass one sees the reflection of oneself, and it is this which, while it gives an everlasting variety to the play, forbids us to feel, as with *Lear* or *Macbeth*, that the centre is solid and holds firm whatever our successive readings lay upon it.

But enough of Shakespeare – let us turn to Augustus Hare. There are people who say that even illness does not warrant these transitions; that the author of *The Story of Two Noble Lives*[15] is not the peer of Boswell; and if we assert that short of the best in literature we like the worst – it is mediocrity that is hateful – will have none of that either. So be it. The law is on the side of the normal. But for those who suffer a slight rise of temperature the names of Hare and Waterford and Canning[16] will always ray out beams of benignant lustre. Not, it is true, for the first hundred pages or so. There, as so often in these fat volumes, we flounder, and threaten to sink in a plethora of aunts and uncles. We have to remind ourselves that there is such a thing as atmosphere; that the masters themselves often keep us waiting intolerably while they prepare our minds for whatever it may be – the surprise, or the lack of surprise. So Hare, too, takes his time; the charm steals upon us imperceptibly; by degrees we become almost one of the family, yet not quite for our sense of the oddity of it all remains, and share the family dismay when Lord Stuart[17] leaves the room – there was a ball going forward – and is next heard of in Iceland. Parties, he said, bored him – such were English aristocrats before marriage with intellect had adulterated the fine singularity of their minds. Parties bore them; they are off to Iceland. Then Beckford's[18] mania for castle building attacked him; and he must lift a French *château* across the channel, and erect pinnacles and towers to serve as servants' bedrooms at vast expense, upon the borders of a crumbling cliff, too, so that the housemaids saw their brooms swimming down the Solent, and Lady Stuart was much distressed, but made the best of it and began, like the high-born lady that she was, planting evergreens in the face of ruin; while the daughters, Charlotte and Louisa, grew up in their incomparable loveliness, with pencils in their hands, for ever sketching, dancing, flirting, in a cloud of gauze. They are not very distinct it is true. For life then was not the life of Charlotte and Louisa. It was the life of families, of groups. It was a web, a net, spreading wide and enmeshing every sort of cousin and dependant, and old retainer. Aunts – Aunt Caledon, Aunt Mexborough – grandmothers – Granny Stuart, Granny Hardwicke[19] – cluster in a kind of chorus, and rejoice and sorrow and eat Christmas dinner together, and grow very old and remain very upright, and sit in hooded chairs cutting flowers, it seems, out of coloured paper. Charlotte married Canning and went to India; Louisa married Lord Waterford and went to Ireland. Then the letters cross vast spaces in slow sailing ships and everything becomes still more protracted and verbose, and there seems no end to the space and the leisure of those early nineteenth century days, and faiths are lost and the life of Hedley Vicars[20] revives them; aunts catch cold but recover; cousins marry; there is the Irish famine and the Indian Mutiny, and both sisters remain, to their great, but silent grief, for in those days there were things that women hid like pearls in their breasts, without children to come after them. Louisa, dumped down in Ireland with

Lord Waterford at the hunt all day, was often very lonely; but she stuck to her post, visited the poor, spoke words of comfort ('I am sorry indeed to hear of Anthony Thompson's loss of mind, or rather of memory; if, however, he can understand sufficiently to trust solely in our Saviour, he has enough')[21] and sketched and sketched. Thousands of notebooks were filled with pen and ink drawings of an evening, and then the carpenter stretched sheets for her and she designed frescoes for schoolrooms, had live sheep into her bedroom, draped gamekeepers in blankets, painted Holy Families in abundance, until the great Watts exclaimed that here was Titian's peer and Raphael's master![22] At that Lady Waterford laughed (she had a generous, benignant sense of humour); and said that she was nothing but a sketcher; had scarcely had a lesson in her life – witness her angel's wings, scandalously unfinished. Moreover, there was her father's house for ever falling into the sea; she must shore it up; must entertain her friends; must fill her days with all sorts of charities, till her Lord came home from hunting, and then, at midnight often, she would sketch him with his knightly face half hidden in a bowl of soup, sitting with her notebook under a lamp beside him. Off he would ride again, stately as a crusader, to hunt the fox, and she would wave to him and think, each time, what if this should be the last? And so it was one morning. His horse stumbled. He was killed. She knew it before they told her, and never could Sir John Leslie[23] forget, when he ran downstairs the day they buried him, the beauty of the great lady standing by the window to see the hearse depart, nor, when he came back again, how the curtain, heavy, Mid-Victorian, plush perhaps, was all crushed together where she had grasped it in her agony.

1–A signed essay in T. S. Eliot's *New Criterion*, January 1926, (Kp C270) reprinted in a shorter version with revisions, as 'Illness: An Unexploited Mine' in *Forum*, April 1926, (see Appendix I) and under its original title, in a slightly revised form (typeset by VW – *III VW Diary*, 16 June 1930) as a Hogarth Press pamphlet (see *V VW Essays*). 'Of course,' VW wrote to Eliot on 3 September 1925, 'I should think it an honour to figure in your first number (by the way, what's the name? Criterion Junior – waiting for the demise of Criterion Senior?) but you'll have to let me know when you want it, and how long, and what is your publication date. I've two or three things promised to America during the next months – a story, an article on something like Painting and Writing, and another undecided – but I should have to say soon if you wanted to print here' (*III VW Letters*, no. 1577). But on 14 September we find her protesting to her diary: 'Tom has treated us scurvily . . . On Monday I get a letter that fawns & flatters, implores me to write for his new 4ly; & proposes to discuss press matters as soon as we get back; on Thursday we read in the Lit Supt. that his new firm is publishing Waste Land & his other poems . . .' which may account, but it seems hard to credit, for the uncharacteristic formality of her letter to Eliot ('Dear Sir' as opposed to 'My dear Tom') of 13 November: 'I am sending my essay tomorrow, Saturday morning, so that I hope it will reach you in time.

'I am sorry to have delayed, but I have been working under difficulties' (*III VW Letters*, no. 1597). She had in fact been ill throughout most of October and November, living a greatly curtailed existence. A postcard from Eliot, mentioned in her diary entry for 7 December, proved discouraging: '. . . *On Being Ill* – an article which I, & Leonard too, thought one of my best: to him characteristic &c: I mean he is not enthusiastic; so, reading the proof just now, I saw wordiness, feebleness, & all the vices in it. This increases my distaste for my own writing, & dejection at the thought of beginning another novel.'

Publication brought her welcome (and not so welcome) praise: '. . . Lytton came up and praised my article in the Criterion tremendously, which, as we never praise each other's writing now, did for a moment illumine me: and Desmond came up and praised it, and this did not much please me, for his mind is all torn up sheets of paper now – such a ragbag . . .' (*III VW Letters*, no. 1617, to Vita Sackville-West, 31 January 1926). Edward Sackville-West approved and she wrote to him: 'I am very glad you liked my article – I was afraid that, writing in bed, and forced to write quickly by the inexorable Tom Eliot I had used too many words' (*ibid.*, no. 1619, 6 February). Two days later she noted in her diary, praise for 'that wonderful essay' from Ottoline Morrell; and a cheque from *Forum*, via Harcourt Brace, amount unspecified. See in addition the introductory paragraph to 'Melodious Meditations', *II VW Essays*: 'The poets of the eighteenth century were fond of making their verses sound dignified by spelling certain qualities with a capital letter . . . We sometimes fancy that these antiquated ghosts merely took ship to America, lodged with the best families, and now walk abroad in those essays which the Americans write so frequently upon Old Age, Old Maids, On Being Ill, and Sorrow'. See Editorial Note, p. xxv. Reprinted: *Mom.*

2 – Cf. *I VW Diary*, 7 March 1919: 'Yesterday I had a tooth out, to which the bag of a large abscess had attached itself. Harrison showed it me, previous to putting it in the fire; a token of much pain he said. The queer little excursion into the dark world of gas always interests me. I came home in the Tube wondering whether any of the people there suspected its existence. I wake from it, or seem rather to step out of it & leave it to go on hurtling through space while the world of Harrison & Dr Trueby engages my attention – "Open your mouth, Mrs Woolf – Now let me take out this little bit of wood." Suppose one woke instead to find the deity himself by one's side! The Christians believe it, I suppose.'

3 – For VW on Thomas De Quincey (1785–1859) and his *Confessions of an English Opium Eater* (1822, 1856), see 'Impassioned Prose' below. Marcel Proust (1871–1922).

4 – The identities of C. L., A. R. and K. T. remain undiscovered (conjecture suggests Charlotte Leaf, Anne [Thackeray] Ritchie and Katherine Thynne, as marginally possible candidates). A 'theorbo' is 'a large kind of lute . . . much in vogue in the 17th century' (*OED*).

5 – Samuel Insull (1859–1938), American financier and business magnate whose empire included a vast network of electricity generating plants. The source of the quotation has not been found.

6–The image of flocking rooks rising and falling net-like is a favourite of VW's. See for example *The Waves* (Hogarth Press, 1931), p. 158: 'the rooks rising and falling and catching the elm-trees in their net.'

7–The Bishop of Lichfield, 1913–37, was the Rt Rev. John Augustine Kempthorne (1864–1946). His views on heaven have regrettably not been discovered in the pages of the *Morning Post*.

8–Edward Gibbon, *The Decline and Fall of the Roman Empire* (1776, 1781, 1788), for VW on whom see 'The Historian and "The Gibbon"' and 'Reflections at Sheffield Place', *VI VW Essays*; Henry James, *The Golden Bowl* (1904), for VW on which see 'Mr Henry James's Novel', *I VW Essays*; Gustave Flaubert, *Madame Bovary* (1856).

9–Milton, *A Mask (Comus)* (1637), ll. 843–4, spoken by the Attendant Spirit, concerning Sabrina.

10–Shelley, *Prometheus Unbound* (1820), II, i, ll. 146–7, spoken by Asia.

11–For VW on Thomas Hardy (1840–1928) see 'Thomas Hardy's Novels' and 'Half of Thomas Hardy' below; Jean de La Bruyère (1645–96).

12–Charles Lamb to Bernard Barton, 25 July 1829, in *The Letters of Charles Lamb*, ed. with an introduction by Alfred Ainger (2 vols, Macmillan and Co. Ltd, 1904), vol. ii, p. 240.

13–Rimbaud, *Une Saison en enfer* (1873) which VW probably read in *Oeuvres de Arthur Rimbaud* [1854–91]. Préface de Paul Claudel [1868–1955] (Paris. Mercure de France, n.d.), p. 295, which has: 'ô chateaux!' and 'sans défauts!'

14–Stéphane Mallarmé (1842–98) upon whose *Vers et Prose* (Paris: Perrin, 1893), probably in 1921, VW made reading notes (MHP, xxxviii).

15–Augustus J. C. Hare (1834–1903), *The Story of Two Noble Lives. Being Memorials of Charlotte, Countess Canning, and Louisa Marchioness of Waterford* (3 vols, George Allen, 1893).

16–Henry, 3rd Marquis of Waterford, and Charles John, Earl Canning (1812–62), governor-general of India.

17–Sir Charles Stuart, Baron Stuart of Rothesay (1779–1845), diplomat, and his wife Elizabeth Margaret, *née* Yorke, were the parents of Charlotte (d. 1861) wife of Charles John, Earl Canning, and Louisa (d. 1891), wife of the 3rd Marquis of Waterford. For Lord Stuart's sudden departure for Iceland, see Hare, vol. i, ch. iii, p. 196.

18–William Beckford (1759–1844), creator of Fonthill Abbey and author of *Vathek* (1786). For Lord Stuart's folly, see Hare, vol. i, ch. ii, p. 170.

19–Catherine, Countess of Caledon; Anne, Countess of Mexborough; Louisa, Lady Stuart; Elizabeth, Countess of Hardwicke.

20–Hedley Shafto Johnstone Vicars (1826–55), officer in the Crimea who underwent an extreme religious conversion and whose story was told by Catherine M. Marsh in *The Memorials of Captain Hedley Vicars* (1855).

21–Hare, vol. iii, p. 43, Louisa, Lady Waterford writing to Canon T. F. Parker, 30 July 1859.

22–*Ibid.*, p. 281: 'It was in this year that Mr Watts and Mr Burne Jones besought Lady Waterford to paint one of her designs on a sufficient scale and with a degree of completeness which should satisfy posterity that "in 1866 there lived an artist as great as Venice ever knew."' G. F. Watts (1817–1904).

23–Sir John (formerly Captain) Leslie, otherwise unidentified.

'Mary Elizabeth Haldane, a Record of a Hundred Years'

Mrs Haldane was publicly famous for two things – the length of her life and the fame of her son. But as many people, whose testimony is worth having, bear witness, she was possessed of a character – serene, judicial, broad-minded – which gave her her own claims to admiration. Yet the century covered by her life was passed in quiet, private living, mostly in the country. In her own autobiographical sketch she depicts a severe and rather dismal upbringing. The terrors of religion were imparted by a governess; cold baths and straw mattresses were the rule; and so Spartan was the discipline that 'she used to wonder why it was a crime to be a child'. Sometimes she escaped, and saw the first locomotive on one occasion, 'a curious, grasshopper-looking machine',[2] at the sight and sound of which her pony bolted. On another she, who was to live through the Great War, saw the first balloon ascend. Her marriage freed her from the misery of adolescence, and she settled down to a life of child-bearing, country pursuits, and neighbourly beneficence, and, though finally bedridden, she became increasingly active-minded. Lord Haldane describes how his mother would read 'difficult philosophical books'[3] in extreme old age, and entered with zeal and intelligence into the talk of the soldiers, writers, and divines who came to Cloan and prized, above all, their visits to the aged lady, sitting up, beautifully dressed, animated and interested, in bed.

1–A notice in the *N&A*, 30 January 1926, (Kp C270.1) of *Mary Elizabeth Haldane. A Record of a Hundred Years (1825–1925)*, edited by her daughter (Hodder & Stoughton, 1926). Mary Elizabeth Burdon-Sanderson married in 1853 Robert Haldane and was the mother of Richard Burdon 1st Viscount Haldane of Cloan (1856–1928), statesman and philosophical writer.
2–For the first quotation, Haldane, ch. ii, p. 86, and for the second, *ibid.*, ch. i, p. 68.
3–*Ibid.*, ch. iii, pp. 123–4.

Robinson Crusoe

This is as handsome an edition of a classic as a classic himself could desire. The three volumes look as if they could be read for ever without shedding a page; as if the print would never grow dim, or the stout binding lose its lustre of red and gold. Then Mr Whibley tells us all we can hope to know about De Foe in the introduction, and there are added those decorous designs by Stothard, engraved by Medland, of trees with innumerable leaves, of waves with crisp curled crests which display so agreeably the simple emotions and careful craftsmanship of the eighteenth century.[2] These words of praise must be uttered firmly and placed conspicuously lest, in the whirl of doubts, questions, and theories which are bound to assail us we forget a proper acknowledgement of our debt.

For there are many ways of approaching these classical volumes. Many professors, many essayists, many reviewers have run up sign-posts with 'To Robinson Crusoe' upon them, but the hesitating reader may well ask which leads quickest to the journey's end? One track meanders delightfully through the heavenly pastures of biography. Who was De Foe? and did he spell his name in one word or two? and which year was he born – 1660 or 1661? The way is delightful: the pastures rich; but whether we shall reach Robinson Crusoe in our lifetime if we follow it is another question. Next, there is a signpost crabbedly and carefully inscribed, 'The Rise and Development of the Novel'. In that land of thickset hedges and bristling brambles we shall learn how the literary tendencies of the seventeenth century were all in favour of the novel; how the spirit of the age had fixed its eye upon fact and detail; how prose had lost its frills and furbelows and become 'close, naked, natural',[3] fitter to express the truth of things than the poetry. Here, too, we might dissipate the waking hours of a happy life, for what will-o'-the-wisp shines brighter or haunts more enchanted forests than the spirit of the age when men of learning, leisure, and enthusiasm scatter all over English literature in her pursuit? Only now and then, as the chase flags, one thinks of the books themselves, somewhere at the end of their avenues, waiting to be read. One begins to wonder whether, if one knew the very hour and moment of De Foe's birth, the colour of his complexion and hair, the history of the origin, rise, growth, development, decline, and fall of the English novel from its conception (say) in Egypt, to its decrease, remote let us hope, in the wilds, perhaps, of Paraguay, one would suck an ounce of additional pleasure from *Robinson Crusoe*, or read it one whit more intelligently.

For however we may wind and wriggle in our approach to books, a lonely battle awaits us at the end. There is a piece of business to be transacted between writer and reader before any further dealings are possible, and to be reminded, in the middle of this, that De Foe's prose owed much to the *Spectator*, or that *Robinson Crusoe* is founded upon the adventures of Alexander Selkirk, is merely a distraction and a worry. It is not detail that we want, but perspective.[4] Until we know how the novelist orders his world, the ornaments of that world, which critics press upon us, the adventures of the writer, to which biographers draw attention, are superfluous possessions of which we can make no use. All alone we must climb upon the novelist's shoulders and gaze through his eyes, until we, too, understand in what order he ranges the large common objects upon which novelists are fated to gaze – man and men, Nature, and, behind or above, the power which is conveniently called God. It is now that the confusion, the misjudgement, and the difficulty begin. For, simple in themselves, these objects can be made monstrous, strange, and indeed unrecognisable by the manner in which they are related to each other. People who live cheek by jowl and breathe the same air yet see trees very large and human beings very small, or the other way about, man vast and trees in miniature. Writers who live at the same moment yet see nothing the same size. Here is Scott, for example, with his mountains looming huge, and his men therefore drawn to scale; Jane Austen picking out the roses on her tea-cups to match the wit of her dialogue; while Peacock bends over Heaven and earth one fantastic distorting mirror, in which the tea-cup may be Vesuvius or Vesuvius a tea-cup.[5] Nevertheless, Scott, Jane Austen, Peacock, lived through the same years; beheld the same world, and are covered, in text-books, by the same curve of history. It is in their perspective that they are different. It is the difference not of time of birth or circumstances, not of those worn old labels, classic and romantic, that distinguishes one writer from another, but the difference in perspective. And if it were granted us to read our writers in the proper focus, then the battle would end in victory, and we could settle down, with the help of critics and historians, to enjoy the fruits.

But here many difficulties arise. For we bring with us a vision of the world which we have taken from reality, composed with our own hands, which is therefore all bound up with our vanities and our loves. It is impossible then not to feel injured and insulted if tricks are played and our own private harmony upset. *Jude the Obscure* appears, or a new volume of Proust, and the papers are flooded with protests.[6] Major Gibbs of Cheltenham would shoot himself tomorrow if life were as Hardy paints it; Miss Wiggs of Hampstead must protest that though Proust's art is wonderful, the real world, thank God, has nothing in common with the distortions of a perverted Frenchman. Both gentleman and lady are trying to control the novelists' perspective so that it shall resemble and reinforce their own. But the great writer – the Hardy, the Proust – goes his way, regardless of private property, and by the sweat of his brow brings order from chaos, plants his tree there, his man here, and lets the robes of the deity flow where he will. In those masterpieces, where his vision is clear and he has achieved order, he inflicts his own perspective upon us so severely and consistently that as often as not we suffer that agony of boredom – we are being wrenched from our supports – tinged with exultation – the view is beautiful all the same – by which we know a great book when we see it.

To return to *Robinson Crusoe* – there are those among us who must admit that it is with tears of boredom, with anguish mixed with exultation that they read it, for it is a masterpiece, and a masterpiece largely because De Foe has throughout kept consistently true to his own sense of perspective. For this reason he thwarts and flouts us at every turn. His subject – a man alone on a desert island – evokes in us who have read Shakespeare and Rousseau,[7] and have our own private idiosyncracy, a vision, shall we say, of sunrises and sunsets, a mind driven to reflect upon society and the soul, in its solitude taking the imprint of every leaf and pebble and yet steeped in the gulfs of its own bitter waters, into which at last burst a troop of man-eating men – some such idea as this rises in outline, and, being false in every particular, has to be corrected at every turn. There are no sunsets and no sunrises; no solitude and no soul. For, as a painter takes his brush and draws a line on the blank canvas to which everything in his picture must conform, so De Foe takes his pen and upon the very first page depicts a large uncompromising solid object, an earthenware pot, a chopping-block –

which we cannot evade or think into non-existence. When we are told, that is to say, where Crusoe got his name, how his father had the gout, and how it was the first of September, 1651, that he set sail, we realise that it is reality, the fact, the substance, that is going to dominate all the rest. So Nature must recede, furl her wings close to her side, and become no fountain of awe and splendour, but the engine of drought or harvest; man be reduced as far as possible to a life-preserving animal; and God shrivel into a magistrate whose seat, cloudy but doubtless convenient, is only a little way above the horizon.

Each sortie of ours in pursuit of information upon those cardinal points of perspective – God, Man, Nature – is snubbed back with ruthless common sense. Robinson Crusoe thinks of God: 'sometimes I would expostulate with myself, why providence should thus completely ruin its creatures ... But something always return'd swift upon me to check these thoughts.'[8] God does not exist. He thinks of Nature, the field 'adorn'd with flowers and grass, and full of very fine woods',[9] but the important thing is that they harbour an abundance of parrots, one of which, if caught, might be tamed and taught to speak. Nature does not exist. He considers the dead, whom he has killed himself. It is of the utmost importance that they should be buried at once, for 'they lay open to the sun and would presently be offensive.'[10] Death does not exist. Nothing exists except an earthenware pot. Finally, that is to say, we are forced back upon what De Foe gives us, and then perceive how, like a great artist, he has forgone this, dared that, in order to bring the prime quality which he knows he possesses to perfection – a sense of reality – into supreme relief. Any enthusiasm for God, any introspection into the soul, any feeling for the beauty of Nature would have weakened the massive effect of fact. As it is, nothing is allowed to move out of its sphere by a hair's breadth; no shadow mitigates the solidity of any object. Every ingenuity is made use of – now a slip in a name, now a detail needlessly given, now a catalogue inserted – to heighten the sense of reality. The result is that we believe implicitly and imbibe without a shadow of doubt the full value of facts; bake, build, dig, and store with a belief in the necessity of all these processes which renews our delight in them until it becomes serious and intent like a child's delight; expand incidents, like those of the wild cat, of the footprint, of the dying goat in the cave, to their full size and importance; and then as the story moves on with a regular normal march, it achieves a certain grandeur by its perfect seriousness, and by the dignity of its truth rouses in us sensations of sublimity and romance for which there is no warrant in the actual facts. None of Stevenson's romances,[11] with all their art, have the same power, for they lack seriousness; no one object is believed in with sufficient conviction to compel the rest to harmony. But De Foe, reiterating that nothing but a plain earthenware pot stands in the foreground, and that to its plainness and earthiness everything else must give way, finally ropes the whole universe into harmony. And is there any reason, we ask ourselves as we shut the book, why the perspective that an earthenware pot requires should not satisfy us as completely, once it is grasped, as man himself, in all his gloom and confusion, with a broken background behind him of Alps and stars?

1–A signed review in the *N&A*, 6 February 1926, (Kp C271) of *The Life and Strange Surprising Adventures of Robinson Crusoe of York. Mariner. Written by Himself* [1719]; *Further Adventures of Robinson Crusoe; Serious Reflections of Robinson Crusoe*. With an introduction by Charles Whibley (3 vols, Constable, 1925) by Daniel Defoe (1660–1731), revised for inclusion in CR2 (see *V VW Essays*). '. . . I read some of the Tempest, to compare with Defoe,' VW wrote to Vita Sackville-West on 7 January 1926, 'But oh my dear Vita, what a rush of delight and relief it is to read poetry after prose!

'So continue your poem: and one day I will explain the torrent of my own emotions about – Shakespeare – compared with Defoe' (*III VW Letters*, no. 1608).

The same issue of the *N&A* contained: LW's 'World of Books' column on 'Mr Pepys and Modernity', discussing *Private Correspondence and Miscellaneous Papers of Samuel Pepys, 1679–1703*, ed. J. R. Tanner; an article on 'The Latest Proust' (*Albertine Disparue*, 1925) by Francis Birrell; and J. M. Keynes on 'Germany's Coming Problem'. See Editorial Note, p. xxv. Reading Notes (Berg, IV). Reprinted CE.

2–Thomas Stothard (1755–1834), painter and illustrator of books by, among others, Swift, Fielding, Smollett, Richardson and Sterne. His designs made 'a new departure in book illustration by their variety of invention, their literary sympathy, their spirit and their grace' (*DNB*). Thomas Medland (d. 1833) whose engravings from Stothard's designs for the 1790 edition of *Robinson Crusoe* were said to be his single most successful work (*DNB*).

3–The source of this quotation and the authorship of 'The Rise and Development of the Novel' (which may perhaps be VW's invention) remain undiscovered.

4–VW's appeal to perspective here recalls her diary entry for 7 December 1925 where she explored theories subsequently developed at length in 'Phases of Fiction' (see *V VW Essays*.) 'I don't think,' she wrote, 'it is a matter of "development" but something to do with prose & poetry, in novels. For instance Defoe at one end: E. Brontë at the other. Reality is something they put at different distances.'

5–Sir Walter Scott (1771–1832); Jane Austen (1775–1817); Thomas Love Peacock (1785–1866) – all three of whom are discussed at some length in 'Phases of Fiction'.

6–Thomas Hardy (1840–1928), *Jude the Obscure* (1895). Marcel Proust (1871–1922) – also discussed in 'Phases of Fiction' – whose *Albertine Disparue* had recently been published (see note 1 above).

7–Jean-Jacques Rousseau (1712–78), author of *Émile* (1762) and *Du Contrat Social* (1762), was a great admirer of *Robinson Crusoe*. For VW and Shakespeare see note 1 above.

8–For the matter up to the ellipsis, Whibley, vol. i, p. 71, and for the remainder, *ibid.*, pp. 71–2.

9–*Ibid.*, p. 126.

10–*Ibid.*, p. 284, which has: 'which lay open to the sun'.

11–Robert Louis Stevenson (1850–94), for VW on whom see 'Phases of Fiction'.

'Queen Alexandra the Well-Beloved'

There can be no doubt that Queen Alexandra was an exquisitely pretty woman. Even the photographs in the present book put that beyond a doubt. Slim, upright, composed, one beautiful little hand clasped tenderly over a lap dog, the other controlling a perfect parasol, she drives through Rotten Row as, Miss Villiers would have us believe, she drove through the greater part of the nineteenth century. At the same time, she is completely dumb, and Miss Villiers is far too well-bred a courtier to break the Royal reserve. We are told nothing about her in the present little book except such facts as befit a lady with a lap dog. She was fond of sketching and music and children. Perhaps her most valuable contribution to her age was that she raised the standard of comfort for dogs. The kennels at Sandringham were famous, and the Queen attended to her pets with her own hands. Volumes, too, might be devoted to the gifts of chocolate boxes and dressing gowns, which descended from the sky, as if by miracle, upon the heads of ecstatic old men and women. But perhaps Miss Villier's most valuable contribution to our knowledge of the Royal Family is the story she tells of a workman who found his way through a drain-pipe into Queen Mary's bedroom. She credits him with loyal motives – he wished to demonstrate, not to eavesdrop – and she recalls, what it is always pleasant to remember, the earlier exploits of the Boy Jones. For in writing the life of Queen Alexandra, it is frequently necessary to talk of something else.

1—A notice in the *N&A*, 6 February 1926, (Kp C271.1) of *Queen Alexandra the Well-Beloved* (Stanley Paul, 1925) by Elizabeth Villiers. Alexandra Caroline Mary Charlotte Louise Julia (b. 1844) of Denmark was queen-consort of Edward VII. She had died on 20 November 1925.

The Life of John Mytton

VW's essay in *Vogue*, early March 1926, (Kp C272) was later revised for inclusion, under the title 'Jack Mytton', in *The Common Reader*: 2nd series (1932). The reader is referred to *V VW Essays*, where the revised version, together with variants in the form of footnotes, is reprinted in its place as part of *The Common Reader*.

'Paradise in Piccadilly'

Paradise in Piccadilly is Albany – Mr Furniss drops the 'The'. The name of that secluded mansion in the corner of your card is said to do more for you than virtue, rank, or riches, or proves that you are the possessor of them all. It was in 1804 that Mr Copland bought from the Duke of York and Albany the house that had originally belonged to Stephen Fox and had been sold by him to Lord Melbourne in 1770.[2] Mr Copland, anticipating the demand for flats, had the brilliant idea of converting the mansion into sets of apartments for gentlemen. As the law of Albany is that no material change can be made without the consent of all the lodgers, and as, until recent years, all the lodgers were men, the building has remained in spirit and in substance precisely as it was in the year 1804. The place has escaped the historian, as indeed it is apt to escape the sightseer. The truth is that once you have commented upon the beauty of the position and referred to the fact that Byron lived there a short, and Lord Macaulay a long time,[3] there is little to be said. One may add that the oil lamps have been replaced by gas, and that it was due to a hoax by Lord Macaulay's niece, who warned him that a robbery was planned, that the present iron gates were hastily provided. Mr Furniss has done his best to fill the book with stories of the occupants, and when these ran thin, has filled up pages with copious quotations from references to Albany in fiction. But this is as it should be. The inhabitants, we have no doubt, much prefer to be left alone.

1–A notice in the *N&A*, 6 March 1926, (Kp C272.1) of *Paradise in Piccadilly. The Story of Albany*. With illustrations from sketches by the author and from photographs (John Lane The Bodley Head Ltd, 1925) by Harry Furniss.
2–Alexander Copland, a businessman, otherwise unidentified, purchased what was originally called 'Piccadilly House' from Frederick, Duke of York and Albany (1763–1827), son of George III. He had obtained the property from the 1st Lord Melbourne, who had bought it from Stephen Fox, 2nd Lord Holland.
3–Lord Byron (1788–1824) was a tenant in 1814–15, Lord Macaulay (1800–59) for fifteen years from 1839.

'Reminiscences of Mrs Comyns Carr'

Mrs Comyns Carr was born in 1850, and thus lived through that curious age when Bohemia, to which she was proud to belong, was beginning, thanks to Lady Lindsay, Lady Lewis, and Lady Jeune,[2] and others, to be admitted to society. But Mrs Comyns Carr did not particularly enjoy admittance, as her sketch of Mrs Wemyss's grim entertainment bears witness. She dabbled in the Princes and the beauties, the Oscar Wildes, Mrs Langtrys, and Prince of Waleses;[3] but with charming spontaneity preferred her own circle, where the men wore peg-top trousers, and the women, following her own leadership, refused to be cumbered with bustles and crinolines. This lively and unembarrassed spirit is perceptible throughout her book. She drew all the writers and painters – Burne-Jones, Sargent, Meredith, Henry James[4] – to her circle, though in her early days the bed had to be made up to look the part of dinner table. Eventually she became dress designer to Ellen Terry, thanks to a happy experiment of hers with a muslin frock and a potato steamer. For some years she was always behind the scenes or sitting with the sarcastic and formidable Irving in the stage box, or awaiting in fear the non-arrival of Ellen Terry.[5] She would dash in two minutes before her call and explain airily that she had been to the Minories to see if a begging letter writer were telling the truth. Irving himself never dared to upbraid her. Off she dashed, draped in Mrs Carr's wondrous gowns of Bohemian silk and beetles' wings. But the charm of the book does not come from its good stories; it comes from the sense it gives that, however grim and gaunt the stock Victorian figures may have been, another life washed at their feet – a life of good fellowship, good eating, merriment, hard work, and ladies, if the portraits are to be trusted, of exquisite grace and charm.

1–A notice in the *N&A*, 20 March 1926, (Kp C272.2) of *Mrs J. Comyns Carr's Reminiscences*. Edited by Eve Adam. With 24 illustrations (Hutchinson & Co. Ltd, 1926). Mrs Comyns Carr, *née* Alice Strettell, wife of the dramatist and critic Jo Comyns Carr, was from 1882 Ellen Terry's dress designer.
2–Lady Lindsay, wife of Sir Coutts Lindsay; Lady Lewis, wife of Sir George Lewis; Lady Jeune, wife of Sir Francis Jeune, Baron St Helier.
3–Millicent Ann Mary Wemyss, of Wemyss Castle, a granddaughter of William IV. Oscar Wilde (1856–1900); Lillie Langtry (1853–1929); Edward VII (1841–1910).
4–Edward Burne-Jones (1833–98); John Singer Sargent (1856–1925); George Meredith (1828–1909); Henry James (1843–1916).
5–Ellen Terry (1847–1928); Henry Irving (1838–1905).

'The Days of Dickens'

This very sprightly and entertaining book collects a mass of information about the early and middle years of Victorian life which certainly bears out the publishers' statement that 'the days of Dickens and Thackeray seem almost as remote as the days of the Stuarts'.[2] One feeling dominates the reader – a sense of escape. For whatever charges may be brought against the present, we could scarcely tolerate one day lived as our great-grandfathers lived it. Consider travel. Early one March morning two of the outside passengers on the Bath Mail were found frozen to death, while a third expired soon afterwards. This was only an exaggeration of the miseries ordinarily suffered in cold weather by the outside fares.

'Postboys were frequently lifted out of their saddles at the point of death.'[3] Or consider sanitation. The drainage of London until 1860 was based on legislation and plans dating from the reigns of Henry VIII and William and Mary. The River Thames was in so disgusting a state that Members of Parliament could hardly bear the smell in the House of Commons. Seven miles of the river in July, 1858 were reported to be in a state of 'putrid fermentation'.[4] In factories children were harnessed to trucks like dogs, and scrambled along on all fours. Little boys were driven up chimneys or shoved down head first. As lately as February, 1864, five pirates were hung in a row outside Newgate. It is true that the splendours of the aristocracy were more solid than they are now, the country more profoundly rural, the mail coaches picturesque, and genius, at least in art and science, prolific. But if the reader wishes to heighten the relish of his own hot baths and electric light, he cannot do better than study *The Days of Dickens* – a book, moreover, stuffed with odds and ends of amusing information.

1–A notice in the *N&A*, 20 March 1926, (Kp C272.3) of *The Days of Dickens. A Glance at Some Aspects of Early Victorian Life in London* (Routledge and Sons, 1926) by Arthur L. Hayward.
2–Hayward, ch. i, p. 1.
3–*Ibid.*, ch. v, p. 79.
4–*Ibid.*, ch. vi, p. 103.

'The Flurried Years'

Many people, of course, will complain that Miss Hunt has outraged decency by speaking so frankly of people still alive, and by revealing so poignantly the sorrows of her own heart. But after all, the hardened reader of memoirs is so well supplied with books stuffed with horsehair that he can hardly help welcoming one made out of the tenderer material of flesh and blood. It is true that blood is a messy liquid; tempers are bound to be ruffled and dignities smeared by writers who dabble their fingers in it. Yet, for all its frankness, Miss Hunt's story is by no means plain sailing. Exactly what happened, and why what happened did so happen, we confess to being still in doubt. 'Like Miss Flite I have haunted for years the law courts of this as well as those of other countries,'[2] says Miss Hunt, and she takes it for granted that the reader is as well versed in legal judgements as she is. It does not very much matter. The book is a novelist's book, and situations are presented as they appear imaginatively, not as they happen prosaically and accurately day by day. Through the glamour and the sordidity (both are well mixed) loom up several of the great Edwardian figures with uncommon brilliancy – Conrad, Hudson, and in particular Henry James.[3] Whether his letters to Miss Hunt have already been published we know not; they are highly and exquisitely characteristic of the unofficial side – the timid, prudish, spinsterly side of that great novelist. Unpleasantness and brilliance are oddly mixed throughout the book, for Miss Hunt has lived her flurried years in the purlieus of letters, and, as we all know, the precincts of genius (but she runs the word to death) are apt to be unsavoury.

1–A notice in the *N&A*, 20 March 1926, (Kp C272.4) of *The Flurried Years*. With sixteen illustrations (Hurst and Blackett Ltd, n.d.) by [Isobel] Violet Hunt (1862–1942), who, from 1911, lived with the author Ford Madox Ford as his wife.
2–Hunt, Part I, 1908, p. 15; Miss Flite, character in Dickens's *Bleak House* (1852–3).
3–Joseph Conrad (1857–1924); W. H. Hudson (1841–1922); Henry James (1843–1916).

'Steeplejacks and Steeplejacking'

Mr Larkins's book is warranted to turn the reader giddy. Often in reading it one has had to cling tightly to the arms of one's chair. For without any literary artifice, simply by telling how he has stood on the tops of chimneys, felt them rock beneath him, or had the lightning playing about his ears while exposed upon a church steeple, he does what writers often vainly attempt – he communicates his own thrill, and we add to it from our own weakness a giddiness which was never his. For he has very seldom lost his nerve, in spite of experiences which one might expect to haunt his pillow for a lifetime. Employed to repair the Nelson column, for instance, he found on reaching the top that the statue stands upon a platform with a sharp slope outwards. It was greasy with soot, and Mr Larkins's foot slipped. Next moment his 'feet and legs hung over the edge ... I only saved myself in the nick of time by using elbows as brakes while lying flat on my back.'[2] Another inch, and he would have been over. The very top of the column serves, he found, as a cemetery for London birds. Further, he is an expert thrower of chimneys, and for a bet will walk along a plank the two ends of which are supported on the two summits of factory chimneys. The moral seems to be that, once you get used to it, climbing a steeple is no whit more dangerous than sitting at a desk. But the reader, being green to the work, will get enough thrills from Mr Larkins's story to break his neck a dozen times over.

1—A notice in the *N&A*, 27 March 1926, (Kp C272.5) of *Steeplejacks and Steeple-jacking* (Jonathan Cape Ltd, 1926) by William Larkins.
2—Larkins, ch. xii, p. 170, which has: 'my elbows'.

A Professor of Life

On a certain Wednesday in March 1889 Walter Raleigh, then aged twenty-eight, gave his first lecture upon English literature in Manchester. It was not his first lecture by any means, for he had already lectured the natives of India on the same subject for two years. After Manchester came Liverpool; after Liverpool, Glasgow; after Glasgow, Oxford.[2] At all these places he lectured incessantly upon English literature. Once he lectured three times a day. He became, indeed, such an adept at the art of lecturing that towards the end 'sometimes he would prepare what he had to say in his half-hour's walk from his home at Ferry Hinksey'.[3] People who heard him said that his lectures stimulated them, opened their eyes, made them think for themselves. '"Raleigh's not always at his best, but when he's good nobody can touch him" – that was the general verdict.'[4] Nevertheless, in the course of two large volumes filled with delightful and often brilliant letters it would be difficult to find a single remark of any interest whatsoever about English literature.

There is necessarily a great deal of talk about the profession of teaching literature, and the profession of writing literary text books, of 'doing Chaucer in six chapters and Wordsworth, better known as Daddy, also in six chapters'.[5] But when one looks for the unprofessional talk, the talk which is talked among friends when business hours are over, one is bewildered and disappointed. Is this all that the Professor of English Literature has to say? 'Scott tomorrow – not a poet I think but fine old man. Good old Scott.'[6] 'The weak point in William [Blake] is not his Reason, which is A.I, but his imagination . . . Wonderful things the inspired old bustard said from time to time in conversation.'[7] 'As for old Bill Wordsworth he is the same old stick-in-the-mud as ever . . . He gets praised chiefly for his celebrated imitation of Shakespeare (which is really very good) and for his admirable reproduction of a bleat. But he has a turn of his own, if only he would do it and be damned to him.'[8] Any clever man at a dinner party anxious not to scare the rowing blue or the city magnate who happens to be within earshot would have talked about books exactly as Raleigh wrote about them at his leisure. There is nothing to suggest that literature was a matter of profound interest to him when he was not lecturing about it. When we read the letters of Keats, the diary of the Goncourts, the letters of Lamb, the casual remarks of that unfashionable poet Tennyson,[9] we feel that, waking or sleeping, these men never stopped thinking about literature. It is kneaded into the stuff of their brains. Their fingers are dyed in it. Whatever they touch is stained with it. Whatever they are doing their minds fill up involuntarily with some aspect of the absorbing question. Nor does it seem to have occurred to them to wonder what the rowing blue will think of them for talking seriously about books. 'I think poetry should surprise by a fine excess and not by singularity; it should strike the reader as a wording of his own highest thoughts and appear almost a remembrance,'[10] wrote Keats, and there is not a damn in the sentence. But the Professor of English Literature could scarcely open his lips without dropping into slang; he could never mention Bill Blake or Bill Shakespeare or old Bill Wordsworth without seeming to apologise for bringing books into the talk at all. Yet there is no doubt, Walter Raleigh was one of the best Professors of Literature of our time; he did brilliantly whatever it is that Professors are supposed to do. How then shall we compose the difference – solve the discrepancy?

In the first place the Professor of English Literature is not there to teach people how to write; he is there to teach them how to read. Moreover, those people include city magnates, politicians, schoolmistresses, soldiers, scientists, mothers of families, country clergymen in embryo. Many of them have never opened a book before. Many will seldom get a chance of opening a book again. They have to be taught – but what? Raleigh himself had no doubts on this point. His business was 'only to get people to love the poets'.[11] 'To make people old or young,' he wrote, 'care for say the principal English poets as much or half as much as I do – that would, I am vain enough to think, be something – if it can be done.'[12] He obstinately refused to stuff his pupils with facts. 'The facts, it is true, tell in examinations. But you will none of you be any nearer Heaven ten years hence for having taken a B.A. degree, while for a love and understanding of Keats you may raise yourself several inches.'[13] He had himself spent no time scraping away the moss, repairing the broken noses on the fabric of English literature; and he did not press that pursuit upon his pupils. He talked his lectures almost out of his head. He joked, he told stories. He made the undergraduates rock with laughter. He drew them in crowds to his lecture room. And they went away loving something or other. Perhaps it was Keats. Perhaps it was the British Empire. Certainly it was Walter Raleigh. But we should be much surprised if anybody went away loving poetry, loving the art of letters.

Nor is it difficult to find the reason. It is written large over Walter Raleigh's books – the *English Novel, Style, Shakespeare*[14] and the rest. They have every virtue; they are readable, just, acute, stimulating and packed with information; they are as firm in style and hard in substance as a macadamised road. But the man who wrote them had no generous measure of the gifts of a writer. The maker of these rather tight, highly academic books had never been outside the critical fence. No novel, no poem, no play had ever lured him away from his prefaces, his summings up, his surveys. The excitement, the adventure, the turmoil of creation were unknown to him. But the critic who makes us love poetry is always sufficiently gifted to have had experiences of his own. He feels his way along a line spun by his own failures and successes. He may stumble; he may stammer; he may be incapable of orderly survey. But it is the Keats, the Coleridge, the Lamb, the Flaubert who get to the heart of the matter. It is in the toil and strife of writing that they have forced the door open and gone within and told us what they have seen there. When Walter Raleigh held a pen in his hand it behaved with the utmost propriety. He never wrote a bad sentence; but he never wrote a sentence which broke down barriers. He never pressed on over the ruins of his own culture to the discovery of something better. He remained trim and detached on the high road, a perfect example of the Professor of Literature who has no influence whatever upon the art of writing. Soon, therefore, for he was by temperament highly adventurous, he began to find literature a little dull. He began to separate literature from life. He began to cry out upon 'culture' and 'culture bugs'.[15] He began to despise critics and criticism. 'I can't help feeling that critical admiration for what another man has written is an emotion for spinsters,'[16] he wrote. He really believed, he said, 'not in refinement and scholarly elegance, those are only a game; but in blood feuds, and the chase of wild beasts and marriage by capture'.[17] In short, being incapable of humbug, a man of entire sincerity and great vitality, Walter Raleigh ceased to profess literature and became instead a Professor of Life.

There is ample evidence in the letters alone that he had a remarkable aptitude for this branch of learning. He seems never to have been bored, never to have been doubtful, never to have been sentimental. He laid hold on things with enviable directness. The whole force of his being seems to have played spontaneously upon whatever he wished and yet to have been controlled by an unerring sense that some things matter and some things do not. His equilibrium was perfect. Whether he was set down in India or Oxford, among the simple or the learned, the aristocrats or the Dons he found his balance at once and got the utmost out of the situation. It is easy to imagine the race and flash of his talk, and what fine unexpected things he said, and what pinnacles of fun he raised and how for all his extravagance and irresponsibility the world that his wit lit up was held steady by his fundamental sanity and good sense. He was the most enchanting of companions – upon that all are agreed.

But the difficulty remained. Once make the fatal distinction between life and letters, once exalt life and find literature an occupation for old maids and inevitably, if one is Walter Raleigh, one becomes discontented with mere praise. Professors must talk; but the lover of life must live. Unfortunately life in the sense of 'blood feuds and the chase of wild beasts, and marriage by capture' was hard to come by in the last years of the nineteenth century. Queen

Victoria was on the throne, Lord Salisbury was in power, and the British Empire was growing daily more robust. A breath of fresh air blew in with the Boer War. Raleigh hailed it with a shout of relief '... the British officer (and man) restores one's joy in the race,'[18] he said. He was coming to feel that there is some close connection between writing and fighting, that in an age like his when the fighter did not write and the writer did not fight, the divorce was unfortunate – especially for literature. 'Were it not better to seek training on a battlefield, and use the first words one learns at mess?'[19] he asked. All his sympathies were tending towards action. He was growing more and more tired of culture and criticism, more definitely of opinion that the 'learned critic is a beast',[20] that 'Education has taken the fine bloom off the writing of books,'[21] less and less attracted by writing at all, until finally, in 1913, he bursts out that he 'can't read Shakespeare any more ... Not that I think him a bad author, particularly' he adds, 'but I can't bear literature'.[22] When the guns fired in August 1914 no one saluted them more rapturously than the Professor of English Literature at Oxford. 'The air is better to breathe than it has been for years,' he exclaimed. 'I'm glad I lived to see it, and sick that I'm not in it.'[23]

It seemed indeed as if his chance of life had come too late. He still seemed fated to praise fighting, but not to fight, to lecture about life but not to live. He did what a man of his age could do. He drilled. He marched. He wrote pamphlets. He lectured more frequently than ever; he practically ceased to read. At length he was made historian of the Air Force.[24] To his infinite satisfaction he consorted with soldiers. To his immense delight he flew to Baghdad. He died within a week or two after his return. But what did that matter? The Professor of English Literature had lived at last.

1–A signed review in *Vogue*, early May 1926, (Kp C273) of *The Letters of Sir Walter Raleigh*, ed. Lady Raleigh, with a Preface by D. Nichol Smith (2 vols, Methuen, 1926), subtitled: 'The Letters of Walter Raleigh, a Brilliant Commentary on the Life and Work of a Great Professor of English Literature'.

VW wrote to Vita Sackville-West, 17 February 1926: 'And, Vita, answer me this: why are all professors of English literature ashamed of English literature? Walter Raleigh calls Shakespeare "Billy Shax" – Blake, "Bill" – a good poem "a bit of all right". This shocks me. I've been reading his letters' (*III VW Letters*, no. 1621). To Clive Bell she wrote on 9 April: 'I am reading Mrs Sidney Webbs autobiography and find it enthralling. As for Walter Raleigh I find him disgusting' (*ibid.*, no. 1627). In her diary, 11 April, she noted: '[Beatrice Webb] taps a great stream of thought. Unlike that self-conscious poseur Walter Raleigh she is much more interested in facts & truth than in what will shock people & what a professor ought not to say.'

Three years later, in *A Room of One's Own*, she 'began to envisage an age to come of pure, of self-assertive virility, such as the letters of professors (take Sir Walter Raleigh's letters, for instance) seem to forbode, and the rulers of Italy have already brought into being' (Triad/Panther, 1977, p. 98). See also 'Trafficks and Discoveries', *I VW Essays*, and 'Romance', *II VW Essays*. Reprinted, as 'Walter Raleigh', *CDB, CE*.

2—Walter Raleigh (1861–1922), knighted 1911, was personal assistant to Professor A. W. Ward at Victoria University, Manchester, March–November 1889, and thereafter, successively, Professor of English Literature at Liverpool – where his relation by marriage Lytton Strachey was for a period his student – Glasgow, and Oxford.

3—Raleigh, vol. i, Preface, p. xviii.

4—*Ibid.*

5—*Ibid.*, to W. P. Ker, 1 December 1900, p. 223: 'I did mean to do Chaucer in six chapters . . .'

6—*Ibid.*, to his sister Jessie, 29 April 1889, p. 125, slightly adapted.

7—*Ibid.*, vol. ii, to John Sampson, 17 November 1905, p. 284, slightly adapted; the square brackets are VW's.

8—*Ibid.*, vol. i, to the same, 16 May 1901.

9—John Keats (1795–1821), for whose letters see next note; Edmond (1822–96) and Jules (1830–70) de Goncourt, *Journal des Goncourts. Mémoires de la vie littéraire* (9 vols, Paris, 1887–96); Charles Lamb (1775–1834), whose letters VW probably read in the edition of Alfred Ainger (2nd ed., 2 vols, Macmillan, 1904); Alfred, Lord Tennyson (1809–92).

10—John Keats, *Letters . . .*, ed. Sidney Colvin (Macmillan, 1891), to John Taylor, 27 February 1818, p. 77.

11—Raleigh, vol. i, to his sister Jessie, 28 November 1889, p. 141, adapted.

12—*Ibid.*, to J. M. Mackay, 30 November 1889, p. 142.

13—*Ibid.*, to his sister Jessie, 29 April 1889, p. 125, which has 'Examination'.

14—*The English Novel* (1891), *Style* (1897), *Shakespeare* (1907).

15—E.g., *ibid.*, to Mrs F. Gotch, 23 August 1903, p. 251, on the birth of his daughter: 'My house *shall* be a fit place for a Lady . . . There ain't going to be no culture, nor nothing horrid like that. If I'm going to give up saying Damn, she mustn't read the works of Carlyle to me – must she?', and *ibid.*, to John Sampson, 6 January 1902, p. 236: 'A simple culture-bug, brought up in superstition. "Educated poet-lovers." Mrs Browning is the priestess of the class. The harm she did to Bob!'

16—*Ibid.*, to John Sampson, 31 December 1904, p. 268: 'Bradley's book on Shakespeare is good . . . Even with it I can't help feeling that critical admiration for what another man has written is an emotion for spinsters. Shakes. didn't want it.'

17—*Ibid.*, to L. J., 5 October 1889, p. 138: 'Culture is what they are after and there is an element of barbarity in my instincts that makes me ill contented in such company. I can talk the lingo, too, in an idle half-hour. But I really believe, not in refinement . . .'

18—*Ibid.*, to his sister Alice, 14 November 1899, p. 213: 'We are both eaten up with

the War, not for itself, but because the British officer (and man)...' Queen
Victoria died in 1901; the Conservative premier Lord Salisbury's third and final
period as prime minister ended in 1902, in which year the South African War also
came to a close.

19—*Ibid.*, to W. P. Ker, 30 March 1897, p. 193, slightly adapted.

20—The source of this quotation remains untraced.

21—Raleigh, vol. ii, to Emile Legouis, 4 October 1911, p. 372.

22—*Ibid.*, to W. Macneile Dixon, 8 September 1913, p. 396: 'The worst of it is, I
can't read Shakespeare any more, so I have to remember the old tags. Not that...'

23—*Ibid.*, to Mrs Walter Crum, 8 August 1914, p. 404.

24—Raleigh was in 1918 commissioned by the Air Ministry to write the official
history of the Royal Air Force, of which he lived to produce one volume: *The War
in the Air* (1922).

The Cinema

People say that the savage no longer exists in us, that we are at the
fag end of civilisation, that everything has been said already and
that it is too late to be ambitious. But these philosophers have presumably forgotten the movies. They have never seen the savages of
the twentieth century watching the pictures. They have never sat
themselves in front of the screen and thought how, for all the
clothes on their backs and the carpets at their feet, no great distance
separates them from those bright-eyed naked men who knocked
two bars of iron together and heard in that clangour a foretaste of
the music of Mozart.

The bars in this case of course are so highly wrought and so
covered over with accretions of alien matter that it is extremely difficult to hear anything distinctly. All is bubble bubble, swarm and
chaos. We are peering over the edge of a cauldron in which fragments seem to simmer, and now and again some vast shape heaves
and seems about to haul itself up out of chaos and the savage in us
starts forward with delight. Yet, to begin with, the art of the cinema
seems a simple and even a stupid art. That is the King shaking hands
with a football team; that is Sir Thomas Lipton's yacht; that is Jack
Horner winning the Grand National.[2] The eye licks it all up instantaneously and the brain, agreeably titillated, settles down to
watch things happening without bestirring itself to think. For the
ordinary eye, the English unaesthetic eye, is a simple mechanism,

which takes care that the body does not fall down coal-holes, provides the brain with toys and sweetmeats and can be trusted to go on behaving like a competent nursemaid until the brain comes to the conclusion that it is time to wake up. What is its surprise then to be roused suddenly in the midst of its agreeable somnolence and asked for help? The eye is in difficulties. The eye says to the brain, 'Something is happening which I do not in the least understand. You are needed.' Together they look at the King, the boat, the horse, and the brain sees at once that they have taken on a quality which does not belong to the simple photograph of real life. They have become not more beautiful, in the sense in which pictures are beautiful, but shall we call it (our vocabulary is miserably insufficient) more real, or real with a different reality from that which we perceive in daily life. We behold them as they are when we are not there. We see life as it is when we have no part in it. As we gaze we seem to be removed from the pettiness of actual existence, its cares, its conventions. The horse will not knock us down. The King will not grasp our hands. The wave will not wet our feet. Watching the antics of our kind from this post of vantage we have time to feel pity and amusement, to generalise, to endow one man with the attributes of a race; watching boats sail and waves break we have time to open the whole of our mind wide to beauty and to register on top of this the queer sensation – beauty will continue to be beautiful whether we behold it or not. Further, all this happened, we are told, ten years ago. We are beholding a world which has gone beneath the waves. Brides are emerging from the Abbey; ushers are ardent; mothers are tearful; guests are joyful; and it is all over and done with. The war opened its chasm at the feet of all this innocence and ignorance. But it was thus that we danced and pirouetted, thus that the sun shone and the clouds scudded, up to the very end. The brain adds all this to what the eye sees upon the screen.

But the picture makers seem dissatisfied with these obvious sources of interest – the wonders of the actual world, flights of gulls, or ships on the Thames; the fascination of contemporary life – the Mile End Road, Piccadilly Circus. They want to be improving, altering, making an art of their own – naturally for so much seems to be within their scope. So many arts at first stood ready to offer their help. For example, there was literature. All the famous novels of the world with their well known characters and their famous scenes only asked to be put on the films. What could be easier, what could be simpler? The cinema fell upon its prey with immense rapacity and to this moment largely subsists upon the body of its unfortunate victim. But the results have been disastrous to both. The alliance is unnatural. Eye and brain are torn asunder ruthlessly as they try vainly to work in couples. The eye says, 'Here is Anna Karenina,'[3] and a voluptuous lady in black velvet wearing pearls comes before us. The brain exclaims, 'That is no more Anna Karenina than it is Queen Victoria!' For the brain knows Anna almost entirely by the inside of her mind – her charm, her passion, her despair, whereas all the emphasis is now laid upon her teeth, her pearls and her velvet. The cinema proceeds, 'Anna falls in love with Vronsky' – that is to say the lady in black velvet falls into the arms of a gentleman in uniform and they kiss with enormous succulence, great deliberation, and infinite gesticulation on a sofa in an extremely well appointed library. So we lurch and lumber through the most famous novels of the world. So we spell them out in words of one syllable written in the scrawl of an illiterate schoolboy. A kiss is love. A smashed chair is jealousy. A grin is happiness. Death is a hearse. None of these things has the least connection with the novel that Tolstoy wrote and it is only when we give up trying to connect the pictures with the book that we guess from some scene by the way – a gardener mowing the lawn outside, for example, or a tree shaking its branches in the sunshine – what the cinema might do if it were left to its own devices.

But what then are its own devices? If it ceased to be a parasite in what fashion would it walk erect? At present it is only from hints and accidents that one can frame any conjecture. For instance at a performance of *Dr Caligari*[4] the other day a shadow shaped like a tadpole suddenly appeared at one corner of the screen. It swelled to an immense size, quivered, bulged and sank back again into nonentity. For a moment it seemed to embody some monstrous diseased imagination of the lunatic's brain. For a moment it seemed as if thought could be conveyed by shape more effectively than by words. The monstrous quivering tadpole seemed to be fear itself, and not the statement 'I am afraid.' In fact, the shadow was accidental, and the effect unintentional. But if a shadow at a certain moment can suggest so much more than the actual gestures, the actual words of men and women in a state of fear, it seems plain that the cinema has within its grasp innumerable symbols for emotions that have so far failed to find expression. Terror has besides its ordinary forms the shape of a tadpole; it burgeons, bulges, quivers, disappears. Anger might writhe like an infuriated worm in black zigzags across a white sheet. Anna and Vronsky need no longer scowl and grimace. They have at their command — but here the imagination fumbles and is baulked. For what characteristics does thought possess which can be rendered visible to the eye without the help of words? It has speed and slowness; dart-like directness and vaporous circumlocution. But it has also an inveterate tendency especially in moments of emotion to make images run side by side with itself, to create a likeness of the thing thought about, as if by so doing it took away its sting, or made it beautiful and comprehensible. In Shakespeare, as everybody knows, the most complex ideas, the most intense emotions form chains of images, through which we pass, however rapidly and completely they change, as up the loops and spirals of a twisting stair. But obviously the poet's images are not to be cast in bronze or traced with pencil and paint. They are compact of a thousand suggestions, of which the visual is only the most obvious or the uppermost. Even the simplest image such as 'My luve's like a red, red rose, that's newly sprung in June'[5] presents us with moisture and warmth and the glow of crimson and the softness of petals inextricably mixed and strung upon the lilt of a rhythm which suggests the emotional tenderness of love. All this, which is accessible to words and to words alone, the cinema must avoid.

But if so much of our thinking and feeling is connected with seeing there must be some residue of visual emotion not seized by artist or painter-poet which may await the cinema. That such symbols will be quite unlike the real objects which we see before us seems highly probable. Something abstract, something moving, something calling only for the very slightest help from words or from music to make itself intelligible — of such movements, of such abstractions the films may in time to come be composed. And once this prime difficulty is solved, once some new symbol for expressing thought is found, the film maker has enormous riches at his command. Physical realities, the very pebbles on the beach, the very quivers of the lips, are his for the asking. His Vronsky and his Anna are there in the flesh. If to this reality he could add emotion, and thought, then he would begin to haul his booty in hand over hand. Then as smoke can be seen pouring from Vesuvius, we should be able to see wild and lovely and grotesque thoughts pouring from men in dress suits and women with shingled heads. We should see these emotions mingling together and affecting each other. We should see violent changes of emotion produced by their collision. The most fantastic contrasts could be flashed before us with a speed which the writer can only toil after in vain. The past could be unrolled, distances could be annihilated. And those terrible dislocations which are inevitable when Tolstoy has to pass from the story of Anna to the story of Levin could be bridged by some device of scenery. We should have the continuity of human life kept before us by the repetition of some object common to both lives.

All this guessing and clumsy turning over of unknown forces points at any rate away from any art we know in the direction of an art which we can only surmise. It points down a long road strewn with obstacles of every sort. For the film maker must come by his convention, as painters and writers and musicians have done before him. He must make us believe that what he shows us, fantastic though it seems, has some relation with the great veins and arteries of our existence. He must connect it with what we are pleased to call reality. He must make us believe that our loves and hates lie that way too. How slow a process this is bound to be, and attended with what pain and ridicule and indifference can easily be foretold when we remember how painful novelty is, how the smallest twig even upon the oldest tree offends our sense of propriety. And here it is not a question of a new twig, but of a new trunk and new roots from the earth upwards.

Yet remote as it is, intimations are not wanting that the emotions are accumulating, the time is coming, and the art of the cinema is about to be brought to birth. Watching crowds, watching the chaos of the streets in the lazy way in which faculties detached from use watch and wait, it seems sometimes as if movements and colours, shapes and sounds had come together and waited for someone to seize them and convert their energy into art; then, uncaught, they disperse and fly asunder again. At the cinema for a moment through the mists of irrelevant emotions, through the thick counterpane of immense dexterity and enormous efficiency one has glimpses of something vital within. But the kick of life is instantly concealed by more dexterity, further efficiency.

For the cinema has been born the wrong end first. The mechanical skill is far in advance of the art to be expressed. It is as if the savage tribe instead of finding two bars of iron to play with had found scattering the sea shore fiddles, flutes, saxophones, grand pianos by Erard and Bechstein,[6] and had begun with incredible energy but without knowing a note of music to hammer and thump upon them all at the same time.

1–A signed essay in *Arts* (New York), June 1926 (Kp C274), also published in *N&A*, 3 July 1926, and, as 'The Movies and Reality', in *NR*, 4 August 1926 (see Appendix II). In a letter written on 3 September 1925 to T. S. Eliot, then establishing the *New Criterion*, VW refers to 'two or three things promised to America' (*III VW Letters*, no. 1577). One of these, still 'undecided', appears possibly to have become the present piece. 'I am so much annoyed to find that the article I sent you,' VW wrote to Virgil Barker, editor of *Arts*, on 27 September 1926, 'has been printed in the New republic. It appeared some time in August, when I was in the country, or I would have written to you before.

'The New republic has an arrangement with the Nation by which it can take certain articles which are sent to it in proof. The Secretary at the Nation is convinced that no proof was sent, and I can only suppose that some one in the New republic took the article in ignorance. We have written to complain. I can only offer you my sincere apologies and hope that as the publication was so much later than yours no harm was done to The Arts' (*VI VW Letters*, no. 1676a). See Editorial Note, p. xxv. Reprinted *CDB*, *CE*.

2–King George V (1865–1936) attended the Football Association Challenge Cup, in which Bolton Wanderers beat Manchester City 1–0, at Wembley Stadium on 24 April 1926, presenting medals to the players and to the winners the Cup. Sir Thomas Johnstone Lipton (1850–1931), grocer and yachtsman, who spent a fortune, between 1899 and 1930, contesting, without success, the America's Cup, was regularly in the news in connection with yachting matters and regattas. 'Jack Horner', owned by C. Schwartz and ridden by W. Storr, won the Grand National at Aintree, on 26 March 1926, by three lengths.

3–Of several silent films based on Tolstoy's novel *Anna Karenina* (1873–7), the first, directed by Gordon J. Edwards, was shown in 1915. The version to which VW refers here has not been traced.

4–*Das Cabinett Des Dr Caligari* (1919), produced by Erich Pommer, screenplay by Carl Mayer and Hans Janowitz, with sets in the Expressionist manner by Herman Warm, Walter Reimann and Walter Roehrig, was showing in London in 1924. According to one commentator . . . *Dr Caligari* made Hollywood 'no longer afraid of shadows' (Carlyle Ellis, 'Art and the Motion Picture', 1926, quoted in *The Classical Hollywood Cinema* (Routledge and Kegan Paul, 1985)).

5–Robert Burns, 'A Red, Red Rose':

> O, my Luve's like a red, red rose
> That's newly sprung in June.
> O, my Luve's like the melodie
> That's sweetly play'd in tune.

6–Sebastian Erard (1752–1831), French piano maker, whose technical innovations are fundamental to the action of the modern grand piano. Friedrich Wilhelm Carl Bechstein (1826–1900) founded the Bechstein firm of piano makers in Berlin in 1853.

Jones and Wilkinson

Whether Jones should come before Wilkinson or Wilkinson before Jones is not a matter likely to agitate many breasts at the present moment, seeing that more than a hundred and fifty years have rolled over the gentlemen in question and diminished a lustre which, even in their own time, round about the year 1750, was not very bright. The Rev. Dr Wilkinson might indeed claim precedence by virtue of his office. He was His Majesty's Chaplain of the Savoy and Chaplain also to his late Royal Highness, Frederick Prince of Wales. But then Dr Wilkinson was transported.[2] Captain James Jones[3] might assert that, as Captain of His Majesty's third regiment of Guards with a residence by virtue of his office in Savoy Square, his social position was equal to the Doctor's. But Captain Jones had to seclude himself beyond the reach of the law at Mortlake. What, however, renders these comparisons peculiarly odious is the fact that the Captain and the Doctor were boon companions whose tastes were congenial, whose incomes were insufficient, whose wives drank tea together, and whose houses in the Savoy were not two hundred yards apart. Dr Wilkinson, for all his sacred offices (he was Rector of Coyty in Glamorgan, stipendiary curate of Wise in Kent, and, through Lord Galway, had the right to 'open plaister-pits in the honour of Pontefract'),[4] was a convivial spirit who cut a splendid figure in the pulpit, preached and read prayers in a voice that was clear, strong and sonorous so that many a lady of fashion never 'missed her pew near the pulpit',[5] and persons of title remembered him many years after misfortune had removed the handsome preacher from their sight.

Captain Jones shared many of his friend's qualities. He was vivacious, witty, and generous, well made and elegant in person, and, if he was not quite as handsome as the doctor, he was perhaps rather his superior in intellect. Compare them as we may, however, there can be little doubt that the gifts and tastes of both gentlemen were better adapted for pleasure than for labour, for society than for solitude, for the hazards and pleasures of the table rather than for the rigours of religion and war. It was the gaming-table that seduced Captain Jones, and here, alas, his gifts and graces stood him in little stead. His affairs became more and more hopelessly embarrassed, so that shortly, instead of being able to take his walks at large, he was forced to limit them to the precincts of St James's, where, by ancient prerogative, such unfortunates as he were free from the attentions of the bailiffs.

To so gregarious a spirit the confinement was irksome. His only resource, indeed, was to get into talk with any such 'park-saunterers'[6] as misfortunes like his own had driven to perambulate the Park, or, when the weather allowed, to bask and loiter and gossip on its benches. As chance would have it (and the Captain was a devotee of that goddess) he found himself one day resting on the same bench with an elderly gentleman of military aspect and stern demeanour, whose ill-temper the wit and humour which all allowed to Captain Jones presumably beguiled, so that whenever the Captain appeared in the Park, the old man sought his company, and they passed the time until dinner very pleasantly in talk. On no occasion, however, did the General – for it appeared that the name of this morose old man was General Skelton[7] – ask Captain Jones to his house; the acquaintance went no further than the bench in St James's Park; and when, as soon fell out, the Captain's difficulties forced him to the greater privacy of a little cabin at Mortlake, he forgot entirely the military gentleman who, presumably, still sought an appetite for dinner or some alleviation of his own sour mood in loitering and gossiping with the park-saunterers of St James's.

But among the amiable characteristics of Captain Jones was a love of wife and child, scarcely to be wondered at, indeed, considering his wife's lively and entertaining disposition and the extraordinary promise of that little girl who was later to become the wife of Lord Cornwallis.[8] At whatever risk to himself, Captain Jones would steal back to revisit his wife and to hear his little girl recite the part of Juliet which, under his teaching, she had perfectly by heart. On one such secret journey he was hurrying to get within the royal sanctuary of St James's when a voice called on him to stop. His fears obsessing him, he hurried the faster, his pursuer close at his heels. Realising that escape was impossible, Jones wheeled about and facing his pursuer, whom he recognised as the Attorney Brown, demanded what his enemy wanted of him. Far from being his enemy, said Brown, he was the best friend he had ever had, which he would prove if Jones would accompany him to the first tavern that came to hand. There, in a private room over a fire, Mr Brown disclosed the following astonishing story. An unknown friend, he said, who had scrutinised Jones's conduct carefully and concluded that his deserts outweighed his misdemeanours, was prepared to settle all his debts and indeed to put him beyond the reach of such tormentors in future. At these words a load was lifted from Jones's heart, and he cried out 'Good God! Who can this paragon of friendship be?'[9] It was none other, said Brown, than General Skelton. General Skelton, the man whom he had only met to chat with on a bench in St James's Park? Jones asked in wonderment. Yes, it was the General, Brown assured him. Then let him hasten to throw himself in gratitude at his benefactor's knee! Not so fast, Brown replied; General Skelton will never speak to you again. General Skelton died last night.

The extent of Captain Jones's good fortune was indeed magnificent. The General had left Captain Jones sole heir to all his possessions on no other condition than that he should assume the name of Skelton instead of Jones. Hastening through streets no longer dreadful, since every debt of honour could now be paid, Captain Jones brought his wife the astonishing news of their good fortune, and they promptly set out to view that part which lay nearest to hand – the General's great house in Henrietta Street. Gazing about her, half in dream, half in earnest, Mrs Jones was so overcome with the tumult of her emotions that she could not stay to gather in the extent of her possessions, but ran to Little Bedford Street, where Mrs Wilkinson[10] was then living, to impart her joy. Meanwhile, the news that General Skelton lay dead in Henrietta Street without a son to succeed him spread abroad, and those who thought themselves his heirs arrived in the house of death to take stock of their inheritance, among them one great and beautiful lady whose avarice was her undoing, whose misfortunes were equal to her sins, Kitty Chudleigh, Countess of Bristol, Duchess of Kingston.[11] Miss Chudleigh, as she then called herself, believed, and who can doubt that with her passionate nature, her lust for wealth and property, her pistols and her parsimony, she believed with vehemence and asserted her belief with arrogance, that all General Skelton's property had legally descended to her. Later, when the will was read and the truth made public that not only the house in Henrietta Street, but Pap Castle in Cumberland and the lands and lead mines pertaining to it, were left without exception to an unknown Captain Jones, she burst out in 'terms exceeding all bounds of delicacy'. She cried that her relative the General was an old fool in his dotage, that Jones and his wife were impudent low upstarts beneath her notice, and so flounced into her coach 'with a scornful quality toss'[12] to carry on that life of deceit and intrigue and ambition which drove her later to wander in ignominy, an outcast from her country.

What remains to be told of the fortunes of Captain Jones can be briefly despatched. Having new furnished the house in Henrietta Street, the Jones family set out when summer came to visit their estates in Cumberland. The country was so fair, the Castle so stately, the thought that now all belonged to them so gratifying that their progress for three weeks was one of unmixed pleasure and the spot where they were now to live seemed a paradise. But there was an eagerness, an impetuosity about James Jones which made him impatient to suffer even the smiles of fortune passively. He must be active – he must be up and doing. He must be 'let down',[13] for all his friends could do to dissuade him, to view a lead mine. The consequences as they foretold were disastrous. He was drawn up, indeed, but already infected with a deadly sickness of which in a few days he died, in the arms of his wife, in the midst of that paradise which he had toiled so long to reach and now was to die without enjoying.

Meanwhile the Wilkinsons – but that name, alas, was no longer applicable to them, nor did the Doctor and his wife any more inhabit the house in the Savoy – the Wilkinsons had suffered more extremities at the hands of Fate than the Joneses themselves. Dr Wilkinson, it has been said, resembled his friend Jones in the conviviality of his habits and his inability to keep within the limits of his income. Indeed, his wife's dowry of two thousand pounds had gone to pay off the debts of his youth. But by what means could he pay off the debts of his middle age? He was now past fifty, and what with good company and good living, was seldom free from duns, and always pressed for money. Suddenly, from an unexpected quarter, help appeared. This was none other than the Marriage Act, passed in 1755, which laid it down that if any person solemnised a marriage without publishing the banns, unless a marriage licence had already been obtained, he should be subject to transportation for fourteen years. Dr Wilkinson, looking at the matter, it is to be feared, from his own angle, and with a view to his own necessities, argued that as Chaplain of the Savoy, which was extra-Parochial and Royal-exempt, he could grant licences as usual – a privilege which at once brought him such a glut of business, such a crowd of couples wishing to be married in a hurry, that the rat-tat-tat never ceased on his street door, and cash flooded the family exchequer so that even his little boy's pockets were lined with gold. The duns were paid; the table sumptuously spread. But Dr Wilkinson shared another failing with his friend Jones; he would not take advice. His friends warned him; the Government plainly hinted that if he persisted they would be forced to act. Secure in what he imagined to be his right, enjoying the prosperity it brought him to the full, the Doctor paid no heed. On Easter Day he was engaged in marrying from eight in the morning till twelve at night. At last, one Sunday, the King's Messengers appeared. The Doctor escaped by a secret walk over the leads of the Savoy, made his way to the river bank, where he slipped upon some logs and fell, heavy and elderly as he was, in the mud; but nevertheless got to Somerset stairs, took a boat, and reached the Kentish shore in safety. Even now he brazened it out that the law was on his side, and came back four weeks later prepared to stand his trial. Once more, for the last time, company overflowed the house in the Savoy; lawyers abounded, and, as they ate and drank, assured Dr Wilkinson that his case was already won. In July 1756 the trial began. But what conclusion could there be? The crime had been committed and persisted in openly in spite of warning. The Doctor was found guilty and sentenced to fourteen years' transportation.

It remained for his friends to fit him out, like the gentleman he was, for his voyage to America. There, they argued, his gifts of speech and person would make him welcome, and later his wife and son could join him. To them he bade farewell in the dismal precincts of Newgate in March 1757. But contrary winds beat the ship back to shore; the gout seized on a body enfeebled by pleasure and adversity; at Plymouth Dr Wilkinson was transported finally and for ever. The lead mine undid Jones; the Marriage Act was the downfall of Wilkinson. Both now sleep in peace, Jones in Cumberland, Wilkinson, far from his friend (and if their failings were great, great too were their gifts and graces) on the shores of the melancholy Atlantic.

1—A signed essay in the *Bermondsey Book*, June 1926, (Kp C274.1) based on *Memoirs of His Own Life* (4 vols, York, 1790) by Tate Wilkinson (1739–1803). See 'How Should One Read A Book?' in *CR* 2 and *V VW Essays*: 'Sometimes a whole story will come together with such beautiful humour and pathos and completeness that it seems as if a great novelist had been at work, yet it is only an old actor, Tate Wilkinson remembering the strange story of Captain Jones ... But we tire of rubbish-reading in the long run. We tire of searching for what is needed to complete the half-truth which is all that the Wilkinsons ... are able to offer us.' Reading Notes (Berg, XVII). Reprinted *DoM, CE*.

2—Rev. John Wilkinson D.D. was transported to America in 1757 for solemnising marriages by his own licence in defiance of the Marriage Act, but died en route at Plymouth. Frederick Louis, Prince of Wales (1707–51).

3—James Jones (d. c.1758) is described in the correspondence of his son-in-law Charles, 1st Marquis of Cornwallis (3 vols, ed. Charles Ross, 1859), as a Captain and Lieutenant-Colonel in the 3rd Foot Guards.

4—Wilkinson, vol. i, p. 2.

5—*Ibid.*, p. 16: '... amongst my father's pious admirers as a preacher, I remember Mrs Graham, late Mrs Yates, never missed her pew near the pulpit.'

6—Cf. *ibid.*, p. 60, which has 'park-frequenters'.

7—Otherwise unidentified.

8—Charles, 1st Marquis and 2nd Earl Cornwallis (1738–1805), governor-general of India and lord-lieutenant of Ireland, and Jemima Tullikens Jones (1747–79) were married in 1768.

9—Wilkinson, vol. i, p. 63.

10—Jane, *née* Doughty, and Wilkinson had married at York in 1768.

11—Elizabeth Chudleigh, Countess of Bristol (1720–88) who, in 1769, bigamously married Evelyn Pierrepoint, 2nd Duke of Kingston.

12—For both quotations, Wilkinson, vol. i, p. 66.

13—*Ibid.*, p. 67.

Romance and the 'Nineties

The reader should not be put off by the apparent discursiveness of Mr le Gallienne's manner. He himself describes his book as 'harmless gossip',[2] but beneath the personalities and the ease and airiness of the style there lies a reasoned and defended point of view. Mr le Gallienne is a profound believer in the importance, to art and letters at least, of the 'nineties. 'Generally speaking, all our present-day developments amount to little more than pale and exaggerated copying of the 'nineties. The amount of creative revolutionary energy packed into that amazing decade is almost bewildering in its variety,' he writes.[3] To most of us this will seem a curious over-statement. The figures of Dowson, Oscar Wilde, Arthur Symons, Aubrey Beardsley, and John Davidson[4] scarcely seem to call for such epithets. We have got into the way of thinking of that 'amazing decade' as the sophisticated, elongated, tapering tail to the body of the robust lion, the Victorian age. But all these classifications are too vague to be valuable. Mr Wells and Mr Bennett and Mr Yeats and Mr Kipling[5] can all be made to fall within the decade if we choose; and, further, it is a fact that death took one after another of these remarkable people at a very early age. At any rate, Mr le Gallienne's conviction serves to shape a very good-tempered, light, and vivacious volume. If residence in America has its share in the romance, still Mr le Gallienne makes us feel that it was genuine. When Mrs Morris[6] gave him a pot of her quince jam, he felt as if Helen of Troy had given it him. He hung about Putney and saw Swinburne steal into a public-house for a forbidden bottle of Burgundy. He visited Pater,[7] and found him looking like a Prussian officer. The glamour that he brought from Liverpool still irradiates his pages.[8]

1−A notice in the *N&A*, 3 July 1926, (Kp C274.2) of *The Romantic '90s* (G. P. Putnam's Sons, 1926) by Richard Le Gallienne (1866–1947), poet and essayist, a founder with W. B. Yeats, Lionel Johnson and others of the Rhymers' Club.
2−Le Gallienne, dedication to Charles Hanson Towne, unnumbered preliminary page.
3−*Ibid.*, ch. 3, pp. 103–4.
4−Ernest Dowson (1867–1900); Oscar Wilde (1854–1900); Arthur Symons (1865–1945), for VW on whom see 'Mr Symons's Essays', *II VW Essays*; Aubrey Beardsley (1872–98); John Davidson (1857–1909), for VW on whom see 'John Davidson', *II VW Essays*.
5−H. G. Wells (1866–1946); Arnold Bennett (1867–1931); W. B. Yeats (1865–1939); Rudyard Kipling (1865–1936).
6−I.e. Jane Morris, wife of William Morris.
7−A. C. Swinburne (1837–1909); Walter Pater (1839–94).
8−Le Gallienne, son of a Birkenhead brewery manager, left his native Liverpool for London in 1888, his literary aspirations having been encouraged by Ralph Waldo Emerson, and by office colleagues who paid for the publication in 1887 of his first book of verse.

'Impassioned Prose'

When he was still a boy, his own discrimination led De Quincey to doubt whether 'his natural vocation lay towards poetry'.[2] He wrote poetry, eloquently and profusely, and his poetry was praised; but even so he decided that he was no poet, and the sixteen volumes of his collected works are written entirely in prose. After the fashion of his time, he wrote on many subjects – on political economy, on philosophy, on history; he wrote essays and biographies and confessions and memoirs. But as we stand before the long row of his books and make, as we are bound to make after all these years, our own selection, the whole mass and range of these sixteen volumes seems to reduce itself to one sombre level in which hang a few splendid stars. He dwells in our memory because he could make phrases like 'trepidations of innumerable fugitives',[3] because he could compose scenes like that of the laurelled coach driving into the midnight market place, because he could tell stories like that of the phantom woodcutter heard by his brother on the desert island. And, if we examine our choice and give a reason for it, we have to confess that, prose writer though he is, it is for his poetry that we read him and not for his prose.

What could be more damaging, to him as writer, to us as readers, than this confession? For if the critics agree on any point it is on this, that nothing is more reprehensible than for a prose writer to write like a poet. Poetry is poetry and prose is prose – how often have we not heard that! Poetry has one mission and prose another. Prose, Mr Binyon wrote the other day, 'is a medium primarily addressed to the intelligence, poetry to feeling and imagination'. And again, 'poetical prose has but a bastard kind of beauty, easily appearing overdressed'.[4] It is impossible not to admit, in part at least, the truth of these remarks. Memory supplies but too many instances of discomfort, of anguish, when in the midst of sober prose suddenly the temperature rises, the rhythm changes, we go up with a lurch, come down with a bang, and wake, roused and angry. But memory supplies also a number of passages – in Browne, in Landor, in Carlyle, in Ruskin, in Emily Brontë[5] – where there is no such jerk, no such sense (for this perhaps is at the root of our discomfort) of something unfused, unwrought, incongruous and casting ridicule upon the rest. The prose writer has subdued his army of facts; he has brought them all under the same law of perspective. They work upon our minds as poetry works upon them. We are not woken; we reach the next point – and it may well be highly commonplace – without any sense of strain.

But, unfortunately for those who would wish to see a great many more things said in prose than are now thought proper, we live under the rule of the novelists. If we talk of prose we mean in fact prose fiction. And of all writers the novelist has his hands fullest of facts. Smith gets up, shaves, has his breakfast, taps his egg, reads *The Times*. How can we ask the panting, the perspiring, the industrious scribe with all this on his hands to modulate beautifully off into rhapsodies about Time and Death and what the hunters are doing at the Antipodes? It would upset the whole proportions of his day. It would cast grave doubt upon his veracity. Moreover, the greatest of his order seem deliberately to prefer a method which is the antithesis of prose poetry. A shrug of the shoulders, a turn of the head, a few words spoken in a hurry at a moment of crisis – that is all. But the train has been laid so deep beneath page after page and chapter after chapter that the single word when it is spoken is enough to start an explosion. We have so lived and thought with these men and women that they need only raise a finger and it seems to reach the skies. To elaborate that gesture would be to spoil it. The whole tendency therefore of fiction is against prose poetry. The lesser novelists are not going to take risks which the greater deliberately avoid. They trust that, if only the egg is real and the kettle boils, stars and nightingales will somehow be thrown in by the imagination of the reader. And therefore all that side of the mind which is exposed in solitude they ignore. They ignore its thoughts, its rhapsodies, its dreams, with the result that the people of fiction bursting with energy on one side are atrophied on the other; while prose itself, so long in service to this drastic master, has suffered the same deformity, and will be fit, after another hundred years of such discipline, to write nothing but the immortal works of Bradshaw and Baedeker.[6]

But happily there are in every age some writers who puzzle the critics, who refuse to go in with the herd. They stand obstinately across the boundary lines, and do a greater service by enlarging and fertilising and influencing than by their actual achievement, which, indeed, is often too eccentric to be satisfactory. Browning did a service of this kind to poetry. Peacock and Samuel Butler[7] have both had an influence upon novelists which is out of all proportion to their own popularity. And one of De Quincey's claims to our gratitude, one of his main holds upon our interest, is that he was an exception and a solitary. He made a class for himself.[8] He widened the choice for others. Faced with the usual problem of what to write, since write he must, he decided that with all his poetic sensibility he was not a poet. He lacked the fire and the concentration. Nor, again, was he a novelist. With immense powers of language at his command, he was incapable of a sustained and passionate interest in the affairs of other people. It was his disease, he said, 'to meditate too much and to observe too little'.[9] He would follow a poor family who went marketing on a Saturday night, sympathetically, but at a distance. He was intimate with no one. Then, again, he had an extraordinary gift for the dead languages, and a passion for acquiring knowledge of all kinds. Yet there was some quality in him which forbade him to shut himself up alone with his books, as such gifts seemed to indicate. The truth was that he dreamed — he was always dreaming. The faculty was his long before he took to eating opium. When he was a child he stood by his sister's dead body and suddenly

a vault seemed to open in the zenith of the far blue sky, a shaft which ran up for ever. I, in spirit, rose as on billows that also ran up the shaft for ever; and the billows seemed to pursue the throne of God; but that also ran before us and fled away continually.[10]

The visions were of extreme vividness; they made life seem a little dull in comparison; they extended it, they completed it. But in what form was he to express this that was the most real part of his own existence? There was none ready made to hand. He invented, as he claimed, 'modes of impassioned prose'. With immense elaboration and art he formed a style in which to express these 'visionary scenes derived from the world of dreams'. For such prose there were no precedents, he believed; and he begged the reader to remember 'the perilous difficulty' of an attempt where 'a single false note, a single word in a wrong key, ruins the whole music'.[11]

Added to that 'perilous difficulty' was another which is often forced upon the reader's attention. A prose writer may dream dreams and see visions, but they cannot be allowed to lie scattered, single, solitary upon the page. So spaced out they die. For prose has neither the intensity nor the self-sufficiency of poetry. It rises slowly off the ground; it reaches its heights by a series of gradual steps; it must be connected on this side and on that. There must be some medium in which its ardours and ecstasies can float without incongruity, from which they receive support and impetus. Here was a difficulty which De Quincey often faced and often failed to solve. Most of his most tiresome and disfiguring faults are the result of the dilemma into which his genius plunged him. There was something in the story before him which kindled his interest and quickened his powers. For example, the Spanish Military Nun, as she descends half-starved and frozen from the Andes, sees before her a belt of trees which promises safety. As if De Quincey had himself reached that shelter and could breathe in safety, he broadens out –

> Oh! verdure of dark olive foliage, offered suddenly to fainting eyes, as if by some winged patriarchal herald of wrath relenting – solitary Arab's tent, rising with saintly signals of peace in the dreadful desert, must Kate indeed die even yet, whilst she sees but cannot reach you? Outpost on the frontier of man's dominions, standing within life, but looking out upon everlasting death, wilt thou hold up the anguish of thy mocking invitation only to betray?[12]

Alas, how easy it is to rise, how dangerous to fall! He has Kate on his hands; he is halfway through with her story; he must rouse himself, he must collect himself, he must descend from these happy heights to the levels of ordinary existence. And, again and again, it is in returning to earth that De Quincey is undone. How is he to bridge the horrid transition? How is he to turn from an angel with wings of flame and eyes of fire to a gentleman in black who talks sense? Sometimes he makes a joke – it is generally painful. Sometimes he tells a story – it is always irrelevant. Most often he spreads himself out in a waste of verbosity, where any interest that there may have been peters out dismally and loses itself in the sand. We can read no more.[13]

It is tempting to say that De Quincey failed because he was not a novelist. He ought to have left Kate alone; he had not a novelist's sense of character and action. To a critic such formulas are helpful; unfortunately, they are often false. For in fact De Quincey can convey character admirably; he is a master of the art of narrative once he has succeeded (and the condition is indispensable for all writers) in adjusting the perspective to suit his own eyesight. It was a sight, it is true, that required a most curious rearrangement of the landscape. Nothing must come too close. A veil must be drawn over the multitudinous disorder of human affairs. It must always be possible, without distressing the reader, to allude to a girl as 'a prepossessing young female'.[14] A mist must lie upon the human face.

The hills must be higher and the distances bluer than they are in the world we know. He required, too, endless leisure and ample elbow-room. He wanted time to soliloquise and loiter; here to pick up some trifle and bestow upon it all his powers of analysis and decoration; here to brush aside such patient discrimination and widen and enlarge and amplify until nothing remains but the level sands and the immense sea. He wanted a subject that would allow him all possible freedom and yet possess enough emotional warmth to curb his inborn verbosity.

He found it, naturally, in himself. He was a born autobiographer. If the *Opium Eater* remains his masterpiece, a longer and less perfect book, the *Autobiographic Sketches*, runs it very close.[15] For here it is fitting that he should stand a little apart, should look back, under cover of his raised hand, at scenes which had almost melted into the past. His enemy, the hard fact, became cloud-like and supple under his hands. He was under no obligation to recite 'the old hackneyed roll-call, chronologically arranged, of inevitable facts in a man's life'.[16] It was his object to record impressions, to render states of mind without particularising the features of the precise person who had experienced them. A serene and lovely light lies over the whole of that distant prospect of his childhood. The house, the fields, the garden, even the neighbouring town of Manchester, all seem to exist, but far away on some island separated from us by a veil of blue. On this background, where no detail is accurately rendered, the little group of children and parents, the little island of home and garden, are all distinctly visible and yet as if they moved and had their being behind a veil. Upon the opening chapters rests the solemnity of a splendid summer's day, whose radiance, long since sunk, has something awful in it, in whose profound stillness sounds strangely reverberate – the sound of hooves on the far-away high road, the sound of words like 'palm', the sound of that 'solemn wind, the saddest that ear ever heard',[17] which was for ever to haunt the mind of the little boy who now heard it for the first time. Nor, so long as he keeps within the circle of the past, is it necessary that he should face the disagreeable necessity of waking. About the reality of childhood still hung some of the charm of illusion. If the peace is broken, it is by an apparition like that of the mad dog which passes and pauses with something of the terror of a dream. If he needs variety, he finds it in describing with a whimsical humour perfectly suited to the subject the raptures and miseries of childhood. He mocks; he dilates; he makes the very small very great;

then he describes the war with the mill hands, the brothers' imaginary kingdoms, his brother's boast that he could walk upon the ceiling like a fly, with admirable particularity. He can rise easily and fall naturally here. Here too, given his own memories to work upon, he can exercise his extraordinary powers of description. He was never exact; he disliked glitter and emphasis; he sacrificed the showy triumphs of the art; but he had to perfection the gift of composition. Scenes come together under his hands like congregations of clouds which gently join and slowly disperse or hang solemnly still. So displayed before us we see the coaches gathering at the post office in all their splendour; the lady in the carriage to whom the news of victory brings only sorrow; the couple surprised on the road at midnight by the thunder of the mail coach and the threat of death; Lamb asleep in his chair; Ann disappearing for ever into the dark London night.[18] All these scenes have something of the soundlessness and the lustre of dreams. They swim up to the surface, they sink down again into the depths. They have, into the bargain, the strange power of growing in our minds, so that it is always a surprise to come upon them again and see what, in the interval, our minds have done to alter and expand.

Meanwhile, all these scenes compose an autobiography of a kind, but of a kind which is so unusual that one is forced to ask what one has learnt from it about De Quincey in the end. Of facts, scarcely anything. One has been told only what De Quincey wished us to know; and even that has been chosen for the sake of some adventitious quality – as that it fitted in here, or was the right colour to go there – never for its truth. But nevertheless there grows upon us a curious sense of intimacy. It is an intimacy with the mind, and not with the body; yet we cannot help figuring to ourselves, as the rush of eloquence flows, the fragile little body, the fluttering hands, the glowing eyes, the alabaster cheeks, the glass of opium on the table. We can guess that no one so gifted with silver speech, so prone to plunge into reverie and awe, held his own imperturbably among his fellows. We can guess at his evasions and unpunctualities; at the hordes of old papers that littered his room; at the courtesy which excused his inability to abide by the ordinary rules of life; at the over-mastering desire that possessed him to wander and dream on the hills alone; at the seasons of gloom and irritability with which he paid for that exquisite fineness of ear that tuned each word to harmony and set each paragraph flowing and following like the waves of the sea. All this we know or guess. But it is odd to reflect how little, after all, we have been admitted to intimacy. In spite of the fact that he talks of confessions and calls the work by which he set most store *Suspiria de Profundis*,[19] he is always self-possessed, secretive and composed. His confession is not that he has sinned but that he has dreamed. Hence it comes about that his most perfect passages are not lyrical but descriptive. They are not cries of anguish which admit us to closeness and sympathy; they are descriptions of states of mind in which, often, time is miraculously prolonged and space miraculously expanded. When in the *Suspiria de Profundis* he tries to rise straight from the ground and to achieve in a few pages without prelude or sequence his own peculiar effects of majesty and distance, his force is not sufficient to bear him the whole distance. There juts up a comment upon the rules of Eton, a note to remind us that this refers to the tobacco States of North America, in the midst of *Levana and Our Ladies of Sorrow*,[20] which puts their sweet-tongued phrases sadly out of countenance.

But if he was not a lyric writer, he was undoubtedly a descriptive writer, a reflective writer, who with only prose at his command – an instrument hedged about with restrictions, debased by a thousand common uses – made his way into precincts which are terribly diffi-cult of approach. The breakfast table, he seems to say, is only a tem-porary apparition which we can think into non-existence, or invest with such associations that even its mahogany legs have their charm. To sit cheek by jowl with our fellows cramped up together is distasteful, indeed repulsive. But draw a little apart, see people in groups, as outlines, and they become at once memorable and full of beauty. Then it is not the actual sight or sound itself that matters, but the reverberations that it makes as it travels through our minds. These are often to be found far away, strangely transformed; but it is only by gathering up and putting together these echoes and frag-ments that we arrive at the true nature of our experience. So think-ing, he altered slightly the ordinary relationships. He shifted the values of familiar things. And this he did in prose, which makes us wonder whether, then, it is quite so limited as the critics say, and ask further whether the prose writer, the novelist, might not capture fuller and finer truths than are now his aim if he ventured into those shadowy regions where De Quincey has been before him.

1–An essay in the *TLS*, 16 September 1926, (Kp C275) based on volumes in *The*

Works of Thomas De Quincey [1785–1859] (2nd ed., 15 vols, Adam and Charles Black, 1862–3). On 6 February 1926, VW wrote in a postscript to Edward Sackville-West: 'I've found out a little about de Quincey' (*III VW Letters*, no. 1619; see also no. 1600, to the same), and this mention may signal her initial preparations for the essay which by 11 May was under way: 'Arguing about the Ar[chbisho]p of Canterbury with Jack Squire at 12 seems now normal, but not – how often do I repeat – nearly as exciting as writing To the Lighthouse or about de Q[uincey]' (*III VW Diary*). By 18 June at least part of her excitement had begun to pall. 'Yes, I do write damned well sometimes,' she confessed to Vita Sackville-West (*III VW Letters*, no. 1649), 'but not these last days, when I've been slogging through a cursed article, and see my novel glowing like the Island of the Blessed far far away over dismal waters, and cant reach land.' A month later, to the same recipient she wrote: '. . . and I'm reading de Quincey, and Richardson, and again de Quincey – again de Quincey, because I'm in the middle of writing about him, and my God Vita, if you happen to know do wire whats the essential difference between prose and poetry – It cracks my poor brain to consider . . .' (*ibid.*, 19? July, no. 1656). And she noted in her diary on 22 July: 'The summer hourglass is running out rapidly & rather sandily. Many nights I wake in a shudder thinking of some atrocity of mine. I bring home pinpricks which magnify in the middle of the night into gaping wounds. However, I drive my pen through de Quincey of a morning, having put The Lighthouse aside till Rodmell . . . Desmond came in and talked about Shakespeare. Now to settle my mind to Suspiria' (*III VW Diary*, 22 July). Finally, on 13 September, she complained: 'I am exacerbated by the fact that I spent 4 days last week hammering out de Quincey, which has been lying about since June; so refused £30 to write on Willa Cather . . .' (*ibid.*). VW read in preparation for her essay Leslie Stephen on 'De Quincey' in *Hours in a Library* (1874); see also Stephen's entry on De Quincey in the *DNB*. She seems too to have used A. H. Japp's *Thomas De Quincey: His Life and Writings* (2 vols, John Hogg and Co., 1877). See also 'The English Mail Coach', *I VW Essays*, Appendix I; 'De Quincey's Autobiography', *CR2* and *V VW Essays*. See Editorial Note p. xxv. Reading Notes (Berg xxv). Reprinted *G&R, CE*.

2 – De Quincey, *Works*, vol. xiv, *Autobiographic Sketches 1790–1833*, ch. vii, 'The Nation of London', p. 197: '. . . I was inclined . . . to doubt whether my natural vocation lay towards poetry.'

3 – *Ibid.*, vol. i, *Confessions of an English Opium Eater*, 'The Pains of Opium', p. 273.

4 – For both quotations, Laurence Binyon, *Tradition and Reaction in Modern Poetry* (The English Association, Pamphlet no. 63, April 1926), pp. 12 and 13, slightly adapted.

5 – For VW on: Sir Thomas Browne (1605–82), see 'Sir Thomas Browne', *III VW Essays*, and see 'The Elizabethan Lumber Room' in *CR1* above; Walter Savage Landor (1775–1864), see 'Landor in Little', *III VW Essays*; Thomas Carlyle (1795–1881); John Ruskin (1819–1900) for VW on whom see 'Ruskin Looks Back on Life'; Emily Brontë (1818–48), see '"Jane Eyre" and "Wuthering Heights"' in *CR1* above.

6 – For a continuation of this discussion, so vital to VW's immediate interests as she worked at *To the Lighthouse* (1927), see for example 'Poetry, Fiction and The Future', effectively her manifesto for *The Waves* (1931), below. George Bradshaw (1801–53), whose *Bradshaw's Railway Guide* was first published in 1839. Karl Baedeker (1801–59), originator of the celebrated series of travel guides.

7–Robert Browning (1812–89), Thomas Love Peacock (1785–1866), Samuel Butler (1835–1902).

8–Cf., Leslie Stephen, *Hours in a Library* (4 vols, new edition with additions, Smith, Elder and Co., Duckworth and Co., 1907), vol. i, 'De Quincey', p. 326: 'He belongs to a genus in which he is the only individual.'

9–De Quincey, Works, vol. i, *The English Opium Eater*, p. 211.

10–*Ibid.*, vol. xix, *Autobiographic Sketches*, pp. 16–17, which has: 'as if on billows' and 'but *that* also ran'.

11–For all four quotations, *ibid.*, vol. i, Preface, p. xvii.

12–*Ibid.*, vol. iii, *The Spanish Military Nun*, p. 55, which has: 'desert – must'.

13–Cf., Stephen, *Hours in a Library*, 'De Quincey', p. 338: 'Impassioned prose may be a very good thing; but when its current is arrested by such incessant stoppages, and the beauty of the English language displayed by showing how many faultless sentences may be expended on an exhaustive description of irrelevant trifles, the human mind becomes recalcitrant.'

14–The source of this allusion has not been traced.

15–See Virginia Woolf. *To the Lighthouse. The original holograph draft*. Transcribed and edited by Susan Dick (Hogarth Press, 1983), Appendix C, p. 255: 'The story of his own life the/expo was his own most congenial subject, for there &/if the Opium Eater is his masterpiece the Autobiographic Sketches which survey a large stretch of his experience, run it very close.' Professor Dick misidentifies this draft as relating to VW's later essay 'De Quincey's Autobiography'.

16–De Quincey writing to James Hogg, 21 September 1850, quoted in *Uncollected Writings* (2 vols, Swan Sonnenschein and Co., 1890), vol. i, p. 358, and by Japp, vol. ii, p. 11.

17–For the significance to De Quincey of the word 'palm', see *Works*, vol. xiv, *Autobiographic Sketches*, ch. i, 'The Afflictions of Childhood', p. 14; and for the 'solemn wind', *ibid.*, p. 15.

18–For De Quincey on Charles Lamb (1775–1834), see *Works*, vol. viii, pp. 108–60; and for 'noble-minded Ann', his 'youthful benefactress', see *ibid.*, vol. i, *Confessions of an English Opium Eater*, pp. 169 ff.

19–De Quincey, *Works*, vol. xvi, *Suspiria De Profundis*. Being a sequel to the Confessions of an English Opium Eater, and Other Miscellaneous Writings.

20–For 'Levana and our Ladies of Sorrow' see *Works*, vol. xvi, *Suspiria De Profundis*, pp. 22–32.

The Cosmos

'"And what is 'Cosmos', Mr Sanderson?" asks Sister Edith. "What is the meaning of the word?" And then I go off like a rocket and explode in stars in the empyrean.'[2] These two large volumes are full of the sparks that fell from that constantly recurring explosion. For Mr Cobden-Sanderson was always trying to explain to somebody –

it might be Professor Tyndall ('I gave him my own view of human destiny, namely, the ultimate coalescence of the human intellect in knowledge with its other self, the Universe'),[3] it might be Mr Churchill,[4] it might be a strange lady whose motor-car had broken down on the road near Malvern – what the word Cosmos meant. He had learnt gradually and painfully himself. For at first the world seemed to him to have no order whatsoever. Everything was wrong. It was wrong for him to become a clergyman; it was wrong to take a degree; it was wrong to remain at the Bar. It was wrong that he, who had three dress suits already, should order another from Poole and pay for it with his wife's money. But what then was right? That was by no means so apparent. 'What was I do to?' he asked himself at three o'clock in the morning in the year 1882, 'aching with exhaustion and nervous horror'.[5] Ought he to live in Poplar and work among the poor? Ought he to devote his life to the work of the Charity Organisation Society? What ought he to give in return for all that he received? For some time – and the candour with which these private struggles are laid bare is no small part of the deep interest of these diaries – he vacillated and procrastinated and drank beef-tea at eleven o'clock in the morning. Lady Carlisle accused him of 'dreamy egotism'.[6] His doctor laughed at his concern for his health. His father was deeply disappointed that he should give up the Bar – and for what? His wife confessed that when she read 'what I wrote about the mountains, and repeated little phrases, she thought me, and had always thought me, at such moments, quite a lunatic!'[7] But once in his early distress he had found that life became suddenly 'rounded off and whole'[8] by a very simple expedient; he had bought a gridiron and cooked a chop. Now, several years later, relief began to filter through from the same channels. Since he enjoyed using his hands, said Mrs Morris when he consulted her, why should he not learn to bind books?[9] He took lessons at once and became, with a speed which astonished him, capable of making 'something beautiful, and, as far as human things can be, permanent'.[10] It was an astonishing relief from attending to the affairs of the London and North Western Railway Company. But the Book Beautiful, as he called it, though tooled magnificently and bound in rose-red morocco, was not an end in itself. It was only a humble beginning – something well made which served to put his own mind and body in order and so in harmony with the greater order which he was beginning, as he pared and gilded, to perceive transcending all human affairs. For there was a unity of the whole in which the virtues and even the vices of mankind were caught up and put to their proper uses. Once attain to that vision, and all things fell into their places. From that vantage ground the white butterfly caught in the spider's net was 'all in the world's plan',[11] and Englishmen and Germans blowing each other's heads off in the trenches were 'brothers not enemies', conspiring to 'create the great emotions which in turn create the greater creation'.[12] To envisage this whole and to make the binding of books and the printing of books and everything one did and said and felt further this end was work enough for one lifetime.

But in addition Mr Cobden-Sanderson felt the inevitable desire to explain the meaning of the word Cosmos to all and sundry, to Sister Edith and to Professor Tyndall. The volumes are full of attempts at explanation. He was not quite certain what he meant; nevertheless, he must 'repeat and repeat' and so 'get relief'.[13] He laboured, too, under a groundless fear that he might catch the contagion of Jane Austen's style. Instead of becoming clearer, therefore, the vision, iterated and reiterated, becomes more and more nebulous, until after two volumes of explanation we are left asking, with Sister Edith, 'But, Mr Sanderson, how does one "fly to the great Rhythm?"[14] What is the extraordinary ring of harmony within harmony that encircles us; what reason is there to suppose that a mountain wishes us well, or that a lake has a profound moral meaning to impart? What, in short, does the word Cosmos mean?' Whereupon the rocket explodes, and the red and gold showers descend, and we look on with sympathy, but feel a little chill about the feet and not very clear as to the direction of the road.

But the man himself who sent his rockets soaring into such incongruous places (he would write a letter about the Ideal to *The Times*)[15] is neither vapid nor insipid nor wrapped round as so many idealists tend to become, in comfortable cotton wool. On the contrary, he was for ever being stung and taunted, as he carried on his business of bookbinder and printer, by the uncompromising creature who was perched upon his shoulders. There were days when the gold would not stick on his lettering; days when on 'turning the leather down at the headband I found it too short'. Then he flew into a passion of rage, 'tore the leather off the board and cut it, and cut it, and slashed it with a knife'.[16] *I* did this, he reflected the next moment, I who have seen the vision can yet fall into ecstasies of vulgar anger! The vision forced him to test everything by its light, no matter what the effort, the unpopularity, the despondency it caused. What did the Coronation mean? he asked, what did the Boer War mean? Nothing could be taken for granted.

But by degrees the ideal got the upper hand. The sense of reality grew fainter. Often he seemed to be passing out of the body into a trance of thought. 'I think I am more related to the hills and the streams ... than to men and women,' he wrote.[17] He roamed off among the mountains to dream and worship. He felt that his part was no longer among the fighters, but among the dreamers. Now and then, chiefly in the Swiss chalet of Lady Russell, he came down to dinner dressed in a dressing gown, with a brush and comb bag on his head, housemaid's gloves on his hands, holding a fan, and was 'very merry'.[18] But his sense of humour seems to have been suffocated by the effort which he made persistently to 'overcome the ordinariness of ordinary life'.[19] The cat was wonderful and the moon; the charwoman and the oak tree; the bread and the butter; the night and the stars. Everything seems to suffer a curious magnification. Nothing exists in itself but only as a means to something else. The solid objects of daily life become rimmed with high purposes, significant, symbolical. The people who drift through these diaries – even Swinburne and Morris[20] – have become curiously thin; we see the stars shining through their backbones. It is in no way incongruous or surprising then to find him in his old age slipping off secretly on dark nights to the river. In his hand he carried a mysterious box swathed round with tape. Looking round him to see that he was not observed he pitched his burden over the parapet into the water. It was thus that he bequeathed the Doves Type to the river; thus that he saved the ideal from desecration. But one night he missed his aim. Two pages wrapped in white paper lodged upon a ledge above the stream. He could see them, but he could not reach them. What was he to do? he asked himself, in bewilderment and amazement. The authorities might send for him; he might be cross-examined. Well, so be it. If they asked him to explain himself he would 'take refuge in the infinitudes'. 'My idea was magnificent; the act was ridiculous,' he said. 'Besides,' he reflected, 'nothing was explicable.'[21] And perhaps he was right.

1–A signed review in the *N&A*, 9 October 1926, (Kp C276) of *The Journals of Thomas James Cobden-Sanderson 1879–1922* (2 vols, Richard Cobden-Sanderson, 1926). 'Curse [Bruce] Richmond, Curse The Times, Curse my own procrastinations & nerves,' VW wrote in her diary on 13 September 1926, 'I shall do Cobden

Sanderson & Mrs Hemans & make something by them however.' The same issue of the *N&A* contained LW's 'World of Books' column, on 'The Publishing Season'; and an article by Clive Bell, on 'The Two Corots'. Reading Notes (Berg, xxv). Reprinted *CDB*, *CE*.

2—Cobden-Sanderson, vol. ii, 8 November 1913, p. 223.

3—*Ibid.*, vol. i, 26 September 1883, p. 120, from a more extensive sentence. John Tyndall (1820–93), professor of natural philosophy, and subsequently superintendent at the Royal Institution.

4—No account of Cobden-Sanderson attempting to explain the word Cosmos to Winston Churchill (1874–1965) has been traced, though the two men certainly were acquainted with each other.

5—Cobden-Sanderson, vol. i, 14 April 1882, p. 77, adapted.

6—*Ibid.*, 11 February 1882, p. 51, quoting a letter from Rosalind Howard, Countess of Carlisle.

7—*Ibid.*, 14 October 1883, p. 143, which has 'when I wrote'. Cobden-Sanderson had married in 1882 Anne Cobden, a daughter of the celebrated politician. He was called to the Bar by the Inner Temple in 1871 and became involved in codifying the powers and obligations of the London and North-Western Railway Company.

8—*Ibid.*, 29 August 1881, p. 31.

9—For Jane Morris's advice, *ibid.*, 24 June 1883, p. 94.

10—*Ibid.*, 10 October 1883, p. 134, punctuation altered.

11—*Ibid.*, vol. ii, 9 August 1908, p. 112.

12—*Ibid.*, 23 June 1918, p. 363, which has 'kindle the great emotions'.

13—*Ibid.*, vol. i, 14 October 1883, p. 143.

14—*Ibid.*, vol. ii, 23 April 1906, pp. 81–2: 'O man, fly to her and to the Vision; fly to the great Rhythm, invisible and inaudible save to the ears and to the eyes of the soul, of the spirit, of the reason enthroned, enthroned in the mind of man.' Sister Edith's questions are extemporised by VW.

15—Cf. *ibid.*, 11 October 1908, p. 126: 'The *Times* has so far taken no notice of my letter on the unemployed. No wonder! Yet I am more than ever convinced of the coming power of voluntary death, as an instrument in the perfection of Life ... those who so sacrifice themselves, themselves shut themselves out from a participation in the future of the ideal, yet share it *in the present*, in the moment of such self-extinction.'

16—*Ibid.*, vol. i, 15 June 1887, p. 260.

17—*Ibid.*, vol. ii, 21 May 1913, p. 215.

18—*Ibid.*, 27 July 1920, p. 397. Lady Russell: formerly Elizabeth von Arnim, *née* Mary Annette Beauchamp (1886–1941), author of *Elizabeth and her German Garden* (1898).

19—*Ibid.*, 10 January 1919, p. 377, which has 'the persistent ordinariness'.

20—Algernon Charles Swinburne (1837–1909); William Morris (1834–96).

21—For the first and third quotations, Cobden-Sanderson, vol. ii, 5 November 1916, p. 303, which has, 'Nothing was explicable.'; for the second, *ibid.*, 28 October 1916, p. 301, which has: 'the act ridiculous'. Founded in 1900 by Cobden-Sanderson, in partnership with Emery Walker, with whom he broke in 1909, the Doves Press finally folded in 1916.

Laughter and Tears

There is an old fallacy which, however often it is scotched, springs up again to the effect that humorous writers are themselves light-hearted men. The opposite would seem to be true; and Mr Jerome's autobiography again reminds us that a humorous writer is for the most part a man with such an insight into hardship that he must perforce laugh. So says Mr Jerome, 'I can see the humorous side of things and enjoy the fun when it comes; but look where I will, there seems to me always to be more sadness than joy in life.' To this 'melancholy and brooding disposition',[2] so much at variance with his appearance (he resembles Lord Oxford,[3] people tell him), a childhood of hardship and poverty contributed. On his first birth-day, his father, who had been a preacher in the Black Country, sat down late at night on his wife's bedside and told her that he was a ruined man. He had lost all his money speculating in coal mines. He set up next as an ironmonger in Limehouse, but the ironmongery failed. One thing after another failed. A few extracts from his wife's diary tell the melancholy story. 'Coals have been eight shillings a ton. It is a fearful prospect. I have asked the Lord to remove it.' 'Coals have gone down again just as we were at the last. "How much better are ye than many sparrows."' But their path remained 'very cloudy and full of sorrow'.[4] The little boy's chief consolation was that his season ticket to school at Chalk Farm allowed him to spend all his holidays exploring the remoter parts of London. Though he was born so lately as 1859 they still 'hunted deer round Highgate'.[5] Hampstead was a pleasant country town. There were real woods and fields and muddy lanes at Walthamstow and Enfield and Edmonton. The future writer learnt more from his season ticket than from his teachers. But his father died, and his mother soon fol-lowed, still hoping that coals would go down in price and that their ship would come in. Then began a life of real solitude and hardship; he slept in doss-houses and shared hay-ricks with tramps; he be-came a clerk at twenty-six pounds a year in the London and North-Western Railway and learnt to drink and smoke, to go to the play, to eat a fried chop with his tea and spend the evening writing. The result *Three Men in a Boat* made *Punch* extremely angry. It referred to him invariably as "'Arry K. 'Arry'; Henley and Max Beerbohm and the rest of the *intelligentsia* derided him.[6] The *Morning Post* said that he 'was an example of the sad results to be expected from the education of the lower orders'.[7] And with his fame and his success and his introduction to literary circles the interest of the chronicle diminishes. For further extracts from his mother's diary we would give all the gossip about Mr Wells and Mr Jacobs.[8] But between the lines of perfunctory story-telling we pick up the impression of a robust, downright character, who has championed Negroes, Germans, Peace, from sheer sympathy with the underdog, and, while enjoying all sports and pleasures ardently, is yet of opinion 'that the one thing certain is that mankind remains a race of low intelligence and evil instincts'.[9]

1–A review in the *N&A*, 16 October 1926, (Kp C276.1) of *My Life and Times* (Hodder and Stoughton, n.d.) by Jerome K. Jerome (1859–1927), author of the comic novel *Three Men in a Boat* (1889), and of the play *The Passing of the Third Floor Back* (1908). The same issue of the *N&A* also contained LW's 'World of Books' column, on *Lord Raingo* by Arnold Bennett.
2–For the first quotation, Jerome, ch. i, pp. 15–16, and for the second, p. 15, which has: 'melancholy, brooding disposition'.
3–For Jerome's resemblance to Lord Oxford (Herbert Henry Asquith, 1852–1928, the former Liberal prime minister), *ibid.*, ch. vi, p. 118.
4–For the first two quotations, ibid., ch. i, p. 18, and for the third, p. 22. Jerome's wife: Georgina Henrietta Stanley, *née* Nesza, daughter of a lieutenant in the Spanish army.
5–*Ibid.*, ch. ii, p. 34.
6–For *Punch*'s anger, and the derision of W. E. Henley (1849–1903), of the *National Observer*, and of Max Beerbohm (1872–1956), *ibid.*, ch. iv, p. 72.
7–*Ibid.*, which has: 'as an example' and 'over-education'.
8–For Jerome on H. G. Wells (1866–1946) and on W. W. Jacobs (1863–1943), *ibid.*, ch. viii, pp. 160–2, 168–72.
9–*Ibid.*, ch. xii, p. 288, which has: 'The one thing certain is . . .'

Julia Margaret Cameron

Julia Margaret Cameron, the third daughter of James Pattle of the Bengal Civil Service, was born on June 11, 1815. Her father was a gentleman of marked, but doubtful, reputation, who after living a riotous life and earning the title of 'the biggest liar in India', finally drank himself to death and was consigned to a cask of rum to await shipment to England.[2] The cask was stood outside the widow's bedroom door. In the middle of the night she heard a violent explosion, rushed out, and found her husband, having burst the lid off the coffin, bolt upright menacing her in death as he had menaced her in life. 'The shock sent her off her head then and there, poor thing, and she died raving.' It is the father of Miss Ethel Smyth who tells the story (*Impressions that Remained*), and he goes on to say that, after 'Jim Blazes' had been nailed down again and shipped off, the sailors drank the liquor in which the body was preserved, 'and, by Jove, the rum ran out and got alight and set the ship on fire! And while they were trying to extinguish the flames she ran on a rock, blew up, and drifted ashore just below Hooghly. And what do you think the sailors said? "That Pattle had been such a scamp that the devil wouldn't let him go out of India!"'[3]

His daughter inherited a strain of that indomitable vitality. If her father was famous for his lies, Mrs Cameron had a gift of ardent speech and picturesque behaviour which has impressed itself upon the calm pages of Victorian biography. But it was from her mother, presumably, that she inherited her love of beauty and her distaste for the cold and formal conventions of English society. For the sensitive lady whom the sight of her husband's body had killed was a Frenchwoman by birth. She was the daughter of Chevalier Antoine de l'Étang, one of Marie Antoinette's pages, who had been with the Queen in prison till her death, and was only saved by his own youth from the guillotine.[4] With his wife, who had been one of the Queen's ladies, he was exiled to India, and it is at Ghazipur, with the miniature that Marie Antoinette gave him laid upon his breast, that he lies buried.

But the de l'Étangs brought from France a gift of greater value than the miniature of the unhappy Queen. Old Madame de l'Étang was extremely handsome. Her daughter, Mrs Pattle, was lovely. Six of Mrs Pattle's seven daughters were even more lovely than she was. 'Lady Eastnor is one of the handsomest women I ever saw in any country,' wrote Henry Greville of the youngest, Virginia.[5] She underwent the usual fate of early Victorian beauty: was mobbed in the streets, celebrated in odes, and even made the subject of a paper in *Punch* by Thackeray, 'On a good-looking lady'.[6] It did not matter that the sisters had been brought up by their French grandmother in household lore rather than in book learning. 'They were artistic in their finger tips, with an appreciation – almost to be called a culte – for beauty.'[7] In India their conquests were many, and when they married and settled in England, they had the art of making round them, whether at Freshwater or at Little Holland House, a society of their own ('Pattledom' it was christened by Sir Henry Taylor[8]), where they could drape and arrange, pull down and build up, and carry on life in a high-handed and adventurous way which painters and writers and even serious men of affairs found much to their liking. 'Little Holland House, where Mr Watts lived, seemed to me a paradise,' wrote Ellen Terry, 'where only beautiful things were allowed to come. All the women were graceful, and all the men were gifted.'[9] There, in the many rooms of the old Dower House, Mrs Prinsep lodged Watts and Burne-Jones,[10] and entertained innumerable friends among lawns and trees which seemed deep in the country, though the traffic of Hyde Park Corner was only two miles distant. Whatever they did, whether in the cause of religion or of friendship, was done enthusiastically.

Was a room too dark for a friend? Mrs Cameron would have a window built instantly to catch the sun. Was the surplice of the Rev. C. Beanlands[11] only passably clean? Mrs Prinsep would set up a laundry in her own house and wash the entire linen of the clergy of St Michael's at her own expense. Then when relations interfered, and begged her to control her extravagance, she nodded her head with its coquettish white curls obediently, heaved a sigh of relief as her counsellors left her, and flew to the writing-table to despatch telegram after telegram to her sisters describing the visit. 'Certainly no one could restrain the Pattles but themselves,' says Lady Troubridge.[12] Once indeed the gentle Mr Watts was known to lose his temper. He found two little girls, the granddaughters of Mrs Prinsep, shouting at each other with their ears stopped so that they could hear no voices but their own. Then he delivered a lecture upon self-will, the vice, he said, which they had inherited from their French ancestress, Madame de l'Étang. 'You will grow up imperious women,' he told them, 'if you are not careful.'[13] Had they not into the bargain an ancestor who blew the lid off his coffin?

Certainly Julia Margaret Cameron had grown up an imperious woman; but she was without her sisters' beauty. In the trio where, as they said, Lady Somers was Beauty, and Mrs Prinsep Dash, Mrs Cameron was undoubtedly Talent.

'She seemed in herself to epitomise all the qualities of a remarkable family,' wrote Mrs Watts, 'presenting them in a doubly distilled form. She doubled the generosity of the most generous of the sisters, and the impulsiveness of the most impulsive. If they were enthusiastic, she was so twice over; if they were persuasive, she was invincible. She had remarkably fine eyes, that flashed like her sayings, and grew soft and tender if she was moved . . .'[14] But to a child she was a terrifying apparition 'short and squat, with none of the Pattle grace and beauty about her, though more than her share of their passionate energy and wilfulness. Dressed in dark clothes, stained with chemicals from her photography (and smelling of them too), with a plump eager face and a voice husky, and a little harsh, yet in some way compelling and even charming,' she dashed out of the studio at Dimbola, attached heavy swans' wings to the children's shoulders, and bade them 'Stand there' and play the part of the Angels of the Nativity leaning over the ramparts of Heaven.[15]

But the photography and the swans' wings were still in the far future. For many years her energy and her creative powers poured themselves into family life and social duties. She had married, in 1838, a very distinguished man, Charles Hay Cameron, 'a Benthamite jurist and philosopher of great learning and ability', who held the place, previously filled by Lord Macaulay,[16] of fourth Member of Council at Calcutta. In the absence of the Governor-General's wife, Mrs Cameron was at the head of European society in India, and it was this, in Sir Henry Taylor's opinion, that encouraged her in her contempt for the ways of the world when they returned to England. She had little respect, at any rate, for the conventions of Putney. She called her butler peremptorily 'Man'.[17] Dressed in robes of flowing red velvet, she walked with her friends, stirring a cup of tea as she walked, halfway to the railway station in hot summer weather. There was no eccentricity that she would not have dared on their behalf, no sacrifice that she would not have made to procure a few more minutes of their society. Sir Henry and Lady Taylor suffered the extreme fury of her affection. Indian shawls, turquoise bracelets, inlaid portfolios, ivory elephants, 'etc.', showered on their heads. She lavished upon them letters six sheets long 'all about ourselves'. Rebuffed for a moment, 'she told Alice [Lady Taylor] that before the year was out she would love her like a sister',[18] and before the year was out Lady Taylor could hardly imagine what life had been without Mrs Cameron. The Taylors loved her; Aubrey de Vere loved her; Lady Monteagle loved her; and 'even Lord Monteagle, who likes eccentricity in no other form, likes her'.[19] It was impossible, they found, not to love that 'genial, ardent, and generous' woman, who had 'a power of loving which I have never seen exceeded, and an equal determination to be loved'.[20] If it was impossible to reject her affection, it was even dangerous to reject her shawls. Either she would burn them, she threatened, then and there, or, if the gift were returned, she would sell it, buy with the proceeds a very expensive invalid sofa, and present it to the Putney Hospital for Incurables with an inscription which said, much to the surprise of Lady Taylor, when she chanced upon it, that it was the gift of Lady Taylor herself. It was better, on the whole, to bow the shoulder and submit to the shawl.

Meanwhile she was seeking some more permanent expression of her abundant energies in literature. She translated from the German, wrote poetry, and finished enough of a novel to make Sir Henry Taylor very nervous lest he should be called upon to read the whole of it. Volume after volume was despatched through the penny post. She wrote letters till the postman left, and then she began her postscripts. She sent the gardener after the postman, the gardener's boy after the gardener, the donkey galloping all the way to Yarmouth after the gardener's boy. Sitting at Wandsworth Station she wrote page after page to Alfred Tennyson until 'as I was folding your letter came the screams of the train, and then the yells of the porters with the threat that the train would not wait for me',[21] so that she had to thrust the document into strange hands and run down the steps. Every day she wrote to Henry Taylor, and every day he answered her.

Very little remains of this enormous daily volubility. The Victorian age killed the art of letter writing by kindness: it was only too easy to catch the post. A lady sitting down at her desk a hundred years before had not only certain ideals of logic and restraint before her, but the knowledge that a letter which cost so much money to send and excited so much interest to receive was worth time and trouble. With Ruskin and Carlyle[22] in power, a penny post to stimulate, a gardener, a gardener's boy, and a galloping donkey to catch up the overflow of inspiration, restraint was unnecessary and emotion more to a lady's credit, perhaps, than common sense. Thus to dip into the private letters of the Victorian age is to be immersed in the joys and sorrows of enormous families, to share their whooping coughs and colds and misadventures, day by day, indeed hour by hour. The standard of family affection was very high. Illness elicited showers of enquiries and kindnesses. The weather was watched anxiously to see whether Richard would be wet at Cheltenham, or Jane catch cold at Broadstairs. Grave misdemeanours on the part of the governesses, cooks, and doctors ('he is guilty of culpable carelessness, profound ignorance', Mrs Camerson would say of the family physician[23]), were detailed profusely, and the least departure from family morality was vigilantly pounced upon and volubly imparted.

Mrs Cameron's letters were formed upon this model; she counselled and exhorted and enquired after the health of dearest Emily with the best; but her correspondents were often men of exalted genius to whom she could express the more romantic side of her nature. To Tennyson she dwelt upon the beauty of Mrs Hambro, 'frolicsome and graceful as a kitten and having the form and eye of an antelope . . . Then her complexion (or rather her skin) is faultless – it is like the leaf of "that consummate flower" the Magnolia – a flower which is, I think, so mysterious in its beauty as if it were the only thing left unsoiled and unspoiled from the garden of Eden . . . We had a standard Magnolia tree in our garden at Sheen, and on a still summer night the moon would beam down upon those ripe rich vases, and they used to send forth a scent which made the soul faint with a sense of the luxury of the world of flowers.'[24] From such sentences it is easy to see why Sir Henry Taylor looked forward to reading her novel with dread. 'Her genius (of which she has a great deal) is too profuse and redundant, not distinguishing between felicitous and infelicitous,' he wrote. 'She lives upon superlatives as upon her daily bread.'[25]

But the zenith of Mrs Cameron's career was at hand. In 1860 the Camerons bought two or three rose-covered cottages at Freshwater, ran them together, and supplemented them with outhouses to receive the overflow of their hospitality. For at Dimbola – the name was taken from Mr Cameron's estate in Ceylon – everybody was welcome. 'Conventionalities had no place in it.'[26] Mrs Cameron would invite a family met on the steamer to lunch without asking their names, would ask a hatless tourist met on the cliff to come in and choose himself a hat, would adopt an Irish beggar woman and send her child to school with her own children. 'What will become of her?' Henry Taylor asked, but comforted himself with the reflection that though Julia Cameron and her sisters 'have more of hope than of reason', still 'the humanities are stronger in them than the sentimentalities',[27] and they generally brought their eccentric undertakings to a successful end. In fact the Irish beggar child grew up into a beautiful woman, became Mrs Cameron's parlour-maid, sat for her portrait, was sought in marriage by a rich man's son, filled the position with dignity and competence, and in 1878 enjoyed an income of two thousand four hundred pounds a year.[28] Gradually the cottages took colour and shape under Mrs Cameron's hands. A little theatre was built where the young people acted. On fine nights they trapesed up to the Tennysons and danced; if it were stormy, and Mrs Cameron preferred the storm to the calm, she paced the beach and sent for Tennyson to come and pace by her side. The colour of the clothes she wore, the glitter and hospitality of the household she ruled reminded visitors of the East. But, if there was an element of 'feudal familiarity', there was also a sense of 'feudal discipline'.[29] Mrs Cameron was extremely outspoken. She could be highly despotic. 'If ever you fall into temptation,' she said to a cousin, 'down on your knees and think of Aunt Julia.'[30] She was caustic and candid of tongue. She chased Tennyson into his tower vociferating 'Coward! Coward!'[31] and thus forced him to be vaccinated. She had her hates as well as her loves, and alternated in spirits 'between the seventh heaven and the bottomless pit'.[32] There were visitors who found her company agitating, so odd and bold were her methods of conversation, while the variety and brilliance of the society she collected round her caused a certain 'poor Miss Stephen' to lament: 'Is there *nobody* commonplace?'[33] as she saw Jowett's four young men drinking brandy and water, heard Tennyson reciting 'Maud',[34] while Mr Cameron wearing a coned hat, a veil, and several coats paced the lawn which his wife in a fit of enthusiasm had created during the night.

In 1865, when she was fifty, her son's gift of a camera gave her at last an outlet for the energies which she had dissipated in poetry and fiction and doing up houses and concocting curries and entertaining her friends. Now she became a photographer. All her sensibility was expressed, and, what was perhaps more to the purpose, controlled in the new born art. The coal-house was turned into a dark room; the fowl-house was turned into a glass-house. Boatmen were turned into King Arthur; village girls into Queen Guenevere. Tennyson was wrapped in rugs: Sir Henry Taylor was crowned with tinsel. The parlourmaid sat for her portrait and the guest had to answer the bell. 'I worked fruitlessly but not hopelessly,'[35] Mrs Cameron wrote of this time. Indeed, she was indefatigable. 'She used to say that in her photography a hundred negatives were destroyed before she achieved one good result; her object being to overcome realism by diminishing just in the least degree the precision of the focus.'[36] Like a tigress where her children were concerned, she was as magnificently uncompromising about her art. Brown stains appeared on her hands, and the smell of chemicals mixed with the scent of the sweet briar in the road outside her house. She cared nothing for the miseries of her sitters nor for their rank. The carpenter and the Crown Prince of Prussia alike must sit as still as stones in the attitudes she chose, in the draperies she arranged, for as long as she wished. She cared nothing for her own labours and failures and exhaustion. 'I longed to arrest all the beauty that came before me, and at length the longing was satisfied,'[37] she wrote. Painters praised her art; writers marvelled at the character her portraits revealed. She herself blazed up at length into satisfaction with her own creations. 'It is a sacred blessing which has attended my photography,' she wrote. 'It gives pleasure to millions.'[38] She lavished her photographs upon her friends and relations, hung them in railway waiting-rooms, and offered them, it is said, to porters in default of small change.

Old Mr Cameron meanwhile retired more and more frequently to the comparative privacy of his bedroom. He had no taste for society himself, but endured it, as he endured all his wife's vagaries, with philosophy and affection. 'Julia is slicing up Ceylon,'[39] he would say, when she embarked on another adventure or extravagance. Her hospitalities and the failure of the coffee crop ('Charles speaks to me of the flower of the coffee plant. I tell him that the eyes of the first grandchild should be more beautiful than any flowers,'[40] she said) had brought his affairs into a precarious state. But it was not business anxieties alone that made Mrs Cameron wish to visit Ceylon. The old philosopher became more and more obsessed with the desire to return to the East. There was peace; there was warmth; there were the monkeys and the elephants whom he had once lived among 'as a friend and a brother'.[41] Suddenly, for the secret had been kept from their friends, the Camerons announced that they were going to visit their sons in Ceylon. Their preparations were made and friends went to say good-bye to them at Southampton. Two coffins preceded them on board packed with glass and china, in case coffins should be unprocurable in the East; the old philosopher with his bright fixed eyes and his beard 'dipt in moonlight'[42] held in one hand his ivory staff and in the other Lady Tennyson's parting gift of a pink rose; while Mrs Cameron, 'grave and valiant,'[43] vociferated her final injunctions and controlled not only innumerable packages but a cow.

They reached Ceylon safely, and in her gratitude Mrs Cameron raised a subscription to present the Captain with a harmonium. Their house at Kalutara was so surrounded by trees that rabbits and squirrels and minah birds passed in and out while a beautiful tame stag kept guard at the open door. Marianne North,[44] the traveller, visited them there and found old Mr Cameron in a state of perfect happiness, reciting poetry, walking up and down the verandah, with his long white hair flowing over his shoulders, and his ivory staff held in his hand. Within doors Mrs Cameron still photographed. The walls were covered with magnificent pictures which tumbled over the tables and chairs and mixed in picturesque confusion with books and draperies. Mrs Cameron at once made up her mind that she would photograph her visitor and for three days was in a fever of excitement. 'She made me stand with spiky coconut branches running into my head ... and told me to look perfectly natural,' Miss North remarked. The same methods and ideals ruled in Ceylon that had once ruled in Freshwater. A gardener was kept, though there was no garden and the man had never heard of the existence of such a thing, for the excellent reason that Mrs Cameron thought his back 'absolutely superb'. And when Miss North incautiously admired a wonderful grass green shawl that Mrs Cameron was wearing, she seized a pair of scissors, and saying: 'Yes, that would just suit you,' cut it in half from corner to corner and made her share it.[45] At length, it was time for Miss North to go. But still Mrs Cameron could not bear that her friends should leave her. As at Putney she had gone with them stirring her tea as she walked, so now at Kalutara she and her whole household must escort her guest down the hill to wait for the coach at midnight. Two years later (in 1879) she died. The birds were fluttering in and out of the open door; the photographs were tumbling over the tables; and, lying before a large open window Mrs Cameron saw the stars shining, breathed the one word 'Beautiful,' and so died.[46]

1–A signed essay introducing *Victorian Photographs of Famous Men and Fair Women* by Julia Margaret Cameron (1815–79), published by the Hogarth Press in November 1926 (see Editorial Note, p. xxv), with an additional introduction by Roger Fry. 'You are urgently needed ...' VW wrote to her sister Vanessa Bell on 18

July 1926, 'to get up a book of Aunt Julia's photographs, among other things' (*III VW Letters*, no. 1650); and in an undated letter of July she wrote again: 'I forgot to ask you the one thing I wanted last night – have you any Aunt Julia letters? I vividly remember reading some, to mother, I think; but can't find any here. I'm now writing about her, and it would be a great advantage to have some of her actual words, which I imagine were extremely profuse, to quote. But I daresay they've all disappeared. I don't want to have to apply to George [Duckworth] or Bee Cameron, if I can help.

'If you *have*, would you ring up tomorrow, and I will come and get them ...' (*ibid.*, no. 1653). See also *ibid.*, nos 1655 and 1693, both to Vita Sackville-West. As Tristram Powell points out in his edition of *Victorian Photographs* ... (Hogarth Press, 1973), the account of James Pattle given here is inaccurate and almost certainly unjust. His reputation for mendacity and intemperance as transmitted by VW via the memoirs of Ethel Smyth and Lady Troubridge belonged more properly to his brother Colonel Pattle. See also '*Guests and Memories*', 'Pattledom', above.

2 – James Pattle (1775–1845). He had married Adeline d L'Étang (1793–1845), daughter of Antoine, Chevalier de L'Étang (d. c. 1840) and Thérèse Blin de Grincourt (1767–1866). The source of the quotation has not been discovered.

3 – For the first and second extensive quotations, Ethel Smyth, *Impressions That Remained. Memoirs* (2 vols, Longmans, Green, and Co., 1920), vol. ii, ch. xliv, pp. 251 and 252 (for VW on 'Ethel Smyth', see *III VW Essays*). Adeline Pattle did not die raving. 'Jim Blazes' does not occur in Smyth and has not been traced elsewhere.

4 – Chevalier de l'Étang, superintendent of the Royal Stud and an officer in Louis XVI's bodyguard, was in fact banished by Louis before the revolution. Nor was his wife, as is subsequently stated, one of Marie Antoinette's ladies. Born in India, she did not visit France until the 1820s.

5 – Greville, *Leaves from the Diary of Henry Greville*, ed. Viscountess Enfield (4 vols, Smith, Elder and Co., 1883–1905), vol. i, 13 March 1852, p. 418, adapted.

6 – W. M. Thackeray, 'The Poser. Essays and Discourses by Dr Solomon Pacifico'. IV 'On a Good-Looking Young Lady', *Punch, or the London Charivari*, 18, 8 June 1850, pp. 223–4. Virginia Pattle (1827–1910), married Lord Eastnor who later became Earl Somers.

7 – Mary S. Watts, *George Frederic Watts. The Annals of an Artist's Life* (2 vols, Macmillan and Co. Ltd, 1912), vol. i, ch. v, p. 122: 'Artistic to their finger-tips, with an appreciation – almost to be called a *culte* – for beauty, the sisters were quickly at home in the studio, and in love with the work and its aims.'

8 – For Sir Henry Taylor (1800–86) and his ascription, see for example Una Taylor, *Guests and Memories. Annals of a Seaside Villa* (OUP, 1924), ch. vi, p. 217, for VW's notice of which see above. Una Taylor had married, as her first husband, Ernest Troubridge, a great-grandson of Sarah Prinsep.

9 – Ellen Terry, *The Story of My Life* (Hutchinson and Co., 1908), ch. ii, p. 53. Ellen Terry (1847–1928).

10 – Sarah Pattle (1816–87), married Henry Thoby Prinsep, an official of the East India Company. G. F. Watts (1817–1904). Edward Burne-Jones (1833–98).

11 – Otherwise unidentified.

12 – Lady Troubridge, *Memories and Reflections* (Heinemann, 1925), ch. iii, p. 53. (Laura Troubridge was a granddaughter of Sarah Prinsep.)

13 – *Ibid.*, p. 52.

14—Watts, vol. i, ch. vii, p. 205; there should be an ellipsis after invincible. The text resumes: '. . . she certainly had remarkably fine eyes'.

15—For the quotations, Troubridge, ch. ii, pp. 33–4.

16—Sir Henry Taylor, *Autobiography of* . . . (2 vols, Longmans Green, 1885), vol. ii, ch. v, p. 48. Charles Hay Cameron (1795–1880), jurist, was appointed to the supreme council of India in 1843. Together with Thomas Babington Macaulay (1800–59), a member of the supreme council 1834–8, he worked upon the codification of the Indian legal system.

17—Anne Thackeray Ritchie, *From Friend to Friend* (John Murray, 1919), ch. i 'From Friend to Friend', p. 4: 'I remember a strange apparition in a flowing red velvet dress, although it was summer, cordially welcoming us to a fine house and some belated meal, when the attendant butler was addressed by her as "man", and was ordered to do many things for our benefit . . .'

18—For the first quotation, Sir Henry Taylor, vol. ii, ch. v, p. 49, and for the second, *ibid.*, ch. vi, p. 54. Taylor had married in 1839 Theodosia Alice Spring-Rice, a daughter of the first Lord and Lady Monteagle (below).

19—*Ibid.*, ch. vi, p. 55. Aubrey de Vere (1788–1846), poet, and a brother-in-law of Thomas Spring-Rice, 1st Baron Monteagle (1790–1866), who married, first, Theodosia Pery (d. 1839) and, second, Marianne Marshall (d. 1889).

20—For the first quotation, *ibid.*, ch. v, p. 49, and for the second, ch. vi, p. 54, which has 'to be beloved'.

21—Ritchie, ch. i, 'From Friend to Friend', p. 23. Alfred, Lord Tennyson (1809–92).

22—John Ruskin (1819–1900), Thomas Carlyle (1795–1881).

23—Ritchie, ch. i, 'From Friend to Friend', p. 6, quoting Sir Henry Taylor: '. . . "Culpable carelessness, profound ignorance," were the least of her criticisms of family physicians whom she had not sent in herself.'

24—*Ibid.*, quoting 'a longer letter written in 1855' from Mrs Cameron to Tennyson, p. 13, which has 'that made the soul faint'. Mrs Hambro, otherwise unidentified.

25—For the first quotation, Una Taylor, ch. vi, p. 225, quoting Henry Taylor, and for the second, *ibid.*, p. 217, also quoting Henry Taylor.

26—Sir Henry Taylor, vol. ii, ch. xiv, p. 184.

27—For all quotations, *ibid.*, p. 186.

28—For an account of Mary Hillier's career, see Troubridge, ch. ii, pp. 35–6.

29—Una Taylor, ch. vi, p. 218: 'Moreover, an element not alone of feudal familiarity, but also of feudal discipline prevailed; and in an atmosphere redolent of India and of the conditions of Indian life, with its lavish hospitalities and spendthrift generosity, no breach of that discipline was suffered unrebuked.'

30—Troubridge, ch. ii, p. 39.

31—*Ibid.*, p. 38.

32—*Ibid.*, ch. vi, p. 217.

33—Anne Thackeray Ritchie, *Letters* . . . (John Murray, 1924), to Walter Senior, Freshwater, Easter, 1865, p. 127. 'Poor Miss Stephen' was VW's aunt Caroline Emelia Stephen (1834–1909) – also quoted in 'The Enchanted Organ', *III VW Essays*.

34—Benjamin Jowett (1817–93), Master of Balliol College. Tennyson's *Maud* was first published in 1855.

35 – Cameron, 'Annals of My Glass House', in a catalogue of her photographs shown at the Cameron Gallery, London, April 1889, quoted by Anne Thackeray Ritchie in *From Friend to Friend*, 'From Friend to Friend', p. 25.

36 – Mary S. Watts, *George Frederic Watts. The Annals of an Artist's Life*, vol. i, ch. vii, p. 206.

37 – Cameron, 'Annals . . .', quoted in Ritchie, p. 25.

38 – Ritchie, p. 26: '"It gives pleasure to millions and a deeper happiness to very many . . ."'

39 – The source of this quotation has resisted all efforts at discovery.

40 – Ritchie, ch. i, 'From Friend to Friend', p. 16, which has 'flower'.

41 – Una Taylor, ch. vi, p. 214.

42 – Hallam Tennyson, *Alfred Lord Tennyson. A Memoir* (2 vols, Macmillan and Co. Ltd, 1897), vol. ii, ch. iii, p. 84, quoting Tennyson.

43 – This quotation remains untraced.

44 – Marianne North (1830–90), flower painter, and intrepid traveller, visited Ceylon during a journey round the world, 1875–7.

45 – For all quotations, North, *Recollections of a Happy Life*, ed. Janet Symonds (2 vols, Macmillan, 1892), vol. i, ch. viii, p. 315: 'She dressed me up in flowing draperies of cashmere wool, let down my hair, and made me stand with spiky cocoa-nut branches running into my head, the noonday sun's rays dodging my eyes between the leaves as the slight breeze moved them, and told me to look perfectly natural (with a thermometer standing at 96°)!'

46 – Ritchie, ch. i, 'From Friend to Friend', p. 37: 'When she lay dying, her bed faced the wide-open window; it was a glorious evening and some big stars were shining. She looked out and just said, "*Beautiful*," and died, her last word, a fitting end to her reverent soul on earth.'

George Eliot

George Eliot lies flattened under the tomb that Mr Cross built over her, to all appearances completely dead.[2] No writer of equal vitality as a writer so entirely lacks vitality as a human being. Yet when the solemnity of the tomb is violated, when her letters are broken into fragments and presented in a volume of modest size, they reflect a character full of variety and full of conflict – qualities that sort ill with the calm composure of death. It is true that Mr Cross so pruned the letters of irrelevances and, for aught we know, so edited the life of indiscretions, that the true George Eliot is hopelessly lost; but enough remains, thanks to Mr Brimley Johnson, when sorted and put artfully in contrast, to show that George Eliot far from being the solemn pedant of legend was a woman of flesh and blood who felt to the full the different currents of her life and time. Nobody changed her skin more completely in the course of sixty-one years. She went from arid Evangelicism to broad Agnosticism, from deploring fiction to writing it, from the depths of agricultural society to the hub of Fleet Street, from lamentations over the worldliness of marriage to an open and irregular liaison with a married man.

It would, of course, be untrue to attribute these changes entirely to her own character. Fate had planted her in such surroundings that it was only by breaking the pot itself that she could escape. It needed no unusual violence to revolt against the pastoral placidity of Griff, against Hannah More's letters, and Doddridge's sermons,[3] and making jelly, and being scolded for not going to church. To dream of seeing 'the bread fruit tree, the fan-palm, and the papyrus',[4] and at last actually to see them at Alton Garden were scarcely enough to fill a life. But there was a strain of impressionability in George Eliot which would have made her uneasy whatever her circumstances. There was something alive and emotional in her which tended to upset the outward solemnity. She had to leave the room overcome with awe when she first saw the beauty of the Sistine Madonna. At one moment she thought that life is a doubtful good and early death to be welcomed; at another she wished to live as long as possible and learn as much as possible. She enjoyed lawn tennis at the age of fifty-eight, and two years after the seemingly fatal blow of Lewes's death[5] she revived and started life afresh with Mr Cross.

But if these vacillations are brought into relief by the broken glimpses we get in this book, we are reminded that with all her sensibility she was also curiously without the sparkling temperament of the impressionable. She was easily depressed. She suffered far more from blame than she was encouraged by praise. 'She had little self-assertion,' Mr Bray said.[6] She was slow and sagacious and inclined to reach out from her own narrow lot towards 'the historical life of the world'.[7] It was a temperament which, though it impeded her in many ways as a writer, made her expose a greater surface to life than any other woman of her time. 'Science, history, poetry — I don't know which draws me most,' she wrote.[8] She rushed 'on the slightest pretext to Sophocles',[9] she filled bottles with zoological wonders on the sea shore; she read philosophy with Mr Lewes; she adored the opera; she dined with Liszt; she discussed the higher education of women with Madame Bodichon.[10] The whole of the nineteenth century seems to be mirrored in the depths of that sensitive and profound mind which lies buried, so far as the life of the body is concerned, under Mr Cross's tomb.

1 – A review in the *N&A*, 30 October 1926, (Kp C276.2) of *The Letters of George Eliot*. Selected with an Introduction by R. Brimley Johnson (Bodley Head Ltd, 1926). See also 'George Eliot' in *CR1* above; 'George Eliot 1819–1880', *III VW Essays*. The same issue of the *N&A* also contained LW's 'World of Books' column on 'Publishers and Old Books'.

2 – J. W. Cross, whom George Eliot married in the last year of her life, published *George Eliot's Life. As Related in her Letters and Journals* in 1884.

3 – Griff, the house on the Arbury Estate in Warwickshire where George Eliot (Mary Ann Evans) lived for the first twenty-one years of her life. Hannah More (1745–1833), religious writer, whose letters were published in 1834. Philip Doddridge (1702–51), Nonconformist divine whose works were published in ten volumes in 1802.

4 – Johnson, letter to Maria Lewis, 23 June 1840.

5 – George Henry Lewes (1817–78) and George Eliot had lived together as man and wife from 1854.

6 – Johnson, Introduction, p. 9, quoting Charles Bray's *Phases of Opinion and Experience During a Long Life* (1884).

7 – *Ibid.*, letter to Edward Burne-Jones, 20 March 1873, p. 165: 'Art works for all whom it can touch. And I want in gratitude to tell you that your work makes life larger and more beautiful to me. I mean that historical life of all the world, in which our little personal share often seems a mere standing-room from which we can look all round, and chiefly backward.'

8 – *Ibid.*, letter to Sara Hennell, 7 December 1866, p. 152, which continues: 'and there is little time left me for any of them'.

9 – *Ibid.*, to the same, 16 April 1857, p. 94.

10 – Ferenc (Franz) Liszt (1811–86); Barbara Leigh Smith Bodichon (1827–91), benefactress of Girton College, Cambridge, who wrote to George Eliot on the publication of *Adam Bede* (1859) recognising it as the work of her friend Mary Ann Evans.

How Should One Read a Book?

At this late hour of the world's history, books are to be found in almost every room of the house – in the nursery, in the drawing-room, in the dining-room, in the kitchen. But in some houses they have become such a company that they have to be accommodated with a room of their own – a reading-room, a library, a study. Let us imagine that we are now in such a room; that it is a sunny room, with windows opening on a garden, so that we can hear the trees rustling, the gardener talking, the donkey braying, the old women gossiping at the pump – and all the ordinary processes of life pursuing the casual irregular way which they have pursued these many hundreds of years. As casually, as persistently, books have been coming together on the shelves. Novels, poems, histories, memoirs, dictionaries, maps, directories; black letter books and brand new books; books in French and Greek and Latin; of all shapes and sizes and values, bought for purposes of research, bought to amuse a railway journey, bought by miscellaneous beings, of one temperament and another, serious and frivolous, men of action and men of letters.

Now, one may well ask oneself, strolling into such a room as this, how am I to read these books? What is the right way to set about it? They are so many and so various. My appetite is so fitful and so capricious. What am I to do to get the utmost possible pleasure out of them? And is it pleasure, or profit, or what is it that I should seek? I will lay before you some of the thoughts that have come to me on such an occasion as this. But you will notice the note of interrogation at the end of my title. One may think about reading as much as one chooses, but no one is going to lay down laws about it. Here in this room, if nowhere else, we breathe the air of freedom. Here simple and learned, man and woman are alike. For though reading seems so simple – a mere matter of knowing the alphabet – it is indeed so difficult that it is doubtful whether anybody knows anything about it. Paris is the capital of France; King John signed the Magna Charta; those are facts; those can be taught; but how are we to teach people so to read *Paradise Lost* as to see that it is a great poem, or *Tess of the D'Urbervilles*[2] so as to see that it is a good novel? How are we to learn the art of reading for ourselves? Without attempting to lay down laws upon a subject that has not been legalised, I will make a few suggestions, which may serve to show you how not to read, or to stimulate you to think out better methods of your own.

And directly we begin to ask how should one read a book we are faced by the fact that books differ; there are poems, novels, biographies on the book shelf there; each differs from the other as a tiger differs from a tortoise, a tortoise from an elephant. Our attitude must always be changing; it is clear. From different books we must ask different qualities. Simple as this sounds, people are always behaving as if all books were of the same species — as if there were only tortoises or nothing but tigers. It makes them furious to find a novelist bring Queen Victoria to the throne six months before her time;[3] they will praise a poet enthusiastically for teaching them that a violet has four petals and a daisy almost invariably ten. You will save a great deal of time and temper better kept for worthier objects if you will try to make out before you begin to read what qualities you expect of a novelist, what of a poet, what of a biographer. The tortoise is bald and shiny; the tiger has a thick coat of yellow fur. So books too differ: one has its fur, the other has its baldness.

Yes; but for all that the problem is not so simple in a library as at the Zoological Gardens. Books have a great deal in common; they are always overflowing their boundaries; they are always breeding new species from unexpected matches among themselves. It is difficult to know how to approach them, to which species each belongs. But if we remember, as we turn to the bookcase, that each of these books was written by a pen which, consciously or unconsciously, tried to trace out a design, avoiding this, accepting that, adventuring the other; if we try to follow the writer in his experiment from the first word to the last, without imposing our design upon him, then we shall have a good chance of getting hold of the right end of the string.

To read a book well, one should read it as if one were writing it. Begin not by sitting on the bench among the judges but by standing in the dock with the criminal. Be his fellow worker, become his accomplice. Even, if you wish merely to read books, begin by writing them. For this certainly is true — one cannot write the most ordinary little story, attempt to describe the simplest event — meeting a beggar, shall we say, in the street, without coming up against difficulties that the greatest of novelists have had to face. In order that we may realise, however briefly and crudely, the main divisions into which novelists group themselves, let us imagine how differently Defoe, Jane Austen,[4] and Thomas Hardy would describe the same incident — this meeting a beggar in the street. Defoe is a master of narrative. His prime effort will be to reduce the beggar's story to perfect order and simplicity. This happened first, that next, the other thing third. He will put in nothing, however attractive, that will tire the reader unnecessarily, or divert his attention from what he wishes him to know. He will also make us believe, since he is a master, not of romance or of comedy, but of narrative, that everything that happened is true. He will be extremely precise therefore. This happened, as he tells us on the first pages of *Robinson Crusoe*, on the first of September. More subtly and artfully, he will hypnotise us into a state of belief by dropping out casually some little unnecessary fact – for instance, 'my father called me one morning into his chamber, where he was confined by the gout.'[5] His father's gout is not necessary to the story, but it is necessary to the truth of the story, for it is thus that anybody who is speaking the truth adds some small irrelevant detail without thinking. Further, he will choose a type of sentence which is flowing but not too full, exact but not epigrammatic. His aim will be to present the thing itself without distortion from his own angle of vision. He will meet the subject face to face, four-square, without turning aside for a moment to point out that this was tragic, or that beautiful; and his aim is perfectly achieved.

But let us not for a moment confuse it with Jane Austen's aim. Had she met a beggar woman, no doubt she would have been interested in the beggar's story. But she would have seen at once that for her purposes the whole incident must be transformed. Streets and the open air and adventures mean nothing to her, artistically. It is character that interests her. She would at once make the beggar into a comfortable elderly man of the upper-middle classes, seated by his fireside at his ease. Then, instead of plunging into the story vigorously and veraciously, she will write a few paragraphs of accurate and artfully seasoned introduction, summing up the circumstances and sketching the character of the gentleman she wishes us to know. 'Matrimony as the origin of change was always disagreeable' to Mr Woodhouse, she says. Almost immediately, she thinks it well to let us see that her words are corroborated by Mr Woodhouse himself. We hear him talking. 'Poor Miss Taylor! – I wish she were here again. What a pity it is that Mr Weston ever thought of her.' And when Mr Woodhouse has talked enough to reveal himself from the inside, she then thinks it time to let us see him through his daughter's eyes. 'You got Hannah that good place. Nobody thought of Hannah till you mentioned her.'[6] Thus she shows us Emma flattering him and humouring him. Finally then, we have Mr Woodhouse's character seen from three different points of view at once; as he sees himself; as his daughter sees him; and as he is seen by the marvellous eye of that invisible lady Jane Austen herself. All three meet in one, and thus we can pass round her characters free, apparently, from any guidance but our own.

Now let Thomas Hardy choose the same theme – a beggar met in the street – and at once two great changes will be visible. The street will be transformed into a vast and sombre heath; the man or woman will take on some of the size and indistinctness of a statue. Further, the relations of this human being will not be towards other people, but towards the heath, towards man as law-giver, towards those powers which are in control of man's destiny. Once more our perspective will be completely changed. All the qualities which were admirable in *Robinson Crusoe*, admirable in *Emma*, will be neglected or absent. The direct literal statement of Defoe is gone. There is none of the clear, exact brilliance of Jane Austen. Indeed, if we come to Hardy from one of these great writers we shall exclaim at first that he is 'melodramatic' or 'unreal' compared with them. But we should bethink us that there are at least two sides to the human soul; the light side and the dark side. In company, the light side of the mind is exposed; in solitude, the dark. Both are equally real, equally important. But a novelist will always tend to expose one rather than the other; and Hardy, who is a novelist of the dark side, will contrive that no clear, steady light falls upon his people's faces, that they are not closely observed in drawing-rooms, that they come in contact with moors, sheep, the sky and the stars, and in their solitude are directly at the mercy of the gods. If Jane Austen's characters are real in the drawing-room, they would not exist at all upon the top of Stonehenge. Feeble and clumsy in drawing rooms, Hardy's people are large-limbed and vigorous out of doors. To achieve his purpose Hardy is neither literal and four-square like Defoe, nor deft and pointed like Jane Austen. He is cumbrous, involved, metaphorical. Where Jane Austen describes manners, he describes Nature. Where she is matter of fact, he is romantic and poetical. As both are great artists, each is careful to observe the laws of his own perspective, and will not be found confusing us (as so many lesser writers do) by introducing two different kinds of reality into the same book.

Yet it is very difficult not to wish them less scrupulous. Frequent are the complaints that Jane Austen is too prosaic, Thomas Hardy too melodramatic. And we have to remind ourselves that it is necessary to approach every writer differently in order to get from him all he can give us. We have to remember that it is one of the qualities of greatness that it brings heaven and earth and human nature into conformity with its own vision. It is by reason of this masterliness of theirs, this uncompromising idiosyncrasy, that great writers often require us to make heroic efforts in order to read them rightly. They bend us and break us. To go from Jane Austen to Hardy, from Peacock to Trollope, from Scott to Meredith, from Richardson to Kipling,[7] is to be wrenched and distorted, thrown this way and then that. Besides, everyone is born with a natural bias of his own in one direction rather than in another. He instinctively accepts Hardy's vision rather than Jane Austen's, and, reading with the current and not against it, is carried on easily and swiftly by the impetus of his own bent to the heart of his author's genius. But then Jane Austen is repulsive to him. He can scarcely stagger through the desert of her novels.

Sometimes this natural antagonism is too great to be overcome, but trial is always worth making. For these difficult and inaccessible books, with all their preliminary harshness, often yield the richest fruits in the end, and so curiously is the brain compounded that while tracts of literature repel at one season, they are appetising and essential at another.

If, then, this is true – that books are of very different types, and that to read them rightly we have to bend our imaginations powerfully, first one way, then another – it is clear that reading is one of the most arduous and exhausting of occupations. Often the pages fly before us and we seem, so keen is our interest, to be living and not even holding the volume in our hands. But the more exciting the book, the more danger we run of over-reading. The symptoms are familiar. Suddenly the book becomes dull as ditchwater and heavy as lead. We yawn and stretch and cannot attend. The highest flights of Shakespeare and Milton become intolerable.[8] And we say to ourselves – is Keats a fool or am I? – a painful question, a question, moreover, that need not be asked if we realised how great a part the art of not reading plays in the art of reading. To be able to read books without reading them, to skip and saunter, to suspend judgement, to lounge and loaf down the alleys and bye-streets of letters is the best way of rejuvenating one's own creative power. All biographies and memoirs, all the hybrid books which are largely made up of facts, serve to restore to us the power of reading real books – that is to say, works of pure imagination. That they serve also to impart knowledge and to improve the mind is true and important, but if we are considering how to read books for pleasure, not how to provide an adequate pension for one's widow, this other property of theirs is even more valuable and important. But here again one should know what one is after. One is after rest, and fun, and oddity, and some stimulus to one's own jaded creative power. One has left one's bare and angular tower and is strolling along the street looking in at the open windows. After solitude and concentration, the open air, the sight of other people absorbed in innumerable activities, comes upon us with an indescribable fascination.

The windows of the houses are open; the blinds are drawn up. One can see the whole household without their knowing that they are being seen. One can see them sitting round the dinner table, talking, reading, playing games. Sometimes they seem to be quarrelling – but what about? Or they are laughing – but what is the joke? Down in the basement the cook is reading a newspaper aloud, while the housemaid is making a piece of toast; in comes the kitchenmaid and they all start talking at the same moment – but what are they saying? Upstairs a girl is dressing to go to a party. But where is she going? There is an old lady sitting at her bedroom window with some kind of wool work in her hand and a fine green parrot in a cage beside her. And what is she thinking? All this life has somehow come together; there is a reason for it; a coherency in it, could one but seize it. The biographer answers the innumerable questions which we ask as we stand outside on the pavement looking in at the open window. Indeed there is nothing more interesting than to pick one's way about among these vast depositories of facts, to make up the lives of men and women, to create their complex minds and households from the extraordinary abundance and litter and confusion of matter which lies strewn about. A thimble, a skull, a pair of scissors, a sheaf of sonnets, are given us, and we have to create, to combine, to put these incongruous things together. There is, too, a quality in facts, an emotion which comes from knowing that men and women actually did and suffered these things, which only the greatest novelists can surpass. Captain Scott, starving and freezing to death in the snow, affects us deeply as any made-up story of adventure by Conrad[9] or Defoe; but it affects us differently. The biography differs from the novel. To ask a biographer to give us the same kind of pleasure that we get from a novelist is to misuse and misread him. Directly he says 'John Jones was born at five-thirty in the morning of August 13, 1862,' he has committed himself, focused his lens upon fact, and if he then begins to romance, the perspective becomes blurred, we grow suspicious, and our faith in his integrity as a writer is destroyed. In the same way fact destroys fiction. If Thackeray, for example, had quoted an actual newspaper account of the Battle of Waterloo in *Vanity Fair*,[10] the whole fabric of his story would have been destroyed, as a stone destroys a bubble.

But it is undoubted that these hybrid books, these warehouses and depositories of facts, play a great part in resting the brain and restoring its zest of imagination. The work of building up a life for oneself from skulls, thimbles, scissors, and sonnets stimulates our interest in creation and rouses our wish to see the work beautifully and powerfully done by a Flaubert or a Tolstoy.[11] Moreover, however interesting facts may be, they are an inferior form of fiction, and gradually we become impatient of their weakness and diffuseness, of their compromises and evasions, of the slovenly sentences which they make for themselves, and are eager to revive ourselves with the greater intensity and truth of fiction.

It is necessary to have in hand an immense reserve of imaginative energy in order to attack the steeps of poetry. Here are none of those gradual introductions, those resemblances to the familiar world of daily life with which the novelist entices us into his world of imagination. All is violent, opposite, unrelated. But various causes, such as bad books, the worry of carrying on life efficiently, the intermittent but powerful shocks dealt us by beauty, and the incalculable impulses of our own minds and bodies, frequently put us into that state of mind in which poetry is a necessity. The sight of a crocus in a garden will suddenly bring to mind all the spring days that have ever been. One then desires the general, not the particular; the whole, not the detail; to turn uppermost the dark side of the mind; to be in contact with silence, solitude, and all men and women and not this particular Richard, or that particular Anne. Metaphors are then more expressive than plain statements.

Thus in order to read poetry rightly, one must be in a rash, an extreme, a generous state of mind in which many of the supports and comforts of literature are done without. Its power of make-believe, its representative power, is dispensed with in favour of its extremities and extravagances. The representation is often at a very far remove from the thing represented, so that we have to use all our energies of mind to grasp the relation between, for example, the song of a nightingale and the images and ideas which that song stirs in the mind. Thus reading poetry often seems a state of rhapsody in which rhyme and metre and sound stir the mind as wine and dance stir the body, and we read on, understanding with the senses, not with the intellect, in a state of intoxication. Yet all this intoxication and intensity of delight depend upon the exactitude and truth of the image, on its being the counterpart of the reality within. Remote and extravagant as some of Shakespeare's images seem, far-fetched and ethereal as some of Keats's, at the moment of reading they seem the cap and culmination of the thought; its final expression. But it is useless to labour the matter in cold blood. Anyone who has read a poem with pleasure will remember the sudden conviction, the sudden recollection (for it seems sometimes as if we were about to say, or had in some previous existence already said, what Shakespeare is actually now saying), which accompany the reading of poetry, and give it its exaltation and intensity. But such reading is attended, whether consciously or unconsciously, with the utmost stretch and vigilance of the faculties, of the reason no less than of the imagination. We are always verifying the poet's statements, making a flying comparison, to the best of our powers, between the beauty he makes outside and the beauty we are aware of within. For the humblest among us is endowed with the power of comparison. The simplest (provided he loves reading) has that already within him to which he makes what is given him — by poet or novelist — correspond.

With that saying, of course, the cat is out of the bag. For this admission that we can compare, discriminate, brings us to this further point. Reading is not merely sympathising and understanding; it is also criticising and judging. Hitherto our endeavour has been to read books as a writer writes them. We have been trying to understand, to appreciate, to interpret, to sympathise. But now, when the book is finished, the reader must leave the dock and mount the bench. He must cease to be the friend; he must become the judge. And this is no mere figure of speech. The mind seems ('seems', for all is obscure that takes place in the mind) to go through two processes in reading. One might be called the actual reading; the other the after reading. During the actual reading, when we hold the book in our hands, there are incessant distractions and interruptions. New impressions are always completing or cancelling the old. One's judgement is suspended, for one does not know what is coming next. Surprise, admiration, boredom, interest, succeed each other in such quick succession that when, at last, the end is reached, one is for the most part in a state of complete bewilderment. Is it good? or bad? What kind of book is it? How good a book is it? The friction of reading and the emotion of reading beat up too much dust to let us find clear answers to these questions. If we are asked our opinion, we cannot give it. Parts of the book seem to have sunk away, others to be starting out in undue prominence. Then perhaps it is better to take up some different pursuit – to walk, to talk, to dig, to listen to music. The book upon which we have spent so much time and thought fades entirely out of sight. But suddenly, as one is picking a snail from a rose, tying a shoe, perhaps, doing something distant and different, the whole book floats to the top of the mind complete. Some process seems to have been finished without one's being aware of it. The different details which have accumulated in reading assemble themselves in their proper places. The book takes on a definite shape; it becomes a castle, a cowshed, a gothic ruin, as the case may be. Now one can think of the book as a whole, and the book as a whole is different, and gives one a different emotion, from the book received currently in several different parts. Its symmetry and proportion, its confusion and distortion can cause great delight or great disgust apart from the pleasure given by each detail as it is separately realised. Holding this complete shape in mind it now becomes necessary to arrive at some opinion of the book's merits, for though it is possible to receive the greatest pleasure and excitement from the first process, the actual reading, though this is of the utmost importance, it is not so profound or so lasting as the pleasure we get when the second process – the after reading – is finished, and we hold the book clear, secure, and (to the best of our powers) complete in our minds.

But how, we may ask, are we to decide any of these questions – is it good, or is it bad? – how good is it, how bad is it? Not much help can be looked for from outside. Critics abound; criticisms pullulate; but minds differ too much to admit of close correspondence in matters of detail, and nothing is more disastrous than to crush one's own foot into another person's shoe. When we want to decide a particular case, we can best help ourselves, not by reading criticism, but by realising our own impression as acutely as possible and referring this to the judgements which we have gradually formulated in the past. There they hang in the wardrobe of our mind – the shapes of the books we have read, as we hung them up and put them away when we had done with them. If we have just read *Clarissa Harlowe*, for example, let us see how it shows up against the shape of *Anna Karenina*.[12] At once the outlines of the two books are cut out against each other as a house with its chimneys bristling and its gables sloping is cut out against a harvest moon. At once Richardson's qualities – his verbosity, his obliqueness – are contrasted with Tolstoy's brevity and directness. And what is the reason of this difference in their approach? And how does our emotion at different crises of the two books compare? And what must we attribute to the eighteenth century, and what to Russia and the translator? But the questions which suggest themselves are innumerable. They ramify infinitely, and many of them are apparently irrelevant. Yet it is by asking them and pursuing the answers as far as we can go that we arrive at our standard of values, and decide in the end that the book we have just read is of this kind or of that, has merit in that degree or in this. And it is now, when we have kept closely to our own impression, formulated independently our own judgement, that we can most profitably help ourselves to the judgements of the great critics – Dryden, Johnson,[13] and the rest. It is when we can best defend our own opinions that we get most from theirs.

So, then – to sum up the different points we have reached in this essay – have we found any answer to our question, how should we read a book? Clearly, no answer that will do for everyone; but perhaps a few suggestions. In the first place, a good reader will give the writer the benefit of every doubt; the help of all his imagination; will follow as closely, interpret as intelligently as he can. In the next place, he will judge with the utmost severity. Every book, he will remember, has the right to be judged by the best of its kind. He will be adventurous, broad in his choice, true to his own instincts, yet ready to consider those of other people. This is an outline which can be filled in at taste and at leisure, but to read something after this fashion is to be a reader whom writers respect. It is by the means of such readers that masterpieces are helped into the world.

If the moralists ask us how we can justify our love of reading, we can make use of some such excuse as this. But if we are honest, we know that no such excuse is needed. It is true that we get nothing whatsoever except pleasure from reading; it is true that the wisest of us is unable to say what that pleasure may be. But that pleasure – mysterious, unknown, useless as it is – is enough. That pleasure is so curious, so complex, so immensely fertilising to the mind of anyone who enjoys it, and so wide in its effects, that it would not be in the least surprising to discover, on the day of judgement when secrets are revealed and the obscure is made plain, that the reason why we have grown from pigs to men and women, and come out from our caves, and dropped our bows and arrows, and sat round the fire and talked and drunk and made merry and given to the poor and helped the sick and made pavements and houses and erected some sort of shelter and society on the waste of the world, is nothing but this: we have loved reading.

1–A signed essay in the *Yale Review*, October 1926, (Kp C277), reprinted very considerably revised in *CR2* and deriving originally from a lecture VW gave on 30 January 1926 at Hayes Court, a private girls' school near Bromley in Kent, at which the daughters of her friends Mary Hutchinson and Helen Anrep were pupils. VW wrote to Vita Sackville-West (early November? 1925): 'I have to write a lecture, for schoolgirls: "how should one read a Book?" and this, by a merciful dispensation, seems to me a matter of dazzling importance and breathless excitement' (*III VW Letters*, no. 1596). 'I grind out a little of that eternal How to read, lecture,' she recorded in her diary on 9 June 1926, 'as the Yale Review has bought it, & cannot conceive what The Lighthouse is all about. I hope to whip my brains up either at Vita's or Rodmell this weekend.' For a transcription of two preliminary pages of VW's lecture see Appendix III.

On 13 July she wrote to Helen McAfee of the *Yale Review*: 'I am sorry for the delay in sending you the essay I spoke of "How should one read a book?" (it is, by the way, really a lecture) but I had an attack of influenza which upset all my plans.

'I enclose it herewith, and hope it will be suitable for your purposes. I should like to see a proof, if possible' (*III VW Letters*, no. 1654). She returned her proofs on 10 August, informing Miss McAfee: 'I . . . have cut out six lines on page 11, at the end of a paragraph, which will I hope meet your wishes. The proofs only reached me last night, as I am staying down in the country' (*ibid*., no. 1661); and see *ibid*., no. 1684 in which VW acknowledges payment. See *CR2* and see 'The Love of Reading', a further adaptation of her essay, in *V VW Essays*. See also 'Reading', 'On Rereading Novels' and 'Byron and Mr Briggs' in *III VW Essays*. See Editorial Note, pp. xxv; Reading Notes (entitled 'How to Read', Berg, XVIII). Reprinted *CE*.

2–For VW on *Tess of the D'Urbervilles* (1891) and 'Thomas Hardy's Novels' in general, see below. John Milton, *Paradise Lost* (1667).

3–Queen Victoria acceded to the throne on 20 June 1837.

4–For VW on Daniel Defoe (1660?–1731) and on Jane Austen (1775–1817), see *CR1* above.

5–Defoe, *The Life and Adventures of Robinson Crusoe* (1719), adapted from the third paragraph of the opening chapter. For VW on this novel see 'Robinson Crusoe' above.

6–For the first quotation, Austen, *Emma* (1816; OUP, ed. R. W. Chapman, 3rd edn, 1923), vol. i, ch. i, p. 7; for the second *ibid*., p. 8; and for the third, *ibid*., p. 9.

7–Thomas Love Peacock (1785–1866); Anthony Trollope (1815–82); Sir Walter Scott (1771–1832), for VW on whom see 'Scott's Character', 'The Antiquary', *III VW Essays*, and 'Gas at Abbotsford', *VI VW Essays*; George Meredith (1828–1909), for VW on whom see 'The Novels of George Meredith' below; Samuel Richardson (1689–1761); Rudyard Kipling (1865–1936).

8–See for example *III VW Diary*, 16 June 1925: '"Them's his words" – this reminds me I must get back to D. Copperfield. There are moments when all the masterpieces do no more than strum upon broken strings. It is very rare – the right mood for reading – in its way as intense a delight as any; but for the most part pain.'

9–For VW on Joseph Conrad (1857–1924), see *CRI* above. Robert Falcon Scott (1868–1912), Antarctic explorer, the tragedy of whose death finds profound expression in the final pages of his journal, published in 1913 as *Scott's Last Expedition*.

10–The Waterloo chapters (xxviii following) in *Vanity Fair* (1847–8) by W. M. Thackeray, who did not claim 'to rank among the military novelists' (*ibid.*, opening to ch. xxx) are drawn from George Robert Gleig's *Story of the Battle of Waterloo* (1847).

11–Gustave Flaubert (1821–80); L. N. Tolstoy (1828–1910).

12–Samuel Richardson, *Clarissa Harlowe* (1747–8); L. N. Tolstoy, *Anna Karenina* (1875–6).

13–John Dryden (1631–1700), Samuel Johnson (1709–84).

Life and the Novelist

The novelist – it is his distinction and his danger – is terribly exposed to life. Other artists, partially, at least, withdraw; they shut themselves up for weeks alone with a dish of apples and a paint box, or a roll of music paper and a piano. When they emerge it is to forget and distract themselves. But the novelist never forgets and is seldom distracted. He fills his glass and lights his cigarette, he enjoys presumably all the pleasures of talk and table, but always with a sense that he is being stimulated and played on by the subject matter of his art. Taste, sound, movement, a few words here, a gesture there, a man coming in, a woman going out, even the motor that passes in the street or the beggar who shuffles along the pavement, and all the reds and blues and lights and shades of the scene claim his attention and rouse his curiosity. He can no more cease to receive impressions than a fish in mid-ocean can cease to let the water rush through his gills.

But if this sensibility is one of the conditions of the novelist's life, it is obvious that all writers whose books survive have known how to master it and make it serve their purposes. They have finished the wine and paid the bill and gone off, alone, into some solitary room where, with toil and pause, in agony (like Flaubert) with struggle and rush, tumultuously (like Dostoevsky)[2] they have mastered their perceptions, hardened them, and changed them into the fabrics of their art.

So drastic is the process of selection that in its final state we can often find no trace of the actual scene upon which the chapter was based. For in that solitary room, whose door the critics are forever trying to unlock, processes of the strangest kind are gone through. Life is subjected to a thousand disciplines and exercises. It is curbed; it is killed. It is mixed with this, stiffened with that, brought into contrast with something else; so that when we get our scene at a café a year later the surface signs by which we remembered it have disappeared. There emerges from the mist something stark, formidable and enduring, the bone and substance upon which our rush of indiscriminating emotion was founded.

Of these two processes, the first – to receive impressions – is undoubtedly the easier, the simpler and the pleasanter. And it is quite possible, provided one is gifted with a sufficiently receptive temperament and a vocabulary rich enough to meet its demands, to make a book out of this preliminary emotion alone. Three quarters of the novels that appear today are concocted of experience to which no discipline, except the mild curb of grammar and the occasional rigours of chapter divisions, has been applied. Is Miss Stern's *A Deputy Was King* another example of this class of writing, has she taken her material away with her into solitude, or is it neither one nor the other, but an incongruous mixture of soft and hard, transient and enduring?

A Deputy Was King continues the story of the Rakonitz family which was begun some years ago in *The Matriarch*.[3] It is a welcome reappearance, for the Rakonitz family is a gifted and cosmopolitan family with the admirable quality, so rare now in English fiction, of belonging to no particular sect. No parish boundary contains them. They overflow the continent. They are to be found in Italy and Austria, in Paris and Bohemia. If they lodge temporarily in some London studio they are not condemning themselves thereby to wear forever the livery of Chelsea, or Bloomsbury or Kensington. Abundantly nourished on a diet of rich meats and rare wines, expensively but exquisitely clothed, enviably though inexplicably flush of ready money, no restraint of class or convention lies upon them if we except the year 1821; it is essential that they should be up to date. They dance, they marry, they live with this man or with that; they bask in the Italian sun; they swarm in and out of each other's houses and studios, gossiping, quarrelling, making it up again. For, after all, besides the constraint of fashion, they lie, consciously or unconsciously, under the bond of family. They have that Jewish tenacity of affection which common hardship has bred in an outcast race. Hence, in spite of their surface gregariousness, they are fundamentally loyal to each other underneath. Toni and Val and Loraine may quarrel and tear each other asunder publicly, but in private the Rakonitz women are indissolubly united. The present instalment of the family history, which, though it introduces the Goddards and relates the marriage of Toni and Giles Goddard, is really the history of a family, and not of an episode, pauses, for the time presumably, in an Italian villa provided with seventeen bedrooms, so that uncles, aunts, cousins, can all come to lodge there. For Toni Goddard, with all her fashion and modernity, would rather shelter uncles and aunts than entertain emperors, and a second cousin whom she has not seen since she was a child is a prize above rubies.

From such materials surely a good novel might be made – that is what one catches oneself saying, before a hundred pages are finished. And this voice, which is not altogether our own, but the voice of that dissentient spirit which may split off and take a line of its own as we read, should be cross-examined instantly, lest its hints should spoil the pleasure of the whole. What, then, does it mean by insinuating this doubtful, grudging sentiment in the midst of our general well-being? Hitherto nothing has interfered with our enjoyment. Short of being a Rakonitz oneself, of actually taking part in one of those 'diamonded evenings', dancing, drinking, flirting with the snow upon the roof and the gramophone braying out 'It's moonlight in Kalua', short of seeing Betty and Colin 'slightly grotesque advancing . . . in full panoply; velvet skirts spread like a huge inverted cup round Betty's feet, as she minced over the pure, sparkling strip of snow, the absurd dangle of plumes on Colin's helmet'[4] – short of taking hold of all this glitter and fantasy with one's own fingers and thumbs, what is better than Miss Stern's report of it?

The grudging voice will concede that it is all very brilliant; will admit that a hundred pages have flashed by like a hedge seen from an express train; but will reiterate that for all that something is wrong. A man can elope with a woman without our noticing it. That is a proof that there are no values. There is no shape to these apparitions. Scene melts into scene; person into person. People rise out of a fog of talk, and sink back into talk again. They are soft and shapeless with words. There is no grasping them.

The charge has substance in it, because it is true, when we consider it, that Giles Goddard can run off with Loraine, and it is to us as if somebody had got up and gone out of the room – a matter of no importance. We have been letting ourselves bask in appearances. All this representation of the movement of life has sapped our imaginative power. We have sat receptive and watched, with our eyes rather than with our minds, as we do at the cinema, what passes on the screen in front of us. When we want to use what we have learnt about one of the characters to urge them through some crisis we realise that we have no steam up; no energy at our disposal. How they dressed, what they ate, the slang they used – we know all that; but not what they are. For what we know about these people has been given us (with one exception) by following the methods of life. The characters are built up by observing the incoherence, the fresh natural sequences of a person who, wishing to tell the story of a friend's life in talk, breaks off a thousand times to bring in something fresh, to add something forgotten, so that in the end, though one may feel that one has been in the presence of life, the particular life in question remains vague. This hand to mouth method, this ladling out of sentences which have the dripping brilliance of words that live upon real lips, is admirable for one purpose; disastrous for another. All is fluent and graphic; but no character or situation emerges cleanly. Bits of entraneous matter are left sticking to the edges. For all their brilliancy the scenes are clouded; the crises are blurred. A passage of description will make both the merit and the defect of the method clear. Miss Stern wants us to realise the beauty of a Chinese coat.

Gazing at it, you might think that you had never seen embroidery before, for it was the very climax of all that was brilliant and exotic. The flower-petals were worked in a flaming pattern round the broad bands of kingfisher blue embroidery; and again round each oval plaque that was woven of a silvery heron with a long green beak, and behind his outstretched wings a rainbow. All among the silver arabesques, butterflies were delicately poised, golden butterflies and black butterflies, and butterflies that were gold and black. The closer you looked the more there was to see; intricate markings on the butterfly wings, purple and grass-green and apricot, . . .[5]

As if we had not enough to see already, she goes on to add how there were tiny stamens springing from every flower, and circles ringing the eye of each separate stork, until the Chinese coat wobbles before our eyes and merges in one brilliant blur.

The same method applied to people has the same result. Quality is added to quality, fact to fact, until we cease to discriminate and our interest is suffocated under a plethora of words. For it is true of every object – coat or human being – that the more one looks the more there is to see. The writer's task is to take one thing and let it stand for twenty: a task of danger and difficulty; but only so is the reader relieved of the swarm and confusion of life and branded effectively with the particular aspect which the writer wishes him to see. That Miss Stern has other tools at her disposal, and could use them if she liked, is hinted now and again, and is revealed for a moment in the brief chapter describing the death of the Matriarch, Anastasia Rakonitz. Here suddenly the flow of words seems to darken and thicken. We are aware of something beneath the surface, something left unsaid for us to find out for ourselves and think over. The two pages in which we are told how the old woman died asking for goose-liver sausage and a tortoise-shell comb, short though they are, hold to my thinking, twice the substance of any other thirty pages in the book.

These remarks bring me back to the question with which I started: the relation of the novelist to life and what it should be. That he is terribly exposed to life *A Deputy Was King* proves once more. He can sit and watch life and make his book out of the very foam and effervescence of his emotions; or he can put his glass down, retire to his room and subject his trophy to those mysterious processes by which life becomes, like the Chinese coat, able to stand by itself – a sort of impersonal miracle. But in either case he is faced by a problem which does not afflict the workers in other arts to the same extent. Stridently, clamorously, life is forever pleading that she is the proper end of fiction and that the more he sees of her and catches of her the better this book will be. She does not add, however, that she is grossly impure; and that the side she flaunts uppermost is often, for the novelist, of no value whatever. Appearance and movement are the lures she trails to entice him after her, as if these were her essence, and by catching them he gained his goal. So believing, he rushes feverishly in her wake, ascertains what foxtrot is being played at the Embassy, what skirt is being worn in Bond

Street, worms and winds his way into the last flings of topical slang, and imitates to perfection the last toss of colloquial jargon. He becomes terrified more than anything of falling behind the times: his chief concern is that the thing described shall be fresh from the shell with the down on its head.

This kind of work requires great dexterity and nimbleness, and gratifies a real desire. To know the outside of one's age, its dresses and its dances and its catchwords, has an interest and even a value which the spiritual adventures of a curate, or the aspirations of a high-minded schoolmistress, solemn as they are, for the most part lack. It might well be claimed, too, that to deal with the crowded dance of modern life so as to produce the illusion of reality needs far higher literary skill than to write a serious essay upon the poetry of John Donne or the novels of M. Proust.[6] The novelist, then, who is a slave to life and concocts his books out of the froth of the moment is doing something difficult, something which pleases, something which, if you have a mind that way, may even instruct. But his work passes as the year 1921 passes, as foxtrots pass, and in three years time looks as dowdy and dull as any other fashion which has served its turn and gone its way.

On the other hand, to retire to one's study in fear of life is equally fatal. It is true that plausible imitations of Addison,[7] say, can be manufactured in the quiet there, but they are as brittle as plaster and as insipid. To survive, each sentence must have, at its heart, a little spark of fire and this, whatever the risk, the novelist must pluck with his own hands from the blaze. His state then is a precarious one. He must expose himself to life; he must risk the danger of being led away and tricked by her deceitfulness; he must seize her treasure from her and let her trash run to waste. But at a certain moment he must leave the company and withdraw, alone, to that mysterious room where his booty is hardened and fashioned into permanence by processes which, if they elude the critic, hold for him so profound a fascination.

1–A signed review in the *NYHT*, 7 November 1926, (Kp C278) of *A Deputy Was King* (Alfred A. Knopf; Chapman and Hall Ltd; 1926) by G. B. [Gladys Bronwyn] Stern (1890–1973). Reprinted *G&R, CE*.
2–Gustave Flaubert (1821–80); Fyodor Dostoevsky (1821–81).
3–*The Matriarch, A Chronicle* (1925), a dramatisation of which, starring Mrs Patrick Campbell, VW later saw at the Royalty Theatre (*III VW Diary*, 11 October 1929).

4—For the quotations, Stern, Part I 'The Good Time', ch. vi, p. 90, which has: 'It had been a diamonded evening, and this was climax'; and: 'grotesque, advancing towards them in full panoply'.

5—*Ibid.*, Part III 'The War of the Chinese Coat', ch. ii, pp. 185–6, which has: 'silken arabesques'.

6—For VW's 'serious essay' on John Donne (1573–1631), 'Donne After Three Centuries' see *CR2*. Marcel Proust (1871–1922).

7—For VW on Joseph Addison (1672–1719) see *CR1* above.

Genius

'Genius,' cried Haydon, darting at his canvas after some momentary rebuff, 'genius is sent into the world not to obey laws, but to give them!'[2] But he need not have said it. Genius is written large all over his memoirs. It is genius of a peculiar kind of course. It is not the Shakespearean but the Victorian genius, not the conscious but the unconscious, not the true, but — let us pause, however, and read Haydon's diaries with attention (they are now reprinted, with a brilliant introduction by Mr Huxley[3]) before we decide what kind of genius his was. That it was violent in its symptoms and remorseless in its severity no one can doubt. Of all those men and women who have been stricken with genius (and the number in the British Isles must be great) none suffered more, or was more terribly its victim than the inspired boy with weak eyes who should have been a bookseller in his father's shop in Plymouth but heard himself summoned to go to London, to be a great painter, to honour his country, and to 'rescue the Art from that stigma of incapacity, which was impressed on it'.[4]

He came to London. He made friends with Wilkie. He lived and painted in one room, and there, night after night, Wilkie, Du Fresne, Dr Millingen, McClaggan, Allan ('the celebrated painter'), and Callender[5] all met and drank his good tea out of his large cups, and argued about art and politics and divinity and medicine and how Marie Antoinette's head was cut off (Du Fresne said he had been present and had flung his red cap into the air), while Liz of Rathbone Place, who loved their talk, but was otherwise cold, sided with one, attacked another, and was found studying Reid on the Human Mind 'with an expression of profound bewilderment'.[6]

'Happy period!' Haydon burst out, 'no servants – no responsibilities – reputation on the bud – ambition beginning, friends untried,'[7] and so things might have gone on had it not been for the demon which possessed him – the devil which made him, even in those early days, indite letters, which Liz applauded, against the might of the Royal Academy, and vow to bring about their humiliation and the triumph of High Art by vast pictures of Dentatus and Macbeth and Solomon[8] which took months to paint, filled his living-room with the reek of oil, required that he should dissect the forequarters of an ass, bring Guardsmen on their horses into his studio, and run into debt for, as he soon found out 'the expenses of a work of High Art in England are dreadful.'[9]

But there was another consequence of his prepossession. High Art being of necessity large art into the bargain, only the great nobles could afford it, and in consequence the simple life with Liz and cups of good tea was abandoned for the life, or at least the dinner tables, of the Mulgraves and the Beaumonts[10] and any other lord or lady who could be hypnotised into the belief that it was their wish to have a vast picture of Achilles in the drawing-room, and to their credit to have a man of genius talking very loud at their board. Haydon, rapt in his burning enthusiasm for the Heroic and for the Elgin Marbles and for himself, took it all seriously. He entertained fashion all day long. Instead of painting, 'I walked about my room, looked into the glass, anticipated what the foreign ambassadors would say,'[11] overheard whispers at parties 'he himself has an antique head',[12] and seriously believed, when the beauties put up their eyeglasses and lisped their admiration, that his fortune was made, and that 'all the sovereigns of Europe would hail with delight an English youth who could paint an heroic picture'.[13] But he was disillusioned. The great, he found, care not for art, but for what people say about pictures. 'Dear Lord Mulgrave',[14] lost his faith in Dentatus when he heard it criticised. Sir George Beaumont shillied and shallied and said at last that Macbeth was too big and Lady Beaumont had no room for it, and 'in fact, Sir George was tired, and wanted another extraordinary young man, for Wilkie was an old story, and I was a nuisance'. 'And so, artists,' he concluded, summing up all that he had borne from his patrons, but letting us infer too how boldly he had corrected them and how terribly he had bored them, 'and so, artists, be humble and discreet!'[15]

He proved the wisdom of his own saying by marrying,[16] in spite of his debts, a widow with two children, and by having, in quick succession, six more children of his own. With all this weight on his shoulders he sank steadily more and more deeply into the mud. For his genius never deserted him. It was always flourishing irresistible subjects before his eyes. He was always rushing at his canvas and 'rubbing in' the head of Alexander 'gloriously',[17] or dashing off some gigantic group of warriors and lions when his room was bare of necessaries, his furniture pawned, his wife screaming in child-birth, and the baby (it was a way they had) sickening of a mortal ill-ness.[18] Where a smaller man would have been content to deal with private difficulties, Haydon took upon himself the cares of the world. He was feverishly interested in politics, in the Reform Bill,[19] in the Trades Union movement, in the success of the British arms. Above all, he was the champion of High Art in England. He must badger Wellington, Peel,[20] and every Minister in turn to employ young English painters to decorate Westminster Hall and the Houses of Parliament. Nor could he let the Royal Academy sleep in peace. His friends begged him to stop: but no. 'The idea of being a Luther or a John Knox in art got the better of my reason[21] . . . I attacked the Academy. I exposed their petty intrigues; I laid open their ungrateful, cruel, and heartless treatment of Wilkie. I annihi-lated Payne Knight's absurd theories against great works. I proved his ignorance of Pliny,'[22] with the result that 'I had brought forty men and all their high connections, on my back at twenty-six years old, and there was nothing left but Victory or Westminster Abbey. I made up my mind for the conflict, and ordered at once a larger can-vas for another work.'[23]

But on the road to Victory and Westminster Abbey lay a more sordid lodging-house, through which Haydon passed four times – the King's Bench prison. Servants and children, he noted, became familiar with the signs of an approaching execution. He himself learnt how to pawn and how to plead, how to flatter the sheriff's officer, how to bombard the great who were certainly generous if they were not clever; how to appeal to the hearts of landlords, whose humanity was extraordinary; but one thing he could not do; deny the demands of his own genius. Portrait painting was an obvious resource. But then how odious to paint a little private in-dividual, a mere Mayor, or Member of Parliament, when one's head was swarming with Solomons and Jerusalems and Pharaohs and Crucifixions[24] and Macbeths! He could scarcely bring himself to do it. One could make them larger than life, it is true, but then the critics sneered, and said that if the ex-Mayor was the size that Haydon painted him he must have stuck in the doorway. It was paltry work. 'The trash that one is obliged to talk! The stuff that one is obliged to copy! The fidgets that are obliged to be borne! My God!'[25]

The name of God was often on his lips. He was on terms of cordial intimacy with the deity. He could not believe that one great spirit could consent to the downfall of another. God and Napoleon and Nelson and Wellington and Haydon were all of the same calibre, all in the grand style. His mind harped on these great names constantly. And, as a matter of fact, though poor Mrs Haydon would smile when he bade her 'trust in God'[26] his trust was often justified. He left his house in the morning with the children fighting, with Mary scolding, with no water in the cistern, to trudge all day from patron to pawn-shop, and came home at night, 'tired, croaking, grumbling, and muddy', when, just as hope seemed extinct, a letter arrived; it was from Lord Grey;[27] it contained a cheque. Once more they were saved.

With it all, he declared, he was a very happy man, pink and plump, in spite of all his worries, when Wilkie who led an abstemious bachelor's life, was cadaverous and plaintive. Now and again they took the children to the sea, or snatched an afternoon in Kensington Gardens, and if they were in the depths of despair on Wednesday, likely enough some stroke of fortune would put them in the seventh heaven by Thursday. He had his friends too – Wordsworth and Scott and Keats and Lamb[28] – with whom he supped and he talked. He had, above all, a mind which was for ever tossing and tumbling like a vigorous and active dolphin in the seas of thought. 'I never feel alone,' he wrote. 'With visions of ancient heroes, pictures of Christ, principles of ancient Art, humorous subjects, deductions, sarcasms against the Academy, piercing remembrance of my dear children all crowding upon me, I paint, I write, conceive, fall asleep ... lamenting my mortality at being fatigued.'[29] The power which drove him to these extremities did at least reward him with some of its delights.

But as the symptoms of inspiration multiply – this passionate joy in creation, this conviction of a divine mission – one asks oneself what then is false, for falsity there certainly seems to be. First there is something in the superabundance of protest, in the sense of persecution which rouses suspicion; next these vast pictures of crowds, armies, raptures, agonies begin, even as he sketches them in words, to scar and wound our eyes; and finally we catch ourselves thinking, as some felicity of phrase flashes out, or some pose or arrangement makes its effect, that his genius is a writer's. He should have held a pen; of all painters, surely he was the best read. 'The truth is I am fonder of books than of anything else on earth,' he wrote.[30] He clung to his Shakespeare and his Homer when his lay figure had to go to the pawnbroker. There was even one moment when he doubted his own vocation and accused the sublime art of hampering his powers. But his instinct to express himself in words was undeniable. Overworked as he was, he always found time to write a diary which is in no way perfunctory, but follows with ease and sinuosity the ins and outs of his life. Phrases form naturally at the tip of his pen. 'He sat and talked easily, lazily, gazing at the sun with his legs crossed,' he says of Chantrey.[31] 'Poor fellow,' he wrote on hearing of the burial of Wilkie at sea, 'I wonder what the fish think of him, with their large glassy eyes in the gurgling deep.'[32] Always his painter's eye lights up his phrases, and scenes which would have been repulsive in paint shape themselves naturally and rightly into words. It was some malicious accident that made him, when he had to choose a medium, pick up a brush when the pen lay handy.

But if accident it was, his genius was unrelenting. Paint he must; paint he did. When his cartoons were rejected he learnt to toss off pictures of Napoleon Musing at the rate of one in two hours and a half. When the public deserted his last exhibition in favour of Tom Thumb next door, he darted at another picture, finished the Saxon Lord, dashed in Alfred, 'worked', he declared, 'gloriously'.[33] But at last even his prayers sound a little hoarse, and his protests without conviction. One morning after quoting Lear and writing out a list of his debts and his thoughts, he put a pistol to his forehead, gashed a razor across his throat, and spattered his unfinished picture of Alfred and the first British Jury with his blood. He was the faithful servant of his genius to the last. If we seek now any relic of all those acres of canvas, those crowds of heroes, we find clean white walls, people comfortably dining, and a vague rumour that a big picture did hang here once, but the management took it away when the place was done up. The pictures are vanished; Allan, 'the celebrated painter', Du Fresne, who saw Marie Antoinette executed, Millingen, Liz of Rathbone Place, are all passed away; but still these pages that he scribbled without thought of Genius or Art or Posterity remain holding vividly before us the struggling, greedy life with all its black smoke and its flame.

1 – A signed review in the *N&A*, 18 December 1926, reprinted in *NR*, 29 December 1926, (Kp C279) of *The Autobiography and Memoirs of Benjamin Robert Haydon (1786–1846). Edited from his Journals by Tom Taylor.* A new edition with an introduction by Aldous Huxley (2 vols, Peter Davies, 1926). 'I should be much obliged,' VW had written to her sister Vanessa Bell in late September 1926, 'if you and Duncan could tell me on a card where I could see some of the historical pictures of Benjamin Haydon? in some restaurant, I think. I have to write about him' (*III VW Letters*, no. 1676). On 27 September she had offered her review ('my fee would be £20') to Virgil Barker, editor of *Arts* (New York), see *VI VW Letters*, Appendix B, no. 1676a.

The same issue of the *N&A* contained LW's 'World of Books' column on 'Cobden and Cobdenism'. See Editorial Note, p. xxv. Reprinted *Mom, CE*.

2 – Huxley, vol. i, ch. vii, quoting the journal, 7 December 1808, p. 81, in which 'Genius' is not repeated.

3 – Aldous Huxley (1894–1963), whose works at this date included *Crome Yellow* (1921) and *Antic Hay* (1923), was an acquaintance of VW and of Bloomsbury.

4 – Huxley, vol. i, ch. ii, p. 18, which has 'art'.

5 – (Sir) David Wilkie (1785–1841), Scottish painter, who found early celebrity with his paintings 'The Village Politicians' (1806) and 'The Blind Fiddler' (1807); (Sir) William Allan (1782–1850), Scottish painter of historical and Russian scenes; Du Fresne, Dr Millingen, McClaggan and Callender otherwise unidentified. Marie Antoinette (1755–93). For the quotation see *ibid.*, ch. iv, p. 56.

6 – *Ibid.*, p. 54. Thomas Reid (1710–96), whose *Inquiry into the Human Mind* was published in 1764.

7 – *Ibid.*, p. 55.

8 – 'Dentatus' was completed in March 1809; 'Macbeth' was begun that year and completed in 1812; 'The Judgment of Solomon', 1812–14.

9 – *Ibid.*, ch. ix, p. 125, quoting the journal, 31 December 1811.

10 – Sir George Beaumont (1753–1827), connoisseur and landscape painter, and his wife Margaret *née* Willes. Henry Phipps, 1st Earl of Mulgrave and Viscount Normanby (1755–1831), statesman, first lord of the admiralty, 1807–10, and master-general of the ordnance, 1810–18, and his wife Martha Sophia, *née* Maling.

11 – Huxley, vol. i, ch. vii, p. 89. The Elgin marbles had been brought to England in 1806.

12 – *Ibid.*, p. 86.

13 – *Ibid.*, p. 89, which has: 'an English youth with delight'.

14 – *Ibid.*, p. 88: 'And yet dear Lord Mulgrave . . . did not possess knowledge sufficient to defend his opinions, and when he heard the picture abused by the Academicians in society he felt his faith in its merits waver.'

15 – For both quotations, *ibid.*, 'Memoirs', 30 June 1825, p. 371; the repetition is VW's.

16 – Haydon married, in October 1821, Mary Hymans, 'a beautiful widow, with whom he had been in love some years' (*DNB*).

17—This appears to be an adaptation: cf., *ibid.*, vol. ii, 'Memoirs', 7 June 1843, p. 750: 'rubbed in Alexander' and, 20 February 1844, p. 764: 'worked gloriously'.

18—Of his several children five did not survive childhood.

19—Of 1832, celebrated by Haydon in 'The Reform Banquet', exhibited in 1834.

20—Arthur Wellesley, 1st Duke of Wellington (1769–1852); Sir Robert Peel (1788–1850).

21—Huxley, vol. i, ch. ix, quoting the journal, 31 December 1811, p. 126.

22—*Ibid.*, p. 127, which has 'intrigues, I laid'. Richard Payne Knight (1750–1824), numismatist.

23—*Ibid.*, p. 130, which has '"Victory or Westminster Abbey"' and 'conflict and ordered'.

24—The paintings referred to and not previously noted are: 'Christ's Entry into Jerusalem' (1820), 'Pharaoh dismissing Moses' (?1826), 'Crucifixion' (began 7 March 1823 but never completed).

25—Huxley, vol. i, 'Memoirs', [? month] 1826, p. 388.

26—*Ibid.*, vol. ii, 'Memoirs', 2 December 1839, p. 667.

27—For the quotation and for Charles Grey, 2nd Earl Grey, Viscount Howick and Baron Grey (1764–1845), statesman, *ibid.*, 26 January 1833, p. 553.

28—William Wordsworth (1770–1850); Sir Walter Scott (1771–1832); John Keats (1795–1821); Charles Lamb (1775–1834).

29—Huxley, vol. ii, 'Memoirs', 10 June 1838, p. 638, which has: 'With visions' and 'and fall asleep'.

30—*Ibid.*, vol. i, 'Memoirs', 23 May 1826, p. 387, which has: 'The truth is, I am'.

31—For the quotation, *ibid.*, 20 January 1827, p. 405, which has 'lazily-gazing'. Sir Francis Chantrey (1781–1841), sculptor (of bequest fame).

32—*Ibid.*, vol. ii, 'Memoirs', 18 May 1841, p. 701, which has 'Poor fellow!' and 'eyes, in'.

33—For Tom Thumb (Charles Sherwood Stratton, 1838–83), the American entertainer who stood less than three feet high, *ibid.*, 13 April 1846, p. 810: 'They rush by thousands to see Tom Thumb. They push, they fight, they scream, they faint, they cry help and murder! and oh! and ah!', and 21 April 1846, p. 811. For the quotation, 17 April 1846, p. 811, which has: 'Worked hard, and got on with my Alfred gloriously;'.

1927

'Victorian Jottings'

It were to be wished that more distinguished men would follow Sir James Crichton-Browne's habit and keep a commonplace book by their side in which to scribble thoughts, incidents, and speculations as they arrive. The book may be as he said, 'without cohesion or concinnity',[2] but for all that it makes excellent mixed reading of a kind that is too rare. Here, indeed, we have the cream of many books. The anecdotes which would have had to be spaced out with dull prose are here offered up cheek by jowl. One can hardly dip into it without finding something to suit one's taste. If one is unlucky, one need not plod along dismally; one is forced to skip. A common thread, of course, runs through it, for Sir James has thought much about medicine and lived much with nervously affected people. We get, therefore, a good many interesting and curious medical anecdotes. The headings will run, Intermittent Mental Trouble, Lord Hampton, Secret Poisoning, Woolner. Then we skip to Melancholy and Adolescence, Gambling, and Huxley. Next we light upon Delusions, My First Coroner's Inquest, and Dr John Brown.[3] Nothing is treated at great length, but the mind which has recorded is so vivacious and has had intercourse with so many interesting people, that the skipping and sipping are a refreshing exercise.

1–A notice in the *N&A*, 12 February 1927, (Kp C279.1) of *Victorian Jottings. From An Old Commonplace Book* (Etchells and MacDonald, 1926) by Sir James

Crichton-Browne (1840–1938), physician, psychologist, lord-chancellor's visitor in lunacy, 1875–1922.
2–Crichton-Browne, Preface, p. v.
3–John Slaney Pakington, 2nd Baron Hampton (d. 1893). Thomas Woolner (1825–92), sculptor. T. H. Huxley (1825–95), man of science. Dr John Brown (1810–82), author of *Rab and His Friends and Other Papers* (1901).

George Gissing

VW's essay in the *N&A*, 26 February 1927, (Kp C280) was later revised and included, under the same title, in *The Common Reader*: 2nd series (1932). The reader is referred to *V VW Essays*, where the revised version, together with variants in the form of footnotes, is reprinted in its place as part of *The Common Reader*.

'The Immortal Isles'

Mr Gordon is one of those enthusiasts who will wait for hours in a cramped position in order to snap a black-throated diver on her nest. Often the author and his wife ran considerable risks crossing from one island to another in a leaky boat to secure a really fine picture of a bird which supposed itself unobserved. The result is a series of those natural and wild-looking pictures of animals in their own surroundings which are among the greatest trophies of the camera. This passion for birds and beasts lends the book a solidity which otherwise it would hardly possess. For the Outer Hebrides provide sunsets and visions and folk-stories rather than history as it is understood on the mainland. What with the extreme loneliness of the islands and the emigration which has been steadily proceeding, it would seem as if the population consisted of seals and gulls and the history was the story of their matings and fightings, Mr Gordon contrives to spin a charming veil of words, however, about the clouds and the gentians and the scabious and the ghosts, and the camera does its part brilliantly.

1—A notice in the *N&A*, 5 March 1927, (Kp C280.1) of *The Immortal Isles* (Williams and Norgate, 1926) by Seton Gordon, illustrated by Finlay Mackinnon.

What Is a Novel?

If there were in England, as there is in France, an Academy of Letters with authority to decide disputed points, one would immediately bring to their notice the chaotic state of fiction.

For three hundred years the human brain has been applying itself with great vigour and fecundity to write novels. Types of the most diverse kinds have come into existence.

Proust, Mr Kipling, Mr de la Mare, Mrs Elinor Glyn, Mr Hardy, Mr Wells are all novelists.[2] But their books differ as the greyhound differs from the bulldog.

So suggestible is the human mind that this repetition of a single word does considerable damage. The reader comes to think that since all these varieties of book have the same name they must have the same nature.

Somewhere at the back of his mind is a vague shape called 'a novel' to which, often with great loss of time and temper, he tries to make the specimen before him conform. Often he is extremely unjust.

A notable instance was lately provided by Mr Wells's *William Chissold*.[3] It was condemned a thousand times not for this fault or for that, but because it was not 'a novel'.

It is high time that this imaginary but still highly potent bogey was destroyed.

And since we are without law-givers, let us implore the novelists themselves to come to our help.

When they write a novel let them define it. Let them say that they have written a chronicle, a document, a rhapsody, a fantasy, an argument, a narrative or a dream.

For there is no such thing as 'a novel'.

1—A signed contribution, displayed in a box, to 'The Three Arts', a column edited by John Austin in the *Weekly Dispatch*, 27 March 1927, (Kp C280.2) reprinted in *Now & Then*, Summer 1927. The column itself was headed 'Novel of London Life' and discussed new novels, by Thomas Burke, Sinclair Lewis and Frances Newman, a new selection of Byron's letters, an exhibition of 19th-century water-colours at the Agnew Galleries, and a book on *Music, Health and Character* by Dr Agnes Savill.

2 – Marcel Proust (1871–1922); Rudyard Kipling (1856–1936); Walter de la Mare (1873–1956); Elinor Glyn (1864–1944), Canadian-born author, whose works include *The Visits of Elizabeth* (1900), *The Career of Katherine Bush* (1917) and *Six Days* (1924); Thomas Hardy (1840–1928), H. G. Wells (1866–1946).

3 – H. G. Wells, *The World of William Clissold* (1926).

A Giant with Very Small Thumbs

In this substantial book Mr Yarmolinsky has collected an immense amount of information about Turgenev, but the value is seriously diminished by the fact that the statements are taken from books which are not accessible to Western readers and no references are given. Mr Yarmolinsky is, if not a disillisioned, still a highly critical biographer. The faults of his subject are very clear to him. But we must be grateful to him for raising the whole question of Turgenev again, and for giving us a profusion of material on which to found our own judgement. Of all the great Russian writers, Turgenev is, perhaps, the one who has had least justice done him in England. It is easy to guess the reason; here is a new country, people said, and therefore its literature must be different, if it is true literature, from any other. They sought out and relished in Tchehov and Dostoevsky[2] those qualities which they supposed to be peculiarly Russian and therefore of peculiar excellence. They welcomed joyously an abandonment to emotion, an introspection, a formlessness which they would have detested in the French or in the English. People drank tea endlessly and discussed the soul without stopping in a room where nothing could be seen distinctly; such was our supposition.

But Turgenev was different altogether. In the first place he was a cosmopolitan, who hunted in England and lived, rather ambiguously, in France. His domestic circumstances indeed were not such as to attach him to his native land. His mother was a woman of extraordinary character.[3] In the heart of Russia she tried to mimic the ceremonies and splendours of the French aristocracy before the

Revolution. She was despotic to the verge of mania. She banished
serfs for neglecting to bow to her. She had her porridge brought hot
by relays of horsemen from a villge where they made it to her liking
ten miles away. A waterfall was turned from its course because it
disturbed her sleep. Whether or not these stories are true, it is certain that she drove her sons from the house. The novelist, in particular, with his democratic sympathies, detested his mother's
behaviour, and being, as he was fond of saying, a man with very
small thumbs, he found it simpler to withdraw. Pauline Viardot[4] received him. He had a seat allotted to him on one of the gilt paws of
the bear skin on which her admirers sat and talked to her between
the acts of the play. Nor was he ever to find another lodging. At the
end of his life he advised young men with melancholy humour to
find a home of their own and not to sit 'on the edge of another
man's nest'.[5] Madame Viardot, it is said, never asked him to come
inside. There he sat, 'a large man with a weak mouth and a skull
padded with fat, who gave the impression of being as soft as butter',[6] until he died in her presence. But for all his melancholy and his
loneliness, it was probable that the arrangement, with its mixture of
freedom and intimacy, was the one that suited him best. The rigours
of domesticity would have thwarted him. He was always late for
meals; he was extremely generous, but very untidy; and he had,
after all, a passion for art.

It is this passion of his that makes him so unlike the English idea
of what a Russian should be. For Turgenev novels might well be the
late ripe fruit on a very old tree. Such restraint, such selection one
attributes to ages of endeavour. All his books are so small in bulk
that one can slip them into one's pocket. Yet they leave behind them
the impression that they contain a large world in which there is
ample room for men and women of full size and the sky above and
the fields around. He is the most economical of writers. One of his
economies is at once obvious. He takes up no room with his own
person. He makes no comments upon his characters. He places
them before the reader and leaves them to their fate. The contact between ourselves and Bazarov,[7] for instance, is peculiarly direct. No
saying is underlined, no conclusion is forced upon us. But the
reader's imagination is perpetually stimulated to work for itself,
and hence each scene and each character has a peculiar vitality.
Hence, too, another peculiarity; we are never able to say that the
point lies here or the point lies there. Return to a definite page, and

the meaning, the power, seems to have fled. For in this highly suggestive art the effect has been produced by a thousand small touches which accumulate, but cannot be pinned down in one emphatic passage or isolated in one great scene. For this reason Turgenev can handle, with a sweetness and wholeness which put our English novelists to shame, such burning questions as the relations of fathers and sons, of the new order and the old. The treatment is of such width and dispassionateness that we are not coerced in our sympathies, and so do not harbour a grudge against the writer which we shall liberate when opportunity serves. After all these years *Fathers and Sons* still keeps its hold on our emotions. In this clarity lie profound depths; its brevity holds in it a large world. For though Turgenev was, according to his present biographer, full of weaknesses and obsessed with a sense of the futility of all things, he held strangely rigorous views on the subject of literature. Be truthful to your own sensations, he counselled; deepen your experience with study; be free to doubt everything; above all, do not let yourself be caught in the trap of dogmatism. Sitting on the edge of another man's nest, he practised these difficult counsels to perfection. Untidy in his habits, a giant with very small thumbs, he was nevertheless a great artist.

1–A signed review in the *N&A*, 2 April 1927, (Kp C281) of *Turgenev. The Man – His Art – And His Age*. Illustrated (Hodder & Stoughton, 1926) by Avrahm Yarmolinsky. Ivan Turgenev (1818–83), reference to the size of whose thumbs has not been traced in Yarmolinsky, but see Lady Ritchie, *Blackstick Papers* (Smith Elder, 1908), No. XII, 'Concerning Tourguénieff', p. 237: 'Mr Tourguénieff came straight up to me at once. "I was so sorry that I could not come and see you," he said, "so very sorry, but I was prevented. Look at my thumbs!" and he held up both his hands with his palms outwards. I looked at his thumbs, but I could not understand. "See how small they are," he went on; "people with such little thumbs can never do what they intend to do, they always let themselves be prevented;" . . .' (and see *'Blackstick Papers'*, *I VW Essays*). See also 'A Glance at Turgenev', *III VW Essays*, 'The Novels of Turgenev', *VI VW Essays*. The same issue of the *N&A* also contained: LW's 'World of Books' column, on 'The Armstrong Case', discussing *Herbert Rowse Armstrong*, ed. Filson Young, a new volume in the Notable British Trials series. Reprinted: *B&P*.
2–Anton Chekhov (1860–1904); Fyodor Dostoevsky (1821–81).
3–Turgenev's tyrannical mother was Varvara Petrovna, *née* Lutovinov.
4–Pauline Viardot-Garcia (1821–1910), mezzo-soprano, sometime pupil of Liszt, friend of George Sand, made her debut in 1837 and retired from the stage in 1863.
5–Yarmolinsky, ch. xxxix, p. 360; the other man, at the edge of whose nest Turgenev sat, was Louis Viardot; he had married Pauline Garcia, a woman less than half his age, in 1840, and thereafter acted as her impresario.

6—*Ibid.*, ch. xv, p. 118.
7—Bazarov is the hero of Turgenev's *Fathers and Sons* (1862), for the influence of which work on English readers, according to VW, see 'On Re-reading Meredith', *II VW Essays.*

Two Women

Up to the beginning of the nineteenth century the distinguished woman had almost invariably been an aristocrat. It was the great lady who ruled and wrote letters and influenced the course of politics. From the huge middle class few women rose to eminence, nor has the drabness of their lot received the attention which has been bestowed upon the splendours of the great and the miseries of the poor. There they remain, even in the early part of the nineteenth century, a vast body, living, marrying, bearing children in dull obscurity until at last we begin to wonder whether there was something in their condition itself – in the age at which they married, the number of children they bore, the privacy they lacked, the incomes they had not, the conventions which stifled them, and the education they never received which so affected them that though the middle class is the great reservoir from which we draw our distinguished men it has thrown up singularly few women to set beside them.

The profound interest of Lady Stephen's life of Miss Emily Davies[2] lies in the light it throws upon this dark and obscure chapter of human history. Miss Davies was born in the year 1830, of middle-class parents who could afford to educate their sons but not their daughters. Her education was, she supposed, much the same as that of other clergymen's daughters at that time. 'Do they go to school? No. Do they have governesses at home? No. They have lessons and get on as they can.'[3] But if their positive education had stopped at a little Latin, a little history, a little housework, it would not so much have mattered. It was what may be called the negative education, that which decrees not what you may do but what you may not do, that cramped and stifled. 'Probably only women who have laboured under it can understand the weight of discouragement produced by being perpetually told that, as women, nothing much is ever expected of them . . . Women who have lived in the atmosphere produced by such teaching know how it stifles and chills; how hard it is to work courageously through it.'[4] Preachers and rulers of both sexes nevertheless formulated the creed and enforced it vigorously. Charlotte Yonge wrote: 'I have no hesitation in declaring my full belief in the inferiority of women, nor that she brought it upon herself.'[5] She reminded her sex of a painful incident with a snake in the garden which had settled their destiny, Miss Yonge said, for ever. The mention of Woman's Rights made Queen Victoria so furious that 'she cannot contain herself'.[6] Mr Greg, underlining his words, wrote that 'the essentials of a woman's being are *that they are supported by, and they minister to, men*'.[7] The only other occupation allowed them, indeed, was to become a governess or a needlewoman, 'and both these employments were naturally overstocked'.[8] If women wanted to paint there was, up to the year 1858, only one life class in London where they could learn. If they were musical there was the inevitable piano, but the chief aim was to produce a brilliant mechanical execution, and Trollope's picture of four girls all in the same room playing on four pianos all of them out of tune seems to have been, as Trollope's pictures usually are, based on fact.[9] Writing was the most accessible of the arts, and write they did, but their books were deeply influenced by the angle from which they were forced to observe the world. Half-occupied, always interrupted, with much leisure but little time to themselves and no money of their own, these armies of listless women were either driven to find solace and occupation in religion, or, if that failed, they took, as Miss Nightingale said, 'to that perpetual day dreaming which is so dangerous'.[10] Some indeed envied the working classes, and Miss Martineau frankly hailed the ruin of her family with delight. 'I, who had been obliged to write before breakfast, or in some private way, had henceforth liberty to do my own work in my own way, for we had lost our gentility.'[11] But the time had come when there were occasional exceptions both among parents and among daughters. Mr Leigh Smith, for example, allowed his daughter Barbara[12] the same income that he gave his sons. She at once started a school of an advanced character. Miss Garrett[13] became a doctor because her parents, though shocked and anxious, would be reconciled if she were a success. Miss Davies had a brother[14] who sympathised and helped her in her determination to reform the education of women. With such encouragement the three young women started in the middle of the nineteenth century to lead the army of the unemployed in search of work. But the war of one sex upon the rights and possessions of the other is by no means a straightforward affair of attack and victory or defeat. Neither the means nor the end itself is clear-cut and recognised. There is the very potent weapon, for example, of feminine charm – what use were they to make of that? Miss Garrett said she felt 'so mean in trying to come over the doctors by all kinds of little feminine dodges'. Mrs Gurney admitted the difficulty, but pointed out that 'Miss Marsh's success among the navvies'[15] had been mainly won by these means, which, for good or for bad, were certainly of immense weight. It was agreed therefore that charm was to be employed. Thus we have the curious spectacle, at once so diverting and so humiliating, of grave and busy women doing fancy work and playing croquet in order that the male eye might be gratified and deceived. 'Three lovely girls' were placed conspicuously in the front row at a meeting, and Miss Garrett herself sat there looking 'exactly like one of the girls whose instinct it is to do what you tell them'.[16] For the arguments that they had to meet by their devious means were in themselves extremely indefinite. There was a thing called 'the tender home-bloom of maidenliness'[17] which must not be touched. There was chastity, of course, and her handmaidens innocence, sweetness, unselfishness, sympathy; all of which might suffer if women were allowed to learn Latin and Greek. The *Saturday Review* gave cogent expression to what men feared for women and needed of women in the year 1864. The idea of submitting young ladies to local university examinations 'almost takes one's breath away', the writer said. If examined they must be, steps must be taken to see that 'learned men advanced in years' were the examiners, and that the presumably aged wives of these aged gentlemen should occupy 'a commanding position in the gallery'. Even so it would be 'next to impossible to persuade the world that a pretty first-class woman came by her honours fairly'. For the truth was, the reviewer wrote, that 'there is a strong and ineradicable male instinct that a learned, or even an accomplished young woman is the most intolerable monster in creation'.[18] It was against instincts and prejudices such as these, tough as roots but intangible as sea mist, that Miss Davies had to fight. Her days passed in a round of the most diverse occupations. Besides the actual labour of raising money and fighting prejudice she had to decide the most delicate moral questions which, directly victory was within sight, began to be posed by the students and their parents. A mother, for example, would only entrust her with her daughter's education on condition that she should come home 'as if nothing had happened', and not 'take to anything eccentric'.[19] The students, on the other hand, bored with watching the Edinburgh express slip a carriage at Hitchin or rolling the lawn with a heavy iron roller, took to playing football, and then invited their teachers to see them act scenes from Shakespeare and Swinburne dressed in men's clothes. This, indeed, was a very serious matter; the great George Eliot was consulted; Mr Russell Gurney was consulted, and also Mr Tomkinson. They decided that it was unwomanly; Hamlet must be played in a skirt.[20]

Miss Davies herself was decidedly austere. When money for the college flowed in she refused to spend it on luxuries. She wanted rooms – always more and more rooms to house those unhappy girls dreaming their youth away in indolence or picking up a little knowledge in the family sitting-room. 'Privacy was the one luxury Miss Davies desired for the student, and in her eyes it was not a luxury – she despised luxuries – but a necessity.'[21] But one room to themselves was enough. She did not believe that they needed arm chairs to sit in or pictures to look at. She herself lived austerly in lodgings till she was seventy-two, combative, argumentative, frankly preferring a labour meeting at Venice to the pictures and the palaces, consumed with an abstract passion for injustice to women which burnt up trivial personalities and made her a litle intolerant of social frivolities. Was is worth while, she once asked, in her admirable, caustic manner, after meeting Lady Augusta Stanley, to go among the aristocracy? 'I felt directly that if I went to Lady Stanley's again, I must get a new bonnet. And is it well to spend one's money in bonnets and flys instead of on instructive books?'[22] she wondered. For Miss Davies perhaps was a little deficient in feminine charm.

That was a charge that nobody could bring against Lady Augusta Stanley. No two women could on the surface have less in common. Lady Augusta, it is true, was no more highly educated in a bookish sense than the middle-class women whom Miss Davies championed. But she was the finest flower of the education which for some centuries the little class of aristocratic women had enjoyed. She had been trained in her mother's drawing-room in Paris. She had talked to all the distinguished men and women of her time – Lamartine, Mérimée, Victor Hugo, the Duc de Broglie, Sainte-Beuve, Renan, Jenny Lind, Turgenev – everybody came to talk to old Lady Elgin[23] and to be entertained by her daughters. There she developed that abounding sensibility, that unquenchable sympathy which were to be so lavishly drawn upon in after years. For she was very young when she entered the Duchess of Kent's household. For fifteen years of her youth she lived there. For fifteen years she was the life and soul of that 'quiet affectionate dull household of old people at Frogmore and Clarence House'.[24] Nothing whatever happened. They drove out and she thought how charming the village children looked. They walked and the Duchess picked heather. They came home and the Duchess was tired. Yet not for a moment, pouring her heart out in profuse letters to her sisters, does she complain or wish for any other existence.

Seen through her peculiar magnifying glass, the slightest event in the life of the Royal family was either harrowing in the extreme or beyond words delightful. Prince Arthur was more handsome than ever. The Princess Helena was so lovely. Princess Ada fell from her pony. Prince Leo was naughty.[25] The Beloved Duchess wanted a green umbrella. The measles had come out, but, alas, they threatened to go in again. One might suppose, to listen to Lady Augusta exclaiming and protesting in alternate rapture and despair, that to read aloud to the old Duchess of Kent was the most exciting of occupations, and that the old ladies' rheumatisms and headaches were catastrophes of the first order. For inevitably the power of sympathy when so highly developed and discharged solely upon personal relations tends to produce a hothouse atmosphere in which domestic details assume prodigious proportions and the mind feeds upon every detail of death and disease with a gluttonous relish. The space devoted in this volume to illness and marriage entirely outweighs any reference to art, literature or politics. It is all personal, emotional, and detailed as one of the novels which were written so inevitably by women.

It was such a life as this and such an atmosphere as this that Mr Greg and the *Saturday Review* and many men who had themselves enjoyed the utmost rigours of education wished to see preserved. And perhaps there was some excuse for them. It is difficult to be sure, after all, that a college don is the highest type of humanity known to us; and there is something in Lady Augusta's power to magnify the common and illumine the dull which seems to imply a very arduous education of some sort behind it. Nevertheless, as one studies the lives of the two women side by side, one cannot doubt that Miss Davies got more interest, more pleasure, and more use out of one month of her life than Lady Augusta out of a whole year of hers. Some inkling of the fact seems to have reached Lady Augusta even at Windsor Castle. Perhaps being a woman of the old type is a little exhausting; perhaps it is not altogether satisfying. Lady Augusta at any rate seems to have got wind of other possibilities. She liked the society of literary people best, she said. 'I had always said that I had wished to be a fellow of a college,'[26] she added surprisingly. At any rate she was one of the first to support Miss Davies in her demand for a University education for women. Did Miss Davies then sacrifice her book and buy her bonnet? Did the two women, so different in every other way, come together over this – the education of their sex? It is tempting to think so, and to imagine sprung from that union of the middle-class woman and the court lady some astonishing phoenix of the future who shall combine the new efficiency with the old amenity, the courage of the indomitable Miss Davies and Lady Augusta's charm.

1–A signed review in the *N&A*, 23 April 1927, reprinted in the *NR*, 18 May 1927, (Kp C282) of *Emily Davies and Girton College* (Constable and Co. Ltd, 1927) by Barbara Stephen, and of *Letters of Lady Augusta Stanley. A Young Lady at Court 1849–1863*. Edited by the Dean of Windsor and Hector Bolitho (Gerald Howe Ltd, 1927). 'I'm writing about Morgan Forster:', VW wrote to Vita Sackville-West on 6 March 1927 (*III VW Letters*, no. 1726), 'I'm writing about street walking; and about novels (in a vulgar rag called The Weekly Dispatch.) None of these, thank God, will you see; and then my hundred's made. I'm well ahead with the world . . .' See also *A Room of One's Own* (1929; Triad/Panther, 1977), ch. 6, p. 96: 'Mr A . . . is therefore impeded and inhibited and self-conscious as Shakespeare might have been if he too had known Miss Clough and Miss Davies'; *Three Guineas* (1938), ch. 3, n. 38; and related references in Reading Notes (MHP, B 2n, B 16f). Reprinted *Mom, CE*.
2–Barbara Stephen, (Margaret Thyra Barbara Shore Smith, later Shore Nightingale, 1872–1945), wife of VW's cousin Sir Harry Lushington Stephen, 3rd Bt. (Sarah) Emily Davies (1830–1921) was the fourth child of the Rev. John Davies D. D. and Mary, *née* Hopkinson. She was an aunt of VW's friend Margaret Llewelyn-Davies.
3–Stephen, ch. ii, p. 25, quoting evidence by Mark Pattison before the Schools Enquiry Commission of 1864.
4–For the quotation up to the ellipsis, *ibid.*, p. 29, which has: 'ever to be expected'; and for the remainder, p. 30; quoting Emily Davies's paper on 'Special Systems of Education for Women'.
5–*Ibid.*, epigraph to ch. i, 'Introduction', p. 1, quoting *Womankind* (1876) by Charlotte M. Yonge (1823–1901).
6–*Ibid.*, p. 17, quoting *Queen Victoria As I Knew Her* (1901) by Sir Theodore Martin. Queen Victoria (1819–1901).
7–*Ibid.*, p. 7, adapted, quoting 'Why are Women Redundant?' in *Social and Literary Judgements* (1868) by W. R. Greg (1809–81), political essayist, described by Stephen as 'an enlightened and philanthropic man of business'.

8—*Ibid.*, adapted.

9—For the four out-of-tune pianists of Anthony Trollope (1815–82) see his *Miss Mackenzie* (1865), referred to by Stephen, ch. i, p. 12.

10—Stephen, ch. i, p. 9: '"We fast mentally, scourge ourselves morally, use the intellectual hair shirt," writes Miss Nightingale, "in order to subdue that perpetual day-dreaming which is so dangerous."' Florence Nightingale (1820–1910).

11—*Ibid.*, p. 6, fn. 2, quoting the *Autobiography* (1877) of Harriet Martineau (1802–76).

12—Barbara Leigh Smith Bodichon (1827–91), daughter of Benjamin Leigh Smith MP and Anne, *née* Longden; she was a close associate of Emily Davies and an indefatigable campaigner in the Girton cause.

13—Elizabeth Garrett Anderson (1836–1917).

14—Rev. John Llewelyn Davies (1826–1916), theologian, Christian Socialist.

15—For both quotations, Stephen, ch. iv, p. 63, quoting Elizabeth Garrett to Emily Davies, 12 April 1861. Emelia Gurney, *née* Batten, a daughter of John Venn of the Clapham Sect, and wife of Russell Gurney (1804–78), QC, noted for the support he gave to the passage of the Married Women's Property Act (1882). Miss Marsh, unidentified.

16—*Ibid.*, ch. vi, p. 90.

17—*Ibid.*, ch. xiii, p. 204, quoting Yonge's *Womankind*.

18—*Ibid.*, ch. vi, p. 91, fn. 1, quoting 'Feminine Wranglers', *Saturday Review*, 23 July 1864, which has: 'one of the most intolerable monsters'.

19—*Ibid.*, ch. xiv, p. 226, which has: 'and not take to teaching or do anything eccentric'.

20—For this amusing episode, which took place during March 1871, see *ibid.*, ch. xiv, pp. 241–3. The performances concerned were of a passage from *Atalanta in Calydon* (1865) by A. C. Swinburne (1837–1909) and from scenes from *Much Ado About Nothing* and *Twelfth Night*. George Eliot (1819–80) was, as might be expected, a staunch supporter of the campaign to found Girton. Henry Richard Tomkinson was secretary to the London Local Examinations Centre.

21—*Ibid.*, ch. xviii, p. 312, which has 'students;'.

22—*Ibid.*, ch. vii, pp. 110–11. Davies met Lady Augusta Stanley of Alderley (1807–95), a leading light in the Women's Liberal-Unionist Association and a member of Girton from 1872 until her death.

23—Alphonse de Lamartine (1790–1869); Prosper Mérimée (1803–70); Victor Hugo (1802–85); probably: Victor, duc de Broglie (1785–1870); Charles-Augustin Sainte-Beuve (1804–69); Ernest Renan (1823–92); Jenny Lind (1820–87), singer, known as the 'Swedish Nightingale'; Ivan Turgenev (1818–83); Lady Augusta's mother: Elizabeth, *née* Oswald, Countess of Elgin.

24—Dean of Windsor and Bolitho, 'Introduction', p. 12; Victoria Mary Louisa, Duchess of Kent (1786–1861).

25—Prince Arthur, third son, and Princess Helena, third daughter of Queen Victoria; Princess Ada, daughter of Princess Hohenlohe; Prince Leopold, youngest son of Queen Victoria.

26—*Ibid.*, ch. xvi, p. 297, 18 October 1863, to Lady Augusta's sister Lady Frances Baillie: 'In religion I could not feel with anyone who was narrow; then the society I like is the society of literary people and the companionship of those much superior to myself; to sit at the feet of someone to whom I could listen and look up, as long ago with Matilda and our Mother. I had always said I should wish to be a Fellow of a College, and I fancied that his [i.e. Dr Stanley's] home would be something like Broomhall long ago.'

The Governess of Downing Street

Lady Oxford has all the qualities of a first-class finishing governess. She is absolutely direct, completely fearless, perfectly self-assured, and entirely unimaginative. No better instructress could be found for young people up to the ages of seventeen or eighteen. As we listen to these short discourses upon Carelessness, Health, Taste, Fashion, Human Nature, Fame, Politics, Opportunity[2] we seem to be back again in the schoolroom; maps are on the walls; grammars upon the table; we are listening submissively to a severe lady who is preparing us in a clear metallic voice for something which is called 'the battle of life'.[3] Her theme this morning is Carelessness: '. . . you will find half the troubles, most of the accidents, and many of the catastrophes come from carelessness,' she tells us. 'Carelessness is a difficult word to analyse. It belongs to no particular category,'[4] and so on. Then, seeing a blank look upon her pupils' faces, she enlivens her discourse by a story about a lady who had a relation who was a professor, and this professor received from a Russian doctor a specimen of the skin of a man who had died from a rare and virulent type of small-pox. The professor placed it in a cardboard box on his mantelpiece. While he was out walking, his wife – looking for something she had left in the room – opened the cardboard box and caught the small-pox. That is the kind of thing that will happen to us if we are careless. The next lesson is on the subject of health. Here Mrs Asquith proves that she is none of those timid suburban spinsters who shirk the disagreeable part of their duties. If spades are spades and primroses are primroses she will call them spades and primroses, and nothing else. 'In this country,' she writes, 'you can write, talk, and speak in public about birth control, unnatural vices, and venereal disease – almost every eschewed subject – but you may not mention constipation.'[5] Mrs Asquith insists upon mentioning constipation. 'You may evade, elude, or fight shy of this proposition [that health depends upon keeping the bowels open], but sooner or later you will have to face it.'[6] What lesson should we draw from the case of the Lord Mayor of Cork?[7] He ate nothing for weeks, yet his doctors had to give him mild aperients. Now, if the intestines of the Lord Mayor of Cork could accumulate poison when he was starving, what, I ask you, is the state of our intestines who have four meals a day? The pupil feels abashed. Ah, adds Mrs Asquith, with that ubiquitous morality which is one of the most valuable assets of a governess, but it is not enough merely to keep your bowels open; you must also forgive your enemies. Open our bowels and forgive our enemies, we murmur; it seems so simple.

But when we come to art and letters it is by no means such plain sailing. The governess wanders; she wobbles; she plunges into the depths and then she scrambles out on to the bank and shakes herself dry as best she may. For example, what is this queer thing Art? 'The function of art is not to awe, teach, stun, or surprise. It is not meant to make you burst out laughing or melt into tears. It appeals to something more fundamental and enduring than emotion...'[8] Somehow one does not feel oneself on firm ground here. Still, 'what I personally find provoking in modern Art is that it is too clever, and lays an insistent emphasis on what is distorted and ugly, which neither the Greeks, Chinese, or Egyptians would have tolerated for a moment'.[9] Did she not once go for a walk with an eminent art critic, and, instead of looking at the sea, did he not look at the pattern on his trousers and talk about the Florentines? Which proves – we scarcely know what.

For the province of a governess is not to reason, but to know; not to persuade, but to dictate. And as the boys and girls sit round the table and listen they will certainly learn that it is better to be good than clever; to play the game; to hunt the fox; to love the beautiful. The little boys will get all the prizes and the little girls will get all the snubs. In the world of the governess little boys are much more satisfactory than little girls; they are so bright, so manly, so chivalrous; above all, they are so amazingly simple. Now a little girl – but Mrs Asquith cannot find anything nice to say about little girls. In this small primitive world, where the rules are so rigid and the rewards are so conventional, little girls are difficult ingredients, apt to elude, to evade, to fight shy. But suddenly we bethink us: this is no schoolroom; this is the great world of politics and power. The boys and girls whom Mrs Asquith addresses are grown men and women; she herself is no governess of limited opportunity, but a woman who has spent her life in the height of luxury at the hub of the universe. This is very strange. Are we to conclude that Downing Street nourishes itself upon copybook maxims that would make a charwoman yawn, that the immortal Souls[10] paid out little platitudes about art and literature which would scarcely ruffle the serenity of a suburban tea-table? Or is Mrs Asquith talking down to us for our good? We do not know. But there remains another fact even stranger. Arid, dogmatic, illogical as these sermons are, they are at the same time irresistible. In every phrase one hears the accent of that penetrating and individual voice which is unlike any other. No one can hear it and remain indifferent. No one can be taught by Mrs Asquith without falling in love with the governess.

1–A review in the *N&A*, 30 July 1927, (Kp C283.1) of *Lay Sermons* (Thornton Butterworth Ltd, 1927) by Margot Asquith, Countess of Oxford and Asquith, *née* Tennant (1864–1945). 'Woman haters depress me,' VW wrote in her diary on 22 June 1927, '& both Tolstoy & Mrs Asquith hate women. I suppose my depression is a form of vanity. But then so are all strong opinions on both sides. I hate Mrs A's hard dogmatic style. But enough: I shall write about her tomorrow: I write every day about something, & have deliberately set apart a few weeks to money making, so that I may put £50 in each of our pockets by September.' See also 'Gipsy or Governess?' above. The same issue of the *N&A* contained LW's 'World of Books' column on 'The Decline and Fall of Monarchy'.
2–Asquith has: 'Opportunities'. There are further sermons on 'Character' and 'Marriage'.
3–The source of this apparent quotation has not been discovered.
4–Asquith, 'Carelessness', pp. 18–19.
5–*Ibid.*, 'Health', p. 40, from a more extensive sentence, which has: 'almost any'.
6–*Ibid.*
7–Alderman Terence Joseph McSwiney, Lord Mayor of Cork, died in Brixton Prison on 25 October 1920, after being on hunger strike.
8–Asquith, 'Taste II', p. 97, which has: 'Art', and: 'Its appeal is to something'.
9–*Ibid.*, 'Taste I', p. 64.
10–For VW on 'that gifted constellation' of friends who flourished in the 1880s see 'Mr Gladstone's Daughter', *II VW Essays*.

Poetry, Fiction and the Future

Far the greater number of critics turn their backs upon the present and gaze steadily into the past. Wisely, no doubt, they make no comment upon what is being actually written at the moment; they leave that duty to the race of reviewers whose very title seems to imply transiency in themselves and in the objects they survey. But one has sometimes asked one's self, must the duty of a critic always be to the past, must his gaze always be fixed backward? Could he not sometimes turn round and, shading his eyes in the manner of Robinson Crusoe on the desert island, look into the future and trace on its mist the faint lines of the land which some day perhaps we may reach? The truth of such speculations can never be proved, of course, but in an age like ours there is a great temptation to indulge in them. For it is an age clearly when we are not fast anchored where we are; things are moving round us; we are moving ourselves. Is it not the critic's duty to tell us, or to guess at least, where we are going?

Obviously the inquiry must narrow itself very strictly, but it might perhaps be possible in a short space to take one instance of dissatisfaction and difficulty, and, having examined into that, we might be the better able to guess the direction in which, when we have surmounted it, we shall go.

Nobody indeed can read much modern literature without being aware that some dissatisfaction, some difficulty, is lying in our way. On all sides writers are attempting what they cannot achieve, are forcing the form they use to contain a meaning which is strange to it. Many reasons might be given, but here let us select only one, and that is the failure of poetry to serve us as it has served so many generations of our fathers. Poetry is not lending her services to us nearly as freely as she did to them. The great channel of expression which has carried away so much energy, so much genius, seems to have narrowed itself or to have turned aside.

That is true only within certain limits of course; our age is rich in lyric poetry; no age perhaps has been richer. But for our generation and the generation that is coming the lyric cry of ecstasy or despair which is so intense, so personal and so limited, is not enough. The mind is full of monstrous, hybrid, unmanageable emotions. That the age of the earth is 3,000,000,000 years; that human life lasts but a second; that the capacity of the human mind is nevertheless boundless; that life is infinitely beautiful yet repulsive; that one's fellow creatures are adorable but disgusting; that science and religion have between them destroyed belief; that all bonds of union seem broken, yet some control must exist — it is in this atmosphere of doubt and conflict that writers have now to create, and the fine fabric of a lyric is no more fitted to contain this point of view than a rose leaf to envelop the rugged immensity of a rock.

But when we ask ourselves what has in the past served to express such an attitude as this – an attitude which is full of contrast and collision; an attitude which seems to demand the conflict of one character upon another, and at the same time to stand in need of some general shaping power, some conception which lends the whole harmony and force, we must reply that there was a form once, and it was not the form of lyrical poetry; it was the form of the drama, of the poetic drama of the Elizabethan age. And that is the one form which seems dead beyond all possibility of resurrection today.

For if we look at the state of the poetic play we must have grave doubts that any force on earth can now revive it. It has been practised and is still practised by writers of the highest genius and ambition. Since the death of Dryden every great poet it seems has had his fling. Wordsworth and Coleridge, Shelley and Keats, Tennyson, Swinburne and Browning[2] (to name the dead only) have all written poetic plays, but none has succeeded. Of all the plays they wrote, probably only Swinburne's *Atalanta* and Shelley's *Prometheus*[3] are still read, and they less frequently than other works by the same writers. All the rest have climbed to the top shelves of our bookcases, put their heads under their wings, and gone to sleep. No one will willingly disturb those slumbers.

Yet it is tempting to try to find some explanation of this failure in case it should throw light upon the future which we are considering. The reason why poets can no longer write poetic plays lies somewhere perhaps in this direction.

There is a vague, mysterious thing called an attitude to life. We all know people – if we turn from literature to life for a moment – who are at loggerheads with existence; unhappy people who never get what they want; are baffled, complaining, who stand at an uncomfortable angle whence they see everything slightly askew. There are others again who, though they appear perfectly content, seem to have lost all touch with reality. They lavish all their affections upon little dogs and old china. They take interest in nothing but the vicissitudes of their own health and the ups and downs of social snobbery. There are, however, others who strike us, why precisely it would be difficult to say, as being by nature or by circumstances in a position where they can use their faculties to the full upon things that are of importance. They are not necessarily happy or successful, but there is a zest in their presence, an interest in their doings. They seem alive all over. This may be partly the result of circumstances – they have been born into surroundings that suit them – but much more is the result of some happy balance of qualities in themselves so that they see things not at an awkward angle, all askew; nor distorted through a mist; but four square, in proportion; they grasp something hard; when they come into action they cut real ice.

A writer too has in the same way an attitude to life, though it is a different life from the other. They, too, can stand at an uncomfortable angle; can be baffled, frustrated, unable to get at what they want as writers. This is true, for example, of the novels of George Gissing.[4] Then, again, they can retire to the suburbs and lavish their interest upon pet dogs and duchesses – prettinesses, sentimentalities, snobberies, and this is true of some of our most highly successful novelists. But there are others who seem by nature or circumstances so placed that they can use their faculties freely upon important things. It is not that they write quickly or easily, or become at once successful or celebrated. One is rather trying to analyse a quality which is present in most of the great ages of literature and is most marked in the work of the Elizabethan dramatists.[5] They seem to have an attitude to life, a position which allows them to move their limbs freely; a view which, though made up of all sorts of different things, falls into the right perspective for their purposes.

In part, of course, this was the result of circumstances. The public appetite, not for books, but for the drama, the smallness of the towns, the distance which separated people, the ignorance in which even the educated then lived, all made it natural for the Elizabethan imagination to fill itself with lions and unicorns, dukes and duchesses, violence and mystery. This was reinforced by something which we cannot explain so simply, but which we can certainly feel. They had an attitude to life which made them able to express themselves freely and fully. Shakespeare's plays are not the work of a baffled and frustrated mind; they are the perfectly elastic envelope of his thought. Without a hitch he turns from philosophy to a drunken brawl; from love songs to an argument; from simple merriment to profound speculation. And it is true of all the Elizabethan dramatists that though they may bore us – and they do – they never make us feel that they are afraid or self-conscious, or that there is anything hindering, hampering, inhibiting the full current of their minds.

Yet our first thought when we open a modern poetic play – and this applies to much modern poetry – is that the writer is not at his ease. He is afraid, he is forced, he is self-conscious. And with what good reason! we may exclaim, for which of us is perfectly at his ease with a man in a toga called Xenocrates, or with a woman in a blanket called Eudoxa? Yet for some reason the modern poetic play is always about Xenocrates and not about Mr Robinson; it is about Thessaly and not about Charing Cross Road. When the Elizabethans laid their scenes in foreign parts and made their heroes and heroines princes and princesses they only shifted the scene from one side to the other of a very thin veil. It was a natural device which gave depth and distance to their figures. But the country remained English; and the Bohemian Prince was the same person as the English noble. Our modern poetic playwrights,[6] however, seem to seek the veil of the past and of distance from a different reason. They want not a veil that heightens but a curtain that conceals; they lay their scene in the past because they are afraid of the present. They are aware that if they tried to express the thoughts, the visions, the sympathies and antipathies which are actually turning and tumbling in their brains in this year of grace 1927 the poetic decencies would be violated; they could only stammer and stumble and perhaps have to sit down or to leave the room. The Elizabethans had an attitude which allowed them complete freedom; the modern playwright has either no attitude at all, or one so strained that it cramps his limbs and distorts his vision. He has therefore to take refuge with Xenocrates, who says nothing or only what blank verse can with decency say.

But can we explain ourselves a little more fully? What has changed, what has happened, what has put the writer now at such an angle that he cannot pour his mind straight into the old channels of English poetry? Some sort of answer may be suggested by a walk through the streets of any large town. The long avenue of brick is cut up into boxes, each of which is inhabited by a different human being who has put locks on his doors and bolts on his windows to insure some privacy, yet is linked to his fellows by wires which pass overhead, by waves of sound which pour through the roof and speak aloud to him of battles and murders and strikes and revolutions all over the world. And if we go in and talk to him we shall find that he is a wary, secretive, suspicious animal, extremely self-conscious, extremely careful not to give himself away. Indeed, there is nothing in modern life which forces him to do it. There is no violence in private life; we are polite, tolerant, agreeable, when we meet. War even is conducted by companies and communities rather than by individuals. Duelling is extinct. The marriage bond can stretch indefinitely without snapping. The ordinary person is calmer, smoother, more self-contained than he used to be.

But again we should find if we took a walk with our friend that he is extremely alive to everything – to ugliness, sordidity, beauty, amusement. He is immensely inquisitive. He follows every thought careless where it may lead him. He discusses openly what used never to be mentioned even privately. And this very freedom and curiosity are perhaps the cause of what appears to be his most marked characteristic – the strange way in which things that have no apparent connection are associated in his mind. Feelings which used to come simple and separate do so no longer. Beauty is part ugliness; amusement part disgust; pleasure part pain. Emotions which used to enter the mind whole are now broken up on the threshhold.

For example: It is a spring night, the moon is up, the nightingale singing, the willows bending over the river. Yes; but at the same time a diseased old woman is picking over her greasy rags on a hideous iron bench. She and the spring enter his mind together; they blend but do not mix. The two emotions, so incongruously coupled, bite and kick at each other in unison. But the emotion which Keats felt when he heard the song of a nightingale is one and entire, though it passes from joy in beauty to sorrow at the unhappiness of human fate. He makes no contrast. In his poem sorrow is the shadow which accompanies beauty.[7] In the modern mind beauty is accompanied not by its shadow but by its opposite. The modern poet talks of the nightingale who sings 'jug jug to dirty ears'.[8] There trips along by the side of our modern beauty some mocking spirit which sneers at beauty for being beautiful; which turns the looking glass and shows us that the other side of her cheek is pitted and deformed. It is as if the modern mind, wishing always to verify its emotions, had lost the power of accepting anything simply for what it is. Undoubtedly this sceptical and testing spirit has led to a great freshening and quickening of soul. There is a candour, an honesty in modern writing which is salutary if not supremely delightful. Modern literature, which had grown a little sultry and scented with Oscar Wilde and Walter Pater, revived instantly from her nineteenth century languor when Samuel Butler and Bernard Shaw[9] began to burn their feathers and apply their salts to her nose. She awoke; she sat up; she sneezed. Naturally the poets were frightened away.

For of course poetry has always been overwhelmingly on the side of beauty. She has always insisted on certain rights, such as rhyme, metre, poetic diction. She has never been used for the common purpose of life. Prose has taken all the dirty work on to her own shoulders; has answered letters, paid bills, written articles, made speeches, served the needs of business men, shopkeepers, lawyers, soldiers, peasants.

Poetry has remained aloof in the possession of her priests. She has perhaps paid the penalty for this seclusion by becoming a little stiff. Her presence with all her apparatus – her veils, her garlands, her memories, her associations – affects us the moment she speaks. Thus when we ask poetry to express this discord, this incongruity, this sneer, this contrast, this curiosity, the quick, queer emotions which are bred in small separate rooms, the wide, general ideas which civilisation teaches, which have kept her at arms' length, she cannot move quickly enough, simply enough, or broadly enough to do it. Her accent is too marked; her manner too emphatic. She gives us instead lovely lyric cries of passion; with a majestic sweep of her arm she bids us take refuge in the past; but she does not keep pace with the mind and fling herself subtly, quickly, passionately into its various sufferings and joys. Byron in *Don Juan*[10] pointed the way; he showed how flexible an instrument poetry might become, but none has followed his example to put his tool to further use. We remain without a poetic play.

Thus we are brought to reflect whether poetry is capable of the task which we are now setting her. It may be that the emotions here sketched in such rude outline and imputed to the modern mind submit more readily to prose than to poetry. It may be possible that prose is going to take over – has, indeed, already taken over – some of the duties which were once discharged by poetry.[11]

If, then, we are daring and risk ridicule and try to see in what direction we who seem to be moving so fast are going, we may guess that we are going in the direction of prose and that in ten or fifteen years' time prose will be used for purposes for which prose has never been used before. That cannibal, the novel, which has devoured so many forms of art will by then have devoured even more. We shall be forced to invent new names for the different books which masquerade under this one heading. And it is possible that there will be among the so-called novels one which we shall scarcely know how to christen. It will be written in prose, but in prose which has many of the characteristics of poetry. It will have something of the exaltation of poetry, but much of the ordinariness of prose. It will be dramatic, and yet not a play. It will be read, not acted. By what name we are to call it is not a matter of very great importance. What is important is that this book which we see on the horizon may serve to express some of those feelings which seem at the moment to be balked by poetry pure and simple and to find the drama equally inhospitable to them. Let us try, then, to come to closer terms with it and to imagine what may be its scope and its nature.

In the first place, one may guess that it will differ from the novel as we know it now chiefly in that it will stand further back from life. It will give, as poetry does, the outline rather than the detail. It will make little use of the marvellous fact-recording power, which is one of the attributes of fiction. It will tell us very little about the houses, incomes, occupations of its characters; it will have little kinship with the sociological novel or the novel of environment. With these limitations it will express the feelings and ideas of the characters closely and vividly, but from a different angle. It will resemble poetry in this that it will give not only or mainly people's relations to each other and their activities together, as the novel has hitherto done, but it will give the relation of the mind to general ideas and its soliloquy in solitude. For under the dominion of the novel we have scrutinised one part of the mind closely and left another unexplored. We have come to forget that a large and important part of life consists in our emotions toward such things as roses and nightingales, the dawn, the sunset, life, death and fate; we forget that we spend much time sleeping, dreaming, thinking, reading, alone; we are not entirely occupied in personal relations; all our energies are not absorbed in making our livings. The psychological novelist has been too prone to limit psychology to the psychology of personal intercourse; we long sometimes to escape from the incessant, the remorseless analysis of falling into love and falling out of love, of what Tom feels for Judith and Judith does or does not altogether feel for Tom. We long for some more impersonal relationship. We long for ideas, for dreams, for imaginations, for poetry.

And it is one of the glories of the Elizabethan dramatists that they give us this. The poet is always able to transcend the particularity of Hamlet's relation to Ophelia and to give us his questioning not of his own personal lot alone but of the state and being of all human life. In *Measure for Measure*, for example, passages of extreme psychological subtlety are mingled with profound reflections, tremendous imaginations. Yet it is worth noticing that if Shakespeare gives us this profundity, this psychology, at the same time Shakespeare makes no attempt to give us certain other things. The plays are of no use whatever as 'applied sociology'. If we had to depend upon them for a knowledge of the social and economic conditions of Elizabethan life we should be hopelessly at sea.

In these respects then the novel or the variety of novel which will be written in time to come will take on some of the attributes of poetry. It will give the relations of man to Nature, to fate; his imagination; his dreams. But it will also give the sneer, the contrast, the question, the closeness and complexity of life. It will take the mould of that queer conglomeration of incongruous things – the modern mind. Therefore it will clasp to its breast the precious prerogatives of the democratic art of prose; its freedom, its fearlessness, its flexibility. For prose is so humble that it can go anywhere; no place is too low, too sordid, or too mean for it to enter. It is infinitely patient, too, humbly acquisitive. It can lick up with its long glutinous tongue the most minute fragments of fact and mass them into the most subtle labyrinths, and listen silently at doors behind which only a murmur, only a whisper, is to be heard. With all the suppleness of a tool which is in constant use it can follow the windings and record the changes which are typical of the modern mind. To this, with Proust and Dostoevsky[12] behind us, we must agree.

But can prose, we may ask, adequate though it is to deal with the common and the complex – can prose say the simple things which are so tremendous? Give the sudden emotions which are so surprising? Can it chant the elegy, or hymn the love, or shriek in terror, or praise the rose, the nightingale, or the beauty of night? Can it leap at one spring at the heart of its subject as the poet does? I think not. That is the penalty it pays for having dispensed with the incantation and the mystery, with rhyme and metre. It is true that prose writers are daring; they are constantly forcing their instrument to make the attempt. But one has always a feeling of discomfort in the presence of the purple patch of the prose poem. The objection to the purple patch, however, is not that it is purple but that it is a patch. Recall for instance Meredith's 'Diversion on a Penny Whistle' in *Richard Feverel*. How awkwardly, how emphatically, with a broken poetic metre it begins: 'Golden lie the meadows; golden run the streams; red gold is on the pine-stems. The sun is coming down to earth and walks the fields and the waters.'[13] Or recall the famous description of the storm at the end of Charlotte Brontë's *Villette*.[14] These passages are eloquent, lyrical, splendid; they read very well cut out and stuck in an anthology; but in the context of the novel they make us uncomfortable. For both Meredith and Charlotte Brontë called themselves novelists; they stood close up to life; they led us to expect the rhythm, the observation, the perspective of fiction; suddenly, violently and self-consciously they change all this for the rhythm, the observation and the perspective of poetry. We feel the jerk and the effort; we are half-woken from that trance of consent and illusion in which our submission to the power of the writer's imagination is most complete.

But let us now consider another book, which though written in prose and by way of being called a novel, adopts from the start a different attitude, a different rhythm, which stands back from life, and leads us to expect a different perspective – *Tristram Shandy*. It is a book full of poetry, but we never notice it; it is a book stained deep purple, which is yet never patchy. Here though the mood is changing always, there is no jerk, no jolt in that change to waken us from the depths of consent and belief. In the same breath Sterne laughs, sneers, cuts some indecent ribaldry and passes on to a passage like this:

Time wastes too fast: every letter I trace tells me with what rapidity life follows my pen; the days and hours of it more precious – my dear Jenny – than the rubies about thy neck, are flying over our heads like light clouds of a windy day, never to return more; everything presses on – whilst thou are twisting that lock – see! It grows grey; and every time I kiss thy hand to bid adieu, and every absence which follows it, are preludes to that eternal separation which we are shortly to make. – Heaven have mercy upon us both!

Chap. IX

Now, for what the world thinks of that ejaculation – I would not give a groat.[15]

And he goes on to my Uncle Toby, the Corporal, Mrs Shandy and the rest of them.

There, one sees, is poetry changing easily and naturally into prose, prose into poetry. Standing a little aloof Sterne lays his hands lightly upon imagination, wit, fantasy; and reaching high up among the branches where these things grow, naturally and no doubt willingly forfeits his right to the more substantial vegetables that grow on the ground. For, unfortunately, it seems true that some renunciation is inevitable. You cannot cross the narrow bridge of art carrying all its tools in your hands. Some you must leave behind, or you will drop them in midstream or, what is worse, over-balance and be drowned yourself.

So, then, this unnamed variety of the novel will be written standing back from life, because in that way a larger view is to be obtained of some important features of it; will be written in prose because prose, if you free it from the beast of burden work which so many novelists necessarily lay upon it of carrying loads of details, bushels of fact – prose thus treated will show itself capable of rising high from the ground, not in one dart, but in sweeps and circles, and of keeping at the same time in touch with the amusements and idiosyncrasies of human character in daily life.

There remains, however, a further question. Can prose be dramatic? It is obvious, of course, that Shaw and Ibsen[16] have used prose dramatically with the highest success, but they have been faithful to the dramatic form. This form one may prophesy is not the one which the poetic dramatist of the future will find fit for his needs. A prose play is too rigid, too limited, too emphatic for his purposes. It lets slip between its meshes half the things that he wants to say. He cannot compress into dialogue all the comment, all the analysis, all the richness that he wants to give. Yet he covets the explosive emotional effect of the drama; he wants to draw blood from his readers, and not merely to stroke and tickle their intellectual susceptibilities. The looseness and freedom of *Tristram Shandy*, wonderfully though they encircle and float off such characters as Uncle Toby and Corporal Trim, do not attempt to range and marshal these people in dramatic contrast together. Therefore it will be necessary for the writer of this exacting book to bring to bear upon his tumultuous and contradictory emotions the generalising and simplifying power of a strict and logical imagination. Tumult is vile; confusion is hateful; everything in a work of art should be mastered and ordered. His effort will be to generalise rather than to split up. Instead of enumerating details he will mould blocks. His characters thus will have a dramatic power which the minutely realised characters of contemporary fiction often sacrifice in the interests of psychology. And then, though this is scarcely visible, so far distant it lies on the rim of the horizon – one can imagine that he will have extended the scope of his interest so as to dramatise some of those influences which play so large a part in life, yet have so far escaped the novelist – the power of music, the stimulus of sight, the effect on us of the shape of trees or the play of colour, the emotions bred in us by crowds, the obscure terrors and hatreds which come so irrationally in certain places or from certain people, the delight of movement, the intoxication of wine. Every moment is the centre and meeting place of an extraordinary number of perceptions which have not yet been expressed. Life is always and inevitably much richer than we who try to express it.

But it needs no great gift of prophecy to be certain that whoever attempts to do what is outlined above will have need of all his courage. Prose is not going to learn a new step at the bidding of the first comer. Yet if the signs of the times are worth anything the need of fresh developments is being felt. It is certain that there are scattered about in England, France and America writers who are trying to work themselves free from a bondage which has become irksome to them; writers who are trying to readjust their attitude so that they may once more stand easily and naturally in a position where their powers have full play upon important things. And it is when a book strikes us as the result of that attitude rather than by its beauty or its brilliancy that we know that it has in it the seeds of an enduring existence.

1–A signed essay published in two instalments in the *NYHT*, 14 and 21 August 1927, (Kp C284), deriving from a paper read to the Oxford University English Club, secretary Aubrey Herbert (see MHP), at St Hugh's College, on 18 May 1927.

VW wrote in her diary on 5 May: 'I know why I am depressed: a bad habit of making up the review I should like before reading the review I get. I am excited about my article on Poetry & Fiction. Writing for an audience always stirs me. I hope to avoid too many jokes. Then Vita will come tomorrow. But I don't want people: I want solitude; Rome.' She stayed in Oxford on the 18th and 19th of the month, accompanied by Vita Sackville-West, and wrote about the visit to her sister on the 22nd (*III VW Letters*, no. 1760): 'Then I went to Oxford to speak to the youth of both sexes on poetry and fiction. They are young; they are callow; they know nothing about either – They sit on the floor and ask innocent questions about Joyce – They are years behind the Cambridge young, it seemed to me; Quentin and Julian could knock them into mud pies. But they have their charm – There was a man called Martin (I think) an adorer and disciple of Roger's, who was the most intelligent. We went on to somebodies [sic] rooms, and there they sat on the floor, and said what a master they thought Roger Fry; . . .They're oddly under our thumb, at the moment – at least this particular group.' See Editorial Note, p. xxv. Reprinted, with minor variations, as 'The Narrow Bridge of Art', *G&R, CE.*

2–John Dryden (1631–1700); William Wordsworth (1770–1850) whose tragedy *The White Doe of Rylstone* written in 1807–8 was published in 1815; S. T. Coleridge (1772–1834) of whose three dramas, *Remorse* was performed at Drury Lane in 1813; P. B. Shelley (1792–1822), see below; John Keats (1795–1821), whose dramatic productions 'King Stephen' and 'Otho the Great' were written in 1819; Alfred, Lord Tennyson (1809–92) wrote several dramas, including *Queen Mary* (1875) and *Becket* (1884); A. C. Swinburne (1837–1909), see below; Robert Browning (1812–89), whose dramas include *Strafford* (1837) and *Colombe's Birthday* (1844), both of which were performed, the latter in 1853 with some success in London and Manchester.

3–Swinburne, *Atalanta in Calydon* (1865); Shelley, *Prometheus Unbound* (1820).

4–For VW on George Gissing (1857–1903) see 'The Novels of George Gissing', *I VW Essays*; 'George Gissing', *CR2* and *V VW Essays.*

5–For VW on which see 'Notes on an Elizabethan Play', *CR1* above.

6–For VW on 'The Poetic Drama', see *I VW Essays*; and see 'Some Poetical Plays', *VI VW Essays*, Appendix.

7–John Keats, 'To a Nightingale', 1819.

8–T. S. Eliot, *The Waste Land* (1922), II 'A Game of Chess', l. 103: '. . . yet there the nightingale / Filled all the desert with inviolable voice / And still she cried, and still the world pursues, / "Jug Jug" to dirty ears.' See also *The Waves* (Hogarth Press, 1931), p. 192: 'Jug, jug, jug, I sing like the nightingale whose melody is crowded in the too narrow passage of her throat.' And see too, John Lyly, *Campaspe* (1584), v, i: 'What bird so sings, yet so does wail? / O 'tis the ravish'd nightingale. / Jug, jug, jug, jug, tereu, she cries, / And still her woes at midnight rise.'

9–Oscar Wilde (1854–1900); Walter Pater (1839–94); Samuel Butler (1835–1902); George Bernard Shaw (1856–1950).

10–Lord Byron (1788–1824), *Don Juan* (1812–24).

11–The first instalment of VW's essay ended here.

12–Marcel Proust (1871–1922), for VW on whom see 'Pictures' above, and 'Phases of Fiction', *V VW Essays*. Fyodor Dostoevsky (1821–81), for VW on whom see 'More Dostoevsky', 'A Minor Dostoevsky', *II VW Essays*; 'Dostoevsky in Cranford', 'Dostoevsky the Father', *III VW Essays.*

13–George Meredith (1828–1909), *The Ordeal of Richard Feverel, A History of a Father and Son* (1859; Memorial Edition, vol. ii, Constable and Company Ltd, 1909), ch. xix, 'A Diversion Played on a Penny-Whistle', which begins: 'Away with Systems! Away with a corrupt World! Let us breathe the air of the Enchanted Island.

'Golden lie the meadows: golden run the streams; red gold is on the pine-stems. The sun is coming down to earth, and walks the fields and the waters.' The first paragraph and part of the second as given here are also quoted in 'The Novels of George Meredith' below.

14—See '"Jane Eyre" and "Wuthering Heights"' in *CR1*, above, where VW writes: 'It is with a description of storm that Charlotte ends her finest novel *Villette*: "The skies hang full and dark – a wrack sails from the west; the clouds cast themselves into strange forms."' Charlotte Brontë (1816–55), *Villette* (1853).
15—Laurence Sterne (1713–68), *The Life and Opinions of Tristram Shandy* (1759–67), vol. ix, conclusion of ch. viii, which begins: 'I will not argue the matter:', and ch. ix in its entirety; punctuation slightly adapted. For VW on 'Sterne' see *I VW Essays*, and see '*The Sentimental Journey*', *CR2* and *V VW Essays*.
16—Henrik Ibsen (1828–1906).

Life Itself

One could wish that the psycho-analysts would go into the question of diary keeping. For often it is the one mysterious fact in a life otherwise as clear as the sky and as candid as the dawn. Parson Woodforde is a case in point – his diary is the only mystery about him. For forty-three years he sat down almost daily to record what he did on Monday and what he had for dinner on Tuesday; but for whom he wrote or why he wrote it is impossible to say. He does not unburden his soul in his diary; yet it is no mere record of engagements and expenses. As for literary fame, there is no sign that he ever thought of it, and finally though the man himself is peaceable above all things, there are little indiscretions and criticisms which would have got him into trouble and hurt the feelings of his friends had they read them. What purpose, then, did the sixty-eight little books fulfil? Perhaps it was the desire for intimacy. When James Woodforde opened one of his neat manuscript books he entered into conversation with a second James Woodforde, who was not quite the same as the reverend gentleman who visited the poor and preached in the church. These two friends said much that all the world might hear; but they had a few secrets which they shared with each other only. It was a great comfort, for example, that Christmas when Nancy, Betsy, and Mr Walker seemed to be in conspiracy against him, to exclaim in the diary, 'The treatment I meet with for my Civility this Christmas is to me abominable.'[2] The second James Woodforde sympathised and agreed. Again, when a stranger abused his hospitality it was a relief to inform the other self who lived in the little book that he had put him to sleep in the attic story, and I treated him as one that would be too free if treated kindly'.[3] It is easy to understand why, in the quiet life of a country parish, these two bachelor friends became in time inseparable. An essential part of him would have died had he been forbidden to keep his diary. And as we read – if reading is the word for it – we seem to be listening to someone who is murmuring over the events of the day to himself in the quiet space which precedes sleep. It is not writing, and, to speak the truth, it is not reading. It is slipping through half a dozen pages and strolling to the window and looking out. It is going on thinking about the Woodfordes while we watch the people in the street below. It is taking a walk and making up the life and character of James Woodforde as we make up our friends' characters, turning over something they have said, pondering the meaning of something they have done, remembering how they looked one day when they thought themselves unobserved. It is not reading; it is ruminating.

James Woodforde, then, was one of those smooth-cheeked, steady-eyed men, demure to look at, whom we can never imagine except in the prime of life. He was of an equable temper, with only such acerbities and touchinesses as are generally to be found in those who have had a love affair in their youth and remained, as they fancy, unwed because of it. The Parson's love affair, however, was nothing very tremendous. Once when he was a young man in Somerset he liked to walk over to Shepton and to visit a certain 'sweet tempered' Betsy White who lived there. He had a great mind 'to make a bold stroke' and ask her to marry him. He went so far, indeed, as to propose marriage 'when opportunity served',[4] and Betsy was willing. But he delayed; time passed; four years passed indeed, and Betsy went to Devonshire, met a Mr Webster, who had five hundred pounds a year, and married him. When James Woodforde met them in the turnpike road he could say little, 'being shy', but to his diary he remarked – and this no doubt was his private version of the affair ever after – 'she has proved herself to me a mere jilt.'[5]

But he was a young man then, and as time went on we cannot help suspecting that he was glad to consider the question of marriage shelved once and for all so that he might settle down with his niece Nancy at Weston Longueville, and give himself simply and solely, every day and all day, to the great business of living. What else to call it we do not know. It seems to be life itself.

For James Woodforde was nothing in particular. Life had it all her own way with him. He had no special gift; he had no oddity or infirmity. It is idle to pretend that he was a zealous priest. God in Heaven was much the same to him as King George upon the throne – a kindly Monarch, that is to say, whose festivals one kept by preaching a sermon on Sunday much as one kept the Royal birthday by firing a blunderbuss and drinking a toast at dinner. Should anything untoward happen, like the death of a boy who was dragged and killed by a horse, he would instantly, but rather perfunctorily exclaim, 'I hope to God the Poor Boy is happy,' and add, 'We all came home singing';[6] just as when Justice Creed's peacock spread its tail – 'and most noble it is' – he would exclaim, 'How wonderful are Thy Works O God in every Being.'[7] But there was no fanaticism, no enthusiasm, no lyric impulse about James Woodforde. In all these pages, indeed, each so neatly divided into compartments, and each of those again filled, as the days themselves were, so quietly and so fully in a hand like the pacing of a well-tempered nag, one can only call to mind a single poetic phrase about the transit of Venus, how 'It appeared as a black patch upon a fair Lady's face.'[8] The words themselves are mild enough, but they hang over the undulating expanse of the Parson's prose with the resplendence of the star itself. So in the fen country a barn or a tree appears twice its natural size against the surrounding flats. But what led him to this palpable excess that summer's night we do not know. It cannot have been that he was drunk. He spoke out too roundly against such failings in his brother Jack to have been guilty himself. Jack was the wild one of the family. Jack drank at the 'Catherine Wheel'. Jack came home and had the impudence to defend suicide to his old father. James himself drank his pint of port, but he was a man who liked his meat. When we think of the Woodfordes, Uncle and Niece, we think of them as often as not waiting with some impatience for their dinner. They gravely watch the joint set upon the table; they swiftly get their knives and forks to work upon the succulent leg or loin, and without much comment, unless a word is passed about the gravy or the stuffing, go on eating. They munch, day after day, year after year, until they have devoured herds of sheep and oxen, flocks of poultry, an odd dozen or so of swans and cygnets, bushels of apples and plums, while the pastries and the jellies crumble and squash beneath their spoons in mountains, in pyramids, in pagodas. Never was there a book so stuffed with food as this one is. To read the bill of fare respectfully and punctually set forth gives one a sense of repletion. It is as if one had lunched at Simpsons daily for a week. Trout and chicken, mutton and peas, pork and apple sauce – so the joints succeed each other at dinner, and there is supper with more joints still to come, all, no doubt, home grown, and of the juiciest and sweetest; all cooked, often by the mistress herself in the plainest English way, save when the dinner was at Weston Hall and Mrs Custance surprised them with a London dainty – a pyramid of jelly, that is to say, with a 'landscape appearing through it'.[9] Then Mrs Custance, for whom James Woodforde had a chivalrous devotion, would play the 'Sticcardo Pastorale', and make 'very soft music indeed';[10] or would get out her work-box and show them how neatly contrived it was, unless indeed Mrs Custance were giving birth to another child upstairs, whom the Parson would baptise and very frequently bury. The Parson had a deep respect for the Custances. They were all that country gentry should be – a little given to the habit of keeping mistresses, perhaps, but that peccadillo could be forgiven them in view of their generosity to the poor, the kindness they showed to Nancy, and their condescension in asking the Parson to dinner when they had great people staying with them. Yet great people were not much to James's liking. Deeply though he respected the nobility, 'One must confess,' he said, 'that being with our equals is much more agreeable.'[11]

He was too fond of his ease, and too shrewd a judge of the values of things to be much troubled with snobbery; he much preferred the quiet of his own fireside to adventuring after dissipation abroad. If an old man brought a Madagascar monkey to the door, or a Polish dwarf or a balloon was being shown at Norwich, the Parson would go and have a look at them, and be free with his shillings, but he was a quiet man, a man without ambition, and it is more than likely that his niece found him a little dull. It is the niece Nancy, to speak plainly, who makes us uneasy. There are the seeds of domestic disaster in her character, unless we mistake. It is true that on the afternoon of April 27th, 1780, she expressed a wish to read Aristotle's philosophy, which Miss Millard had got of a married woman, but she is a stolid girl; she eats too much, she grumbles too much, and she takes too much to heart the loss of her red box. No doubt she was sensible enough; we will not blame her for being pert and saucy, or for losing her temper at cards, or even for hiding the parcel that came by post when her Uncle longed to know what was in it, and had never done such a thing by her. But when we compare her with Betsy Davy we realise that one human being has only to come into the room to raise our spirits, and another sets us on edge merely by the way she blows her nose. Betsy, the daughter of that frivolous wanton Mrs Davy (who fell downstairs the day Miss Donne swallowed the barley corn with its stalk), Betsy the shy little girl, Betsy livening up and playing with the Parson's wig, Betsy falling in love with Mr Walker, Betsy receiving the present of a fox's brush from him, Betsy compromising her reputation with a scamp, Betsy bereaved of him – for Mr Walker died at the age of twenty-three and was buried in a plain coffin – Betsy left, it is to be feared, in a very scandalous condition – Betsy always charms; we forgive Betsy anything. The trouble with Nancy is that she is beginning to find Weston dull. No suitor has yet appeared. It is but too likely that the ten years of Parson Woodforde's life that still remain will often have to record how Nancy teased him with her grumbling.

The ten years that remain – one knows, of course, that it must come to an end. Already the Custances have gone to Bath; the Parson has had a touch of gout; far away, with a sound like distant thunder, we hear the guns of the French Revolution. But it is comforting to observe that the imprisonment of the French King and Queen and the anarchy and confusion in Paris are only mentioned after it has been recorded that Thomas Ram has lost his cow, and that Parson Woodforde has 'brewed another Barrell of Table Beer today'.[12] We have a notion, indeed – and here it must be confessed that we have given up reading Parson Woodforde altogether, and merely tell over the story on a stroll through fields where the hares are scampering and the rooks rising above the elm trees – we have a notion that Parson Woodforde does not die. Parson Woodforde goes on. It is we who change and perish. It is the Kings and Queens who lie in prison. It is the great towns that are ravaged with anarchy and confusion. But the river Wensum still flows; Mrs Custance is brought to bed of yet another baby; there is the first swallow of the year. The spring comes and summer with its hay and its strawberries; then autumn when the walnuts are exceptionally fine, though the pears are poor; so we lapse into winter, which is indeed boisterous, but the house, thank God, withstands the storm; and then again there is the first swallow and Parson Woodforde takes his greyhounds out a-coursing.

1–A signed review in the *N&A*, 20 August 1927, (Kp C285) also published in the

NR, 17 August, of vol. iii of *The Diary of a Country Parson. The Reverend James Woodforde* [1740–1803]. Ed. John Beresford (1927; 5 vols, OUP, 1924–31), subsequently revised and expanded for inclusion under the title 'Two Parsons' ('James Woodforde') in *CR*2. See Editorial Note, p. xxv. The same issue of the *N&A* contained LW's 'World of Books' column, on 'The Revolt Against Europe', discussing Arnold J. Toynbee on *The Islamic World Since the Peace Settlement* (Survey of International Affairs, vol. i, 1925). See also *V VW Essays*. Reading Notes (Berg, xv, xix; and see LXIX). Reprinted *CDB*, ('James Woodforde') *CE*.

2–Woodforde, vol. iii, 3 January 1789, p. 77.

3–*Ibid.*, vol. ii, 4 August 1784, p. 145.

4–For the first two quotations, *ibid.*, vol. i, 25 September 1771, p. 111, which has: 'She is a sweet tempered girl indeed, and I like her much, and I think would make a good wife, I do not know but I shall make a bold stroke that way'; and for the third, *ibid.*, 28 May 1774, p. 132, which has 'an opportunity'.

5–*Ibid.*, 16 September 1775, p. 168.

6–*Ibid.*, 11 July 1765, pp. 48–9.

7–*Ibid.*, 9 May 1768, p. 75.

8–*Ibid.*, 3 June 1769, p. 86.

9–*Ibid.*, vol. ii, 28 March 1782, p. 15.

10–*Ibid.*, vol. i, 9 September 1778, p. 235.

11–*Ibid.*, vol. ii, 7 November 1783, p. 104.

12–*Ibid.*, vol. iii, 16 October 1789, p. 146: 'I breakfasted, dined &c again at home. To a poor old man of Hockering by name of Thomas Ram, having lost a Cow gave 0.2.6. Brewed another Barrell of Table Beer today. Sad news from France all anarchy and Confusion. The King, Queen and Royal Family confined at Paris. The Soldiers joined the People, many murdered.'

A Terribly Sensitive Mind

The most distinguished writers of short stories in England are agreed, says Mr Murry, that as a writer of short stories Katherine Mansfield was *hors concours*.[2] No one has succeeded her, and no critic has been able to define her quality. But the reader of her journal is well content to let such questions be. It is not the quality of her writing or the degree of her fame that interest us in her diary, but the spectacle of a mind – a terribly sensitive mind – receiving one after another the haphazard impressions of eight years of life. Her diary was a mystical companion. 'Come my unseen, my unknown, let us talk together'[3] she says on beginning a new volume. In it she noted facts – the weather, an engagement; she sketched scenes; she analysed her character; she described a pigeon or a dream or a conversation. Nothing could be more fragmentary; nothing more private. We feel that we are watching a mind which is alone with itself; a mind which has so little thought of an audience that it will make use of a shorthand of its own now and then, or, as the mind in its loneliness tends to do, divide into two and talk to itself. Katherine Mansfield about Katherine Mansfield.

But then as the scraps accumulate we find ourselves giving them, or more probably receiving from Katherine Mansfield herself, a direction. From what point of view is she looking at life as she sits there, terribly sensitive, registering one after another such diverse impressions? She is a writer; a born writer. Everything she feels and hears and sees is not fragmentary and separate; it belongs together as writing. Sometimes the note is directly made for a story. 'Let me remember when I write about that fiddle how it runs up lightly and swings down sorrowful; how it *searches*,'[4] she notes. Or, '*Lumbago*. This is a very queer thing. So sudden, so painful, I must remember it when I write about an old man. The start to get up, the pause, the look of fury, and how, lying at night, one seems to get locked.'[5]

Again, the moment itself suddenly puts on significance, and she traces the outline as if to preserve it. 'It's raining, but the air is soft, smoky, warm. Big drops patter on the languid leaves, the tobacco flowers lean over. Now there is a rustle in the ivy. Wingly has appeared from the garden next door; he bounds from the wall. And delicately, lifting his paws, pointing his ears, very afraid the big wave will overtake him, he wades over the lake of green grass.'[6] The Sister of Nazareth 'showing her pale gums and big discoloured teeth' asks for money. The thin dog, so thin that his body is like 'a cage on four wooden pegs', runs down the street.[7] In some sense, she feels the thin dog is the street. In all this we seem to be in the midst of unfinished stories; here is a beginning; here an end. They only need a loop of words thrown round them to be complete.

But then, the diary is so private and so instinctive that it allows another self to break off from the self that writes and to stand a little apart watching it write. The writing self was a queer self; sometimes nothing would induce it to write. 'There is so much to do and I do so little. Life would be almost perfect here if only when I was *pretending* to work I always was working. Look at the stories that wait and wait just at the threshold . . . *Next day*. Yet take this morning, for instance. I don't want to write anything. It's grey; its heavy, and dull. And short stories seem unreal and not worth doing. I don't want to write; I want to *live*. What does she mean by that? It's not easy to say. But there you are!'[8]

What does she mean by that? No one felt more seriously the importance of writing than she did. In all the pages of her journal, instinctive, rapid as they are, her attitude to her work is admirable; sane, caustic and austere. There is no literary gossip; no vanity; no jealousy. Although during her last years she must have been aware of her success she makes no allusion to it. Her own comments upon her work are always penetrating and disparaging. Her stories wanted richness and depth; she was only 'skimming the top – no more'.[9] But writing, the mere expression of things adequately and sensitively, is not enough. It is founded upon something unexpressed; and this something must be solid and entire. Under the desperate pressure of increasing illness she began a curious difficult search, of which we catch glimpses only and those hard to interpret, after the crystal clearness which is needed if one is to write truthfully. 'Nothing of any worth can come of a disunited being,'[10] she wrote. One must have health in one's self. After five years of struggle she gave up the search after physical health not in despair, but because she thought the malady was of the soul and that the cure lay not in any physical treatment, but in some such 'spiritual brotherhood' as that at Fontainebleau,[11] in which the last months of her life were spent. But before she went she wrote the summing up of her position with which the journal ends.

She wanted health, she wrote; but what did she mean by health? 'By health,' she wrote, 'I mean the power to live a full, adult, living, breathing life in close contact with what I love – the earth and the wonders thereof – the sea – the sun . . .[12] Then I want to work. At what? I want so to live that I work with my hands and my feeling and my brain. I want a garden, a small house, grass, animals, books, pictures, music. And out of this, the expression of this, I want to be writing. (Though I may write about cabmen. That's no matter.)'[13] The diary ends with the words 'All is well.'[14] And since she died three months later it is tempting to think that the words stood for some conclusion which illness and the intensity of her own nature drove her to find at an age when most of us are loitering easily among those appearances and impressions, those amusements and sensations, which none had loved better than she.

1—A signed review in the *N&A*, 10 September 1927, reprinted in *NYHT*, 18 September, (Kp C286) of the *Journal of Katherine Mansfield 1914–1922*, ed. J. Middleton Murry (Constable and Co. Ltd, 1927). 'I've been reading Katherine Mansfield,' VW wrote to Vita Sackville-West, on 7 August 1927, 'with a mixture of sentiment and horror. What odd friends I've had – you and she –' (*III VW Letters*, no. 1797). See Editorial Note, p. xxv. Reprinted *G&R, CE*.

2—John Middleton Murry (1889–1957), critic, editor and author, had married Katherine Mansfield (1888–1923) in 1918, in which year her story *Prelude* was published by the Woolfs, as the Hogarth Press's third publication. VW's friendship with Mansfield, in which natural affection, literary rivalry, and a certain social unease on VW's part, were inextricably mixed, is intriguingly revealed in the latter's diary.

3—Mansfield, 13 November 1921, p. 195, which has: 'Come, my unseen'.

4—*Ibid.*, [?December] 1920, p. 170.

5—*Ibid.*, 22 January 1922, p. 221, which has: 'so painful. I must remember' and '– the pause – the look of fury –'.

6—*Ibid.*, 1919, 'Wingley', p. 117, which has: 'that big wave'.

7—For the Sister of Nazareth, *ibid.*, 1917, p. 68; and for the thin dog, 1918, p. 94.

8—*Ibid.*, 13 July 1921, p. 182, which has: 'There is so much to do, and'; 'always was working. But that is surely not too hard. Look at the stories'.

9—*Ibid.*, 1 February 1922, p. 226: 'Yes, that's it. To do anything, to be anything, one must gather oneself together and "one's faith make stronger". Nothing of any worth can come from a disunited being. It's only by accident that I write anything worth a rush, and then it's only skimming the top – no more.'

10—*Ibid.*, see previous note.

11—*Ibid.*, Murry's concluding note. Mansfield, dying of advanced gonorrhoeal infection and tuberculosis, spent her last months at George Gurdjieff's Institute for the Harmonious Development of Man, at Fontainebleau, the object of which society, 'at least as she understood it' (p. 252), was, according to Murry, 'to help its members to achieve a spiritual regeneration'.

12—*Ibid.*, 10 October 1922, p. 250.

13—*Ibid.*, p. 251.

14—*Ibid.*

An Essay in Criticism

Human credulity is indeed wonderful. There may be good reasons for believing in a King or a Judge or a Lord Mayor. When we see them go sweeping by in their robes and their wigs, with their heralds and their outriders, our knees begin to shake and our looks to falter. But what reason there is for believing in critics it is impossible to say. They have neither wigs nor outriders. They differ in

no way from other people if one seem them in the flesh. Yet these insignificant fellow creatures have only to shut themselves up in a
room, dip a pen in the ink and call themselves 'we' for the rest of us
to believe that they are somehow exalted, inspired, infallible. Wigs
grow on their heads. Robes cover their limbs. No greater miracle
was ever performed by the power of human credulity. And, like
most miracles, this one, too, has had a weakening effect upon the
mind of the believer. He begins to think that critics, because they
call themselves so, must be right. He begins to suppose that something actually happens to a book when it has been praised or
denounced in print. He begins to doubt and conceal his own sensitive, hesitating apprehensions when they conflict with the critics'
decrees.

And yet, barring the learned (and learning is chiefly useful in
judging the work of the dead), the critic is rather more fallible than
the rest of us. He has to give us his opinion of a book that has been
published two days, perhaps, with the shell still sticking to its head.
He has to get outside that cloud of fertile, but unrealised sensation
which hangs about a reader, to solidify it, to sum it up. The chances
are that he does this before the time is ripe; he does it too rapidly
and too definitely. He says that it is a great book or a bad book. Yet,
as he knows, when he is content to read only, it is neither. He is
driven by force of cicumstances and some human vanity to hide
those hesitations which beset him as he reads, to smooth out all
traces of that crab-like and crooked path by which he has reached
what he chooses to call 'a conclusion'. So the crude trumpet blasts
of critical opinion blow loud and shrill, and we, humble readers
that we are, bow our submissive heads.

But let us see whether we can do away with those pretences for a
season and pull down the imposing curtain which hides the critical
process until it is complete. Let us give the mind a new book, as one
drops a lump of fish into a cage of fringed and eager sea anemones,
and watch it pausing, pondering, considering its attack. Let us see
what prejudices affect it; what influences tell upon it. And if the
conclusion becomes in the process a little less conclusive, it may, for
that very reason, approach nearer to the truth. The first thing that
the mind desires is some foothold of fact upon which it can lodge
before it takes flight upon its speculative career. Vague rumours
attach themselves to people's names. Of Mr Hemingway, we know
that he is an American living in France, an 'advanced' writer, we

suspect, connected with what is called a movement, though which of the many we own that we do not know. It will be well to make a little more certain of these matters by reading first Mr Hemingway's earlier book, *The Sun Also Rises*,[2] and it soon becomes clear from this that if Mr Hemingway is 'advanced', it is not in the way that is to us most interesting. A prejudice of which the reader would do well to take account is here exposed; the critic is a modernist. Yes, the excuse would be because the moderns make us aware of what we feel subconsciously; they are truer to our own experience; they even anticipate it, and this gives us a particular excitement. But nothing new is revealed about any of the characters in *The Sun Also Rises*. They come before us shaped, proportioned, weighed, exactly as the characters of Maupassant[3] are shaped and proportioned. They are seen from the old angle; the old reticences, the old relations between author and character are observed.

But the critic has the grace to reflect that this demand for new aspects and new perspectives may well be overdone. It may become whimsical. It may become foolish. For why should not art be traditional as well as original? Are we not attaching too much importance to an excitement which, though agreeable, may not be valuable in itself, so that we are led to make the fatal mistake of overriding the writer's gift?

At any rate, Mr Hemingway is not modern in the sense given; and it would appear from his first novel that this rumour of modernity must have sprung from his subject matter and from his treatment of it rather than from any fundamental novelty in his conception of the art of fiction. It is a bare, abrupt, outspoken book. Life as people live it in Paris in 1927 or even in 1928 is described as we of this age do describe life (it is here that we steal a march upon the Victorians), openly, frankly, without prudery, but also without surprise. The immoralities and moralities of Paris are described as we are apt to hear them spoken of in private life. Such candour is modern and it is admirable. Then, for qualities grow together in art as in life, we find attached to this admirable frankness an equal bareness of style. Nobody speaks for more than a line or two. Half a line is mostly sufficient. If a hill or a town is described (and there is always some reason for its description) there it is, exactly and literally built up of little facts, literal enough, but chosen, as the final sharpness of the outline proves with the utmost care. Therefore, a few words like these: 'The grain was just beginning to ripen and the fields were full of poppies. The pasture land was green and there were fine trees, and sometimes big rivers and châteaux off in the trees'[4] – which have a curious force. Each word pulls its weight in the sentence. And the prevailing atmosphere is fine and sharp, like that of winter days when the boughs are bare against the sky. (But if we had to choose one sentence with which to describe what Mr Hemingway attempts and sometimes achieves, we should quote a passage from a description of a bullfight: 'Romero never made any contortions, always it was straight and pure and natural in line. The others twisted themselves like corkscrews, their elbows raised and leaned against the flanks of the bull after his horns had passed, to give a faked look of danger. Afterwards, all that was faked turned bad and gave an unpleasant feeling. Romero's bullfighting gave real emotion, because he kept the absolute purity of line in his movements and always quietly and calmly let the horns pass him close each time.')[5] Mr Hemingway's writing, one might paraphrase, gives us now and then a real emotion, because he keeps absolute purity of line in his movements and lets the horns (which are truth, fact, reality) pass him close each time. But there is something faked, too, which turns bad and gives an unpleasant feeling – that also we must face in course of time.

And here, indeed, we may conveniently pause and sum up what point we have reached in our critical progress. Mr Hemingway is not an advanced writer in the sense that he is looking at life from a new angle. What he sees is a tolerably familiar sight. Common objects like beer bottles and journalists figure largely in the foreground. But he is a skilled and conscientious writer. He has an aim and makes for it without fear or circumlocution. We have, therefore to take his measure against somebody of substance, and not merely line him, for form's sake, beside the indistinct bulk of some ephemeral shape largely stuffed with straw. Reluctantly we reach this decision, for this process of measurement is one of the most difficult of a critic's tasks. He has to decide which are the most salient points of the book he has just read; to distinguish accurately to what kind they belong, and then, holding them against whatever model is chosen for comparison, to bring out their deficiency or their adequacy.

Recalling *The Sun Also Rises*, certain scenes rise in memory: the bullfight, the character of the Englishman, Harris; here a little landscape which seems to grow behind the people naturally; here a long, lean phrase which goes curling round a situation like the lash of a whip. Now and again this phrase evokes a character brilliantly, more often a scene. Of character, there is little that remains firmly and solidly elucidated. Something indeed seems wrong with the people. If we place them (the comparison is bad) against Tchehov's[6] people, they are flat as cardboard. If we place them (the comparison is better) against Maupassant's people they are crude as a photograph. If we place them (the comparison may be legitimate) against real people, the people we liken them to are of an unreal type. They are people one may have seen showing off at some café, talking a rapid, high-pitched slang, because slang is the speech of the herd, seemingly much at their ease, and yet if we look at them a little from the shadow not at their ease at all, and, indeed, terribly afraid of being themselves, or they would say things simply in their natural voices. So it would seem that the thing that is faked is character; Mr Hemingway leans against the flanks of that particular bull after the horns have passed.

After this preliminary study of Mr Hemingway's first book, we come to the new book, *Men Without Women*, possessed of certain views or prejudices. His talent plainly may develop along different lines. It may broaden and fill out; it may take a little more time to go into things – human beings in particular – rather more deeply. And even if this meant the sacrifice of some energy and point, the exchange would be to our private liking. On the other hand, his is a talent which may contract and harden still further! it may come to depend more and more upon the emphatic moment; make more and more use of dialogue, and cast narrative and description overboard as an encumbrance.

The fact that *Men Without Women* consists of short stories, makes it probable that Mr Hemingway has taken the second line. But before we explore the new book, a word should be said which is generally left unsaid, about the implications of the title. As the publisher puts it ... 'the softening feminine influence is absent – either through training, discipline, death, or situation.'[7] Whether we are to understand by this that women are incapable of training, discipline, death, or situation, we do not know. But it is undoubtedly true, if we are going to persevere in our attempt to reveal the processes of the critic's mind, that any emphasis laid upon sex is dangerous. Tell a man that this is a woman's book, or a woman that this is a man's, and you have brought into play sympathies and antipathies which have nothing to do with art. The greatest writers lay no stress upon sex one way or the other. The critic is not reminded as he reads them that he belongs to the masculine or the feminine gender. But in our time, thanks to our sexual perturbations, sex consciousness is strong, and shows itself in literature by an exaggeration, a protest of sexual characteristics which in either case is disagreeable. Thus Mr Lawrence, Mr Douglas, and Mr Joyce[8] partly spoil their books for women readers by their display of self-conscious virility; and Mr Hemingway, but much less violently, follows suit. All we can do, whether we are men or women, is to admit the influence, look the fact in the face, and so hope to stare it out of countenance.

To proceed then – *Men Without Women* consists of short stories in the French rather than in the Russian manner. The great French masters, Mérimée[9] and Maupassant, made their stories as self-sufficient and compact as possible. There is never a thread left hanging; indeed so contracted are they, that when the last sentence of the last page flares up, as it so often does, we see by its light the whole circumference and significance of the story revealed. The Tchehov method is, of course, the very opposite of this. Everything is cloudy and vague, loosely trailing rather than tightly furled. The stories move slowly out of sight like clouds in the summer air, leaving a wake of meaning in our minds which gradually fades away. Of the two methods, who shall say which is the better? At any rate, Mr Hemingway, enlisting under the French masters, carries out their teaching up to a point with considerable success.

There are in *Men Without Women* many stories which, if life were longer, one would wish to read again. Most of them indeed are so competent, so efficient, and so bare of superfluity that one wonders why they do not make a deeper dent in the mind than they do. Take the pathetic story of the major whose wife died – 'In Another Country'; or the sardonic story of a conversation in a railway carriage – 'A Canary for One'; or stories like 'The Undefeated', and 'Fifty Grand' which are full of the sordidness and heroism of bullfighting and boxing – all of these are good trenchant stories, quick, terse and strong. If one had not summoned the ghosts of Tchehov, Mérimée and Maupassant, no doubt one would be enthusiastic. As it is, one looks about for something, fails to find something, and so is brought again to the old familiar business of ringing impressions on the counter, and asking what is wrong?

For some reason the book of short stories does not seem to us to go as deep or to promise as much as the novel. Perhaps it is the excessive use of dialogue, for Mr Hemingway's use of it is surely excessive. A writer will always be chary of dialogue because dialogue puts the most violent pressure on the reader's attention. He has to hear, to see, to supply the right tone, and to fill in the background from what the characters say without any help from the author. Therefore, when fictitious people are allowed to speak it must be because they have something so important to say that it stimulates the reader to do rather more than his share of the work or creation. But, although Mr Hemingway keeps us under the fire of dialogue constantly, his people, half the time, are only saying what the author could say much more economically for them. At last we are inclined to cry out with the little girl in 'Hills Like White Elephants', 'Would you please please please please please please stop talking.'[10]

And probably it is this superfluity of dialogue which leads to that other fault which is always lying in wait for the writer of short stories: the lack of proportion. A paragraph in excess will make these little craft lopsided and will bring about that blurred effect which, when one is out for clarity and point, so baffles the reader. And both these faults, the tendency to flood the page with unnecessary dialogue and the lack of sharp, unmistakable points by which we can take hold of the story, come from the more fundamental fact that though Mr Hemingway is brilliantly and enormously skilful, he lets his dexterity, like the bullfighter's cloak, get between him and the fact. For in truth story writing has much in common with bullfighting. One may twist one's self like a corkscrew and go through every sort of contortion so that the public thinks one is running every risk and displaying superb gallantry. But the true writer stands close up to the bull and lets the horns – call them life, truth, reality, whatever you like, – pass him close each time.

Mr Hemingway, then, is courageous; he is candid; he is highly skilled; he plants words precisely where he wishes; he has moments of bare and nervous beauty; he is modern in manner but not in vision; he is self-consciously virile; his talent has contracted rather than expanded; compared with his novel his stories are a little dry and sterile. So we sum him up. So we reveal some of the prejudices, the instincts and the fallacies out of which what it pleases us to call criticism is made.

1–A signed review in the *NYHT*, 9 October 1927, (Kp C287) of *Men Without*

Women (Charles Scribner's Sons, 1927) by Ernest Hemingway (1898–1961). 'It aint so much that I'm a bad writer though that I am, as that I'm a sold soul,' VW wrote to Vita Sackville-West on 2 September 1927 (*III VW Letters*, no. 1805), 'The body to Lady G[erald]. W[ellesley]: the soul to Mrs Van Doren [Irita van Doren, who edited the *NYHT*'s 'Weekly Book Supplement']. Here I am bound hand and foot to write an article on the works of a man called Hemingway. There are 3 more to follow. For this I shall be paid £120 . . . write for the Americans again, write for money again, I will not.' On 13 September she told Harold Nicolson (*ibid.*, no. 1811) how 'One polishes off Hemingway and without a second's pause plunges into Shelley's; and on 20 September she noted in her diary: 'And Quentin came & the Keynes's came, & Morgan came. All of this I meant, perhaps, to describe: but then how hard I drive my pen through one article after another – Hemingway, Morgan, Shelley; & now Biography.'

For his reaction to VW's review see Hemingway's letter to Max Perkins, his editor at Scribner's, written from Paris, c. 1 November 1927 (Carlos Baker, ed. *Ernest Hemingway, Selected Letters*, Scribner's, 1981), pp. 264–5. Professor Michael Reynolds, Hemingway's biographer, has kindly told me that Hemingway omitted to relate to Perkins that 'when he read the review in Sylvia Beach's bookshop – Shakespeare and Company – he was so furious that he punched a lamp and broke it. Sylvia billed him for the lamp. (Beach Collection, Firestone Library, Princeton).' See also note 7 below.

See 'American Fiction' above. Reading Notes (Berg xxv). Reprinted *G&R*, *CE*.

2 – *The Sun Also Rises* (1926).

3 – Guy de Maupassant (1850–93).

4 – Hemingway, *The Sun Also Rises* (Charles Scribner's Sons, 1926), Book II, ch. ix, p. 89, which has: 'green, and there were fine'.

5 – *Ibid.*, ch. xv, p. 174, which has: 'their elbows raised, and' and 'Afterward'.

6 – Anton Chekhov (1860–1904).

7 – The publisher's account has not been traced to either a blurb or other form of promotion, but as Professor Reynolds points out it clearly echoes a letter to Perkins (14 February 1927, *Selected Letters*, p. 245): 'In all these, almost, the softening feminine influence through training, discipline, death or other causes, being absent.' Concerning this, Hemingway's letter of c. 1 November, is interesting: 'The deliberate twisting of the blurb was what angered me – that and the imputation that I faked and cheated etc. I was glad I did not get it when I was having one of those hellish depressions when you feel you can never write again' (*ibid.*, p. 265).

8 – For VW on: D. H. Lawrence (1885–1930), see 'Postscript or Prelude?', *III VW Essays* (also 'Modern Fiction' in *CR1* above); James Joyce (1882–1941), see 'Modern Fiction'; Norman Douglas (1868–1952) see 'South Wind', *II VW Essays*.

9 – Prosper Mérimée (1803–70).

10 – *Men Without Women* (Charles Scribner's Sons, 1927), 'Hills Like White Elephants', p. 76, where 'please' is repeated seven, not six, times.

Is Fiction An Art?

That Fiction is a lady, and a lady who has somehow got herself into trouble from which many gallant gentlemen are ready to rescue her without precisely knowing how, is a thought that must have struck her admirers. First, Sir Walter Raleigh plotted out her pedigree and tidied up her family history with scrupulous skill; then Mr Lubbock went most carefully into the nature of her constitution;[2] now Mr Forster, who has had the advantage of close intimacy with her for many years, lets us into a good many of her secrets and tells us some unpleasant home truths. None of the three quite gets her out of her scrape; but, as one might expect, Mr Forster is far the most at his ease, and if the atmosphere of the lecture room – the book is a series of lectures delivered at Cambridge[3] – brews rather more heartiness than seems necessary in daily life, few books about fiction have the wit or the subtlety to get as far or go as quickly as this one.

But before we begin to consider what Mr Forster has to tell us about fiction, we must make sure where he stands. He makes it plain from the start that his is not the scholar's attitude. He cannot lecture chronologically on the word because he has not read enough and does not know enough. On the other hand, he is resolved not to adopt the methods of the pseudo-scholar who will relate a book to any fact or person or tendency rather than read it. 'Books written before 1847, books written after it, books written after or before 1848. The novel in the reign of Queen Anne, the pre-novel, the ur-novel, the novel of the future'[4] – such books are the books that the pseudo-scholar writes, and we can do without them. But there is a point of view which the unscholarly lecturer can adopt usefully, if modestly. He can, as Mr Forster puts it, 'visualise the English novelists not as floating down that stream which bears all its sons away unless they are careful, but as seated together in a room, a circular room – a sort of British Museum, reading room – all writing their novels simultaneously. They do not, as they sit there, think "I live under Queen Victoria, under Anne" – the fact that their pens are in their hands is far more vivid to them. They are half-mesmerised, their sorrows and joys are pouring out through the ink, they are approximated by the act of creation'[5] – so much so indeed that they forget all that the professors have done for them and persist in writing out of their turn. Richardson insists that he is contemporary with Henry James. Wells will write a passage which might have been written by Dickens.[6]

Being a novelist himself, Mr Forster is not annoyed at this discovery. He knows from experience what a muddled and illogical machine the brain of a writer is. He knows how little writers think about methods; how completely they forget their grandfathers; how absorbed they tend to become in some vision of their own. Thus, though the scholars have all his respect, his sympathies are with the untidy and harassed people who are scribbling away at their books. And looking down on them, not from any great height, but, as he says, over their shoulders, he makes out, as he passes, that certain shapes and ideas tend to recur in their minds whatever their period. Since story-telling began, stories have always been made out of much the same elements; and these which he calls The Story, People, Plot, Fantasy, Prophecy, Pattern and Rhythm he now proceeds to examine.

But the word 'examine' is unfortunate.[7] It suggests a professor, a corps and pupils. Mr Forster is never professional, and his subject, far from being extended on a board, is a lady of charm and variety who lets Mr Forster come close up to her and engages in animated conversation with him. As for the pupils, they are certainly attentive, but they do not hesitate to disagree. They exercise this right, indeed, at the earliest opportunity, in the first chapter, about the art of story-telling and Sir Walter Scott.

According to Mr Forster's arrangement the story is the first element in the novel. It runs 'like a backbone, or, may I say, a tapeworm, for its beginning and end are arbitrary' through all fiction. It is a 'low atavistic form'[8] which one could well wish different. How much better, for example, if melody or perception of truth had been the highest factor common to all novels and not the story. The exemplar of story-telling whom Mr Forster chooses is Scott. Scott, he says, owes his fame, such of it as is genuine and not due to the fact people connect him sentimentally with youth or gastronomically with oatcakes, to the fact that he can tell a story. 'He cannot construct. He has neither artistic detachment nor passion, and how can a writer who is devoid of both create characters who will move us deeply?'[9] There rise in memory, as Mr Forster speaks, all those muddled, imperfect works *Waverley, Red Gauntlet, The Bride of*

Lammermoor.[10] It is true, then, that our liking is sentimental? Is there nothing but cardboard in the mountains and cotton wool in the human hearts? Are we tricked into tolerating these people only because they jog forward, and we ask, as we ask at the 'movies', what is going to happen next? Surely not. For what we remember is first a prodigious power of creation, in itself impressive, whether the creations are flimsy or solid; and some, the humorous and low born, we maintain, are as solid as need be. Next a romantic force such as Stevenson[11] was always trying to capture but never achieved, the sense of valleys, mountains, plumes, heroes, death, disaster, all composed and rightly ordered, so that we feel assuaged, relieved, satisfied, without precisely knowing why. But as a story-teller Scott is imperfect. Defoe, Arnold Bennett, George Moore[12] all surpass him there. Only his romance and his humour carry him through.

So having roused us, as he expected and doubtless hoped, Mr Forster proceeds to assemble the parts of fiction and to comment upon their use and nature. He glances at Jane Austen's people and at Defoe's, shows us how 'the perfect novelist', Jane Austen, Richardson or Defoe, 'seems to pass the creative finger down every sentence and into every word';[13] observes that Dickens and Wells are much alike in that their characters tend to be flat as gramophone records, but both have such immense vitality of their own that the part of their novels which is alive 'galvanises the part that is not and causes the characters to jump about and speak in a convincing way';[14] remarks, 'in music fiction is likely to find its nearest parallel';[15] tells us that the reason why we cannot imagine Moll Flanders in daily life is because we know so much more about her than about real people, for the people of fiction 'are people whose secret lives are visible or might be visible; we are people whose secret lives are invisible. And that is why novels, even when they are about wicked people, can solace us; they suggest a more comprehensible, and thus a more manageable human race; they give us the illusion of perspicacity and power.'[16] It is tempting to quote further to show Mr Forster as he plays round his subject and darts in and out and says in his ordinary speaking voice things which sink airily enough into the mind and then unexpectedly stay and begin to unfurl like those Japanese flowers which open up in the depths of the water.

But greatly though these sayings intrigue us, we want to call a halt at some definite stopping place; we want to make Mr Forster stand and deliver. For possibly, if fiction is, as we suggest, in difficulties, it may be because nobody grasps her firmly and defines her severely. She has had no rules drawn up for her. And though rules may be wrong, and must be broken, they have this advantage – they confer dignity and order upon their subject; they admit her to a place in civilised society. But this part of his duty, if it is his duty, Mr Forster expressly disowns. He is not going to theorise about fiction except incidentally; he doubts even whether she is to be approached by a critic, and if so, with what critical equipment. All we can do is to edge him into a position which is definite enough for us to see where he stands by noticing what he likes and dislikes. And perhaps the best way to do this is to quote his summaries of three great figures – Meredith, Hardy,[17] and Henry James.

> Meredith is not the great name he was twenty years ago when much of the universe and all Cambridge trembled ... His philosophy has not worn well. His heavy attacks upon sentimentality – they bore the present generation ... And his visions of Nature – they don't endure like Hardy's, there is too much Surrey about them, they are fluffy and lush ... When he get serious and noble minded, there is a strident overtone – a bullying that becomes distressing. I feel indeed that he was like Tennyson in one respect: through not taking himself quietly enough he strained his inside. And his novels: most of the social values are faked. The tailors are not tailors, the cricket matches are not cricket ...[18]

Next, Hardy. Hardy is 'far greater than Meredith but less successful as a novelist'.[19] And the reason is that the characters have been

> required to contribute too much to the plot; except in their rustic humours, their vitality has been impoverished, they have gone thin and dry. This, as far as I can make out, is the flaw running through Hardy's novels: he has emphasised causality more strongly than his medium permits.[20]

Finally, Henry James.

> The beauty that suffuses the *Ambassadors* is the reward due to a fine artist for hard work. James knew exactly what he wanted. He pursued the narrow path of aesthetic duty, and success to the full extent of his possibilities has crowned him; ... But at what sacrifice? So enormous is the sacrifice that many readers can't get interested in James ... They can't grant his premise, which is that most of human life has to disappear before he can do us a novel. He has in the first place a very short list of characters ... In the second place, the characters, besides being few in number, are constructed on very stingy lines ... Maimed creatures can alone breathe in Henry James's pages – maimed yet specialised. They remind one of the exquisite deformities who haunted Egyptian art in the region of Akhnaton – huge heads and tiny legs but nevertheless charming. In the following reign they disappear.[21]

Now, if we look at these judgements and place beside them certain significant admissions and omissions, we shall see that though we cannot pin Mr Forster down to a theory or a creed, we are able to commit him to a point of view. He has in his mind's eye something – we hesitate to be more precise – which he calls 'life',[22] and it is to this that he brings the Egoist, Tess, or the Golden Bowl for comparison.[23] Meredith's social values are faked, he says; Hardy's people shrivel because their life has been sucked by philosophy. Henry James prefers a pattern to humanity. Always their failure is some failure in relation to life. This indeed is expressed with singular wit and insight. It is the humane as opposed to the aesthetic view. It maintains that the novel is 'sogged with humanity'; that 'human beings have their great chance in the novel';[24] it implies that it is the duty of a novel to be as life-like, to keep as close to life, to absorb as much of life as possible. It leads, as in the quotation given, to a notably harsh judgement of Henry James. For Henry James brought into the novel something besides human beings. He created patterns which, though beautiful in themselves, are hostile to humanity. And it is for his neglect of human life, says Mr Forster, that he will perish.

At this point perhaps the pertinacious pupil will demand 'but what is this "life" that keep on cropping up so mysteriously in books about fiction? Why is it absent in a pattern and present in a tea party? Why, if we get a keen and genuine pleasure from the pattern in the Golden Bowl, is it less valuable than the emotion which Trollope[25] gives us when he describes a lady drinking tea in a parsonage? Surely the definition of life is too arbitrary and requires to be expanded? Why, again, should the final test of plot, character, story and the other ingredients of a novel lie in their power to imitate life? Why should a real chair be better than an imaginary elephant?' To all of this, Mr Forster would reply presumably that he lays down no laws; he is merely telling us what moves him and what leaves him cold. There is no other criterion.

In short, we are back in the old bog; nobody knows anything, about the laws of fiction. We can only trust our instincts, and if instinct leads one reader to call Scott a story-teller and another to call him a master of romance; if one reader desires reality in a novel, and another is satisfied by something, which he calls proportion, each is right and each can pile a card house of theory on top of his opinion as high as he can go. But the assumption that fiction is more intimately and humbly attached to the service of human beings than the other arts leads to a further position which Mr Forster's book again illustrates. It is unnecessary to dwell upon fiction's aesthetic functions because they are so feeble that they can safely be ignored. Thus, though it is impossible to imagine a book on painting in which not a word should be said about the medium in which a painter works, a wise and brilliant book, like Mr Forster's, can be written about fiction without saying more than a sentence or two about the medium in which a novelist works. Almost nothing is said about words. One might suppose, unless one had read them, that a sentence means the same thing and is used for the same purposes by Sterne and by Wells. One might conclude that Tristram Shandy[26] gains nothing from the language in which it is written.

So with the other aesthetic qualities. Pattern, as we have seen, is recognised but severely censured for her tendency to obscure the human features. Beauty occurs, but she is suspect. She makes one furtive appearance – 'Beauty at which a novelist should never aim, though he fails if he does not achieve it'[27] – and the possibility that she may emerge again as rhythm is briefly discussed in a few interesting pages at the end. But for the rest, Fiction is treated as a parasite which draws her sustenance from life, and must, in gratitude, resemble life or perish. In poetry, in drama, words may excite and stimulate and deepen; but in fiction they must, first and foremost, hold themselves at the service of the teapot and a pug dog, and to be found wanting is to be found lacking.

Yet, strange though this unaesthetic attitude would be in the critic of any other art, it does not surprise us in the critic of fiction. For one thing, the problem is extremely difficult. A book fades like a mist, like a dream. How are we to take a stick and point to that tone, that relation, in the vanishing pages, as Mr Roger Fry[28] points with his wand at a line or a colour in the picture displayed before him? Moreover, a novel has roused a thousand ordinary human feelings in its progress. To drag in art in such a connection seems priggish and cold-hearted. It may well compromise the critic as a man of feeling and domestic ties. And so, while the painter and the musician and the poet come in for their share of criticism, the novelist escapes untouched. His character will be discussed; his morality will be examined; his attitude to life will be scrutinised, but his writing will go scot free. There is not a critic alive now who will say that a novel is a work of art and that as such as he will judge it.

And perhaps, as Mr Forster insinuates, the critics are right. In

England, at any rate, a novel is not a work of art. 'It is most distinctively one of the moister areas of literature, irrigated by a hundred rills and occasionally degenerating into a swamp.'[29] There are no English novels to stand beside *War and Peace*, the *Brothers Karamazov* and *A la Recherche du Temps Perdu*.[30] But while we accept the fact we cannot suppress one last conjecture. In France and Russia they take fiction seriously. Flaubert[31] will spend a month looking for a phrase to describe a cabbage; Tolstoy will write *War and Peace* seven times over. Something of their pre-eminence may be due to the pains they take and something to the severity with which they are judged. If the English critic were less domestic, less punctilious about the shades and grades of niceness and gentility, the novelist might be encouraged to be bolder. He might cut adrift from the eternal tea table and the plausible but preposterous formulas which are still supposed to represent life, love and other human adventures. But then the story might wobble; the plot might crumble; ruin might seize upon the characters. It might be necessary to enlarge our idea of the novel. Such are the dreams that Mr Forster leads us to cherish. For his is a book to encourage dreaming. None more suggestive has been written about the poor lady whom, with mistaken chivalry perhaps, we still persist in calling the art of fiction.

1–A signed review in the NYHT, 16 October 1927, (Kp C288) of *Aspects of the Novel* (Edward Arnold and Co., 1927) by E. M. Forster (1879–1970), a condensed version of which was published in the *N&A*, 12 November 1927 (see Appendix IV). 'And Quentin came, & the Keynes's came, & Morgan came,' VW noted in her diary on 20 September 1927. 'All of this I meant, perhaps, to describe: but then how hard I drive my pen through one article after another – Hemingway, Morgan, Shelley; & now Biography.' For Forster's reaction to VW's review, written on 13 November, see *II QB*, pp. 134–5; and for her response see *ibid.*, and *III VW Letters*, nos 1832 and 1835. VW's critical energies in the preceding months had been much absorbed by Forster: see 'The Novels of E. M. Forster' below, an essay written in fact before the present review. See also 'A Room with a View', *I VW Essays*; *VI VW Essays*, Appendix; and see Editorial Note, p. xxv. Reading Notes (Berg, xxv). Reprinted: *Mom, CE*.

2–Walter Raleigh, *The English Novel* (1883); Percy Lubbock, *The Craft of Fiction* (1921), for VW's more extended views on which see 'On Re-reading Novels', *III VW Essays*.

3–Forster's Clark Lectures were delivered in the spring of 1927 (under the auspices of Trinity College, Cambridge).

4–Forster, I 'Introductory', p. 22.

5–*Ibid.*, pp. 18–19, which has: '"I live under Queen Victoria, I under Anne, I carry

on the tradition of Trollope, I am reacting against Aldous Huxley." The fact . . .';
and which continues: '". . . act of creation", and when Professor Elton says, as he
does, that "after 1847 the novel of passion was never to be the same again," none
of them understand [sic] what he means.'

6 – Samuel Richardson (1689–1761); Henry James (1843–1916); H. G. Wells
(1866–1946); Charles Dickens (1812–70).

7 – Cf., Forster, I 'Introductory', p. 38: 'Principles and systems may suit other
forms of art, but they cannot be applicable here – or if applied their results must be
subjected to re-examination. And who is the re-examiner? Well, I am afraid it will
be the human heart . . . The final test of a novel will be our affection for it, as it is
the test of our friends, and of anything else which we cannot define.'

8 – For both quotations, *ibid.*, II 'The Story', p. 41, punctuation adapted.

9 – *Ibid.*, p. 47, punctuation adapted.

10 – Sir Walter Scott (1771–1832), *Waverley (1814)*, *Redgauntlet (1824)*, *The Bride
of Lammermoor* (1819).

11 – Robert Louis Stevenson (1850–94).

12 – Daniel Defoe (1660?–1731), for VW on whom see 'Defoe' in *CR 1* and 'Robinson Crusoe' above. Arnold Bennett (1867–1931), for VW on whom see 'Mr Bennett
and Mrs Brown' and 'Character in Fiction', *III VW Essays*. George Moore (1852–
1933), for VW on whom see 'George Moore' above.

13 – Forster, IV 'People', p. 99. For VW on Jane Austen (1775–1817), see 'Jane Austen' in *CR1* above.

14 – *Ibid.*, p. 99, punctuation adapted.

15 – *Ibid.*, VIII 'Pattern and Rhythm', p. 216.

16 – *Ibid.*, III 'People', p. 89, which begins a new paragraph at 'And that is why . . .'
and ends: 'the illusion of perspicacity and of power'. Daniel Defoe, *The Fortunes
and Misfortunes of the Famous Moll Flanders* (1722).

17 – George Meredith (1828–1909), for VW on whom see 'The Novels of George
Meredith' below. Thomas Hardy (1840–1928), for VW on whom see 'Thomas
Hardy's Novels' and 'Half of Thomas Hardy' below.

18 – Forster, V 'The Plot', pp. 120–1, which has 'they do not endure'; punctuation
adapted. Alfred, Lord Tennyson (1809–92).

19 – *Ibid.*, p. 125, which has: 'Meredith, and yet less successful'.

20 – *Ibid.*, p. 126, which has 'dry and thin'.

21 – *Ibid.*, VIII 'Pattern and Rhythm', pp. 204–6, which has: 'But at what sacrifice!'; 'cannot get interested' and 'cannot grant his premise'; punctuation adapted.
Henry James, *The Ambassadors* (1903).

22 – Cf., *ibid.*, II 'The Story', p. 44: 'So daily life, whatever it may be really, is practically composed of two lives – the life in time and the life by values – and our conduct reveals a double allegiance.' And, p. 45: 'And what the entire novel does – if it
is a good novel – is to include the life by values as well . . .'

23 – George Meredith, *The Egoist* (1879); Thomas Hardy, *Tess of the d'Urbervilles, A Pure Woman* (1891); Henry James, *The Golden Bowl* (1904), for VW on
which see 'Mr Henry James's Latest Novel', *I VW Essays*.

24 – For the first quotation, *ibid.*, I 'Introductory', p. 38; and for the second, VIII
'Pattern and Rhythm', p. 216.

25 – Anthony Trollope (1815–82).

26 – Laurence Sterne (1713–68), *The Life and Opinions of Tristram Shandy* (1759–

67), for VW on whom see 'Sterne', *I VW Essays*, and 'A Sentimental Journey', *CR* 2 and *V VW Essays*.

27–Forster, V 'The Plot', p. 119.

28–Roger Eliot Fry (1866–1934), whose most profound influence upon VW's aesthetic finds its expression in *To the Lighthouse* (the book she considered and regretted not dedicating to Fry) published in May of this year.

29–Forster, I 'Introductory', p. 14, punctuation adapted.

30–L. N. Tolstoy (1828–1910), *War and Peace* (1865–72); Fyodor Dostoevsky (1821–81), *The Brothers Karamazov* (1880). For VW on the Russians, see, for example, 'The Russian Point of View' in *CR 1* above. Marcel Proust, *À la recherche du temps perdu* (1913–27).

31–Gustave Flaubert (1821–80).

Not One of Us

Professor Peck does not apologise for writing a new life of Shelley, nor does he give any reason for doing what has been so thoroughly done already, nor are the new documents that have come into his hands of any great importance. And yet nobody is going to complain that here are two more thick, illustrated, careful and conscientious volumes devoted to the re-telling of a story which every one knows by heart. There are some stories which have to be retold by each generation, not that we have anything new to add to them, but because of some queer quality in them which makes them not only Shelley's story but our own. Eminent and durable they stand on the skyline, a mark past which we sail, which moves as we move and yet remains the same.

Many such changes of orientation toward Shelley have been recorded. In his own lifetime all except five people looked upon him, Shelley said, 'as a rare prodigy of crime and pollution, whose look even might infect'.[2] Sixty years later he was canonised by Edward Dowden. By Matthew Arnold he was again reduced to the ordinary human scale.[3] How many biographers and essayists have since absolved him or sentenced him, it is impossible to say. And now comes our turn to make up our minds what manner of man Shelley was; so that we read Professor Peck's volumes, not to find out new facts, but to get Shelley more sharply outlined against the shifting image of ourselves.

If such is our purpose, never was there a biographer who gave his readers more opportunity to fulfil it than Professor Peck. He is singularly dispassionate, and yet not colourless. He has opinions, but he does not obtrude them. His attitude to Shelley is kind but not condescending. He does not rhapsodise, but at the same time he does not scold. There are only two points which he seems to plead with any personal partiality; one, that Harriet was a much wronged woman;[4] the other, that the political importance of Shelley's poetry is not rated sufficiently high. Perhaps we could spare the careful analysis of so many poems. We scarcely need to know how many times mountains and precipices are mentioned in the course of Shelley's works. But as a chronicler of great learning and lucidity, Professor Peck is admirable. Here, he seems to say, is all that is actually known about Shelley's life. In October he did this; in November he did that; now it was that he wrote this poem; it was here that he met that friend. And, moulding the enormous mass of the Shelley papers with dexterous fingers, he contrives tactfully to embed dates and facts in feelings, in comments, in what Shelley wrote, in what Mary wrote,[5] in what other people wrote about them, so that we seem to be breasting the full current of Shelley's life and get the illusion that we are, this time, seeing Shelley, not through the rosy glasses or the livid glasses which sentiment and prudery have fixed on our forerunners' noses, but plainly, as he was. In this, of course, we are mistaken; glasses we wear, though we cannot see them. But the illusion of seeing Shelley plain[6] is sufficiently exhilarating to tempt us to try to fix it while it lasts.

There is an image of Shelley's personal appearance in everybody's picture gallery. He was a lean, large-boned boy, much freckled, with big, rather prominent blue eyes. His dress was careless, of course, but it was distinguished; 'he wore his clothes like a gentleman'.[7] He was courteous and gentle in manner, but he spoke in a shrill, harsh voice and soon rose to the heights of excitement. Nobody could overlook the presence of this discordant character in the room, and his presence was strangely disturbing. It was not merely that he might do something extreme, he might, somehow, make whoever was there appear absurd. From the earliest days normal people had noticed his abnormality and had done their best, following some obscure instinct of self-preservation, to make Shelley either toe the line, or else quit the society of the respectable. At Eton they called him 'mad Shelley'[8] and pelted him with muddy balls. At Oxford he spilt acid over his tutor's carpet, 'a new purchase, which he thus completely destroyed',[9] and for other and more serious differences of opinion he was expelled.

After that he became the champion of every down-trodden cause and person. Now it was an embankment; now a publisher; now the Irish nation; now three poor weavers condemned for treason; now a flock of neglected sheep. Spinsters of all sorts who were oppressed or aspiring found in him their leader. The first years of his youth thus were spent in dropping seditious pamphlets into old women's hoods; in shooting scabby sheep to put them out of their misery; in raising money; in writing pamphlets; in rowing out to sea and dropping bottles into the water which when broken open by the Town Clerk of Barnstable were found to contain a seditious paper, 'the contents of which the mayor has not yet been able to ascertain'.[10] In all these wanderings and peregrinations he was accompanied by a woman, or perhaps by two women, who either had young children at the breast, or were shortly expecting to become mothers. And one of them, it is said, could not contain her amusement when she saw the pamphlet dropped into the old woman's hood, but burst out laughing.

The picture is familiar enough; the only thing that changes is our attitude towards it. Shelley, excitable, uncompromising, atheistical, throwing his pamphlets into the sea in the belief that he is going to reform the world, has become a figure which is half-heroic and wholly delightful. On the other hand, the world that Shelley fought has become ridiculous. Somehow the untidy, shrill-voiced boy, with his violence and his oddity has succeeded in making Eton and Oxford, the English government, the Town Clerk and Mayor of Barnstable, the country gentlemen of Sussex and innumerable obscure people whom we might call generically, after Mary's censorious friends, the Booths and the Baxters[11] – Shelley has succeeded in making all these look absurd.

But, unfortunately, though one may make bodies and institutions look absurd, it is extremely difficult to make private men and women look anything so simple. Human relationships are too complex; human nature is too subtle. Thus contact with Shelley turned Harriet Westbrook, who should have been the happy mother of a commonplace family, into a muddled and bewildered woman, who wanted both to reform the world and yet to possess a coach and bonnets, and was finally drawn from the Serpentine on a winter's morning, drowned in her despair. And Mary and Miss Hitchener, and Godwin and Claire, and Hogg and Emilia Viviani, and Sophia Stacey and Jane Williams[12] – there is nothing tragic about them, perhaps; there is, indeed, much that is ridiculous. Still, their association with Shelley does not lead to any clear and triumphant conclusion. Was he right? Were they right? The whole relationship is muddy and obscure; it baffles; it teases.

One is reminded of the private life of another man whose power of conviction was even greater than Shelley's, and more destructive of normal human happiness. One remembers Tolstoy and his wife. The alliance of the intense belief of genius with the easy-going, non-belief or compromise of ordinary humanity must, it seems, lead to disaster and to disaster of a lingering and petty kind in which the worst side of both natures is revealed. But while Tolstoy might have wrought out his philosophy alone or in a monastery, Shelley was driven by something yielding and enthusiastic in his temperament to entangle himself with men and women. 'I think one is always in love with something or other,' he wrote.[13] But this 'something or other', besides lodging in poetry and metaphysics and the good of society in general, had its dwelling in the bodies of human beings of the opposite sex. He saw 'the likeness of what is perhaps eternal'[14] in the eyes of Mary. Then it vanished, to appear in the eyes of Emilia; then there it was again manifesting itself indisputably in Sophia Stacey or in Jane Williams. What is the lover to do when the will o' the wisp shifts its quarters? One must go on, said Shelley, until one is stopped. And what is to stop one? Not, if one is Shelley, the conventions and superstitions which bind the baser part of mankind; not the Booths and the Baxters. Oxford might expel him, England might exile him, but still, in spite of disaster and derision, he sought the 'likeness of what is perhaps eternal'; he went on being in love.

But as the object of his love was a hybrid creature, half-human, half-divine, so the manner of his love partook of the same ambiguous nature. There was something inhuman about Shelley. Godwin, in answer to Shelley's first letter, noticed it. He complained of the 'generalising character' of Shelley's style, which, he said, had the effect of making him 'not an individual character' to him.[15] Mary Shelley, musing over her life when Shelley was dead, exclaimed, 'What a strange life mine has been. Love, youth, fear and fearlessness led me early from the regular routine of life and I united myself to this being who, not one of *us*, though like us, was pursued by numberless miseries and annoyances, in all of which I shared.'[16] Shelley was 'not one of *us*'. He was, even to his wife, 'a being', someone who came and went like a ghost, seeking the eternal. Of the transitory, he had little notion. The joys and sorrows from whose threads are woven the warm cocoon of private life in which most men live, had no hold upon him. A strange formality stiffens his letters; there is no intimacy in them and no fun.

At the same time it is perfectly true, and Professor Peck does well to emphasise the fact, that Shelley loved humanity if he did not love this Harriet or that Mary. A sense of the wretchedness of human beings burnt in him as brightly and as persistently as his sense of the divine beauty of Nature. He loved the clouds and the mountains and the rivers more passionately than any other man loved them; but at the foot of the mountain he always saw a ruined cottage; there were criminals in chains, hoeing up the weeds in the pavement of St Peter's Square; there was an old woman shaking with ague on the banks of the lovely Thames. Then he would thrust aside his writing, dismiss his dreams and trudge off to physic the poor with medicine or with soup. Inevitably there collected around him, as time went on, the oddest assortment of pensioners and protégés. He took on himself the charge of deserted women and other people's children; he paid other persons' debts and planned their journeys and settled their relationships. The most ethereal of poets was the most practical of men.

Hence, says Professor Peck, from this union of poetry and humanity springs the true value of Shelley's poetry. It was the poetry of a man who was not a 'pure poet',[17] but a poet with a passion for reforming the wrongs of men. Had he lived, he would have reconciled poetry and the statement of 'the necessity of certain immediate reforms in politics, society and government'.[18] He died too young to be able to deliver his message; and the difficulty of his poetry arises from the fact that the conflict between poetry and politics rages there unresolved. We may not agree with Professor Peck's definition, yet we have only to read Shelley again to come up against the difficulty of which he speaks. It lies partly in the disconcerting fact that we had thought his poetry so good and we find it indeed so poor. How are we to account for the fact that we remember him as a great poet and find him on opening his pages a bad one? The explanation seems to be that he was not a 'pure poet'. He did not concentrate his meaning in a small space; there is nothing in Shelley's poetry as rich and compact as the odes of Keats.[19] His taste could be sentimental; he had all the vices of the album makers; he was unreal, strained, verbose. The lines which Professor Peck quotes with admiration: 'Good night? No, love! The night is ill,'[20] seems to us a proof of it. But if we pass from the lyrics, with all their exquisite beauty, and read ourselves into one of the longer poems, *Epipsychidion* or *Prometheus Unbound*,[21] where the faults have space to lose themselves, we again become convinced of his greatness. And here again we are confronted by a difficulty. For if we were asked to extract the teaching from these poems we should be at a loss. We can hardly say what reform in 'politics, society and government' they advocate. Their greatness seems to lie in nothing so definite as a philosophy, in nothing so pure as perfection of expression. It lies rather in a state of being. We come through skeins of clouds and gusts of whirlwind out into a space of pure calm, of intense and windless serenity. Defensibly or not, we make a distinction – 'The Skylark', the 'Ode to the West Wind' are poems,[22] – the *Prometheus*, the *Epipsychidion* are poetry.

So if we outline our relationship to Shelley from the vantage ground of 1927 we shall find that his England is a barbarous place where they imprison journalists for being disrespectful to the Prince Regent, stand men in stocks for publishing attacks upon the Scriptures, execute weavers upon the suspicion of treason, and, without giving proof of strict religious belief themselves, expel a boy from Oxford for avowing his atheism.[23] Politically, then, Shelley's England has already receded, and his fight, valiant though it is, seems to be with monsters who are a little out of date, and therefore slightly ridiculous. But privately he is much closer to us. For alongside the public battle wages, from generation to generation, another fight which is as important as the other, though much less is said about it. Husband fights with wife and son with father. The poor fight the rich and the employer fights the employed. There is a perpetual effort on the one hand to make all these relationships more reasonable, less painful and less servile; on the other, to keep them as they are. Shelley, both as son and as husband, fought for reason and freedom in private life, and his experiments, disastrous as they were in many ways, have helped us to greater sincerity and happiness in our own conflicts. The Sir Timothys of Sussex[24] are no longer so prompt to cut their sons off with a shilling; the Booths and the Baxters are no longer quite so sure that an unmarried wife is an unmitigated demon. The grasp of convention upon private life is no longer quite so coarse or quite so callous because of Shelley's successes and failures.

So we see Shelley through our particular pair of spectacles – a shrill, charming, angular boy; a champion riding out against the forces of superstition and brutality with heroic courage; at the same time blind, inconsiderate, obtuse to other persons' feelings. Rapt in his extraordinary vision, ascending to the very heights of existence, he seems, as Mary said, 'a being', 'not one of us', but better and higher and aloof and apart. Suddenly there comes a knock at the door; the Hunts and seven children are at Leghorn; Lord Byron has been rude to them; Hunt is cut to the heart.[25] Shelley must be off at once to see that they are comfortable. And, rousing himself from his rapture, Shelley goes.

1–A signed review in the *NYHT*, 23 October 1927, (Kp C289) of *Shelley* [1792–1822] *His Life and Work* (2 vols, Ernest Benn Ltd, 1927) by Walter Edwin Peck. 'I am so bothered with these articles,' VW wrote to Harold Nicolson, 13 September 1927, 'that I dont think its worth it, even for the money. One polishes off Hemingway and without a second's pause plunges into Shelley ...' (*III VW Letters*, no. 1811). A week later in her diary we find her still detained by the *NYHT*: 'And Quentin came, & the Keynes's came, & Morgan came. All of this I meant, perhaps, to describe: but then how hard I drive my pen through one article after another – Hemingway, Morgan, Shelley; & now Biography.' See also her diary entry for 25 September: 'On the opposite page I wrote notes for Shelley, I think by mistake for my writing book.' See also 'Shelley and Elizabeth Hitchener', *I VW Essays*. Reading Notes (Berg, Diary xv, reproduced in *III VW Diary*, p. 158, no. 12; also Berg, xxv). Reprinted: *DoM, CE*.

2–Peck, vol. ii, ch. xv, p. 120, quoting Shelley writing to Thomas Love Peacock, 6 April 1819.

3–Edward Dowden, *The Life of Percy Bysshe Shelley* (2 vols, Kegan Paul, 1886). Matthew Arnold, *Essays in Criticism. Second Series* (Macmillan & Co., 1888), 'Byron', wherein is passed a famous judgement: 'Shelley, beautiful and ineffectual angel, beating in the void his luminous wings in vain' (p. 203).

4–Harriet, *née* Westbrook, who married Shelley in 1811 and bore him a son, and who, in 1816, abandoned and again pregnant, committed suicide by drowning in the Serpentine.

5–Mary, *née* Wollstonecraft Godwin (1797–1851) married Shelley as his second wife, in 1816, and wrote the gothic classic *Frankenstein, or the Modern Prometheus* (1818).

6–Robert Browning, 'Memorabilia': 'Ah, did you once see Shelley plain' (in *Men and Women*, 1855).

7–Cf. Dowden, vol. i, ch. ii, p. 83: 'He always dressed "like a gentleman", says Hogg, "handsomely indeed".'

8–*Ibid.*, vol. i, ch. i, p. 23: 'Singly they dared not attack "Mad Shelley"; there still was in him something dangerous which their wisdom feared ...'

9–Peck, vol. i, ch. iv (continued), p. 107, quoting an account by Elizabeth Grant:

'He began his career by every kind of wild prank at Eton [sic], and when remonstrated with by his tutor, repaid the well-meant private admonition by spilling an acid over the carpet of that gentleman's study, a new purchase, which he thus completely destroyed. He did no deed so mischievous at University, but...'

10–*Ibid.*, ch. vii (continued), p. 271, quoting a letter from Henry Drake, town clerk of Barnstaple, to Lord Sidmouth.

11–I.e. Isabel (who became Mrs David Booth) and Christy, daughters of William Baxter of Dundee, whose relations with Shelley, severed abruptly by Baxter, are explored in Shelley's poem *Rosalind and Helen* (1819).

12–Elizabeth Hitchener, schoolmistress, object of Shelley's precipitate admiration and, equally precipitate, his extreme aversion, 1811–12. William Godwin (1756–1836), Shelley's father-in-law. Clara Mary Jane (Claire) Clairmont (1798–1879), Godwin's daughter by his second wife. Thomas Jefferson Hogg (1792–1862), friend and biographer of Shelley. (Teresa) Emilia Viviani, daughter of an Italian count, was consigned to a convent by the machinations of her stepmother; her plight provided the inspiration for Shelley's *Epipsychidion* (1821). Sophia Stacey, a ward of Shelley's uncle-by-marriage Robert Parker. Jane Williams, wife of Edward Ellerker Williams, the friend who drowned with Shelley in the bay of Spezzia.

13–Peck, vol. ii, ch. xiv, p. 76, quoting a letter written by Shelley 'within a month of his death' (recipient unidentified), which continues: '; the error, and I confess it is not easy for spirits cased in flesh and blood to avoid it, consists in seeking in a mortal image the likeness of what is perhaps eternal.'

14–See previous note.

15–For both quotations, Peck, vol. i, ch. vi, p. 209.

16–From 'Mrs Shelley's Private Journal', 7 October 1822, in *Shelley Memorials*, ed. Lady [Jane] Shelley (Smith, Elder, 1859), p. 234, punctuation adapted, and which has: 'in all which I shared'.

17–Adapted from Peck, vol. ii, ch. xv, pp. 116–17.

18–*Ibid.*, p. 117.

19–John Keats (1795–1821).

20–Peck, vol. ii, ch. xv, pp. 162–3.

21–*Epipsychidion* (1821); *Prometheus Unbound* (1820).

22–'To a Skylark' (1821), 'Ode to the West Wind' (1819).

23–Leigh Hunt (1784–1859) was fined and imprisoned for certain reflections on the Prince Regent, published in his paper the *Examiner*. Shelley was sent down from (University College) Oxford in 1811, for circulating his pamphlet on 'The Necessity of Atheism'.

24–Timothy Shelley, the poet's father, succeeded *his* father, Sir Bysshe, as baronet in 1815.

25–Leigh Hunt, his wife Marianne and their seven children arrived at Leghorn from England on 1 July 1822 (just a week before Shelley's death) and removed to Pisa to stay with Lord Byron (1788–1824).

The New Biography

'The aim of biography,' said Sir Sidney Lee, who had perhaps read and written more lives than any man of his time, 'is the truthful transmission of personality,'[2] and no single sentence could more neatly split up into two parts the whole problem of biography as it presents itself to us today. On the one hand there is truth; on the other, there is personality. And if we think of truth as something of granite-like solidity and of personality as something of rainbow-like intangibility and reflect that the aim of biography is to weld these two into one seamless whole, we shall admit that the problem is a stiff one and that we need not wonder if biographers have for the most part failed to solve it.

For the truth of which Sir Sidney speaks, the truth which biography demands, is truth in its hardest, most obdurate form; it is truth as truth is to be found in the British Museum; it is truth out of which all vapour of falsehood has been pressed by the weight of research. Only when truth had been thus established did Sir Sidney Lee use it in the building of his monument; and no one can be so foolish as to deny that the piles he raised of such hard facts, whether one is called Shakespeare or another King Edward the Seventh,[3] are worthy of all our respect. For there is a virtue in truth; it has an almost mystic power. Like radium, it seems able to give off for ever and ever grains of energy, atoms of light. It stimulates the mind, which is endowed with a curious susceptibility in this direction as no fiction, however artful or highly coloured can stimulate it. Truth being thus efficacious and supreme, we can only explain the fact that Sir Sidney's life of Shakespeare is dull, and that his life of Edward the Seventh is unreadable, by supposing that though both are stuffed with truth, he failed to choose those truths which transmit personality. For in order that the light of personality may shine through, facts must be manipulated; some must be brightened; others shaded: yet, in the process, they must never lose their integrity. And it is obvious that it is easier to obey these precepts by considering that the true life of your subject shows itself in action which is evident rather than in that inner life of thought and emotion which meanders darkly and obscurely through the hidden channels of the soul. Hence, in the old days, the biographer chose the easier path. A life, even when it was lived by a divine, was a series of exploits. The biographer, whether he was Izaak Walton or Mrs Hutchinson[4] or that unknown writer who is often so surprisingly eloquent on tombstones and memorial tablets, told a tale of battle and victory. With their stately phrasing and their deliberate, artistic purpose, such records transmit personality with a formal sincerity which is perfectly satisfactory of its kind. And so, perhaps, biography might have pursued its way, draping the robes decorously over the recumbent figures of the dead, had there not arisen toward the end of the eighteenth century one of those curious men of genius who seem able to break up the stiffness into which the company has fallen by speaking in his natural voice. So Boswell spoke. So we hear booming out from Boswell's page the voice of Samuel Johnson. 'No, sir; stark insensibility,'[5] we hear him say. Once we have heard those words we are aware that there is an incalculable presence among us which will go on ringing and reverberating in widening circles however times may change and ourselves. All the draperies and decencies of biography fall to the ground. We can no longer maintain that life consists in actions only or in works. It consists in personality. Something has been liberated beside which all else seems cold and colourless. We are freed from a servitude which is now seen to be intolerable. No longer need we pass solemnly and stiffly from camp to council chamber. We may sit, even with the great and good, over the table and talk.

Through the influence of Boswell, presumably, biography all through the nineteenth century concerned itself as much with the lives of the sedentary as with the lives of the active. It sought painstakingly and devotedly to express not only the outer life of work and activity but the inner life of emotion and thought. The uneventful lives of poets and painters were written out as lengthily as the lives of soldiers and statesmen. But the Victorian biography was a parti-coloured, hybrid, monstrous birth. For though truth of fact was observed as scrupulously as Boswell observed it, the personality which Boswell's genius set free was hampered and distorted. The convention which Boswell had destroyed settled again, only in a different form, upon biographers who lacked his art. Where the Mrs Hutchinsons and the Izaak Waltons had wished to prove that their heroes were prodigies of courage and learning the Victorian biographer was dominated by the idea of goodness. Noble, upright, chaste, severe; it is thus that the Victorian worthies are presented to us. The figure is almost always above life size in top hat and frock coat, and the manner of presentation becomes increasingly clumsy and laborious. For lives which no longer express themselves in action take shape in innumerable words. The conscientious biographer may not tell a fine tale with a flourish, but must toil through endless labyrinths and embarrass himself with countless documents. In the end he produces an amorphous mass, a life of Tennyson or of Gladstone,[6] in which we go seeking disconsolately for voice or laughter, for curse or anger, for any trace that this fossil was once a living man. Often, indeed, we bring back some invaluable trophy, for Victorian biographies are laden with truth; but always we rummage among them with a sense of the prodigious waste, of the artistic wrong headedness of such a method.

With the twentieth century, however, a change came over biography, as it came over fiction and poetry. The first and most visible sign of it was in the difference of size. In the first twenty years of the new century biographies must have lost half their weight. Mr Strachey compressed four stout Victorians into one slim volume; M. Maurois boiled the usual two volumes of a Shelley life into one little book the size of a novel.[7] But the diminution of size was only the outward token of an inward change. The point of view had completely altered. If we open one of the new school of biographies its bareness, its emptiness makes us at once aware that the author's relation to his subject is different. He is no longer the serious and sympathetic companion, toiling even slavishly in the footsteps of his hero. Whether friend or enemy, admiring or critical, he is an equal. In any case, he preserves his freedom and his right to independent judgement. Moreover, he does not think himself constrained to follow every step of the way. Raised upon a little eminence which his independence has made for him, he sees his subject spread about him. He chooses; he synthesises; in short, he has ceased to be the chronicler; he has become an artist.

Few books illustrate the new attitude to biography better than *Some People*, by Harold Nicolson. In his biographies of Tennyson and of Byron[8] Mr Nicolson followed the path which had been already trodden by Mr Strachey and others. Here he has taken a step on his own initiative. For here he has devised a method of writing about people and about himself as though they were at once real and imaginary. He has succeeded remarkably, if not entirely, in making the best of both worlds. *Some People* is not fiction because it has the substance, the reality of truth. It is not biography because it has the freedom, the artistry of fiction. And if we try to discover how he has won the liberty which enables him to present us with these extremely amusing pages we must in the first place credit him with having had the courage to rid himself of a mountain of illusion. An English diplomat is offered all the bribes which usually induce people to swallow humbug in large doses with composure. If Mr Nicolson wrote about Lord Curzon[9] it should have been solemnly. If he mentioned the Foreign Office it should have been respectfully. His tone toward the world of the Bognors and Whitehall should have been friendly but devout. But thanks to a number of influences and people, among whom one might mention Max Beerbohm and Voltaire,[10] the attitude of the bribed and docile official has been blown to atoms. Mr Nicolson laughs. He laughs at Lord Curzon; he laughs at the Foreign Office; he laughs at himself. And since his laughter is the laughter of the intelligence it has the effect of making us take the people he laughs at seriously. The figure of Lord Curzon concealed behind the figure of a drunken valet is touched off with merriment and irreverence; yet of all the studies of Lord Curzon which have been written since his death none makes us think more kindly of that preposterous but, it appears, extremely human man.

So it would seem as if one of the great distinctions, one of the great advantages, of the new school to which Mr Nicolson belongs is the lack of pose, humbug, solemnity. They approach their bigwigs fearlessly. They have no fixed scheme of the universe, no standard of courage or morality to which they insist that he shall conform. The man himself is the supreme object of their curiosity. Further, and it is this chiefly which has so reduced the bulk of biography, they maintain that the man himself, the pith and essence of his character, shows itself to the observant eye in the tone of a voice, the turn of a head, some little phrase or anecdote picked up in passage. Thus in two subtle phrases, in one passage of brilliant description, whole chapters of the Victorian volume are synthesised and summed up. *Some People* is full of examples of this new phase of the biographer's art. Mr Nicolson wants to describe a governess and he tells us that she had a drop at the end of her nose and made him salute the quarterdeck. He wants to describe Lord Curzon, and he makes him lose his trousers and recite 'Tears, Idle Tears'.[11] He does not cumber himself with a single fact about them. He waits till they have said or done something characteristic, and then he pounces on it with glee. But, though he waits with an intention of pouncing which might well make his victims uneasy if they guessed it, he lays suspicion by appearing himself in his own proper person in no flattering light. He has a scrubby dinner jacket, he tells us; a pink bumptious face, curly hair and a curly nose. He is as much the subject of his own irony and observation as they are. He lies in wait for his own absurdities as artfully as for theirs. Indeed, by the end of the book we realise that the figure which has been most completely and most subtly displayed is that of the author. Each of the supposed subjects holds up in his or her small bright diminishing mirror a different reflection of Harold Nicolson. And though the figure thus revealed is not noble or impressive or shown in an heroic attitude, it is for these very reasons extremely like a real human being. It is thus, he would seem to say, in the mirrors of our friends that we chiefly live.

To have contrived this effect is a triumph not of skill only, but of those positive qualities which we are likely to treat as if they were negative – freedom from pose, from sentimentality, from illusion. And the victory is definite enough to leave us asking what territory it has won for the art of biography. Mr Nicolson has proved that one can use many of the devices of fiction in dealing with real life. He has shown that a little fiction mixed with fact can be made to transmit personality very effectively. But some objections or qualifications suggest themselves. Undoubtedly the figures in *Some People* are all rather below life size. The irony with which they are treated, though it has its tenderness, stunts their growth. It dreads nothing more than that one of these little beings should grow up and become serious or perhaps tragic. And, again, they never occupy the stage for more than a few brief moments. They do not want to be looked at very closely. They have not a great deal to show us. Mr Nicolson makes us feel, in short, that he is playing with very dangerous elements. An incautious movement and the book will be blown sky high. He is trying to mix the truth of real life and the truth of fiction. He can only do it by using no more than a pinch of either. For though both truths are genuine, they are antagonistic; let them meet and they destroy each other. Even here, where the imagination is not deeply engaged, when we find people whom we know to be real like Lord Oxford or Lady Colefax, mingling with Miss Plimsoll and Marstock,[12] whose reality we doubt, the one casts suspicion upon the other. Let it be fact, one feels, or let it be fiction; the imagination will not serve under two masters simultaneously.

And here we again approach the difficulty which, for all his ingenuity, the biographer still has to face. Truth of fact and truth of fiction are incompatible; yet he is now more than ever urged to combine them. For it would seem that the life which is increasingly real to us is the fictitious life; it dwells in the personality rather than in the act. Each of us is more Hamlet, Prince of Denmark, than he is John Smith, of the Corn Exchange. Thus, the biographer's imagination is always being stimulated to use the novelist's art of arrangement, suggestion, dramatic effect to expound the private life. Yet if he carries the use of fiction too far, so that he disregards the truth, or can only introduce it with incongruity, he loses both worlds; he has neither the freedom of fiction nor the substance of fact. Boswell's astonishing power over us is based largely upon his obstinate veracity, so that we have implicit belief in what he tells us. When Johnson says 'No, sir; stark insensibility,' the voice has a ring in it because we have been told, soberly and prosaically, a few pages earlier, that Johnson 'was entered a Commoner of Pembroke, on the 31st of October, 1728, being then in his nineteenth year'.[13] We are in the world of brick and pavement; of birth, marriage and death; of Acts of Parliament; of Pitt and Burke and Sir Joshua Reynolds.[14] Whether this is a more real world than the world of Bohemia and Hamlet and Macbeth we doubt, but the mixture of the two is abhorrent.

Be that as it may we can assure ourselves by a very simple experiment that the days of Victorian biography are over. Consider one's own life; pass under review a few years that one has actually lived. Conceive how Lord Morley would have expounded them; how Sir Sidney Lee would have documented them; how strangely all that has been most real in them would have slipped through their fingers. Nor can we name the biographer whose art is subtle and bold enough to present that queer amalgamation of dream and reality, that perpetual marriage of granite and rainbow. His method still remains to be discovered. But Mr Nicolson with his mixture of biography and autobiography, of fact and fiction, of Lord Curzon's trousers and Miss Plimsoll's nose, waves his hand airily in a possible direction.[15]

1–A signed review in the *NYHT*, 30 October 1927, (Kp C290) of *Some People*

(Constable, 1927) by Harold Nicolson (1886–1968), diplomatist, husband of Vita Sackville-West. 'It was more than angelic of you to send me an early copy of your book,' VW wrote to Nicolson on 15 June 1927 (*III VW Letters*, no. 1775): 'It is now half past ten: Leonard is saying we must go to bed; but I must scribble a line in haste to say how absolutely delightful I think it – how I laughed out loud to myself again and again. Yet at the same time it is rather serious – I can't make out how you combine the advantages of fact and fiction as you do. I am also jealous – I cant help it – that all these things should have happened to you, not to me. And also, for some reason I feel profoundly and mysteriously shy. What this arises from I have not yet discovered: some horror of the past no doubt: but I think it is a great tribute to a book when it makes one fumble in ones own inside. I was so glad to find poor dear Bloomsbury playing its games in its corner – Sibyl Colefax popping in for one moment. You must write another, and for goodness sake, send them to the Wolves.' Again, on 13 September (*ibid.*, no. 1811), she wrote: 'Yes, the flattery was delicious, exquisite, charming and certainly would have been effective, had I not already written to the Tribune and said I would do your book: But I'm rather nervous. You say its out on *Sept* 16th: you dont mean October, I suppose? If it is Sept: I am afraid they may have done it already. However they are proving so incompetent, that I'm taking the law into my own hands, and will do it unless they positively forbid. I'm afraid though that I shall have to mush you up with Harriet Martineau and some general reflections, as it is to be a general review, a commentary or whatever they call it. I am so bothered with these articles that I dont think its worth it, even for the money. One polishes off Hemingway and without a second's pause plunges into Shelley: and I find it difficult to get up indignation about Harriet, or even to care whether she spells her name with two ts. Anyhow, – this is genuine, because I'm not, at the moment, asking you for anything, though no doubt I soon shall – I shall be very happy to write about a real book, (I mean *Some People*) instead of these Stuffed Americans.' See also *III VW Diary*, 20 September 1927; and see *Orlando* (1928), *passim*. Reading Notes (Berg, XIV). Reprinted: *G&R, CE*.

2 – Sidney Lee, *Principles of Biography* (CUP, 1911), ch. iv, pp. 25–6, which has: 'The aim of biography is not the moral edification which may flow from the survey of either vice or virtue; it is the truthful transmission of personality.' Sir Sidney Lee (1859–1926) had succeeded Sir Leslie Stephen as editor of the *DNB* in 1891.

3 – Lee, *A Life of William Shakespeare* (1899), *King Edward VII* (1925, 1927).

4 – Izaak Walton (1593–1683), biographer of among others John Donne, Sir Henry Wotton and George Herbert. Lucy Hutchinson (b. 1620) whose *The Memoirs of the Life of Colonel Hutchinson* was published in 1806.

5 – James Boswell, *The Life of Samuel Johnson Ll.D.* (1791; ed. R. W. Chapman, OUP, 1980), p. 45: 'Aetat. 19 ... Thursday, 31 October 1728': '"I had no notion that I was wrong or irreverent to my tutor." BOSWELL: "That, Sir, was great fortitude of mind." JOHNSON: "No, Sir; stark insensibility."'

6 – Hallam Tennyson, *Life of Alfred Tennyson* (2 vols, 1897); John Morley, *Life of Gladstone* (3 vols, 1903).

7 – Lytton Strachey, *Eminent Victorians* (1918); André Maurois, *Ariel* (1923).

8 – Nicolson, *Tennyson: Aspects* (1923), *Byron. The Last Journey* (1924).

9 – George Nathaniel Curzon, Marquess Curzon of Kedleston (1859–1925), as foreign secretary, 1919–24, presided influentially over the Lausanne Conference, 1922–3. Nicolson was to write about him further in *Curzon, the Last Phase* (1934).

10–Max Beerbohm (1872–1956); Voltaire (François Marie Aronet, 1694–1778).

11–For Lord Curzon's trousers and his recitation of Tennyson's poem, Nicolson, 'Artekall', pp. 212–13.

12–For H. H. Asquith (Lord Oxford, 1852–1928), Liberal prime minister, 1908–16, see Nicolson, 'Professor Malone', p. 172; and for the society hostess Lady Sibyl Colefax (d. 1950), see 'Miriam Codd', p. 220.

13–Boswell, 'Aetat. 19 . . . Thursday, 31 October 1728', p. 45.

14–William Pitt, 1st Earl of Chatham (1708–78). Edmund Burke (1729–97) and Sir Joshua Reynolds (1723–92) were both original members of Johnson's literary 'Club'.

15–'Granite and rainbow' and 'trousers' (albeit appropriated by the constabulary) make an interesting occurrence in *Orlando* (1928) – in the 'Preface' to which Nicolson is acknowledged (see, Penguin 1975, pp. 54–5): 'Nature, who has played so many queer tricks upon us, making us so unequally of clay and diamonds, of rainbow and granite, and stuffed them into a case, often of the most incongruous, for the poet has a butcher's face and the butcher a poet's; nature who delights in muddle and mystery, so that even now (1 November 1927) we know not why we go upstairs, or why we come down again . . . nature, who has so much to answer for besides the perhaps unwieldy length of this sentence, has further complicated her task and added to our confusion by providing not only a perfect ragbag of odds and ends within us – a piece of policeman's trousers lying cheek by jowl with Queen Alexandra's wedding veil – but has contrived that the whole assortment shall be lightly stitched together by a single thread.'

Street Haunting: A London Adventure

No one perhaps has ever felt passionately towards a lead pencil. But there are circumstances in which it can become supremely desirable to possess one; moments when we are set upon having an object, a purpose, an excuse for walking half across London between tea and dinner. As the foxhunter hunts in order to preserve the breed of horses, and the golfer plays in order that open spaces may be preserved from the builders, so when the desire comes upon us to go street rambling the pencil does for a pretext, and getting up we say, 'Really I must buy a pencil,' as if under cover of this excuse we could indulge safely in the greatest pleasure of town life in winter – rambling the streets of London.

The hour should be evening and the season winter, for in winter the champagne brightness of the air and the sociability of the streets are grateful. We are not then taunted as in summer by the longing for shade and solitude and sweet airs from the hayfields. The evening hour, too, gives us the irresponsibility which darkness and lamplight bestow. We are no longer quite ourselves. As we step out of the house on a fine evening between four and six we shed the self our friends know us by and become part of that vast republican army of anonymous trampers, whose society is so agreeable after the solitude of one's own room. For there we sit surrounded by objects which perpetually express the oddity of our own temperaments and enforce the memories of our own experience. That bowl on the mantelpiece, for instance, was bought at Mantua on a windy day. We were leaving the shop when the sinister old woman plucked at our skirts and said she would find herself starving one of these days, but 'Take it!' she cried, and thrust the blue and white china bowl into our hands as if she never wanted to be reminded of her quixotic generosity. So, guiltily, but suspecting nevertheless how badly we had been fleeced, we carried it back to the little hotel where, in the middle of the night, the innkeeper quarrelled so violently with his wife that we all leant out into the courtyard to look, and saw the vines laced about among the pillars and the stars white in the sky. The moment was stabilised, stamped like a coin indelibly, among a million that slipped by imperceptibly. There, too, was the melancholy Englishman, who rose among the coffee cups and the little iron tables and revealed the secrets of his soul – as travellers do. All this – Italy, the windy morning, the vines laced about the pillars, the Englishman and the secrets of his soul – rise up in a cloud from the china bowl on the mantelpiece. And there, as our eyes fall to the floor, is that brown stamp on the carpet. Mr Lloyd George made that. 'The man's a devil!' said Mr Cummings, putting the kettle down with which he was about to fill the teapot so that it burnt a brown ring on the carpet.

But when the door shuts on us, all that vanishes. The shell-like covering which our souls have excreted to house themselves, to make for themselves a shape distinct from others, is broken, and there is left of all these wrinkles and roughness a central oyster of perceptiveness, an enormous eye. How beautiful a street is in winter! It is at once revealed and obscured. Here vaguely one can trace symmetrical straight avenues of doors and windows; here under the lamps are floating islands of pale light through which pass quickly bright men and women, who for all their poverty and shabbiness wear a certain look of unreality, an air of triumph, as if they had given life the slip, so that life, deceived of her prey, blunders on without them. But, after all, we are only gliding smoothly on the surface. The eye is not a miner, not a diver, not a seeker after buried treasure. It floats us smoothly down a stream, resting, pausing, the brain sleeps perhaps as it looks.

How beautiful a London street is then, with its islands of light, and its long groves of darkness, and on one side of it perhaps some tree-sprinkled, grass-grown space where night is folding herself to sleep naturally and, as one passes the iron railing, one hears those little cracklings and stirrings of leaf and twig which seem to suppose the silence of fields all round them, an owl hooting, and far away the rattle of a train in the valley. But this is London, we are reminded; high among the bare trees are hung oblong frames of reddish yellow light — windows; there are points of brilliance burning steady like low stars — lamps; this empty ground which holds the country in it and its peace is only a London square, set about by offices and houses where at this hour fierce lights burn over maps, over documents, over desks where clerks sit turning with wetted forefingers the files of endless correspondences; or more suffusedly the firelight wavers and the lamplight falls upon the privacy of some drawing-room, its easy chairs, its papers, its china, its inlaid table, and the figure of a woman, accurately measuring out the precise number of spoons of tea which — She looks at the door as if she heard a ring downstairs and somebody asking, is she in?

But here we must stop peremptorily. We are in danger of digging deeper than the eye approves; we are impeding our passage down the smooth stream by catching at some branch or root. At any moment, the sleeping army may stir itself and wake in us a thousand violins and trumpets in response; the army of human beings may rouse itself and assert all its oddities and sufferings and sordidities. Let us dally a little longer, be content still with surfaces only — the glossy brilliance of the motor omnibuses; the carnal splendour of the butchers' shops with their yellow flanks and their purple steaks; the blue and red bunches of flowers burning so bravely through the plate glass of the florists' windows.

For the eye has this strange property: it rests only on beauty; like a butterfly it seeks out colour and basks in warmth. On a winter's night like this, when Nature has been at pains to polish and preen itself, it brings back the prettiest trophies, breaks off little lumps of emerald and coral as if the whole earth were made of precious

stone. The thing it cannot do (one is speaking of the average unprofessional eye) is to compose these trophies in such a way as to
bring out their more obscure angles and relationships. Hence after a
prolonged diet of this simple, sugary fare, of beauty pure and un-
composed, we become conscious of satiety. We halt at the door of
the boot shop and make some little excuse, which has nothing to do
with the real reason for folding up the bright paraphernalia of the
streets and withdrawing to some duskier chamber of the being
where we may ask, as we raise our left foot obediently upon the
stand, 'What, then, is it like to be a dwarf?'

She came in escorted by two women who, being of normal size,
looked like benevolent giants beside her. Smiling at the shop girls,
they seemed to be at once disclaiming any lot in her deformity and
assuring her of their protection. She wore the peevish yet apologetic
expression usual on the faces of the deformed. She needed their
kindness, yet she resented it. But when the shop girl has been summoned and the giantesses, smiling indulgently, had asked for shoes
for 'this lady' and the girl had pushed the little stand in front of her,
the dwarf stuck her foot out with an impetuosity which seemed to
claim all our attention. Look at that! Look at that! she seemed to
demand of us all, as she thrust her foot out, for behold it was the
shapely, perfectly proportioned foot of a well-grown woman. It was
arched; it was aristocratic. Her whole manner changed as she
looked at it resting on the stand. She looked soothed and satisfied.
Her manner became full of self-confidence. She sent for shoe after
shoe; she tried on pair after pair. She got up and pirouetted before a
glass which reflected the foot only in yellow shoes, in fawn shoes, in
shoes of lizard skin. She raised her little skirts and displayed her
little legs. She was thinking that, after all, feet are the most important part of the whole person; women, she said to herself, have been
loved for their feet alone. Seeing nothing but her feet, she imagined
perhaps that the rest of her body was of a piece with those beautiful
feet. She was shabbily dressed, but she was ready to lavish any
money upon her shoes. And as this was the only occasion upon
which she was not afraid of being looked at but positively craved
attention, she was ready to use any device to prolong the choosing
and fitting. Look at my feet, look at my feet, she seemed to be saying, as she took a step this way and then a step that way. The shop
girl good-humouredly must have said something flattering, for suddenly her face lit up in an ecstasy. But, after all, the giantesses, benevolent though they were, had their own affairs to see to; she must

make up her mind; she must decide which to choose. At length, the pair was chosen and, as she walked out between her guardians, with the parcel swinging from her finger, the ecstasy faded, knowledge returned, the old peevishness, the old apology came back, and by the time she had reached the street again she had become a dwarf.

But she had changed the mood; she had called into being an atmosphere which, as we followed her out into the street, seemed actually to create the humped, the twisted, the deformed. Two bearded men, brothers apparently, stone-blind, supporting themselves by resting a hand on the head of a small boy between them, marched down the street. On they came with the unyielding yet tremulous tread of the blind, which seems to lend to their approach something of the terror and inevitability of the fate that has overtaken them. As they passed, holding straight on, the little convoy seemed to cleave asunder the passers-by with the momentum of its silence, its directness, its disaster. Indeed, the dwarf had started a hobbling grotesque dance to which everybody in the street now conformed: the stout lady tightly swathed in shiny sealskin; the feeble-minded boy sucking the silver knob of his stick; the old man squatted on a doorstep as if, suddenly overcome by the absurdity of the human spectacle, he had sat down to look at it – all joined in the hobble and tap of the dwarf's dance.

In what crevices and crannies, one might ask, did they lodge, this maimed company of the halt and the blind? Here, perhaps, in the top rooms of these narrow old houses between Holborn and the Strand, where people have such queer names, and pursue so many curious trades, are gold beaters, accordion pleaters, cover buttons, or others who support life, with even greater fantasticality, upon a traffic in cups with saucers, china umbrella handles, and highly coloured pictures of martyred saints. There they lodge, and it seems as if the lady in the sealskin jacket must find life tolerable, passing the time of day with the accordion pleater, or the man who covers buttons; life which is so fantastic cannot be altogether tragic. They do not grudge us, we are musing, our prosperity; when, suddenly, turning the corner, we come upon a bearded Jew, wild, hunger-bitten, glaring out of his misery; or pass the humped body of an old woman flung abandoned on the step of a public building with a cloak over her like the hasty covering thrown over a dead horse or donkey. At such sights, the nerves of the spine seem to stand erect; a sudden flare is brandished in our eyes; a question is asked which is never answered. Often enough these derelicts choose to lie not a stone's throw from theatres, within hearing of barrel organs, almost, as night draws on, within touch of the sequined cloaks and bright legs of diners and dancers. They lie close to those shop windows where commerce offers to a world of old women laid on doorsteps, of blind men, of hobbling dwarfs, sofas which are supported by the gilt necks of proud swans; tables inlaid with baskets of many coloured fruit, sideboards paved with green marble the better to support the weight of boars' heads, gilt baskets, candelabra; and carpets so softened with age that their carnations have almost vanished in a pale green sea.

Passing, glimpsing, everything seems accidentally but miraculously sprinkled with beauty, as if the tide of trade which deposits its burden so punctually and prosaically upon the shores of Oxford Street had this night cast up nothing but treasure. With no thought of buying, the eye is sportive and generous; it creates; it adorns; it enhances. Standing out in the street, one may build up all the chambers of a vast imaginary house and furnish them at one's will with sofa, table, carpet. That rug will do for the hall. That alabaster bowl shall stand on a carved table in the window. Our merrymakings shall be reflected in that thick round mirror. But, having built and furnished the house one is happily under no obligation to possess it; one can dismantle it in the twinkling of an eye, build and furnish another house with other chairs and other glasses. Or let us indugle ourselves at the antique jewellers, among the trays of rings and the hanging necklaces. Let us choose those pearls, for example, and then imagine how, if we put them on, life would be changed. It becomes instantly between two and three in the morning; the lamps are burning very white in the deserted streets of Mayfair. Only motor-cars are abroad at this hour, and one has a sense of emptiness, of airiness, of secluded gaiety. Wearing pearls, wearing silk, one steps out on to a balcony which overlooks the gardens of sleeping Mayfair. There are a few lights in the bedrooms of great peers returned from Court, of silk-stockinged footmen, of dowagers who have pressed the hands of statesmen. A cat creeps along the garden wall. Love-making is going on sibilantly, seductively in the darker places of the room behind thick green curtains. Strolling sedately as if he were promenading a terrace beneath which the shires and counties of England lie sun-bathed, the aged Prime Minister recounts to Lady So-and-So with the curls and the emeralds the true history of some great crisis in the affairs of the land. We seem to be riding on the top of the highest mast of the tallest ship; and yet at the same time we know that nothing of this sort matters, love is not proved thus, nor great achievements completed thus; so that we sport with the moment and preen our feathers in it lightly, as we stand on the balcony watching the moonlit cat creep along Princess Mary's garden wall.

But what could be more absurd? It is, in fact, on the stroke of six; it is a winter's evening; we are walking to the Strand to buy a pencil. How then are we also on a balcony, wearing pearls in June? What could be more absurd? Yet it is Nature's folly, not ours. When she set about her chief masterpiece, the making of man, she should have thought of one thing only. Instead, turning her head, looking over her shoulder, into each one of us she let creep instincts and desires which are utterly at variance with his main being, so that we are streaked, variegated, all of a mixture; the colours have run. Is the true self this which stands on the pavement in January, or that which bends over the balcony in June? Am I here, or am I there? Or is the true self neither this nor that, neither here nor there, but something so varied and wandering that it is only when we give the rein to its wishes and let it take its way unimpeded that we are indeed ourselves? Circumstances compel unity; for convenience' sake a man must be a whole. The good citizen when he opens his door in the evening must be banker, golfer, husband, father; not a nomad wandering the desert, a mystic staring at the sky, a debauchee in the slums of San Francisco, a soldier heading a revolution, a pariah howling with scepticism and solitude. When he opens his door, he must run his fingers through his hair and put his umbrella in the stand like the rest.

But here, none too soon, are the second-hand bookshops. Here we find anchorage in these thwarting currents of being; here we balance ourselves after the splendours and miseries of the streets. The very sight of the bookseller's wife with her foot on the fender, sitting beside a good coal fire, screened from the door, is sobering and cheerful. She is never reading, or has only the newspaper; her talk when it leaves bookselling, as it does so gladly, is about hats; she likes a hat to be practical, she says, as well as pretty. Oh no, they don't live at the shop; they live at Brixton; she must have a bit of green to look at. In summer a jar of flowers grown in her own garden is stood on the top of some dusty pile to enliven the shop. Books are everywhere; and always the same sense of adventure fills us. Second-hand books are wild books, homeless books; they have come together in vast flocks of variegated feather, and have a charm which the domesticated volumes of the library lack. Besides, in this random, miscellaneous company we may rub against some complete stranger who will, with luck, turn into the best friend we have in the world. There is always a hope, as we reach down some greyish-white book from an upper shelf, directed by its air of shabbiness and desertion, of meeting here with a man who set out on horseback over a hundred years ago to explore the woollen market in the midlands and Wales; an unknown traveller, who stayed at inns, drank his pint, noted pretty girls and serious customs, wrote it all down stiffly, laboriously for sheer love of it (the book was published at his own expense); was infinitely prosy, busy, and matter-of-fact, and so let flow in without his knowing it the very scent of the hollyhocks and the hay together with such a portrait of himself as gives him forever a seat in the warm corner of the mind's inglenook. One may buy him for eighteen pence now. He is marked three and sixpence, but the bookseller's wife, seeing how shabby the covers are and how long the book has stood there since it was bought at some sale of a gentleman's library in Suffolk, will let it go at that.

Thus, glancing round the bookshop, we make other such sudden capricious friendships with the unknown and the vanished whose only record is, for example, this little book of poems, so fairly printed, so finely engraved, too, with a portrait of the author. For he was a poet and drowned untimely, and his verse, mild as it is and formal and sententious, sends forth still a frail fluty sound like that of a piano organ played in some back street resignedly by an old Italian organ-grinder in a corduroy jacket. There are travellers, too, row upon row of them, still testifying, indomitable spinsters that they were, to the discomforts that they endured and the sunsets they admired in Greece when Queen Victoria was a girl; a tour in Cornwall with a visit to the tin mines was thought worthy of voluminous record; people went slowly up the Rhine and did portraits of each other in Indian ink, sitting reading on deck beside a coil of rope; they measured the pyramids; were lost to civilisation for years; converted negroes in pestilential swamps. This packing up and going off, exploring deserts and catching fevers, settling in India for a lifetime, penetrating even to China and then returning to lead a parochial life at Edmonton, tumbles and tosses upon the dusty floor like an uneasy sea, so restless the English are, with the waves at their very door. The waters of travel and adventure seem to break upon little islands of serious effort and lifelong industry stood in jagged column upon the bookshop floor. In these piles of puce-bound volumes with gilt monograms on the back, thoughtful clergymen expound the gospels; scholars are to be heard with their hammers and their chisels chipping clear the ancient texts of Euripides and Aeschylus. Thinking, annotating, expounding, goes on at a prodigious rate all round us and over everything, like a punctual, everlasting tide, washes the ancient sea of fiction. Innumerable volumes tell how Arthur loved Laura and they were separated and they were unhappy and then they met and they were happy ever after, as was the way when Victoria ruled these islands.

The number of books in the world is infinite, and one is forced to glimpse and nod and go on after a moment of talk, a flash of understanding, as, in the street outside, one catches a word in passing and from a chance phrase fabricates a lifetime. It is about a woman called Kate that they are talking, how 'I said to her, quite straight last night . . . if you don't think I'm worth a penny stamp, I said . . .' But who Kate is, and to what crisis in their friendship the penny stamp refers, we shall never know; for Kate sinks under the warmth of their volubility; and here, at the street corner, another page of the volume of life is laid open by the sight of two men consulting under the lamp post. They are spelling out the latest wire from Newmarket in the stop press news. Do they think, then, that fortune will ever convert their rags into fur and broad-cloth, sling them with watch chains, and plant diamond pins where there is now a ragged open shirt? But the main stream of walkers at this hour sweeps too fast to let us ask such questions. They are wrapt, in this short passage from work to home, in some narcotic dream, now that they are free from the desk, and have the fresh air on their cheeks. They put on those bright clothes which they must hang up and lock the key upon all the rest of the day, and are great cricketers, famous actresses, soldiers who have saved their country at the hour of need. Dreaming, gesticulating, often muttering a few words aloud, they sweep over the Strand and across Waterloo Bridge whence they will be swung in long rattling trains, still dreaming, to some prim little villa in Barnes or Surbiton where the sight of the clock in the hall and the smell of the supper in the basement puncture the dream.

But we are come to the Strand now, and as we hesitate on the curb, a little rod about the length of one's finger begins to lay its bar across the velocity and abundance of life. 'Really I must – really I must' – that is it. Without investigating the demand, the mind cringes to the accustomed tyrant. One must, one always must, do something or other; it is not allowed one simply to enjoy oneself. Was it not for this reason that, some time ago, we fabricated that excuse, and invented the necessity of buying something? But what was it? Ah, we remember, it was a pencil. Let us go then and buy this pencil.[2] But just as we are turning to obey the command, another self disputes the right of the tyrant to insist. The usual conflict comes about. Spread out behind the rod of duty we see the whole breadth of the River Thames – wide, mournful, peaceful. And we see it through the eyes of somebody who is leaning over the Embankment on a summer evening, without a care in the world. Let us put off buying the pencil; let us go in search of this person (and soon it becomes apparent that this person is ourselves). For if we could stand there where we stood six months ago, should we not be again as we were then – calm, aloof, content? Let us try then. But the river is rougher and greyer than we remembered. The tide is running out to sea. It brings down with it a tug and two barges, whose load of straw is tightly bound down beneath tarpaulin covers. There is too, close by us, a couple leaning over the balustrade murmuring with that curious lack of self-consciousness which lovers have, as if the importance of the affair they are engaged on claims without question the indulgence of the human race. The sights we see and the sounds we hear now have none of the quality of the past; nor have we any share in the serenity of the person who, six months ago, stood precisely where we stand now. His is the happiness of death; ours the insecurity of life. He has no future; the future is even now invading our peace. It is only when we look at the past and take from it the element of uncertainty that we can enjoy perfect peace. As it is, we must turn, we must cross the Strand again, we must find a shop where, even at this hour, they will be ready to sell us a pencil.

It is always an adventure to enter a new room; for the lives and characters of its owners have distilled their atmosphere into it, and directly we enter it we breast some new wave of emotion. Here, without a doubt, in the stationer's shop people had been quarrelling. Their anger shot through the air. They both stopped; the old woman – they were husband and wife evidently – retired to a back room; the old man whose rounded forehead and globular eyes would have looked well on the frontispiece of some Elizabethan folio, stayed to serve us. 'A pencil, a pencil,' he repeated, 'certainly, certainly.' He spoke with the distraction yet effusiveness of one whose emotions have been roused and checked in full flood. He began opening box after box and shutting them again. He said that it was very difficult to find things when they kept so many different articles. He launched into a story about some legal gentleman who had got into deep waters owing to the conduct of his wife. He had known him for years; he had been connected with the Temple for half a century, he said, as if he wished his wife in the back room to overhear him. He upset a box of rubber bands. At last, exasperated by his incompetence, he pushed the swing door open and called out roughly, 'Where d'you keep the pencils?' as if his wife had hidden them. The old lady came in. Looking at nobody, she put her hand with a fine air of righteous severity upon the right box. There were the pencils. How then could he do without her? Was she not indispensable to him? In order to keep them there, standing side by side in forced neutrality, one had to be particular in one's choice of pencils; this was too soft, that too hard. They stood silently looking on. The longer they stood there, the calmer they grew; their heat was going down, their anger disappearing. Now, without a word said on either side, the quarrel was made up. The old man who would not have disgraced Ben Jonson's title-page, reached the box back to its proper place, bowed profoundly his good night to us, and they disappeared. She would get out her sewing; he would read his newspaper; the canary would scatter them impartially with seed. The quarrel was over.

During these minutes in which a ghost had been sought for, a quarrel composed, and a pencil bought, the streets had become completely empty. Life had withdrawn to the top floor, and lamps were lit. The pavement was dry and hard; the road was of hammered silver. Walking home through the desolation one could tell oneself the story of the dwarf, of the blind men, of the party in the Mayfair mansion, of the quarrel in the stationer's shop. Into each of these lives one could penetrate a little way, far enough to give oneself the illusion that one is not tethered to a single mind but can put on briefly for a few minutes the bodies and minds of others. One could become a washerwoman, a publican, a street singer. And what greater delight and wonder can there be than to leave the straight lines of personality and deviate into those footpaths that lead beneath brambles and thick tree trunks into the heart of the forest where live those wild beasts, our fellow men?

That is true: to escape is the greatest of pleasures; street haunting in winter the greatest of adventures. Still as we approach our own doorstep again, it is comforting to feel the old possessions, the old prejudices, fold us round, and shelter and enclose the self which has been blown about at so many street corners, which has battered like a moth at the flame of so many inaccessible lanterns. Here again is the usual door; here the chair turned as we left it and the china bowl and the brown ring on the carpet. And here – let us examine it tenderly, let us touch it with reverence – is the only spoil we have re-trieved from the treasures of the city, a lead pencil.

1–A signed essay in the *Yale Review*, October 1927, (Kp C291). VW wrote to Helen McAfee, managing editor of the review, on 29 March 1927, offering her essay, and adding: '. . . I should be much obliged if you would tell me when you propose to publish it so that I may arrange for simultaneous publication over here' (*III VW Letters*, no. 1740). (There was no simultaneous publication in a British journal.) VW wrote again on 1 May to say she was glad McAfee liked her essay and to ask for two sets of proofs 'in good time' because 'There are some passages I should like to alter' (*ibid.*, no. 1749). On 19 July she wrote: 'I am so sorry that you had the trouble of cabling to me. I have been delayed by illness, but I hope I have been able to improve the essay a little. I shall be very grateful for the double set of proofs which you are good enough to promise . . .

'Please accept my apologies for the delay . . .' (*ibid.*, no. 1787). On 17 August she welcomed her proofs and added: 'I have returned one, with a few very slight cor-rections which will not affect the length. I have let the title stand as you altered it. I agree with you in thinking it an improvement' (*ibid.*, no. 1799). (For a typescript with holograph corrections and a subsequent draft of this essay see Beinecke Rare Book and Manuscript Collection, Yale University.) Acknowledging her cheque and copies of the *Yale Review*, VW wrote again to McAfee on 14 November, adding, in answer to the latter's enquiry about the possibility of another contribution: 'I am afraid I put rather a higher price on my stories than on my articles – that is to say I would ask £30 instead of £20; and I daresay this is more than the Yale Review would be able to give' (*ibid.*, no. 1830). Reprinted *DoM, CE*.

2–The passage here seems to echo T. S. Eliot's *flâneur* J. Alfred Prufrock.

The Novels of E. M. Forster

I

There are many reasons which should prevent one from criticising the work of contemporaries. Besides the obvious uneasiness – the fear of hurting feelings – there is too the difficulty of being just.[2] Coming out one by one, their books seem like parts of a design which is slowly uncovered. Our appreciation may be intense, but our curiosity is even greater. Does the new fragment add anything to what went before? Does it carry out our theory of the author's talent, or must we alter our forecast? Such questions ruffle what should be the smooth surface of our criticism and make it full of argument and interrogation. With a novelist like Mr Forster this is specially true, for he is in any case an author about whom there is considerable disagreement. There is something baffling and evasive in the very nature of his gifts. So, remembering that we are at best only building up a theory which may be knocked down in a year or two by Mr Forster himself, let us take Mr Forster's novels in the order in which they were written, and tentatively and cautiously try to make them yield us an answer.

The order in which they were written is indeed of some import-ance, for at the outset we see that Mr Forster is extremely suscep-tible to the influence of time. He sees his people much at the mercy of those conditions which change with the years. He is acutely con-scious of the bicycle and of the motor-car; of the public school and of the university; of the suburb and of the city. The social historian will find his books full of illuminating information. In 1905 Lilia learned to bicycle, coasted down the High Street on Sunday even-ing, and fell off at the turn by the church.[3] For this she was given a talking to by her brother-in-law which she remembered to her dying day. It is on Tuesday that the housemaid cleans out the drawing-room at Sawston. Old maids blow into their gloves when they take them off. Mr Forster is a novelist, that is to say, who sees his people in close contact with their surroundings. And therefore the colour and constitution of the year 1905 affect him far more than any year in the calendar could affect the romantic Meredith or the poetic Hardy.[4] But we discover as we turn the page that observation is not an end in itself; it is rather the goad, the gadfly driving Mr Forster to provide a refuge from this misery, an escape from this meanness. Hence we arrive at that balance of forces which plays so large a part in the structure of Mr Forster's novels. Sawston implies Italy; timid-ity, wildness; convention, freedom; unreality, reality. These are the villains and heroes of much of his writing. In *Where Angels Fear to*

Tread the disease, convention, and the remedy, Nature, are provided if anything with too eager a simplicity, too simple an assurance, but with what a freshness, what a charm! Indeed it would not
be excessive if we discovered in this slight first novel evidence of
powers which only needed, one might hazard, a more generous diet
to ripen into wealth and beauty. Twenty-two years might well have
taken the sting from the satire and shifted the proportions of the
whole. But, if that is to some extent true, the years have had no
power to obliterate the fact that, though Mr Forster may be sensitive to the bicycle and the duster, he is also the most persistent devotee of the soul. Beneath bicycles and dusters, Sawston and Italy,
Philip, Harriet, and Miss Abbott, there always lies for him – it is
this which makes him so tolerant a satirist – a burning core. It is the
soul; it is reality; it is truth; it is poetry; it is love; it decks itself in
many shapes, dresses itself in many disguises. But get at it he must;
keep from it he cannot. Over brakes and byres, over drawing-room
carpets and mahogany sideboards, he flies in pursuit. Naturally the
spectacle is sometimes comic, often fatiguing; but there are
moments – and his first novel provides several instances – when he
lays his hands on the prize.

Yet, if we ask ourselves upon which occasions this happens and
how, it will seem that those pages which are least didactic, least
conscious of the pursuit of beauty, succeed best in achieving it.
When he allows himself a holiday – some phrase like that comes to
our lips; when he forgets the vision and frolics and sports with the
fact; when, having planted the apostles of culture in their hotel, he
creates airily, joyfully, spontaneously, Gino the dentist's son sitting
in the café with his friends, or describes – it is a masterpiece of
comedy – the performance of *Lucia di Lammermoor*[5], it is then that
we feel that his aim is achieved. Judging, therefore, on the evidence
of this first book, with its fantasy, its penetration, its remarkable
sense of design, we should have said that once Mr Forster had
acquired freedom, had passed beyond the boundaries of Sawston,
he would stand firmly on his feet among the descendants of Jane
Austen and Peacock. But the second novel, *The Longest Journey*,[6]
leaves us baffled and puzzled. The opposition is still the same: truth
and untruth; Cambridge and Sawston; sincerity and sophistication.
But everything is accentuated. He builds his Sawston of thicker
bricks and destroys it with stronger blasts. The contrast between
poetry and realism is much more precipitous. And now we see much

more clearly to what a task his gifts commit him. We see that what might have been a passing mood is in truth a conviction. He believes that a novel must take sides in the human conflict. He sees beauty – none more keenly; but beauty imprisoned in a fortress of brick and mortar whence he must extricate her. Hence he is always constrained to build the cage – society in all its intricacy and triviality – before he can free the prisoner. The omnibus, the villa, the suburban residence, are an essential part of his design. They are required to imprison and impede the flying flame which is so remorselessly caged behind them. At the same time, as we read *The Longest Journey* we are aware of a mocking spirit of fantasy which flouts his seriousness. No one seizes more deftly the shades and shadows of the social comedy; no one more amusingly hits off the comedy of luncheon and tea party and a game of tennis at the rectory. His old maids, his clergy, are the most life-like we have had since Jane Austen laid down the pen. But he has into the bargain what Jane Austen had not – the impulses of a poet. The neat surface is always being thrown into disarray by an outburst of lyric poetry. Again and again in *The Longest Journey* we are delighted by some exquisite description of the country; or some lovely sight – like that when Rickie and Stephen send the paper boats burning through the arch[7] – is made visible to us for ever. Here, then, is a difficult family of gifts to persuade to live in harmony together: satire and sympathy; fantasy and fact; poetry and a prim moral sense. No wonder that we are often aware of contrary currents that run counter to each other and prevent the book from bearing down upon us and overwhelming us with the authority of a masterpiece. Yet if there is one gift more essential to a novelist than another it is the power of combination – the single vision. The success of the masterpieces seems to lie not so much in their freedom from faults – indeed we tolerate the grossest errors in them all – but in the immense persuasiveness of a mind which has completely mastered its perspective.

II

We look then, as time goes on, for signs that Mr Forster is committing himself; that he is allying himself to one of the two great camps to which most novelists belong. Speaking roughly, we may divide them into the preachers and the teachers, headed by Tolstoy and Dickens, on the one hand, and the pure artists, headed by Jane Austen and Turgenev,[8] on the other. Mr Forster, it seems, has a strong impulse to belong to both camps at once. He has many of the instincts and aptitudes of the pure artist (to adopt the old classification) – an exquisite prose style, an acute sense of comedy, a power of creating characters in a few strokes which live in an atmosphere of their own; but he is at the same time highly conscious of a message. Behind the rainbow of wit and sensibility there is a vision which he is determined that we shall see. But his vision is of a peculiar kind and his message of an elusive nature. He has no great interest in institutions. He has none of that wide social curiosity which marks the work of Mr Wells.[9] The divorce law and the poor law come in for little of his attention. His concern is with the private life; his message is addressed to the soul. 'It is the private life that holds out the mirror to infinity; personal intercourse, and that alone, that ever hints at a personality beyond our daily vision.'[10] Our business is not to build in brick and mortar, but to draw together the seen and the unseen. We must learn to build the 'rainbow bridge that should connect the prose in us with the passion. Without it we are meaningless fragments, half-monks, half-beasts.'[11] This belief that it is the soul that is eternal, runs through all his writing. It is the conflict between Sawston and Italy in *Where Angels Fear to Tread*; between Rickie and Agnes in *The Longest Journey*; between Lucy and Cecil in *A Room with a View*.[12] It deepens, it becomes more insistent as time passes. It forces him on from the lighter and more whimsical short novels past that curious interlude, *The Celestial Omnibus*, to the two large books, *Howards End* and *A Passage to India*, which mark his prime.[13]

But before we consider those two books let us look for a moment at the nature of the problem he sets himself. It is the soul that matters; and the soul, as we have seen, is caged in a solid villa of red brick somewhere in the suburbs of London. It seems, then, that if his books are to succeed in their mission his reality must at certain points become irradiated; his brick must be lit up; we must see the whole building saturated with light. We have at once to believe in the complete reality of the suburb and in the complete reality of the soul. In this combination of realism and mysticism his closest affinity is, perhaps, with Ibsen.[14] Ibsen has the same realistic power. A room is to him a room, a writing table a writing table, and a waste-paper basket a waste-paper basket. At the same time, the paraphernalia of reality have at certain moments to become the veil through which we see infinity. When Ibsen achieves this, as he certainly does, it is not by performing some miraculous conjuring trick at the critical moment. He achieves it by putting us into the right mood from the very start and by giving us the right materials for his purpose. He gives us the effect of ordinary life, as Mr Forster does, but he gives it us by choosing a very few facts and those of a highly relevant kind. Thus when the moment of illumination comes we accept it implicitly. We are neither roused nor puzzled; we do not have to ask ourselves, What does this mean? We feel simply that the thing we are looking at is lit up, and its depths revealed. It has not ceased to be itself by becoming something else.

Something of the same problem lies before Mr Forster – how to connect the actual thing with the meaning of the thing and to carry the reader's mind across the chasm which divides the two without spilling a single drop of its belief. At certain moments on the Arno, in Hertfordshire, in Surrey, beauty leaps from the scabbard, the fire of truth flames through the crusted earth; we must see the red brick villa in the suburbs of London lit up. But it is in these great scenes which are the justification of the huge elaboration of the realistic novel that we are most aware of failure. For it is here that Mr Forster makes the change from realism to symbolism; here that the object which has been so uncompromisingly solid becomes, or should become, luminously transparent. He fails, one is tempted to think, chiefly because that admirable gift of his for observation has served him too well. He has recorded too much and too literally. He has given us an almost photographic picture on one side of the page; on the other he asks us to see the same view transformed and radiant with eternal fires. The bookcase which falls upon Leonard Bast in *Howards End*[15] should perhaps come down upon him with all the dead weight of smoke-dried culture; the Marabar caves should appear to us not real caves but, it may be, the soul of India. Miss Quested should be transformed from an English girl on a picnic to arrogant Europe straying into the heart of the East and getting lost there. We qualify these statements, for indeed we are not quite sure whether we have guessed aright. Instead of getting that sense of instant certainty which we get in *The Wild Duck* or in *The Master Builder*,[16] we are puzzled, worried. What does this mean? we ask ourselves. What ought we to understand by this? And the hesitation is fatal. For we doubt both things – the real and the symbolical: Mrs Moore, the nice old lady, and Mrs Moore, the sibyl. The conjunction of these two different realities seems to cast doubt upon them both. Hence it is that there is so often an ambiguity at the heart of Mr Forster's novels. We feel that something has failed us at the critical moment; and instead of seeing, as we do in *The Master Builder*, one single whole we see two separate parts.

The stories collected under the title of *The Celestial Omnibus* represent, it may be, an attempt on Mr Forster's part to simplify the problem which so often troubles him of connecting the prose and poetry of life. Here he admits definitely if discreetly the possibility of magic. Omnibuses drive to Heaven; Pan is heard in the brushwood; girls turn into trees. The stories are extremely charming. They release the fantasticality which is laid under such heavy burdens in the novels. But the vein of fantasy is not deep enough or strong enough to fight single-handed against those other impulses which are part of his endowment. We feel that he is an uneasy truant in fairyland. Behind the hedge he always hears the motor horn and the shuffling feet of tired wayfarers, and soon he must return. One slim volume indeed contains all that he has allowed himself of pure fantasy. We pass from the freakish land where boys leap into the arms of Pan and girls become trees to the two Miss Schlegels, who have an income of six hundred pounds apiece and live in Wickham Place.

III

Much though we may regret the change, we cannot doubt that it was right. For none of the books before *Howards End* and *A Passage to India* altogether drew upon the full range of Mr Forster's powers. With his queer and in some ways contradictory assortment of gifts, he needed, it seemed, some subject which would stimulate his highly sensitive and active intelligence, but would not demand the extremes of romance or passion; a subject which gave him material for criticism, and invited investigation; a subject which asked to be built up of an enormous number of slight yet precise observations, capable of being tested by an extremely honest yet sympathetic mind; yet, with all this, a subject which when finally constructed would show up against the torrents of the sunset and the eternities of night with a symbolical significance. In *Howards End* the lower-middle, the middle, the upper-middle classes of English society are so built up into a complete fabric. It is an attempt on a larger scale than hitherto, and, if it fails, the size of the attempt is largely responsible. Indeed, as we think back over the many pages of this elaborate and highly skilful book, with its immense technical accomplishment, and also its penetration, its wisdom, and its beauty, we may wonder in what mood of the moment we can have been prompted to call it a failure. By all the rules, still more by the keen interest with which we have read it from start to finish, we should have said success. The reason is suggested perhaps by the manner of one's praise. Elaboration, skill, wisdom, penetration, beauty — they are all there, but they lack fusion; they lack cohesion; the book as a whole lacks force. Schlegels, Wilcoxes, and Basts, with all that they stand for of class and environment, emerge with extraordinary verisimilitude, but the whole effect is less satisfying than that of the much slighter but beautifully harmonious *Where Angels Fear to Tread*. Again we have the sense that there is some perversity in Mr Forster's endowment so that his gifts in their variety and number tend to trip each other up. If he were less scrupulous, less just, less sensitively aware of the different aspects of every case, he could, we feel, come down with greater force on one precise point. As it is, the strength of his blow is dissipated. He is like a light sleeper who is always being woken by something in the room. The poet is twitched away by the satirist; the comedian is tapped on the shoulder by the moralist; he never loses himself or forgets himself for long in sheer delight in the beauty or the interest of things as they are. For this reason the lyrical passages in his books, often of great beauty in themselves, fail of their due effect in the context. Instead of flowering naturally — as in Proust,[17] for instance — from an overflow of interest and beauty in the object itself, we feel that they have been called into existence by some irritation, are the effort of a mind outraged by ugliness to supplement it with a beauty which, because it originates in protest, has something a little febrile about it.

Yet in *Howards End* there are, one feels, in solution all the qualities that are needed to make a masterpiece. The characters are extremely real to us. The ordering of the story is masterly. That indefinable but highly important thing, the atmosphere of the book, is alight with intelligence; not a speck of humbug, not an atom of falsity is allowed to settle. And again but on a larger battlefield, the struggle goes forward which takes place in all Mr Forster's novels — the struggle between the things that matter and the things that do not matter, between reality and sham, between the truth and the lie. Again the comedy is exquisite and the observation faultless. But again, just as we are yielding ourselves to the pleasures of the imagination a little jerk rouses us. We are tapped on the shoulder. We are to notice this, to take heed of that. Margaret or Helen, we are made to understand, is not speaking simply as herself; her words have another and a larger intention. So, exerting ourselves to find out the meaning, we step from the enchanted world of imagination, where our faculties work freely, to the twilight world of theory, where only our intellect functions dutifully. Such moments of disillusionment have the habit of coming when Mr Forster is most in earnest, at the crisis of the book, where the sword falls or the bookcase drops. They bring, as we have noted already, a curious insubstantiality into the 'great scenes' and the important figures. But they absent themselves entirely from the comedy. They make us wish, foolishly enough, to dispose Mr Forster's gifts differently and to restrict him to write comedy only. For directly he ceases to feel responsible for his characters' behaviour, and forgets that he should solve the problem of the universe, he is the most diverting of novelists. The admirable Tibby and the exquisite Mrs Hunt in *Howards End*, though thrown in largely to amuse us, bring a breath of fresh air in with them. They inspire us with the intoxicating belief that they are free to wander as far from their creator as they choose. Margaret, Helen, Leonard Bast, are closely tethered and vigilantly overlooked lest they may take matters into their own hands and upset the theory. But Tibby and Mrs Munt go where they like, say what they like, do what they like. The lesser characters and the unimportant scenes in Mr Forster's novels thus often remain more vivid than those with which, apparently, most pain has been taken. But it would be unjust to part from this big, serious, and highly interesting book without recognising that it is an important if unsatisfactory piece of work which may well be the prelude to something as large but less anxious.

IV

Many years passed before *A Passage to India* appeared. Those who hoped that in the interval Mr Forster might have developed his technique so that it yielded rather more easily to the impress of his whimsical mind and gave freer outlet to the poetry and fantasy which play about in him were disappointed. The attitude is precisely the same four-square attitude which walks up to life as if it were a house with a front door, puts its hat on the table in the hall, and proceeds to visit all the rooms in an orderly manner. The house is still the house of the British middle classes. But there is a change from *Howards End*. Hitherto Mr Forster has been apt to pervade his books like a careful hostess who is anxious to introduce, to explain, to warn her guests of a step here, of a draught there. But here, perhaps in some disillusionment both with his guests and with his house, he seems to have relaxed these cares. We are allowed to ramble over this extraordinary continent almost alone. We notice things, about the country especially, spontaneously, accidentally almost, as if we were actually there; and now it was the sparrows flying about the pictures that caught our eyes, now the elephant with the painted forehead, now the enormous but badly designed ranges of hills. The people too, particularly the Indians, have something of the same casual, inevitable quality. They are not perhaps quite so important as the land, but they are alive; they are sensitive. No longer do we feel, as we used to feel in England, that they will be allowed to go only so far and no further lest they may upset some theory of the author's. Aziz is a free agent. He is the most imaginative character that Mr Forster has yet created, and recalls Gino the dentist in his first book, *Where Angels Fear to Tread*. We may guess indeed that it has helped Mr Forster to have put the ocean between him and Sawston. It is a relief, for a time, to be beyond the influence of Cambridge. Though it is still a necessity for him to build a model world which he can submit to delicate and precise criticism, the model is on a larger scale. The English society, with all its pettiness and its vulgarity and its streak of heroism, is set against a bigger and a more sinister background. And though it is still true that there are ambiguities in important places, moments of imperfect symbolism, a greater accumulation of facts than the imagination is able to deal with, it seems as if the double vision which troubled us in the earlier books was in process of becoming single. The saturation is much more thorough. Mr Forster has almost achieved the great feat of animating this dense, compact body of observation with a spiritual light. The book shows signs of fatigue and disillusionment; but it has chapters of clear and triumphant beauty, and above all it makes us wonder, What will he write next?

1 – A signed essay in the *Atlantic Monthly*, November 1927, (Kp C292) reprinted in the *Saturday Review of Literature*, 17 December 1927. E. M. Forster (1879–1970).

'I've *not* got a cold in my head,' VW wrote to Vita Sackville-West on 31 January 1927 (*III VW Letters*, no. 1711), 'but its like having a cold in the head, sitting here writing to you and everything at sixes and sevens. I feel dissipated and aimless for some reason. I've got to read all Morgan's novels, and so far cant open a book without being interrupted. Then its you being away.' (See also no. 1726, to the same, 6 March 1927.) On 12 February she confided in her diary: 'For the rest – its been a gay tropical kind of autumn, with so much Vita & Knole & staying away ... I'm reading & writing at a great pace; mean to "do" Morgan; have a fling at my book on fiction; & make all the money we want for Greece & a motor car.' To her sister Vanessa Bell she remarked, on 25 May 1927 (*III VW Letters*, no. 1762): '... I ought to be writing an article on Morgan's novels, which I cannot finish'; and in her diary entry for 23 July she noted: 'Bruce Richmond is coming to tea on Monday to discuss an article on Morgan; & I am going to convey to him the fact that I can't always refuse £60 in America for the *Times*' £10.' See 'Is Fiction Art?' above, and Appendix IV; and see '*A Room With a View*', *I VW Essays*. Editorial Note, p. xxv. Reading Notes (Berg, xv). Reprinted *DoM, CE.*

2–Such considerations, further complicated by their close friendship, led VW in June to show Forster a draft of her essay, just as he had shown her 'The Novels of Virginia Woolf', prior to its publication in the *New Criterion*, April 1926 (reprinted as 'The Early Novels of Virginia Woolf', *Abinger Harvest*, 1936). He responded on 28 June: '*I don't believe my method's wrong! ...*' (*II EMF Letters*, no. 259); see also no. 260, 9 August, to Leonard Woolf: '... Be sure that she does not spoil the article by softening down or omitting anything; there is no individual phrase that I "mind" in the least.'; and see no. 261, same day, to T. E. Lawrence. VW noted in her diary on 10 August: 'An odd incident, psychologically as the vanished Kot[eliansky] used to say, has been Morgan's serious concern about my article on him. Did I care a straw what he said about me? Was it more laudatory? Yet here is this self-possessed, aloof man taking every word to heart, cast down to the depths, apparently, because I do not give him superlative rank, & writing again & again to ask about it, or suggest about it, anxious that it shall be published in England, & also that more space shall be given to the Passage to India. Had I been asked, I should have said that of all writers he would be the most indifferent & cool under criticism. And he minds a dozen times more than I do, who have the opposite reputation.'

3–For Lilia Theobold's adventure see *Where Angels Fear to Tread* (1905, ch. i; Penguin, 1959, p. 10).

4–George Meredith (1828–1909); Thomas Hardy (1840–1928).

5–For the comic performance of Donizetti's opera see *Where Angels Fear to Tread*, ch. 6.

6–*The Longest Journey* (1907). Jane Austen (1775–1817); Thomas Love Peacock (1785–1866).

7–See the conclusion to ch. xxxiii: 'But they played as boys who continued the nonsense of the railway carriage. The paper caught fire from the match, and spread into a rose of flame. "Now gently with me," said Stephen and they laid it flower-like on the stream. Gravel and tremulous weeds leapt into sight, and then the flower sailed into deep water, and up leapt the two arches of a bridge. "It'll strike!" they cried; "no, it won't; it's chosen the left," and one arch became a fairy tunnel, dropping diamonds. Then it vanished for Rickie; but Stephen, who knelt in the water, declared that it was still afloat, far through the arch, burning as if it would burn for ever.'

8–L. N. Tolstoy (1828–1910); Charles Dickens (1812–70); Ivan Turgenev (1818–83).

9–H. G. Wells (1866–1946).

10–Forster, *Howards End* (Edward Arnold, 1910), ch. x, p. 78.

11–*Ibid.*, ch. xxii, p. 183, which has: 'Margaret greeted her lord with peculiar tenderness on the morrow. Mature as he was, she might yet be able to help him to the building of the rainbow bridge that should connect the prose in us with the passion. Without it we are meaningless fragments, half monks, half beasts, unconnected arches that have never joined into a man.'

12–*A Room With a View* (1908).

13–*The Celestial Omnibus* (1911); *A Passage to India* (1924).

14–Henrik Ibsen (1828–1906).

15–For Leonard Bast's demise, see the conclusion to chapter xli: 'The man took him by the collar and cried, "bring me a stick." Women were screaming. A stick, very bright descended. It hurt me, not where it descended, but in the heart. Books fell over him in a shower. Nothing had sense.

'. . . They laid Leonard, who was dead, on the gravel; Helen poured water over him.

"That's enough," said Charles.

"Yes, murder's enough," said Miss Avery, coming out of the house with the sword.'

16–*The Wild Duck* (1884); *The Master Builder* (1892).

17–Marcel Proust (1871–1922).

Ruskin Looks Back on Life

That an abridgement of *Modern Painters* should lately have been published,[2] may be held to prove that while people still want to read Ruskin, they have no longer the leisure to read him in the mass. Happily, for it would be hard to let so great a writer recede from us, there is another and much slighter book of Ruskin's, which contains as in a teaspoon the essence of those waters from which the many coloured fountains of eloquence and exhortation sprang.*

Praeterita – 'outlines of scenes and thoughts perhaps worthy of memory in my past life' as he called it – is a fragmentary book, written in a season of great stress towards the end of his life and left unfinished. It is for these reasons, perhaps, less known than it should be; yet if anybody should wish to understand what sort of man Ruskin was, how he was brought up, how he came to hold the views he did, he will find it all indicated here; and if he wishes to feel for himself the true temper of his genius, these pages, though much less eloquent and elaborate than many others, preserve it with exquisite simplicity and spirit.[3]

Ruskin's father was 'an entirely honest'[4] wine merchant, and his mother was the daughter of the landlady of the Old King's Head, at Croydon. The obscurity of his birth is worth notice, because he paid some attention to it himself and it influenced him much. His natural inclination was to love the splendour of noble birth and the glamour of great possessions. Sitting between his father and mother when they drove about England in their chariot taking orders for sherry, he loved best to explore the parks and castles of the aristocracy. But he admitted manfully, if with a tinge of regret, that his own uncle was a tanner and his own aunt a baker's wife. Indeed, if he reverenced aristocracy and what it stood, or should stand for, he reverenced still more the labours and virtues of the poor. To work hard and honestly, to be truthful in speech and thought, to make one's watch or one's table as well as tables and watches can be made, to keep one's house clean and pay one's bills punctually were qualities that won his enthusiastic respect.

The two strains are to be found conflicting in his life and produce much contradiction and violence in his work. His passion for the great French cathedrals conflicted with his respect for the suburban chapel. The colour and warmth of Italy fought with his English puritanical love of order, method and cleanliness. Though to travel abroad was a necessity to him, he was always delighted to return to Herne Hill and home.[5]

Again the contrast finds expression in the marked varieties of his style. He is opulent in his eloquence, and at the same time meticulous in his accuracy. He revels in the description of changing clouds and falling waters, and yet fastens his eye to the petals of a daisy with the minute tenacity of a microscope. He combined – or at least there fought in him – the austerity of the puritan, and the sensuous susceptibility of the artist. Unluckily for his own peace of mind, if nature gave him more than the usual measure of gifts and mixed them with more than her usual perversity, his parents brought him up to have far less than the usual power of self-control.

Mr and Mrs Ruskin were both convinced that their son John was to become a great man, and in order to ensure it they kept him, like any other precious object, in a cardboard box wrapped in cotton wool. Shut up in a large house with very few friends and very few toys, perfectly clothed, wholesomely nourished and sedulously looked after, he learnt, he said, 'Peace, obedience, faith,' but on the other hand 'I had nothing to love . . . I had nothing to endure, . . . I was taught no precision nor etiquette of manners . . . Lastly, and chief of evils, my judgment of right and wrong, and power of independent action, were entirely undeveloped; because the bridle and blinkers were never taken off me.'[6][†]

He grew therefore, a shy, awkward boy, who was intellectually so highly precocious that he could write the first volume of *Modern Painters* before he was twenty-four, but was emotionally so stunted that, desperately susceptible as he was, he did not know how to amuse a lady for an evening. His efforts to ingratiate himself with the first of those enchanting girls who made havoc of his life, reminded him, he said, of the efforts of a skate in an aquarium to get up the glass.[7] Adèle was Spanish-born, Paris-bred and Catholic-hearted, he notes, yet he talked to her of the Spanish Armada, the Battle of Waterloo and the doctrine of Transubstantiation.

Some such pane of glass or other impediment was always to lie between him and the freedom of ordinary intercourse. Partly the boyish days of anxious supervision were to blame. He had much rather go away alone and look at things, he said, than stay at home and be looked at. He did not want friends; he marvelled that anyone should be fond of a creature as impersonal and self-contained as a camera lucida or an ivory foot rule. And then he was still further withdrawn from the ordinary traffic of life by Nature who, to most people only the background, lovely or sympathetic, to their own activities, was to him a presence mystic, formidable, sublime, dominating the little human figures in the foreground.

Though she thus rapt him from his fellows, Nature did not console him.[‡] The cataract and the mountain did not take the place of hearth and lamplight and children playing on the rug; the beauty of the landscape only made more terrible to him the wickedness of man. The rant and fury and bitterness of his books seem to spring not merely from the prophetic vision, but from a sense of his own frustration. More eloquent they could hardly be; but we cannot help guessing that had little John cut his knees and run wild like the rest of us, not only would he have been a happier man, but instead of the arrogant scolding and preaching of the big books we should have had more of the clarity and simplicity of *Praeterita*.

For in *Praeterita*, happily, there is little left of these old rancours.

At last Ruskin was at peace; his pain was no longer his own, but everybody's pain; and when Ruskin is at peace with the world it is surprising how humorously, kindly, and observantly he writes of it.[8]

Never were portraits more vividly drawn than those of his father and mother; the father, upright, able, sensitive, yet vain too, and glad that his clerk's incompetence should prove his own capacity; the mother, austere and indomitably correct, but with a dash of 'the Smollettesque'[9] in her, so that when a maid toppled backwards over a railing in full view of a monastery, she laughed for a full quarter of an hour. Never was there a clearer picture of English middle-class life when merchants were still princes and suburbs still sanctuaries. Never did any autobiographer admit us more hospitably and generously into the privacy of his own experience.

That he should go on for ever talking and that we should still listen, is all we ask; but in vain. Before the book is finished the beautiful stream wanders out of his control and loses itself in the sands. Limpid as it looks, that pure water was distilled from turmoil; and serenely as the pages run, they resound with the echoes of thunder and are lit with the reflections of lightning. For the old man who sits now babbling of his past, was a prophet once and had suffered greatly.

— *T. P.'s Weekly* has 'sprung'; I have adopted the more grammatical 'sprang' as found in *NR*.

[†] — *NR* continues with: 'He was not taught to swim, that is to say, but only to keep away from the water.'

[‡] — *NR* has: 'But though she thus rapt him from his fellows, Nature did not console him.'

1—A signed essay in *T. P.'s Weekly*, 3 December 1927, (Kp C293), reprinted as 'Praeterita', with revisions as shown in *NR*, 28 December 1927, based on *Praeterita. Outlines of Scenes and Thoughts perhaps Worthy of Memory in my Past Life* (1885–9; 3 vols, George Allen, 1899) by John Ruskin (1819–1900); references are here located in *Praeterita and Dilecta*, ed. E. T. Cook and Alexander Wedderburn (vol. xxxv, *The Complete Works of John Ruskin. Library Edition*, George Allen, 1908).

The essay appeared in 'T. P.'s Training in Literature' series; it bore the subtitle and by-line: '"Praeterita": Serene Thoughts with the Echoes of Thunder/By Virginia Woolf (Author of "To the Lighthouse")'; and with it was reproduced a plate from Ruskin's drawing in *The Seven Lamps of Architecture* (1849): 'Pierced Ornaments from Lisieux, Bayeux, Verona and Padua, including the spandril from the entrance to the Cathedral of Lisieux'. Further 'training' was provided in the form of two paragraphs from *Praeterita*, under the title 'A Cameo of Prose', affording 'an intimate glimpse of Ruskin's home-life as a child'. See also 'Ruskin', *VI VW Essays*. Reading Notes (Berg, XIV). See Editorial Note, p. xxv. Reprinted (*NR* version): *B&P*.

2—John Ruskin, *Modern Painters* (1843, −46, −56, −60), abridged and edited by A. J. Finberg (G. Bell, 1927).

3—There follows in *T. P.'s Weekly* a subheading: 'Seeing England by Chariot'.

4—Ruskin, vol. i, ch. i, p. 15: 'I ... have written on the granite slab over his grave that he was "an entirely honest merchant"'. Ruskin's parents were John James Ruskin (1785–1864), son of an Edinburgh calico merchant, and Margaret Cox (1781–1871), 'daughter of a skipper in the herring fishery' (*DNB*).

5—There follows in *T. P.'s Weekly* a subheading: 'Changing Clouds and Falling Waters'.

6—For the quotations up to the first ellipsis, Ruskin, vol. i, ch. ii, p. 44; for the two subsequent quotations, p. 45; and for the last, p. 46, which has: 'powers' and 'were left entirely undeveloped'.

7—*Ibid.*, ch. x, p. 180; the first of Ruskin's 'enchanting girls' and Adèle Domecq, to whom, according to Quentin Bell (*Ruskin*, Oliver and Boyd Ltd, 1963, ch. ii, p. 23), Ruskin 'wrote his most successful poetry'.

8—There follows in *T. P.'s Weekly* a subheading: 'Picture of the Middle Class'.

9—Ruskin, vol. i, ch. viii, p. 144: 'For on the contrary, there was a hearty, frank, and sometimes even irrepressible, laugh in my mother! Never sardonic, yet with a very definitely Smollettesque turn in it! ... Much more she could exult in a harmless bit of Smollettesque reality.'

1928

Thomas Hardy's Novels

When we say that the death of Thomas Hardy leaves the art of fiction in England without a head we are speaking the most obvious of truths. So long as Hardy lived there was not a writer who did not feel that his calling was crowned by the unworldly and simple old man who made not the slightest effort to assert his sovereignty, yet stood for more to this generation than it is possible for any single voice to say. The effect of such a presence is indeed incalculable. His greatness as a writer, his standing among the great of other ages, will be judged perhaps more truly by critics of a later day. But it is for the living to bear witness to another sort of influence, hardly less important, though bound in the nature of things more quickly to disappear. His was a spiritual force; he made it seem honourable to write, desirable to write with sincerity; so long as he lived there was no excuse for thinking meanly of the art he practised. His genius, his age, his distance might remove all possibility of intercourse; the plainness and homeliness of his life lent him an obscurity which neither legend nor gossip disturbed; but it is no exaggeration to say that while he lived there was a king among us and now we are without. Of no one, however, would it be more unfitting to write in terms of rhetorical eulogy. His only demand upon us, and there is none more exacting, was that we should speak the truth.

Our task, then, as we consider the seventeen volumes of fiction which he has left us, is not to attempt to grade them in order of merit or to assign them to their final station in English literature.

Rather we must try to discover the broad outlines of his genius, to distinguish between those qualities which are and those which are not still forces in the life of the present moment, to content ourselves with conjectures rather than attempt the more exact and measured estimate which time will bring within our reach. Let us go back to the beginning, to the year 1871, to the first novel, *Desperate Remedies*, and make our starting point there. Here is a young man, as he says in his preface, 'feeling his way to a method';[2] a young man of powerful imagination and of sardonic turn; book-learned in a home-made way; who can create characters but cannot control them; obviously hampered by the difficulties of his technique and driven both by maladroitness and by an innate desire to pit his human figures against forces outside themselves, to shape his book by an extreme and even desperate use of coincidence. He is already possessed of the conviction that a novel is not a toy, or an argument, but can deal faithfully with life, and record a truthful, if not a pleasing, account of the destinies of men and women. Had there been in those days a critic of abnormal perspicacity he might have said that the most remarkable thing in this first book was not character or plot or humour, but the sound that echoed and boomed through its pages of a waterfall. It is the first manifestation of that power which was to grow to such huge dimensions later. It is not the power of observing Nature, though already Hardy knew how the rain falls differently on roots and arable, how the wind sounds differently through the branches of different trees; it is the power of making a symbol of Nature, of summoning a spirit from down or mill-wheel or moor which can sympathise or can mock or can remain a passive and indifferent spectator of the drama of man. Already that gift was his; already in this crude story the involved fortunes of Miss Aldclyffe and Cytherea[3] are watched by the eyes of the gods and worked out in the presence of Nature. That he was a poet should have been obvious; that he was a novelist might still have been held uncertain. But the year after, when *Under the Greenwood Tree*[4] appeared, it was clear that much of the effort of 'feeling for a method' had been overcome. Something of the stubborn originality of the earlier book was lost. The second is accomplished, charming, idyllic compared with the first. The writer, it seems, may well develop into one of our English landscape painters, whose pictures are all of cottage gardens and old peasant women, who lingers to collect and preserve from oblivion the old-fashioned ways and words which are rapidly falling into disuse. And yet what kindly lover of antiquity, what naturalist with a microscope in his pocket, what scholar solicitous for the changing shapes of language, ever heard the cry of a small bird killed in the next wood by an owl with such intensity? The cry 'passed into the silence without mingling with it'.[5] Again we hear, very far away, like the sound of a gun out at sea on a calm summer's morning, a strange and ominous echo. But as we read these early books there is a sense of waste. There is a feeling that Hardy's genius was obstinate and perverse; first one gift would have its way with him and then another. They would not consent to run together easily in harness. Such indeed was likely to be the fate of a writer who was at once poet and realist, a faithful son of field and down, yet tormented by the doubts and despondencies bred of book-learning; a lover of old ways and plain countrymen, yet doomed to see the faith and flesh of his forefathers turn to thin and spectral transparencies before his eyes.

To this contradiction Nature had added another element likely to disorder a symmetrical development. Some writers (as readers we know it, though as critics we may fail to explain it) are born conscious of everything, others unconscious of many things. Some, like Henry James and Flaubert,[6] are able not merely to make the best use of the spoil their gifts bring in, but beyond that they control their genius in the act of creation, they remain aware and awake and are never taken by surprise. The unconscious writers, on the other hand, like Dickens and Scott,[7] seem suddenly and without their own consent to be lifted up and swept onwards. The wave sinks and they cannot say what has happened or why. Among them – it is the source of his strength and the source of his weakness – we must place Hardy. His own word, 'moments of vision',[8] exactly describes those passages of astonishing beauty and force which are to be found in every book that he wrote. With a sudden quickening of power which we cannot foretell, nor he, it seems, control, a single scene breaks off from the rest. We see, as if it existed alone and for all time, the wagon with Fanny's dead body inside travelling along the road under the dripping trees; we see the bloated sheep struggling among the clover; we see Troy flashing his sword round Bathsheba where she stands motionless, cutting the lock off her head and spitting the caterpillar on her breast.[9] Vivid to the eye, but not to the eye alone, for every sense participates, such scenes dawn upon us and their splendour remains. But the power goes as it comes. The moment of vision is succeeded by long stretches of plain daylight, nor can we believe that any craft or skill could have caught the wild power and turned it to the best advantage. The novels therefore are full of inequalities; they are hewn rather than polished; and there is always about them that little blur of unconsciousness, that halo of freshness and margin of the unexpressed which often produce the most profound sense of satisfaction. It is as if Hardy himself were not quite aware of what he did, as if his consciousness held more than he could produce, and he left it for his readers to make out his full meaning and to supplement it from their own experience.

For these reasons Hardy's genius was uncertain in development, uneven in accomplishment, but, when the moment came, magnificent in achievement. The moment came, completely and fully, in *Far from the Madding Crowd*. The subject was right; the method was right; the poet and the countryman, the sensual man, the sombre reflective man, the man of learning, all enlisted to produce a book which, however fashions may chop and change, must remain one of the great English novels. There is, in the first place, that sense of the physical world which Hardy more than any novelist can bring before us; the sense that the little prospect of man's existence is ringed by a landscape which, while it exists apart, yet confers a deep and solemn beauty upon his drama. The dark downland, marked by the barrows of the dead and the huts of shepherds, rises against the sky, smooth as a wave of the sea, but solid and eternal, rolling away to the infinite distance, but sheltering in its folds quiet villages whose smoke rises in frail columns by day, whose lamps burn in the immense darkness by night. Gabriel Oak tending his sheep up there on the back of the world is the eternal shepherd; the stars are ancient beacons; and for ages he has watched beside his sheep.

But down in the valley the earth is full of warmth and life; the farms are busy, the barns stored, the fields loud with the lowing of cattle and the bleating of sheep. Nature is prolific, splendid and lustful; not yet malignant and still the Great Mother of labouring men. And now for the first time Hardy gives full play to his humour, where it is freest and most rich, upon the lips of countrymen. Jan Coggan and Henry Fray and Joseph Poorgrass gather in the malthouse when the day's work is over and give vent to that halfshrewd, half-poetic humour which has been brewing in their brains and finding expression over their beer since the pilgrims tramped the Pilgrims' Way; which Shakespeare and Scott and George Eliot[10] all loved to overhear, but none loved better or heard with greater understanding than Hardy. But it is not the part of the peasants in the Wessex novels to stand out as individuals. They compose a pool of common wisdom, a fund of perpetual life. They comment upon the actions of the hero and heroine, but while Troy or Oak or Fanny or Bathsheba come in and out and pass away, Jan Coggan and Henry Fray and Joseph Poorgrass remain. They drink by night and they plough the fields by day. They are eternal. We meet them over and over again in the novels, and they always have something typical about them, more of the character that marks a race than of the features which belong to an individual. The peasants are the great sanctuary of sanity, the country the last stronghold of happiness. When they disappear, there is no hope for the race.

With Oak and Troy and Bathsheba and Fanny Robin we come to the men and women of the novels at their full stature. In every book three or four figures predominate, and stand up like lightning conductors to attract the force of the elements. Oak and Troy and Bathsheba; Eustacia, Wildeve and Venn; Henchard, Lucetta and Farfrae, Jude, Sue Bridehead and Phillotson.[11] There is even a certain likeness between the different groups. They live as individuals and they differ as individuals; but they also live as types and have a likeness as types. Bathsheba is Bathsheba, but she is woman and sister to Eustacia and Lucetta and Sue; Gabriel Oak is Gabriel Oak, but he is man and brother to Henchard, Venn, and Jude. However lovable and charming Bathsheba may be, still she is weak; however stubborn and ill-guided Henchard may be, still he is strong. This is fundamental; this is the core of Hardy's vision, and drawn from the deepest sources of his nature. The woman is the weaker and the fleshlier, and she clings to the stronger and obscures his vision. How freely, nevertheless, in his greater books life is poured over the unalterable framework! When Bathsheba sits in the wagon among her plants, smiling at her own loveliness in the little looking-glass, we may know, and it is proof of Hardy's power that we do know, how severely she will suffer and cause others to suffer before the end. But the moment has all the bloom and beauty of life. And so it is, time and time again. His characters, both men and women, were creatures to him of an infinite attraction. For the women he shows a more tender solicitude than for the men, and in them, perhaps, he takes a keener interest. Vain might their beauty be and terrible their fate, but while the glow of life is in them their step is free, their laughter sweet, and theirs is the power to sink into the breast of Nature and become part of her silence and solemnity, or to rise and put on them the movement of the clouds and the wildness of the flowering woodlands. The men who suffer, not like the women through dependence upon other human beings, but through conflict with fate, enlist our sterner sympathies. For such a man as Gabriel Oak we need have no passing fears. Honour him we must, though it is not granted us to love him quite so freely. He is firmly set upon his feet and can give as shrewd a blow, to men at least, as any he is likely to receive. He has a prevision of what is to be expected that springs from character rather than from education. He is stable in his temperament, steadfast in his affections, and capable of open-eyed endurance without flinching. But he, too, is no puppet. He is a homely, humdrum fellow on ordinary occasions. He can walk the street without making people turn to stare at him. In short, nobody can deny Hardy's power – the true novelist's power – to make us believe that his characters are fellow-beings driven by their own passions and idiosyncrasies, while they have – and this is the poet's gift – something symbolical about them which is common to us all.

And it is at this point, when we are considering Hardy's power of creating men and women, that we become most conscious of the profound differences that distinguish him from his peers. We look back at a number of these characters and ask ourselves what it is that we remember them for. We recall their passions. We remember how deeply they have loved each other and often with what tragic results. We remember the faithful love of Oak for Bathsheba; the tumultuous but fleeting passions of men like Wildeve. Troy and Fitzpiers; we remember the filial love of Clym[12] for his mother, the jealous paternal passion of Henchard for Elizabeth Jane. But we do not remember how they have loved. We do not remember how they talked and changed and got to know each other, finely, gradually, from step to step and from stage to stage. Their relationship is not composed of those intellectual apprehensions and subtleties of perception which seem so slight yet are so profound. In all the books love is one of the great facts that mould human life. But it is a catastrophe; it happens suddenly and overwhelmingly, and there is little to be said about it. The talk between the lovers when it is not passionate is practical or philosophic, as though the discharge of their daily duties left them with more desire to question life and its purpose than to investigate each other's sensibilities. Even if it were in their characters to analyse their emotions, life is too stirring to give them time. They need all their strength to deal with the downright blows, the freakish ingenuity, the gradually increasing malignity of fate. They have none to spend upon the subtleties and delicacies of the human comedy.

Thus there comes a time when we can say with certainty that we shall not find in Hardy some of the qualities that have given us most delight in the works of other novelists. He has not the perfection of Jane Austen, or the wit of Meredith, or the range of Thackeray, or Tolstoy's amazing intellectual power.[13] There is in the work of the great classical writers a finality of effect which places certain of their scenes, apart from the story, beyond the reach of change. We do not ask what bearing they have upon the narrative, nor do we make use of them to interpret problems which lie on the outskirts of the scene. A laugh, a blush, half a dozen words of dialogue, and it is enough; the source of our delight is perennial. But Hardy has none of this concentration and completeness. His light does not fall directly upon the human heart. It passes over it and out on to the darkness of the heath and upon the trees swaying in the storm. When we look back into the room the group by the fireside is dispersed. Each man or woman is battling with the storm, alone, revealing himself most when he is least under the observation of other human beings. We do not know them as we know Pierre or Natasha or Becky Sharp.[14] We do not know them in and out and all round as they are revealed to the casual caller, to the Government official, to the great lady, to the general on the battlefield. We do not know the complication and involvement and turmoil of their thoughts. Geographically, too, they remain fixed to the same stretch of the English countryside, and it is seldom, and not with happy results, that Hardy leaves the yeoman or farmer to describe the class above theirs in the social scale. In the drawing-room and clubroom and ballroom, where people of leisure and education come together, where comedy is bred and shades of character revealed, he is awkward and ill at ease. But the opposite is equally true. If we do not know his men and women in their relations to each other, we know them in their relations to time, death and fate. If we do not see them in quick agitation against the lights and crowds of cities, we see them against the earth, the storm and the seasons. We know their attitude towards some of the most tremendous problems that can confront mankind. They take on a more than mortal size in memory. We see them, not in detail but enlarged and dignified. We see Tess reading the baptismal service in her nightgown 'with an impress of dignity that was almost regal'. We see Marty South, 'like a being who had rejected with indifference the attribute of sex for the loftier quality of abstract humanism',[15] laying the flowers on Winterbourne's grave. Their speech has a Biblical dignity and poetry. They have a force in them which cannot be defined, a force of love or of hate, a force which in the men is the cause of rebellion against life, and in the women implies an illimitable capacity for suffering, and it is this which dominates the character and makes it unnecessary that we should see the finer features that lie hid. This is the tragic power; and, if we are to place Hardy among his fellows, we must call him the greatest tragic writer among English novelists. Thus, if we are to appreciate him truly we must look at the outer conflict, not at the inner; we must read him for his scenes, not for his sentences; for his poetry, not for his prose.

But let us, as we approach the danger-zone of Hardy's philosophy, be on our guard. Nothing is more necessary, in reading an imaginative writer, than to keep at the right distance above his page. Nothing is easier, especially with a writer of marked tendency, than to fasten on opinions, convict him of a creed, tether him to a consistent point of view. Nor was Hardy any exception to the rule that the mind, which is most capable of receiving impressions is very often the least capable of drawing conclusions. It is for the reader, steeped in the impression, to supply the comment. It is his part to know when to put aside the writer's conscious intention in favour of some deeper intention of which perhaps he may be unconscious. Hardy himself was aware of this. A novel 'is an impression, not an argument', he has warned us, and, again: 'Unadjusted impressions have their value, and the road to a true philosophy of life seems to lie in humbly recording diverse readings of its phenomena as they are forced upon us by chance and change.'[16] Certainly it is true to say of him that, at his greatest, he gives us impressions; at his weakest, arguments. In *The Woodlanders, The Return of the Native, Far from the Madding Crowd*, and, above all, in *The Mayor of Casterbridge*, we have Hardy's impression of life as it came to him without conscious ordering. Let him once begin to tamper with his direct intuitions and his power is gone. 'Did you say the stars were worlds, Tess?' asks little Abraham as they drive to market with their beehives. Tess replies that they are like 'the apples on our stubbard-tree, most of them splendid and sound – a few blighted'. 'Which do we live on – a splendid or a blighted one?' 'A blighted one,'[17] she replies, or rather the mournful thinker who has assumed her mask speaks for her. The words protrude, cold and raw, like the springs of a machine where we had seen only flesh and blood. We are crudely jolted out of that mood of sympathy which is renewed a moment later when the little cart is run down and we have a concrete instance of the ironical methods which rule our planet.

That is the reason why *Jude the Obscure* is the most painful of all Hardy's books, and the only one against which we can fairly bring the charge of pessimism. In *Jude the Obscure* argument is allowed to dominate impression, with the result that though the misery of the book is overwhelming it is not tragic. As calamity succeeds calamity we feel that the case against society is not being argued fairly or with profound understanding of the facts. Here is nothing of that width and force and knowledge of mankind which, when Tolstoy criticises society, makes his indictment formidable. Here we have revealed to us the petty cruelty of men, not the large injustice of the gods. It is only necessary to compare *Jude the Obscure* with *The Mayor of Casterbridge* to see where Hardy's true power lay. Jude carries on his miserable contest against the deans of colleges and the conventions of sophisticated society. Henchard is pitted, not against another man, but against something outside himself which is opposed to men of his ambition and power. No human being wishes him ill. Even Farfrae and Newson and Elizabeth Jane whom he has wronged all come to pity him, and even to admire his strength of character. He is standing up to fate, and in backing the old Mayor whose ruin has been largely his own fault, Hardy makes us feel that we are backing human nature in an unequal contest. There is no pessimism here. Throughout the book we are aware of the sublimity of the issue, and yet it is presented to us in the most concrete form. From the opening scene in which Henchard sells his wife to the sailor at the fair to his death on Egdon Heath the vigour of the story is superb, its humour rich and racy, its movement large-limbed and free. The skimmity ride, the fight between Farfrae and Henchard in the loft, Mrs Cuxsom's speech upon the death of Mrs Henchard, the talk of the ruffians at Peter's Finger with Nature present in the background or mysteriously dominating the foreground, are among the glories of English fiction. Meagre and scanty, it may be, is the measure of happiness allowed to each, but so long as the struggle is, as Henchard's was, with the decrees of fate and not with the laws of man, so long as it is in the open air and calls for activity of the body rather than of the brain, there is greatness in the contest, and the death of the broken corn merchant in his cottage on Egdon Heath is comparable to the death of Ajax lord of Salamis. The true tragic emotion is ours.

Before such power as this we are made to feel that the ordinary tests which we apply to fiction are futile enough. Do we insist that a great novelist shall be a master of melodious prose? Hardy was no such thing. He feels his way by dint of sagacity and uncompromising sincerity to the phrase he wants, and it is often of unforgettable pungency. Failing it, he will make do with any homely or clumsy or old-fashioned turn of speech, now of the utmost plainness, now of a bookish elaboration. No style in literature, save Scott's, is so difficult to analyse; it is on the face of it so bad, yet it achieves its aim so unmistakably. As well might one attempt to rationalise the charm of a muddy country road, or of a plain field of roots in winter. And then, like Dorsetshire itself, out of these very elements of stiffness and angularity his prose will put on greatness; will roll with a Latin sonority; will shape itself in a massive and monumental symmetry like that of his own bare downs. Then again, do we require that a novelist shall observe the probabilities, and keep close to reality? To find anything approaching the violence and convolution of Hardy's plots one must go back to the Elizabethan drama. Yet we accept his story completely as we read it; and, more than that, it becomes obvious that his violence and his melodrama, when they are not due to a curious peasantlike love of the monstrous for its own sake, are part of that wild spirit of poetry which saw with intense irony and grimness that no reading of life can possibly outdo the strangeness of life itself, no symbol of caprice and unreason be too extreme to represent the astonishing circumstances of our existence.

But as we consider the great structure of the Wessex novels it seems irrelevant to fasten on little points – this character, that scene, this phrase of deep and poetic beauty. It is something larger that Hardy has bequeathed to us. Like every great novelist, he gives us not merely a world which we can liken to the world we know, but an attitude towards it, an atmosphere surrounding it, which is of far greater importance and lasts long after the world which the novelist portrays has vanished for ever. This spirit, though it is in the scene, exists apart from the scene. It is in the life and character of the writer, as well as in the art and language that he uses. The greater the writer, the more completely the different elements are fused into one. That is why the effect of a great novel is so commanding, so complete, and yet so extremely difficult to analyse in words. When we read the Wessex novels we have to free ourselves from the cramp and pettiness imposed by life. Our imaginations have to expand and soar; our humour has to laugh out; we have to drink deep of the beauty of the earth. But also we have to enter the shade of a sorrowful and brooding spirit which even in its saddest mood still bore itself with a grave uprightness and never, even when most moved to anger, lost its simple tenderness for the sufferings of men and women. Thus it is no mere transcript of life at a certain time and place that Hardy has given us. It is a vision of the world and of man's lot as they revealed themselves to an astonishing imagination, a profound and poetic genius, a gentle and humane soul. It is for this, a gift of lasting and inexhaustible value, that we have to thank him today.

1—A commemorative essay upon the death on 11 January 1928 of Thomas Hardy (b. 1840) in the *TLS*, 19 January 1928, (Kp C294), which VW subsequently revised for inclusion as 'The Novels of Thomas Hardy' in *CR2*. Bruce Richmond had written to her as early as 14 February 1919 (MHP) asking her to be ready to write on Hardy whenever the 'evil hour' of his death should come. 'But oh, dear, what a lot I've got to read!' she exclaimed in her diary on 5 March 1919, 'The entire works of Mr James Joyce, Wyndham Lewis, Ezra Pound, so as to compare them with the entire works of Dickens & Mrs Gaskell; besides that George Eliot; & finally Hardy.' Her reading list had changed by 12 July completely but for Hardy: '. . . why do I let myself imagine spaces of leisure at Monks House? I know I shall have books that must be read there too, just as here & now I should be reading Herman Melville, & Thomas Hardy, not to say Sophocles . . .' And Hardy remained a perennial: 'I have muddled away these 3 days, as far as writing is concerned, & intend to write nothing in Cornwall; but to read the classics. Candide: Shakespeare – historical plays: Adolphe: Keats' Letters: Thomas Hardy: & perhaps Hudibras. I shall find some old biography or 10th rate novel & read only that. Never mind' (22 March 1921). On 9 August 1921 she noted in her diary: 'Indeed I am reading Hardy for my famous article – the one I'm always talking about. I ransack public libraries & find them full of sunk treasure.' By 15 November following she urged she 'must do Hardy'. Ten days later, with a hint of desperation in her voice, she wrote: '. . . I wake in the night & think that I haven't written Hardy; & I shall open my paper & find him dead –' Then on 11 December: 'I mark that for perhaps the 50th time, I am frustrated as I mean to write poor T. Hardy. I pray that he sits safe & sound by his fireside at this moment. May all bicycles, bronchitises, & influenzas keep far from him.' By 18 December she was able to write that she was 'at last starting on Hardy, & saying to myself, not for the first time, This at least is going to be first rate.' Her entry for 3 January informs us that 'In the morning I wrote with steady stoicism my posthumous article upon Hardy.' On 22 January she was in a position to 'fancy I shall finish Hardy tomorrow'. Her visit to see Hardy (who had known and had written for Leslie Stephen when the latter was editor of the *Cornhill Magazine*) is recorded in a celebrated diary entry for 25 July 1926. On 17 January 1928 she described Hardy's funeral, which the Woolfs had attended the previous day, and concluded with remarks on 'the pressure of writing two articles on Meredith & furbishing up Hardy.' See also *LW Letters*, to Vanessa Bell, 7 February 1928, p. 230: 'Hardy and Meredith between them very nearly did for V. At any rate they succeeded in giving her a headache. However she was sensible, and it seems to have gone now.' See 'Half of Thomas Hardy' below. Reading Notes (Berg, xx; MHP, B 2j). Reprinted *CE*.

2—*Desperate Remedies. A Novel* (1871; The Wessex Novels, vol. xii, Macmillan, 1896), Prefatory Note, dated January 1889, p.v: 'The following story, the first published by the author, was written nineteen years ago, at a time when he was feeling his way to a method. The principles observed in its composition are, no doubt, too exclusively those in which mystery, entanglement, surprise, and moral obliquity are depended on for excitement.'

3—Cytherea Graye, the heroine, and lady's maid to Miss Aldclyffe whose illegitimate son Aeneas Mauston she marries in *Desperate Remedies*.

4—*Under the Greenwood Tree. A Rural Painting of the Dutch School* (1872).

5—*Under the Greenwood Tree* (The Wessex Novels, vol. xvi, 1896), Part the Fourth. Autumn. ch. ii, p. 207: 'Dick said nothing; and the stillness was disturbed only by some small bird that was being killed by an owl in the adjoining wood, whose cry passed into the silence without mingling with it.'

6—Henry James (1843–1916); Gustave Flaubert (1821–80).

7—Charles Dickens (1812–70); Sir Walter Scott (1771–1832).

8—'Moments of Vision', the title of a poem and of a volume of poems (1917) by Hardy.

9—Fanny Robin, Sergeant Troy and Bathsheba Everdene in *Far from the Madding Crowd* (1874), a novel originally serialised in the *Cornhill Magazine* by Leslie Stephen.

10—George Eliot (1819–80), for VW on whom see above.

11—Eustacia Vye, Damon Wildeve, and Diggory Venn, characters in *The Return of the Native* (1878); Michael Henchard, Lucetta Le Seur and Donald Farfrae, in *The Mayor of Casterbridge* (1886); Jude Fawley, Sue Bridehead and Richard Phillotson in *Jude the Obscure* (1894–5).

12—Edred Fitzpiers in *The Woodlanders* (1887); Clym Yeobright in *The Return of the Native*.

13—Jane Austen (1775–1817), for VW on whom see above; George Meredith (1828–1909), for VW on whom see below. W. M. Thackeray (1811–63); L. N. Tolstoy (1828–1910).

14—Pierre Bezuhov and Natasha Rostov in Tolstoy's *War and Peace* (1863–9); Becky Sharp in Thackeray's *Vanity Fair* (1847–8).

15—For the first quotation, *Tess of the D'Urbervilles. A Pure Woman* (1891; The

Wessex Novels, vol. i, 1895), 'Maiden No More', ch. xiv, p. 119, which has 'which was almost regal'; and for the second *The Woodlanders* (The Wessex Novels, vol. vii, 1896), ch. xlviii, p. 459, penultimate paragraph of the book, which has 'almost like'.

16 – For the first quotation, Preface, dated July 1892, to *Tess of the d'Urbervilles*; and for the second quotation, Preface, dated 1901, to *Poems of the Past and Present* (1902).

17 – *Tess of the d'Urbervilles*, 'The Maiden', ch. iv, p. 35, which has: 'stubbard-tree. Most of them . . .'

The Sun and The Fish

It is an amusing game especially for a dark winter's morning. One says to the eye Athens; Segesta; Queen Victoria; and one waits, as submissively as possible, to see what will happen next. And perhaps nothing happens, and perhaps a great many things happen, but not the things one might expect. The old lady in horn spectacles – our late Queen – is vivid enough; but somehow she has allied herself with a soldier in Piccadilly who is stooping to pick up a coin; with a yellow camel who is swaying through an archway in Kensington Gardens; with a kitchen chair and a distinguished old gentleman waving his hat. Dropped years ago into the mind, she has become stuck about with all sorts of alien matter. When one says Queen Victoria, one draws up the most heterogeneous collection of objects, which it will take a week at least to sort. On the other hand one may say to oneself Mont Blanc at dawn; the Taj Mahal in the moonlight; and the mind remains a blank. For a sight will only survive in the queer pool in which we deposit our memories if it has the good luck to ally itself with some other emotion by which it is preserved. Sights marry, incongruously, morganatically (like the Queen and the camel) and so keep each other alive. Mont Blanc, the Taj Mahal, sights which we travelled and toiled to see, fade and perish and disappear because they failed to find the right mate. On our death-beds it is possible we shall see nothing more majestic than a cat and an old woman in a sun-bonnet. The great sights will have died for lack of mates.

So, on this dark winter's morning, when the real world has faded, let us see what the eye can do for us. Show me the eclipse, we say to the eye; let us see that strange spectacle again. And we see at once –

but the mind's eye is only by courtesy an eye; it is a nerve which hears and smells, which transmits heat and cold, which is attached to the brain and rouses the mind to discriminate and speculate – it is only for brevity's sake that we say that we 'see' at once a railway station at night. A crowd is gathered at a barrier; but how curious a crowd! Mackintoshes are slung over their arms; in their hands they carry little cases. They have a provisional, extemporised look. They have that moving and disturbing unity which comes from the consciousness that they (but here it would be more proper to say 'we') have a purpose in common.[2] Never was there a stranger purpose than that which brought us together that June night in Euston Railway Station. We were come to see the dawn. Trains like ours were starting all over England at that very moment to see the dawn. All noses were pointing North. When for a moment we halted in the depths of the country, there were the pale yellow lights of motor-cars also pointing North. There was no sleep, no fixity in England that night. All were travelling North. All were thinking of the dawn. As the night wore on the sky, which was the object of so many million thoughts, assumed greater substance and prominence than usual. The consciousness of the whitish soft canopy above us increased in weight as the hours passed. When in the chill early morning we were turned out on a Yorkshire road-side, our senses had orientated themselves differently from usual. We were no longer in the same relation to people, houses and trees; we were related to the whole world. We had come, not to lodge in the bedroom of an Inn; we were come for a few hours of disembodied intercourse with the sky.

Everything was very pale. The river was pale and the fields, brimming with grasses and tasselled flowers which should have been red, had no colour in them, but lay there whispering and waving round colourless farm-houses. Now the farm-house door would open and out would step to join the procession the farmer and his family in their Sunday clothes, neat, dark and silent as if they were going up hill to church; or sometimes women merely leant on the window sills of the upper rooms watching the procession pass with amused contempt, it appeared, – they have come such hundreds of miles, and for what? they seemed to say – in complete silence.[3] We had an odd sense of keeping an appointment with an actor of such vast proportions that he would come silently and be everywhere.

By the time we were at the meeting place, on a high fell where the hills stretched their limbs out over the flowing brown moorland below, we had put on too – though we were cold and with our feet stood in red bog water were likely to be still colder, though some of us were squatted on mackintoshs among cups and plates, eating, and others were fantastically accoutred and none were at their best – still we had put on a certain dignity. Rather, perhaps, we had put off the little badges and signs of individuality. We were strung out against the sky in outline and had the look of statues standing prominent on the ridge of the world. We were very, very old; we were men and women of the primeval world come to salute the dawn. So the worshippers at Stonehenge must have looked among tussocks of grass and boulders of rock. Suddenly from the motor-car of some Yorkshire Squire, there bounded four large lean, red dogs, hounds of the ancient world, hunting dogs, they seemed, leaping with their noses close to the ground on the track of boar or deer.[4] Meanwhile, the sun was rising. A cloud glowed as a white shade glows when the light is slowly turned up behind it. Golden wedge-shaped streamers fell down from it and marked the trees in the valley green and the villages blue-brown. In the sky behind us there swam white islands in pale blue lakes. The sky was open and free there, but in front of us a soft snow bank had massed itself. Yet, as we looked, we saw it proving worn and thin in patches. The gold momentarily increased, melting the whiteness to a fiery gauze, and this grew frailer and frailer till, for one instant, we saw the sun in full splendour. Then there was a pause. There was a moment of suspense, like that which precedes a race. The starter held his watch in his hand counting the seconds. Now they were off.

The sun had to race through the clouds and to reach the goal, which was a thin transparency to the right, before the sacred seconds were up. He started. The clouds flung every obstacle in his way. They clung, they impeded. He dashed through them. He could be felt flashing and flying, when he was invisible. His speed was tremendous. Here he was out and bright; now he was under and lost. But always one felt him flying and thrusting through the murk to his goal. For one second he emerged and showed himself to us through our glasses, a hollowed sun, a crescent sun. It was a proof perhaps that he was doing his best for us. Now he went under his last effort. Now he was completely blotted out. The moments passed. Watches were held in hand after hand. The sacred twenty-four seconds were begun. Unless he could win through before the last one was over he was lost. Still one felt him tearing and racing behind the clouds to win free; but the clouds held him. They spread; they thickened; they slackened, they muffled his speed. Of the twenty-four seconds only five remained and still he was obscured. And, as the fatal seconds passed and we realised that the sun was being defeated, had now indeed lost the race, all the colour began to go from the moor. The blue turned to purple; the white became livid as at the approach of a violent but windless storm. Pink faces went green, and it became colder than ever. This was the defeat of the sun then, and this was all, so we thought, turning in disappointment from the dull cloud blanket in front of us to the moors behind. They were livid, they were purple; but suddenly one became aware that something more was about to happen; something unexpected, awful, unavoidable. The shadow growing darker and darker over the moor was like the heeling over of a boat, which, instead of righting itself at the critical moment, turns a little further and then a little further; and suddenly capsizes. So the light turned and heeled over and went out. This was the end. The flesh and blood of the world was dead and only the skeleton was left. It hung beneath us, frail; brown; dead; withered. Then, with some trifling movement, this profound obeisance of the light, this stooping down and abasement of all splendour was over. Lightly, on the other side of the world up it rose; it sprang up as if the one movement, after a second's tremendous pause, completed the other and the light which had died here, rose again elsewhere. Never was there such a sense of rejuvenescence and recovery. All the convalescences and respite of life seemed rolled into one.[5] Yet at first, so pale and frail and strange the light was sprinkled rainbow-like in a hoop of colour, that it seemed as if the earth could never live decked out in such frail tints. It hung beneath us, like a cage, like a hoop, like a globe of glass. It might be blown out; it might be stove in. But steadily and surely our relief broadened and our confidence established itself as the great paint brush washed in woods, dark on the valley, and massed the hills blue above them. The world became more and more solid; it became populous; it became a place where an infinite number of farmhouses, of villages, of railway lines have lodgment; until the whole fabric of civilisation was modelled and moulded. But still the memory endured that the earth we stand on is made of colour; colour can be blown out; and then we stand on a dead leaf; and we who tread the earth securely now have seen it dead.

But the eye has not done with us yet. In pursuit of some logic of its own, which we cannot follow immediately, it now presents us with a picture, or generalised impression rather, of London on a hot summer day, when, to judge by the sense of concussion and confusion the London season is at its height. It takes us a moment to realise first that we are in some public gardens, next from the asphalt and the paperbags strewn about that it must be the Zoological Gardens, and then without further preparation we are presented with the complete and perfect effigy of two lizards. After destruction calm; after ruin steadfastness – that perhaps is the logic of the eye. At any rate one lizard is mounted immobile on the back of another, with only the twinkle of a gold eye-lid or the suction of a green flank to show that they are living flesh, and not made of bronze. All human passion seems furtive and feverish beside this still rapture. Time seems to have stopped and we are in the presence of immortality. The tumult of the world has fallen from us like a crumbling cloud. Tanks cut in the level blackness enclose squares of immortality, worlds of settled sunshine, where there is neither rain nor cloud. There the inhabitants perform for ever evolutions whose intricacy, because it has no reason, seems the more sublime. Blue and silver armies, keeping a perfect distance for all their arrow-like quickness, shoot first this way, then that. The discipline is perfect, the control absolute; reason there is none. The most majestic of human evolutions seems feeble and fluctuating compared with the fishes'. Each of these worlds too, which measures perhaps four feet by five is as perfect in its order as in its methods. For forests, they have half a dozen bamboo canes; for mountains, sand-hills; in the curves and crinkles of a sea-shell lie for them all adventure, all romance. The rise of a bubble, negligible elsewhere, is here an event of the highest performance. The silver drop bores its way up a spiral staircase through the water to burst against the sheet of glass which seems laid flat across the top. Nothing exists needlessly. The fish themselves seem to have been shaped deliberately and slipped into the world only to be themselves. They neither work nor weep. In their shape is their reason. For what other purpose, except the sufficient one of perfect existence, can they have been thus made, some so round, some so thin, some with radiating fins upon their backs, others lined with red electric light, others undulating like white pancakes on a frying pan, some armoured in blue mail, some given prodigious claws, some outrageously fringed with huge whiskers?

More care has been spent upon half a dozen fish than upon the races of mankind. Under our tweed and silk is nothing but a monotony of pink nakedness. Poets are not transparent to the backbone as these fish are. Bankers have no claws. Kings and Queens themselves wear neither ruffs nor frills. In short, if we were to be turned naked, into an Aquarium – but enough. The eye shuts now. It has shown us a dead world and an immortal fish.

1–A signed essay on the 'Miscellany' page of *Time and Tide*, 3 February 1928, re-printed in *NR*, 6 February, (Kp C296) drawing upon an excursion to Richmond in North Yorkshire to see from Bardon Fell the total eclipse of the sun, on 29 June 1927. For VW's original account of this historic occasion, see her diary entry for 30 June (*III VW Diary*). On 15 May VW had written to her sister Vanessa Bell: 'We are, by the way, taking a first class carriage to see the Eclipse in June. Will you share? It stops in Yorkshire as the sun disappears, for 5 seconds; we all get out and look up; hot coffee is then served and we return to London . . .' (*III VW Letters*, no. 1756; see also *ibid.*, no. 1761, to Vita Sackville-West). See also *'Day In, Day Out'* below. See Editorial Note, p. xxv. Reprinted *CDB, CE*.

2–VW's immediate travelling companions were Leonard Woolf, Quentin Bell, Harold Nicolson, Vita Sackville-West, Saxon Sydney-Turner and Edward Sackville-West.

3–Cf., *III VW Diary*, 30 June 1927: 'Pale & grey too were the little uncompromising Yorkshire farms. As we passed one, the farmer, & his wife & sister came out, all tightly & tidily dressed in black, as if they were going to church. At another ugly square farm, two women were looking out of the upper windows.'

4–Cf., *ibid.*, '. . . the setters were racing round; everyone was standing in long lines, rather dignified, looking out. I thought how we were like very old people, in the birth of the world – druids on Stonehenge:'.

5–Cf., *ibid.*: 'Nothing could be seen through the cloud. The 24 seconds were passing. Then one looked back again at the blue: & rapidly, very very quickly, all the colours faded; it became darker & darker as at the beginning of a violent storm; the light sank & sank: we kept saying this is the shadow; & we thought now it is over – this is the shadow when suddenly the light went out. We had fallen. It was extinct. There was no colour. The earth was dead. That was the astonishing moment: & the next when as if a ball had rebounded, the cloud took colour on itself again, only a sparky aetherial colour & so the light came back. I had very strongly the feeling as the light went out of some vast obeisance; something kneeling down, & low & suddenly raised up, when the colours came. They came back astonishingly lightly & quickly & beautifully in the valley & over the hills – at first with a miraculous glittering & aetheriality, later normally almost, but with a great sense of relief. It was like recovery. We had been much worse than we had expected. We had seen the world dead. This was within the power of nature. Our greatness had been apparent too.'

The Novels of George Meredith

Twenty years ago the fame of George Meredith was at its height.[2] His novels had won their way to celebrity through all sorts of difficulties, and their fame was all the brighter and the more singular for what it had subdued. Then, too, it was generally discovered that the maker of these splendid books was himself a splendid old man. Visitors who went down to Box Hill reported that they were thrilled as they walked up the drive of the little suburban house by the sound of a voice booming and reverberating within. The novelist, seated among the usual knick-knacks of the drawing-room, was like the bust of Euripides to look at. Age had worn and sharpened the fine features, but the nose was still acute, the blue eyes still keen and ironical. Though he had sunk immobile into an armchair, his aspect was still vigorous and alert. It was true that he was almost stone-deaf, but this was the least of afflictions to one who was scarcely able to keep pace with the rapidity of his own ideas. Since he could not hear what was said to him, he could give himself wholeheartedly to the delights of soliloquy. It did not much matter, perhaps, whether his audience was cultivated or simple. Compliments that would have flattered a duchess were presented with equal ceremony to a child. Never did he lapse into commonplace colloquialism. But all the time this highly wrought, artificial conversation, with its crystallised phrases and its high-piled metaphors, moved and tossed on a current of laughter. His laugh curled round his sentences as if he himself enjoyed their humorous exaggeration. The master of language was splashing and diving in his element of words. So the legend grew; and the fame of George Meredith, who sat with the head of a Greek poet on his shoulders in a suburban villa beneath Box Hill, pouring out poetry and sarcasm and wisdom in a voice that could be heard almost on the high road, made his fascinating and brilliant books seem more fascinating and brilliant still.

But that is twenty years ago. His fame as a talker is necessarily dimmed, and his fame as a writer seems also under a cloud. On none of his successors is his influence now marked. When one of them whose work has given him the right to be heard chances to speak his mind on the subject, it is not flattering. 'Meredith,' writes Mr Forster in his 'Aspects of Fiction', 'is not the great name he was twenty years ago ... His philosophy has not worn well. His heavy attacks on sentimentality – they bore the present generation[3] ... When he gets serious and noble-minded there is a strident overtone, a bullying that becomes distressing ... What with the faking, what with the preaching, which was never agreeable and is now said to be hollow, and what with the home counties posing as the universe, it is no wonder Meredith now lies in the trough.'[4] The criticism is not, of course, intended to be a finished estimate; but in its conversational sincerity it condenses accurately enough what is in the air when Meredith is mentioned. No, the general conclusion would seem to be, Meredith has not worn well. But the value of centenaries lies in the occasion they offer us for solidifying such airy impressions. Talk, mixed with half-rubbed-out memories, forms a mist by degrees through which we scarcely see plain. To open the books again, to try to read them as if for the first time, to try to free them from the rubbish of reputation and accident – that, perhaps, is the most acceptable present we can offer to a writer on his hundredth birthday.

And since the first novel is always apt to be an unguarded one, where the author displays his gifts without knowing how to dispose of them to the best advantage, we may do well to open *Richard Feverel* first.[5] It needs no great sagacity to see that the writer is a novice at his task. The style is extremely uneven. Now he twists himself into iron knots; now he lies flat as a pancake. He seems to be of two minds as to his intention. Ironic comment alternates with long-winded narrative. He vacillates from one attitude to another. Indeed, the whole fabric seems to rock a little unsecurely. The baronet wrapped in a cloak; the county family; the ancestral home; the uncles mouthing epigrams in the dining-room; the great ladies flaunting; the jolly farmers slapping their thighs; all liberally, yet spasmodically, sprinkled with dried aphorisms from a pepper-pot called the Pilgrim's Scrip – what an odd conglomeration it is! But the oddity is not on the surface. It is not simply that whiskers and bonnets have gone out of fashion; or that Proust and Henry James[6] have given the novel a twist in another direction. The oddity lies deeper, where indeed, with a writer of any standing, it must lie: not in his outward bearing, but in his attitude as a whole. And when we say that Meredith's attitude is a strange one we mean that it combines in the most paradoxical way a romantic wildness and a starched artificiality. For what purpose has he knocked down all the usual staircases and dissolved all the usual stucco mansions? Verisimilitude is violated on every page. The atmosphere crackles with unreality. The airs and the graces, the capital letters and the quotations, the formal 'Sirs' and 'Ma'ams' of the dialogue are all there to create an atmosphere unlike that of daily life: an atmosphere in which astonishing things can happen, in which exotic characters can seem natural. And behold, after all this preparation, there enter a baronet, a hero, a bad woman, a good woman, a landlady and a butler. There is an indescribable conventionality about them which makes them fit their ready-made clothing precisely. For what, then, we may ask, has he sacrificed the substantial advantages of plain common sense? For the sake, perhaps, not of his characters, who have gained little, but of his scenes. One after another he creates scenes which we can name abstractly by such titles as the Birth of Love, Youth, the Power of Nature. We are galloped to them over every obstacle on the pounding hoofs of rhapsodical prose. 'Away with Systems! Away with a corrupt World! Let us breathe the air of the Enchanted Island! Golden lie the meadows; golden run the streams; red gold is on the pine stems.'[7] But we have not yet exhausted the elements of this strange book, for we have to reckon with the ubiquitous author. He is by no means merged in his characters. He has a mind stuffed with ideas, hungry from argument. His boys and girls may spend their time picking daisies in the meadows, but they breathe, however unconsciously, an air brittle with electricity. On a dozen occasions these incongruous elements strain and threaten to break apart. The book is cracked through and through with unreality. Yet it succeeds in holding miraculously together: not certainly by the depth or originality of its character drawing, but by the vigour of its intellectual power and by its lyrical intensity.

Let him write another book or two; get into his stride; control his crudities; and we will open *Harry Richmond*[8] and see what has happened now. Of all the things that might have happened this surely is the strangest. All trace of immaturity is gone; but with it every trace of the uneasy adventurous mind has gone too. The story bowls smoothly along the road which Dickens[9] has already trodden of autobiographical narrative. It is a boy speaking, a boy thinking, a boy adventuring. For that reason, no doubt, the author has curbed his redundance and pruned his speech. The style is the most rapid possible. It runs smooth, without a kink in it. Stevenson,[10] one feels, must have learnt much from this supple narrative, with its precise adroit phrases, its fir-trees, its landscapes, its gypsies, its exact quick glance at visible things.

Plunged among dark green leaves, smelling wood-smoke, at night; at morning waking up, and the world alight, and you standing high, and marking the hills where you will see the next morning and the next, morning after morning, and one morning the dearest person in the world surprising you just before you wake: I thought this a heavenly pleasure.[11]

It goes gallantly, but a little self-consciously. He hears himself talking. Doubts begin to rise and hover and settle at last (as in *Richard Feverel*) upon the human figures. These boys are no more real boys than the sample apple which is laid on top of the basket is a real apple. They are too simple, too gallant, too adventurous to be of the same unequal breed as David Copperfield, for example.[12] They are sample boys, novelist's specimens; and again we encounter the extreme conventionality of Meredith's mind where we found it, to our surprise, before. With all his boldness (and there is no risk that he will not run with probability) there are a dozen occasions on which a reach-me-down character will satisfy him well enough. But just as we are thinking that the young gentlemen are altogether too pat, and the adventures which befall them altogether too slick, the shallow bath of illusion closes over our heads and we sink with Richmond Roy and the Princess Ottilia[13] into the world of fantasy and romance, where all holds together and we are able to put our imagination at the writer's service without reserve. That such surrender is above all things delightful: that it adds spring-heels to our boots: that it fires the cold scepticism out of us and makes the world glow in lucid transparency before our eyes, needs no showing, as it certainly submits to no analysis. That Meredith can induce such moments proves him possessed of an extraordinary power. Yet it is a capricious power and highly intermittent. For pages all is effort and agony; phrase after phrase is struck and no light comes. Then, just as we are about to drop the book, the rocket roars into the air; the whole scene flashes into light; and the book, years after, is recalled by that sudden splendour.

If, then, this intermittent brilliancy is Meredith's characteristic excellence, it is worth while to look into it more closely. And perhaps the first thing we shall discover is that these scenes which catch the eye and remain in memory have little psychological value. Richard and Lucy, Harry and Ottilia, Clara and Vernon, Beauchamp and

Renée[14] are shown us on board some yacht, under some cherry tree, on some river bank. Always the landscape makes part of the emotion. The sea or the sky or the wood is brought forward so as to symbolise what the human beings are feeling or looking. 'The sky was bronze, a vast furnace dome. The folds of lights and shadow everywhere were satin rich. That afternoon the bee hummed of thunder and refreshed the ear.'[15] That is a description of a state of mind. 'These winter mornings are divine. They move on noiselessly. The earth is still as if waiting. A wren warbles, and flits through the lank, drenched branches; hillside opens green; everywhere is mist, everywhere expectancy.'[16] That is a description of a woman's face. But only some states of mind and some expressions of face can be described in imagery – only those which are so highly wrought as to be simple and, for that reason, will not submit to analysis. This is a limitation; for though we may be able to see these people, very brilliantly, in a moment of illumination, the light sinks and leaves us in darkness. We have no such intuitive knowledge of Meredith's characters as we have of Stendhal's, Tchehov's, Jane Austen's.[17] Indeed, our knowledge of such characters is so intimate that we can almost dispense with 'great senses' altogether. Some of the most emotional scenes in fiction are the quietest. We have been wrought upon by nine hundred and ninety little touches; the thousandth, when it comes, is as slight as the others, but the effect is prodigious. But with Meredith there are no touches; there are hammer strokes only, so that our knowledge of his characters is partial, spasmodic and intermittent.

Meredith, then, is not among the great psychologists – that would seem to be true if we consider only the characters that are created by the lyrical and poetical side of his genius. But a mind which is so self-conscious, so sophisticated, is not likely to remain lyrical for long. He does not sing only; he dissects. Even in his most poetical scenes there is a hint of irony, a sneer curling its lash round the phrases and laughing at their extravagance. The comic spirit when it is allowed to dominate the scene licked the world to a very different shape. *The Egoist*, for example, at once modifies our theory that Meredith is pre-eminently the master of great scenes. Here there is none of that precipitate hurry which has rushed us up to and over obstacles to the summit of one emotional peak after another. The case is one that needs argument; argument needs logic; Sir Willoughby, 'our original male in giant form',[18] is turned slowly round before a steady fire of scrutiny and criticism which allows no twitch on the victim's part to escape it. At the same time Meredith pays us the supreme compliment; we are civilised people, he seems to say. He raises us to a seat beside him on the bench. He imputes to us the same disinterestedness, the same maturity, that he has himself. So seldom are we asked to think, so often are we asked to feel, so implicit is the novelist's assumption that thinking is the death of living, that when Meredith asks us openly to put our minds at his service in *The Egoist* we are at first bewildered and then delighted. Indeed, his comic spirit is a far more penetrating goddess than his lyrical. It is she who cuts a clear path through the jungle of his manner; she who surprises us again and again with the depth of her observations; she who creates the dignity, the intellectual vitality of Meredith's world, its seriousness, its solidity. Had Meredith, one is tempted to reflect, lived in an age or a country where civilisation was high enough to allow of comedy, he might never have contracted those airs of intellectual superiority, that manner of oracular solemnity which it is, he points out, the use of the comic spirit to correct.

But now when it comes to making a whole of these scattered impressions, to shaping from many books one composite volume upon which to pronounce judgement – and with most writers that happy illusion is reached when two or three books have been read carefully – something eludes us. Never was there a harder task. It is as if the one quality which binds and concentrates and commits us to an opinion had been omitted. Nothing but a brilliant but disintegrated mass is left. The books change shape and colour even as we look at them. *Richard Feverel, Harry Richmond, The Egoist*, each differs profoundly from the other. They are at once tragic and comic; didactic and lyric; flamboyant and severe. They change so quickly and so completely that we almost accuse the author of acting a part, of assuming a character to deceive us. And even if we could reduce our total impressions to order, we are reminded by an excuse here, an irritation there, that Meredith is hedged off from us by a thicket of thorns, and the sympathy between us is torn and imperfect. And it is, perhaps, because he rouses these antipathies that we are a little more anxious than usual to cross-examine our impressions, to turn back and amplify some of those notes which were hastily scribbled in the margin of the mind in reading. His conventionality, for instance, disconcerted us. There was, we felt, something of pose and artificiality about his people. The hero was a hero and the butler was a butler. It is not, let us quickly insist, that we require the surface realism which is usually called life. A novelist, we say, can be as fantastic as he likes or as real as he likes provided that he observes his own laws of perspective. When Meredith asks us to grant him an atmosphere which, compared with Trollope's, is tropical in the extreme, we grant it willingly; only we ask that the emotion shall be consistent. For, more especially when the emotion is high pitched, we dread the wrong contrast, the wrong relief, that will rouse us and make us feel ridiculous in proportion to our exaltation. The emotion in Meredith is always at fever-heat. Dip into his pages, and we find that his ordinary narrative prose is so highly strung that he will go out of his way to avoid simple words like laughter or sewing. He prefers to say 'gave his lungs full play' or 'tasking the intricacies of the needle'.[19] And when the pitch of feeling is at this height, it is natural that a novelist should lapse, not into dullness, as Trollope would have done in the same case, but into the meretricious and the false. The big phrases roll up, but there is no emotion to fill them. It is natural, because it is natural that a novelist's invention should flag, and that his imagination should cool. A novel, moreover, is a great many pages in length, and there is no help to be had by the novelist from outside. The poet and the dramatist can invoke rhyme and metre and the artifices of the theatre. For them both emotion is roused in advance and the atmosphere warmed and made ready. But the novelist, above all the lyrical novelist of Meredith's type, has it all to raise with his own hands from the ground. His inadequacy as a writer of narrative, the huddle and confusion of his manner, the daubed and bombastic nature of his characters and the over-emphasis of his speech are due in part to the ambitious nature of his undertaking. It is unfair to ask of him the same integrity that we have the right to demand of the plodding novelist, when he has given us so much else.

For if he has neglected the usual amenities of fiction, is it not that he may give us what the ordinary novelist ignores – philosophy, poetry, the fine comedy which induces not laughter but a smile? Of the philosophy it is difficult to speak, and perhaps we resent the necessity of having to speak of it at all. For philosophy should not be separable from fiction. It is a view of life which has buried itself in flesh and blood, and it should be buried beyond the possibility of exhumation. No one can dispense with it; the simplest story has its view of life behind it; but the great, it would seem, the Shakespeares, the Tolstoys,[20] the Tchehovs, the Jane Austens, with their profundity and their fire and their humility and their patience, assimilate it so completely that nothing is left unconsumed. Otherwise, when a few years have passed, the teaching sticks out from the body of the book, annoying us by its irrelevances as if the builder had left his scaffolding when the building was finished. The fact that we can go through Meredith's novels underlining this passage with a pencil, cutting out that sentence with a pair of scissors, and pasting the whole into a system, is against them. It is not that the philosophy is empty; on the contrary, it is packed and muscular and high minded and sincere. But it is addressed to men in whiskers and to women in poke bonnets. The souls of these people no doubt stood in need of this particular medicine about the year 1870; in 1928 ours look over the medicine bottle out of the window somewhere else. Perhaps we are chiefly repelled by the fact that Meredith's teaching is based on optimism, an optimism which seems to us arrived at rather by self-assertion than by sympathy. At the sound of the thundering hoofs of his phrases, all the more subtle and secret sensibilities steal away. He cannot, even to hear the profoundest secret, suppress his own opinion. His own opinion, and he has one on every topic, is often highly original and brilliantly phrased; but as Vernon Whitford said of Mrs Mountstuart Jenkinson, the phrase makers 'are so bent on describing brilliantly'[21] they see very little of what goes on before them. So Meredith himself is so anxious to illumine the path of wisdom that he scarcely lets us take a step in any direction. He is always twitching at our sleeves, tugging at our arms, and belabouring us with so many fine phrases that we never escape into that solitude where the imagination is most awake.

As for the poetry in Meredith's novels, there are people who suspect poetry in novels and hold, not without reason, that the perfect novelists are those fortunate writers whose gifts can be poured, smooth and entire, into the form provided. Defoe, Fielding, Trollope, what need had they of poetry?[22] Was not their prose indeed the richer for its exclusion? Or if poetry must come in, let it steal over us imperceptibly without the raising of the voice or the swelling of the sound. There is poetry in Turgenev,[23] in Tchehov, in Jane Austen, we shall find if we do not look for it. But Meredith's poetry never steals imperceptibly; it bursts at full blast. 'Away with

Systems! Away with a Corrupt World! Let us breathe the air of the Enchanted Island!' At one jump we have landed right in the middle of the lawn, crashed into the thick of the fantastic grove, are among rapturous lovers, see adventurers astride marble horses, while the sun dazzles orange and purple in our eyes, and the spires of Venice glitter on the horizon. It is outrageous, but it is sublime. Meredith is at his best when he is most Meredithian. To get on to any sort of terms with him we must concede him the rights of complete fantasy. After all, our long and forced diet upon Russian fiction skinned in translation of its style and thus made negative and neutral should not lead us to forget that the English character is often eccentric and the English language often exuberant. Meredith's flamboyancy has a great ancestry behind it; we cannot avoid all memory of Shakespeare.

Meredith's interest for us certainly, then, does not lie in his philosophy and, though largely, not entirely in his poetry. It lies in his comedy – in the assumption which is explicitly stated in the 'Essay on Comedy' and inspires the *Egoist* and *Diana of the Crossways*[24] that there is a self-conscious society: a group of men and women who think, who criticise, who laugh at each other. To have conceived such an audience, to have written for it, is a remarkable achievement, if we consider how seldom the actors in fiction are allowed any relationship except of the simplest; how passive, how personal, how animal they are. Meredith, on the other hand, not only dares himself to be brilliant, but insists that life is an affair which calls for the vigorous use of the brain. His most memorable phrases, like Clara's 'I must be myself to be of any value to you, Willoughby,'[25] are memorable for their penetrating sanity. It is by their thinking that his people live; it is the brain that defines them, and it is the brain, of course, that desiccates them. They have no halo round them, no atmosphere. Everything is clear, sharp, vibrant, and a little dry. For Meredith was too pugnacious, and too much of a preacher to let down into the mind any of those tremulous sensitive sentences which seem to be washed hither and thither in the tides of the consciousness and to be drawn up coated with rubbish or with pearl. He stood alert on the surface. He was conscious in the extreme.

It is for such reasons as these, then, that while we are stimulated and roused and irritated it is difficult to take kindly and instinctively to Meredith's novels at the moment. Nevertheless Meredith is still a power, booming, reverberating with his own unmistakable accent, if behind a partition. He was a master in his own right. He took his way undaunted through obstacles which were more formidable then than they are now. He refused to concern himself with mere accuracy of representation. By every device of style, by metaphor, by elision, by rhythm he strove to shore up and concentrate the billowy form of the novel, and to substitute starlight or limelight for the prosaic light of midday. The effort of bringing the unwieldy world of fiction into a state that allows of great poetic or comic intensity was exhausting, so that his characters are apt to be artificial and the style in its tension becomes tedious. But by these means he achieved great beauty, great intensity, great and abundant fantasy. Had he been able to hold aloof with the fixity of such writers as Turgenev or Flaubert,[26] he might have achieved that completeness for lack of which his splendid gifts and his amazing energy now sometimes run to waste. But, as he wrote himself of Carlyle, of whom he so often reminds us, 'if he did no perfect work he had lightning's power to strike out marvellous pictures and reach to the inmost of men with a phrase'.[27] The riot and confusion of the books; the sudden changes of perspective; the disconcerting mixture of the soaring and the didactic, disturb but do not destroy their power and their insight. And always as we read we feel that we are in the presence of a Greek god who sits incongruously surrounded by innumerable ornaments in a suburban drawing-room; who talks incessantly at the top of his voice; who is deaf to the lower tones of the human spirit; who is a little rigid and immobile perhaps, but at the same time marvellously alive and alert. This brilliant and uneasy figure has his place rather with the great eccentrics than with the great masters. His books are like the freakish blossoms which flower suddenly and strangely upon an old tree. He will be read, one may guess, by fits and starts. By many he will be found repellent, and by a few he will be idolised. But he will not be forgotten.

1 – A centenary essay in the *TLS*, 9 February 1928, (Kp C297), reprinted as 'George Meredith: Feb. 12, 1828', in *NYHT*, 12 February 1928, and, in part, as 'The Novels of George Meredith' in *CR*2, see *V VW Essays*. 'Yesterday we went to Hardy's funeral,' VW wrote in her diary on 17 January 1928, '. . . After dinner at Clive's Lytton protested that the great man's novels are the poorest of poor stuff; & cant read them . . . Over all this broods for me, some uneasy sense, of change & mortality, & how partings are deaths; & then a sense of my own fame – why should this come over me? – & then of its remoteness; & then the pressure of writing two articles on Meredith & furbishing up Hardy.' On 12 February she wrote to Edward

Sackville-West: 'I am disinclined for fiction of all kinds. But then I was forced to read all Meredith in a week. I did get through three of them; and feel like an old sheep which has torn off half its fleece, in a hedge' (*III VW Letters*, no. 1859). And see *LW Letters*, to Vanessa Bell, 7 February: 'Hardy and Meredith between them very nearly did for V.' See also 'On Re-Reading Meredith', *II VW Essays*; 'Small Talk About Meredith', 'Memories of Meredith', *III VW Essays*; 'Phases of Fiction: "The Poets"', *V VW Essays*. See Editorial Note, p. xxv. Reading Notes (MHP, B 2n). Reprinted *G&R and CE*.

2—For VW on George Meredith (1828–1909) 'twenty years ago' see *EJ*, Italy, 1908, pp. 391–2: 'I read Harry Richmond at Siena. I complain that Meredith fails to satisfy me, at the same time that I recognise a remarkable brain. Instead of sup-porting his fabric, as Hardy does, with an intricate wire netting, Meredith contents himself, as I think, with flimsy vapour, shot with all the colours of the sunset, but without substance where there should be substance. His mind seems to be so stuffed with conceits that he never allows himself to dispense with them, to look quite frankly, or perhaps, is conscious that his power is not for seeing things, but for covering them with a light of his own. So, at those times when sharp emotion requires that peoples [sic] characters should be distinct, that you may understand their action & feel its force, a fiery rhapsody obscures them completely. Has he really made so sure of his subjects that he can exhibit them in a crisis? The tempta-tion is great I imagine to cover them with brilliant generalities; explorers of poetry – epigrams – aphorisms; birthday book compilers will find such pages in Meredith full of treasure. I doubt though that the patient reader takes away one complete character, consistently developed. This failure is due to the intense centralisation of Merediths mind; all its power seems pent up within his own forehead, & turned upon the singular objects to be found there. In his novels, then, we get the shadow of something magnificent, & without likeness; red silhouettes of men, extravagant grotesques, an earth & sky all on fire as in perpetual sunset. It is a world of his own, as one says of the great writers; & so far, he too is a great writer. But now & again, as in Harry & Ottilia's love scene by the lake, in the adventures of the Pris-cilla, & the final catastrophe, there is something surely not of Merediths world, or of our world; cardboard mountains have been lifted from the stage, light is made of time; I suppose that supreme cleverness, long underrated, tempts him to such im-position. The public he thinks is too stupid to find out, & by degrees he deceives himself.'

3—E. M. Forster, *Aspects of the Novel* (Edward Arnold, 1927), V, 'The Plot', p. 120.

4—*Ibid.*, p. 121.

5—*The Ordeal of Richard Feverel* (1859).

6—Marcel Proust (1871–1922), Henry James (1843–1916), for VW on whom see especially 'Phases of Fiction: "The Psychologists"', *V VW Essays* and *G&R*.

7—*The Ordeal of Richard Feverel* (3 vols, Chapman and Hall, 1859), vol. ii, ch. iv, 'A Diversion Played on a Penny-Whistle', p. 41, chapter opening.

8—*The Adventures of Harry Richmond* (1871).

9—Charles Dickens (1812–70).

10—Robert Louis Stevenson (1850–94).

11—*The Adventures of Harry Richmond* (3 vols, Smith, Elder and Co., 1871), vol. i, ch. vi, 'A Tale of a Goose', p. 103.

12—Dickens's novel *David Copperfield* was first published in 1849–50.

13—Richmond Roy, the hero's father, and Princess Ottilia of Eppenwelzen-Sarkeld, in *Harry Richmond*.

14—Richard Feverel and Lucy Desborough; Harry Richmond and Princess Ottilia; Clara Middleton and Vernon Whitford (drawn from Leslie Stephen) in *The Egoist* (1879); Nevil Beauchamp and Renée de Croisnel in *Beauchamp's Career* (1875, 1876).

15—*The Adventures of Harry Richmond*, vol. ii, ch. ix, 'A Summer Storm, and Love', p. 101: 'The sky was bronze, a vast furnace dome. The folds of light and shadow everywhere were satin-rich; shadows perforce of blackness had light in them, and the light a sword-like sharpness over their edges. It was inanimate radiance. The laurels sparkled as with frost-points; the denser foliage drooped burning brown: a sickly saint's-ring was round the heads of the pines. That afternoon the bee hummed of thunder, and refreshed the ear.'

16—*Ibid.*, ch. xii, 'What Came of a Shilling', p. 145, which has: 'Those winter mornings are divine. They move on noiselessly. The earth is still as if waiting. A wren warbles, and flits through the lank drenched brambles; hill-side opens green; elsewhere is mist, everywhere expectancy. They bear the veiled sun like a zangreal aloft to the wavy marble flooring of stainless cloud.'

17—Stendhal (Henri Beyle, 1783–1842), for VW on whom see 'Stendhal', *III VW Essays*. Anton Chekhov (1860–1904), for VW on whom see 'Tchehov's Questions', *II VW Essays*; 'The Russian Background', '*The Cherry Orchard*', *III VW Essays*; 'The Russian Point of View' above. Jane Austen (1775–1817), see above.

18—*The Egoist* (3 vols, C. Kegan Paul and Co., 1879), vol. ii, ch. v, 'Treats of Union of Temper and Policy', p. 108: 'The Egoist, who is our original male in giant form, had no bleeding victim beneath his paw, but there was the sex to mangle.'

19—*The Ordeal of Richard Feverel*, vol. i, ch. vii, 'Arson', p. 111, which has: 'Richard gave his lungs loud play'; and *ibid.*, ch. xiv, 'In Which the Last Act of Bakewell Comedy is Closed in a Letter', p. 202, which has: 'Mama Thompson and her submissive brood sat tasking the swift intricacies of the needle, and emulating them with the tongue...'

20—L. N. Tolstoy (1828–1910).

21—*The Egoist*, vol. ii, ch. xii, 'Treating of the Dinner-Party at Mrs Mountstuart Jenkinson's', p. 263.

22—Daniel Defoe (1660–1731), for VW on whom see 'Defoe' and 'Robinson Crusoe' above. Henry Fielding (1707–54); Anthony Trollope (1815–82).

23—Ivan Turgenev (1818–83), for VW on whom see 'A Giant With Very Small Thumbs', above; 'A Glance at Turgenev', *III VW Essays*; and 'The Novels of Turgenev', *VI VW Essays*.

24—'The Idea of Comedy and the Uses of the Comic Spirit', a lecture given in 1877 and published in 1897; *Diana of the Crossways* (1885).

25—*The Egoist*, vol. i, ch. 6, 'His Courtship', p. 86.

26—Gustave Flaubert (1821–80).

27—*The Letters of George Meredith* (3 vols, ed. C. L. Cline, OUP, 1970), vol. ii, letter no. 744, to André Raffalovich, 23 May 1882, p. 661. Thomas Carlyle (1795–1881).

'Memories and Notes'

Mr Anthony Hope's Memoirs stand out from the ruck by the distinction of their manner and the modesty of their tone. Nature seems to have contrived that he should never settle down and take himself too seriously. First he wished to be an actor; but won a Balliol scholarship and so learnt the classics instead. Then, after leaving Oxford, he went to the Bar, and was just making a comfortable connection there when the slut Fiction, as he ungallantly calls her, induced him to write two or three highly successful novels, and to desert the Bar. That in outline is the story of what he calls 'an uneventful life'.[2] But it is told with a deftness, a humour, and an economy which make it much more than a mere record, or a mere anecdote. The men he knew he knew well. Some were as famous as Jowett, others as little known but as well remembered as Arthur Llewellyn Davies.[3] Mr Hope brings them before us with quiet skill. When it comes to speaking of himself – and it does not often come to that – he tells us that as a novelist he is 'inured to long and increasingly long periods of barrenness', which explains the rarity of his fiction. Also, 'my mind is intractable and does not readily accept tuition'[4] – in other words, he has a great gift for doing what he likes. He likes reading Jane Harrison – 'a great writer',[5] he calls her. He likes the study of anthropology and the history of religion. And for our part we should like a second volume of *Memories and Notes*.

1–A notice in the *N&A*, 11 February 1928, (Kp C297.1) of *Memories and Notes*. With a photograph of the author (Hutchinson and Co. Ltd, 1927) by Anthony Hope. Sir Anthony Hope Hawkins (1863–1933), author of *The Prisoner of Zenda* (1894). See 'Preferences' below. See also *IV VW Diary*, 15 September 1935.
2–Hope, ch. xv, p. 246, which has 'a very quiet and uneventful life'.
3–Benjamin Jowett (1817–93), Master of Balliol; (Roland) Arthur Llewelyn-Davies, killed in action 4 October 1918, while serving as a lieutenant in the Royal Fusiliers; he and Hawkins had been contemporaries at Marlborough.
4–For both quotations, Hope, ch. xv, p. 247.
5–*Ibid.*, ch. xv, p. 249. Jane Ellen Harrison (1850–1928), Greek scholar and from 1898 Lecturer in Classical Archaeology at Newnham College, Cambridge. The Hogarth Press published her *Reminiscences of a Student's Life* in 1925.

'The Cornish Miner'

It is impossible in a brief notice to give an adequate idea of the deep interest and, indeed, fascination of this book. Mr Jenkin has gone to the original sources, and has produced a book of genuine historical importance upon a theme which is rich in interest both for the student and for the general reader. The history both of the Cornish mines and of the Cornish miners is extremely varied and picturesque. The records go back for two thousand years. The industry has always been subject to extreme fluctuations of fortune. The demand for tin varies as social habits change. When pewter is in demand, the mines flourish; when earthenware comes in they suffer. Even so, the natives of China may take to burning tin leaf before their idols, and so the natives of Cornwall prosper again. Then science steps in, and with the new machinery new seams of copper are discovered, and an age of vast prosperity in the first half of the nineteenth century is inaugurated. The tinners, meanwhile, continue to be a race apart. They look upon the mines as the peasants in other parts of England look upon the great squire and the landlord. They seldom strike. They are the most savage of wreckers, and as time goes on the most devout of Wesleyans. They endure great suffering stoically. For when copper was introduced from abroad, the British industry almost collapsed, and the Cornish mine was known to most tourists as a derelict slag heap rusting to decay. In the past few years, however, tin has once more been found beneath the copper, and, with new methods of mining, it is probable that the industry is entering upon another lease of vigorous prosperity. Mr Jenkins tells the story, whose interest it is impossible to summarise, with great ability and skill.

1—A notice in the *N&A*, 25 February 1928, (Kp C297.2) of *The Cornish Miner* (Allen and Unwin, 1927) by A. K. Hamilton Jenkin.

An English Aristocrat

VW's essay in the *TLS*, 8 March 1928, (Kp C298) was later revised for inclusion, under the title 'Lord Chesterfield's Letters to His Son', in *The Common Reader*: 2nd series (1932). The reader is referred to *V VW Essays*, where the revised version, together with variants in the form of footnotes, is reprinted in its place as part of *The Common Reader*.

'Stalky's Reminiscences'

By far the most interesting part of this book is that devoted to the writer's schooldays. As everyone knows, General Dunsterville was at Westward Ho with Mr Kipling. He tells us a little about the celebrated author, who had already it seems found his style, for one of his first efforts was called 'Ave Imperatrix', and it was written in French class at the end of a French text-book.[2] Kipling, he says, must have been a difficult youth to manage. When the master raged at him, 'I remember Kipling . . . merely removing his glasses, polishing them carefully, replacing them on his nose, and gazing with placid bewilderment at the thundering tyrant, with a look that suggested, "There, there. Don't give way to your little foolish tantrums."'[3] There is a very interesting description of the headmaster Cormell Price[4] and his methods.

1—A notice in the *N&A*, 7 April 1928, (Kp C298.1) of *Stalky's Reminiscences* (Jonathan Cape, 1928) by Major-General L. C. Dunsterville, lifelong friend of Rudyard Kipling (1865–1936) from their schooldays together at the United Services College, Westward Ho!, and model for the hero in the latter's tales of schoolboy life *Stalky and Co.* (1899).
2—Dunsterville, ch. iii, 'Stalky & Co.', pp. 49–50.
3—*Ibid.*, p. 50.
4—A friend of Kipling's family and known to him as Uncle Crom; Cormell Price and his school, founded in 1874, specialised in coaching for the Army Entrance Examination.

Waxworks at the Abbey

Nobody but a very great man could have worn the Duke of Wellington's top hat. It is as tall as a chimney, as straight as a ramrod, as black as a rock. One could have seen it a mile off advancing indomitably down the street. It must have been to this emblem of incorruptible dignity that the Duke raised his two fingers when passers-by respectfully saluted him. One is almost tempted to salute it now.

The connexion between the waxworks in the Abbey and the Duke of Wellington's top hat is one that the reader will discover if he goes to the Abbey when the waxworks are shut. The waxworks have their hours of audience like other potentates. And if that hour is four and it is now a trifle past two, one may spend the intervening moments profitably in the United Services Museum in Whitehall, among cannon and torpedos and gun-carriages and helmets and spurs and faded uniforms and the thousand other objects which piety and curiosity have saved from time and treasured and numbered and stuck in glass cases for ever. When the time comes to go, indeed, there is not as much contrast as one would wish, perhaps, between the Museum at one end of Whitehall and the Abbey at the other. Too many monuments solicit attention with outstretched hands; too many placards explain this and forbid that; too many sightseers shuffle and stare for the past and the dead and the mystic nature of the place to have full sway. Solitude is impossible. Do we wish to see the Chapels? We are shepherded in flocks by gentlemen in black gowns who are forever locking us in or locking us out; round whom we press and gape; from whom drop raucously all kinds of dry unappetising facts; how much beauty this tomb has; how much age that; when they were destroyed; by whom they were restored and what the cost was – until everybody longs to be let off a tomb or two and is thankful when the lesson hour is over. However, if one is very wicked, and very bored, and lags a little behind; if the key is left in the door and turns quite easily, so that after all it is an open question whether one has broken one's country's laws or not, then one can slip aside, run up a little dark staircase and find oneself in a very small chamber alone with Queen Elizabeth.[2]

The Queen dominates the room as she once dominated England.

Leaning a little forward so that she seems to beckon you to come to her, she stands, holding her sceptre in one hand, her orb in the other. It is a drawn, anguished figure, with the pursed look of someone who goes in perpetual dread of poison or of trap; yet forever braces herself to meet the terror unflinchingly. Her eyes are wide and vigilant; her nose thin as the beak of a hawk; her lips shut tight; her eyebrows arched; only the jowl gives the fine drawn face its massiveness. The orb and the sceptre are held in the long thin hands of an artist, as if the fingers thrilled at the touch of them. She is immensely intellectual, suffering, and tyrannical. She will not allow one to look elsewhere.

Yet in fact the little room is crowded. There are many hands here holding other sceptres and orbs. It is only beside Queen Elizabeth that the rest of the company seems insignificant. Flowing in velvet they fill their glass cases, as they once filled their thrones, with dignity. William and Mary are an amiable pair of monarchs; bazaar-opening, hospital-inspecting, modern; though the King, unfortunately, is a little short in the legs. Queen Anne fondles her orb in her lap with plump womanly hands that should have held a baby there. It is only by accident that they have clapped a great crown on her hair and told her to rule a kingdom, when she would so much rather have flirted discreetly – she was a pretty woman; or run to greet her husband smiling – she was a kindly one. Her type of beauty in its homeliness, its domesticity, comes down to us less impaired by time than the grander style. The Duchess of Richmond, who gave her face to Britannia on the coins, is out of fashion now.[3] Only the carriage of the little head on the long neck, and the simper and the still look of one who has always stood still to be looked at assure us that she was beautiful once and had lovers beyond belief. The parrot sitting on its perch in the corner of the case seems to make its ironical comment on all that. Once only are we reminded of the fact that these effigies were moulded from the dead and that they were laid upon coffins and carried through the streets. The young Duke of Buckingham who died at Rome of consumption is the only one of them who has resigned himself to death.[4] He lies very still with the ermine on his shoulders and the coronet on his brows, but his eyes are shut; his nose is a great peak between two sunk cheeks; he has succumbed to death and lies steeped in its calm. His aloofness compares strangely with the carnality of Charles the Second round the corner. King Charles still seems quivering with the passions and the

greeds of life. The great lips are still pouting and watering and asking for more. The eyes are pouched and creased with all the long
nights they have watched out – the torches, the dancing, and the
women. In his dirty feathers and lace he is the very symbol of volup-
tuousness and dissipation, and his great blue-veined nose seems an
irreverence on the part of the modeller, as if to set the crowd, as the
procession comes by, nudging each other in the ribs and telling
merry stories of the monarch.

And so from this garish bright assembly we run downstairs again
into the Abbey, and enter that strange muddle and miscellany of
objects both hallowed and ridiculous. Yet now the impression is less
tumultuous than before. Two presences seem to control its incoherence, as sometimes a chattering group of people is ordered and
quieted by the entry of someone before whom, they know not why,
they fall silent. One is Elizabeth, beckoning; the other is an old top-
hat.

1–An essay in the NR, 11 April 1928, (Kp C299), also published as 'The Waxworks at the Abbey' in Eve, 23 May 1928. Reprinted G&R, CE.
2–The wax funeral effigy of Elizabeth I (probably not the original but a replace-
ment commissioned by the Abbey's Lay Clerks in 1760) was at this date kept, together with other effigies, in the Upper Islip Chapel (now known as the Nurses'
Chapel). The effigies can today be seen at the Undercroft Museum.
3–Frances Teresa Stuart, Duchess of Richmond and Lennox (1647–1702), known
as 'La Belle Stuart' and famously pursued by Charles II, figured as Britannia on
numerous medals and on the halfpenny coin issued in 1672 to a design by John
Roettiers.
4–Edmund (Sheffield), Duke of Buckingham and Normanby, Marquess of Normanby, Earl of Mulgrave, and Baron Sheffield of Butterwicke (1716–1735), died at
Rome of rapid consumption, aged 19, and was buried at Westminster Abbey.

Preferences

Your request that I should name some books that have interested
me during the past winter sets me rummaging through my memory
– a proceeding which proves perhaps that I have read nothing
which made a very deep impression on me. But I must immediately
add that my reading has been neither deep nor wide and, as is
always the case with current books, much at the mercy of chance.

Thus some of the most admired books of the winter have, for one reason or another, escaped me. I have been constantly advised to read Miss Bowen's *The Hotel*, but have not yet come across it. I have heard Mr Wilder's *The Bridge of San Luis Rey* and Mr Julien Green's *Avarice House*[2] discussed whenever books were mentioned. Some critics declare them both to be novels of high and lasting merit; others find in them only skilful imitations of good books. So one waits for the dust to settle. For my own part I would like to praise one novel and one book of short stories, but as both were published at my instance by the Hogarth Press I must refrain. I have also bought and propose to read should my life last long enough the final volumes of Proust's masterpiece.[3] The advance guard who have been to the journey's end speak in the highest praise of it, but for such an expedition time and courage are needed.

As I trace the course of my winter's reading I find it irregular, as it is leading steadily away from fiction in the direction of poetry and biography. The most interesting winter's biography has been undoubtedly Monsieur Jean-Aubry's life of Conrad.[4] It is neither a work of art nor a psychological document, but it contains a mass of information from which one can create Conrad for one's self, and for that one must be grateful. Gertrude Bell's Letters[5] interested me profoundly. Chance and choice combined to let me read many obscure autobiographies. The most notable are George Sturt's *Small Boy in the Sixties*, Lord Ribblesdale's Memoirs, which have a fine dashing style of their own, Mr Anthony Hope's Memoirs, a model of modesty and concision, and the first volume of Lord Curzon's Life.[6] But it is the poets who have given me the greatest pleasure. One is Lady Winchilsea, whose poems are many winters old but have lived in such obscurity that their beauty seems new, and another is Mr Yeats. Mr Yeats improves poetically as he grows older. *The Tower*[7] contains his best, deepest and most imaginative work. When I say nothing has impressed me deeply I must except that for which alone the winter was memorable.

But as I look through the crowded lists I feel with some distress how likely it is that in the press and scuffle the book I should most have enjoyed has been trampled under foot and will only be found reprinted when 'I have lain for centuries dead.'[8]

1–A contribution to the *NYHT*, 15 April 1928, (Kp C300), under the heading 'Preferences of Four Critics'. The other contributors were: G. B. Stern (1890–1973), for

VW on whom see 'Life and the Novelist' above; Rebecca West (1892–1983); and Ellen Glasgow (1874–1945).

2–Elizabeth Bowen, *The Hotel* (1927); Thornton Wilder, *The Bridge of San Luis Rey* (1927); Julien Green, *Avarice House*, translated by M. A. Best (1927).

3–Marcel Proust, *À la recherche du temps perdu* (1913–27). Proust had died in 1922; *Le Temps retrouvé*, the last two volumes of his novel, appeared in 1927.

4–G. Jean Aubry, *Joseph Conrad. Life and Letters* (1927).

5–Gertrude Bell, *The Letters of Gertrude Bell*, selected and edited by Lady [Florence] Bell (1927).

6–George Sturt, *A Small boy in the Sixties* (1927); Thomas Lister, Baron Ribblesdale, *Impressions and Memories* (1927); Anthony Hope, *Memories and Notes* (1927), for VW on which see above; Laurence J. L. Dundas, *The Life of Lord Curzon* (3 vols, 1928).

7–Lady Anne Winchelsea, *Poems ... 1661–1720*, selected by John Middleton Murry (1928); for VW on Lady Anne see *A Room of My Own* (1929), ch. iv; W. B. Yeats, *The Tower* (1928), for VW on which see 'Mr Yeats' below.

8–This quotation, which possibly derives from a classical source, is echoed by (or else echoes) Tennyson, *Maud*, pt. I, xxii, xi: 'Had I lain for a century dead'.

Mr Yeats

> Did all old men and women, rich and poor,
> Who trod upon these rocks or passed this door,
> Whether in public or in secret rage
> As I do now against old age?[2]

So Mr Yeats asks in one of the poems in *The Tower*, and the thought of his age and the impediments it brings recurs again and again. Hence perhaps the remarkable vitality of this last book of poems. Instead of the acquiescence of old age we have the exacting self-tormenting mood of a man who resents and fights old age, and instead of yielding to it supinely is spurred by it to greater animation than before. Whatever the cause, Mr Yeats has never written more exactly and more passionately.

So rare is it for the poet to have mastered the art of dealing with everyday emotions, while he yet keeps them remote, that we have got into the habit of turning to the prose writers to express what we feel. But Mr Yeats is at once very close and very aloof. He is able by some supremely difficult combination of art and emotion to speak quite simply and yet in the universal language. Now we seem almost to hear some one talking, the verse runs so nervously, so idiomatically; and now we are given lines all grown together with meaning, massive, and incapable of disintegration. Here he is as vivid as a novelist:

> There lurches past, his great eyes without thought,
> Under the shadow of striped straw-pale lock,
> That insolent fiend Robert Artisson;[3]

and now, in 'Leda and the Swan' he carves as remote and impersonal an image of beauty as if we were made of spirit and wanted only loveliness to look at:

> How can those terrified vague fingers push
> The feathered glory from her loosening thighs?
> And how can body, laid in that white rush
> But feel the strange heart beating where it lies?[4]

And, instead of cutting off his mind and letting language soar, as the English language will do after all these years of teaching almost by itself, his intellect is always active and at work. The reader has to read very cautiously lest he overrun his signals. The poems are difficult, not through obscurity of language, but because the thought lies deep and turns strangely.

Possibly then – the thought has its encouragement – this is an age when poets only become mature when they are old. The poet's task is harder than it was. He requires an austerity which is difficult for the young; must have felt the lure of language and not yielded to it; and must have said so many things in so many ways that at last – being always vigilant and not self-satisfied – he can use his natural voice in speaking and be still musical. At any rate, years seem to have dried up the Celtic mists, to have braced the nerves and sharpened the senses of this particular poet, so that he reverses the usual order and is a better poet in his age than in his youth.

1–An unsigned review in the *N&A*, 21 April 1928, (Kp C301) of *The Tower* (Macmillan and Co. Ltd, 1928) by W. B. Yeats (1865–1939). On 6 March VW had written to Vita Sackville-West about an encounter with the Irish writer James Stephens who told her that 'Yeats spent 20 years writing Leda [and the Swan]; and used to say it over and over, till the weight of every word was right: sometimes he would take one out, and then next year put it in again' (*III VW Letters*, no. 1868). For a portrait of Yeats by VW see *III VW Diary*, 8 November 1930. See also 'Preferences' above and see 'Some Poetical Plays', where VW discusses Yeats's *Deirdre* (1907), (*Guardian*, 1 January 1908) in *VI VW Essays*, Appendix.

2–Yeats, 'The Tower', II, pp. 10–11.
3–*Ibid.*, 'Nineteen Hundred and Nineteen', VI, p. 41, which has 'stupid straw-pale locks,'.
4–*Ibid.*, 'Leda and the Swan', p. 51.

'Behind the Scenes with Cyril Maude'

This is a kindly autobiography. It follows amiably in the well-worn footsteps of such works, and tells story after story until we should almost welcome dullness as a relief. And Mr Maude himself gets a little tired of the theatre and its incessant gossip before the end. 'I hope never to have to play again,' he writes, 'but to live my life down in Devon mostly,' where by a stroke of luck he has found 'an ideal little country house by the sea'.

1–A notice in the *N&A*, 28 April 1928, (Kp C301.1) of *Behind the Scenes with Cyril Maude*. By Himself (John Murray, 1928). Cyril Francis Maude (1862–1951), actor-manager. For the quotations, Maude, ch. xxiii, pp. 318 and 314 respectively.

'Behind the Brass Plate'

A doctor is in an unrivalled position for observing human life and a doctor who observes shrewdly and can write efficiently is bound to produce a delightful, an amusing, a memorable book. Dr Schofield's book is all three. And it has the further advantage that it is not the book of a specialist, confined to the treatment of one disease. Dr Schofield has been a general practitioner in life. He was an atheist, and in the twinkling of an eye became the most devout of Christians – but never a solemn one. He was for many years a man of business; but just as his business flourished, certain practices tolerated in business, but not in private life, disgusted him and he threw up his career as his father had done before him. He came thus to medicine with more experiences than fall to the usual lot. For this reason perhaps he seems to have known every sort of person, and to have heard every sort of queer story. No student of Carlyle's life ought to neglect the very amusing description of Louisa Lady Ashburton as she appeared when she was not perhaps on her best behaviour.[2] We have seldom read a more vivid and accurate account of the vagaries of a great lady of the Victorian age. And at the same time one can see by what spells it was that she captivated the peasant of genius and nearly ruined his life.

1—A notice in the *N&A*, 5 May 1928, (Kp C301.2) of *Behind the Brass Plate* (Sampson Low, 1928) by Dr A. T. Schofield.
2—Thomas Carlyle (1795–1881) proved famously susceptible to the charms of Harriet (not Louisa) Mary, Lady Ashburton, *née* Montagu (d. 1857), wife of William Bingham Baring, 2nd Baron Ashburton, so causing his wife Jane Welsh Carlyle the deepest distress.

'The Book of Catherine Wells'

Mrs Wells was herself a writer. But the fact that she was married to a writer of the eminence and popularity of Mr Wells acts upon her as it would act upon a shy and sensitive woman. 'She sent her work to various periodicals from a different address and through various agents so as not to be identified with me,'[2] her husband writes. Many of the stories – the Emerald in particular – show that she was genuinely gifted with the writer's temperament. She was, it is clear, aware of something which she could only express by writing it down. The work is remarkably expressive for an untrained pen, and, what is more remarkable, shows, one would say, no trace of her husband's influence. But perhaps the chief interest of the stories is that they help to consolidate the very interesting suggestion which Mr Wells makes as to his wife's peculiar and complex temperament. She had two personalities, one christened Jane, the other Catherine. Jane was practical, an able 'shopper'; 'she helped people in difficulties and stood no nonsense from the plumber.'[3] Catherine was a dreamer, mystical, aloof. Both combined, with many others, to form a personality which was one of singular charm and humanity. The book, indeed, indicates a whole character and outlook in a most attractive way.

1—A notice in the *N&A*, 26 May 1928, (Kp C301.3) of *The Book of Catherine*

Wells. With an introduction by her husband H. G. Wells [1866–1946] (Chatto and Windus, 1928). For VW on meeting Amy Catherine ('Jane') Wells, *née* Robbins (1872–1927), see *III VW Diary*, 1 July 1926; and for an account of Catherine Wells's funeral see *ibid.*, 27 October 1927 (see also *III VW Letters*, no. 1820).

2–Wells, Introduction, p. 4.

3–*Ibid.*, p. 6.

'On the Stage: An Autobiography'

The first chapter of Mr Arliss's book, which describes Bloomsbury, London, W.C., England, about 1880, is enough to show that Mr Arliss has the picturesque power of a real writer. He isolates a scene and savours its delicious peculiarities. He writes far better than an actor who has been busy in his profession all his life has a call to. In short, if only he had not had to cram in so many stories and changes of scene and facts about this play and that, if he could have let himself go, and stood rather further off from his page, he would have written a real book; as it is he has written a book which vacillates in the strangest manner from an actor's scrap-book to a genuine autobiography.

1–A notice in the *N&A*, 30 June 1928, (Kp C301.4) of *On the Stage: An Autobiography* (John Murray, 1928) by George Arliss (1868–1946).

An Introduction to *Mrs Dalloway*

It is difficult – perhaps impossible – for a writer to say anything about his own work. All he has to say has been said as fully and as well as he can in the body of the book itself. If he has failed to make his meaning clear there it is scarcely likely that he will succeed in some pages of preface or postscript. And the author's mind has another peculiarity which is also hostile to introductions. It is as inhospitable to its offspring as the hen sparrow is to hers. Once the young birds can fly, fly they must; and by the time they have fluttered out of the nest the mother bird has begun to think perhaps of another brood. In the same way once a book is printed and published it ceases to be the property of the author; he commits it to the care of other people; all his attention is claimed by some new book which not only thrusts its predecessor from the next but has a way of subtly blackening its character in comparison with its own.

It is true that the author can if he wishes tell us something about himself and his life which is not in the novel; and to this effort we should do all that we can to encourage him. For nothing is more fascinating than to be shown the truth which lies behind those immense façades of fiction — if life is indeed true, and if fiction is indeed fictitious. And probably the connection between the two is highly complicated. Books are the flowers or fruit stuck here and there on a tree which has its roots deep down in the earth of our earliest life, of our first experiences. But here again to tell the reader anything that his own imagination and insight have not already discovered would need not a page or two of preface but a volume or two of autobiography. Slowly and cautiously one would have to go to work, uncovering, laying bare, and even so when everything had been brought to the surface, it would still be for the reader to decide what was relevant and what not. Of *Mrs Dalloway* then one can only bring to light at the moment a few scraps, of little importance or none perhaps; as that in the first version Septimus, who later is intended to be her double, had no existence; and that Mrs Dalloway was originally to kill herself, or perhaps merely to die at the end of the party. Such scraps are offered humbly to the reader in the hope that like other odds and ends they may come in useful.

But if one has too much respect for the reader pure and simple to point out to him what he has missed, or to suggest to him what he should seek, one may speak more explicitly to the reader who has put off his innocence and become a critic. For though criticism, whether praise or blame, should be accepted in silence as the legitimate comment which the act of publication invites, now and again a statement is made without bearing on the book's merits or demerits which the writer happens to know to be mistaken. One such statement has been made sufficiently often about *Mrs Dalloway* to be worth perhaps a word of contradiction. The book, it was said, was the deliberate offspring of a method. The author, it was said, dissatisfied with the form of fiction then in vogue, was determined to beg, borrow, steal or even create another of her own. But, as far as it is possible to be honest about the mysterious process of the mind, the facts are otherwise. Dissatisfied the writer may have been; but her dissatisfaction was primarily with nature for giving an idea, without providing a house for it to live in. The novelists of the preceding generation had done little – after all why should they? – to help. The novel was the obvious lodging, but the novel it seemed was built on the wrong plan. Thus rebuked the idea started as the oyster starts or the snail to secrete a house for itself. And this it did without any conscious direction. The little note-book in which an attempt was made to forecast a plan was soon abandoned, and the book grew day by day, week by week, without any plan at all, except that which was dictated each morning in the act of writing. The other way, to make a house and then inhabit it, to develop a theory and then apply it, as Wordsworth did and Coleridge, is, it need not be said, equally good and much more philosophic. But in the present case it was necessary to write the book first and to invent a theory afterwards.

If, however, one singles out the particular point of the book's methods for discussion it is for the reason given – that it has been made the subject of comment by critics, not that in itself it deserves notice. On the contrary, the more successful the method, the less it attracts attention. The reader it is to be hoped will not give a thought to the book's method or to the book's lack of method. He is concerned only with the effect of the book as a whole on his mind. Of that most important question he is a far better judge than the writer. Indeed, given time and liberty to frame his own opinion he is eventually an infallible judge. To him then the writer commends *Mrs Dalloway* and leaves the court confident that the verdict whether for instant death or for some years more of life and liberty will in either case be just.

1 – VW's introduction to an impression of the first American edition of her novel *Mrs Dalloway* (1925), published by Random House as vol. 96 in 'The Modern Library of the World's Best Books', 24 December 1928 (Kp A9c). The piece is signed as having been written in: 'London. June 1928'. See Editorial Note, p. xxv.

'Clara Butt: Her Life Story'

Miss Butt is six foot two, and her stature is faithfully reflected in her biography. Her biographer makes us feel that Miss Butt is a great deal bigger than the ordinary human being. She writes in a strain of adulation which is fitted for a giantess. And in some respects undoubtedly this is an accurate view of anyone with a voice of the calibre of Miss Butt's. Ordinary limits cease to have any meaning for them. When her voice boomed out everything went down before it. The middle-class girl – she is descended from Theodore Hook[2] by the way – became the friend of Empresses. She mixed familiarly with Kings and Princes. She seems possessed not only of the height but of the temper of the Gods. Wherever she goes people fall down before her. All her efforts are crowned with success. Yet Miss Ponder writes well enough to give us the impression that Clara Butt is no lay figure. She is obviously a woman of gigantic vitality. She was able to hold her own with conductors and professors long before she had her fame to back her. Nothing annoys her more than the legend that she takes her work easily. Few people could have sung 'Abide with me' as she did, with a fly stuck in her throat.[3] But while the book gives a lively and enthusiastic account of Clara Butt, it is strange how seldom music is mentioned. The Empress of Germany is much more important.

1–A notice in the N&A, 14 July 1928, (Kp C301.5) of *Clara Butt: Her Life Story*. With a foreword by Dame Clara Butt [1872–1936], and twenty-four illustrations (George G. Harrap and Co. Ltd, 1928) by Winifred Ponder.
2–Theodore Edward Hook (1788–1841), author of light verse and popular novels, sometime editor of *John Bull*.
3–For this incident, Ponder, ch. xiii, p. 172. 'Abide with me...' was originally composed for Butt by Samuel Liddle, her pianist.

'Day In, Day Out'

Mrs Le Blond, who is the author of a well-known book on Italian gardens, was first married to the famous Colonel Burnaby. She is descended from many races. Hence, perhaps, she has had many experiences. Her memories begin with the Prince of Wales's set and hunting in Ireland. Mrs Le Blond has been very lucky in her sightseeing. She has seen most people of importance in the last fifty years or so, most quarters of the globe, and her luck did not fail her last summer when she was one of the few people who had a perfect view of the eclipse.[2]

1–A notice in the *N&A*, 11 August 1928, (Kp C301.6) of *Day In, Day Out* with twenty-nine illustrations (John Lane The Bodley Head Ltd, 1928) by Mrs Aubrey Le Blond (*née* Elizabeth Alice Frances Hawkins Whitshed), whose first husband was Colonel Frederick Gustavus Burnaby (1842–85), traveller and soldier, who died in the campaign to relieve General Gordon at Khartoum.
2–Mrs Le Blond travelled to Southport in Lancashire to see the total eclipse on 29 June 1927 which VW saw from Yorkshire (see 'The Sun and the Fish' above).

'A Sentimental Journey'

VW's essay in the *NYHT*, 23 September 1928, (Kp C303) was later revised to serve as an introduction to the World's Classics edition of Sterne's novel and included as 'The "Sentimental Journey"' in *The Common Reader*: 2nd series (1932). The reader is referred to V VW Essays, where the revised version, together with variants in the form of footnotes, is reprinted in its place as part of *The Common Reader*.

'The Diaries of Mary, Countess of Meath'

This volume of Lady Meath's diaries is limited to the account of her philanthropic undertakings and travels between the years 1874 and 1900. It cannot therefore be taken as a full record of her life, but it gives nevertheless a very curious account of the charitable life of a Victorian great lady. It was strenuous in the extreme. Lady Meath never ceased to found homes for Epileptic Women; for Aged Ladies; to start schemes for the good of people in workhouses; to improve cottages and to build workmen's dwellings on her husband's estate. When she went abroad, she and Lord Meath bought vast numbers of musical boxes – over nine hundred in one shop indeed – and oleographs, which they distributed in hospitals and workhouse infirmaries. Her visits to the houses of other great ladies always included prayer meetings and religious discussions. 'On the way there and back Lady Ailsa talked to me almost entirely on receiving Christ . . . Drove over to Maybole . . . Lady Ailsa goes there once a week to read and pray with some who were drunkards.'² And so it goes on, both in England and in foreign countries. Once she met Lady Russell, who was anxious that her grandson (Lady Amberley's boy) should 'turn out all that is nice'.³ This is perhaps the first reference to Mr Bertrand Russell.

1–A notice in the N&A, 29 September 1928, (Kp C303.1) of *The Diaries of Mary, Countess of Meath. Edited by her Husband*. With twenty-eight illustrations (vol. i, 1874–99, Hutchinson and Co. Ltd, 1928). Lady Mary Jane (d. 1918), daughter of Thomas Maitland, 11th Earl of Lauderdale, had married in 1868 Reginald Brabazon, 12th Earl of Meath (1841–1929), diplomat and philanthropist.
2–For the quotation up to the first ellipsis, Meath, 6 November 1881, p. 40, and for the remainder, *ibid.*, 7 November, p. 41, adapted.
3–*Ibid.*, 3 September 1881, p. 35. Bertrand Russell (1872–1970), son of Viscount (d. 1876) and Lady Amberley (d. 1874), was, upon his father's death, brought up under the guardianship of his paternal grandmother, second wife and after 1878 widow of the 1st Earl Russell, in whose 'firm and unremitting care' (*DNB*) he remained until he went up to Cambridge in 1890.

Dorothy Osborne's Letters

It is pleasant to find the Clarendon Press putting its fine print and paper at the service of Dorothy Osborne, and Mr Moore-Smith bestowing on her such scholarship and devotion that there is scarcely a date lacking where dates were very dubious and scarcely a reference left obscure where references were very elusive. Thus she enters among the classics. Thus a new generation confirms the insight of Judge Parry by whose perspicacity her letters were first brought to light,² and proves the truth of Macaulay's contention that 'the mutual relations of the two sexes seem to us to be at least as important as the mutual relations of any two governments in the world'.[3] Dorothy Osborne indeed has a twofold claim upon our sympathy. She was the heroine of what she called a 'romance story',[4] for she loved William Temple and they were poor and they were separated and were united at last; and she was also a woman of charm enough and of wit enough to make us read her letters for the sheer pleasure of reading them.

In our day, no doubt, a Dorothy Osborne with Dorothy Osborne's gift for writing would have written books. In her day – she was born in 1627 and died in 1694[5] – the thought of a woman writing a book had something monstrous about it. Only madcaps like the crazy Duchess of Newcastle wrote books. 'Sure the poore woman is a little distracted' was Dorothy's comment upon the authoress. 'If I should not sleep this fortnight, I should not come to that.'[6] Women's art was the art of letter writing, an occupation one could carry on at odd moments, by a father's sick bed, among a thousand interruptions, anonymously as it were, and often with the pretence that it served some useful purpose. Into these innumerable letters, for the most part irretrievably lost, to our great impoverishment, went those powers of observation and wit that were later to take rather a different shape in *Evelina* and *Pride and Prejudice*.[7] The women letter writers were the true forerunners of the women novelists. Without any special education, Dorothy had clear views upon the art of letter writing. '. . . great Schollers are not the best writer's (of letters I mean, of books perhaps they are) . . . all letters mee thinks should be free and easy as one's discourse.'[8] Indeed, she was in agreement with an old uncle of hers, who threw his standish at his secretary's head for saying 'put pen to paper' instead of simply 'wrote'.[9] Later, it is true, with the Bible and Shakespeare running in her head, she reflects that there is a difference between the spoken word and what can be written even in a letter. '. . . many pritty things shuffled together'[10] do better spoken than in a letter.

And so we come by a form of literature, if Dorothy Osborne will let us call it so, easy yet formal, which is different from any other, and which we may well regret now that it is gone from us, as true letter writing seems gone from us, for ever. For Dorothy Osborne, as she filled her great sheets with this fine prose, gave us a record of life seen from the chimney corner day in and day out, and imparted freely to a public of one. In such a manner and to such an audience, things can be said with an ease and intimacy that the novelist can never know. She gossips, she tells a story, she makes love, she reflects. Since it is her business to keep her lover informed of what passes in her home, she must sketch the solemn Sir Justinian Isham – Sir Soloman Justinian she calls him – the pompous widower, with four daughters and a great gloomy house in Northamptonshire, who wished to marry her. 'Lord what would I give that I had a Lattin letter of his for you,' she exclaims, in which he gave an Oxford friend a character of her, specially commending her that she was 'capable of being company and conversation for him';[11] she must sketch her Cousin Molle waking up one morning in fear of the dropsy and taking coach in a hurry to his doctor in Cambridge; and describe rhapsodically the lovely Lady Diana Rich whose mind was even more charming than her body. Any gossip that comes her way is sent on to amuse her lover. Lady Sunderland, for instance, has condescended to marry plain Mr Smith,[12] who treats her like a princess, which Sir Justinian thinks a bad example for wives. But Lady Sunderland tells everyone she married him out of pity and that, Dorothy comments, 'was the pittyfull'st sayeing that ever I heard'.[13] Soon we have picked up enough about her friends to relish any further addition to the portraits that are forming in her mind's eye. Indeed, our glimpses of the society of Bedfordshire in the seventeenth century are all the more intriguing because we never know whether Sir Justinian will pop in again or whether Lady Diana cured the eyes that had slain so many, or what became of Mr Smith and his lady. In they come and out they go, for all the world like living people. But with all this intermittency the letters, like the letters of born letter writers, provide their own continuity. They make us feel soon that we have our seat at the centre of the pageant, in the depths of Dorothy's mind, which unfolds itself page by page as we read. For she possessed indisputably the gift which counts for more in letter writing than wit or brilliance or traffic with great people; she gave herself away merely by being herself without a word of emphasis or analysis, and thus envelops all these odds and ends in the mesh of her own personality. It was a character both original and attractive. Phrase by phrase we come closer into touch with it.

Of the womanly virtues that befitted her age we hear indeed very little. She says nothing of sewing or of baking. She was perhaps a little indolent by temperament. She browsed casually on vast French romances. She roamed the commons, loitered to hear the milkmaids singing their ballads, and walked her garden by night smelling sweet scented jasmine and wishing that Temple were with her. She was apt to fall silent and sit dreaming over the fire, inattentive to what was said, till some talk of flying, perhaps, roused her, and she made her brother laugh by asking what they were saying about flying, for the thought had struck her, would that she could fly to London and be with Temple! This pensive strain was dominant in rousing her to a sense of fortune and its tyranny, making her feel the vanity of things, and the littleness of man, and the uselessness of effort. A vein of melancholy and some turn for letters ran, it seems, in the family. Her sister, she notes, who had 'a great deal of Witt and was thought to write as well as most Women in England . . . was a melancholy retir'd woman and besydes the company of her husband and her book's never sought any,' and again she quotes her mother, 'whoe (if it may be allow'd mee to say it) was counted as wise a woman as most in England' – telling her 'I have lived to see that 'tis almost impossible to think People worse than they are and soe will you.'[14] Dorothy indeed, had to assuage her spleen by drinking water that steel had been stood in, and by visiting the wells at Epsom.

With all this melancholy her humour naturally took the form of irony rather than of wit. She loved to mock her lover, and to pour a fine raillery over the pomps and ceremonies of existence. Pride of birth she laughed at. Pompous old men were fine subjects for her satire. A dull sermon moved her to laughter. She saw through fine clothes and fine speeches to the greed or the snobbery beneath. But with this fastidiousness went a fear of ridicule, a hatred of publicity almost morbid in their intensity. The interference of a brother or an aunt under the guise of affection exasperated her. 'I would live in a hollow Tree,' she said, 'to avoyde them.' A husband kissing his wife in public seemed to her as 'ill a sight as one would wish to see'. Though she disdained the good opinion of the world and cared no more for their praise of her wit or beauty than 'whether they think my name Eliz: or Dor:'[15] any gossip about her private life set her in a quiver. A faithful friend, a moderate fortune, a retired life – those were the ends of her ambition.

Thus, when it came to action, when it came to proving in the eyes of the world the depth and the tenderness of her love, to which her dreams by night and her thoughts by day bore witness, she could not bring herself to do it. There was a timidity, a deep-seated fear of ridicule in her which made her afraid to risk censure by marrying a penniless man like Temple. 'I confesse that I have an humor will not suffer mee to Expose myself to People's Scorne,'[16] she wrote. Clear-sighted as she was, and unworldly, she shrank from any extravagance that could draw the eyes of the gossips upon her. It was a weakness for which Temple had sometimes to reprove her. For Temple's character emerges more and more clearly – it is a proof of Dorothy's gift as a correspondent. A good letter writer so takes the colour of his correspondent that from reading the one we can imagine the other. As she argues, as she reasons, we hear Temple almost as clearly as we hear Dorothy herself. He was in many ways the opposite of her. He drew out her melancholy by rebutting it. He made her defend her dislike of marriage by opposing it. Temple, it is clear, though but one of his letters to her remains, was by far the more positive and resolute of the two. Yet there is perhaps something a little hard, a little conceited in him, that justified her brother's dislike of him. Henry Osborne, though his jealous love for his sister and his desire for her worldly advantage make him a partial witness, called him, Dorothy says, the 'proudest imperious insulting ill-natured man that ever was'.[17] But to Dorothy undoubtedly Temple had qualities that none of her other suitors possessed. He was not a mere country gentleman; nor a pompous justice of the peace; nor a pedantic lawyer; nor a town gallant making love to every woman he met; nor a travelled Monsieur; nor, in short, was he in any way a fool. For had he been any one of these things, Dorothy, with her quick sense of the ridiculous, would have dispatched him instantly. Some charm he had, some fineness of sympathy which lets her write to him whatever comes into her head, sense or nonsense, and makes her feel herself at her best with him. He was a man of taste, too, and could praise her letters so as to give her, who disliked praise mostly, some of the joys of fame. No two people, it would seem, were better fitted to marry each other. Yet suddenly she declared that marry him she would not.

The passion which inspires marriage is the most vile and tyrannical of our senses, she argued. Passion had made Lady Anne Blount the 'talk of all the footmen and Boy's in the street'.[18] Passion had been the undoing – of the lovely Lady Izabella – what should she do with beauty now, married to 'that beast with all his estate?'[19] If people knew each other before marriage there would be no more marrying, she thought. Indeed, torn asunder by her brother's anger, by Temple's jealousy and that queer shrinking of hers at the thought of the world's laughter, she wished for nothing but to be left to herself and to find 'an early, and a quiet grave'.[20] That Temple overcame her scruples and overrode her brother's ill will is much to the credit of his character. Yet it is an act that we can scarcely help deploring. Married to Temple, Dorothy wrote no more. Perhaps she was too happy; perhaps she was too dull. All is open to conjecture, for with a reticence that became her well, Lady Temple said nothing.

1—A signed review in the *NR*, 24 October 1928, (Kp C304) and (as 'Dorothy Osborne') in the *TLS*, 25 October (see Appendix V), of *The Letters of Dorothy Osborne* [1627–95] *to William Temple* [1628–99]. Ed. G. C. Moore-Smith (OUP, 1928), incorporated in part in 'Dorothy Osborne's "Letters"', *CR2* (see Editorial Note, p. xxv; and *V VW Essays*). 'And I felt this is the heart of England – this wedding in the country [at Rodmell]:', VW observed in her diary on 22 September 1928, 'history I felt; Cromwell; The Osbornes; Dorothy's shepherdesses singing: of all of whom Mr & Mrs Jarrad seem more descendants than I am: as if they represented the unconscious breathing of England & L & I, leaning over the wall, were detached, unconnected ... Down here I have flung myself tooth & nail on my fiction book, & should have finished the first draft but for Dorothy Osborne whom I'm dashing off ... And there were the Russell Cookes ... A woman is in some ways so much better than a man – more natural, juicy, unfettered. But then he is a bounder ... I must use that cliché because I must do my Osborne article. & it is getting cold out here.' See also *III VW Letters*, no. 1927, 25 September, to LW (from Saulieu in France) and *LW Letters*, to VW, 25 and 26 September (pp. 233, 234). Reading Notes (MHP, B 2n and B 3c).
2—*Letters from Dorothy Osborne to Sir William Temple 1652–1654* Ed. E. A. Parry (1888).
3—Thomas Babington Macaulay, *Critical and Historical Essays* (2 vols, J. M. Dent, 1907), vol. i, 'Sir William Temple', p. 209.
4—Moore-Smith, Letter 54, 13–15 January 1653/4, p. 130: 'but noe I saw you, when I shall doe it againe god only know's; can there bee a more Romance Story then ours would make if the conclusion should prove happy?'
5—The *DNB* gives the year of Dorothy Osborne's death as 1695. In his pedigrees of the Osborne and Temple families, Moore-Smith provides no year for her death but does give her year of birth as 1627.
6—Moore-Smith, Letter 17, 14 April 1653, p. 37. For VW on Margaret Cavendish, Duchess of Newcastle (1623–73), see 'The Duchess of Newcastle' above.
7—Fanny Burney, *Evelina* (1778); Jane Austen, *Pride and Prejudice* (1813).
8—Moore-Smith, Letter 40, September 1653, p. 90.
9—*Ibid.*, p. 91.
10—*Ibid.*, Letter 60, 25 February 1653/4. p. 153.
11—*Ibid.*, Letter 6, 29 January 1652/3, p. 15. Sir Justinian Isham (1610–74), MP for Northamptonshire after the Restoration; his first wife Jane, *née* Garrard, died in

childbirth in 1638–9. The 'Emperor' as Osborne also referred to him, was eventually remarried, in 1653, to Vere, daughter of Lord Leigh of Stoneleigh.

12 – Lady Dorothy Sidney (Waller's 'Sacharissa'), widow of the Earl of Sunderland (d. 1643), married in 1652 plain Robert Smith, Esq., of Bounds Park, Tonbridge, whose titular inadequacy was made good by the award of a baronetcy after the Restoration. Henry Molle (1597–1658), Fellow of King's College, Cambridge, author of light verse and prose 'characters', was distantly related to the Osborne family. Lady Diana Rich, youngest daughter of Henry, Earl of Holland, and Isabel née Cope.

13 – Moore-Smith, Letter 6, 29 January 1652/3, p. 16.

14 – For the first quotation, *ibid.*, Letter 40, September 1653, pp. 89–90; and for the two subsequent quotations, Letter 59, 19 February 1653/4, p. 150 and p. 151 respectively. Osborne's sister referred to here was Elizabeth, Lady Peyton (1610–42); her mother, Dorothy née Danvers (d. 1650 or 1651).

15 – For the first quotation, *ibid.*, Letter 21, 14 May 1653, p. 43; for the second, Letter 41, October 1653, p. 95; and the third, Letter 45, 23 October 1653, p. 110.

16 – *Ibid.*, Letter 53, 8 January 1653/4, p. 128.

17 – *Ibid.*, Letter 62, 2 April 1654, p. 157; Sir Henry Osborne (1619–75).

18 – *Ibid.*, Letter 48, 16 December 1653, p. 118, which has 'Blunt'. (In April 1654 Lady Anne Blunt or Blount, daughter of the Earl of Newport, *aetat* 17, would petition the Protector, asserting that she had *not* in fact contracted marriage with one William Blount, a recusant Papist.)

19 – *Ibid.*, Letter 43, October 1653, p. 100. Lady Isabella Rich was married to Sir James Thynne.

20 – *Ibid.*, Letter 48, 16 December 1653, p. 119.

The Niece of an Earl

There is an aspect of fiction of so delicate a nature that less has been said about it than its importance deserves. One is supposed to pass over class distinctions in silence; one person is supposed to be as well born as another; and yet English fiction is so steeped in the ups and downs of social rank that without them it would be unrecognisable. Where Meredith, in the *Story of General Ople and Lady Camper*, remarks 'He sent word that he would wait on Lady Camper immediately, and betook himself forthwith to his toilette. She was the niece of an Earl',[2] all of British blood accept the statement unhesitatingly, and know that Meredith is right. A General in those circumstances would certainly have given his coat an extra brush.

For though the General might have been, we are given to understand that he was not, Lady Camper's social equal. He received the
shock of her rank upon a naked surface. No Earldom, baronetage,
or knighthood protected him. He was an English gentleman merely,
and a poor one at that. Therefore, to British readers even now it
seems unquestionably fitting that he should 'betake himself to his
toilette' before appearing in the lady's presence.

It is useless to suppose that social distinctions have vanished.
Each may pretend that he knows no such restrictions, and that the
compartment in which he lives allow him the run of the world. But
it is an illusion. The idlest stroller down summer streets may see for
himself the charwoman's shawl shouldering its way among the silk
wraps of the successful; he sees shop-girls pressing their noses
against the plate glass of motor-cars; he sees radiant youth and
august age waiting their summons within to be admitted to the presence of King George.[3] There is no animosity, perhaps, but there is
no communication. We are enclosed, and separate, and cut off.
Directly we see ourselves in the looking-glass of fiction we know
that this is so. The novelist, and the English novelist in particular,
knows and delights, it seems, to know that Society is a nest of glass
boxes one separate from another, each housing a group with special
habits and qualities of its own. He knows that there are Earls and
that Earls have nieces; he knows that there are Generals and that
Generals brush their coats before they visit the nieces of Earls. But
this is only the ABC of what he knows. For in a few short pages,
Meredith makes us aware not only that Earls have nieces, but that
Generals have cousins; that the cousins have friends; that the
friends have cooks; that the cooks have husbands, and that the husbands of the cooks of the friends of the cousins of the Generals are
carpenters. Each of these people lives in a glass box of his own, and
has peculiarities of which the novelist must take account. What
appears superficially to be the vast equality of the middle classes is,
in truth, nothing of the sort. All through the social mass run curious
veins and streakings separating man from man and woman from
woman, mysterious prerogatives and disabilities too ethereal to be
distinguished by anything so crude as a title, yet impeding and dis-
ordering the great business of human intercourse. And even so,
when we have threaded our way carefully through all these grades
from the niece of the Earl to the friend of the cousin of the General,
we are still faced with an abyss; a gulf yawns before us; on the other

side are the working classes. The writer of perfect judgement and taste, like Jane Austen, does no more than glance across the gulf; she restricts herself to her own special class and finds infinite shades within it. But for the brisk, inquisitive, combative writer like Meredith, the temptation to explore is irresistible. He runs up and down the social scale; he chimes one note against another; he insists that the Earl and the cook, the General and the farmer shall speak up for themselves and play their part in the extremely complicated comedy of English civilised life.

It was natural that he should attempt it. A writer touched by the comic spirit relishes these distinctions keenly; they give him something to take hold of; something to make play with. English fiction without the nieces of Earls and the cousins of Generals would be an arid waste. It would resemble Russian fiction. It would have to fall back upon the immensity of the soul and upon the brotherhood of man. Like Russian fiction, it would lack comedy. But while we realise the immense debt that we owe the Earl's niece and the General's cousin, we doubt sometimes whether the pleasure we get from the play of satire on these broken edges is altogether worth the price we pay. For the price is a high one. The strain upon a novelist is tremendous. In two short stories Meredith gallantly attempts to bridge all gulfs, and to take half a dozen different levels in his stride. Now he speaks as an Earl's niece; now as a carpenter's wife. It cannot be said that his daring is altogether successful. One has a feeling (perhaps it is unfounded) that the blood of the niece of an Earl is not quite so tart and sharp as he would have it. Aristocracy is not, perhaps, so consistently high and brusque and eccentric as, from his angle, he would represent it. Yet his great people are more successful than his humble. His cooks are too ripe and rotund; his farmers too ruddy and earthy. He overdoes the pith and the sap; the fist-shaking and the thigh-slapping. He has got too far from them to write of them with ease.

It seems, therefore, that the novelist, and the English novelist in particular, suffers from a disability which affects no other artist to the same extent. His work is influenced by his birth. He is fated to know intimately, and so to describe with understanding, only those who are of his own social rank. He cannot escape from the box in which he has been bred. A bird's-eye view of fiction shows us no gentlemen in Dickens; no working men in Thackeray. One hesitates to call Jane Eyre a lady. The Elizabeths and the Emmas of Miss Austen could not possibly be taken for anything else.[4] It is vain to look for dukes or for dustmen – we doubt that such extremes are to be found anywhere in fiction. We are, therefore, brought to the melancholy and tantalising conclusion not only that novels are poorer than they might be, but that we are very largely prevented – for after all, the novelists are the great interpreters – from knowing what is happening either in the heights of Society or in its depths. There is practically no evidence available by which we can guess at the feelings of the highest in the land. What does a King feel? What does a Duke think? We cannot say. For the highest in the land have seldom written at all, and have never written about themselves. We shall never know what the Court of Louis XIV looked like to Louis XIV himself.[5] It seems likely indeed that the English aristocracy will pass out of existence, or be merged with the common people without leaving any true picture of themselves behind.

But our ignorance of the aristocracy is nothing compared with our ignorance of the working classes. At all times the great families of England and France have delighted to have famous men at their tables, and thus the Thackerays and the Disraelis and the Prousts have been familiar enough with the cut and fashion of aristocratic life to write about it with authority. Unfortunately, however, life is so framed that literary success invariably means a rise, never a fall, and seldom, what is far more desirable, a spread in the social scale. The rising novelist is never pestered to come to gin and winkles with the plumber and his wife. His books never bring him into touch with the cat's-meat man, or start a correspondence with the old lady who sells matches and bootlaces by the gate of the British Museum. He becomes rich; he becomes respectable; he buys an evening suit and dines with peers. Therefore, the later works of successful novelists show, if anything, a slight rise in the social scale. We tend to get more and more portraits of the successful and the distinguished. On the other hand, the old rat-catchers and ostlers of Shakespeare's day are shuffled altogether off the scene, or become what is far more offensive, objects of pity, examples of curiosity. They serve to show up the rich. They serve to point the evils of the social system. They are no longer, as they used to be when Chaucer wrote, simply themselves.[6] For it is impossible, it would seem, for working men to write in their own language about their own lives. Such education as the act of writing implies at once makes them self-conscious, or removes them from their own class. The anonymity, the unconsciousness in the shadow of which writers write most happily, are the prerogatives of the middle class alone. It is from the middle class that writers spring, because it is in the middle class only that the practice of writing is as natural and habitual as hoeing a field or building a house. Thus it must have been harder for Byron to be a poet than Keats; and it is as impossible to imagine that a Duke could be a great novelist as that *Paradise Lost* could be written by a man behind a counter.[7]

But things change; class distinctions were not always so hard and fast as they have now become. The Elizabethan age was far more elastic in this respect than our own; we, on the other hand, are far less hidebound than the Victorians. Thus it may well be that we are on the edge of a greater change than any the world has yet known. In another century or so, none of these distinctions may hold good. The Duke and the agricultural labourer as we know them now may have died out as completely as the bustard and the wild cat. Only natural differences such as those of brain and character will serve to distinguish us. General Ople (if there are still Generals) will visit the niece (if there are still nieces) of the Earl (if there are still Earls) without brushing his coat (if there are still coats). But what will happen to English fiction when it has come to pass that there are neither Generals, nieces, Earls nor coats, we cannot imagine. It may change its character so that we no longer know it. It may become extinct. Novels may be written as seldom and as unsuccessfully by our descendants as the poetic drama by ourselves. The art of a truly democratic age will be – what?

1–A signed essay in Desmond MacCarthy's *Life and Letters*, October 1928, (Kp C305), reprinted in CR2. See Editorial Note, p. xxv.
2–George Meredith (1828–1909), 'The Case of General Ople and Lady Camper' (1898; Memorial Edition of the Works of George Meredith, Constable, 1910, vol. XXI), ch. 2, p. 130. For VW on Meredith see 'The Novels of George Meredith' above.
3–George V reigned 1910–36.
4–Charles Dickens (1812–70); W. M. Thackeray (1811–63); Charlotte Brontë, *Jane Eyre* (1847); Elizabeth Bennet in Jane Austen, *Pride and Prejudice* (1813) and Emma Woodhouse in *Emma* (1816).
5–Louis XIV reigned 1643–1715.
6–For VW on Geoffrey Chaucer see 'The Pastons and Chaucer' in CR1 above.
7–George Gordon, Lord Byron (1788–1824); John Keats (1795–1821). John Milton, *Paradise Lost* (1667).

Plays and Pictures

Of the three pieces given at the ADC at Cambridge last week, Stravinsky's 'The Tale of a Soldier'[2] is, of course, the most famous, and to those who saw it for the first time the most difficult. Like all highly original work, it begins by destroying one's conceptions, and only by degrees builds them up again. Therefore the chance which so rarely occurs of seeing and hearing it was unusually welcome. The acting, save that of Madame Lopokova, was amateur, but on the whole that lent a sincerity to the performance which was of advantage to it. There was no suspicion of fatigue, or routine, or conventionality. Mr Redgrave was particularly effective as the Soldier, and Mr Arundell was successful as the reader.[3] But in some ways, the performance of Shakespeare's 'A Lover's Complaint' (for the first time) was the most interesting of the pieces. The poem seemed to be neither acted nor read aloud, but presented from another angle in another medium. Mr Grant[4] exquisitely emphasised the visual side of the poem by his decorations, and suggested how curiously the sister arts might illustrate each other if they chose. Here Madame Lopokova showed genuine dramatic talent, and her accent was no more foreign than that of the Elizabethans would have been. Indeed, it would be delightful if she would employ her sympathy, imagination, and wit in thus translating for us other famous poems. Finally, Mr Hedley Briggs danced some very witty and fantastic measures. Altogether the evening, if unequal, was one of unusual exhilaration.

1–A notice in the *N&A*, 17 November 1928, (Kp C305.1), of a production, from 7 November, at the Cambridge ADC's small theatre in Park Street, to which the Woolfs went on 10 November.

2–'The Soldier's Story' (*L'Histoire du Soldat*, a short entertainment with four characters by G. F. Ramuz, 1917) music by Igor Stravinsky (1882–1971).

3–A correspondent in *The Times*, 9 November 1928, reported: 'The A.D.C. have ... departed from their usual tradition by introducing professional players in Mr Hedley Briggs [otherwise unidentified] and Mr Michael Redgrave [1908–85].' Lydia Lopokova (1891–1981), the Russian ballet dancer who in 1925 had married Maynard Keynes. She had performed in the same work at the Arts Theatre Club in July 1927 (see *III VW Diary*, 11 July 1927).

4–Duncan Grant (1885–1978) had this month also designed scenery for an ADC production by George Rylands of Milton's *Comus*.

Memories

After living eighty-two years and after writing fifty novels or so, Mr Hawthorne turns from fiction to fact, and summons before us, with all the craft of the experienced writer and the trained eye of a novelist, pictures of real people and scenes from his own life. But no editor could be more ruthless to the manuscripts of the verbose than Mr Hawthorne to the multiplicity of his own memories. He admits in the first place only those that relate to England, and among these he selects and arranges so that instead of the slow pace of a conscientious narrative we have a bird's-eye view; instead of plodding every foot of the way we circle and skip and alight where fancy chooses. Is not fancy, after all, the only guide? Does not fancy always keep what is worth keeping and drop the rest? We step first into England in the 'fifties; we lodge with Mrs Blodgett in Liverpool,[2] where the beds are four-posters and the candlesticks are of brown metal, and from this vantage ground we survey the world through the eyes of a small American boy whose father the great novelist, is of all strange things, the American Consul at that port.[3] Since Hawthorne is the shyest, and most nocturnal of great writers, it is exciting to catch a glimpse of him as in his office refusing to look at the scar which is offered for his inspection on the old sea-captain's head; and next as a father telling his little boy stories about General Quattlebum, 'a powerful magician',[4] and flying from an infuriated goat. But soon, owing to the caprice of memory, Liverpool and Mrs Blodgett, who fed twenty American sea-captains royally every day more from love of good cheer than from wish to make a living, and the little Major, who had been at Waterloo and swung his sword in the drawing-room to show how with that identical sword he had cut down a trooper on the battlefield, disappear and give place to London in the 'seventies; that is to say, to Mr Hepworth Dixon, to Mrs Langtry, and to Lord Houghton with his alcove of improper books which shocked Henry James; and Mr Procter who had known Lord Byron;[5] and Temple Bar and the antiquated horse omnibus. All this Mr Hawthorne observed with a relish which still tingles, though he must look back fifty years, and it is not the hansom cab that he hears now, but only the Pacific pounding at his doors. And then through the dimness his eyes light upon memorable faces; he sees Lord Leighton 'in black velvet lounging sack and pearl-grey pantaloons ... he was almost too beautiful ... He would stroke his sable-silvered beard as he conversed ... His eyes ... were a trifle too small';[6] and then in would come Henry James, mild and urbane, 'watching his ideas develop on the ceiling ... his thoughts apparently outpacing his words, as a child's hoop bowls away from him before the wind...';[7] and then there is Browning 'like a rich banker, a perfected butler',[8] and Mrs Browning 'fine as an insect, immense eyes burning through thick black curls; ... nervously smiling through a mouth so large that no portrait painter had dared be truthful about it'.[9]

In short, Mr Hawthorne saw everybody in London, and he saw them keenly, ironically, graphically as befits a man who walked to his parties on his own feet all the way from Twickenham and cooled his excitement in the dawn walking back. On one occasion the search for a white tie brought to light twenty-five forgotten sovereigns hoarded in the tie box so that he could take a train. But in those days to walk was practicable and enjoyable. The roads were white; they wound in and out; they led to pleasant quiet places; they were not scourged and scraped by incessant motor-cars.[10] Yet though this sentence paves a way for the peroration that is all regret and retrospect, Mr Hawthorne warrants no such lachrymosity. He loves England as she is, here and now; and looking at her from the shores of the Pacific sees 'John Bull as my kin, and as the incarnation of a great human spirit on earth'.[11] He sees us more flatteringly than we see ourselves, but he sees us very amusingly, very vividly, going about our ways in London in the 'seventies.

1 – A review in the N&A, 17 November 1928, (Kp C305.2) of *Shapes That Pass. Memories of Old Days* (John Murray, 1928) by Julian Hawthorne (1846–1934), author of numerous novels, and biographer of his father the American novelist Nathaniel Hawthorne (1804–64).

VW wrote to LW on 28 September 1928, from the Hotel de la Poste, Vezelay, Yonne: 'So I am going to write to Tom [Eliot] and Saxon [Sydney-Turner] and to Florence Bishop, and perhaps review Julian Hawthorne, who turns out to be rather amusing in a dry way' (*III VW Letters*, no. 1932). Reading Notes (MHP, B 2n).

2 – Mrs Blodgett's boarding house stood in Duke Street, Liverpool.

3 – Nathaniel Hawthorne was US Consul at Liverpool, 1853–8.

4 – Hawthorne, ch. iii, p. 25: 'The General was a creation who grew and expanded as his history progressed. It appeared that he and my father were powerful magicians ...'

5 – William Hepworth Dixon (1821–79), editor of the *Athenaeum*, 1853–69, briefly

notorious when charged with indecency following publication of *Spiritual Wives* (1868), his study of Mormon marriage. Lillie Langtry (1852–1929), actress. Richard Monckton Milnes, 1st Baron Houghton (1809–85), author and philanthropist; for his improper books and their effect on Henry James (1843–1916), see Hawthorne, ch. iv, pp. 53–4. Bryan Waller Procter, pseud. Barry Cornwall (1787–1874), poet and dramatist, had been a contemporary of Byron at Harrow.

6–Hawthorne, ch. ix, p. 175; Sir Frederic Leighton, cr. Baron Leighton of Stretton, 1896 (1830–96), artist, from 1878 president of the Royal Academy of Arts.

7–*Ibid.*, ch. vii, p. 136.

8–*Ibid.*, p. 140, which has: 'he was a rich banker, he was a perfected butler'. Robert Browning (1812–89).

9–*Ibid.*, ch. v, p. 68; the subject of this sentence is in fact Mrs Henry S. King, wife of a London publisher, fancied by Hawthorne to resemble Elizabeth Barrett Browning (1806–61), whom he subsequently describes as being Browning's 'little black-haired wife, like a witch etching by Dulac' (*ibid.*, p. 140).

10–Hawthorne was indeed a devoted walker and belonged to the Sunday Tramps, that Victorian fraternity of long-distance pedestrians formed under the muscular leadership of the reviewer's father, Leslie Stephen (1832–1904). See Hawthorne, ch. xi, pp. 233–4.

11–Hawthorne, ch. xvi, p. 358.

Half of Thomas Hardy

Thomas Hardy, it is not surprising to learn, had not sufficient admiration for himself to record his recollections and not enough interest in himself to brood over his own character. 'A naturalist's interest in the hatching of a queer egg or germ is the utmost introspective consideration you should allow yourself,'[2] he wrote, and the observation was made in a pocket-book which nobody but himself was to read. Hence, though he was forced to agree that a life of him must be written, it is by his wish a life so devoid of artifice, so simple in its structure that it resembles nothing so much as the talk of an old man over the fire about his past. Much of it indeed was written down by Mrs Hardy as he spoke it. Many of the phrases are unmistakably his own. And whatever it may lack in substance or in symmetry is more than made up for by the sound of the speaking voice and the suggestiveness which it carries with it. Indeed, by no other method could Mrs Hardy have kept so close to her husband's spirit.

For Hardy was the last person to be subjected to the rigours of biography. Never was anyone less stereotyped, less formalised, less flattened out by the burden of fame and the weight of old age. He sprang up effortlessly, unconsciously, like a heather root under a stone, not by imposing his views or by impressing his personality, but by being simply and consistently himself. Everything he wrote – it is a quality that makes up for a thousand faults – had this integrity ingrained in it. One finds it again pervading his life. Fantastic as it sounds, one can scarcely help fancying that it was Hardy who imagined it all – the fiddling father, the mother who loved reading, the house 'between woodland and heathland'; the old English family, with its legends of Monmouth and Sedgemoor, and its 'spent social energies', who had come down in the world – 'So we go down, down, down,'[3] said Hardy, meeting the head of his family trudging beside a common spring trap in the road. Everything takes on the colour of his own temperament. His memories have the quality of moments of vision. He could remember coming home at three in the morning from fiddling with his father – for the Hardys had fiddled in church and farm for generations without taking a penny for it, and little Tom was a dancer and a fiddler from his birth – and seeing 'a white human figure without a head'[4] in the hedge – a man almost frozen to death. He could remember the farm-women at the harvest supper 'sitting on a bench against the wall in the barn and leaning against each other as they warbled,

> Lie there, lie there, thou false-hearted man,
> Lie there instead o' me.'[5]

He could remember how his father, the music-loving builder, would stroll on to the heath alone with the telescope that had belonged to some sea-faring Hardy and 'stay peering out into the distance by the half-hour'.[6] He could remember how he had once stood on the heath and put that same brass telescope to his eye and seen a man in white fustian on the gallows at Dorchester. At that moment the figure 'dropped downward and the faint note of the town clock struck eight',[7] and he seemed alone on the heath with the hanged man. But more distinctly than anything else he could remember lying on his back as a small boy and thinking how useless he was and how he did not wish to grow up – 'he did not want at all to be a man, or to possess things, but to remain as he was in the same spot, and to know no more people than he already knew (about half a dozen). Yet . . . he was in perfect health and happy circumstances.'[8]

So the memories succeed each other, like poems, visualised and complete. It was thus, perhaps, that Hardy's mind worked when it was most at its ease, flashing its light fitfully and capriciously like a lantern swinging in a hand, now on a rose-bush, now on a tramp frozen in the hedge. He has none of that steady and remorseless purpose that people would attribute to him. It was by chance that he saw things, not by design. He puts the telescope to his eye and there is a man on the gallows. He walks in Dorchester High Street and sees the gipsy girls with their big brass earrings in the light from a silversmith's shop. At once these sights shape themselves into poems and set themselves to some old tune that has been running in his mind. He stops to muse upon their meaning. He cannot hold firmly on his way. Indeed, he 'cared for life only as an emotion and not as a scientific game';[9] he did not want to grow up and possess things. Hence the doubts and the fluctuations of his career. He might have gone to Cambridge had he chosen, but he did not make the effort. He fumbled about with architecture, pulled down the old churches that he loved and built new ones. Now he was going to devote himself to poetry, now to fiction. One result of this vacillation seems to have been that he lay singularly open to influence. He wrote a satirical novel in the manner of Defoe, and because Meredith advised him to write another with a more complicated plot, he sat down and wrote *Desperate Remedies* with a plot as complicated as a mediaeval mouse-trap.[10] When the *Spectator* said that the novel (because there is a rich spinster in it with an illegitimate child) was rightly anonymous, for even a nom-de-plume might 'at some future time disgrace the family name, and still more the Christian name, of a repentant and remorseful novelist',[11] Hardy sat on a stile and wished himself dead. It was in deference to another critic, John Morley, that he wrote *Under the Greenwood Tree* in the pastoral manner; and it was in reply to the jibes of the journalists, who said that he was a house decorator, that he put aside the first version of *The Woodlanders* and proved his sophistication by writing *The Hand of Ethelberta*.[12]

All this deference to authority, which contrasts so queerly with the perfectly uncompromising character of his genius, comes no doubt from some inertness of temper in the descendant of a spent race; but it rose, too, from a fact which Hardy himself noticed, that he came to maturity much later than most men. His gifts lay hidden far longer than is usual. Poems dropped now and again into a drawer. But the desire to write poetry seems to have been fitful and dubious even when he was at the most poetic age. Bread and butter had to be earned, however, and therefore reluctantly and hesitatingly, without the illusions or the hot-headedness of the born novelist he stumbled into a calling for which he had little respect, and for which, if he had magnificent gifts, he had also great disabilities.

For though it was all very well to write novels like *Far from the Madding Crowd*[13] upon chips of wood or white leaves or even upon flat stones out of doors, he was persuaded that a novelist, to be successful, must describe manners and customs. He must live in town. He must frequent dinners, and clubs and crushes. He must keep a note-book. And so, though Hardy could not bear the touch of an arm upon his shoulder, and a note-book in his pocket made him 'barren as the Sahara',[14] he faced the position squarely; rented a house in Upper Tooting, bought a note-book, and dined out nightly. 'Certainly,' exclaimed Miss Thackeray, when he consulted her, 'a novelist must necessarily like society!'[15]

Society seen from Upper Tooting looked a little queer. He put the brass telescope to his eye and saw the strangest sights. Men and women were being hung even in the gayest streets. He mused upon the passions and sorrows that raged in the breasts of the crowd at the Marble Arch. He lay in bed at Upper Tooting and could not sleep because he lay so close 'to a monster who had four heads and eight million eyes'.[16] He sat next Lady Camperdown at dinner 'and could not get rid of the feeling that I was close to a great naval engagement'.[17] But he also noted down the correct things. He met Matthew Arnold, who 'had a manner of having made up his mind upon everything years ago',[18] and Henry James, 'who has a ponderously warm manner of saying nothing in infinite sentences';[19] and old Mrs Proctor, 'who swam about through the crowd like a swan';[20] and Byron's Ianthe, 'a feeble beldame muffled up in black and furs';[21] and the Carnarvons and the Salisburys and the Portsmouths[22] – and of all this he took note as a novelist should. Moreover, when the books were finished he did whatever the editors required him to do to make them saleable. Book after book appeared in magazines with passages cut out or with incidents put in to please the British public. For if the whole thing – in this case the whole thing was *The Mayor of Casterbridge* – was 'mere journey work',[23] did it very much matter what compromise he made? Fiction was a trade like another – off he went to the Crawford-Dilke case, note-book in hand.[24] Yet now and then the note-

book would record a state of mind or a thought that was quite un-
suitable for fiction. For instance: '. . . when I enter into a room to
pay a simple morning call I have unconsciously the habit of regarding the scene as if I were a spectre not solid enough to influence
my environment; only fit to behold and say, as another spectre said,
"Peace be unto you." '[25] Or again he mused, 'People are somnam-
bulists – the material is not the real – only the visible, the real being
invisible optically.'[26]

For a while with one-half of his mind Hardy noted down what a
successful novelist ought to observe, the other half remorselessly
saw through these observations and turned them to moonshine.
Hardy, of course, might have suppressed the second half; he might
have succeeded in writing agreeable cynical novels of London life
like any other. But that obstinate conviction that made him for all
his efforts an outsider, that faculty for putting the telescope to his
eye and seeing strange, grim pictures – if he went to a First-Aid lecture he saw children in the street behind a skeleton, if he went to a
French play he saw a cemetery behind the players' heads – all this
fecundity and pressure of the imagination brought about at last not
a compromise but a solution. Why run about with note-books
observing manners and customs when his mind involuntarily
flooded itself with strange imaginations and sung itself scraps of old
ballads? Why not simplify, make abstract, give the whole rather
than the detail? Again the note-book records certain ideas that
would be out of place in a novel. 'The "simple natural" is interesting no longer. The much decried, mad, late-Turner rendering
is now necessary to create my interest. The exact truth as to material fact ceases to be of importance in art – I want to see the deeper
reality underlying the scenic, the expression of what are sometimes
called abstract imaginings.'[27] But it was a question how far abstract
imagination could be expressed in a novel. Would not realities
fatally conflict with that observation of manners and customs which
Hardy, so simply and so modestly, had accepted as the staple of the
novelist's trade?

The first half of Hardy's life ends with that note of interrogation.
We have reached the year 1891. He has written *Tess of the D'Urbervilles*. It has appeared in the *Graphic*. At the editor's request, Hardy
has omitted the christening scene; he has allowed the milkmaids to
be wheeled across the lane in a wheelbarrow instead of being
carried in Clare's arms; and, although one father of daughters still

objects that the bloodstain on the ceiling is indecent – 'Hardy could never understand why'[28] – the book is a great success. But, we ask ourselves, what is going to happen next?

1–A signed review in the *N&A*, 24 November 1928, reprinted in the *NR*, 5 December, (Kp C306) of *The Early Life of Thomas Hardy 1840–1891* (Macmillan and Co. Ltd, 1928) by Florence Emily Hardy (1879–1937). 'Just to solace myself before correcting Hardy & Gissing,' wrote VW in her diary on 8 November, 'I will note that we went to Karin's party last night.' The same issue of the *N&A* also contained LW's 'World of Books' column on *The Diary of Tolstoy's Wife 1860–1891*, trans. Alexander Werth, and *The Diary of Dostoevsky's Wife*, trans. from the German by Madge Pemberton; and an article by Raymond Mortimer on 'Mr Strachey's New Book', a review of *Elizabeth and Essex: A Tragic History*. See also 'Thomas Hardy's Novels' above. See Editorial Note, p. xxv. Reading Notes (Berg, XIV). Reprinted *CDB*.
2–Hardy, ch. xvi, p. 267, note-book entry dated 5 January 1888: 'Be rather curious than anxious about your own career; for whatever result may accrue to its intellectual and social value, it will make little difference to your personal well-being. A naturalist's interest . . .'
3–For the first quotation, *ibid.*, ch. i, p. 3; for the second, p. 5; and for the third, from a note-book entry dated 30 September 1888, p. 281. Hardy's parents: Thomas (1811–92) and Jemima, *née* Hand (1813–1904).
4–*Ibid.*, ch. i, p. 30.
5–*Ibid.*, p. 26, which has 'warbled the Dorset version of the ballad [known variously as 'The Outlandish Knight', 'Mary Colvine', 'The Western Tragedy'], which differed a little from the northern:'; the quatrain continues: 'For six pretty maidens thou has a-drown'd here, / But the seventh hath drown-ed thee!'
6–*Ibid.*, p. 27.
7–*Ibid.*, ch. ii, p. 37, which has: 'dropped downwards,'.
8–*Ibid.*, ch. i, pp. 19–20, which has: 'as he was, in the same spot', and: 'Yet this early evidence of that lack of social ambition which followed him through life was shown when he was . . .'
9–*Ibid.*, ch. iii, p. 70, which has: 'He constitutionally shrank from the business of social advancement, caring for life as an emotion rather than for life as a science of climbing . . .'
10–Hardy's unpublished satirical novel in the manner of Daniel Defoe was *The Poor Man and the Lady*, completed in 1868. George Meredith (1828–1909); *Desperate Remedies* (1871).
11–Hardy, ch. vi, pp. 110–11, quoting the *Spectator*, 22 April 1871.
12–John Morley (1838–1923), 1st Viscount, statesman, editor of the *Fortnightly Review*, 1867–82, and of the *Pall Mall Gazette* 1881–3. *Under the Greenwood Tree* (1872); *The Woodlanders* (1887); *The Hand of Ethelberta* (1876), which was serialised in the *Cornhill Magazine* by Leslie Stephen (1832–1904).
13–*Far from the Madding Crowd* (1874), also serialised in the *Cornhill* by Stephen.
14–Hardy, ch. vii, p. 127.
15–*Ibid.*, p. 138; Anne Thackeray Ritchie (1837–1919), daughter of W. M. Thackeray, and VW's 'Aunt Anny'.

16 – *Ibid.*, ch. x, p. 179, which has 'a monster whose body had four million heads and eight million eyes'.

17 – *Ibid.*, ch. xiv, p. 237; Lady Camperdown, widow of the 2nd Earl of Camperdown.

18 – *Ibid.*, ch. x, p. 175; Matthew Arnold (1822–88).

19 – *Ibid.*, ch. xiv, p. 237; Henry James (1843–1916).

20 – *Ibid.*, ch. xiii, p. 217; Anne Benson Procter [sic], widow of the poet who wrote under the pseudonym 'Barry Cornwall'.

21 – *Ibid.*, ch. x, p. 172; Byron's Ianthe: Lady Charlotte Bacon, formerly Lady Charlotte Harley, dedicatee of the first and second cantos of *Childe Harold's Pilgrimage* (1812–18).

22 – These were: Lady Carnarvon and the 4th Earl of Carnarvon (1831–90), statesman; Lady Salisbury and the 3rd Marquis of Salisbury (1830–1903), statesman; Lady and the 5th Lord Portsmouth.

23 – Hardy, ch. xiv, p. 235: 'However, as at this time he called his novel-writing "mere journeywork" he cared little about it as art . . .' *The Mayor of Casterbridge* (1886).

24 – *Ibid.*, ch. xiv, pp. 239–40. In 1886 Donald Crawford, Liberal MP for Lanark, sued his wife for divorce after she freely confessed to adultery with Sir Charles Wentworth Dilke, the Liberal member for Chelsea, who steadfastly denied any such involvement.

25 – *Ibid.*, ch. xvi, p. 275, quoting Hardy's note-book, June 1888.

26 – *Ibid.*, ch. xiv, p. 243, quoting Hardy's note-book, 13 February 1887, which has: 'that the material is not the real'.

27 – *Ibid.*, pp. 242–3, note-book, January 1887, adapted. J. M. W. Turner (1775–1851).

28 – *Ibid.*, ch. xvii, p. 291. The Grundyan editor of the *Graphic* was Arthur Locker (1828–93), whose paper began serialisation of *Tess of the d'Urbervilles* in July 1891.

Lady Strachey

There are some people who without being themselves famous seem to sum up the qualities of an age and to represent it at its best. Lady Strachey, who died last week at the age of eighty-eight, was among them. She seemed the type of the Victorian woman at her finest – many-sided, vigorous, adventurous, advanced. With her large and powerful frame, her strongly marked features, her manner that was so cordial, so humorous, and yet perhaps a little formidable, she seemed cast on a larger scale, made of more massive material than the women of today. One could not but be aware even to look at her that she was in the line of a great tradition. She came of a family famous for its administrators and public servants; she married into one of the great Anglo-Indian families of the nineteenth century. One could easily imagine how, had she been a man, she would have ruled a province or administered a Government department. She had all that instinct for affairs, that broad-minded grasp of politics that made the great public servant of the nineteenth century. But, in addition, like all Victorian women of her stamp, she was emphatically a mother and a wife. Even while she wrote dispatches at her husband's dictation and debated – for she was in the counsels of the men who governed India – this problem, that policy, she was bringing up, now in India, now in England, a family of ten children. She was presiding over one of those vast Victorian households which, chaotic as they seem now, had a character and a vitality about them which it is hard to suppose will ever be matched again. Memory provides a picture of the many-roomed house; of people coming and going; of argument; of laughter; of different voices speaking at once; of Lady Strachey herself a little absent-minded, a little erratic, but nevertheless the controller and inspirer of it all, now wandering through the rooms with a book, now teaching a group of young people the steps of the Highland reel, now plunging into ardent debate about politics or literature, now working out, with equal intentness, some puzzle in a penny paper which if solved would provide her with thirty shillings a week and a workman's cottage for life.

In her old age she wrote down a few memories of the past which show, very briefly, how naturally, how as a matter of course, she was in touch with the great figures of the Victorian world.[2] She joked with Huxley; she exchanged spectacles with Tennyson;[3] she was a special favourite with George Eliot, and, 'though much ashamed of my vanity in recording it', could not help remembering how 'Lewes told a friend of mine that I was his idea of Dorothea in Middlemarch.'[4] She sat up to all hours of the night, 'eagerly discussing every aspect of humanity',[5] with the most distinguished men of her time, openly but impersonally, rather as if they were in full evening dress, so it seems to a less formal age. For together with her keen interest in public questions, particularly in the education and emancipation of women, went an interest as vigorous in music and the drama, and especially in literature. She had a vast capacity for enthusiasm which fed happily and confidently as was common with the Victorians upon her own contemporaries and their works. She had no doubts whatever about the greatness of the men she knew and the lasting importance of their books. When she met Browning for the first time at a concert she wrote on her programme:

> And did you once see Browning plain?
> And did he stop and speak to you?[6]

and kept it, a sacred relic. She counted it one of her great pieces of good luck that she was born contemporary with Salvini.[7] She went to the theatre every night on which he acted. But she was not only attracted by the great figures of her own age. She was an omnivorous reader. She had her hands upon the whole body of English literature, from Shakespeare to Tennyson, with the large loose grasp that was so characteristic of the cultivated Victorian. She had a special love for the Elizabethan drama, and for English poetry – Beddoes[8] was one of the obscure writers whom she championed and discovered – a little incongruously perhaps, for her own affinities seemed rather with the age of reason and the robust sense of the great English prose writers. She was, above all things, rational, positive, agnostic, like the distinguished men who were her friends. Later in life, after her husband's death, when her activities were somewhat lessened, though they were still varied enough to have filled the life of a younger woman, she would spend an entire winter's afternoon in reading an Elizabethan play from end to end. For reading aloud was one of her great natural gifts. She read with fire and ardour, and with a great clarity and distinction of utterance. Often she would pause to point out the beauty of some passage, or propound with extreme ingenuity some emendation, or impart a curious illustration that had stuck in her mind from her wide and miscellaneous foraging among books. Then, when the reading was over, she would launch out into stories of the past; of Lord Lytton and his sky-blue dressing gown; of Lord Roberts helping to mend her sewing machine; of Lawrence and Outram (she never passed the statue of Outram without making a salute, she said); of Pattles and Prinseps;[9] of bygone beauties and scandals – for though she observed the conventions she was not in the least a prude; of Indian society fifty years, eighty years, a hundred years ago. For she had the Scottish love of following family histories and tracing the friendships and alliances of the present back to their roots in the past. Thus a haphazard party would come in her presence to have a patriarchal air, as she recalled the memories and the marriages that had bound parents and grandparents together years ago, in the distant past.

Gradually, though the vigour of her mind was as great as ever, it seemed to withdraw from modern life and to focus itself more and more upon the past. She did not remember clearly what had happened the week before, but Calcutta in 1870, Robert Browning's laugh, some saying of George Eliot's, were as clear, as dear, and as vivid as ever. It was her hard fate to lose her sight almost entirely some years before she died. She could no longer go foraging and triumphing through English literature – for it seemed as if she carried on even the passive act of reading with something of the vigour with which she strode the streets, peering forward with her short-sighted eyes, or tossed her head high in a shout of laughter. But she could talk, she could argue, she could join in the disputes of the younger generation and follow with pride the successes of her children. Her mind was still busy with literature, still active with suggestions for reviving forgotten plays, for editing old texts, for bringing to light some hidden splendour in those old books which she could no longer read herself, but almost commanded the younger generation to love as she had loved them. Her memory, grown to be the strongest part of her, still kept unimpaired in its depths some of the loveliest things in English poetry. When she was past eighty, she stopped one summer evening under a tree in a London square and recited the whole of 'Lycidas'[10] without a fault. Last summer, though too weak to walk any more, she sat on her balcony and showered down upon the faces that she could not see a vast maternal benediction. It was as if the Victorian age in its ripeness, its width, with all its memories and achievements behind it were bestowing its blessing. And we should be blind indeed if we did not wave back to her a salute full of homage and affection.

1–An obituary bearing its author's initials in the *N&A*, 22 December 1928, (Kp C307) of Lady Strachey (b. 1840), *née* Jane Maria Grant, who died on 15 September 1928, wife of General Sir Richard Strachey (1817–1908). 'I was switched off to write a eulogy of Lady Strachey,' VW noted in her diary on 18 December, 'burnt yesterday with a bunch of our red & white carnations on top of her. It is odd how little her death means to me – for this reason. About a year ago she was said to be dying; & at once (Adrian told me) I made up my visualisations; felt the whole emotion of Lady Strachey's passing – her memories & so on – that night; & then she did not die; & now when she does die, not a vision, not an emotion comes my way. These little tricks of psychology amuse me.' To Lytton Strachey, her eulogy was 'perfect' and 'superb' and on 21 December he wrote from Ham Spray to tell her so. See *Virigina Woolf and Lytton Strachey. Letters*, ed. Leonard Woolf and James Strachey (Hogarth Press, 1956, p. 116) and for VW's reply (*ibid.*, p. 117; and *III VW Letters*, no. 1971, 25 December): 'It was the greatest relief, getting your letter, dearest Lytton. I was so afraid I had said only commonplace things. One can't say the things that matter – and it all seemed rather unreal. She was very real to me – oddly so, seeing how little I saw her; and I keep thinking of her. She used to descend upon me sometimes in Fitzroy Square and talk about you.' Reprinted *B&P*.

2–Published in the *N&A*, 5 January, 23 February, 12 July, and 30 August 1924, as 'Some Recollections of a Long Life', an output so relatively slight as to serve as a warning to the would-be memoirist, as VW noted towards the end of her own life as she began 'A Sketch of the Past': 'Two days ago – Sunday 16th April 1939 to be precise – Nessa said that if I did not start writing my memoirs I should soon be too old. I should be eighty-five, and should have forgotten – witness the unhappy case of Lady Strachey' (*Moments of Being*, Hogarth Press, 1985, p. 64).

3–For Lady Strachey and T. H. Huxley (1825–95), see 'Some Recollections . . .' III, *N&A*, 12 July 1924, p. 473; and for Tennyson (1809–92), and his spectacles, *ibid.*, IV, 30 August 1924, p. 664.

4–For George Eliot (1819–80) and G. H. Lewes (1817–78), *ibid.*, III, p. 474. Eliot's *Middlemarch, a Study of Provincial Life* was published in 1871–2.

5–*Ibid.*, IV, p. 665.

6–For Robert Browning (1812–89), *ibid.*, III, pp. 473–4. The quotation is adapted from Browning's 'Memorabilia': 'Ah, did you once see Shelley plain, / And did he stop and speak to you / And did you speak to him again?'

7–For Tommaso Salvini (1829–1916), Italian actor, see *ibid.*, IV, 30 August 1924, p. 664.

8–Thomas Lovell Beddoes (1803–49), author of *Death's Jest-Book* (1850).

9–For Edward Robert Bulwer Lytton (1831–91), Viceroy of India, and for Frederick Sleigh Roberts, 1st Earl Roberts (1832–1914), field marshal, see 'Some Recollections . . .' II, *N&A*, 23 February 1924, p. 731; for (probably) John Laird Mair Lawrence, 1st Baron Lawrence (1811–79), governor-general of India, see *ibid.*, IV, 30 August, 1924; and for Sir James Outram (1803–63), lieutenant general in the Indian Army, see *ibid.*, I, 5 January 1924, p. 515. The statue of Outram which Lady Strachey never failed to salute is that by Matthew Noble on the Thames Embankment. For VW on the Pattles and Prinseps, families variously connected with India, see 'Guests and Memories', 'Pattledom' and 'Julia Margaret Cameron' above.

10–John Milton's 'Lycidas' was written in 1637.

Appendices

APPENDIX I

Illness – An Unexploited Mine

The following signed essay, published in *Forum*, April 1926, is a condensed version of 'On Being Ill', VW's essay in the *New Criterion*, January 1926, (Kp C270). See above and see Editorial Note, p. xxv.

Considering how common illness is, how tremendous the spiritual change that it brings, how astonishing, when the lights of health go down, the undiscovered countries that are then disclosed, what wastes and deserts of the soul a slight attack of influenza brings to light, what precipices and lawns sprinkled with bright flowers a little rise of temperature reveals, what ancient and obdurate oaks are uprooted in us in the act of sickness, how we go down into the pit of death and feel the waters of annihilation close above our heads and wake thinking to find ourselves in the presence of the angels and the harpers when we have a tooth out and come to the surface in the dentist's arm-chair and confuse his 'Rinse the mouth – rinse the mouth' with the greeting of the Deity stooping on the floor of Heaven to welcome us, – when we think of this and in-finitely more as we are so frequently forced to think of it, it becomes strange indeed that illness has not taken its place with love, battle, and jealousy among the prime themes of literature. Novels, one would have thought, would have been devoted to Influenza; epic poems to Typhoid; odes to Pneumonia, Appendicitis, and Cancer; lyrics to Toothache. But no; with a few exceptions, – De Quincey attempted something of the sort in *The Opium Eater*; there must be a volume or two about disease scattered through the pages of Proust, – literature does its best to maintain that its concern is with the mind; that the body is a sheet of plain glass through which the soul looks straight and clear, and, save for one or two passions such as desire and greed, is null and negligible and non-existent.

On the contrary, the very opposite is true. All day, all night the body intervenes; blunts or sharpens, colours or discolours; turns us to wax in the warmth of June, hardens us to tallow in the murk of February. The creature within can only gaze through the pane – smudged or rosy; it cannot separate off from the body like the sheath of a knife or the pod of a pea for a single instant; it must go through the whole unending procession of changes, heat and cold, comfort and discomfort, hunger and satisfaction, health and illness, until there comes the inevitable catastrophe: the body smashes itself to smithereens, and the soul (it is said) escapes.

But of all this daily drama of the body there is no record. People write always about the doings of the mind, the thoughts that come to it; its noble plans; how it has civilised the universe. They show it ignoring the body in the philosopher's turret; or kicking the body, like an old leather football, across leagues of snow and desert in the pursuit of conquest or discovery. Those great wars which it wages by itself, with the mind a slave to it in the solitude of the bedroom against the assault of fever or the oncome of melancholia, are neglected. Nor is the reason far to seek. To look these things squarely in the face would need the courage of a lion tamer, – of ten thousand lion tamers, – for these lions are within us not without; and a robust philosophy; and a reason rooted in the bowels of the earth. Short of these, this monster, this miracle, of the body and pain, will soon make us taper into mysticism, or rise with rapid beats of the wings into the raptures of transcendentalism.

More practically speaking, the public would say that a novel devoted to influenza lacked plot; they would complain that there was no love in it, wrongly however, for illness often takes on the disguise of love, and plays the same odd tricks, investing certain faces with divinity, setting us to wait hour after hour with pricked ears for the creaking of a stair, and wreathing the faces of the absent (plain enough in health, Heaven knows) with a new significance, while the mind sports with them, and concocts legends and romances about them for which it has not time nor liberty in health.

Finally, among the drawbacks of illness as matter for literature there is the poverty of the language. English which can express the thoughts of Hamlet and the tragedy of Lear has no words for the shiver and the headache. It has all grown one way. The merest schoolgirl, when she falls in love, has Shakespeare, Donne, Keats to speak her mind for her; but let a sufferer try to describe a pain in his head to a doctor, and language at once runs dry. There is nothing ready-made for him. He is forced to coin words himself, and, taking his pain in one hand and a lump of pure sound in the other (as perhaps the inhabitants of Babel did in the beginning), so to crush them together that a brand new word in the end will emerge, and it will be something laughable. For who of English birth can take liberties with the language? It is a sacred thing to us and therefore doomed to die, unless the Americans, whose genius is so much happier in the making of new words than in the artful disposition of the old, will come to our help, and set the springs aflow again.

But it is not only a new language that we need, – primitive, subtle, sensual, obscene, – but a new hierarchy of the passions; love must be deposed in favour of a temperature of 104 degrees; jealousy give place to the pangs of sciatica; sleeplessness play the part of villain, and the hero become a white liquid with a sweet taste, that mighty prince with the moth's eyes and the feathered feet, one of whose names is Chloral.

But to return to the invalid. 'I am in bed with influenza,' he says, and actually complains that he gets no sympathy at all. 'I am in bed with influenza,' but what does that convey of the great experience: how the world has changed its shape; the tools of business have grown remote; the sounds of festival romantic become like a merry-go-round across the fields; and friends have changed, some putting on a strange beauty, others deformed to the squatness of toads while the whole landscape of life lies remote, fair, silent, like the shore seen from a ship out at sea; and he is now exalted on a peak and needs no help from man or God, and now grovels supine on the floor glad of a kick from a housemaid. The experience cannot be imparted and, as is always the way with these dumb things, his own suffering serves but to wake memories in his friends' minds of their influenzas, their aches and pains which went unwept last February, and now cry out, desperately, clamorously, for the divine relief of sympathy.

But sympathy we cannot have. Wisest Fate says no. If her children, whose lot is hard enough already, were to take on them that burden too, adding in imagination others' pains to their own, buildings would cease to rise, roads would peter out into grassy tracks, there would be an end of music and of painting; one great sigh alone would rise to Heaven, and the only attitudes for men and women would be those of horror and despair. As it is, there is always some little distraction – an organ grinder at the corner of the Hospital, a shop with a book or a picture to decoy one past the prison or the workhouse, some absurdity of cat or dog to prevent one from turning the old beggar's hieroglyphic of misery into volumes of sordid suffering – and the vast effort of sympathy which those barracks of pain and discipline, those dried symbols of sorrow, ask us to exert on their behalf is uneasily shuffled off for another time.

Sympathy nowadays is dispensed chiefly by the laggards and failures, women for the most part (in whom the obsolete exists so strangely side by side with anarchy and newness) who, having dropped out of the race, have time to spend upon fantastic and unprofitable excursions; C. L. for example who, sitting by the stale sickroom fire, builds up with touches at once sober and imaginative the nursery fender, the loaf, the lamp, barrel organs in the West, and all the simple old wives' tales of pinafores and escapades; A. R. the rash, the magnanimous, who if you fancied a giant tortoise to solace you, and a theorbo to cheer you, would ransack the markets of London and procure them somehow, wrapped in paper, before the end of the day; the frivolous K. T. who, dressed in silks and feathers, painted and powdered (which takes time too) as if for a banquet of Kings and Queens, spends her whole brightness in the gloom of the sick room, and makes the medicine bottles ring and the flames shoot up with her gossip and her mimicry.

But such follies have had their day; civilisation points to a different goal; if the cities of the Middle West are to blaze with electric light, Mr Insull 'must keep twenty or thirty engagements every day of his working months,' – and then what place is there for the tortoise and the theorbo?

There is, let us confess it (and illness is the great confessional), a childish outspokenness in illness; things are said, truths blurted out, which the cautious respectability of health conceals. About sympathy for example; we can do without it. That illusion of a world so shaped that it echoes every laugh, every tear, of human beings so tied together by common needs and fears that a twitch of one wrist jerks another, where however far you penetrate into your own mind someone has been there before you – is all an illusion. We do not know our own souls, let alone the souls of others. Human beings do not go hand in hand the whole stretch of the way. There is a virgin forest, tangled, pathless, in each; a snow field where even the print of a birds' feet is unknown. Here we go alone, and like it better so. Always to have sympathy, always to be accompanied, always to be understood would be intolerable. But in health the genial pretence must be kept up and the effort renewed – to communicate, to civilise, to share, to cultivate the desert, educate the native, to work by day together and by night to sport.

In illness this make-believe ceases. Directly the bed is called for, or sunk deep among pillows in one chair we raise our feet even an inch above the ground on another, we cease to be soldiers in the army of the upright; we become deserters. They march to battle. We float with the sticks on the stream; helter-skelter with the dead leaves on the lawn, irresponsible and disinterested, and able perhaps for the first time for years, to look round, to look up – to look at the sky, for example.

The first impression of that extraordinary spectacle is strangely overcoming. Ordinarily to look at the sky for any length of time is impossible. Pedestrians would be impeded and disconcerted by a public sky gazer. What snatches we get of it are mutilated by chimneys and churches, serve as a background for man, signify wet or fine weather, daub windows gold, and, filling in the branches, complete the pathos of dishevelled autumnal plane trees in London squares. Now, become as the leaf or the daisy, lying recumbent, staring straight up, the sky is discovered to be something so different from this that really it is a little shocking. This then has been going on all the time without our knowing it! This incessant making up of shapes and casting them down, this buffeting of clouds together, and drawing vast trains of ships and wagons across the sky, this incessant ringing up and down of curtains of light and shade, this interminable experiment with gold shafts and blue shadows, with veiling the sun and unveiling it, with making rock ramparts and wafting them away, this endless activity with the waste of Heaven-knows-how-many million horse power of energy has been left to work its will year in year out, and we have not known it. The fact seems to call for comment and indeed for censure. Use should be made of it. One could not let this gigantic cinema play perpetually to an empty house.

But watch a little longer, and another emotion drowns the stirrings of civic ardour. Divinely beautiful it is also divinely heartless. Immeasurable resources are used for some purpose which has nothing to do with human pleasure or human profit. If we were all laid prone, frozen, stiff, still the sky would be experimenting with its blues and golds. Perhaps, then, looking down at something very small and close and familiar we shall find sympathy. Let us examine the rose. We have seen it so often flowering in bowls, connected it so often with beauty in its prime, or June, or youth, that we have forgotten how it stands still and steady throughout an entire afternoon in the earth. It preserves a demeanour of perfect dignity and self-possession. The suffusion of its petals is of inimitable rightness. Now perhaps one deliberately falls; now all the flower, the voluptuous purple, the creamy, in whose waxen flesh a spoon has left a swirl of cherry juice, gladioli, dahlias, lilies, sacerdotal, ecclesiastical, flowers with prim cardboard collars tinged apricot and amber, all gently incline their heads to the breeze – all, with the exception of the heavy sunflower, who proudly acknowledges the sun at midday, and perhaps at midnight rebuffs the moon. There they stand; and it is of these, the stillest, the most self-sufficient of all things that human beings have made companions; these that symbolise their passions, decorate their festivals, and lie (as if they knew sorrow) upon the pillows of the dead. Wonderful to relate, poets have found religion in nature; people live in the country to learn virtue from plants. It is in their indifference that they are comforting. That snowfield of the mind, where man has not been, rejoices in the cloud itself perhaps, in the upright rose, as, in another sphere, it is the great artists, the Miltons, the Popes, who console, not by thinking of us, but by forgetting us entirely.

Meanwhile, with the heroism of the ant or the bee, however indifferent the sky may be or disdainful the flowers, the army of the upright marches to battle. Mrs Jones catches her train, Mr Smith mends his motor. The cows are driven home to be milked. Men thatch the roof. The dogs bark. The rooks rising in a net fall in a net upon the elm trees. The wave of life flings itself out indefatigably. It is only the recumbent who know what, after all, Nature is at no pains to conceal – that she in the end will conquer; the heat will leave the world; stiff with frost we shall cease to drag our feet about the fields; ice will lie thick upon factory and engine; the sun will go out. Even so, when the whole earth is sheeted with ice, some undulation, some irregularity of surface will mark the boundary of an ancient garden, and there, thrusting its head up undaunted in the starlight the rose will flower, the crocus will burn.

But with the hook of life within us still we must wriggle. We cannot stiffen peaceably into glassy mounds. Even the recumbent spring up at the mere imagination of frost about the toes and stretch out to avail themselves of the universal hope – Heaven, immortality. Surely, since men have been wishing all these ages they will have wished something into existence; there will be some green isle for the mind to rest on even if the foot cannot plant itself there. The co-operative imagination of mankind will have drawn some firm outline. But no such thing. One opens the *Morning Post* and reads the Bishop of Lichfield on Heaven – a vague discourse, weak, watery, inconclusive. One watches the churchgoers file to church, those gallant temples where, on the bleakest day in the wettest fields, lamps will be burning, bells punctually ringing, and however the autumn leaves may shuffle and the winds sigh, hopes and desires will be changed to beliefs and certainties. Do they look serene? Are their eyes filled with the light of their sublime conviction? Would one of them dare leap straight into Heaven off Beachy Head?

None but a simpleton would ask such questions; they lag and drag and pry and gossip; the mother is worn, the children fidget, the father is tired. The Bishops are tired too. Frequently we read in the same paper how the Diocese has presented its Bishop with a motor car, how at the presentation some leading citizen has remarked, with obvious truth, that the Bishop has more need of motor cars than any of his flock. But this making Heaven available needs time and concentration. It needs the imagination of a poet. Left to ourselves we can but trifle with it – imagine Pepys in Heaven, adumbrate little interviews with celebrated people on tufts of thyme, soon fall into gossip about such of our friends as have stayed in Hell, or, worse still, revert again to earth and choose, since there is no harm in choosing, to live over and over, now as man, now as woman, as sea captain, court lady, Emperor, farmer's wife, in splendid cities and remote moors, in Teheran and Tunbridge Wells, at the time of Pericles or Arthur, Charlemagne or George the Fourth – to live and live till we have lived out those embryo lives which attend about us in early youth and fade in the shadow of that tyrannical 'I' who has conquered so far as this world is concerned but shall not, if wishing can alter it, usurp Heaven too, and condemn us who have played our parts here as Mr Jones or Mrs Smith to remain Mr Jones and Mrs Smith for ever. Left to ourselves we speculate thus carnally. We need the poets to imagine for us. The duty of Heaven-making should be attached to the office of Poet Laureate.

Indeed, it is to the poets that we turn. Illness makes us disinclined for the long campaigns that prose exacts. We cannot command all our faculties and keep our reason and our judgement and our memory at attention while chapter swings on top of chapter, and, as one settles into place, we must be on the watch for the coming of the next, until the whole structure – arches, towers, battlements – stands firm on its foundations. The *Decline and Fall of the Roman Empire* is not the book for influenza, nor *The Golden Bowl*, nor *Madame Bovary*. On the other hand, with responsibility shelved and reason in abeyance – for who is going to exact criticism from an invalid or sound sense from the bedridden? – other tastes assert themselves; sudden, fitful, intense. We rifle the poets of their flowers. We break off a line or two and let them open in the depths of the mind, spread their bright wings, swim like coloured fish in green waters:

> ... and oft at eve
> Visits the herds along the twilight meadows
> Wandering in thick flocks along the mountains
> Shepherded by the slow, unwilling wind –

Or there is a whole three-volume novel to be mused over and spread out in a verse of Hardy's, or a sentence of La Bruyère's. We dip in Lamb's Letters (some prose writers are to be read as poets) and find, 'I am a sanguinary murderer of time, and would kill him inch-meal just now. But the snake is vital', and who shall explain the delight of that? or open Rimbaud and read

> O saisons, o châteaux
> Quelle âme est sans défauts?

and who shall rationalise the charm? In illness words seem to possess a mystic quality. We grasp what is beyond their surface meaning, gather instinctively this, that, and the other – a sound, a colour, a stress, a pause which the poet, knowing words to be meagre in comparison with ideas, has strewn about his page to evoke, when collected, a state of mind which is not in one word or in one sentence, nor can the reason explain it. Incomprehensibility has an enormous power over us, more legitimately perhaps than the upright will allow. In health, meaning has encroached upon sound. Our intelligence domineers over our senses. But in illness, with the police off duty, we creep beneath some obscure poem by Mallarmé or Donne, some phrase in Latin or Greek, and the words give out their scent, and ripple like leaves, and chequer us with light and shadow, and then if at last we grasp the meaning it is all the richer for having travelled slowly up with all the bloom upon its wings. Foreigners to whom the tongue is strange have us at a disadvantage. The Chinese must know better what *Antony and Cleopatra* sounds like than we do.

APPENDIX II

The Cinema/The Movies and Reality

The following signed essay was published in the *N&A*, 3 July 1926, as 'The Cinema', and in the *NR*, 4 August 1926, as 'The Movies and Reality', and is a variant version of 'The Cinema', *Arts*, June 1926, (Kp C274). See p. 348 above and see Editorial Note, p. xxv.

People say that the savage no longer exists in us, that we are at the fag-end of civilisation, that everything has been said already, and that it is too late to be ambitious. But these philosophers have presumably forgotten the movies. They have never seen the savages of the twentieth century watching the pictures. They have never sat themselves in front of the screen and thought how, for all the clothes on their backs and the carpets at their feet, no great distance separates them from those bright-eyed, naked men who knocked two bars of iron together and heard in that clangour a foretaste of the music of Mozart.

The bars in this case, of course, are so highly wrought and so covered over with accretions of alien matter that it is extremely difficult to hear anything distinctly. All is hubble-bubble, swarm and chaos. We are peering over the edge of a cauldron in which fragments of all shapes and savours seem to simmer; now and again some vast form heaves itself up, and seems about to haul itself out of chaos. Yet, at first sight, the art of the cinema seems simple, even stupid. There is the King shaking hands with a football team; there is Sir Thomas Lipton's yacht; there is Jack Horner winning the Grand National. The eye licks it all up instantaneously, and the brain, agreeably titillated, settles down to watch things happening without bestirring itself to think. For the ordinary eye, the English unaesthetic eye, is a simple mechanism, which takes care that the body does not fall down coal-holes, provides the brain with toys and sweetmeats to keep it quiet, and can be trusted to go on behaving like a competent nursemaid until the brain comes to the conclusion that it is time to wake up. What is its surprise, then, to be roused suddenly in the midst of its agreeable somnolence and asked for help? The eye is in difficulties. The eye wants help. The eye says to the brain, 'Something is happening which I do not in the least understand. You are needed.' Together they look at the King, the boat, the horse, and the brain sees at once that they have taken on a quality which does not belong to the simple photograph of real life. They have become not more beautiful, in the sense in which pictures are beautiful, but shall we call it (our vocabulary is miserably insufficient) more real, or real with a different reality from that which we perceive in daily life? We behold them as they are when we are not there. We see life as it is when we have no part in it. As we gaze we seem to be removed from the pettiness of actual existence. The horse will not knock us down. The King will not grasp our hands. The wave will not wet our feet. From this point of vantage, as we watch the antics of our kind, we have time to feel pity and amusement, to generalise, to endow one man with the attributes of the race. Watching the boat sail and the wave break, we have time to open our minds wide to beauty and register on top of it the queer sensation – this beauty will continue, and this beauty will flourish whether we behold it or not. Further, all this happened ten years ago, we are told. We are beholding a world which has gone beneath the waves. Brides are emerging from the Abbey – they are now mothers; ushers are ardent – they are now silent; mothers are tearful; guests are joyful; this has been won and that has been lost, and it is over and done with. The war sprung its chasm at the feet of all this innocence and ignorance, but it was thus that we danced and pirouetted, toiled and desired, thus that the sun shone and the clouds scudded up to the very end.

But the picture-makers seem dissatisfied with such obvious sources of interest as the passage of time and the suggestiveness of reality. They despise the flight of gulls, ships on the Thames, the

Prince of Wales, the Mile End Road, Piccadilly Circus. They want
to be improving, altering, making an art of their own – naturally,
for so much seems to be within their scope. So many arts seemed to
stand by ready to offer their help. For example, there was literature.
All the famous novels of the world, with their well known characters, and their famous scenes, only asked, it seemed, to be put on the
films. What could be easier and simpler? The cinema fell upon its
prey with immense rapacity, and to this moment largely subsists
upon the body of its unfortunate victim. But the results are disastrous to both. The alliance is unnatural. Eye and brain are torn
asunder ruthlessly as they try vainly to work in couples. The eye
says: 'Here is Anna Karenina.' A voluptuous lady in black velvet
wearing pearls comes before us. But the brain says: 'That is no more
Anna Karenina than it is Queen Victoria.' For the brain knows
Anna almost entirely by the inside of her mind – her charm, her passion, her despair. All the emphasis is laid by the cinema upon her
teeth, her pearls, and her velvet. Then 'Anna falls in love with Vronsky' – that is to say, the lady in black velvet falls into the arms of a
gentleman in uniform, and they kiss with enormous succulence,
great deliberation, and infinite gesticulations on a sofa in an extremely well-appointed library, while a gardener incidentally mows
the lawn. So we lurch and lumber through the most famous novels
of the world. So we spell them out in words of one syllable written,
too, in the scrawl of an illiterate schoolboy. A kiss is love. A broken
cup is jealousy. A grin is happiness. Death is a hearse. None of these
things has the least connection with the novel that Tolstoy wrote,
and it is only when we give up trying to connect the pictures with
the book that we guess from some accidental scene – like the gardener mowing the lawn – what the cinema might do if it were left to
its own devices.

But what, then, are its devices? If it ceased to be a parasite, how
would it walk erect? At present it is only from hints that one can
frame any conjecture. For instance, at a performance of *Doctor
Caligari* the other day, a shadow shaped like a tadpole suddenly
appeared at one corner of the screen. It swelled to an enormous size,
quivered, bulged, and sank back again into nonentity. For a
moment it seemed to embody some monstrous, diseased imagination of the lunatic's brain. For a moment it seemed as if thought
could be conveyed by shape more effectively than by words. The
monstrous, quivering tadpole seemed to be fear itself, and not the

statement, 'I am afraid.' In fact, the shadow was accidental, and the effect unintentional. But if a shadow at a certain moment can suggest so much more than the actual gestures and words of men and women in a state of fear, it seems plain that the cinema has within its grasp innumerable symbols for emotions that have so far failed to find expression. Terror has, besides its ordinary forms, the shape of a tadpole; it burgeons, bulges, quivers, disappears. Anger is not merely rant and rhetoric, red faces and clenched fists. It is perhaps a black line wriggling upon a white sheet. Anna and Vronsky need no longer scowl and grimace. They have at their command – but what? Is there, we ask, some secret language which we feel and see, but never speak, and, if so, could this be made visible to the eye? Is there any characteristic which thought possesses that can be rendered visible without the help of words? It has speed and slowness; dartlike directness and vaporous circumlocution. But it has also, especially in moments of emotion, the picture-making power, the need to lift its burden to another bearer; to let an image run side by side along with it. The likeness of the thought is, for some reason, more beautiful, more comprehensible, more available than the thought itself. As everybody knows, in Shakespeare the most complete ideas form chains of images through which we mount, changing and turning, until we reach the light of day. But, obviously, the images of a poet are not to be cast in bronze, or traced by pencil. They are compact of a thousand suggestions of which the visual is only the most obvious or the uppermost. Even the simplest image: 'My luve's like a red, red rose, that's newly sprung in June,' presents us with impressions of moisture and warmth and the glow of crimson and the softness of petals inextricably mixed and strung upon the lilt of a rhythm which is itself the voice of the passion and hesitation of the lover. All this, which is accessible to words, and to words alone, the cinema must avoid.

Yet if so much of our thinking and feeling is connected with seeing, some residue of visual emotion which is of no use either to painter or to poet may still await the cinema. That such symbols will be quite unlike the real objects which we see before us seems highly probable. Something abstract, something which moves with controlled and conscious art, something which calls for the very slightest help from words or music to make itself intelligible, yet justly uses them subserviently – of such movements and abstractions the films may, in time to come, be composed. Then, indeed, when some new symbol for expressing thought is found, the film-maker has enormous riches at his command. The exactitude of reality and its surprising power of suggestion are to be had for the asking. Annas and Vronskys – there they are in the flesh. If into this reality he could breathe emotion, could animate the perfect form with thought, then his booty could be hauled in hand over hand. Then, as smoke pours from Vesuvius, we should be able to see thought in its wildness, in its beauty, in its oddity, pouring from men with their elbows on a table; from women with their little handbags slipping to the floor. We should see these emotions mingling together and affecting each other.

We should see violent changes of emotion produced by their collision. The most fantastic contrasts could be flashed before us with a speed which the writer can only toil after in vain; the dream architecture of arches and battlements, of cascades falling and fountains rising, which sometimes visits us in sleep or shapes itself in half-darkened rooms, could be realised before our waking eyes. No fantasy could be too far-fetched or insubstantial. The past could be unrolled, distances annihilated, and the gulfs which dislocate novels (when, for instance, Tolstoy has to pass from Levin to Anna, and in doing so jars his story and wrenches and arrests our sympathies) could, by the sameness of the background, by the repetition of some scene, be smoothed away.

How all this is to be attempted, much less achieved, no one at the moment can tell us. We get intimations only in the chaos of the streets, perhaps, when some momentary assembly of colour, sound, movement suggests that here is a scene waiting a new art to be transfixed. And sometimes at the cinema in the midst of its immense dexterity and enormous technical proficiency, the curtain parts and we behold, far off, some unknown and unexpected beauty. But it is for a moment only. For a strange thing has happened – while all the other arts were born naked, this, the youngest, has been born fully clothed. It can say everything before it has anything to say. It is as if the savage tribe, instead of finding two bars of iron to play with, had found, scattering the seashore, fiddles, flutes, saxophones, trumpets, grand pianos by Erard and Bechstein, and had begun with incredible energy, but without knowing a note of music, to hammer and thump upon them all at the same time.

APPENDIX III

'How Should One Read a Book?' – Manuscript Draft

What follows is a transcript of a preliminary draft (Berg, Diary XIV) for VW's lecture 'How Should One Read a Book?', which was later published as an essay in the *Yale Review* (Kp C277). See above and see Editorial Note, p. xxv.

⸺

This is a great pleasure, I think; this making up lives & fishing out of these vast bran pies of biographies little pieces of real feeling or humour or oddity with which to decorate them. Only I would have you notice that it is not reading in the sense that reading a novel is reading. We are using different faculties; we are getting a different kind of pleasure. And I go on to suggest that a play ~~show~~ has its own

But now there comes a point again, when one gets tired of people. One gets tired of being on the look out for oddities, ~~& one wishes that~~ tired of the slovenly ~~word~~ untidy messy [?] way in which these large slipshod books are written. What does one want then? ~~Poetry I think~~. Lady Waterford & Lady Canning drive one straight into the arms of Milton. ~~For there are in the world~~ we are so made that we get tired of each other. We want to be alone; we want to be alone partly in order that we may think more closely – quietly about people; & ~~about~~ also about the sky, trees, birds, flowers, things we have seen, ideas that come to us. This is the kind of mood, I

597

imagine, in which it is natural to go to the shelf & find a poet. I said Milton, because he is in some ways the purest, the least personal of poets. ~~It~~ Milton ~~would not have cared to~~ scarcely realised the existence of Lady Waterford & Lady Canning & all the fun & gossip & oddity of daily life. To read poetry I think you want to [be] in this rather solitary frame of mind. You want to be able to concentrate your mind very intensely; ~~upon~~ & to ~~break these faculties~~ look out for all those qualities which we must also look out for in a novel; only we must find them squeezed together, packed into an acorn instead of spreading over a whole large room. Everything is heightened. ~~Eve~~ All a poets tools are very dangerous & very powerful. Take metre for example. If we tried to write a little of our story about the woman who cheated us of five shillings in metre we should see at once what an emotional effect we should gain.

intensified
packed
together

> At the windy corner of the dreary Street ~~you~~
> A woman ~~stood, Her sto~~ stopped me. O O ~~thou~~, she said,
> ~~Whose Who~~ You who pass by, consider my poor feet,
> And how from dawn to night, in search of bread,
> ~~They carry me from~~

Well — I am not a poet; & I do not see how to tell that story in verse. ~~What I m But~~ Nevertheless, I spend a good deal of time reading it, observing how a poet ~~does~~ in a very small space, leaving out all the details, using language in a particular way, & getting the metre to enforce it, does produce emotions wh.

APPENDIX IV

The Art of Fiction

The following signed essay, published in the *N&A*, 12 November 1927, is a condensed version of 'Is Fiction an Art', VW's review in *NYHT*, 16 October 1927, (Kp C288), of E. M. Forster's *Aspects of the Novel* (see above and see Editorial Note, p. xxv).

That fiction is a lady and a lady who has somehow got herself into trouble is a thought that must often have struck her admirers. Many gallant gentlemen have ridden to her rescue, chief among them Sir Walter Raleigh and Mr Percy Lubbock. But both were a little ceremonious in their approach; both, one felt, had a great deal of knowledge of her, but not much intimacy with her. Now comes Mr Forster, who disclaims knowledge but cannot deny that he knows the lady well. If he lacks something of the other's authority, he enjoys the privileges which are allowed the lover. He knocks at the bedroom door and is admitted when the lady is in slippers and dressing gown. Drawing up their chairs to the fire they talk easily, wittily, subtly, like old friends who have no illusions, although in fact the bedroom is a lecture-room, and the place the highly austere city of Cambridge.

This informal attitude on Mr Forster's part is, of course, deliberate. He is not a scholar; he refuses to be a pseudo-scholar. There remains a point of view which the lecturer can adopt usefully if

modestly. He can, as Mr Forster puts it, 'visualise the English novelists, not as floating down that stream which bears all its sons away
unless they are careful, but as seated together in a room, a circular
room – a sort of British Museum reading-room – all writing their
novels simultaneously'. So simultaneous are they, indeed, that they
persist in writing out of their turn. Richardson insists that he is contemporary with Henry James. Wells will write a passage which
might be written by Dickens. Being a novelist himself, Mr Forster is
not annoyed at this discovery. He knows from experience what a
muddled and illogical machine the brain of a writer is. He knows
how little they think about methods; how completely they forget
their grandfathers; how absorbed they tend to become in some
vision of their own. Thus though the scholars have all his respect,
his sympathies are with the untidy and harassed people who are
scribbling away at their books. And looking down on them not
from any great height, but, as he says, over their shoulders, he
makes out, as he passes, that certain shapes and ideas tend to recur
in their minds whatever their period. Since story-telling began,
stories have always been made out of much the same elements; and
these, which he calls The Story, People, Plot, Fantasy, Prophecy,
Pattern, and Rhythm, he now proceeds to examine.

Many are the judgements that we would willingly argue, many
are the points over which we would willingly linger, as Mr Forster
passes lightly on his way. That Scott is a story-teller and nothing
more; that a story is the lowest of literary organisms; that the novelist's unnatural preoccupation with love is largely a reflection of his
own state of mind while he composes – every page has a hint or a
suggestion which makes us stop to think or wish to contradict.
Never raising his voice above the speaking level, Mr Forster has the
art of saying things which sink airily enough into the mind to stay
there and unfurl like those Japanese flowers which open up in the
depths of the water. But greatly though these sayings intrigue us we
want to call a halt at some definite stopping place; we want to make
Mr Forster stand and deliver. For possibly, if fiction is, as we suggest, in difficulties, it may be because nobody grasps her firmly and
defines her severely. She has had no rules drawn up for her, very
little thinking done on her behalf. And though rules may be wrong,
and must be broken, they have this advantage – they confer dignity
and order upon their subject; they admit her to a place in civilised
society; they prove that she is worthy of consideration. But this part

of his duty, if it is his duty, Mr Forster expressly disowns. He is not going to theorise about fiction except incidentally; he doubts even whether she is to be approached by a critic, and if so, with what critical equipment. All we can do is to edge him into a position which is definite enough for us to see where he stands. And perhaps the best way to do this is to quote, much summarised, his estimates of three great figures – Meredith, Hardy, and Henry James. Meredith is an exploded philosopher. His vision of Nature is 'fluffy and lush'. When he gets serious and noble, he becomes a bully. 'And his novels; most of the social values are faked. The tailors are not tailors, the cricket matches are not cricket.' Hardy is a far greater writer. But he is not so successful as a novelist because his characters are 'required to contribute too much to the plot; except in their rustic humours, their vitality has been impoverished, they have gone thin and dry – he has emphasised causality more strongly than his medium permits.' Henry James pursued the narrow path of aesthetic duty and was successful. But at what a sacrifice? 'Most of human life has to disappear before he can do us a novel. Maimed creatures can alone breathe in his novels. His characters are few in number and constructed on stingy lines.'

Now if we look at these judgements and place beside them certain admissions and omissions, we shall see that, if we cannot pin Mr Forster to a creed, we can commit him to a point of view. There is something – we hesitate to be more precise – which he calls 'life'. It is to this that he brings the books of Meredith, Hardy, or James for comparison. Always their failure is some failure in relation to life. It is the humane as opposed to the aesthetic view of fiction. It maintains that the novel is 'sogged with humanity'; that 'human beings have their great chance in the novel'; a triumph won at the expense of life is, in fact, a defeat. Thus we arrive at the notably harsh judgement of Henry James. For Henry James brought into the novel something besides human beings. He created patterns which, though beautiful in themselves, are hostile to humanity. And for his neglect of life, says Mr Forster, he will perish.

But at this point the pertinacious pupil may demand, 'What is this "Life" that keeps on cropping up so mysteriously and so complacently in books about fiction? Why is it absent in a pattern and present in a tea party? Why is the pleasure that we get from the pattern in The Golden Bowl less valuable than the emotion which Trollope gives us when he describes a lady drinking tea in a parsonage? Surely the definition of life is too arbitrary and requires to be expanded.' To all of this Mr Forster would reply, presumably, that he lays down no laws; the novel somehow seems to him too soft a substance to be carved like the other arts; he is merely telling us what moves him and what leaves him cold. Indeed, there is no other criterion. So then we are back in the old bog; nobody knows anything about the laws of fiction; or what its relation is to life; or to what effects it can lend itself. We can only trust our instincts. If instinct leads one reader to call Scott a story-teller, another to call him a master of romance; if one reader is moved by art, another by life, each is right, and each can pile a card-house of theory on top of his opinion as high as he can go. But the assumption that fiction is more intimately and humbly attached to the service of human beings than the other arts leads to a further position which Mr Forster's book again illustrates. It is unnecessary to dwell upon her aesthetic functions because they are so feeble that they can safely be ignored. Thus, though it is impossible to imagine a book on painting in which not a word should be said about the medium in which a painter works, a wise and brilliant book, like Mr Forster's, can be written about fiction without saying more than a sentence or two about the medium in which a novelist works. Almost nothing is said about words. One might suppose, unless one had read them, that a sentence means the same thing and is used for the same purposes by Sterne and by Wells. One might conclude that *Tristram Shandy* gains nothing from the language in which it is written. So with the other aesthetic qualities. Pattern, as we have seen, is recognised, but severely censured for her tendency to obscure the human features. Beauty occurs, but she is suspect. She makes one furtive appearance 'beauty at which a novelist should never aim, though he fails if he does not achieve it' – and the possibility that she may emerge again as rhythm is briefly discussed in a few interesting pages at the end. But for the rest, fiction is treated as a parasite, which draws its sustenance from life, and must, in gratitude, resemble life or perish. In poetry, in drama, words may excite and stimulate and deepen without this allegiance; but in fiction they must, first and foremost, hold themselves at the service of the teapot and the pug dog, and to be found wanting is to be found lacking.

Strange though this unaesthetic attitude would be in the critic of any other part, it does not surprise us in the critic of fiction. For one thing, the problem is extremely difficult. A book fades like a mist, like a dream. How are we to take a stick and point to that tone, that relation, in the vanishing pages, as Mr Roger Fry points with his wand at a line or a colour in the picture displayed before him? Moreover, a novel in particular has roused a thousand ordinary human feelings in its progress. To drag in art in such a connection seems priggish and cold-hearted. It may well compromise the critic as a man of feeling and domestic ties. And so, while the painter, the musician, and the poet come in for their share of criticism, the novelist goes unscathed. His character will be discussed; his morality, it may be his genealogy, will be examined; but his writing will go scot-free. There is not a critic alive now who will say that a novel is a work of art and that as such he will judge it.

And perhaps, as Mr Forster insinuates, the critics are right. In England, at any rate, the novel is not a work of art. There are none to be stood beside *War and Peace, The Brothers Karamazov,* or *A la Recherche du Temps Perdu.* But while we accept the fact, we cannot suppress one last conjecture. In France and Russia they take fiction seriously. Flaubert spends a month seeking a phrase to describe a cabbage. Tolstoy writes *War and Peace* seven times over. Something of their pre-eminence may be due to the pains they take, something to the severity with which they are judged. If the English critic were less domestic, less assiduous to protect the rights of what it pleases him to call life, the novelist might be bolder too. He might cut adrift from the eternal tea table and the plausible and preposterous formulas which are supposed to represent the whole of our human adventure. But then the story might wobble; the plot might crumble; ruin might seize upon the characters. The novel in short might become a work of art.

Such are the dreams that Mr Forster leads us to cherish. For his is a book to encourage dreaming. None more suggestive has been written about the poor lady whom, with perhaps mistaken chivalry, we still persist in calling the art of fiction.

APPENDIX V

Dorothy Osborne

The following essay in the *TLS*, 25 October 1928, (Kp C304) varies too considerably from the *NR* version printed above for its substantive difference to be sensibly accounted for other than by reproducing it in its entirety. See Editorial Note, p. xxv.

It is pleasant to find the Oxford Press putting its fine print and paper at the services of Dorothy Osborne and Mr Moore Smith bestowing on her such scholarship and devotion that there is scarcely a date lacking where dates were very dubious, and scarcely a reference left obscure where references were very elusive. Thus she enters among the classics: thus a new generation confirms the insight of Judge Parry, by whose perspicacity the letters were first brought from their long obscurity to the light. Dorothy Osborne, indeed, has a twofold hold upon our sympathy. She was the heroine of what she called 'a romance story', for she loved Temple; they were separated, they quarrelled, they came together again; and she was also a woman of character enough and of wit enough to make us read her letters for the mere pleasure of reading them.

No doubt in our day a Dorothy Osborne, with Dorothy Osborne's gifts, instead of writing letters would have written books. But in her day – she was born in 1627 and wrote these letters from 1652 to 1654 – the thought of a woman writing a book had something monstrous about it. Only madcaps like the crazy Duchess of

Newcastle wrote books. 'Sure the poore woman is a little distracted' was Dorothy's comment upon one of them. 'If I should not sleep this fortnight I should not come to that.' The art that a woman might practise was an art that could be carried on at odd moments, by a father's sick-bed, among a thousand interruptions, anonymously as it were, and often with the pretence that it served some useful purpose. Yet into these innumerable letters, lost now for the most part to our great impoverishment, went powers of observation and of wit that were later to take rather a different shape in *Evelina* and in *Pride and Prejudice*. They were only letters, yet some pride went to their making. Dorothy, without admitting it, took pains with her own writing and had views as to the nature of it: '. . . great Scholler's are not the best writer's (of Letters I mean, of books perhaps they are) . . . all letters mee thinks should be free and easy as one's discourse.' She was in agreement with an old uncle of hers who threw his standish at his secretary's head for saying 'put pen to paper' instead of simply 'wrote'. Yet there were limits, she reflected, to free-and-easiness: '. . . many pritty things shuffled together' do better spoken than in a letter. And so we come by a form of literature, if Dorothy Osborne will let us call it so, which is distinct from any other, and much to be regretted now that it has gone from us, as it seems, for ever.

For Dorothy Osborne, as she filled her great sheets by her father's bed or by the chimney corner gave a record of life, gravely yet playfully, formally yet with intimacy, to a public of one, but to a fastidious public, as the novelist can never give it, or the historian either. Since it is her business to keep her lover informed of what passes in her home she must sketch the solemn Sir Justinian Isham – Sir Soloman Justinian, she calls him – the pompous widower with four daughters and a great gloomy house in Northamptonshire who wished to marry her. 'Lord what would I give that I had a Lattin letter of his for you,' she claims, in which he described her to an Oxford friend and specially commended her that she was 'capable of being company and conversation for him'; she must sketch her valetudinarian Cousin Molle waking one morning in fear of the dropsy and hurrying to the doctor at Cambridge; she must draw her own picture wandering in the garden at night and smelling the 'Jessomin', 'and yet I was not pleased' because Temple was not with her. Any gossip that comes her way is sent on to amuse her lover. Lady Sunderland, for instance, has condescended to marry plain Mr

Smith, who treats her like a princess, which Sir Justinian thinks a bad precedent for wives. But Lady Sunderland tells everyone she married him out of pity, and that, Dorothy comments, 'was the pittyfull'st sayeing that ever I heard'. Soon we have picked up enough about all her friends to snatch eagerly at any further addition to the picture which is forming in our mind's eye.

Indeed, our glimpse of the society of Bedfordshire in the seventeenth century is the more intriguing for its intermittency. In they come and out they go – Sir Justinian and Lady Diana and Mr Smith and his countess – and we never know when or whether we shall hear of them again. But with all this haphazardry, the letters, like the letters of all born letter-writers, provide their own continuity. They make us feel soon that we have our seat at the heart of the pageant in the depths of Dorothy's mind, which unfolds itself page by page as we read. For she possessed indisputably the gift which counts for more in letter-writing than wit or brilliancy or traffic with great people. By being herself without effort or emphasis she envelops all these odds and ends in the flow of her own personality. It was a character that was both attractive and a little obscure. Phrase by phrase we come closer into touch with it. Of the womanly virtues that befitted her age she shows little trace. She says nothing of sewing or baking. She was a little indolent by temperament. She browsed casually on vast French romances. She roams the commons, loitering to hear the milkmaids sing; she walks in the garden by the side of a small river, 'where I sitt downe and wish you were with mee'. She was apt to fall silent in company and dream over the fire till some talk of flying, perhaps, roused her, and she made her brother laugh by asking what they were saying about flying, for the thought had struck her, if she could fly she could be with Temple. Gravity, melancholy were in her blood. She looked, her mother used to say, as if all her friends were dead. She is oppressed by a sense of fortune and its tyranny and the vanity of things and the uselessness of effort. Her mother and sister were grave women too, the sister famed for her letters, but fonder of books than of company, the mother 'counted as wise a woman as most in England', but sardonic. 'I have lived to see that 'tis almost impossible to think People worse than they are and soe will you' – Dorothy could remember her mother saying that. To assuage her spleen Dorothy herself had to visit the wells at Epsom and to drink water that steel had stood in.

With such a temperament her humour naturally took the form of irony rather than of wit. She loved to mock her lover and to pour a fine raillery over the pomps and ceremonies of existence. Pride of birth she laughed at. Pompous old men were fine subjects for her satire. A dull sermon moved her to laughter. She saw through parties; she saw through ceremonies; she saw through worldliness and display. But with all this clear-sightedness there was something that she did not see through. She dreaded with a shrinking that was scarcely sane the ridicule of the world. The meddling of aunts and brothers exasperated her. 'I would live in a hollow Tree,' she said, 'to avoyde them.' A husband kissing his wife in public seemed to her as 'ill a sight as one would wish to see'. Though she cared no more whether people praised her beauty or her wit than whether 'they think my name Eliz: or Dor': a word of gossip about her own behaviour would set her in a quiver. Thus when it came to proving before the eyes of the world that she loved a poor man and was prepared to marry him she could not do it. 'I confesse that I have an humor that will not suffer mee to Expose myself to People's Scorne,' she wrote. She could be 'sattisfyed within as narrow a compasse as that of any person liveing of my rank', but ridicule was intolerable to her. She shrank from any extravagance that could draw the censure of the world upon her. It was a weakness for which Temple had sometimes to reprove her.

For Temple's character emerges more and more clearly as the letters go on – it is a proof of Dorothy's gift as a correspondent. A good letter-writer so takes the colour of the reader at the other end that from reading the one we can imagine the other. As she argues, as she reasons, we hear Temple almost as clearly as we hear Dorothy herself. He was in many ways the opposite of her. He drew out her melancholy by rebutting it; he made her defend her dislike of marriage by opposing it. Of the two Temple was by far the more robust and positive. Yet there was perhaps something – a little hardness, a little conceit – that justified her brother's dislike of him. He called Temple the 'proudest imperious insulting ill-natured man that ever was'. But, in the eyes of Dorothy, Temple had qualities that none of her other suitors possessed. He was not a mere country gentleman, nor a pompous Justice of the Peace, nor a town gallant, making love to every woman he met, nor a travelled Monsieur; for had he been any one of the these things Dorothy, with her quick sense of the ridiculous, would have had none of him. To her he had

608

some charm, some sympathy, that the others lacked; she could write to him whatever came into her head; she was at her best with him; she loved him; she respected him. Yet suddenly she declared that marry him she would not. She turned violently against marriage indeed, and cited failure after failure. If people knew each other before marriage, she thought, there would be an end of it. Passion was the most brutish and tyrannical of all our senses. Passion had made Lady Anne Blount the 'talk of all the footmen and Boy's in the street'. Passion had been the undoing of the lovely Lady Izabella – what use was her beauty now married to 'that beast with all his estate'? Torn asunder by her brother's anger, by Temple's jealousy, and by her own dread of ridicule, she wished for nothing but to be left to find 'an early, and a quiet grave'. That Temple overcame her scruples and over-rode her brother's opposition is much to the credit of his character. Yet it is an act that we can scarcely help deploring. For, married to Temple, Dorothy wrote to him no more. Perhaps they were too happy; perhaps – dare we hint it? – they were too dull. All is open to conjecture, for, with a reticence that suits her well, Lady Temple says nothing.

APPENDIX VI

Notes on the Journals

With the publication of *The Common Reader*, 1st series, VW found herself 'getting pushed into criticism' (*III VW Diary*, 27 June 1925). She wrote a very great many reviews and notices for the *Nation & Athenaeum* and received commissions to write for, or requests to co-publish articles in, a new range of journals, especially in the USA. Most notable is the huge decline in the number of contributions to the *Times Literary Supplement* (1919–24 saw almost seventy; in 1925–8 there were seven). As in the preceding volumes of this edition the appendix here provides notes on the editors and their editorial policies as available from the journals themselves, from the *Newspaper Press Directory* (*NPD*), from biographical studies, including the *DNB*, and from John Gross's *The Rise and Fall of the Man of Letters* (Weidenfeld & Nicolson, 1969). Information has also been taken from Frank Luther Mott's *A History of American Magazines* (5 vols, Harvard University Press, 1930–68). Against each periodical are given details of VW's contributions.

Arts (New York)

Based at 19 East 59th Street, New York, *Arts* was edited by Forbes Watson with the assistance of his European editor Virgil Barker. In an undated letter, but one clearly written in the early summer of 1925 (MHP), Barker wrote to VW referring to 'Pictures', her recent essay in the *N&A*, and soliciting contributions he sought to pursue personally during a visit to London, 5–14 September. Whether Barker succeeded in meeting his author is not recorded. Her essay duly appeared in *Arts*, but some weeks later another version of the essay appeared, under the title 'The Movies and Reality', in the *NR*. Barker was clearly upset by this. VW's apologetic reply to his subsequent complaint (*VI VW Letters*, no. 1676a, 27 September 1926) is of especial value because it casts light on the nature of co-publication arrangements between the *N&A* and *NR* (for an account of which see Editorial Note). VW's contribution: *1926*: 'Cinema' (June 1926) ['Cinema', *N&A*; 'The Movies and Reality', *NR*].

Atlantic Monthly

Founded in 1857 with J. R. Lowell, VW's so-called godfather, its first editor, the *Atlantic Monthly* was acquired in 1909 by Ellery Sedgwick (1872–1960) and the Atlantic Monthly Company, which Sedgwick founded with MacGregor Jenkins. Under Sedgwick's editorship (1909–38) it gradually threw off the conservativism into which it had sunk by the end of the nineteenth century and became and remained a leading review of literature, art and politics, publishing articles of often quite controversial character (for example, in the March 1927 issue, its coverage of the Sacco-Vanzetti Case). In the 'Contributors' Column' for the issue concerned VW, paying tribute 'to the genius of her countryman, E. M. Forster', was described as 'perhaps the most accomplished woman novelist of today'. The journal opened with an article, by several hands, on 'The Question of the Women's Colleges', said to be 'nearing crisis' and needing to 'attain equality with the colleges for men or be condemned to permanent inferiority'. VW's contribution: *1927*: 'The Novels of E. M. Forster' (November) [*Saturday Review of Literature*].

Bermondsey Book

A quarterly review 'devoted to all phases of life and literature' and published for the Bermondsey Bookshop, Bermondsey Street, South London. The *Bermondsey Book* sought 'to make its appeal primarily as a link between the two worlds which lie North and South of London River'. As its manifesto declared, it included work by leading writers 'side by side with articles descriptive of the life, work, and ambitions of those living across the bridges'. In this instance, VW, Aldous Huxley (interviewed), Julian Huxley, John Drinkwater and Humbert Wolfe were the celebrities. VW's contribution: *1926*: 'Jones and Wilkinson' (June).

Eve

A glossy magazine, incorporating *The Women's Supplement*, *The Gentlewoman* and *Modern Life*. The cover of the issue concerned here bore a photograph of 'Lady Annaly and the Hon. Elizabeth [a child] White'. VW's piece opened adjacent to a photographic feature on the Kempton races and was illustrated by 'A pen picture of the Past – inspired by the effigies of the Lordly Ones – shifting from the sublime to the ridiculous, from a beckoning Queen to an old top hat' (decoration by John Austen). She herself was billed as 'Winner of the much-coveted "Femina" Prize with her brilliant novel "The Lighthouse" [sic]'. VW's contribution: *1928*: 'The Waxworks at the Abbey' (23 May) ['Waxworks at the Abbey', *NR*].

Forum (New York)

A quarterly review, founded in 1886, and edited during 1923–40 by Henry Goddard Leach (1880–1970), author and educator. Concerned with contemporary national and international questions, it also published general articles and, during 1925–36, fiction. VW's contribution: *1926*: 'Illness: An Unexploited Mine' (April) ['On Being Ill', *New Criterion*]; *1927*: 'The New Dress' (May – see *CSF*); *1928*: 'Slater's Pins Have No Points' (January – see *CSF*).

Life and Letters

A monthly financed by Oliver Brett (later 3rd Viscount Esher), founded in 1928 and edited until 1934 by Desmond MacCarthy (1877–1952), with Brett his sub-editor. In his opening editorial MacCarthy told readers they could not expect 'to perceive any marked tendency in its pages' and could anticipate 'a varied diet'. A certain tendency may be discerned, however, in a list of its regular contributors, among whom were Clive Bell, Peter Quennell and Cyril Connolly. The issue concerned included pieces by Aldous Huxley ('Wordsworth in the Tropics') and Hilaire Belloc ('Belinda', continued from the previous issue), as well as book reviews and an editorial by MacCarthy on censorship, entitled 'Literary Taboos'. VW's contribution: *1928*: 'The Niece of an Earl' (October).

Nation & Athenaeum

Edited by Hubert Henderson (see Appendix IV, *III VW Essays*) with LW as his (increasingly reluctant) literary editor, the *N&A* provided VW with a great deal of workaday reviewing. VW's contributions: *1925*: 'Coming back to London...' (14 March): *'This for Remembrance'* (28 March): 'The Two Samuel Butlers' (11

April): 'Guests and Memories' (11 April): 'Mainly Victorian' (11 April): 'John Addington Symonds' (18 April): 'Further Reminiscences' (18 April): 'The Letters of Mary Russell Mitford' (18 April): 'Pictures' (25 April): 'What the bloods of the 'nineties used to say...' (25 April): 'A Player Under Three Reigns' (25 April): 'The Tragic Life of Vincent Van Gogh' (9 May): 'Gipsy or Governess?' (16 May): 'Celebrities of Our Times' (16 May): 'Harriette Wilson' (13 June) ['On the Wrong Side of the Sword' NR]: 'Pattledom' (1 August): 'Unknown Essex' (8 August): 'In My Anecdotage' (8 August): 'Time, Taste and Furniture' (15 August): 'David Copperfield' (22 August): 'A brilliant Englishwoman writes to me...' (5 September): 'In any family save the Darwins...' (26 September): 'Congreve' (17 October): 'Twenty Years of My Life' (17 October): 'Sterne's Ghost' (7 November): 'Saint Samuel of Fleet Street' (14 November): 'Melba' (5 December): 'Some of the Smaller Manor Houses of Sussex' (5 December): 'From Hall-Boy to House-Steward' (26 December); 1926: 'Mary Elizabeth Haldane' (30 January): 'Robinson Crusoe' (6 February): 'Queen Alexandra the Well-Beloved' (6 February): 'Paradise in Piccadilly' (6 March): 'Reminiscences of Mrs Comyns Carr' (20 March): 'The Days of Dickens' (20 March): 'The Flurried Years' (20 March): 'Steeplejacks and Steeplejacking' (27 March): 'Cinema' (3 July) ['Cinema', Arts; 'The Movies and Reality', NR]: 'Romance and the 'Nineties' (3 July): 'The Cosmos' (9 October): 'Laughter and Tears' (16 October): 'George Eliot' (30 October): 'Genius' (18 December) [NR]; 1927: 'Victorian Jottings' (12 February): 'George Gissing' (26 February) [NR]: 'The Immortal Isles' (5 March): 'A Giant With Very Small Thumbs' (2 April): 'Two Women' (23 April): 'The Governess of Downing Street' (30 July): 'Life Itself' (20 August) [NR]: 'A Terribly Sensitive Mind' (10 September) [NYHT]: 'The Art of Fiction' (12 November) [NYHT]; 1928: 'Memories and Notes' (11 February): 'The Cornish Miner' (25 February): 'Stalky's Reminiscences' (7 April): 'Mr Yeats' (21 April): 'Behind the Scenes with Cyril Maude' (28 April): 'Behind the Brass Plate' (5 May): 'The Book of Catherine Wells' (26 May): 'On the Stage: An Autobiography' (30 June): 'Clara Butt: Her Life Story' (14 July): 'Day In, Day Out' (11 August): 'The Diaries of Mary, Countess of Meath' (29 September): 'Plays and Pictures' (17 November): 'Memories' (17 November): 'Half of Thomas Hardy' (24 November): 'Lady Strachey' (22 December).

New Criterion

A continuation of T. S. Eliot's *Criterion*, now with backing from Faber & Gwyer (see Appendix IV, *III VW Essays*). VW's contribution: 1926: 'On Being Ill' (January) ['Illness: An Unexploited Mine', *Forum*].

New Republic

A weekly journal of opinion and liberal views, founded in 1914 by Willard D. Straight, and edited by Herbert Croly (1869–1930), associate editor to 1927, Robert Littell (1896–1963). Most of the pieces concerned were reprinted from the *N&A* (see Editorial Note). VW's contributions: *1925:* 'Olive Schreiner' (18 March): 'John Addington Symonds' (3 June) [*N&A*]: 'Pictures' (13 May): 'On the Wrong Side of the Sword' (24 June) ['Harriette Wilson', *N&A*]; *1926:* 'The Movies and Reality' (4 August) ['Cinema', *Arts, N&A*]: 'Genius' (29 December) [*N&A*]; *1927: 'George Gissing'* (2 March) [*N&A*]: 'Two Women' (18 May) [*N&A*]: 'Life Itself' (17 August) [*N&A*]: 'Praeterita' (28 December) ['Ruskin Looks Back', *T.P.'s Weekly*]; *1928:* 'The Sun and the Fish' (8 February) [*Time and Tide*]: 'Waxworks at the Abbey' (11 April) ['The Waxworks at the Abbey', *Eve*]: 'Dorothy Osborne's Letters' (24 October) ['Dorothy Osborne', *TLS*]: 'Half of Thomas Hardy' (5 December) [*N&A*].

New York Herald Tribune

A major newspaper with an extensive 'Weekly Book Supplement' edited, 1926–63, by Irita van Doren (1891–1966), who had previously been literary editor of the American *Nation*, 1923–4, and of *Books*, 1924–6. 'It aint so much that I'm a bad writer though that I am, as that I'm a sold soul . . . to Mrs Van Doren,' VW wrote on 2

September 1927 to Vita Sackville-West (*III VW Letters*, no. 1805).
'Here am I bound hand and foot to write an article on the works of
a man called Hemingway. There are three more to follow. For this I
shall be paid £120. Not a penny more do I earn as long as I live; so
help me God ... write for the Americans again, write for money
again, I will not.' VW's contributions: *1926*: 'Life and the Novelist'
(7 November); *1927*: 'Poetry, Fiction and the Future' (14 August):
'A Terribly Sensitive Mind' (18 September) [*N&A*]: 'An Essay in
Criticism' (9 October): 'Is Fiction an Art?' (16 October) [*N&A*]:
'Not One of Us' (23 October): 'The New Biography' (30 October);
1928: 'George Meredith' (12 February) ['The Novels of George
Meredith', *TLS*]: 'Preferences' (15 April): 'A Sentimental Journey'
(23 September).

Now and Then

A periodical of books and personalities published occasionally,
from Eleven Gower Street by Jonathan Cape (subsequently from
Thirty Bedford Square), and founded in 1921 when its editorial
declared it to have 'no interest in politics, unless it be the politics of
world authorship and printing'. Other contributors to the issue concerned included G. B. Stern, Mrs Belloc Lowndes and Ethel Man-
nin. VW's contribution: *1927*: 'What Is a Novel?' (Summer, no. 24)
[*Weekly Dispatch*].

Saturday Review of Literature

Founded in 1924 and edited until 1936 by Henry Seidal Canby
(1878–1961), critic and author, with whom VW had previously
published in the *Literary Review of the New York Evening Post*,
where Canby was literary editor 1920–4 (see Appendix IV, *III VW
Essays*). VW's contributions: *1925*: 'American Fiction' (1 August);
1927: 'The Novels of E. M. Forster' (17 December) [*Atlantic
Monthly*].

Time and Tide

Independent weekly founded in 1920 and for many years edited by Margaret Haig, Viscountess Rhondda (1883–1958), a feminist, who sought to change the nation's 'habit of mind' and establish 'a fresher, more liberal climate of opinion'. VW's contribution: *1928*: 'The Sun and the Fish' (3 February) [*NR*].

Times Literary Supplement

Still under the editorship of Bruce Lyttelton Richmond (1871–1964), the *TLS* published considerably fewer pieces by VW than hitherto. A large part of the explanation for this must lie in her involvement with the *N&A*. Another factor appears to have been money: 'Bruce Richmond is coming to tea on Monday to discuss an article on Morgan;' VW noted in her diary on 23 July 1927, '& I am going to convey to him the fact that I can't always refuse £60 in America for the Times' £10.' VW's contributions: *1925*: 'Notes on an Elizabethan Play' (5 March): 'Swift's Journal to Stella' (24 September); *1926*: 'Impassioned Prose' (16 September); *1928*: 'Thomas Hardy's Novels' (19 January): 'The Novels of George Meredith' ['George Meredith', *NYHT*] (9 February): 'An English Aristocrat' ['Lord Chesterfield and the Graces', *NR*] (8 March): 'Dorothy Osborne' ['Dorothy Osborne's Letters', *NR*] (25 October).

T.P.'s Weekly

Established in 1902 by the journalist and (originally Parnellite) politician Thomas Power O'Connor (1848–1929). A popular literary paper dealing with 'men, women and books' (*NPD*), it possessed, according to the *DNB*, 'more than ordinary merit'. VW's contribution: *1927*: 'Ruskin Looks Back on Life' (3 December) ['Praeterita', *NR*].

Vogue

Fashion magazine, edited during the period 1922–6 by Dorothy Todd (see Appendix IV, *III VW Essays*). VW's contributions: *1925*: 'George Moore' (early June): '*The Tale of the Genji*' (late July); *1926*: 'The Life of John Mytton' (early March): 'A Professor of Life' (early May).

Weekly Dispatch

A national Sunday paper, established in 1810 and published by Associated Newspapers, it devoted 'special attention to articles by famous people' and dealt 'fully with home affairs, amusements and sport' (*NPD*). VW's contribution: *1927*: 'What Is a Novel?' (27 March) [*Now and Then*].

Yale Review

A quarterly published by Yale University Press. Founded in 1892 and reorganised in 1911, it was edited by Wilbur L. Cross (1862–1948), whose *The Life and Times of Laurence Sterne* (1909) VW reviewed in the *TLS*, 12 August 1909 (*I VW Essays*). However, VW appears to have dealt only with Helen McAfee, the review's managing editor (MHP). VW's contributions: *1926*: 'How Should One Read a Book?' (October); *1927*: 'Street Haunting' (October).

Bibliography

For bibliographical details concerning other works by Virginia Woolf, and for related biographical works, see under Abbreviations, p. xxxi.

WORKS BY VIRGINIA WOOLF

A Passionate Apprentice. The Early Journals (Hogarth Press, 1990; Harcourt Brace Jovanovich, 1990) edited by Mitchell A. Leaska

To The Lighthouse. The original holograph draft transcribed and edited by Susan Dick (Hogarth Press, 1983).

Unrecorded Times Literary Supplement Reviews introduced by B. J. Kirkpatrick, *Modern Fiction Studies*, 38, 1, spring 1992

Women & Fiction. The manuscript versions of A Room of One's Own (Shakespeare Head Press, 1992) edited by S. P. Rosenbaum

WORKS OF REFERENCE

Virginia Woolf's Reading Notebooks (Princeton University Press, Princeton, New York, 1983) by Brenda R. Silver

Virginia Woolf's Literary Sources and Allusions. A Guide to the Essays (Garland, New York, 1983) by Elizabeth Steele

Virginia Woolf's Rediscovered Essays. Sources and Allusions (Garland, New York, 1987) by Elizabeth Steele

Virginia Woolf: The Critical Heritage (Routledge and Kegan Paul, 1975) edited by Robin Majumdar and Allen McLaurin

INDEX

This index has been compiled upon the same principles as those employed and outlined in the previous volumes of *The Essays*. Thematic entries have been included under the following heads: Americans; Aristocracy; Art; Autobiography; Beauty; Biography; Character; Cinema; Class distinction; Common reader; Critics and criticism; Diarists and diaries; Eclipse; Egotism; Elizabethan drama; Elizabethans; Emotion; Essays; Eyelessness; Genius; Granite and rainbow; Greek; Greek literature; History; Illness; Impressions; Letter-writing; Lighthouse; Literature; Metaphor; Modern, the (modernism, modernity, moderns); Moment; Narrow bridge of art; Nature; 'Only believe'; Nightingale; Novels; Patrons and patronage; Perspective; Poetry; Press, the; Prose; Psychology; Reading; Reality; Reviewers and reviewing; Russian literature; Solitude; Soul; Telephone, the; Translation; Transparency; Victorians; War; Whole, artistic; Women; Working classes. References to places in London have been grouped together under London.

Abbott, Caroline, Forster's character, 493
Acton, Lord: on George Eliot, 171; *Letters of Lord Acton to Mary, Daughter of the Right Hon. W. E. Gladstone*, ed. Herbert Paul, 180n4
Ada, Princess, 423, 425n25
Adam, Eve: ed. *Mrs J. Comyns Carr's Reminiscences*, notice, 338–9, 339n1
Addison, Joseph: lives on, well worth reading, 108; and Pope, 108, 111, 112, 117n5; Thackeray on, 108, 117n5; barriers between VW's era and, 109, 110–11; still readable, 111; on 'the fair sex', his clear notion of fine writing, 112; his conversation, 112–13, 118n20; a lutanist, 113; his perfect essays, 113–15; rendered prose prosaic, 115; and Swift, 293; plausible imitations of, 405; 42, 219, 220; *Cato*, 108, 117n6; quoted, 110, 117n8, n9; 'Addison', by Samuel Johnson, 108, 110; 'The Life and Writings of Addison', by Lord

Macaulay, quoted, 107–8, 116n2, n3; *The Works of the Right Honourable Joseph Addison*, ed. Richard Hurd, essay, 107–15, 117n7
Aelfred, 265, 268n2
Aelfric, 264–5, 268n2
Aeschylus: and Butler, 8, 219; death of 39, 51n3; and use of metaphor, 44; and the far side of language, 45, 48, 50, 140n; *The Agamemnon . . .*, trans. A. W. Verrall, 44, quoted, 45, 52n15, n17
Agathon, 46
Agincourt, battle of, 21
Ainger, Canon Alfred: on Johnson, 311, 312n6; ed. *The Letters of Charles Lamb*, 324, 329n12, 343, 347n9
Ajax, 42, 141n, 516
Alcibiades, 46
Aldclyffe, Miss, Hardy's character, 508, 518n3
Alexander the Great, 76

Ford, John: Havelock Ellis on, 65, 70n10; *see also* Dekker, Thomas; *The Broken Heart*, quoted, 66, 70n13; 68, 70n20; *'Tis Pity She's a Whore*, 65–6; *John Ford*, ed. Havelock Ellis, 65, 70n10

Forster, E. M.: VW commands him to read Defoe, 105n1; asks VW to lunch, 299n1; not a scholar, 457–8; on Scott, 458–9; on Jane Austen, Defoe, Dickens, Richardson and Wells, 459; on Hardy and James, 460–1; on Meredith, 460–1, 525–6; and humane v. aesthetic view, 461, 461–3; his gifts baffling and evasive, 492; both preacher and pure artist, 494–5; his affinity with Ibsen, 495–6; his admirable gift for observation, 496; his gifts trip each other up, 498; VW would restrict him to comedy, 499; his concern over VW's essay, 501n2; xvi, xvii; *Aspects of the Novel*, review, xviii, 457–63, 463n1; 525–6, 535n3, n4; *see also* Appendix IV; *The Celestial Omnibus*, 495, 497; *Howards End*, quoted, 495, 502n10, n11; 496, 502n15, 497–9; 500; *The Longest Journey*, 493–4, 501n6, n7; 495; *A Passage to India*, 495, 497, 499–500; *A Room With a View*, 495; *Where Angels Fear to Tread*, 492–3, 501n3, n5; 495, 498, 500; *and see* Appendix IV

Fortnightly Review, periodical, xiv, 217, 226n7, 572n12

Forum (New York), periodical, xvii, 614

Fox, Charles James, 3

Fray, Henry, Hardy's character, 510, 511

French Revolution, 445

Frend, Sophia Elizabeth, *see* De Morgan, Sophia Elizabeth

Frend, William, 121, 142n10

Froude, James Anthony, as superb essayist, 216; *English Seamen in the Sixteenth Century*, 53, 60n3

Fry, Roger Eliot, and the aesthetics of the novel, 462; 440n1, 465n28; 'Chinese Art', 9n1; intro. to *Victorian Photographs . . .* , by Julia Cameron, 383n1

Fujitsubo, 267, 268n10

Furniss, Harry: *Paradise in Piccadilly. The Story of Albany*, notice, 337–8, 338n1

Gairdner, James: ed. *The Paston Letters*, essay, 20–6, 33–5, 36n1

Galsworthy, John: a disappointment, 158; a materialist, 158, 159; and the use of 'brother', 183; *Beyond*, 164n3; 'The First and Last' (in *Five Tales*), 183, 189n5

Garland, Herbert: trans. *The Tragic Life of Vincent Van Gogh* by Louis Piérard, notice, 249–50, 250n1

Garnett, Constance: trans. *The Lady with the Dog and Other Stories*, by Chekhov, 184, 190n7; *The Wife and Other Stories*, by Chekhov, 185, 190n12; *The Witch and Other Stories*, by Chekhov, 162–3, 165n12, n13; 184, 190n8, n9

Garnett, David: a natural story–teller, 27; 37n17

Gaskell, Elizabeth, 179n1

Gatrill, Rev. J. M., 14&n2

Gauguin, Paul, 250

Genius: and Olive Schreiner, 5; and Sophocles, 41–2; and Plato, 47; Sir Thomas Browne's sublime, 58; Elizabethan word-coining, 67; and diaries, and posterity, 91; Evelyn not a, 96; Defoe's peculiar, 101; Addison's, 110; . . . a boy of, 126; Swift's, 128; required atmosphere for, and Austen, 143; Austen's comic, 151; fatal alloy in Wells's, 158; Charlotte Brontë's, 166; power of George Eliot's, 176; impact of, 183; men of . . . brawling about Greek, 198; Conrad's, 227; ungenerous distrust of contemporary, 234; age of, succeeded by endeavour, 237; and Van Gogh, 249; Rodin on, 254&n4; in Pattledom, 280; Dickens and, 286; of American word-coiners, 319; flurried years in the precincts of, 380; De Quincey's, 364; Mrs Cameron and men of, 380; reading to the bent of the author's, 393; Haydon's, 406ff; curious men of, and the natural voice, 474; and Shelley, 468; Ruskin's, 503; Hardy's, 507, 509, 517

George III, King, 202

George V, King, 348, 353n2, 560

George, Henry, 253, 254n2

Gibbon, Edward: *The Decline and Fall of the Roman Empire*, 324, 329n8

Gibbons, Grinling, 94, 97n9

Gilbert, Ann (*née* Taylor): and life in Colchester, 119–20; and James Montgomery, 120; 142n2; *Autobiography and Other Memorials of Mrs Gilbert . . .* , ed. Josiah Gilbert, essay, 119–20, 141n1

Gilbert, Sir Humfrey, 54, 60n6, n8

Gilbert, Rev. Joseph, 120, 142n2

Gilbert, Josiah: ed. *Autobiography and Other Memorials of Mrs Gilbert . . .* , essay, 119–20, 141n1

Gilfils, the, George Eliot's characters, 174, 181n22

Gimson, Ernest, 284

Gino, Forster's character, 493, 500

Girton College, Cambridge, campaign to found, 421–2, 424, 425nn20–2

Gissing, George, Defoe of his school, 104; 107n23, 431

quoted, 31; *The Excursion*, 237; *Lyrical Ballads*, 193; *The Prelude*, xxiiin32; *The White Doe of Rylstone*, 430, 440n2

Working classes, the: of Sheffield and Archbishop Thomson, 207; from hall-boy to house-steward, 315–16; steeplejacks, 341–2; reverenced by Ruskin, 503; Cornish tinners, 538; Meredith's not successful, 561; and Thackeray, 561; ignorance of, and the rising novelist, no longer themselves, 562

Wray, Sir William, 97, 98n20

Wren, Sir Christopher, 97n8; and John Evelyn, 94

Wright, Sir Charles Hagberg, 190n6; intro. to *The Village Priest* ... , (by Militsina and Saltikov, trans. B. Tollemache), 183, 189n4, n6

Wright, Thomas, 99: *The Life of Daniel Defoe*, 106n3, n4, n6, n7

Wycherley, William, 49, 302, 310

Xenocrates, 432

Yale Review, quarterly, xvi–xvii, 399n1, 619

Yarmolinsky, Avrahm: *Turgenev. The Man – His Art – And His Age*, review, 416–18, 418n1

Yeats, W. B.: and George Moore, like a crow, 263; 237, 360&n1; 'Leda and the Swan', 545n1, quoted, 545, 546n4; *The Tower*, 543; review, xxi, 544–5, 545n1

Yeobright, Clym, Hardy's character, 512, 518n12

Yonge, Charlotte M.: *Womankind*, quoted, 420, 424n5; 421, 425n17

York and Albany, Frederick, Duke of, 337, 338n2

Yūgao, 267, 268n10

Printed in the United States
127946LV00004B/37/P

9 780156 035224